A Geography of Mankind

*"I could perhaps understand New England without knowing the land,
but never without knowing the Puritan immigrants."*

FRIEDRICH RATZEL

MC GRAW-HILL SERIES IN GEOGRAPHY

JOHN C. WEAVER, *Consulting Editor*

Bennett: Soil Conservation
Broek and Webb: A Geography of Mankind
Carlson: Africa's Lands and Nations
Cressey: Asia's Lands and Peoples
Cressey: Land of the 500 Million: A Geography of China
Fryer: World Economic Development
Murphy: The American City: An Urban Geography
Pounds: Europe and the Soviet Union
Pounds: Political Geography
Raisz: General Cartography
Raisz: Principles of Cartography
Thoman: The Geography of Economic Activity
Trewartha: An Introduction to Climate
Trewartha, Robinson, and Hammond: Elements of Geography: Physical and Cultural
Trewartha, Robinson, and Hammond: Physical Elements of Geography
  (A republication of Part I of the above)
Trewartha, Robinson, and Hammond: Fundamentals of Physical Geography
Van Riper: Man's Physical World

Vernor C. Finch was Consulting Editor of this series from its inception in 1934 to 1951.

A Geography of Mankind

Jan O. M. Broek

Department of Geography
University of Minnesota

John W. Webb

Department of Geography
University of Minnesota

Cartographic design by
Mei-Ling Hsu
Department of Geography
University of Minnesota

McGraw-Hill Book Company

New York, St. Louis, San Francisco
Toronto, London, Sydney

A Geography of Mankind

ISBN 07-007999-4

7890   CR   BP   743210

Cover photograph: *Mass meeting in Pakistan,* used
with permission of Josephine Powell.

Preface

It is told that the first president of Cuba sent his brother to Switzerland to study democracy and bring it home. "That's all very well," said the brother, "but where in Cuba are we going to find the Swiss?"

Geographers would readily agree to the need of recognizing differences in behavior, attitude, and value patterns when comparing countries. Yet, curiously enough, many fail to deal explicitly with the traits that give human groups their distinctive character and that condition the manner in which each group perceives and uses its habitat. This book attempts to fill that gap by emphasizing the socio-cultural diversity of mankind as an essential requisite to geographic understanding.

Another feature of this volume is its topical, or thematic, presentation. Although the geographer seeks to understand the character of places, it need not follow that he must begin by dividing the earth into segments or regions, such as continents, climatic provinces, economic, or political units. He can also proceed analytically by inquiring into the nature and distribution of various features—e.g., population, cultural attributes, types of economy—that shape the earth's variety and interdependence. This topical approach permits deeper probing into general concepts and principles than the regional procedure allows. It also has the merit of making the reader a partner in the quest for an intelligible spatial order, instead of handing him a preconceived regional system in which to pigeonhole the geographic data. Furthermore, the thematic treatment responds to the increasing interest all social sciences are taking in comparative or cross-cultural studies.

Traditionally, space and time have been sundered and awarded to geography and history respectively. But it is increasingly realized that all events occur in specific places, and that all places derive their character from changes through time. Concern with process, that is, the interaction of forces through time, has particular relevance to social and cultural geography. Observing where peoples and things are leads to questions about their place of origin, their routes of dispersal, and their transformation within the present location. Accordingly, the authors have freely reached into the past to trace sequences through time and space.

Writing an introductory treatise of this kind is like painting a canvas with broad strokes: Many details must be sacrificed to highlight main contours. To counteract the danger of overgeneralization, a number of case studies provide a closer look at particular areas. Many of the maps, too, present specific patterns on a large scale. Above all, we hope that the student will go beyond this book and profit from the sources suggested in the bibliographies that accompany the chapters.

The map is the basic tool of the geographer, a graphic shorthand for what otherwise would require long verbal descriptions of location and arrangement. More important, comparison of distributional patterns often uncovers significant spatial relationships. As the neophyte in geography learns to use these cartographic devices, he soon realizes that they are an integral part of the book.

The order of presentation, reflecting the authors' objectives, may be summarized as follows:

Part I introduces fundamental geographic concepts, draws attention to the present population distribution, and surveys the origin and diffusion of skills and tools by which societies in different parts of the world have transformed their habitat.

Part II goes to the heart of the argument by examining race, language, religion, and nation as categories of thought patterns and institutions that unite or separate human groups. After this analysis follows a provisional synthesis that arranges the earth into broad culture realms.

Part III presents the diverse forms of economy prevailing in tribal, traditional, and modern societies, and evaluates their levels of development. It will be noted that these economic patterns correlate fairly well with the culture realms of the second part.

Part IV compares the forms of settlement in different culture realms, from farmstead and village to town and city, and explores the emerging structure of the metropolitan region with its perplexing problems.

Part V returns to the topic of population, but now considers its dynamic aspects of natural growth and movement as seen against the background of spatial variety in cultural tradition, type of economy, and degree of urbanization.

The Epilogue reviews the great forces of change in our era and how they affect the various culture realms. The earth becomes ever more "One World," but not necessarily a uniform world modeled after the Occidental civilization.

Obviously a survey of this kind incorporates many ideas and facts from other sources, but does not lend itself to detailed documentation. The debt is largely acknowledged in the Citations and in the Further Readings, listed at the end of each chapter. The courtesy of those who permitted reproduction of photographs and use of maps is deeply appreciated; recognition is given in the appropriate places. The authors are especially grateful for the constructive comments from colleagues who read one or more sections; to mention names would be unjust to those thoughtful anonymous critics who reviewed the entire manuscript when it was close to completion.

The graphic materials were prepared in the Cartographic Laboratory of the Department of Geography at the University of Minnesota under the general supervision of our colleague, Dr. Mei-Ling Hsu. To her the authors express their keen appreciation for designing the maps and graphs, while reserving for themselves the responsibility for any factual errors that remain. Miss Patricia

Kangel and Mr. I-Shou Wang not only skillfully drafted these materials, but also made valuable suggestions for improvement.

During the long preparation of this book our wives have been loyal and patient—though not silent—partners. The presentation has greatly profited from their frank comments.

Minneapolis
September, 1967

Jan O. M. Broek
John W. Webb

Contents

List of Maps and Graphs

List of Maps and Graphs

Part I. Introduction

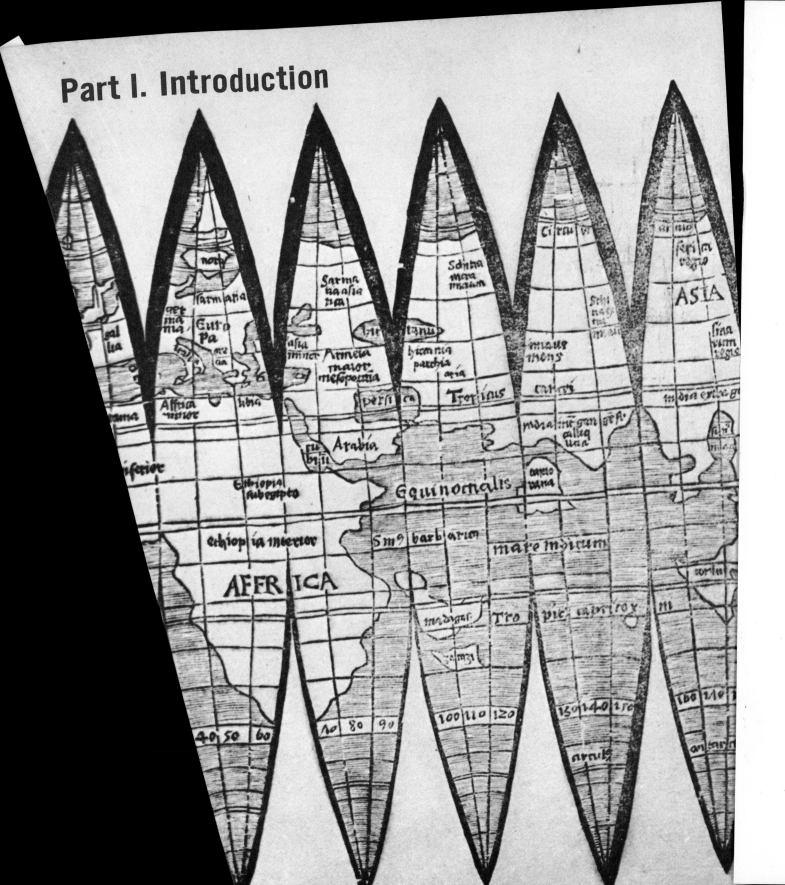

*List of Maps
and Graphs*

Part I. Introduction

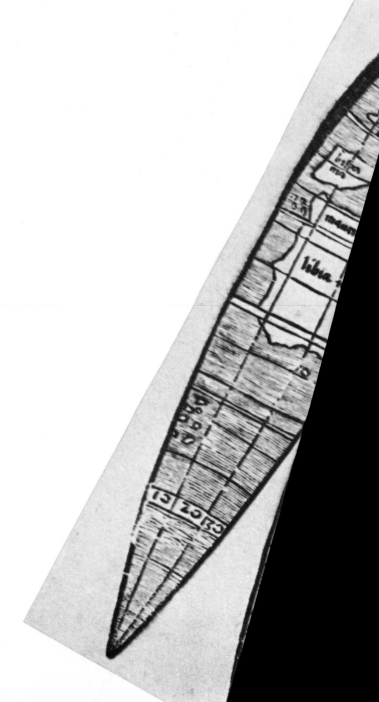

This introductory section serves to lay some general foundations for the more specialized parts that follow. Chapters 1 and 2 attempt to explain what geography, especially in its sociocultural aspects, is all about. If some of the concepts appear vague we hope they will become more meaningful when put to work in the body of the text.

This book has its focus on man's present world, but current conditions can be understood only by recognizing them as a phase in a perpetual transformation. Chapter 3 provides a useful historical perspective by tracing origins and dispersals of technology as the means of man's increasing control over energy and as a driving force—though certainly not the only one—in the rise and spread of civilizations.

I. Introduction

1. The Geographic Viewpoint

The Value of Geography

In London one can visit the quarters where Winston Churchill guided the war effort in Britain's darkest hours. The walls of his own room in this underground shelter are covered with maps. They show the lay of the land in the actual and potential battle zones, the locations of cities and manufacturing districts, and reveal at a glance the position of strategic key points in the network of the world's shipping, air, and land routes. This room demonstrates the crucial value of geography in a nation's effort to survive: knowledge of lands and peoples, and of their interrelations.

The average citizen is not likely to find himself in a position where he must make decisions that directly affect the national welfare. But as a member of a democracy he should be well informed so that he can judge current issues, whether of worldwide or local significance, and cast his vote in a responsible manner. Yet, how many Americans understood the vital importance of Greece and Turkey when, after World War II, Russian pressure toward the Mediterranean Sea was mounting; or the strategic location of Korea when that distant war burst upon us in 1950?

Quite often we ignore reports about the progress of the multinational effort to develop the resources of the Mekong River basin and about petroleum and gas discoveries in Queensland or western Europe because we lack the background to grasp the significance of the story. Or we are surprised by news of rebellion in Sudan and extremist violence in Italian Tyrol because we were not aware of smoldering resentment among ethnic minorities. We are puzzled and dismayed that billions of American dollars apparently have failed to stimulate economic development in backward countries, but we rarely know enough about those countries to get at the social and cultural roots of the trouble.

Geographic ignorance is also common in domestic affairs. As citizens we are concerned with such matters as floods and water shortages, air and stream pollution, chaotic growth of metropolitan areas, legislative reapportionment, and pockets of poverty; but all too seldom do we clearly understand these problems in their regional context.

Geography is not merely useful. It is exciting for its own sake. Anyone who takes the trouble to study maps and read books about the places he will visit finds his route of travel much more meaningful. The urge to understand a country makes every traveler into an explorer. He becomes alert to the variety in farming types and house forms, to the extent of man-caused erosion, the effect of a new dam, or whatever else may intrigue him about a people and their land.

If we cannot go and see Africa for ourselves, we can travel in thought with George Kimble while he explains that continent's problems and prospects. If we are interested in Mexico, we can learn much about its personality from Carl Sauer, whose writings are based on many years of close observation. The era of discovering new continents is past, but the discovery of new truths about old countries goes on forever.

The Purpose of Geography

Geography is organized knowledge of the earth as the world of man. It deals with organic and inorganic phenomena, not for their own sake, but as they help to understand the earth as the place where people live, work, meet, and mingle, transforming its surface into their habitat.

To speak of "the earth" as a unit fails to bring out its variety of features. Next to terrestrial integration—an ever more meaningful concept in this era of shrinking distances—we should give equal attention to earth differentiation. Geographers want to understand the character of countries, regions, areas—let us say "places" for short—but they realize that no place can be understood by itself. The wealth and welfare of the Dakota grain farmer are linked not only to the precarious rainfall of the northern plains and his methods of farming, but equally, or more, to government decisions in Washington or to the movement of grain prices on the world's exchanges. The character of a place is, therefore, always determined by the interplay of both local and distant factors. Taking account of the notions of variety and relationships, we can now restate the aim of geography. It is: to understand the earth as the world of man, with particular reference to the differentiation and integration of places.

This statement may surprise some readers. They may hold the notion that geography is vaguely akin to geology and should study plains and mountains, seas and rivers. Or they may think that it is geography's task to demonstrate how nature influences man in different environments. Still others, understanding that geography deals with location, believe that its goal is to map the distribution of any and all phenomena over the earth's surface. Quite true, geographers are interested in landforms, in the effect of environment on man, and in the location of peoples and things. But these tasks are *means,* not the *end.* They all must serve the purpose of geography as described above.

The Main Concepts of Geography

Geography is a meaningful way of looking at the earth, not a mere inventory of its contents. This geographic viewpoint rests upon a number of fundamental, intertwined concepts. These basic ideas and propositions guide the geographer in his research as well as in teaching. A brief preview will help the reader to spot these concepts as they appear in the following chapters.

Location. "Where," as the point of reference, is the first thing the geographer wants to know. To find where something is requires defining its spatial relationship to other points. To locate is to relate. The mathematical position of a specific place can be found on globe or map by means of the grid of meridians and parallels which serve as coordinates. Knowing the mathematical position of a place is like having the address of a person. It only tells you where to find him, but nothing about his home and surroundings. Geographical insight comes only with knowledge of the place itself, that is, its *site,* and its relations with other areas, its *situation.*

Site stands for that aspect of place that has to do with the local forces and processes and their interrelations. For instance, one might describe how man has organized his life in an oasis in Central Asia by noting the interrelations of climate, soil, water supply, agriculture, and town life.

Situation, also called relative location or geographic position, shows how a place is related to other places. It recognizes that a locality is not an island unto itself, but has contacts with other places, which may in part

List of Maps and Graphs

Part I. Introduction

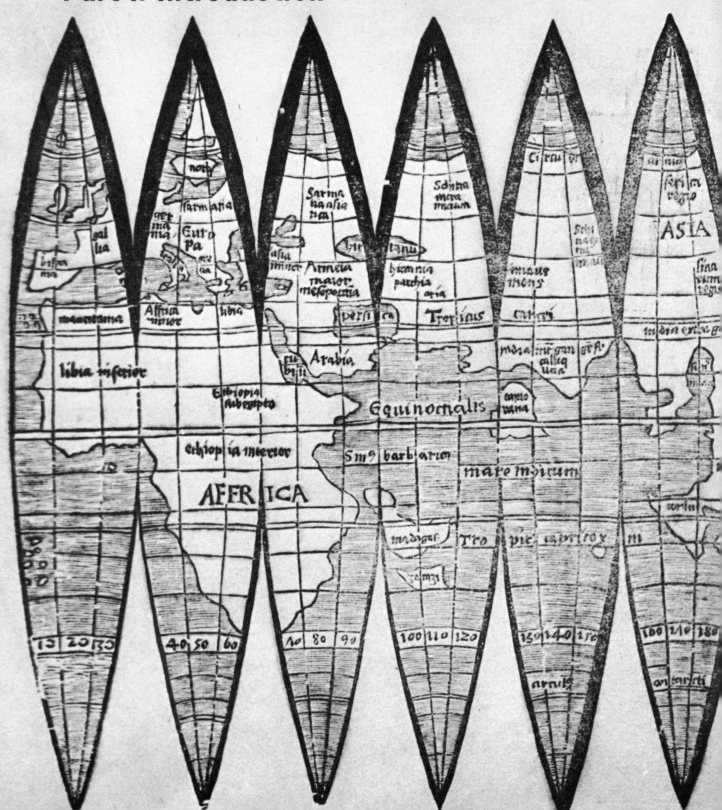

This introductory section serves to lay some general foundations for the more specialized parts that follow. Chapters 1 and 2 attempt to explain what geography, especially in its sociocultural aspects, is all about. If some of the concepts appear vague we hope they will become more meaningful when put to work in the body of the text.

This book has its focus on man's present world, but current conditions can be understood only by recognizing them as a phase in a perpetual transformation. Chapter 3 provides a useful historical perspective by tracing origins and dispersals of technology as the means of man's increasing control over energy and as a driving force—though certainly not the only one—in the rise and spread of civilizations.

Part-opening photograph: Martin Waldseemüller's Globe Map of 1507, the first of its kind to show the name America. [Courtesy of James Ford Bell Collection, University of Minnesota]

I. Introduction

1. The Geographic Viewpoint

The Value of Geography

In London one can visit the quarters where Winston Churchill guided the war effort in Britain's darkest hours. The walls of his own room in this underground shelter are covered with maps. They show the lay of the land in the actual and potential battle zones, the locations of cities and manufacturing districts, and reveal at a glance the position of strategic key points in the network of the world's shipping, air, and land routes. This room demonstrates the crucial value of geography in a nation's effort to survive: knowledge of lands and peoples, and of their interrelations.

The average citizen is not likely to find himself in a position where he must make decisions that directly affect the national welfare. But as a member of a democracy he should be well informed so that he can judge current issues, whether of worldwide or local significance, and cast his vote in a responsible manner. Yet, how many Americans understood the vital importance of Greece and Turkey when, after World War II, Russian pressure toward the Mediterranean Sea was mounting; or the strategic location of Korea when that distant war burst upon us in 1950?

Quite often we ignore reports about the progress of the multinational effort to develop the resources of the Mekong River basin and about petroleum and gas discoveries in Queensland or western Europe because we lack the background to grasp the significance of the story. Or we are surprised by news of rebellion in Sudan and extremist violence in Italian Tyrol because we were not aware of smoldering resentment among ethnic minorities. We are puzzled and dismayed that billions of American dollars apparently have failed to stimulate economic development in backward countries, but we rarely know enough about those countries to get at the social and cultural roots of the trouble.

Geographic ignorance is also common in domestic affairs. As citizens we are concerned with such matters as floods and water shortages, air and stream pollution, chaotic growth of metropolitan areas, legislative reapportionment, and pockets of poverty; but all too seldom do we clearly understand these problems in their regional context.

Geography is not merely useful. It is exciting for its own sake. Anyone who takes the trouble to study maps and read books about the places he will visit finds his route of travel much more meaningful. The urge to understand a country makes every traveler into an explorer. He becomes alert to the variety in farming types and house forms, to the extent of man-caused erosion, the effect of a new dam, or whatever else may intrigue him about a people and their land.

If we cannot go and see Africa for ourselves, we can travel in thought with George Kimble while he explains that continent's problems and prospects. If we are interested in Mexico, we can learn much about its personality from Carl Sauer, whose writings are based on many years of close observation. The era of discovering new continents is past, but the discovery of new truths about old countries goes on forever.

is to map the distribution of any and all phenomena over the earth's surface. Quite true, geographers are interested in landforms, in the effect of environment on man, and in the location of peoples and things. But these tasks are *means,* not the *end.* They all must serve the purpose of geography as described above.

The Purpose of Geography

Geography is organized knowledge of the earth as the world of man. It deals with organic and inorganic phenomena, not for their own sake, but as they help to understand the earth as the place where people live, work, meet, and mingle, transforming its surface into their habitat.

To speak of "the earth" as a unit fails to bring out its variety of features. Next to terrestrial integration—an ever more meaningful concept in this era of shrinking distances—we should give equal attention to earth differentiation. Geographers want to understand the character of countries, regions, areas—let us say "places" for short—but they realize that no place can be understood by itself. The wealth and welfare of the Dakota grain farmer are linked not only to the precarious rainfall of the northern plains and his methods of farming, but equally, or more, to government decisions in Washington or to the movement of grain prices on the world's exchanges. The character of a place is, therefore, always determined by the interplay of both local and distant factors. Taking account of the notions of variety and relationships, we can now restate the aim of geography. It is: to understand the earth as the world of man, with particular reference to the differentiation and integration of places.

This statement may surprise some readers. They may hold the notion that geography is vaguely akin to geology and should study plains and mountains, seas and rivers. Or they may think that it is geography's task to demonstrate how nature influences man in different environments. Still others, understanding that geography deals with location, believe that its goal

The Main Concepts of Geography

Geography is a meaningful way of looking at the earth, not a mere inventory of its contents. This geographic viewpoint rests upon a number of fundamental, intertwined concepts. These basic ideas and propositions guide the geographer in his research as well as in teaching. A brief preview will help the reader to spot these concepts as they appear in the following chapters.

Location. "Where," as the point of reference, is the first thing the geographer wants to know. To find where something is requires defining its spatial relationship to other points. To locate is to relate. The mathematical position of a specific place can be found on globe or map by means of the grid of meridians and parallels which serve as coordinates. Knowing the mathematical position of a place is like having the address of a person. It only tells you where to find him, but nothing about his home and surroundings. Geographical insight comes only with knowledge of the place itself, that is, its *site,* and its relations with other areas, its *situation.*

Site stands for that aspect of place that has to do with the local forces and processes and their interrelations. For instance, one might describe how man has organized his life in an oasis in Central Asia by noting the interrelations of climate, soil, water supply, agriculture, and town life.

Situation, also called relative location or geographic position, shows how a place is related to other places. It recognizes that a locality is not an island unto itself, but has contacts with other places, which may in part

Poor farming practices made this rolling Texas country
part of the "dust bowl" in the 1930s. Now water and wind
erosion are checked by contour plowing, strip farming, terracing,
and planting windbreaks. [Courtesy of U.S. Department of Agriculture]

explain the character of the place. For instance, in the case of the oasis, the town may be the market for exchange of products between farmer and nomad from the surrounding steppe.

Evaluation of an area must always take into account both site and situation, though one may prove to be more important than the other. Extensive ruins in central Asian oases suggest that several hundred years ago there was a much larger and wealthier urban population. Some geographers seek the main cause for the decay in increased aridity which made irrigation more and more difficult; in other words,

they hold a local *site* factor responsible. But others deny the evidence of long-range climatic deterioration. They point out that the former wealth of oasis cities rested on their function as trade centers along the caravan routes of inner Asia. When trade was interrupted or shifted to sea routes, the cities lost their source of prosperity. The latter view stresses the change in *situation* as the fundamental cause for the decline.

Site and situation present two aspects of place: site the internal, situation the external. What is "internal" and what "external" de-

*1. The
Geographic
Viewpoint*

7

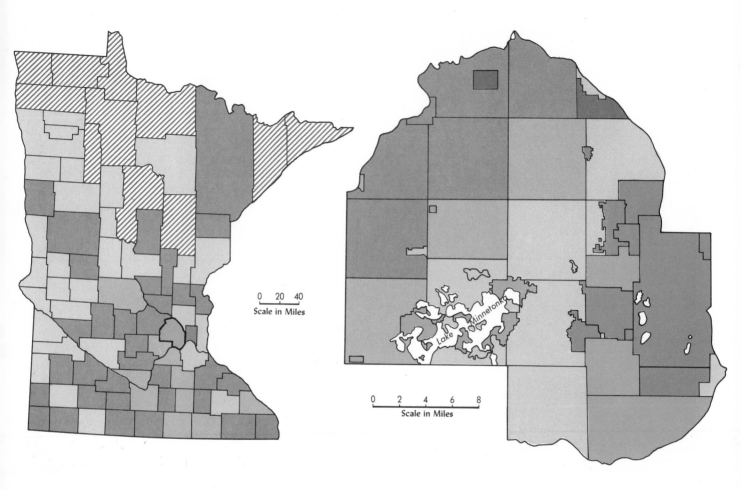

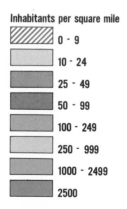

Inhabitants per square mile

▨	0 - 9
░	10 - 24
▦	25 - 49
▓	50 - 99
▤	100 - 249
▢	250 - 999
▨	1000 - 2499
■	2500

Figure 1–1. SCALE AND POPULATION DENSITY

Minnesota had an average population density of 43 per square mile in 1960. At the county scale (map on the left) densities ranged from 2 per square mile in Cook County in the extreme northeast to 2,641 in Ramsey County, which contains the city of St. Paul. At the scale of minor civil divisions—cities, villages, townships, etc.—Hennepin County, with an average density of 1,492 per square mile, had local densities ranging from 28 per square mile in a western township to 8,940 in the city of Minneapolis, the large rectangular area at the east edge (map on the right). Data from *U.S. Census of Population, 1960.*

I. Introduction

pends on how the area is defined. In buying a home the qualities of the house and lot represent the site, the character and facilities of the neighborhood the situation. In evaluating the strategic position of the United States in the world, the country is the site, the surrounding lands and seas the situation. In each case we are thinking of places and their surroundings, but in the framework of different scales.

The Meaning of Scale. Scale, a familiar term in cartographic presentation, expresses the proportional relationship between map and earth reality. It has important bearing on geographic thought, because the size of the area we observe affects not only the intensity of perception, but also the kind of generalizations that can be made about the area (Figure 1–1).

The field worker who wants to record what he observes in a small area makes use of a large-scale map on which, for instance, one inch represents a quarter mile in reality, expressed numerically as a scale of 1:15,840. At this scale he can mark each field, footpath, and house, though he must generalize a bit on shapes. If he wants to cover an area four times as wide and long but on the same size paper, he uses the smaller scale of one inch to the mile (1:63,360). On this scale he must omit many details; that is, he reduces the individual features into more general patterns of cropland, pasture, house blocks, and roads. By decreasing the scale still further—and keeping the map size constant—he finally arrives at a map of the earth which can only show the gross surface configurations, the larger rivers, and the biggest cities.

Another type of map represents only one category of facts as distributed over part or all of the earth. If such a "thematic" or "topical" map, say of population, is on a very large scale, it can show one dot for each enumerated person at the exact location of his residence, but as the scale decreases one dot must stand for one hundred, one thousand, or even more persons.

We cannot say that one scale is better than another, because its value depends on what the map is for. But it is important to realize that the level of general conclusions will differ with the scale of the map. There would not be so many disputes about the validity of generalizations if people took careful note of the scale of investigation on which the findings were based. For example, while one might conclude from the study of a small area that the location of manufacturing plants is strongly conditioned by taxes, zoning, and terrain, these factors would carry little weight in generalizations about the location of industries in the United States or the world as a whole.

Spatial Interaction. Interaction between places implies mobility of things, ideas, or people over the earth's surface. Movements of air masses make the local weather, ocean currents condition the temperature and salinity of the sea, and runoff from the highlands affects the lowlands. In human affairs migration brings strangers into new lands, and diffusion of an invention carries a novel idea beyond its area of origin. Division of labor makes people dependent on each other. Territorial specialization demands the exchange of goods and services with other areas. Thus, spatial differentiation goes together with spatial interaction. This interaction requires overcoming distance through communication and transportation or—to adopt a French term covering all forms of movement—through "circulation." Accessibility measures the degree to which a place is approachable from other places by means of circulation (Figure 1–2).

Central location is usually an advantage because it signifies that a place is accessible from all directions, the focus for the surrounding area, its market, its forum, from where in turn goods and ideas radiate. Being in the center of things is not always a blessing, as in a war or tornado. Apart from such destructive forces, however, great advantages accrue to being in the middle of events. We see this easily when we contrast central and marginal locations in a city, a country, or a wider realm. Marginal in the sense here used means being offside, removed from the flow of circulation. Backwaters tend to be stagnant. It is no accident that—

Figure 1–2. THE LAND HEMISPHERE

Instead of the conventional northern and southern
hemispheres, divided by the equator, one can
bisect the earth in such manner that one half
contains as much as possible of the land surface.
The pole of this land, or principal, hemisphere, lies
in northwestern France. This presentation demonstrates an aspect of relative location. The shaded
areas on each side of the North Atlantic Ocean
form the world's main industrial-commercial zone.

before the Europeans came—the southern tips
of South America and Africa, as well as
Australia and Tasmania, were the homes of
very primitive peoples. Knowledge of new ideas
and tools hardly reached these remote dead
ends (Figure 1–3).

I. Introduction

10

Distance from the centers of innovation is
not the only factor. Any barrier to circulation
lessens accessibility and thus acts to preserve
traditional ways. The rain forests of the Congo
Basin, the jungle-covered uplands of central
India, and the "green desert" of the Amazon
lowland hide tribes of a much lower level of
culture than the people in surrounding regions.
Even the inhabitants of the Appalachians, the
Scottish Highlands, and the marshes of Poland
and of western Russia have a retarded economy
compared to their compatriots in more accessible areas. All suffer more or less from isolation.

Spatial Distribution. Each individual place has
its specific location on the earth's surface. If we
select one element or property of that place to
compare it with the location of like elements or
properties in other places, we record a *distribution.* For instance, there is only one Keokuk,
Iowa. But if we think of it as a river town, and
now record the location of all river towns in the
central United States, we have a map of a distribution (Figure 1–4). The same can be done
with all other elements or properties that give
character to a place, be they distribution of
precipitation in Kansas, of Puerto Ricans in
New York, of Chinese in Malaya, or of cotton
in Egypt.

Analysis of distributions is a highly important
part of geographic study. Some geographers
declare it to be the hallmark of geography, but
this seems an error. The purpose of geography
is to understand the character of places; the
study of distributions is one of the means to
pursue that end. Many other disciplines also
use distributions. The plant pathologist who
studies wheat diseases certainly will make a
map of their occurrence. While doing that, he
is not suddenly transformed into a geographer.
The geographer, however, who is investigating
the wheat regions in the United States will
welcome his map.

By presenting distributions on a map we can
detect areal associations. For instance, we may
note the presence of fruit orchards near the
shores of Lake Ontario in those areas where
late spring and early autumn frosts are rare. In

Figure 1–3. THE WORLD ON A NORTH POLAR ZENITHAL PROJECTION

This projection distorts the shapes of the landmasses and oceans. However, it emphasizes the propinquity of the northern continents and the relative isolation of southern South America, southern Africa, and Australasia.

Polar Azimuthal Equidistant Projection

some cases visual comparison of different distributional patterns may suffice, but in others much more sophisticated statistical methods are needed to establish as exactly as possible the extent of areal correlation between different phenomena. High correlation between two variables is no proof of causal relationship; it is possible that the correspondence in areal extent of the two variables is the unrelated result of a third, unknown, factor. Or the association may be coincidental and of little significance, as in the case where a geographer observed a close correspondence between the American manufacturing belt and the area where Ben Davis apples are grown.

Spatial distribution presents three aspects: density, dispersion, and pattern. The drawings in Figure 1–5 illustrate these distinctions. *Density* is defined as the overall frequency of occurrence of a phenomenon within the area under study, relative to the size of this area. *Dispersion* refers to the extent of the spread of the feature relative to the size of the study area. *Pattern* means the geometric arrangement

Figure 1–4. RIVER TOWNS OF MID-AMERICA

"Places" have many and diverse characteristics. The towns shown on this map all have one property in common: they belong to the generic class of "river towns."

without regard to the size of the study area. These distinctions are vital to the correct understanding of distribution. To illustrate, compare the state of Kuwait on the Persian Gulf with an area of equal size (6,000 square miles) in northern Iowa. Both units have about the same density of population (55 people per square mile). However, the dispersion of population is very different. In Kuwait by far the greater part is concentrated in the old city of Al-Kuwait and the modern oil-company town of Ahmadi, with minor clusters at the oil fields in the desert; in Iowa the spread is much wider over small towns and farmsteads. The patterns too show decided contrasts: the rectangular arrangement of settlement in Iowa reflects the land-survey system, while in Kuwait the pattern appears without any order, except for the recent oil developments. In Kenya, the map of population distribution shows different densities, dispersions, and patterns from one part of the country to another (Figure 1–6).

The Regional Concept. The places geographers study are of two kinds. First of all, place means a specific individual locality identified by its given name, be it San Francisco or Paris,

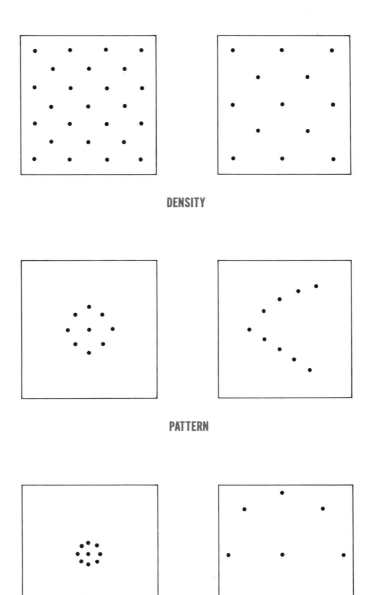

Figure 1–5. DENSITY, PATTERN, AND DISPERSION

Based on a diagram by E. N. Thomas.

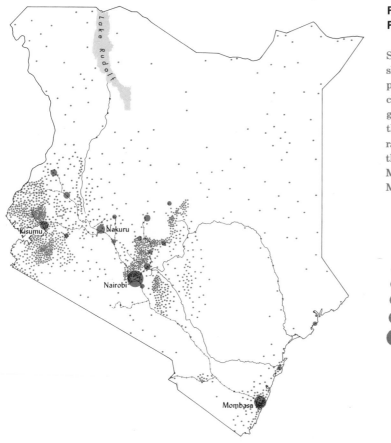

Figure 1–6. KENYA: DISTRIBUTION OF POPULATION, 1962

Small dots show rural population, large circles show towns. The uneven distribution of rural population reflects not only the influences of soil, climate, terrain, and vegetation, but also tribal groupings and the history of land allocation during the European settlement earlier in this century. The railroads link together the populated areas. Note the large size of Nairobi (the capital city) and Mombasa (the main port) compared to other towns. Modified from Survey of Kenya, 1962, map 25A.

5,000 Persons

Persons in Towns

- 5,000 - 10,000
- 10,000 - 20,000
- 20,000 - 50,000
- 50,000 - 100,000
- 100,000 - 250,000
- Over 250,000

Arizona or Alsace. These places are "given." They are instituted by official action and have well-defined boundaries. Less well defined but also recognizable as place-individuals are such concrete natural features as Mount Whitney, the Baltic Sea, or Cuba—less well defined because where exactly does a mountain begin, and where is the boundary between land and sea?

Examples of the second kind of place are the Cotton Belt, the tundra, the American manufacturing belt, the Great Plains. Such places are not "given." Many people deny that there is a "Cotton Belt," and while most would concede that the Great Plains exist, no two fully agree as to their exact extent (Figure 1–7). We are dealing here with mental constructs formulated to arrange earth features in some abstract order. The layman who looks at, say, a map showing climatic regions is apt to take it as a discovery of science, like the table of atomic weights. Instead, he should think of it as a more or less adequate tool, designed to bring order into the infinite variety of climatic conditions.

A region, then, is a part of the earth that is

I. Introduction

Figure 1–7. THE GREAT PLAINS REGION DEFINED

Four different ways of defining the Great Plains: (A) as a "physiographic province" according to Fenneman, 1916; (B) as an "agricultural region" acording to Baker, 1923; (C) as a "semi-arid, treeless, and level environment" by Webb, 1931; (D) as a "geographical region" by White and Foscue, 1943.

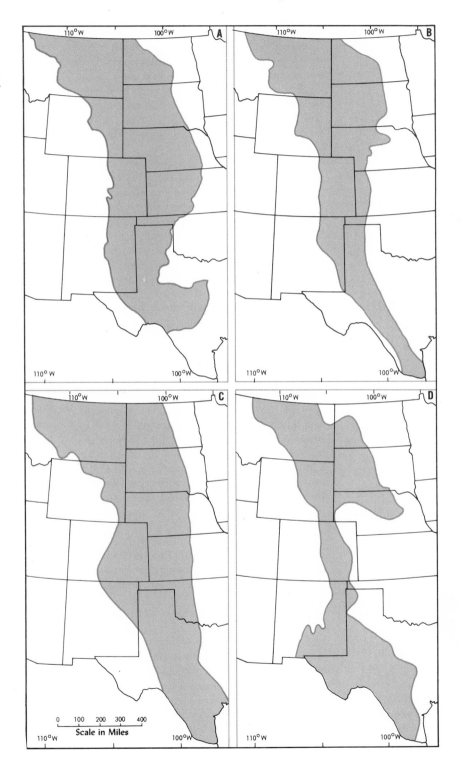

alike in terms of the specific criteria chosen to delimit it from other regions. A certain place-individual can be in different regions according to the generic order employed—generic in the sense of order by genus or class. Illinois belongs climatically to the humid continental region of North America, agriculturally to the mixed-farming belt, and industrially to the main manufacturing zone.

The examples just mentioned have in common that they are regions defined by the likeness or even homogeneity of features or forms. This so-called "formal" region differs from the "nodal" or "functional" region. The latter type is conceived as a spatial entity functioning around a central city through a network of circulation. Denver lies between two very different formal regions, the Rocky Mountains and the Great Plains, but it is the node of an inland "empire" which includes segments of the mountains as well as the plains, and such diverse activities as mining, ranching, and crop farming. The limits of Denver's supporting and tributary area, or hinterland, can be determined by the extent and intensity of spatial interaction, such as the in-and-out flow of goods, travel, long-distance telephone calls, newspaper circulation, wholesale deliveries, and so on. Figure 1–8 shows the tributary region of Minneapolis–St. Paul (the Twin Cities) as another example. In a worldwide view, sovereign states assume the character of functional regions. France exemplifies how highly diverse formal regions function as an integrated whole around Paris as the national hub.

In summary, regions do not exist in reality; they are mental constructs. The regional concept is a necessary and valuable device to order the earth's particular places into meaningful general frames.

Internal Coherence. There are many heterogeneous things that make a country: people, terrain, climate, soil, vegetation, minerals, crops, factories, trade and other services, town and country. If these elements were independent odds and ends, an observer could do no more than make an inventory, like listing the contents of a department store. Actually, each region has an interplay of forces, an interdependence and arrangement of elements, and a common imprint which permits rational inspection and comprehension. This internal consistency unites the particles into a whole, what the French call an *ensemble* and the Germans a *Gestalt*. To be sure, we must verify the assumption that such internal integration exists. The anthropologist who thinks that there is more to culture than a hodgepodge of unrelated traits uses a similar approach to his subject. The historian too, when he faces the multitude of events in some bygone period, takes it for granted that there are relationships.

Biologists use the term *ecology* for the study of the mutual relations between all organisms living together in a particular habitat.* The organisms depend on their environment, both physical and biological and, in turn, affect and modify that environment. The mutual interaction between organisms and environment can be conceived as a functioning spatial organization and is called an "ecosystem." The concept of the ecosystem serves as a useful analogy to illustrate the geographic notion of internal coherence. "Analogy" is the word rather than "identity," because we cannot safely transfer these biological concepts to the world of man. True, man depends on nature, transforms it, is part of it, but at the same time apart from it—because of his culture (see Chapter 2).

The study of elements in their interaction does not presuppose that all are part of one great chain of causality. Obviously the major landforms result from entirely different forces than climate. Climate, though affecting the distribution of organisms and soil types, does not explain their origin and evolution. Nor is man merely a product of his physical environment. Clearly, many and disparate processes combine to create the earth and its parts. How

---

*The term ecology, coined in 1884 by the German biologist Ernst H. Haeckel, derives from *oikos,* meaning "house" or "household," and *logos,* meaning "word" or, in this context, "knowledge" or "science."

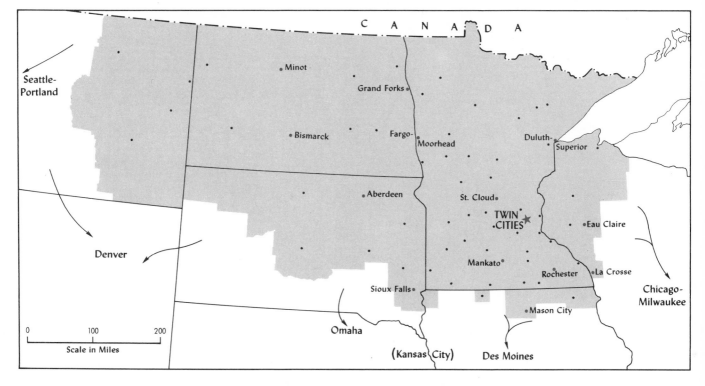

Figure 1–8. THE TWIN CITIES (MINNEAPOLIS–ST. PAUL) TRADE REGION

This functional region extends from western Wisconsin to Montana. Medium-sized and small trade centers within the region are also shown. After a map in Borchert and Adams, 1963, 25.

then can we hope to find internal coherence in an area where diverse forces happen to meet? The answer lies in viewing man, or actually human society, as the organizer of its habitat. Each society molds the forces and features of its biophysical environment to its singular purpose. In this way it organizes space into a coherent entity such as a country, a region—in short, a place.

This seems a good opportunity to point out the difference in viewpoint between the so-called systematic sciences (economics, sociology, biology, geology, and such), and geography.

The workers in each of those disciplines extract from reality one particular set of phenomena to study. Some of them criticize geographers because they are interested in all things at once and thus constantly trespass into fields already neatly divided among the systematic sciences. They do not understand that the geographer studies peoples, industries, cities, climates not for their own sake, but because he perceives them as parts of a whole that give character to a place. In this holistic position geography resembles history. The historian, too, uses any and all facts—a constitution, a muddy battle-

1. The Geographic Viewpoint

17

The Netherlands: Dike village of Zuid-Scharwoude,
23 miles north of Amsterdam. Almost all farm plots grow
vegetables. Because for centuries farmers have dredged the
drainage ditches to spread the fertile mud over the fields, one-fourth
of the surface is water. [Photograph KLM Aerocarto, Airport Amsterdam]

field, a statesman's ulcer—to explain a historic event. Both history and geography take a comprehensive view of mankind and earth, one stressing time bonds, the other place bonds. This approach counterbalances artificial partitions. Geographers feel that the greater the fragmentation of knowledge the more the need for putting the bits together again in an orderly way, to understand the reality of places.

The Theme of Change.   To say that geography deals with place and history with time is only part of the truth. The historian always treats events in specific places, be it colonial rule in India or feudalism in western Europe. And the geographer perceives each place as the product of change through time.

"The abiding earth" is a comforting phrase, but reality is different. Everything is in process of change. Even an equilibrium is maintained only by dynamic forces, like that of a rider on a bicycle. The word *process* refers to an interplay of forces that causes a series of changes through time. The process of erosion creates a valley. The process of urbanization swallows up the countryside. To understand the nature, direction, and rate of change requires knowledge of the process that causes the change. We must view events in time scales appropriate to the process. For instance, weather is subject to daily and seasonal cycles; climate has fluctuated around a relatively constant mean over the last several thousand years, but has actually changed over much longer time spans. Confusion of time scales leads to errors (much like confusion of area scales), such as interpreting the succession of a few cold years as the advent of a new ice age.

In human affairs there are similar short- and long-term changes, though even the longest are brief compared to the geologic time scale. Some are part of daily, seasonal, and annual cycles or fluctuations (e.g., commuter traffic, livestock drives, manufacturing output); others are long-term processes modifying the way of life and the landscape (such as the European migrations or the so-called Industrial Revolution).

Old cities like Rome and Istanbul are living exhibits of what different societies have contributed to city building and architecture. Elsewhere, and particularly in the countryside, the impact of the past may be less striking; nevertheless, it is there and affects the present. Property lines, for instance, are very stubborn space dividers. In coastal California, alignment of farms and house lots quite commonly conforms to the pattern of Spanish land grants. In each case, an action in the remote past is to be reckoned with today.

The legacy of the past plagues many cities. The problem often is one of site. The first white settlers found the small island of Manhattan and the narrow hilly peninsula at the Golden Gate suited to their needs. They could hardly foresee the modern metropolitan centers that would evolve on these sites.

Changing geographic situations also affect, often severely, the fortunes of cities, countries, and even larger parts of the earth. The New York and San Francisco metropolitan regions, in spite of cramped sites for their central cities, have prospered because they commanded, and still command, the funnels of trade between ocean and continent. But Samarkand and Venice are only shadows of their glorious past when they were on the world's main trade routes. In the rise of the ancient civilizations the favorable situation of the Middle East was an important factor. Here, at the junction of land and sea routes, peoples, ideas, and goods mingled. Later the centers of progress moved to the shores of the Mediterranean Sea. When the positional advantage shifted to the ocean boards, western Europe became the center of innovation. The Mediterranean became a backwater after the Great Discoveries, but regained some of its former value when the Suez Canal was opened.

In the historical perspective, regions may be conceived as expanding and contracting entities, perhaps even migrating ones. Somewhere a certain type of economy or a culture trait starts (nomadic herding, irrigation, the cotton plantation), puts its mark on society and landscape, then spreads from there as far as conditions favor its expansion. But a new resource may be discovered, or a different economy invade and transform the area. The new forces may even overgrow and smother the old regional pattern until at last only some relict forms of the old order remain.

Even if the geographer concentrates on current conditions, he must always remember that the present is but an interim phase in an ever-changing existence. Behind the dominant features he will note the inheritance of the past; but he also may detect mutations or innovations that point toward new directions in the way of life and the use of the habitat.

The seven concepts we have discussed in this introduction express the geographic turn of mind. One theme, the relationship between man and nature, has been repeatedly mentioned, but not explicitly examined. In the following chapter we will look more closely at this relationship.

1. The Geographic Viewpoint

Citations

Baker, O. E. "The Agriculture of the Great Plains Region," *Annals of the Association of American Geographers,* 13 (1923): 109–168. [Map]

Borchert, J. R., and Adams, R. B. "Trade Centers and Trade Areas of the Upper Midwest," Upper Midwest Economic Study, *Urban Report No. 3,* Minneapolis, Minn. (1963). [Map]

Fenneman, N. M. "Physiographic Divisions of the United States," *Annals of the Association of American Geographers,* 6 (1916): 19–98. [Map]

Survey of Kenya, *Atlas of Kenya,* Nairobi, 1962. [Map]

Webb, W. P. *The Great Plains,* New York, 1931. [Map]

White, C. L., and Foscue, E. S. *Regional Geography of Anglo-America,* New York, 1943. [Map]

Further Readings

Ackerman, E. A. *Geography as a Fundamental Research Discipline,* University of Chicago, Department of Geography Research Paper no. 53, Chicago, 1956.

Ad Hoc Committee on Geography, Earth Sciences Division, National Academy of Sciences—National Research Council, *The Science of Geography,* Washington, D.C., 1965. This report contains suggestions for new avenues of research, particularly in theoretical and deductive studies.

Broek, J. O. M. *Compass of Geography,* Columbus, Ohio, 1966. A brief, nontechnical introduction. Also published as *Geography, Its Scope and Spirit,* Columbus, Ohio, 1965, with an additional chapter suggesting methods for elementary and secondary teachers.

Chorley, R. J., and Haggett, P. *Frontiers of Geographical Teaching,* London, 1965.

Freeman, T. W. *One Hundred Years of Geography,* London, 1961.

Haggett, P. *Locational Analysis in Human Geography,* London, 1966.

Hartshorne, R. *The Nature of Geography,* Lancaster, Pa., 1939 (and several later editions). A survey of geographic thought in the light of the past. Difficult for the neophyte.

———. *Perspective on the Nature of Geography,* Chicago, 1959. A more concise treatment than the previous title.

Hettner, A. *Die Geographie, ihre Geschichte, ihr Wesen und ihre Methoden,* Breslau, 1927. Fundamental work on the history of geography from the orthodox viewpoint.

Howarth, O., and Dickinson, R. E. *The Making of Geography,* London, 1933.

James, P. E., and Jones, C. F. (eds.) *American Geography: Inventory and Prospect,* Syracuse, N.Y., 1954. A collective survey by a number of geographers, covering most branches of the field.

Taylor, G. T. (ed.) *Geography in the Twentieth Century,* New York and London, 1957. Essays on various aspects of the discipline.

Wooldridge, S. W., and East, W. G. *The Spirit and Purpose of Geography,* London, 1951.

Important Geographical Periodicals

Annales de géographie (six issues yearly), Librairie Armand Colin, 103 Boulevard St. Michel, Paris 5e, France, 1891–.

Annals of the Association of American Geographers (quarterly), Association of American Geographers, 1146 16th St. N.W., Washington, D.C., 1911–. High-quality journal with many articles of a philosophical and methodological nature.

Bibliographie géographique internationale (annual), Centre National de la Recherche Scientifique, Paris, 1891–. Annotated bibliography covering a vast amount of geographical literature.

Canadian Geographer—Géographe canadien (quarterly), Canadian Association of Geographers, Morrice Hall, McGill University, Montreal 2, P.Q. Canada, 1951–. Professional journal of Canadian geographers.

Current Geographical Publications, Additions to the Research Catalogue of the American Geographical Society (monthly, except July and August), American Geographical Society, Broadway and 156th St., New York, N.Y., 1938–.

Economic Geography (quarterly), Clark University, Worcester, Mass., 1925–. The scope of articles is broader than the title would suggest.

Erdkunde (quarterly), Geographisches Institut der Universität, Franziskanerstrasse 2, 53 Bonn, German Federal Republic, 1947–.

Focus (monthly, except July and August), American Geographical Society of New York, New York, 1950–. Pamphlets with background information on countries and topics of current interest.

Geographical Journal (quarterly), Royal Geographical Society, London, 1893–. Published under other titles since 1830.

Geographical Review (quarterly), American Geographical Society of New York, New York, 1916–. Contains articles and reviews of high quality.

Geographische Zeitschrift (quarterly), Geographisches Institut der Universität, Neue Universität, 69 Heidelberg, German Federal Republic, 1895–1944, 1963–. Recently revived West German periodical, particularly important for articles on human geography.

Journal of Geography (monthly, except June, July, and August), National Council for Geographic Education, Chicago, Ill., 1902–. Devoted to articles on the teaching of geography in primary and secondary schools.

Landscape (3 issues yearly), J. B. Jackson, Santa Fe, N.Mex., 1951–. Concerned with man's impact on the earth.

New Geographical Literature and Maps (biannually), Royal Geographical Society, London, 1951–. Selective bibliographies.

Petermann's Geographische Mitteilungen (quarterly), Justus Perthes Strasse 3–9, Gotha, German Democratic Republic, 1855–. An old and internationally respected scholarly journal.

Professional Geographer (bimonthly), Association of American Geographers. For address, see *Annals of the Association of American Geographers*, 1949–. Contains articles, news of members and centers of geographic work, and official notices.

Scottish Geographical Magazine (quarterly), Royal Scottish Geographical Society, Edinburgh, 1885–.

Transactions and Papers of the Institute of British Geographers (biannually),

Institute of British Geographers, G. Philip and Son, Ltd., Victoria Road, London, N.W. 10, England, 1935–.

Other important periodicals include: *University of California, Publications in Geography; University of Chicago, Department of Geography, Research Papers; Die Erde; Geografiska Annaler; Geography; Tijdschrift voor Economische en Sociale Geografie; Revue de Géographie Alpine; Geographia Polonica; Soviet Geography; Geographical Review of India; Lund Studies in Geography; Geographical Bulletin; Pacific Viewpoint; Journal of Tropical Geography; Geographica Helvetica.*

2. Nature and Culture

Influences of the Natural Environment

Ever since man became thinking man—*Homo sapiens*—he must have reflected on how the world around him affected his daily life. He tried to placate the spirits, ghosts, or gods that controlled the forces of the environment. Although modern man seems far removed from those crude fears and practices, he too must reckon with nature. One might think offhand that science has provided a clear view on the relationships between man and nature, but this is not true. Some people claim that science will give almost complete control over the environment, promising a bright future for mankind as soon as the new techniques are widely put to use: solar or nuclear energy, mining the oceans, air conditioning the tropics, rainmaking over deserts, or irrigation with desalinated sea water, all these and many more inventions will free man from nature's tyranny. Others argue that our massive interference with nature has brought erosion of soils, depletion of groundwater, exhaustion of mines, pollution of air and water, and destruction of wildlife, all pointing up the lack of control over the environment which, if continued, may lead to catastrophe.

In trying to understand the character of places, the geographer must face the issue of environmental relations. Boiled down to its essence, current geographic thought denies that nature is the active force and man the passive subject. To the contrary, man is the active

agent, nature passive. And, most important, "man" is always part of a specific society. Each society perceives and interprets its biophysical surroundings through the prism of its own way of life, its culture. Only within this perceptual framework can the physical environment affect man.

The statement needs elaboration, but it will be understood better if we examine first another position, the so-called environmentalist view.

Environmentalism

In geography environmentalism refers to the view that man's activities are strongly conditioned or even determined by his biophysical environment.

A clear doctrine of the influence of the natural environment on man appears to have been formulated first in the book *Airs, Waters, Places,* ascribed to Hippocrates, who lived in the latter half of the fifth century B.C. This work was written by a physician for colleagues going abroad, and might be called the archetype of treatises on environmental health. It presents therefore a medical rather than a geographical theory. The author described the influence of each natural habitat on the people. For instance, because the climate of Europe is more variable than that of Asia (as known to

Hippocrates) "the physique of Europeans varies more than that of Asians." The same reasoning applies also to character. "In such a [European] climate arise wildness, unsociability and spirit. For the frequent shocks to the mind impart wildness, destroying tameness and gentleness." In contrast, the uniformity of the seasons in "Asia" explains why its inhabitants are less warlike.

Aristotle repeated the generalization about national character and added the political element: "The nations inhabiting the cold places and those of Europe are full of spirit but somewhat deficient in intelligence and skill, so that they continue comparatively free, but lacking in political organization and capacity to rule their neighbors. The peoples of Asia on the other hand are intelligent and skillful in temperament, but lack spirit, so that they are in continuous subjection and slavery. But the Greek race participates in both characters, just as it occupies the middle position geographically" (van Paassen, 1957, 324–328).

The theme reappeared in the Renaissance and found strong support by the French political philosopher Jean Bodin (1530–1596). He, too, attributed the main differences between peoples to three climatic belts. The northern cold zone produced a physically vigorous but mentally slow type, tending toward democratic government; the hot south had lazy people, intelligent but politically passive, and thus satisfied to live under despotism; in between, in the temperate zone, natural conditions brought about the right mixture of intelligence and industry, and favored the existence of the true monarchy. The influence of Aristotle is obvious, except that Bodin claims France to be representative of the ideal climatic conditions, thereby underscoring neatly the subjectivity of the generalization.

The works of eighteenth-century writers such as Montesquieu (*The Spirit of Laws,* 1748), Buffon (*Natural History of Man,* 1749), and Voltaire (*Essay on the Customs and the Spirit of Nations,* 1756) reveal similar environmental notions. A century later Henry Buckle in his *History of Civilization* (1857–1861) applied the method of the natural sciences to historical problems. Although his analysis was more rigorous than that of the earlier writers, he came to much the same conclusions. In Buckle's view the mild and moist climate of England had distinct advantages over either Scandinavia or Spain, because in the latter two countries year-round work was interrupted by cold, dark winters or dry, hot summers, leading to irregular work habits and vaccilation, in contrast to the steady work and perseverance of the English.

None of these men were geographers. Nevertheless, the layman usually thinks that it is the special task of geography to study how environmental conditions shape human life. Common use of the term "geographic" reinforces this misunderstanding. In correct usage the adjective "geographic" refers not only to influences of the physical environment, but to any factor that makes areas different from or related to each other.

The popular view of geography is mainly a carry-over from ideas in the late nineteenth century. The theory of evolution through adaptation to the environment appeared to explain why human societies developed individually. Geographers always had found it difficult to determine what caused the coherence between a people and its habitat. Now "adaptation to the physical environment" gave—or rather seemed to give—the scientific answer. It was in this period that the emphasis in geography shifted from the study of places to the study of environmental influences. In the United States the preoccupation with environmentalism lasted until the 1920s, when professional geographers turned away from it. The old notions, however, survived much longer in primary and secondary school education (Rostlund, 1956).

The fault of the environmentalists lay not in the issue they raised—How do the physical surroundings affect man?—but in the sweeping generalizations they drew from scattered data, often ignoring contrary evidence. Having defined geography as the study of environmental influences on man, they concentrated on proving the doctrine rather than objectively examining the facts. A favorite theme was the effect of climate (Figure 2–1). The variable but never extreme weather of northwestern Europe was

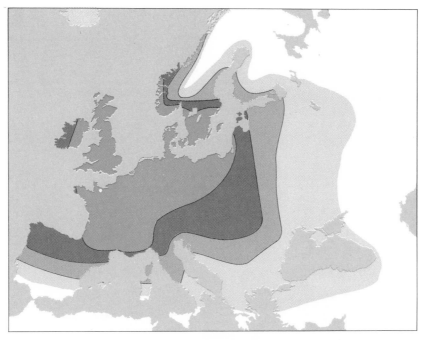

Figure 2–1. CLIMATIC EFFICIENCY IN EUROPE, BY ELLSWORTH HUNTINGTON

Based on a map in Van Valkenburg and Huntington, 1935, 23.

presented as stimulating mental activity and thus as the fundamental cause of progress in that area. To answer the question why and how other civilizations could have arisen in less favorable climates, the proponents of the theory suggested that climates probably had changed substantially in the last five thousand years. Others linked the birth of Judaic-Christian monotheism to the desert environment, and the beginnings of free democracy to the landforms and climate of Greece.

Modern geographers have become wary of such grand but simple explanations. Instead of reasoning from physical environment to human worth, they now ask how a particular society at a given time perceives its physical milieu and exploits the resources. This more sophisticated view has led in recent years to a renewed interest in the investigation of environmental factors. The term *human ecology* has now become fashionable for this type of study, but in essence it is a welcome revitalization of the traditional geographic concern with the interrelations between society and habitat.

The Nature of Culture

The terms *society* and *culture* defy exact definition and lead to circular arguments. A society is an organized group of human individuals possessing a distinct culture. This shifts the burden to the definition of culture. Anthropologists, to whom the concept is obviously of particular importance, have discussed it at length, without coming to general agreement (Kroeber and Kluckhohn, 1952). Perhaps it is simplest to say that a specific culture is the total way of life of a people. Or, if one wants to stress the idealized standards rather than the practice, one might say that a culture is a people's design for living. The content of each culture includes

2. Nature and Culture

25

The oasis of Rustaq in Oman, at the southeast corner of the Arabian peninsula.
Walls are made of sun-dried bricks, roofs are flat. Irrigation allows
cultivation of date palms, some near the village, but mainly on the alluvial
fans at the mountains' edge, in background. [A Shell photograph]

systems of belief (ideology), social institutions (organization), industrial skills and tools (technology), and material possessions (resources). A composite and more explicit characterization of a culture is: a historically derived system of standardized forms of behavior, which is acquired by the individual as a member of a society. This statement stresses that culture consists of learned behavior, in contrast to the direct response to inherited biologic drives which are common to all animals including man.

Cultures are dynamic; they are in constant process of change. Essentially change comes in two ways: by invention within the society, or by introduction of something new from without. Of course, the group must accept these innovations before they can become part of its culture.

Invention. The question whether local invention or borrowing from other cultures more effectively shapes the ways of life should be resolved by facts. But preconceived notions of man's inherent creative aptitude, or, just the opposite, of man's limited inventive ability, doubtless influence the interpretation of what facts we have. Consider, for instance, the effect of the environmentalist doctrine. One who believes that the natural environment conditions, if not determines, the way of life, probably will emphasize local invention as man's response to nature's challenge.

Our modern Occidental society, with its purposeful drive for technical innovations, makes it seem that invention is the obvious and major starter of change, everywhere and at all times. The truth, however, is very different, as

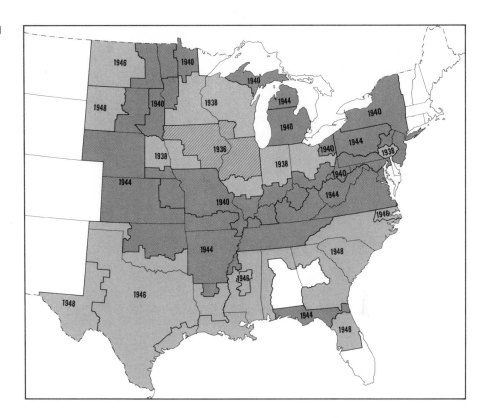

Figure 2–2. THE SPREAD OF HYBRID CORN

Areas with Hybrid Corn

By 1936

By 1938

By 1944

By 1948

Innovations spread rapidly in modern societies, especially if they improve the economic position of individuals, and if governmental information agencies propagate them.

demonstrated in numerous anthropological studies. Indeed, one must conclude that, on the whole, introductions from without, not local inventions, bring about most cultural changes.

Diffusion. The spread of culture elements or complexes from one society to another is called *diffusion*. The manner of its transfer may be by direct contact between peoples or by indirect transmission through a chain of intermediaries. As an example of the latter form, it is well known that the Indian tribes of the northern Great Plains adopted the horse as well as the art of riding and much that went with it without ever having met a Spaniard. Innumerable ideas and things which we now consider as our European heritage actually came into Europe from cradlelands in the Middle East or even China or India. In turn, many culture traits of the modern Occidental world—be they soft drinks, atomic energy, or even the idea of progress itself—spread to other peoples. The same thing happens within our own society with

new inventions. A good example, well documented by various studies, is the diffusion of hybrid corn from its area of origin in Iowa to other states during the 1930s and 1940s (Figure 2–2).

Acculturation

The study of diffusion is concerned with the spread of a culture trait or complex. However, one can also focus attention on a specific culture and see how it is affected by the adoption of foreign traits. The result of the transmission may range from a relatively minor change to virtual assimilation. Somewhere in between these two extremes lies *acculturation,* a useful concept if one can accept its somewhat indeterminate position. The term is most commonly used for "the process of interaction between two societies by which the culture of the society in the subordinate position is drastically modi-

2. Nature and Culture

27

fied to conform to the culture of the dominant society" (Hoebel, 1966, 559).

The dominant society—for instance, the Spanish or Portuguese in Latin America—is usually called the donor; the dominated one—i.e., the Indians—the recipient. However, these positions are not absolute, because the donor group is also a recipient to the extent that it accepts elements (a tool, a food plant, a word) from the other party. Nevertheless, it is in the nature of the definition that the donor society makes the real impact on the other. Even so, the entire culture of the donor may not be available to the recipient, or the latter may not accept all that is offered. A people do not take a foreign element like a patient swallowing a pill from his doctor. Rather, they chew on it, adding their own juices to make it digestible—or they chew it around and reject it.

The present century witnesses great modifications in non-Occidental cultures under the impact of Western civilization. In Japan acculturation has gone quite far. If the term acculturation implies interaction *in process,* most would agree that non-Occidental peoples are largely in the position of recipients, thus becoming more similar to Occidental peoples. However, if we want to judge acculturation by the *result* achieved, we must reserve judgment. The process has not yet run its course; there may be recoils and reversals; and conditions vary greatly from society to society. With the degree of acculturation-in-the-end so uncertain, complete cultural assimilation (resulting in conformity) seems most unlikely. We live in "One World," but it is not likely to become a uniform world. This may be all to the good. Mankind has, on the whole, profited from diversity of ideas and customs. It will continue to do so in the future.

The Concept of Culture in Geography

Though a former generation of geographers emphasized environmentalism, the conclusion need not be that geography ignored cultural factors until recently. One of the founders of modern geography, Alexander von Humboldt (1769–1859), though mainly known for his studies of landforms, climate, and vegetation in Latin America, also examined cultural differences. For instance, he noted that no pastoral nomads inhabited pre-Columbian America, and therefore questioned the popular view that this form of existence is a universal stage in social evolution.

Another outstanding German geographer, Carl Ritter (1779–1859), was primarily interested in the historical growth of cultures in different parts of the world. He thought that divine will had created the earth as a school for man, in which he would advance from crude barbarism to spiritual greatness. Different "natural regions" (mainly defined by landforms) each served a specific purpose in this march of progress. Although this teleological approach (that is, the concern with ultimate ends) is foreign to modern scientific attitude, much remains of value today in Ritter's writings.

Even when Darwinistic notions of adaptation to the environment were at their height, not all geographers subscribed to this view. Friedrich Ratzel (1844–1904), a geographer and ethnologist, was at first beguiled by environmentalism, but afterwards saw the flaws in the argument. In one of his essays he underscored the paramount significance of the cultural factor by declaring: "I could perhaps understand New England without knowing the land, but never without knowing the Puritan immigrants" (Ratzel, 1904, 407).

The founder of modern French geography, Paul Vidal de la Blache (1845–1918), consistently expressed outright opposition to environmental determinism. According to him the earth does not dictate man's behavior. It only offers opportunities. Human society makes the choice. To use his own words:

One must start from the notion that a land is a reservoir containing dormant energies of which nature has planted the seed, but whose use depends on man. It is he who by molding them to his purpose demonstrates his individuality. Man establishes the connection between disparate elements by substituting a purposeful organization of forces for the random effects of local

A census taker (back to camera) in an Andean highland village
in Peru. Some seven million Indians live in isolation, at altitudes between
9,000 and 15,000 feet, in Peru, Ecuador, and Bolivia. The census is
part of a development program jointly undertaken by the three
governments concerned and five international organizations.
[Courtesy of United Nations]

circumstance. In this manner a region acquires identity differentiating it from others, till at length it becomes, as it were, a medal struck in the likeness of a people (Vidal, 1903, 8).

The "choice" man makes is not a free and arbitrary one. It is guided and restrained by the mental and social patterns of the group and its level of technology, in short, its culture. Man conceives the nature of his habitat through the filter of his habits. Vidal's ideas have been refined and new ones added, but he deserves our appreciation for placing the human group and

its way of life, or its life style (*genre de vie*), in the center of geographic study.

The fundamental truth of his observations becomes clear to anyone who reflects on the vastly different ways in which succeeding societies have used the same area. For instance, the physical features of the Upper Great Lakes area are now virtually the same as they were four hundred years ago. Yet, it saw in succession Indian tribes, French fur traders, American lumbermen, miners, and dairy farmers. Today, the opportunity for recreation is one of its main assets. A comparison of land use in modern

Israel with that of less than fifty years ago provides another instructive example.

Perception of the Environment

Culture shapes what men see in their surroundings. Studies of environmental perception, quite fashionable now, have their roots in ideas expressed some fifty years ago by Vidal de la Blache and others of his generation. The British geographer Halford J. Mackinder, for instance, wrote in 1918: "The influence of geographical conditions upon human activities has depended . . . not merely on the realities as we now know them to be and to have been, but even in greater degree on what men imagined in regard to them. . . . Each century has its own geographic perspective" (Mackinder, 1942, 28–30).

When the Portuguese on their initial voyages along the west coast of Africa approached the equator they worried about the hazard of the boiling seas, much the same as airplane builders and pilots discussed the sound barrier not many years ago. Columbus planned his voyage to Asia believing the earth to be much smaller than it is. Americans early in the nineteenth century thought the western interior of their country to be a great desert. The familiar Mercator world map, showing the Americas separated from the Old World by broad ocean moats, bolstered American isolationism.

Environment-as-perceived is called the *operational* environment, to distinguish it from the *cognized* environment, which is as objective science knows it from all available facts. The difference becomes clear if one compares the operational Atlantic of Columbus's voyage with the cognized Atlantic today. The former explains why Columbus decided to sail and why he thought he had reached the Indies; the latter shows what he actually accomplished.

Divergent cultural views often cause misunderstanding when technicians from Western countries, coming into another culture area, introduce new tools or practices. Occidental culture looks upon nature as a physical matter to be manipulated for man's material comfort or power. Many other cultures regard man as part of nature; he does not dominate it, but must conform to the rules. An innovation that may threaten the cosmic harmony is apt to be viewed with suspicion. For instance, in various parts of Indonesia rice is harvested with a little knife no larger than a safety-razor blade. According to local beliefs this preserves the soul of the rice or appeases the rice goddess. Any other way of harvesting is bound to bring disaster. In East Africa, cattle ownership gives prestige, and the more cattle, the higher the social status. Very little direct economic benefit is derived from the half-wild animals; worse, the large herds overgraze the land and cause serious soil erosion. Sound land use demands a reduction in livestock, but the cultural attitude is an obstacle to better resource management. It is easier to see the mote in another man's eye than the beam in one's own. Surely, Occidental culture is not without its own restrictive attitudes which thwart better use of resources. In the United States the tradition of self-government for small units creates much friction in the efficient organization of metropolitan areas. For instance, in the metropolitan area of the Twin Cities Minneapolis–St. Paul there are not less than 300 units of local government with taxing authority.

The perceptual approach clarifies the meaning of a "natural resource." It is an element or property of the earth that is useful to man. Man's economic needs and technical skills determine what is useful; in other words, his cultural appraisal decides what constitutes a natural resource. Obsidian was just a glassy volcanic rock, no resource, until prehistoric man discovered its value as a cutting tool. Acorns were a major resource to the Californian Indians, but have very little value now. Rare metals and other substances unknown or ignored fifty years ago, such as uranium and thorium for nuclear fuel, are eagerly sought for today. Districts and whole regions rise or decline when natural resources are discovered, exhausted, or replaced by cheaper substitutes. But even things long known can take on new meaning as a resource. For instance, skiing and water sports have brought prosperity to many mountain and lake districts. A natural resource, then, is a relative concept, relative to culture. It is a cultural achievement.

The Cultural Landscape

Instead of asking how the earth influences man one can reverse the question: How has man changed the earth? The surface of the earth, as modified by human action, is called the cultural landscape.

Creation myths of many peoples express the thought that the earth was designed for man. The Old Testament contains the same idea: the Creator commands man to take possession of the earth. Opinions differ on how well man has managed his domain. For many centuries the dominant thought was that man and nature lived in harmony, although more critical views were not lacking. Already Plato observed that Attica had become "a skeleton of a body wasted by disease" due to man-caused soil erosion. In modern times the theme of man as a destructive agent was eloquently expressed by the American statesman and scholar George Perkins Marsh (1801–1881) in his book *Man and Nature, or Physical Geography as Modified by Human Action* (1864). In his view, it was not the earth that made man, but man who made the earth, and worse, who despoiled it by ruthless exploitation. He warned Americans to exercise restraint in taming their vast new domain, lest it be turned into a wasteland like parts of the Old World. For this reason Marsh has been called "the fountainhead of the conservation movement in the United States" (Mumford, 1931, 78).

Whether man acts in a destructive or in a constructive manner, there is no doubt that his actions transform the earth surface. Man must be ranked with the forces of the physical and biotic world as a landscape-forming agent. The American geographer who is mainly responsible for the modern interest in the study of the cultural landscape is Carl O. Sauer (born 1889), for many years professor of geography at the University of California, Berkeley. He and his pupils stress the need to understand the present landscape as the result of long-time processes involving the changing relations between man and land. Sequent occupance by different cultures has left its marks. Each new generation of inhabitants must take into account what its predecessors have wrought. What we call so glibly "natural prairie," "primeval forest," and "wildlife" actually are ecosystems induced or at least modified by man in the course of thousands if not hundreds of thousands of years. And such "natural disasters" as floods and dust storms are often in part due to man's intervention with nature.

In addition to the intellectual satisfaction of comprehending the earth as the home of man, there is great practical worth in the study of the cultural landscape. Regional and city planning aim to bring harmony and efficiency to our environment, with "a place for everything and everything in its place." A prerequisite for any plan is full knowledge of the existing landscape so that we may preserve what is of value and change what is obsolete. It is no wonder that many geographers here and abroad find careers in regional planning.

The Distribution of Mankind

Even a cursory inspection of the distribution of the world's population makes readily apparent the complexity of interrelations between culture and nature (Figure 2–3). Most of the 3,400 million human beings crowd together in only a few parts of the earth, while vast areas remain virtually empty. The three major areas of concentration are East Asia, South Asia, and Europe; two minor ones are Southeast Asia and the central-east part of North America. These lands together contain some 2,500 million people, or about three-quarters of the world's population. Adding a few scattered small clusters in Africa, Southwest Asia, Latin America, and on the west coast of the United States brings the proportion of those living in areas of relatively high density to more than four-fifths of the total population (Figure 2–4, Table 2–1).

2. Nature and Culture

Figure 2–3. WORLD: POPULATION DISTRIBUTION

Dot-and-circle population distribution maps have an advantage over density maps in that they show the actual locations and concentrations of people. A careful observer of the map can infer the relative densities of population groupings in different parts of the earth.

100,000 Persons

City Populations in millions

- •   0.5 - 1
- •   1 - 2
- ●   2 - 5
- ⬤   over 5

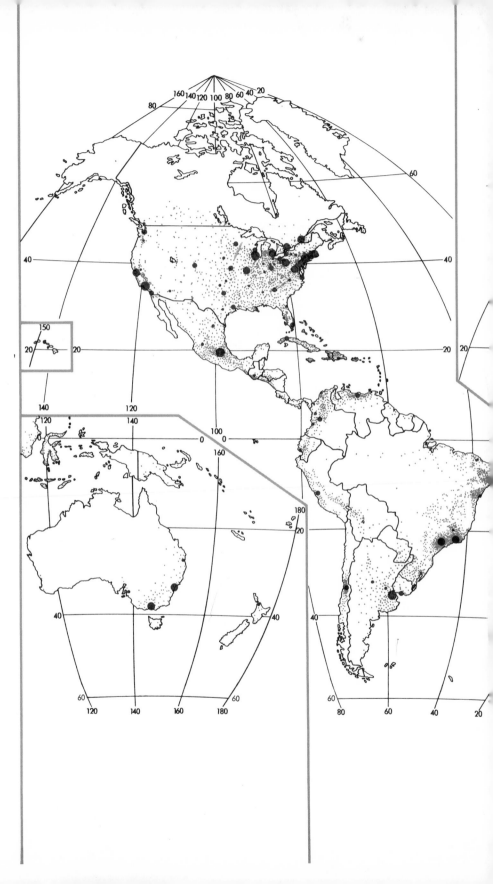

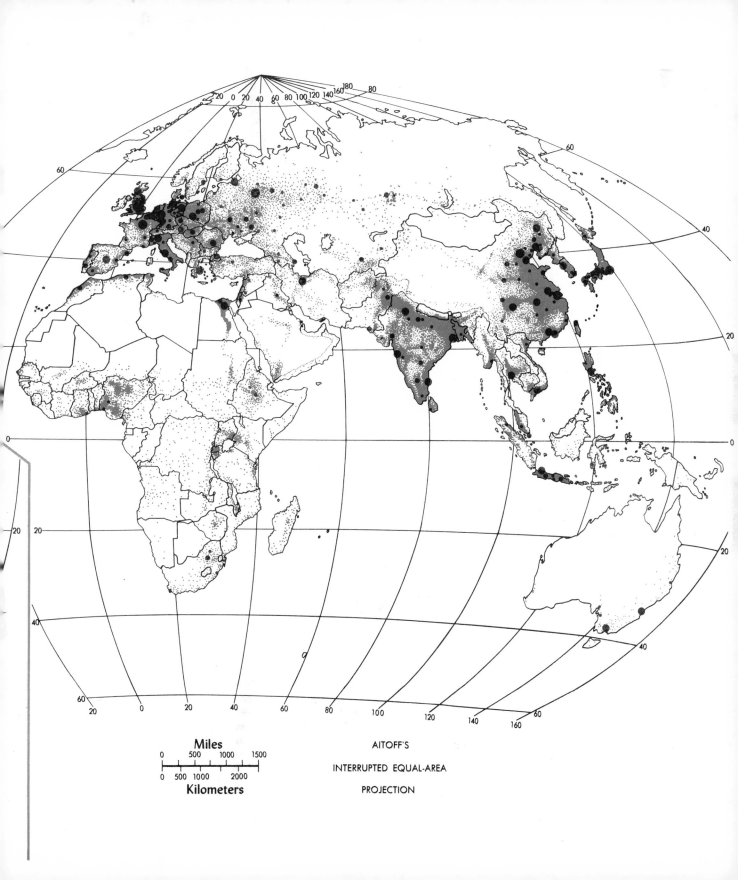

Miles

0   500   1000   1500

0   500   1000   2000

Kilometers

AITOFF'S

INTERRUPTED EQUAL-AREA

PROJECTION

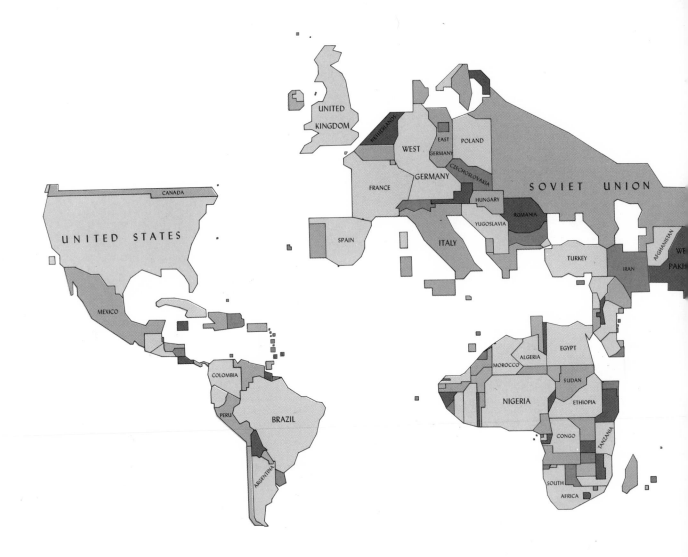

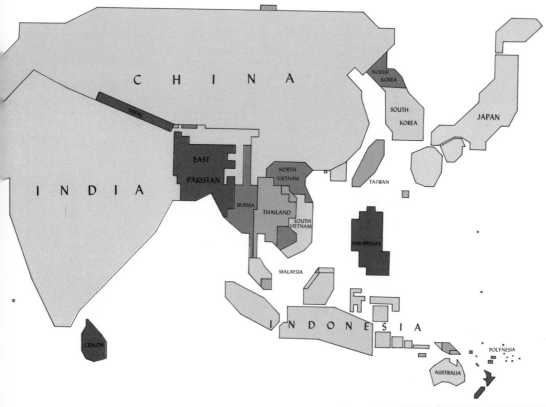

One Million Population

Figure 2–4. WORLD: NATIONAL POPULATIONS

The area occupied by each country is proportional to its population as estimated for 1965. This cartogram is a good antidote for the hypnotic effect of the conventional map showing the surface area of countries. Some countries are highly distorted in shape, and others do not touch their proper neighbors. The marked east-west extension of the cartogram is due to (1) relatively small populations in the southern hemisphere, and (2) small populations in northern latitudes of the northern hemisphere, except for northwestern Europe. All countries with over ten million inhabitants in 1965 are named.

*2. Nature
and
Culture*

It is tempting to link this gross distribution to the physical alignments of the earth. Indeed, there are broad correlations between the arrangement of the population and the features of the earth (Figures 2–5 and 2–6). Lands deficient in moisture (deserts) and those deficient in heat (polar ice caps, tundras, and subpolar forests) are very sparsely occupied, if at all. In equatorial lowlands, the opposite condition—abundant moisture and heat throughout the year—also appears to deter settlement. Mountain lands, whether because of inaccessibility, low oxygen content of the air, low temperatures, or stony soils, also tend to be areas of light settlement. In contrast, the lowlands of the humid mid-latitudes and subtropics are, on the whole, the habitats of most of the world's population.

But closer scrutiny of the map points up many situations which cannot be squared with environmental factors. For example, in the wet tropical lowlands the population densities are in general highest in Asia, lower in Africa, and

Table 2–1. Areas of Population Concentration (millions)

East Asia		*South Asia*		*Europe**	
China, mainland	720	India	495	Southern Europe	103
Taiwan	13	Pakistan	105	Central Europe	132
North Korea	12	Ceylon	12	Northwestern Europe	212
South Korea	29	Nepal	10	Soviet Union in Europe	170
Japan	99	Other states	2		
Hong Kong	4				
TOTAL	877		624		617
Percent of world population	25.8		18.4		17.9

Southeast Asia†		*Central-east of North America*		*Other Clusters*	
Mainland	112	Northeast United States	98	United States Pacific Coast	20
Islands	143	Southeast Canada	15	Central Mexico	30
				Southeast South America	90
				Northwest Africa	25
				East African Highlands	35
				Nigeria	58
				Levant‡	42
TOTAL	255		113		300
Percent of world population	7.5		3.3		8.8

* Southern Europe: Portugal, Spain, Italy, Albania, and Greece. Central Europe: Finland, Austria, and the "People's Democracies." Northwestern Europe: Scandinavia, British Isles, Low Countries, West Germany, France, and Switzerland.
† Mainland: Burma, Thailand, Laos, Cambodia, North and South Vietnam, Malaya, and Singapore. Islands: Indonesia, Philippines, Sabah, Brunei, Sarawak, and Portuguese Timor.
‡ Levant: Egypt, Israel, Lebanon, and Syria.

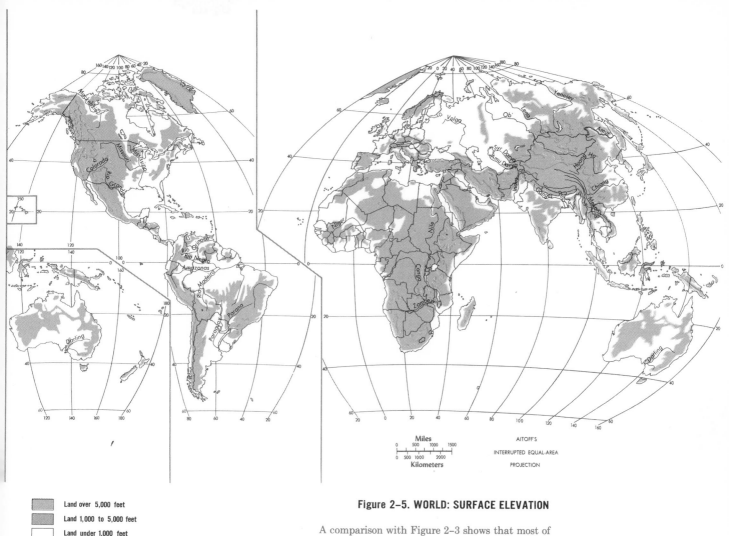

Land over 5,000 feet

Land 1,000 to 5,000 feet

Land under 1,000 feet

Figure 2–5. WORLD: SURFACE ELEVATION

A comparison with Figure 2–3 shows that most of
the world's population lives at low elevations,
whether plains or hill lands. However, note significant
exceptions, especially in the tropical highlands of
Africa and Central and South America.

quite low in South America. Many of India's
teeming millions live in a hot climate with a
short and uncertain rainy season, not much different from the almost empty wet-and-dry savanna lands of Brazil. Or, within Asia, there
is a striking contrast between the crowded con-

ditions in India, China, North Vietnam, and
Java, and the moderate to low density that
prevails in most of Southeast Asia. The ice-
scoured subpolar forest lands of northern Europe support a population which, though sparse,
greatly exceeds that of the similar environment

*2. Nature
and
Culture*

37

in North America, which is still virtually out-side the *ecumene* (the inhabited world). In many parts of Central and South America more people live in highlands than in lowlands.

These anomalies—and many more could be cited—support the contention that we must consider the quality of the habitat in the con-text of a society's capacities and needs. Among these cultural factors the level of technology and form of economy are the immediate and concrete forces through which societies manipu-late their environments. Less tangible but none-theless important are the spiritual forces that shape cultural values and attitudes. These affect economic behavior and, in turn, are condi-tioned by the economy. Furthermore, historical circumstance always must be taken into ac-count. Many contrasts between Europe and the Americas in density, dispersion, and pattern of population are due to the fact that the New World was colonized only recently.

With these thoughts in mind, the inspection of a population map becomes more than learn-ing mere data on the whereabouts of people. It should raise a multitude of exciting questions about the ways different societies have met the challenge of their particular physical environ-ments. The next chapter suggests answers to some of these questions by examining the role of technology in the rise of civilizations.

Figure 2–6. WORLD: CLIMATES

A comparison with Figure 2–3 shows a fair correla-tion between population concentrations and the humid mid-latitude climates. However, there are numerous and significant exceptions, demonstrating that climate is not the determinant of population distribution.

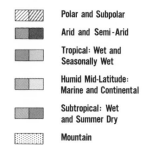

Polar and Subpolar

Arid and Semi-Arid

Tropical: Wet and Seasonally Wet

Humid Mid-Latitude: Marine and Continental

Subtropical: Wet and Summer Dry

Mountain

Citations

Hoebel, E. A. *Anthropology,* New York, rev. ed. 1966.

Kroeber, A. L., and Kluckhohn, C. "Culture: A Critical Review of Concepts and Definitions," *Papers of the Peabody Museum of Archaeology and Eth-nology,* 47 (1952): no. 1.

Mackinder, H. J. *Democratic Ideals and Reality,* London, 1942 (first issued in 1918).

Marsh, G. P. *Man and Nature, or Physical Geography as Modified by Human Action,* New York, 1864; 2d ed. *The Earth as Modified by Human Action,* New York, 1874.

Mumford, L. *The Brown Decades,* New York, 1931.

Ratzel, F. "Einige Aufgaben einer politischen Ethnographie," *Zeitschrift für Sozialwissenschaft,* 3 (1900): 1–19. Reprinted in Helmolt, H. *Kleine Schriften von Friedrich Ratzel* 2, München-Berlin, 1904.

Rostlund, E. "Twentieth Century Magic," *Landscape,* 5 (1956): 23–26. Re-

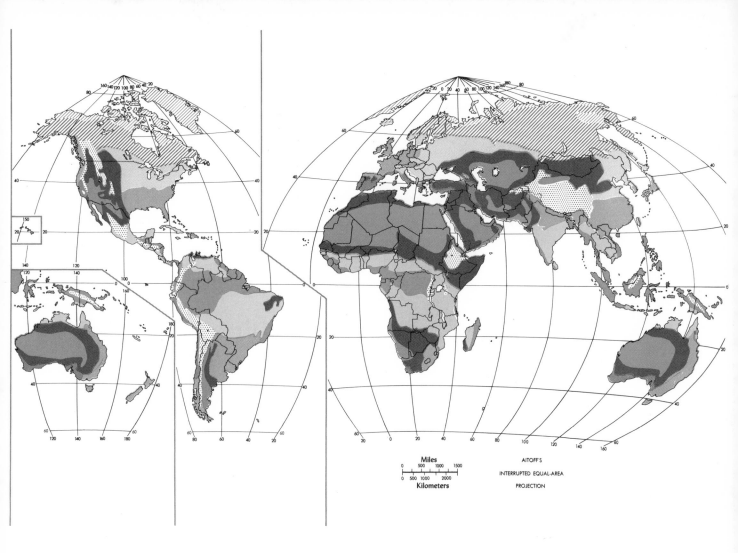

Miles

0   500   1000   1500

0   500 1000   2000

Kilometers

AITOFF'S

INTERRUPTED EQUAL-AREA

PROJECTION

printed in Wagner, P. L., and Mikesell, M. W. (eds.) *Readings in Cultural Geography,* Chicago, 1962, 48–53.

van Paassen, C. *The Classical Tradition in Geography,* Groningen, Netherlands, 1957.

Van Valkenburg, S., and Huntington, E. *Europe,* New York, 1935. [Map]

Vidal de la Blache, P. *Tableau de la géographie de la France,* Paris, 1903.

Further Readings

For a discussion or a sampling of the (translated) thoughts of the founding fathers of modern geography:

Brunhes, J. *Human Geography,* New York and Chicago, 1952. (A translation

2. Nature and Culture

39

of an abridged French edition of 1947; this classic was first published in 1910.) While Vidal stressed the *genre de vie,* Brunhes emphasized the impress of the way of life on the landscape.

Harrison Church, R. J. "The French School of Geography," in Taylor, G. T. (ed.) *Geography in the Twentieth Century,* London and New York, 1957. An informative and analytical survey.

Humboldt, A. von *Views of Nature* or *Aspects of Nature.* (Translated from *Ansichten der Natur,* Stuttgart, 1808, 1849.)

Ritter, C. *Comparative Geography* (translated by W. L. Gage), New York, 1865.

————. *Geographical Studies* (translated by W. L. Gage), New York, 1861.

Sorre, M. *Les Fondements de la géographie humaine,* Paris, 1943–1952. (Vol. 1, *Fondements biologiques;* vol. 2, *Les Techniques;* vol. 3, *L'habitat.*)

————. "The Concept of Genre de Vie," in Wagner, P. L., and Mikesell, M. W. (eds.) *Readings in Cultural Geography,* Chicago, 1962, 399–415. Originally printed in *Annales de géographie,* 57 (1948): 97–108, 193–204.

Stoddart, D. S. "Darwin's Impact on Geography," *Annals of the Association of American Geographers,* 56 (1966): 683–698.

Vidal de la Blache, P. *Principles of Human Geography,* New York, 1926; London, 1959. These translations of an incomplete and posthumously published manuscript give a fairly good idea of Vidal's views.

Wanklyn, H. *Friedrich Ratzel, A Biographical Memoir and Bibliography,* Cambridge and New York, 1961. In the absence of translations of Ratzel's writings, this is a valuable introduction to the father of "anthropogeography."

Wrigley, E. A. "Changes in the Philosophy of Geography," in Chorley, R. J., and Haggett, P. (eds.) *Frontiers of Geographical Teaching,* London, 1965, 3–20. Useful overview of important shifts in geographical thinking since the eighteenth century.

Representative on "environmentalism":

Brigham, A. P. *Geographic Influences in American History,* New York, 1903.

Bryan, P. W. *Man's Adaptation to Nature,* London, 1933.

Huntington, E. *Civilization and Climate,* New York, 1920.

————, and Cushing, S. W. *Principles of Human Geography,* New York, 1934.

————. *Mainsprings of Civilization,* New York, 1945. Reprinted in paperback edition.

Markham, S. F. *Climate and the Energy of Nations,* New York, 1942.

Semple, E. C. *American History and Its Geographic Conditions,* Boston and New York, 1903.

————. *Influences of Geographic Environment,* New York, 1911.

Taylor, G. T. *Environment and Nation: Geographical Factors in the Cultural and Political History of Europe,* Toronto and Chicago, 1936.

Comments on "environmentalism":

Febvre, L. *A Geographical Introduction to History,* London, 1950. (Translation of *La Terre et l'évolution humaine,* Paris, 1923.)

Rostlund, E. "Twentieth Century Magic," see above.

Sauer, C. O. "Cultural Geography," *Encyclopaedia of the Social Sciences,* 6 (1931): 621–623. Reprinted in Wagner, P. L., and Mikesell, M. W. (eds.) *Readings in Cultural Geography,* Chicago, 1962, 30–34.

Sorre, M. "The Role of Historical Explanation in Human Geography," in Wagner, P. L., and Mikesell, M. W. (eds.) *Readings in Cultural Geography,* Chicago, 1962, 44–47.

Spate, O. H. K. "Toynbee and Huntington: A Study in Determinism," *Geographical Journal,* 118 (1952): 406–428.

Tatham, G. "Environmentalism and Possibilism," in Taylor, G. T. (ed.) *Geography in the Twentieth Century,* London and New York, 1957.

Other studies on the relation of man and environment, including some recent work on the ecological approach in geography:

Bates, M. *Where Winter Never Comes,* New York, 1952. An optimistic view of the tropical lands.

Eyre, S. R. "Determinism and the Ecological Approach to Geography," *Geography,* 49 (1964): 369–376.

——, and Jones, S. R. J. (eds.) *Geography as Human Ecology: Methodology by Example,* New York, 1966.

Gourou, P. *The Tropical World,* London, 1953. A pessimistic view of the tropical lands.

Herbertson, A. J. "The Major Natural Regions: An Essay in Systematic Geography," *Geographical Journal,* 25 (1902): 300ff.

Meggers, B. T. "Environmental Limitations on the Development of Culture," *American Anthropologist,* 56 (1954): 801–824.

Stoddart, D. R. "Geography and the Ecological Approach: The Ecosystem as a Geographic Principle and Method," *Geography,* 50 (1965): 242–251.

U.S. Department of Agriculture. *Climate and Man,* Washington, D.C., 1941. (*Yearbook of Agriculture,* 1941.)

The concept of culture has been discussed by numerous anthropologists. Especially helpful in relation to geography are:

Benedict, R. *Patterns of Culture,* New York, 1934. Also in paperback reprint.

Forde, C. D. *Habitat, Economy, and Society,* London, 1934.

Foster, G. M. *Culture and Conquest: America's Spanish Heritage,* New York, 1960. A discussion of "conquest culture," culture transfer, and acculturation.

Goldschmidt, W. *Man's Way,* Cleveland and New York, 1959.

Hall, E. T. *The Silent Language,* New York, 1959.

Keesing, F. M. *Cultural Anthropology: The Science of Custom,* New York, 1958.

Kluckhohn, C. *Mirror for Man,* New York, 1949. Also in paperback reprint.

Kroeber, A. L. *Anthropology,* New York, 1948.

Social Science Research Council " 'Acculturation': An Explanatory Formulation," *American Anthropologist,* 56 (1954): 973–1002.

White, L. A. *The Science of Culture,* New York, 1949. Also in paperback reprint.

From the large and growing literature on cultural, social, and historical geography a few titles have been selected on their own merit as well as a guide to further reading:

Bobek, H. "The Main Stages in Socioeconomic Evolution from a Geographical Point of View," reprinted in Wagner, P. L., and Mikesell, M. W. (eds.) *Readings in Cultural Geography,* Chicago, 1962, 218–247.

Brown, R. H. *Mirror for Americans: Likeness of the Eastern Seaboard, 1810,* New York, 1943. A fascinating portrait of the Atlantic coast, seen through the eyes of a fictitious geographer of the period.

———. *Historical Geography of the United States,* New York, 1948.

Clark, A. H. "Historical Geography," in James, P. E., and Jones, C. F. (eds.) *American Geography: Inventory and Prospect,* Syracuse, 1954, 70–105.

Darby, H. C. (ed.) *An Historical Geography of England before 1800,* London, 1936.

——— (ed.) *The Domesday Geography of England,* 5 vols., London, 1952–.

East, W. G. *An Historical Geography of Europe,* London, 1948.

Gauld, W. A. *Man, Nature, and Time,* London, 1946.

Gulley, J. L. M. "The Turnerian Frontier: A Study in the Migration of Ideas," *Tijdschrift voor Economische en Sociale Geografie,* 50 (1959): 65–72, 81–91.

Hägerstrand, T. "The Propagation of Innovation Waves," in Wagner, P. L., and Mikesell, M. W. (eds.) *Readings in Cultural Geography,* Chicago, 1962, 355–368. Originally printed in *Lund Studies in Geography, Series B, Human Geography,* 4 (1952).

Lowenthal, D. "Geography, Experience, and Imagination: Toward a Geographical Epistemology," *Annals of the Association of American Geographers,* 51 (1961): 241–260.

Lukermann, F. "The Concept of Location in Classical Geography," *Annals of the Association of American Geographers,* 51 (1961): 194–210.

Sauer, C. O. "Foreword to Historical Geography," *Annals of the Association of American Geographers,* 31 (1941): 1–24. Also reprinted in the following title.

———. *Land and Life: A Selection from the Writings of Carl Ortwin Sauer* (edited, with introduction, by John Leighly), Berkeley and Los Angeles, 1963. An excellent collection of stimulating essays on historical and cultural geography by one of America's leading scholars.

Thomas, W. L. (ed.) *Man's Role in Changing the Face of the Earth,* Chicago, 1956. An international symposium in the footsteps of G. P. Marsh.

Wagner, P. L. *The Human Use of the Earth,* New York, 1960.

———, and Mikesell, M. W. (eds.) *Readings in Cultural Geography,* Chicago, 1962. A valuable collection of papers on social and cultural geography.

Wheatley, P. *The Golden Khersonese: Studies in the Historical Geography of the Malay Peninsula before* A.D. *1580,* Kuala Lumpur, 1961.

Whittlesey, D. "Sequent Occupance," *Annals of the Association of American Geographers,* 19 (1929): 162–165.

Zimmermann, E. W. *Resources and Industries,* New York, 1933, rev. ed. 1951. An excellent analysis of the concept of resources. The first ten chapters have been reissued as Hunker, H. L. (ed.) *Erich W. Zimmermann's Introduction to World Resources,* New York, 1964.

Works on population distribution, including maps:

Ahmad, E. "The Rural Population of Bihar," *Geographical Review,* 51 (1961): 253–276.

Ahmad, N. "The Pattern of Rural Settlement in East Pakistan," *Geographical Review,* 46 (1956): 388–398.

Beaujeu-Garnier, J. *Géographie de la population,* 2 vols., Paris, 1956 and 1958.

Burgdorfer, F. (ed.) *World Atlas of Population,* Hamburg, 1954–. A loose-leaf atlas of small-scale dot population maps for major regions of the world.

Hooson, D. J. M. "The Distribution of Population as the Essential Geographical Expression," *Canadian Geographer,* 17 (1960): 10–20.

James, P. E. "The Geographic Study of Population," in James, P. E., and Jones, C. F. (eds.) *American Geography: Inventory and Prospect,* Syracuse, N.Y., 106–122.

Lowenthal, D. "Population Contrasts in the Guianas," *Geographical Review,* 50 (1960): 41–58.

Monkhouse, F. J., and Wilkinson, H. R. *Maps and Diagrams: Their Compilation and Construction,* New York, 1963. Contains much information on the mapping of distributions and densities.

Trewartha, G. T. "A Case for Population Geography," *Annals of the Association of American Geographers,* 43 (1953): 71–97.

———, and Zelinsky, W. "Population Distribution and Change in Korea," *Geographical Review,* 44 (1954): 1–26.

——— and ———. "Population Patterns in Tropical Africa; the Population Geography of Belgian Africa," *Annals of the Association of American Geographers,* 44 (1954): 135–193.

———. "New Population Maps of Uganda, Kenya, Nyasaland, and Gold Coast," *Annals of the Association of American Geographers,* 47 (1957): 41–58.

———. "New Population Maps of China," *Geographical Review,* 47 (1957): 234–239.

Witthauer, K. "Die Bevölkerung der Erde: Verteilung und Dynamik," *Petermanns Geographische Mitteilungen,* Supplement 265, Gotha, 1958. Impressive collection of population statistics, worldwide in scope.

Wright, J. K. "Some Measures of Distribution," *Annals of the Association of American Geographers,* 27 (1937): 177–211.

Zelinsky, W. *Prologue to Population Geography,* Englewood Cliffs, N.J., 1966.

3. Technology: Origins and Diffusion

Tools and skills are part of culture. They are the means to control and transform nature and to increase productivity. Progress in making tools set the ancestors of man apart from other primates. Tremendous technical achievements distinguish the modern Western world from other cultures. Singling out technology for special attention at this point is not to say that it is the mainspring in the progress and the differentiation of human groups. Certainly, technology affects other facets of culture, but the reverse is equally true. Tools, after all, are not just things. They express the inner world of ideas, which comprises the total experience of a culture.

The purpose of this chapter is (1) to review the conquest of nature by early societies, especially those of the Middle East, but also America and China; (2) to describe briefly the emergence of the West to a position of technological dominance in the modern era. Essentially, the technical assemblage that ancient civilizations achieved governed the ceiling of productivity for many centuries—until the advent of modern science and industry. In sequence, different places at different times led in technical progress. Ideas spread from the centers of invention to other parts of the world, but not all. The contrast between "developed" and "underdeveloped" countries, of which we are now so keenly aware, has persisted throughout human history.

I. Introduction

The Old Stone Age (Paleolithic)

The Pleistocene period is thought to have lasted about a million years, ending around ten thousand years ago. In this time span, periods of widespread glaciation alternated with retreat of the glaciers. Advance of the ice cover resulted from more snow accumulating in winter than melting in summer. Winters were not extremely cold—otherwise there would have been little precipitation—and summers were short, cloudy, rainy, and cool. Areas of arid climate were relatively small. As the ice held more and more water, sea levels dropped, exposing the continental shelves. Rivers increased in velocity as they descended to the lower sea levels and cut deeply into valleys, leaving terraces to show the former height of the valley floors.

During the interglacial periods the climate was drier and warmer, causing glaciers to shrink and deserts to expand. The released waters returned to the oceans, raising their levels and causing large coastal plains to disappear below the sea. Rivers flowed more slowly and covered their floodplains with large swamps.

Plants, animals, and early man had to adjust to the slow but drastic alterations of their habitat. It is far from clear how man evolved into a species so different from other primates. Using only the feet for walking freed his hands

44

as manipulative organs. One may further reason that the larger head—to accommodate a larger brain—required the infant to be born earlier, necessitating long postnatal care outside the mother, who carried it in her arms. These changes by themselves, however, would only have created another animal, not man.

Speech, tools, and fire have been called "the tripod of culture." To master all three must have taken a long time. Articulate speech, a function of the brain, means using sound clusters to express symbols, a very different matter from the sounds apes make to transmit direct experience. Language enabled man to communicate his thoughts to his companions, to exchange and accumulate experience, and to unite a group in a common world of meanings and values. Not only could man learn from others, but his reflective generalizing thought made it possible for him to improve on what he had learned, to innovate, reorganize, and create.

Apes sometimes use tools—a stick to reach a fruit, a stone to kill a scorpion—but man became a *toolmaking* creature. Manual skills, too, depend primarily on initiation and coordination in the brain. Tools supplemented hands and teeth, thus greatly increasing man's ability to use his environment. The first things he made were wooden clubs, pointed shafts for spears, and rough-shaped stones with sharp edges for cutting, scraping, and chopping. Though no evidence survives, early man may have used sinews or cordage for snaring animals and for lashing in general.

Man must have used fire first by capturing it from natural conflagrations: volcanic activity, lightning, burning coal or gas seepages, or from spontaneous combustion. Keeping the hearth fire burning was probably the task of the woman and mother, kept close to the home base by the need to care for helpless infants. When it came to *making* fire, man had to depend on tools. The widely different devices employed by primitive peoples today suggest that fire making was invented independently in various places.

What kind of life did early man lead? Women naturally assumed the task of protecting and nurturing children during the protracted state of immaturity. They did, however, forage around the campsite for roots, seeds, berries, and edible leaves, as well as grubs and other easily caught creatures. The men were the hunters, roaming over much wider areas, banding together to overpower the prey, and sharing the kill among themselves and their families. Here we notice further important distinctions between apes and man: division of labor between the sexes, and sharing of the food supply. Fire, used for food preparation, widened the range of edibles and caused changes in nutrition through chemical transformation of organic matter. Fire also provided light, thus lengthening the workday and extending man's living space into deep caves which hitherto he had avoided.

There is much speculation whether early man was essentially a hunter and thus carnivorous, or chiefly a plant gatherer and eater like his simian ancestors. More likely he was both; emphasis on one or the other source depended on where he lived. In the tropical forest few game animals were available on the ground level accessible to man, but there were plenty of tubers and other edible plant parts. In contrast, subpolar steppes (tundra) and woodlands were relatively poor in plants fit for human consumption, but rich in game animals. Tidal beaches, river and lakeshores too must have provided a fairly large and secure animal protein intake.

During the early and middle Paleolithic, man's progress was slow. However, during the late Old Stone Age, which coincides with the last 100,000 to 50,000 years of the Pleistocene, he made great advances. In this period the modern type of man—*Homo sapiens*—developed. He fashioned specialized tools in a great variety for hunting, fishing, and gathering and for domestic tasks. He had used flint for toolmaking for a long time, since it occurred in many places, but now he also adapted bone and ivory. Tools found hundreds of miles from their raw material source prove that there was long-distance trade in special stones for the ancient crafts.

Archaeologic discoveries of Upper Paleolithic

3. Technology: Origins and Diffusion

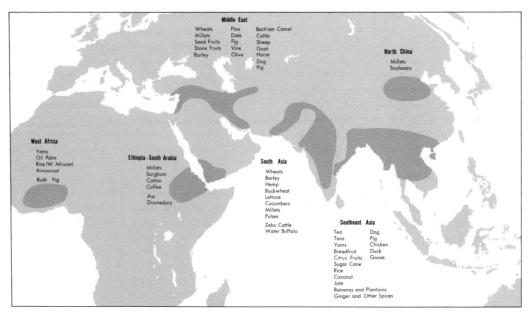

Figure 3–1. OLD WORLD: PLANT AND ANIMAL DOMESTICATION

The place of origin of many agricultural plants and animals is not known for certain. The map therefore shows names of several domesticates as originating in more than one place. Based in part on Sauer, 1952.

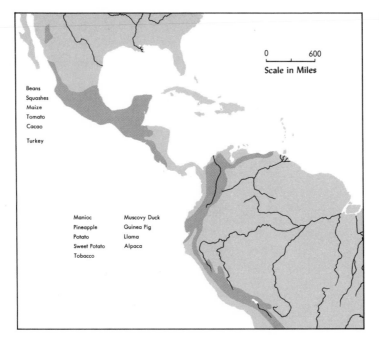

Figure 3–2. NEW WORLD: PLANT AND ANIMAL DOMESTICATION

Based in part on Sauer, 1952.

Figure 3–3. THE FERTILE CRESCENT

The dark area is the Fertile Crescent. The Persian Gulf penetrated further inland in ancient times than it does now. The dots indicate locations where evidence of earliest agriculture has been found (in the north and around the Dead Sea); also the sites of the earliest cities, in the lower Tigris and Euphrates Valley.

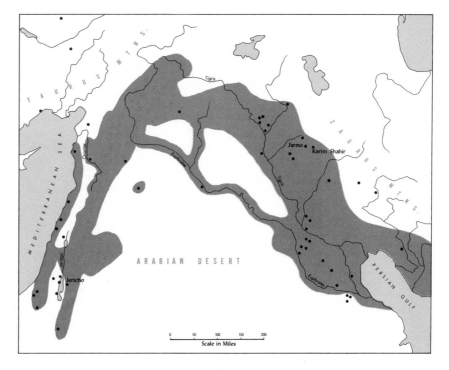

sites in western Europe—variously estimated at ten to twenty thousand years old—indicate that the hunting peoples of that time lived in comparative comfort and had a fairly complex social life. Their possession of the bow, and probably the spear-thrower, enabled them to kill ample numbers of the large mammals that roamed the tundralike steppes and open woodlands south of the retreating ice cap. The cave paintings in southern France, probably intended as hunting magic, are not only impressive as art, but also give an idea how these hunters lived.

The New Stone Age (Neolithic)

The Paleolithic was the era of hunting and gathering with chipped stone tools. The term Neolithic formerly referred to the cultural stage when man learned to grind and polish stone, but present-day usage emphasizes the achievement of agriculture and often also pottery.

Intensive archaeologic research has revealed to us the cradles of Middle Eastern and American civilizations. Present evidence points to these regions as the earliest sites of agriculture. This does not exclude, though, the possibility of early and independent origins elsewhere. Some scholars argue that Southeast Asia and West Africa were hearths of early crop cultivation; this may well be true, but proof of their relative antiquity is lacking (Figures 3–1 and 3–2). India and China had early civilizations, but it is not known whether their initial agriculture was an indigenous achievement or derived from other lands (Harris, 1967).

The Middle East

Surrounding the Syrian desert lies a sickle-shaped zone traditionally called the Fertile Crescent (Figure 3–3). It curves from the coastal areas of Palestine and Syria eastward to the

3. Technology: Origins and Diffusion

47

alluvial plain of the Euphrates and Tigris and is backed by the heights of the Lebanon-Taurus-Zagros mountains. Recent archaeologic finds indicate that the origin of agriculture lay not in the bottomlands of the great rivers but at some 2,500- to 5,000-feet altitude in the intermontane basins and valleys. These uplands receive some 10 to 25 inches of rain, mainly in winter; it appears that the precipitation some ten thousand years ago was approximately the same. In the open woodlands roamed the wild ancestors of goats, sheep, and cattle, and among the grasses were the forebears of wheat and barley.

This hilly zone offered a great variety of natural habitat niches, each with its own complex of plant and animal communities. It was almost like a natural field experiment station for early man as he approached the threshold of agriculture. How the domestication of plants and animals got started is not known. The people of this period, still mainly food collectors, learned how to manipulate some biotic elements of their environment to their benefit. Indisputable evidence of village farming communities appears in recent excavations at Jarmo, on the inward slopes of the Zagros mountains of Kurdistan, at Haçilar and Çatal Hüyük in southwestern Turkey, and near Jericho, Jordan. By means of the radiocarbon 14 method these sites have been dated at 7000–6500 B.C. Here were found remains of six-row barley, three varieties of domesticated wheat, two kinds of pea, and bones of domesticated goats, sheep, and possibly cattle and pigs (Braidwood, 1960, 134; Harris, 1967, 93). Tools made of obsidian point to external trade, since this material must have been brought from Anatolia, well to the north.

The Beginnings of Civilization. Early agriculture in the uplands depended on rainfall. The small gardening plots, worked by hand tools, were probably abandoned after a few years for new clearings of fresh fertility. Before 5000 B.C. cultivators began to move down the mountain flanks into the lowland of the Tigris and Euphrates. Here they had to adjust to a very different set of environmental conditions.

As the meltwater from the mountains runs off, the rivers flood the lower plain in April or May and deposit their silt. The fertility of the soil, however, is countered by the arid climate and the fierce summer heat. Crops planted in the fall need irrigation from the rivers, which by that time have retreated to their channels. It is not known exactly how and when the lowland farmers devised the system of canals and ditches to divert river water to their fields, but it is likely that water management allowed the use of permanent fields instead of the shifting cultivation as practiced in the hills. Another important advance came with the invention of the plow and the use of oxen to pull it. The triad of grain, plow, and draft animal established field agriculture in its essentials.

The arts of pottery and probably weaving were already known in the early farming communities. Metallurgy came later. It started with the use of native copper, followed by silver and gold. More important for practical purposes was the discovery, around 3500 B.C., that a mixture of copper and tin produced the hard alloy, bronze. But tin was scarce, and it is likely that bronze weapons and tools were for the rich only, while the common man continued to use stone, wood, and bone, or baked brick. In time most of the tin had to be brought from large deposits in the Danube Basin and along the coasts of western Europe. This attests to the existence of long-distance commerce. Doubtless goods other than tin—as well as ideas—spread along these trade routes (Figure 3–4).

Transportation had relied on man and beast as pack carriers and on rowing vessels until between 3500 and 3000 B.C. Then the wheel came into use for vehicles and the sail for ships, both permitting greater loads. The Minoans of Crete and the Phoenicians rose to importance chiefly because they served as middlemen between the civilizations of the south and east and the barbarians—we would now say underdeveloped peoples—of the north and west who produced raw materials.

The horse was a relative latecomer in the field of transportation. It may have been domesticated in the grasslands of Hungary, southern Russia, or Central Asia, and was introduced

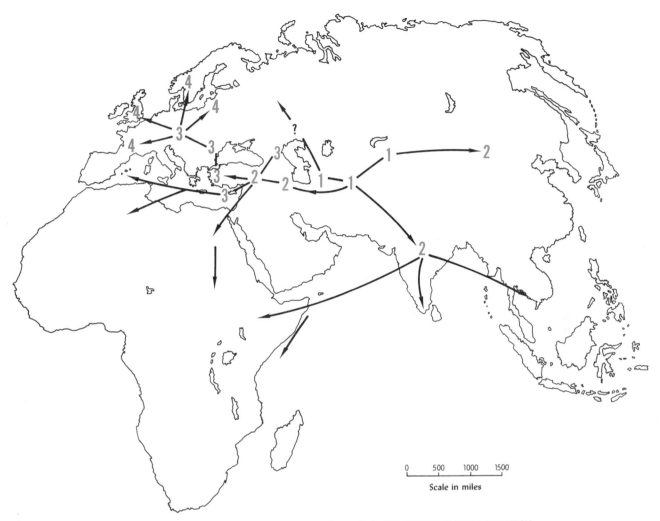

1 Earliest Centers in Middle East
2 Spread to Middle East, India, and China
3 Eastern Mediterranean, Balkans, and Central Europe
4 Northern and Western Europe

Figure 3–4. THE DIFFUSION OF METALLURGY
IN THE OLD WORLD

After Forbes, 1958.

*3. Technology:
Origins and
Diffusion*

into the ancient civilizations early in the second millennium B.C. when Indo-European peoples invaded the Middle East from the north. From then on, the man on the chariot, and later on horseback, dominated the battlefield as well as the ceremonial procession.

With improvements in agricultural techniques and in transportation, populations increased and occupations became more specialized. Nonfarming people concentrated in towns, even large cities. By 4000 B.C. the trend toward urban living was well under way, especially in lower Mesopotamia, that is, south of the present Baghdad. In these urban centers resided the priest-rulers, who used large labor battalions to build monumental temples and palaces. Writing, mathematics, astronomy, and a calendar attest further to the intellectual level of this culture, which truly can be called a civilization.

In presenting the chain of events in early history, the technological and economic links have been stressed at the expense of other factors. Actually the civilizing process must have been one of mutually interacting elements. Economic change had social and political consequences, but in turn was conditioned, as it is now, by spiritual, social, and political forces. For instance, the use of canal irrigation was a highly important innovation, but it would not have been possible without some tradition of cooperative enterprise. In the same way, before cities could grow there had to be a food surplus, but in turn the sociopolitical power of the urban ruling group may well have initiated new ways toward greater production. Societies are interacting organizations. No exclusive ultimate cause—environmental, religious, economic, or political—can fully explain them.

Two later achievements of importance deserve mention. One was the development of a successful method for extracting iron in quantity and its conversion, as wrought iron, into a multitude of things, from pots to swords and plowshares. Now for the first time a metal came within reach of the working folk. The place of origin was in eastern Anatolia or Armenia, the date about 1500 B.C.

The second great achievement, also about this time, was the alphabet; it was devised by Semitic peoples living in the Palestine-Sinai area. This marked a great step forward over the cuneiform and hieroglyphic writing systems of Mesopotamia and Egypt. It could be learned more quickly and thus, in Kroeber's words, served as a democratizing agent. Eventually this alphabet, with minor modifications, displaced all other kinds of writing except the Sinitic.

From the Middle East, ideas and things radiated, although not all of them, nor at the same speed. Agricultural village life reached Egypt by 5000 B.C. or somewhat later and developed from then onward into a civilization with a style of its own. Middle Eastern accomplishments spread north and then east through Turkestan and the oases of Central Asia to northern China. Here, near the confluence of the Huang (Yellow) and Fen rivers, evidence has been found that grain cultivation, cattle and sheep raising, and pottery making were well established by 3000 B.C. But not all traits or techniques filtered through the Asian heartland and some that did may have been rejected. For instance, milking did not become part of the agricultural complex of China or, for that matter, of East and Southeast Asia as a whole. Early presence in China of indigenous cultivated plants, such as kaoliang (a kind of sorghum) and millets, suggests local development, but the question remains open whether this preceded the borrowing from the Middle East (Figure 3–5).

The dry climate of inner Asia and North Africa discouraged crop production beyond the stream-fed areas. Here the ancient association of livestock and grain farming broke down and was replaced by nomadic herding. In its earliest phase the pastoral nomads depended on sheep and goats, with the ass as beast of burden. All are well adapted to spare brush and scrub vegetation. Bovine cattle were important only in the less dry areas where grass was available for pasture. The Old Testament gives us glimpses of this precarious life on the steppe and desert, and of the yearning for a more settled existence in the land of milk and honey.

Domestication of the horse and later the camel gave nomadic herding a boost. Both provided a powerful means of transportation. The camel was particularly well adapted to the

Figure 3–5. CHINESE CULTURE HEARTH

The arrows represent the generalized spread of some Chinese cultural traits.

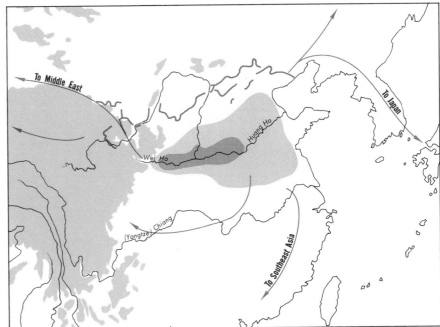

▓	Chinese Culture Hearth, about 2,000 B.C.
▒	Chinese Culture Hearth, about 1,000 B.C.
░	Land over 2,000 meters
·········	Great Wall of China
◄───	Directions of Spread of Chinese Culture

desert, the horse to the steppe. Moreover, the horse and the dromedary—the one-humped camel—proved valuable in forming fast-moving armies. The mounted nomads gained military superiority over settled farming communities and became capable of controlling large empires. Although livestock herding spread southward into Africa over the eastern highlands, neither the horse nor camel followed it. The Meso-African always remained a herdsman-on-foot.*

Archaeologic evidence from India suggests that many Middle Eastern innovations, including agriculture, had reached the Indus Valley by 3000 B.C., if not earlier. Europe also turned to agriculture, but beyond the Alpine ranges cooler and wetter conditions changed its character. Moreover, it appears that European forest dwellers, who had developed a relatively efficient form of intensive food collecting, resisted and slowed down the progress of farming.

*"Meso-Africa" is used in this book in preference to Negro-Africa. See Chapter 8.

Even so, some crops were grown in the lands near the North Sea as early as 4000 B.C. But stock raising predominated, with crop cultivation a poor second, both supplemented by the old and well-established skills of fishing and hunting.

In Africa the Sahara formed a severe barrier to the dispersal of new ideas. The Nile Valley, however, offered a route southward to central Africa. Several crops spread by that route into the Sudan. Others may have come overseas from India and even the Malay Archipelago. The practice of migratory agriculture and the prevalence of the tsetse fly (see p. 231) discouraged the use of draft animals and the plow (Figure 3–6). To this day the main field tool of the Meso-African farmer is the hoe.

In perspective, it is truly remarkable what the peoples of the Middle East wrought in the time span from 8000 to 1500 B.C. The following centuries saw few if any additional basic inventions and discoveries. Even the Greek and Roman civilizations, whatever their achievements in other spheres, were technologically

3. Technology: Origins and Diffusion

51

Figure 3–6. THE LIMITS OF PLOW CULTIVATION IN A.D. 1492

In the pre-Columbian world the use of the plow coincided fairly well with the spheres of influence of the major civilizations of the Old World.

The advance toward civilization occurred in two areas. The one generally called Meso-America comprised central and south Mexico, Guatemala, El Salvador, British Honduras, and part of Honduras (Figure 3–7). The other was the central Andes area, including the high plateaus of Peru and the near corner of Bolivia, the valley-dissected western mountain slope and the adjacent narrow coastal lowland (Figure 3–8). Each had its peripheral zones, such as the Southwest of the present United States and the Andes region between the two centers. It is also possible that the intermediate Andes region and adjacent lowlands, say about the present Colombia, had the earliest agriculture, from where it spread north and south (Sauer, 1952). However that may be, the two nuclei had interconnections, though they matured somewhat independently into centers of civilization.

The physical environment in Meso-America was more diverse than that of the Middle East. It varied from moist tropical lowlands to semi-arid temperate tablelands and high volcanoes. In the central Andes it ranged from the hot and dry coast to the cold and arid plateaus. Even more than in the Middle East it offered a wide choice of places to live and plants to cultivate.

Meso-America. It appears that by 7000 B.C. inhabitants of Mexico supplemented their gathering and hunting activities by growing a few crops: pumpkin or squash, and chili pepper. Later they domesticated the frijol bean (ancestor to many of our varieties of garden beans), the lima bean, maize, the bottle gourd, and cotton. Village life, polished-stone tools, and pottery were slow to develop as compared to their early association with agriculture in the Middle East. Not before 1500 B.C. did most of Meso-America have well-established agricultural communities, depending mainly on the cultivation of squash, beans, and especially, much improved varieties of maize. Apparently the fields were cleared by the slash-and-burn method, and abandoned after a few years to make new clearings. One would not think that such land use could support a dense population, and certainly not a large nonfarming one. Yet,

only extensions and proliferations of the Middle Eastern accomplishment.

Ancient Civilizations in the Americas

The first human immigrants entered the Americas perhaps some 30,000 years ago by way of the land corridor now occupied by the Bering Strait. They possessed techniques and equipment typical for north Asian Paleolithic hunters and gatherers, such as the use of fire, stone tools, and the dog. As they spread southward they adjusted their ways of life to different environments. They hunted big game in the forests and grasslands of humid North America, but in the semiarid and arid southwestern parts they necessarily emphasized seed and plant collecting.

Figure 3–7. MESO-AMERICAN CULTURE HEARTH

The lightly shaded areas represent regions of advanced culture, darker areas represent the cores of the Mexican and Mayan societies. Dots show the locations of important archeological sites where evidence of early or incipient agriculture has been found. From a map in Braidwood and Willey, 1962. By permission of Aldine Publishing Company.

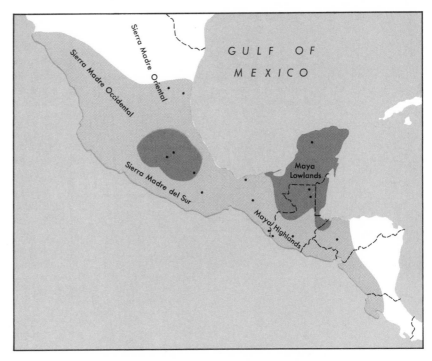

after 1000 B.C. massive public ceremonial structures were erected. Probably these centers had only a small resident population, but drew large crowds during religious festivals and on market days.

From 300 B.C. onward, cities developed. The largest one, Teotihuacan in the Valley of Mexico, at one time may have had at least 100,000 inhabitants. It seems reasonable to assume that irrigation was used then, though direct proof of this is lacking. We know for certain that when the Spaniards arrived in 1520 irrigation was being practiced in the Valley of Mexico and other highland basins. The lowland Maya of Yucatan and adjacent areas seem to have retained migratory-field (*milpa*) agriculture. If this is true, their grandiose temple complexes are not necessarily evidence of a well-developed urban life. Instead, they may have been only ceremonial centers for a largely agrarian Mayan population.

The social superstructure built on this Meso-American economic base was in many ways impressive. It included a priestly hierarchy and other forms of social stratification. Astronomy, mathematics, and a calendar system were well developed, especially by the Maya. There was a system of writing, but its application to daily economic and administrative tasks came quite late. Sculpture and pottery show great creativity. Metallurgy was slow to develop and remained restricted to gold, silver, and copper, with little use in fashioning tools. Among the few domesticated animals were the dog and the turkey. The wheel was unknown, apart from its use in toys.

The Central Andes Region. Excavations on the northern desert coast of Peru have disclosed the existence of sedentary village communities at 2500 B.C., and perhaps as early as 4000 B.C. The settlements, located at the river mouths, depended more on fishing and hunting than on farming. But they cultivated squash, chili pepper, lima beans, and cotton, the latter perhaps used with gourds to provide materials for net fishing. Tuberous crops such as manioc,

3. Technology: Origins and Diffusion

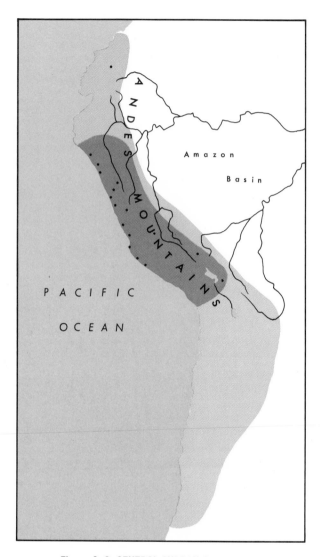

Figure 3–8. CENTRAL ANDEAN CULTURE HEARTH

The lightly shaded area represents the region of advanced culture, the darker area the core of Andean society. Dots show important sites where evidence of incipient or early agriculture has been found. From a map in Braidwood and Willey, 1962. By permission of Aldine Publishing Company.

potato, and sweet potato may have been introduced around 2500 B.C. Maize (from the north?) and peanuts were added about 1400 B.C. After 750 B.C. agricultural villages spread inland; in leaving behind the moist river bottoms near the coast they must have relied more and more on irrigation. The early presence of monumental architecture suggests that these interior settlements had a surplus of food available for the full-time employment of craftsmen, artists, and priests. From then on, gradually, agriculture intensified, the population increased in density, the social organization became more elaborate. State formation and class-structured society came into being nearly two thousand years ago. Real cities developed late—after A.D. 800—and never reached the size of those in Mexico. The famed road system with its efficient courier service dates back no further than A.D. 900.

Little is known about the order of events in the intermontane valleys and on the plateaus. We do have proof that fields were terraced and fertilized with guano and that irrigation was intensively practiced. The potato was domesticated in the highlands. Compared to Meso-America, animal husbandry was important. The llama served mainly as a pack animal and the alpaca was prized for wool. Weaving and metal casting developed after the beginning of the present era; copper tools and weapons had wider use than in Meso-America. The technique of bronze making became known later, and this alloy was much used during the last centuries of the pre-Columbian era.

The complete absence of a writing system—in contrast to Meso-America—helps explain the weak development in mathematics, astronomy, and calendrics. By A.D. 900, however, a numerical notation system by means of knotted strings had been devised, which served to keep the statistical and fiscal records for the elaborate organization of the Inca Empire.

American Civilizations and the Old World. The development of American civilizations shows many parallels with the Old World, though progress from incipient agriculture to real civilization seems to have been slower. This raises

The ruins of the fifteenth-century Inca fortress town of Machu Picchu, near Cuzco, Peru, a silent reminder of the Andean civilization. [Courtesy of United Nations]

the question whether the stimulus toward higher levels of culture came from the Old World to the Americas. The discussion around this problem is too complex for full exposition, but we must set forth a few pro and con arguments.

Those who favor the notion that many New World culture traits were introduced from the Old World minimize the ocean barrier by pointing to the Malayo-Polynesian voyages far eastward into the Pacific, the successful *Kon-Tiki* expedition by raft westward across that ocean,

3. Technology: Origins and Diffusion

and the not infrequent drifting of fishing vessels from Japan to the west coast of North America. And, of course, they note the numerous similarities between New and Old Worlds before Columbus, from alcoholic beverages to the zodiac. The trouble is that so much of this material consists of isolated items that do not fit into a consistent process of diffusion. Why could not men in different parts of the world have hit on the same idea?

But there is one sector of civilization where man's creative thought is not enough. He cannot invent plants, and this is the trump card of the diffusionists. Plant domesticates present in both parts of the world in pre-Columbian times are the sweet potato, bottle gourd, coconut, and cotton. There have been various arguments raised against accepting these crops as evidence of pre-Columbian trans-Pacific cultural contacts, but least effectively against the sweet potato. This plant (not to be confused with the Old World yam) is apparently of American origin. When the first whites visited New Zealand, the Maoris were using the sweet potato as a common food crop. If this is valid evidence, one can hardly rule out the possibility of movements in the other, eastward, direction. But were these movements infrequent and accidental, or part of a constant trickle, if not flow, of men and ideas? The latter must be postulated if it is to support the hypothesis that much of the American civilizations originated in the Old World. But if many advanced culture traits were imported, why were other, equally valuable, ideas not transferred, or not accepted? If America got the notion of the zero and zodiac from the civilizations in Asia, why did not such eminently useful inventions as the wheel for pottery and transportation, the plow, manufacture of iron, and more advanced forms of writing cross the ocean?

The present state of knowledge appears to favor the concept of a largely independent cultural evolution in the Americas. Nevertheless, it may be wise to agree with an observer who concluded that "a verdict of 'not proven' must . . . be accepted by all but convinced diffusionists—and their equally convinced opponents" (Singer, 1954, vol. 1, 84).

China and the West

We must now return to the Old World, first to consider briefly the influence of China on western Eurasia, second to outline the emergence and spread of modern technology. We have seen that several innovations moved from west to east into China, thereby contributing much to its early agricultural assemblage. Chinese culture developed a character of its own and independently made important advances in technology. These inventions filtered slowly south and westward by land and sea routes. There can be little doubt that much of the spurt in technical progress during the European Renaissance was due to the introduction of ideas or skills that originated in China. These included papermaking, printing with blocks and movable type, gunpowder, the crossbow, suspension bridge, canal lock, watertight compartments for ships, and the use of the magnetized needle in navigation.

In this transmission, the Islamic world of the Middle East and Central Asia played the key role. This may be illustrated by the diffusion of papermaking (Figure 3–9). About A.D. 100 the Chinese invented paper, using a process similar to that of today. In 751 the Chinese attacked Samarkand, a trade center astride the route between China and the West. The Arab garrison successfully defended it and even took Chinese prisoners. Among them were some papermakers who taught the Arabs their trade. Within two centuries paper mills had been established at Baghdad and Cairo. Diffusion to Europe came by way of Moorish-dominated Iberia and Sicily. Paper mills were set up in Toledo and Valencia by 1150. Moorish papermakers helped to found a mill in Hérault in southern France. By the fourteenth century papermaking had spread to northern Italy, from where Italian artisans carried their craft over the Alps into Germany. England had its first mill probably in the fifteenth century. Across the Atlantic papermaking began in Mexico City in 1575, and in 1690 a German migrant to Philadelphia began business in nearby Germantown. After that, papermaking spread throughout the colonies.

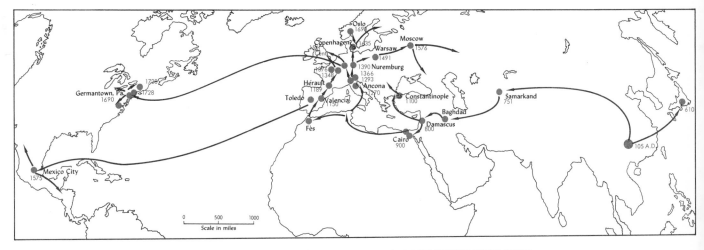

Figure 3–9. THE DIFFUSION OF PAPERMAKING FROM CHINA TO THE WEST

Papermaking spread through the Moslem world from Samarkand and reached Christian Europe in 1189. It crossed the Atlantic to Mexico City in 1575 and to Pennsylvania (Germantown) in 1690. Based in part on information in Blum, 1946.

The Modern Technological Revolution

In the last two centuries a new kind of society has joined the old tribal and traditional farming economies. As industrial life began in Europe and spread to America and elsewhere, it transformed patterns of organization, sparked new theories of economic management, and stimulated political thought regarding the distribution of wealth.

Modern man, instead of being subject to nature, attempts to dominate and control it. No longer is he tied to his "station in life" or to any single locality. Communication, transportation, and sources of energy in manifold forms give him freedom never before imagined. Science and technology unlock the way to well-being and progress. A. R. Hall writes of the change in attitude that accompanied the Industrial Revolution: "Men looked to the future now, not to the past, and perhaps for the first time in history had some inkling of the road to be traversed in time to come. They saw science as the inspiration of technology, and technology as the key to a life of richness and prosperity" (Singer, 1954, vol. 3, 721).

The New Transportation Technology

The most spectacular results of science and technology have been those involving transport of goods, men, and ideas: the ocean-going sailing ship; the steam engine as used in the railway locomotive; the internal combustion engine of car, truck, and plane; knowledge of electromagnetic impulses, as employed in telephone, radio, television; perhaps soon, atomic power applied to space flight. These carriers by their very nature spread their use, together with other technical paraphernalia, far from their points of origin. They enabled Europeans, and later Americans, to invade all parts of the globe,

3. Technology: Origins and Diffusion

——————	Portuguese
– – – – –	Russian
——————	British
——————	Spanish
– – – – –	French
··············	Dutch

Figure 3–10. THE EUROPEAN DISCOVERY OF THE EARTH, A.D. 1400–1800

The shaded area represents the regions well known to Europeans in 1400. The search for sea routes from Europe to Asia dominated the age of discovery. The Portuguese worked their way down the west coast of Africa, rounded the Cape of Good Hope, and crossed to India and Southeast Asia. The Spanish, searching for another way to Asia, crossed the Atlantic and found instead a New World. Later they uncovered the vastness of the Pacific Ocean. The English and Dutch dominated the search for passages to the Orient around the north of Eurasia and North America. The Dutch were the first to set foot on Australia and discover New Zealand. The Russians traveled overland eastward, laid open the Siberian wastes, and uncovered the relationships between northeastern Asia and northwestern North America. Later others, especially the British and French, discovered the vastness of the southern oceans.

The numbers on the map refer to the century of first European exploration in the modern era.

I. Introduction

and with armaments, trading companies, and colonial administrations, to control regional and world politics and to shape economies to their own ends. The West rose to dominance through its command of new means of circulation.

Ocean Sailing. The fifteenth century saw European sailing ships venture from coasts and enclosed seas out into the open oceans. The Portuguese, putting together many technical improvements in ship construction, built the three-masted caravel, the type of ship used by Columbus, da Gama, Magellan, and other seamen of the great age of discovery. Concurrently they improved navigation methods, originally learned from the Arabs, and developed from earlier Mediterranean examples the arts of chart and map making. During the period from 1400 to 1800 when Europeans explored the land and sea configuration of the earth (Figure 3–10) and brought its peoples into new contact with one another, the sailing ship was the most complex and ingenious invention man had achieved.*

Portugal founded a sea empire in the southern Atlantic and around the Indian Ocean as far as the Moluccas and China. Seamanship, zeal for exploration, a knack for commerce, and religious fervor changed her from a small peripheral European state into the mistress of a great empire. Spain appropriated most of the New World and reached across the Pacific to claim the Philippines. This Iberian world hegemony waned by the end of the sixteenth century as the English, Dutch, and French challenged the joint Spanish-Portuguese monopoly of overseas dominion. The Dutch, having wrenched independence from their Spanish masters, took to the oceans and carved an empire of their own from Portuguese possessions, mostly in Southeast Asia. The Dutch held the world's stage during the mid-seven-

teenth century, for a time keeping other empire seekers in check.

The English under their vigorous Tudor sovereigns made conquest of the sea and colonization a national concern. They settled along the Atlantic coast of North America and undertook commercial and imperial ventures that led to the creation of an Indian empire. France also entered the competition, sent settlers to North America, and acquired a trading empire in the Orient. While the Dutch managed to hold onto most of their East Indian possessions, the French lost their claims in India and in America to the British, who emerged in the nineteenth century as masters of the seas and arbiters of world affairs.

All these enterprises combined to expand trade in spices and condiments, sugar, slaves, tobacco, and the more valuable metals. Western Europe became the geographical focus for the new ocean trade that increasingly concentrated in the "narrow seas," the seas bounded by England, France, and the Netherlands. This trade, together with the burgeoning farm production at home, brought wealth to the rising populations of western Europe, though the distribution of these new riches varied considerably.

To found commercial empires with distant sea connections was one thing; to settle permanently overseas was another. First Spain, then Portugal, England, France, and the Netherlands, and to a lesser extent Denmark, Sweden, Germany, and other European nations sent out a growing number of colonists, who created overseas societies from New Spain, New France, New England, and New Netherlands to New Zealand and New South Wales.

The age of discovery had barely closed when iron ships propelled by steam engines revolutionized ocean transportation in the first half of the nineteenth century. Before long, goods in enormous quantities were being carried between the Americas and Europe, and between southern Asia and Europe. The opening of the Suez Canal in 1869 and of the Panama Canal in 1914 greatly reduced the length of ocean voyages.

The Europeans became expert in channeling their own work and abilities into profitable

*The same could be said of the subsequent steam-driven ocean-going warship and liner. In our day the spaceship continues the theme that the most advanced forms of technology develop in transportation systems.

3. Technology: Origins and Diffusion

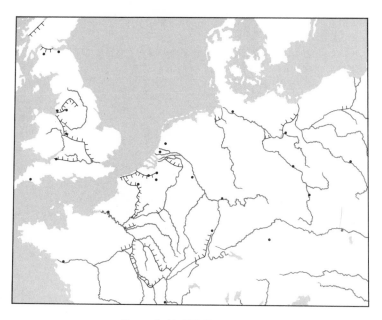

Figure 3–11. EUROPE: CANALS BUILT BY 1840

⊔⊔⊔⊔ Canals built by 1840

• Cities with over 50,000 Population in 1815

• Cities with over 500,000 Population in 1815

land highways, though coastal routes also were used. The Rhine, Elbe, Danube, and rivers further east carried heavy traffic. This was also true in North America, where most of the settlements depended on river or coastal traffic.

The need to improve land transportation brought about the grading and surfacing of roads with binding materials to subdue dust and enhance drainage. The well-constructed toll road (turnpike) became a common feature in the late eighteenth and early nineteenth centuries in western Europe and along the Atlantic Seaboard of North America. Some countries developed a system of fast horse-drawn coaches to carry mail and passengers overland.

Another way of breaking the bottleneck of land transportation was by digging canals. China, Italy, and the Netherlands had long supplemented their rivers in this manner. The need for transporting bulky goods inland brought about a canal-building era that reached its high point late in the eighteenth century and lasted until about 1840 (Figure 3–11). England connected the industrial towns of the Midlands with the seaports of London and Liverpool; France joined her principal rivers; the United States attempted, with only partial success, to unite the eastern seaboard with rivers and lakes of the interior. These prodigious feats in canal building alleviated, for a time, the paucity of inland transportation.

The railroad dramatically improved the accessibility of landlocked places. Soon after the reciprocating steam engine became the prime power for industrial machines, the steam locomotive was developed by adapting it to wheels. England built the first steam railway in the 1820s; soon rails began to extend over western Europe and eastern North America. Not since the time of the mounted-nomad society in Central Asia had it been possible to link together and develop large inland areas as economic units. Now railways connected seaboard with interior in Europe, North America, southern South America, Australia, and, to a lesser extent, India and Russia (Figure 3–12). Cities no longer needed to locate on important waterways. Americans could settle in their Midwest

ways and in harnessing the energy of other peoples to their advantage. They formed a market, not only for the old luxuries, but also for vast quantities of meat, wheat, and other foods, for cotton and wool, metal ores, and industrial raw materials. In return, Europe sent out manufactured goods, capital for investment in plantations, mines, and railways, and armies of administrators, engineers, and soldiers to manage and protect the colonial enterprises.

Land and Air Transportation. Land transportation until the nineteenth century remained primitive as compared to that of ocean ship and river boat. Indeed, most of the roads were mere tracks; even the heavily traveled ones were less well constructed than those left by the Romans. Rivers still served as the chief in-

I. Introduction

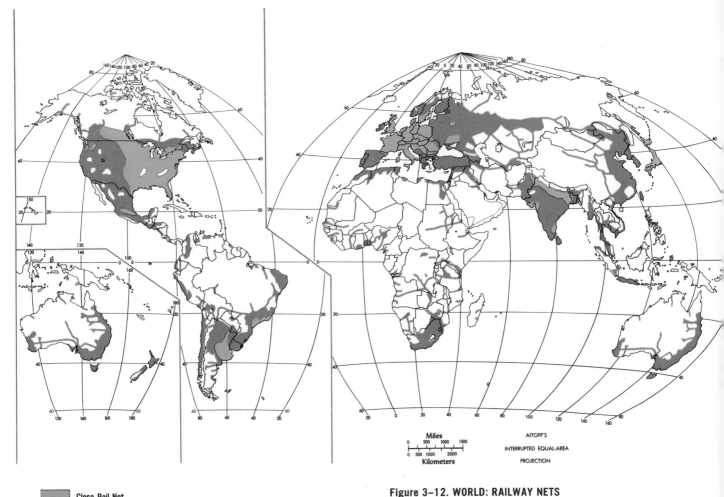

Figure 3–12. WORLD: RAILWAY NETS

Based on a map in
Introduction to Geography by H. M. Kendall, R. M. Glendinning,
and C. H. MacFadden, 1962, 569. Copyright 1951, © 1958, 1962, by
Harcourt, Brace, and World Inc., and reproduced with their permission.

Close Rail Net

Open Rail Net (Or Single Lines)

No Railroads

and Great Plains, yet feel that their lives and economy were tied by railroad to the Atlantic Coast, and ultimately with overseas markets and suppliers. In Russia, industry and cities developed more slowly than in western Europe. The coming of the railroad emancipated what industry there was and stimulated expansion as far east as the Ural Mountains.

The advent of the motor vehicle around 1900 brought a whole new type of transportation

into being. Since then the car and truck have furnished a personal and ubiquitous way of getting from one place to another. After the automobile diffused throughout Anglo-America and western Europe it spread to other countries. Figure 3–13 shows that regions of early invention and development still have most of the motor vehicles, but now other areas are beginning to manufacture or import cars in considerable quantities. The densest road networks,

*3. Technology:
Origins and
Diffusion*

The electric pylon symbolizes the spread of Occidental technology in West Bengal, India. With international assistance the Damodar River and its tributaries, which often caused disastrous floods, have been regulated through dams and reservoirs. Controlled irrigation aids the farmer, who tends his rice field with bullocks and simple plow; hydroelectricity powers the steel, aluminum, and chemical plants in what is called "the Ruhr of India." [Courtesy of United Nations]

I. Introduction

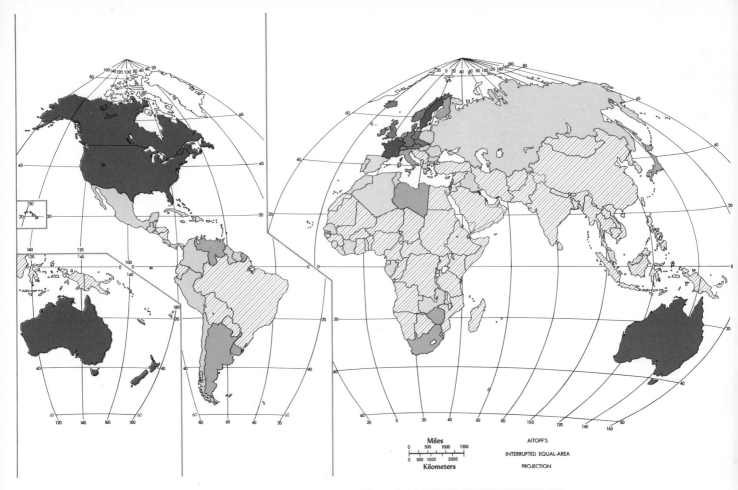

Motor Vehicles per Thousand Persons

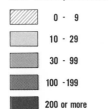

(hatched)	0 - 9
(light gray)	10 - 29
(medium gray)	30 - 99
(darker gray)	100 - 199
(black)	200 or more

Figure 3–13. WORLD: MOTOR VEHICLES PER THOUSAND POPULATION, 1962

By 1970 many countries will have moved up a category or two. Data from United Nations, *Statistical Yearbook 1964,* table 148, 391ff.

too, still lie in western Europe and North America, which also have many excellent superhighways (Figures 3–14 and 3–15).

In all economically advanced countries the use of the car for personal transportation and the truck for freight increases rapidly. Indeed, in some countries freight transportation by road expands faster than private-car use, notably in planned economies like the Soviet Union and the central European republics. Trucks offer more flexibility than freight cars for terminals and routes, which often enables them to capture new markets and offer special services. In the United States and western Europe the railroads are readjusting to functions they are best able to perform in the new competitive situation.

3. Technology: Origins and Diffusion

63

Figure 3–14. EUROPE: SUPERHIGHWAYS, MID-1960s

National differences are evident from the map. Much of the German system dates from the 1930s and 1940s. The Dutch and Italian roads are relatively new. France, long known for its fine highway system, has not yet felt the need to build many long superhighways. Other roads, not shown on this map, were completed in the late 1960s, among them those through central Yugoslavia and along the Dalmatian coast.

Logically, the same regions that developed the railroad and automobile produced the airplane. Airlines transport passengers and some high-value goods, but it may be decades before they rival the truck, railway car, or ship as freight carriers.

Cultures vary in how they utilize technological advances. Japan has built a dense railway web, and its road traffic is increasing rapidly. Countries where economic development began to accelerate only two or three decades ago may never acquire a complete railway system. More probably, roads complemented by air routes will serve most of their needs. Airplane and helicopter afford immediate access to spots in trackless deserts, rain forests, and mountains. They demonstrate once more the vital significance of transportation in man's conquest of the earth.

Power and the Manufacturing Revolution

The Industrial Revolution introduced great changes in sources of energy. Late in the eighteenth century the steam engine, after much experimentation, began to replace waterwheel and muscle as a prime mover of machines. Before long, James Watt's designs were copied and installed in many places in Britain. Early in the nineteenth century British engineers

Figure 3–15. NORTH AMERICA: SUPERHIGHWAYS, 1965

Construction of the United States "interstate and defense highway system" began in 1956. By 1965 about half of the system was completed. The map includes these highways as well as some built by state authorities. Canada has some superhighways, especially in Ontario. Short sections near Sydney, Nova Scotia, and Halifax, Nova Scotia, are not shown. Based in part on a map published in *The New York Times*.

helped to set up the first steam engines on the European continent near Liège in the Meuse Valley. Soon thereafter France and Germany followed, then the United States and other countries.

Prior to the steam engine, spinning and weaving were carried on in small rooms, often in farm homes. In contrast, a steam engine of sufficiently advanced design could turn the spindles and looms of a whole factory. Soon other power-driven tools were invented to melt, bore, shape, and test. Manufacturing became a series of processes concentrated at point locations. Groups of "mills" located near one an-

*3. Technology:
Origins and
Diffusion*

other, surrounded by dwellings for the workers. Thus began a new kind of settlement aggregation: the industrial town (Chapter 13). First in Britain, then Belgium, later northern France, eastern United States, and western Germany, these industrial towns usually located at or near coalfields where they had cheap fuel to supply the boilers of the steam engines. Often factories were grafted onto the outskirts of already existing towns. As manufacturing and service industries attracted more labor, the proportion of people living in urban areas surpassed, for the first time in history, that in the countryside.

Development of Modern Agriculture

The same application of science and technology also created a modern "agricultural revolution." Many advances came to the landed estates of the northwestern European countries during the seventeenth and eighteenth centuries when capital earned overseas was invested in land reclamation and in new methods of production (see Chapter 12). Improvements in farming included, briefly: crop rotation to replace medieval fallowing of fields; introduction of disease-resistant plant varieties and better qualities of seed and breeding stock; also the use of chemical fertilizers. Machinery took over many farm jobs. The agricultural transformation greatly increased the productivity per worker. Scientific forestry ensured and conserved timber supplies and reduced soil erosion. Marketing arrangements and transportation facilities efficiently moved products to the consumer. Regional and worldwide networks of production, trade, and consumption replaced the localized patterns of earlier times.

Massive increase in population and a revolution in political and social affairs accompanied these developments in industry and agriculture. The profits from factory, farm, and commerce became the right of many to enjoy, no longer the prerogative of the wealthy few. From Europe and America, where the ideas of social justice first flowered, they spread to other parts of the world with varying degrees of emphasis.

Today the most advanced forms of technology appear in the application of atomic science to armaments, space exploration, power production, and medicine; in the use of high-speed computers and other "thinking machines"; and in the introduction of automation in the process of manufacturing. The North Atlantic countries that spearheaded the drive toward industrial maturity lead the others by far, though the Soviet Union valiantly endeavors to catch up in certain sectors. Newly developing nations just entering the industrial age are finding it more and more difficult to lessen the gap between their simple economies and those of the highly developed countries where scientific and technologic complexities speed ahead at an unprecedented rate.

Citations

Blum, A. *La Route du papier,* Grenoble, 1946. [Map]

Braidwood, R. J. "The Agricultural Revolution," *Scientific American* (September, 1960): 130–148.

————, and Willey G. R. (eds.) *Courses toward Urban Life: Archaeological Considerations of Some Cultural Alternatives,* Viking Fund Publications in Anthropology, no. 32, New York, 1962. [Maps]

Forbes, R. J. *Man the Maker,* New York and London, 1958. [Map]

Harris, D. R. "New Light on Plant Domestication and the Origins of Agriculture: A Review," *Geographical Review,* 57 (1967): 90–107.

Kendall, H. M., Glendinning, R. M., and MacFadden, C. H. *Introduction to Geography,* New York, 1962. [Map]

Sauer, C. O. *Agricultural Origins and Dispersals,* Bowman Memorial Lectures, series 2, American Geographical Society, New York, 1952.

Singer, C., Holmyard, E. J., Hall, A. R., and Williams, T. N. (eds.) *A History of Technology,* 5 vols., London, 1954–1958.

Further Readings

Ashton, T. S. *The Industrial Revolution,* London, 1950.

Bennett, W. C., and Bird, J. B. *Andean Culture History,* American Museum of Natural History, Handbook Series no. 15, New York, 1949.

Boxer, C. R. *The Dutch Seaborne Empire,* London, 1965.

Burkill, I. H. "Habits of Man and the Origins of Cultivated Plants of the Old World," in Wagner, P. L., and Mikesell, M. W. (eds.) *Readings in Cultural Geography,* Chicago, 1962, 248–281. Originally published in *Proceedings of the Linnean Society of London,* 164 (1951–1952): 12–42.

Butzer, K. W. *Environment and Archeology: An Introduction to Pleistocene Geography,* Chicago, 1965.

Carter, G. F. "Plant Evidence for Early Contacts with America," *Southwestern Journal of Anthropology,* 6 (1950): 161–182.

———— . "Movement of People and Ideas across the Pacific," in Barrau, J. (ed.) *Plants and the Migrations of Pacific Peoples,* Honolulu, 1963.

Childe, V. G., *Man Makes Himself,* London, 1936, 1941, 1951. Also in paperback edition.

Clark, G. *World Prehistory: An Outline,* Cambridge, 1961.

————, and Piggott, S. *Prehistoric Societies,* London, 1965. A fine introduction to the subject. The first volume of the "History of Human Society" series.

Cutler, H. C. "Food Sources in the New World," in Wagner, P. L., and Mikesell, M. W. (eds.) *Readings in Cultural Geography,* Chicago, 1962, 282–289. Originally published in *Agricultural History,* 28 (1954): 43–49.

Daniel, A. G. *Ancient Peoples and Places,* London and New York, various dates. A multivolume series, each book of which deals with a particular society in ancient and prehistoric times. Among the most interesting are Powell, T. G. E. *The Celts;* Harden, D. *The Phoenicians;* Talbot-Rice, T. *The Scythians;* Bloch, R. *The Etruscans;* Wheeler, M. *Early India and Pakistan;* and Bushnell, G. H. S. *Peru.*

Hawkes, J. *Prehistory,* in *History of Mankind, Cultural and Scientific Development,* vol. 1, part 1, New York, 1963. The first volume of a multivolume series on the history of mankind; sponsored and published by UNESCO.

Jefferson, M. "The Civilizing Rails," *Economic Geography,* 4 (1928): 217–231.

———— . "The Geographic Distribution of Inventiveness," *Geographical Review,* 19 (1929): 649–661.

Kramer, F. L. "Eduard Hahn and the End of the 'Three Stages of Man,'" *Geographical Review,* 57 (1967): 73–89.

Lüthy, H. "Colonization and the Making of Mankind," *Economic History,* 21 (1961): 483–495.

Marsak, L. M. (ed.) *The Rise of Science in Relation to Society,* New York, 1964.

3. Technology: Origins and Diffusion

McNeill, W. H. *The Rise of the West: A History of the Human Community,* Chicago, 1963. Also in paperback edition.

Mellaart, J. *Earliest Civilizations of the Near East,* London, 1965.

Needham, J. *Science and Civilization in China,* 4 vols., London, 1954–1962.

Nef, J. U. *Cultural Foundations of Industrial Civilization,* New York, 1960.

Parry, J. H. *The Establishment of the European Hegemony,* New York, 1961. Also in paperback.

———. *The Spanish Seaborne Empire,* London, 1966.

Penrose, B. *Travel and Discovery in the Renaissance, 1420–1620,* Cambridge, Mass., 1955.

Plumb, J. H. *The British Seaborne Empire, 1600–1800,* London, 1967.

Price, A. G. *The Western Invasions of the Pacific and Its Continents: A Study of Moving Frontiers and Changing Landscapes, 1513–1958,* London, 1963.

Reed, C. A. "Animal Domestication in the Prehistoric Near East," *Science,* 130 (1959): 1629–1639.

Sauer, C. O. "The End of the Ice Age and Its Witnesses," *Geographical Review,* 47 (1957): 29–43. Reprinted in Leighly, J. (ed.) *Land and Life,* Berkeley and Los Angeles, 1963, 271–287.

Skelton, R. A. *Explorers' Maps: Chapters in the Cartographic Record of Geographical Discovery,* New York, 1958.

Steward, H. H., et al. *Irrigation Civilizations: A Comparative Study,* Pan-American Union Social Science Monographs no. 1, Washington, D.C., 1955.

Sykes, P. *A History of Exploration,* New York, 1961. Also in paperback edition.

Thompson, J. E. *The Rise and Fall of Maya Civilization,* Norman, Okla., 1956.

Vaillant, G. C. *The Aztecs of Mexico,* American Museum of Natural History Science Series, vol. 2, New York, 1941. Also in paperback edition.

Vavilov, N. I. "The Origin, Variation, Immunity, and Breeding of Cultivated Plants: Selected Writings of N. I. Vavilov" (translated from the Russian by K. S. Chester) *Chronica Botanica,* 13 (1951): 1–366.

Washburn, S. L. (ed.) *Social Life of Early Man,* Viking Fund Publications in Anthropology no. 31, New York, 1961.

Willey, G. R. (ed.) *Prehistoric Settlement Patterns in the New World,* Viking Fund Publications in Anthropology no. 23, New York, 1956.

Wright, J. K. *Human Nature in Geography,* Cambridge, Mass., 1966.

Part II. Cultural Diversity

Part II. Cultural Diversity

The word *culture* commonly embraces the entire way of life of a people. However, it can also be used in a more limited sense for the manifestations of the inner world of the spirit. Culture in the latter meaning forms the subject of this part. Its main themes are race, language, religion, and nation.

Race as such is a biological concept, but it has cultural implications. Religious and political ideologies condition, if not determine, consciously held beliefs and unconscious assumptions and, in turn, reflect cultural traditions. Language is the main instrument for transmitting culture within a group, and at the same time is one of its important characteristics. These traits in various combinations provide the psychic energy of people and bind them together in a society set apart, though not isolated, from other societies.

The last chapter of this part proposes a division of the earth into broad culture realms and briefly describes each of them. It paves the way to apprehending economic and demographic differences, which will be examined in subsequent sections.

*II. Cultural
Diversity*

Part-opening photograph: Funeral procession in Bali, Indonesia.
[Courtesy of Ruth Broek]

4. Race: Biological Facts and Social Attitudes

The geographer considers "race" from two different angles. In the scientific view, race concerns the physical variety of men as inherited and passed on from generation to generation and manifested in the biologically distinct groups living in different parts of the earth. This scientific approach differs sharply from the popular notion of what constitutes "race." Each human group perceives its own racial character and that of others through the lens of its culture. These sentiments, however ill-conceived, are social realities. Since race relations may deeply affect the social and economic fabric of a country, they fall within the purview of human geography.

Geography and Genetics

Biologically speaking mankind is a single species, that is, an interbreeding population descended from a single source. Differences among humans result from diversification and remixing within the species. How these differences emerged and became typical of groups with distinct geographical locations are questions which genetics, the branch of the biological sciences that deals with heredity, can help answer.

Geneticists tell us that man inherits from his parents such characteristics as the shape of nose, skin color, hair form, and so on. The units of inheritance are called genes; thousands of pairs of genes, arranged in order in pairs of chromosomes, form the nuclei of human cells. But each reproductive cell of the male and female carries only one of each pair of genes. These join at fertilization, producing in each cell of the offspring the same number of pairs of genes as found in the parents' cells. For example, assuming for the moment that hair color results from the operation of a single gene, a child will receive two genes for hair color, one from each parent. If both genes signal "brown hair" the child will have brown hair. If one gene calls for "brown hair" and the other for "red hair," one gene (in this case "brown hair") will predominate over its alternate. The determining gene is *dominant,* the losing gene *recessive.* The genetic signals do not merge or integrate; they remain independent or *segregated.*

Table 4–1 shows the dominant-recessive nature of a group of important features. Its contents should be accepted with reservation since the research is far from complete. Actually, most features result from not one but several genes.

Dominant genes can come from either parent, thus giving each generation an *independent assortment* of inherited characteristics. Barnett

Table 4–1. Some Human Traits Inherited according to the Rules of Segregation

Trait	Dominant	Recessive
Head shape	Round	Long
Stature	Short	Tall
Chin	Straight	Receding
Eye color	Brown	Blue-gray
Eyelid	Epicanthic fold	No fold
Hair amount	Abundant	Scanty
Hair form	Woolly Curly Straight	Straight Straight Wavy
Nose shape	Convex Straight	Straight Concave
Skin color	Dark	Light

SOURCE: Adapted from Whitney, 1942.

sums up a discussion of human physical inheritance:

Genetic effects are determined by individual particles, the genes, and the genes may appear in any combination in different individuals. This re-combination is the origin of much of the variation between people that we see around us. Even a group of people living in a small community and with very similar environments may show great variation in appearance and in other small characteristics. Though part of the variation may be due to small environmental differences, a great deal comes from the mixing and reshuffling of the genes at each generation. (Barnett, 1950, 28–29)

New variety is added by *mutation,* a permanent structural change in a gene—as in the rearrangement of atoms in a complex molecule —resulting in the loss or alteration of some feature. Accumulation of mutations in a group can bring about striking changes. The conditions that perpetuate mutations are *selection* and *isolation,* in both of which relative location is an essential factor.

The principle of *natural selection* is that all species contain some individuals more able to survive than others because they cooperate better with the conditions of life. Those who adjust best become established as "normal," those less fitted gradually disappear. Environments select in the sense that their conditions may suit some mutations and combinations, not in the sense that they cause mutations. An environment tends to preserve those preadapted to it and to eliminate those not adapted.

Dark-skinned people are not susceptible to sunburn, but light-skinned people are. Broad noses with wide nostrils may suit the tropics, where the air does not chill the linings of the respiratory organs; high and narrow noses with small openings may be an advantage in a cool climate, for they warm the air before it reaches the lungs. From such adaptations a variety of human types has evolved, able to exploit particular opportunities.

In *social selection,* artificial barriers regulate unions and do away with random breeding. Until recently, for example, parts of the United States forbade by law marriage between whites and Negroes. Some religious groups do not permit, or at least discourage, outside marriages. In India, marriages between persons of different stations in life (castes) are frowned on. Such rules obviously affect the distribution of genes among populations in a region.

Sexual selection probably did not much affect the early development of mankind, but it is significant in some modern societies. In the long run the skin color of North Americans with Negro ancestry tends to change because they prefer to mate with those of lighter skin. Marriages between brunet whites and blond whites are quite common and thus preserve the balance of such types.

Isolation, in the genetic sense, is the separation of one breeding group from another in the same species. All isolated communities if not too large will after a time become physically different whether or not they live in the same environment, for mutation is random. In a small isolated population, mutations of no particular advantage diffuse throughout the group; this is called *genetic drift*. If small groups occupy unlike environments the chance is they will become even more distinct physically because the effect of natural selection is added to that of genetic drift. In this way segregated peoples become breeds or races with evenly spread *(homozygous)* genetic patterns. When two or more such homozygous communities meet and blend, a *heterozygous* population emerges which, because of its mixed genetic patterns, is physically diverse.

Environmental conditions and relative location strongly affect the biological processes of natural selection and the formation of homozygous and heterozygous groups. Distinct features, evolved during the ages when mankind lived in more or less isolated groups, in widely different environments, have through subsequent dispersion and mixing become characteristic of large populations. Most human beings belong to heterozygous groups.

Problems of Classification

Peoples differ not only in appearance but also physiologically in blood types and susceptibility to specific diseases. Genes determine traits, but the frequency of certain genes varies from group to group. Ideally speaking, races are populations with similar individual genetic patterns. Because little is known about the genetic origins of most features *(genotypes)*, race classification must necessarily rely on the features themselves *(phenotypes)*.

Two problems immediately arise. (1) Phenotypes rarely covary by groups. For example, mankind can be broadly divided into groups with different skin colors, but these groups fail to match with the divisions according to hair form. Only by carefully selecting certain traits and by excluding some human groups can we find an approximate covariation. (2) Because

Arab from Qatar peninsula, on the Persian Gulf, representative of the Mediterranean type of Caucasoid. [A Shell photograph]

most phenotypes derive from many genes, with independent assortment, they divide into subclasses that merge gradually into each other. This makes it virtually impossible to divide races by hard-and-fast lines. This is especially true for skin pigmentation, the yardstick most people use for race. Some traits (for example, the A B O blood types) are inherited through the presence or absence of a single gene. In these cases there is no merging of phenotypes;

4. Race:
Biological
Facts and
Social
Attitudes

unfortunately these traits do not covary with others from group to group.

Some Physical Traits

People differ greatly in *stature*. Most striking are the Pygmies, who average less than 5 feet. (But this average covers much variation—some Pygmies are taller than some New Yorkers.) Observations of other peoples indicate that stature increases with better food, medical care, and hygiene. For instance, the postwar generation of Japanese is taller than their parents. One could therefore argue that the small stature of the Pygmies is due to their difficult life, debilitating diseases, and poor diet.

In contrast, some peoples are tall in spite of hard life; among them are the Shilluk in the Sudd. In the United States the tallest recruits for the army in 1917 came from the poorest communities in the Appalachians. In the Congo the Watusi, who average almost 6 feet, live side by side with the Pygmies. Evidently genetic factors are important, but we know so little about them and the effect of living conditions that height is of little use to classify races.

The *shape of the head* was once thought the best indicator of race. Environment seldom modifies it. What we know of prehistoric man necessarily depends on skeletal remains, of which the skull provides easy measurement. There are, indeed, marked differences in head shape from group to group, but they do not covary with other traits. Among light-skinned peoples most Russians have broad heads and most Norwegians long heads; Mongols have broad heads but most Japanese long heads; Negroes and West Europeans have long heads.

Blood types are referred to as A, B, AB, and O, the last indicating an absence of A and B, the substances that cause agglutination (clotting) of the red blood cells when mixed with blood that does not contain them. The A and B genes are both dominant over O, but neither A nor B is dominant over the other; a person with A and B genes has blood type AB. The types are carried by a single gene and follow the laws of segregation; thus the blood types do not merge: an individual with type AB has both substances and not a blend of them.*

Figure 4–1 shows that the blood types are fairly well regionalized. The O gene occurs in high percentages among western Europeans, Australian aborigines, peoples of northeastern Asia, American Indians, and some African populations. Lower O gene frequencies occur in East and Central Asia and in the Middle East. The A gene is less easy to regionalize; high proportions are found in some outlying European populations, among North American Indians, among some Balkan and Middle Eastern peoples, and among some groups of Australian aborigines. Type A is almost absent in Middle and South America, with low frequencies in Africa, South Asia and northeastern Asia. The gene for blood type B is most common in Central and Southeast Asia and in some parts of Africa.

These distributions pose problems as yet unsolved. Some scholars think that all mankind was of type O early in its history but that, since O is recessive, the A and B genes have pushed it into regions marginal to the center of human dispersion. This hypothesis presupposes that there was one center of dispersion over a long time. In this line of thought, A was an early mutation pushing outward and replacing O. Type B was a later mutation and followed the same course. The higher incidence of B in eastern Europe as against A in western Europe and a similar division between northern and southern India can be explained in terms of nomadic armies from Central Asia with high B frequencies invading the agricultural peripheries of Eurasia and subsequently breeding with O and A peasant peoples. Type B is thus associated with groups often referred to as Mongoloid,† but at a later stage of their evolution, for B is uncommon among American Indians.

---

*Each individual has at least nine other genetically independent systems of blood types, including the MN groups and the Rh factor.

†The suffix *-oid,* from the Greek, means "having the form of," "like."

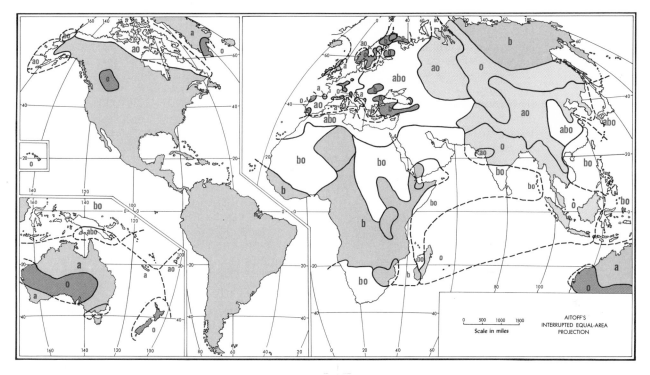

Frequency of the ABO Genes

A over 30 per cent

B over 20 per cent

O over 70 per cent

a   A 10 to 30 per cent

b   B 10 to 20 per cent

o   O 50 to 70 per cent

Figure 4–1. DISTRIBUTION OF THE A B O BLOOD GROUP GENES IN THE ABORIGINAL POPULATIONS OF THE WORLD

The frequency categories used in this map reflect the much higher proportion of blood type O and the lower proportions of blood types A and B in the human population. Based on maps and data in Mourant et al., 1958.

Such sweeping explanations fail to account for the existence of B genes in central Africa, the Pacific Islands, and among some groups in the Americas. It seems unlikely that independent but parallel mutations occurred among peoples so remote from each other. Perhaps early migrations were more extensive than so far realized, including, for instance, widespread diffusion of Mongolian features among African populations.

In short, the meaning of the distribution of blood types is not yet clear. Before their value in tracing man's migrations can be understood

there must be much patient sifting of serological clues. In the present state of knowledge, blood types can only be used to supplement classifications based on other data.

Skin color is to most people the hallmark of race. The more pigmentation, the darker the skin. Pigments protect blood and tissues from exposure to radiation. It may therefore be assumed that dark skins evolved from natural selection in tropical regions where radiation from the sun is highest. Since pigmentation results from the operation of many genes, the

4. Race: Biological Facts and Social Attitudes

color shades of skin range from very fair to black. Any attempt to divide this continuum into sections is arbitrary.

Color subdivisions maintain themselves because marriages between members of different color groups are infrequent as compared to those within each group. Color persistence also depends on relative isolation and on social selection. In the modern era, as distances are overcome and new contacts made, color distinctions in some regions are blurring. For example, in Latin America there is much intermarriage between persons of American, African, and European ancestry.

Hair form and texture show significant racial differences. Between the straight hair of the Mongol and the fine woolly hair of the West African there are intermediate forms of wavy and curly hair, as found among Europeans and North Africans. Though environment and manipulation may temporarily change hair form, basically heredity controls it, and the forms do not seem to merge. The selective propensities of the different kinds of hair are unknown and attempts to explain them remain speculative.

Among some African and Australian peoples *prognathism*—protrusion of the jaw—is common. But prognathism is recessive. Thus in North America the jutting jaw of the Negro has largely disappeared because of interbreeding with Europeans. The broadest *noses* are found in West Africa, the narrowest in northern Europe, and those of intermediate width in Asia. The long and high nose, which is usually associated with Armenians and Jews, is actually widespread in Asia Minor and the Balkan countries. The nose of the American Indian is often higher and longer than that of the East Asian, perhaps resulting from a dominant aquiline form mixing with a shorter East Asian type.

A distinctive trait among many groups in Eastern and Central Asia, Southeast Asia, and among many Indians in the Americas is the *epicanthic* or *Mongolian eye fold*. It covers the upper eyelid and has selective value against sun glare. The Bushmen and Hottentots of southern Africa have a slightly different form; here the fold may be due to independent natural selection in an environment where the sunlight is as intense as in Mongolia.

The conclusion, as these examples show, is that any classification of the human species into racial groups is bound to be artificial and to some degree arbitrary. Nature gives us no classification. What we call "human races" are statistical averages. The problem is not new. Blumenbach, founder of modern physical anthropology, wrote in 1775:

Although there seems to be [such a] difference between widely separated nations, that you might easily take the inhabitants of the Cape of Good Hope, the Greenlanders, and the Circassians for so many species of men, yet when the matter is thoroughly considered, you see that all do so run into one another, and that one variety of mankind does so sensibly pass into another, that you cannot mark out the limits between them. (Blumenbach, 1865, 99)

A meaningful classification of human groups will take into account not only the distribution of important physical traits, but also the origin and genetic nature of distinctive human groups. A modern anthropologist, Ashley Montagu, expresses the same idea:

Within the divisions of mankind there exist many local types, but most of these local types are very much mixed, so that only in a very small number of cases is it possible to distinguish distinctive local types or ethnic groups among them. . . . Not one of the great divisions of mankind is unmixed, nor is any one of its ethnic groups pure; all are, indeed, much mixed and of exceedingly complex descent. . . . The differences between the great divisions of man and between the ethnic groups comprising them represent merely a distribution of variations which, for reasons which may be fairly clearly understood, occur more frequently in one group than they do in another. (Montagu, 1942, 5–6)

It is no wonder, then, that many different classifications have been proposed. In the eighteenth century Blumenbach, using skin color as a differentiating feature, identified five races; a century later Deniker listed 29 races based on hair form, skin color, and nose shape; in 1946 Hooton recognized three main racial stocks

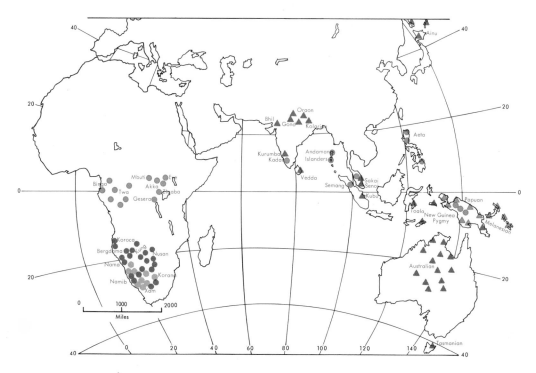

Figure 4–2. ISOLATED PEOPLES

The symbols indicate locations of groups genetically isolated from the main mass of mankind until recent times.

with 23 primary subraces, giving some consideration to mixtures. Certain classifications give the impression that they refer to sharp divisions, implying that each has arisen from "pure" types (*Scientific American*, 1960, 118–120). Still others assume that the evolution of man has somehow reached a stable situation, while in fact race formation continues into the present (*Scientific American*, 1960, 206–217).

Isolated Peoples

Easiest to classify are several small isolated groups. Their isolation means that their genes play only a minor role in determining the physique of the mass of mankind. Figure 4–2 and Table 4–2 summarize the nature and location of these peoples. It has been suggested that such peoples represent the prototypes of modern man, resembling the human beings from whom have developed the present main racial stocks outlined below. The widespread distribution of the Australoids (and also the Negritoids) lends credence to this idea. On the other hand, slight differences within each of these isolated groups suggest either a series of roughly parallel developments in different places or migration to their present locations during a relatively recent stage of human evolution. Perhaps the Negritoids originated in southern Asia, spread widely, then were pushed back to their present refuge areas by invaders.

4. Race: Biological Facts and Social Attitudes

Table 4–2. Isolated Peoples

Group	Features	Examples	
Negritoid	Yellow to brown skin Black spiral (peppercorn) hair Short stature Negrito and Negrillo have different blood types	Congo River and Upper Nile Pygmy	Negrillo
		Andaman Islanders Semang of Malaya New Guinea Pygmy Aeta of Luzon	Negrito
Bushmanoid	Hair and skin like Negritoid Flat face Epicanthic eye fold Steatopygy in females	Bushmen and Hottentots of southern Africa	
Australoid	Dark skin and eyes Dark wavy hair Broad nose Full lips Long head Hirsute A and O blood types (no B)	Australian aborigines Ainu of Hokkaido and Sakhalin Vedda of Ceylon Sakai of Malaya Kurumba of Deccan Plateau Bhil, Gond of Deccan Plateau Oraon of Chota Nagpur	
Papuan- Melanesian	Much like the Australoid, but more frizzly hair	Papuans of New Guinea Melanesians of Solomons	

The Bushmen pose a riddle with their eye folds and slanting eyes, which resemble those of Asians. Formerly there were many throughout southern Africa; only a few survive. The more numerous Hottentots appear to derive some traits from types now living in southeastern Africa.

The Main Racial Stocks

The great mass of men belong to the heterogeneous peoples with variable genetic structures. Although the physical types merge imperceptibly into one another, we can identify three distinct sets of genetic features which allow a broad division into Negroid, Mongoloid, and Caucasoid racial stocks.

The Negroid set includes black skin and black woolly hair, dark eyes, broad and flat nose, thick and everted lips, long head, prognathous jaw, and stocky body build. The regions of selection appear to have been the hot, bright savanna lands of West Africa.

The Mongoloid set includes light yellow to brown skin, brown eyes, straight and coarse black hair, flat face and nose, broad head, epicanthic eye fold, high cheekbones, and short and stocky build. The regions of selection were probably the dry and bright mid-latitude steppes with pronounced summer and winter seasons of Central Asia.

The Caucasoid set includes fair skin and eyes, light and wavy hair, prominent and narrow nose, thin lips, and abundance of body hair. The regions of selection most likely were the damp, cool, cloudy tundras and forests of western Eurasia.

The climatic-vegetational environments here

mentioned do not describe the present, but the ecological conditions during the last glaciation. In that period the mountain belts from Anatolia to Kamchatka became impassable. Between these barriers and the deserts of North Africa and Southwest Asia lay a zone of more genial climate. We can postulate that mankind (probably only a few scattered thousands) originally lived in this central belt, but that some groups moved into outlying regions where they were overtaken by climatic change. Where isolated for long periods in extreme environments, the people were modified by natural selection and genetic drift. Distinctive adaptations became common to each of the isolated groups: for example, black skin, hair, and eyes, the eye fold and flat face, the fair hair and skin.

In the central belt, it can be further conjectured, the peoples continued to maintain a pool of diverse hereditary factors. Toward the end of the glaciation when climatic conditions ameliorated, contacts were reestablished between the formerly extreme areas and the central belt. Much migration and intermixing took place, especially along the margins of the regions where specialized types had evolved. This explains why peoples of the central belt are hardest to classify. Here groups, probably quite diverse to begin with, have absorbed over a long time features from the Caucasoids, Mongoloids, and Negroids.

As an example, let us see how Mongoloid traits may have spread, according to a team of experts on racial origins (Coon, Garn, and Birdsell, 1950, 83–84):

When the climate of the boreal zone of the Northern Hemisphere warmed up, the survivors of the cold had every chance to increase in numbers, to fill up their cradle area, and spill out beyond its former barriers. The earliest post-glacial populations of which we know in north and central China, Mongolia, and Siberia were Mongoloid. Some of them went across Bering Strait and the Aleutian chain to North America, where unspecialized peoples of the same basic stock had preceded them. Or so all evidence now at hand would indicate.

During the third millennium B.C. farming people of Mediterranean-Caucasoid stock moved eastward through Asia from oasis to

oasis, and spread into the Yellow River Valley of northern China. There they mixed to some extent with the aborigines, and thus acquired a partially Mongoloid character. As the Chinese pushed southward they drove ahead of them most of the indigenous Mongoloid tribes who, in turn, invaded Southeast Asia's mainland "over a period of more than a thousand years, from about 400 B.C. to 800 A.D."

Mongoloid groups also moved into the Malay Archipelago—from perhaps as early as 2000 B.C. onward—and absorbed some of the earlier inhabitants. The mixture produced a local Mongoloid variety, the ancestors of the Polynesians.

A series of migrations of Caucasoid peoples from the north into the Mediterranean region and southwestern Asia infused lighter color into the populations of these areas. Some Negroid traits from West Africa spread through the southern and northern sections of the continent and reached even parts of southern Europe and southwestern Asia. Figure 4–3 summarizes the main directions of these Old World migrations up to historic times. The diagram (Figure 4–4) shows as an example the presumed relations of ethnic groups within the Negroid division. The lines that connect the various groups do not imply descent as from parent to child on a genealogical table; rather, they represent unmarked scales of increasing and decreasing gene frequencies.

Present Distribution of the Main Races

The "true" Negro lives in West Africa. This region and that further to the east was probably the area where the natural selection of distinctive Negroid features occurred. As we move away from West Africa we meet many types that have some Negroid features, but also traits common to peoples of the Mediterranean and southwestern Asia (Figure 4–4). Black skin gives way to brown and lighter shades, broad flat nose to narrow nose, stocky to slender build, tightly curled hair to wavy or even straight, thick lips to thin.

A clue to the explanation comes from the

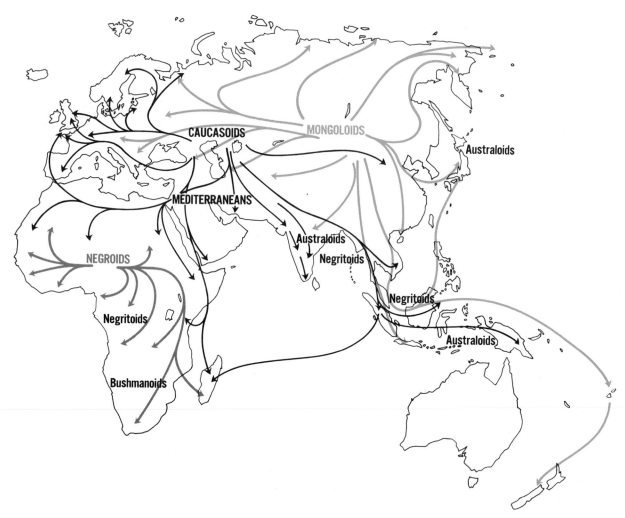

Figure 4–3. EARLY HUMAN MIGRATIONS

The map shows, in diagrammatic form, the direction of migrations of
Negroid, Caucasoid, and Mongoloid raciál elements into regions occupied
by Negritoid, Bushmanoid, and Australoid peoples.

descendants of the Negroes brought as slaves
to the New World from West Africa. We know
for a fact that in the Americas many people
from Europe interbred with their slaves. From
this an American Negro population developed
possessing on the average numerous Caucasoid
features. We can assume that also in Africa

populations exhibiting such mixtures of traits
result from similar interbreeding.

The "classic" Mongoloid individual is found
today in Mongolia. In this region, isolated by
mountain ranges and ice sheets, his distinctive features evolved through "climatic engineering." As in the case of the Negroid peoples,

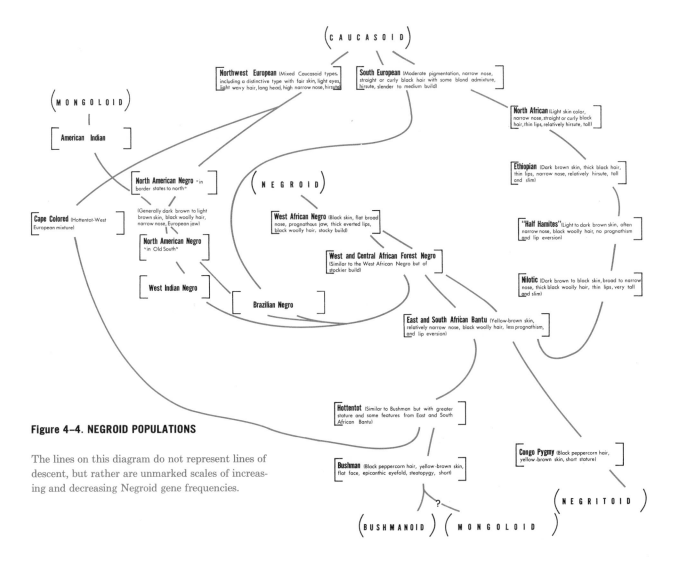

Figure 4–4. NEGROID POPULATIONS

The lines on this diagram do not represent lines of descent, but rather are unmarked scales of increasing and decreasing Negroid gene frequencies.

there are strong indications that Mongoloid genes decrease in frequency as one moves away from the area of origin. The North Chinese is often slim in build, and the facial features of a significant proportion (perhaps one in twenty) remind us of Mediterranean–Southwest Asian types. In southern China the epicanthic eye fold is less evident. Contrasting with the round-faced, relatively hairless and stocky Mongolian, the Japanese is often narrow-faced, hirsute, and slightly built. The Eskimo has many Mon-

goloid features, but a prominent narrow nose. American Indians, often lumped together as a variety of Mongoloid, actually are diverse in physique, some with almost pure Mongoloid features, others resembling Southeast Asians.

It is not so easy to divide the Caucasoid peoples into distinct subgroups living in separate regions. This is particularly true of Europe, where many migrations have resulted in much mixing and remixing. Three principal types can be recognized, however: (1) *Nordic* people have

4. Race: Biological Facts and Social Attitudes

Indians of Ecuador. Like all indigenous peoples of the Americas they are of Mongoloid racial stock, though altered by circumstance of time and place. [A Shell photograph]

fair skin, wavy blond or red hair, blue eyes, narrow noses, and long heads; they form only a bare majority of the Scandinavians, a large minority in the British Isles, North Germany, and the Low Countries, and occur in still lower proportions farther afield. (2) The *Alpines* have broad heads, thick-set bodies, light skin, and straight to wavy brown hair; they too are found in varying proportions throughout Europe, with a wedgelike zone of concentration from Central Asia penetrating into western France. One view claims that Alpine traits represent a blend of Nordic and Mediterranean features with those of prehistoric European populations. Another view contends that they evolved from an intermixing of Nordic with Mongoloid after invasions from Central Asia. (3) The *Mediterranean* type occupies lands from Portugal and Morocco to the Indian subcontinent. The nose is generally large, the head long, eyes dark, and facial features smooth. But other traits show considerable range: the skin from light olive to dark, and the hair from brown to very dark brown and from straight to wavy. In North and East Africa, Mediterranean features shade into Negroid. Complexions become darker in India, almost black in south India, although many other features are similar to those of the lighter folk further north. Mediterranean traits gradually fade away in Southeast Asia and the islands of the Pacific Ocean; they are replaced by those of Mongoloid peoples and by characteristics associated with Australoid and perhaps Negritoid peoples.

The white populations of South Africa, Australia, and New Zealand are similar to their counterparts in northwestern Europe, while those of North America reflect the more diverse racial origins of its immigrants. In South America the peoples of European background are principally Mediterranean in physique. In Siberia the white settlers, having come from eastern Europe, show high proportions of Alpine features.

In each of these cases the Europeans have mixed to a greater or lesser extent with peoples of other genetic background. The offspring from Anglo-Americans and Negroes are referred to as Negro and generally classed with those of solely Negro ancestry. South African whites mating with Hottentots created the Cape Coloreds, most of whom live in Cape Province. Latin Americans of European origin combined with indigenous American stock to produce the Mestizos, who are very numerous and form the bulk of the population in several Latin American countries.

Race versus Culture

Often one can observe some correspondence between physical and cultural characteristics: the English are Caucasoid, the Chinese Mongoloid, the Ghanaians Negroid. A common saying is, "He looks like a Frenchman (Mexican, Filipino)." This is understandable, because both biological inheritance and learned behavior stem mostly from parents. Some people, though, are not aware of the essential difference between race and culture. They carelessly use such terms as "German race," "Jewish race," and "Arab race," instead of "nation," "religious community," and "cultural group." Others go much further; they assert that race determines culture. To them the achievements of Western civilization are due to the superiority of the white race, while the low levels of living in Asia and Africa, or among the Negroes in the United States, result from inborn inferiority of the "colored races."

It is nonsense to say that skin color is a key to mental worth. A physical trait cannot express or affect mental qualities one way or the other. But it is possible that the inheritance of mental qualities varies from one physically distinct group to another. Are general intelligence, artistic sense, or an energetic disposition inherited in different degrees or forms by different racial groups? A satisfactory answer is impossible. To experiment is extremely difficult, because the influences of nurture cannot be stripped away to discover what is nature. Tests that try to distinguish inborn mental traits or capabilities of racial groups only succeed in being gauges of economic or social opportunity.

The history of civilized man shows no evidence that race determines the level of technical achievement. For instance, the many inventions in agriculture originated among various races. As Pasternak writes: "Mankind does not live in a state of nature, but in history." An individual's attainments appear to be governed by the culture in which he is embedded rather than by the racial group to which he belongs. Confucius put it more simply: "Men's natures are alike; it is their habits that carry them far apart." Regarding the American Negro, an anthropologist writes:

So far as he has been permitted [the American Negro] has acquired the cultural traits of the white population among which he lives, while the white population have acquired some of his traits. This is not due to physical mixture but to cultural intermixture. If the physical mixture were responsible then we should observe a blending of Negro and white cultural traits,

This Indonesian boy is fairly representative of the Southeast Asian type of Mongoloid, also called Oceanic Mongoloid. [A Shell photograph]

but we observe nothing of the sort. The original cultures of the African Negro ancestors survive in Africa, but have been to a large extent lost among many Negro groups in America, having been completely eroded by the dominant white culture. This could not have occurred had the genes been responsible for the development of either "soul" or "culture." (Montagu, 1951, 362–363)

Racial Tensions

The geographer's concern with racial relations follows from his interest in the comparative study of places: Why do racial tensions occur where they do and how do they affect the character of a country? Racial relations derive from attitudes that are part of culture. Knowledge of the biological character of ethnic groups in a region of racial tension provides no answer to these questions. It only serves to set the stage for investigating the locational, historical, and social conditions that may account for the conflict.

In modern history, colonization by Europeans has often created situations conducive to race prejudice. But colonization itself is not the cause of racial tension, for there have been cases where racial discord has not followed it. In Brazil, for example, the Portuguese imposed a colonial system on the American Indians and later imported large numbers of Negro slaves; despite these events, that country has minimal race prejudice, although it doubtless exists.

The emergence of racial bias, then, depends on the specific nature and circumstances of the encounter between ethnic groups. Confrontations have occurred in different ways: in colonial settlement, like that of Europeans in the Americas, Africa, Australia, and Siberia; through economic enterprise as represented by European and American trading companies and plantations in less developed tropical regions; or in colonial imperialism as, for instance, the division of Africa between European powers in the nineteenth century.

On the whole, contacts in the economic sphere have been, and are, most common. Here the different levels of cultural attainment of various racial groups turn into a division of work along ethnic lines. The use of cheap labor came to be justified on the grounds that the workers were of an inferior race and thus worthy only of menial tasks. The dominant group used the same rationalization to support their political control—the inferior should be governed by the superior. Such views, of course, are not confined to peoples of European culture.

Much racial prejudice has the same kind of economic and political motivation as class prejudice, and the two may be related in origin. In former times, and in some places today, intolerance was directed toward class. The ruling class considered the lower classes as "born to their station in life." As long as an economy required a force of "hewers of wood and drawers of water" the menial workers could be perpetuated by treating them as a race apart. Rigid class if not caste systems with strictly confined marriage circles are, or have been, common to many societies regardless of racial character.

In Europe, when the eighteenth-century Enlightenment promoted the idea of human equality, class barriers began to crumble, leading to more or less "open societies." In this respect the United States, less burdened by tradition than Europe, took the lead.

Unfortunately race prejudice appears to have taken the place of class prejudice. Thus, although slavery was abolished in Western countries in the nineteenth century, attitudes held toward the lower classes were transferred to the descendants of slaves, especially those of African ancestry. The motivation was still one of economic and political power, but the test of who belonged to the low-caste laboring group became skin color. This explanation of racial relations is not all-inclusive, to be sure, but it helps to understand the situation in countries like the United States, Rhodesia, and South Africa.

Interbreeding

In almost all cases of race prejudice the final argument of those who favor segregation is that the children of mixed marriages are inferior.* They may well be inferior in their upbringing or accomplishments if they are discriminated against. There is no evidence that they are biologically inferior. Indeed, it is likely that crossbreeding results in biologically superior specimens. As L. C. Dunn puts it:

The limited amount of in-breeding which occurs within a marriage circle tends to produce gene differences between different circles. When members of different circles marry, the children are liable to contain more gene pairs with unlike partners than the

*"Race mixture" and "miscegenation" are misleading terms since true races in the sense of homozygous populations rarely are involved in interbreeding, at least in modern times. The terms "mixed-blood," "half-blooded," and "full-blooded" are liable to misinterpretation (although perhaps justified by continuous usage) because each individual's blood is his own. As pointed out before, blood types cut across the normally used racial divisions of mankind.

parents. In some animals and plant populations this condition appears to be conducive to greater biological vigor—the "mixed bloods" or hybrids are superior in some respects to either parent stock. In fact it may be that variety is good because it makes unlike combinations commoner. We know very little about this sort of thing in man, but the very mixed biological make-up of all present day human individuals and groups suggests that there may be something in it.

Biologically then, men belong to one mating circle, and share in a common pool of genes. Thus there is no biological justification for race hatred or prejudice. One should be careful to recognize this prejudice for what it is, and not try to conceal it behind a "scientific" rationalization.

The conditions of the modern world, deplorable as they are for many peoples over whom hangs the threat of insecurity and war, are nevertheless just those which tend to remove and reduce the factors which created biological race differences. If given a chance to continue in operation, they have the power to restore the unity which the human race lost by geographical dispersion. (UNESCO, 1952, 283–284)

It has been suggested that the status of "half-breeds" indicates the degree of assimilation between the two parent groups. The offspring of European-Asian mixing (often called "Eurasians") usually have not been fully accepted either by Asians or by Europeans, thus pointing up the marked cleavage between the colonized and the colonizers. On the other hand, people of mixed parentage in Hawaii and Brazil meet with little racial discrimination.

Table 4–3 shows the ethnic composition in a number of countries where the inhabitants are of different racial origin. The table is of less value for its figures, which should be used with caution, than for the heterogeneity of ethnic or racial concepts it reveals. The explanatory footnotes demonstrate again how significant cultural perception is in the classification of racial groups.

Negroes in the United States

The United States Census divides the population into "Whites" and "Nonwhites," and the

Table 4–3. Mixed Populations in Selected Political Units*

Political Unit	Date	Description	Population Thousands	Percent
Angola	1950	White	79	1.9
		Mixed	30	0.7
		Negro	4,036	97.4
Cape Verde Islands	1950	White	3	8.1
		Mixed	103	65.3
		Negro	42	26.6
Southwest Africa	1951	White	49	11.7
		Others	17	4.1†
		Bantu	349	84.2
South Africa	1951	White	2,642	20.8
		Asiatic	367	2.9
		Bantu	8,556	67.6
		Others	1,103	8.7†
Kenya	1948	Indian	91	1.7
		Colored	1	
		Arab	24	0.5
		African	5,251	97.1
		European	30	0.6
		Goans	7	0.1
Cuba	1953	White	4,244	73.0
		Mixed	843	14.5
		Negro	725	12.5

* From table 7 (Population by Ethnic Composition and Sex), United Nations *Demographic Yearbook 1956,* New York, 1956. The book contains a discussion of this and other compilations. "The heterogeneity of the concepts used in collecting these data is their basic defect. This lack of uniformity is evidenced by the variety of terms used: ('nationality,' 'race,' 'color,' 'race and color,' 'color and geography,' 'stock,' 'origin,' 'socio-economic characteristics,' etc.). Furthermore, different shades of meaning have been attached to these words, so that the connotations range from a rough biological concept . . . to a question of cultural affiliation. . . . In addition, more than one concept has sometimes been

Political Unit	Date	Description	Population	
			Thousands	Percent
Windward Islands	1946	White	3	1.2
		Colored	89	35.3
		Black	151	60.0
		Indian	8	3.2
Dominican Republic	1950	White	601	28.1
		Mulatto	1,289	60.4
		Negro	245	11.5
Brazil‡	1950	White	32,038	61.7
		Colored	13,787	26.5
		Unknown	108	0.2
		Black	5,693	10.9
		Yellow	329	0.7
Hawaii	1950	Caucasian	115	23.0
		Hawaiian	86	17.2
		Filipino	61	12.2
		Puerto Rican	10	2.0
		Negro	3	0.6
		Japanese	185	37.0
		Chinese	32	6.4
		Korean	7	1.4
New Zealand	1951	European	1,791	92.6
		Chinese	6	0.3
		Indian	2	0.1
		Maori	115	5.9
		Polynesian	3	0.2

employed in a single distribution, so that, for instance, 'French' and 'Negro' may appear as two of the items in a classification. . . . It goes without saying that the terms and figures of the table should be treated with circumspection."

† "Persons not of pure European, Asiatic or Bantu stock, including *inter alia* Hottentots, Cape Malays, Cape Coloureds, Bushmen, Griquas, Namaquas, Korannas, and St. Helena Islanders."

‡ "Excluding Indian jungle population (number unknown) and 31,960 schedules not tabulated by ethnic group and sex."

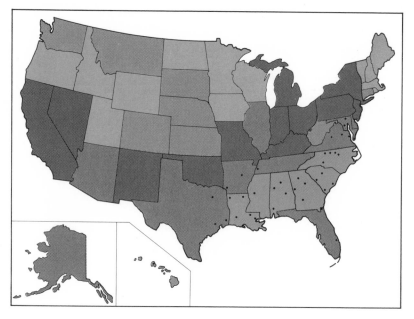

Percentage Nonwhite

 Under 2.5

2.5 - 4.9

5.0 - 9.9

10.0 - 24.9

25.0 and over

Figure 4–5. UNITED STATES: NONWHITE POPULATIONS AS A PERCENTAGE OF TOTAL POPULATION

The dots represent urban areas (over 50,000 population) with over 20 percent of their population nonwhite. The vast majority of "nonwhites" are Negroes. Higher percentages in the southwest are partly due to concentrations of Mexicans and American Indians; the latter are also numerous in the north central portion and Alaska. Compiled from data in U.S. Bureau of the Census *County and City Data Book, 1962* (A Statistical Abstract Supplement), Washington, D.C., 1962.

II. Cultural Diversity

latter into "Nonwhite Races," among whom are "Negro, American Indian, Japanese, Chinese, Filipino, Korean, Asian Indian, and Malayan." For the Bureau of the Census, "the concept of race is derived from that which is commonly accepted by the general public. . . . [It] does not reflect clear-cut definitions of biological stock, and several categories obviously refer to national origin" (U.S. Census, 1960). In responding to census questions, individuals have to assign themselves to one category or another. Presumably, many individuals of mixed ancestry make the decision on sociocultural grounds.

According to the census, Negroes number over 20 million, comprising about 11 percent of the national population. Table 4–4 shows how their distribution has changed since 1790. The table is largely self-explanatory and only needs a few comments. The northern border states of the South were the first to experience a relative decline in their Negro population. In the twentieth century, losses spread to rural districts of other Southern states. The cities of the South maintained and, in the case of the large cities, even increased their proportion of Negroes. Since the Civil War the shares of the Northeast and Middle West and, in more recent times, of the Pacific Coast states have steadily grown.

The dominant feature of change at mid-twentieth century is the migration of the Negro to the cities. Figure 4–6 shows two things: the large numbers moving from the South to northern cities, and the relationship between southern areas of origin and northern cities of destination. The proportion of the national Negro population in each of three pairs of regions—South Atlantic–Northeast, Central South–Midwest, Southwest-Pacific—has remained almost constant since 1890 (Hart, 1960).

The majority of American Negroes exhibit physical characteristics derived from both African and European ancestry. Most of the interbreeding took place before the emancipation of the slaves. The institution of slavery was succeeded by the color bar. Many states, especially in the South, have laws forbidding the marriage of Negroes and whites. In many Southern states the color bar is drawn in law

Table 4–4. United States: Percentage of Total Negro Population in Selected Regions, 1790–1960

Region	1790	1860	1910	1960
Northeast	24.3	8.2	9.1	21.8
East North Central	1.0	1.4	3.1	15.3
Pacific		0.1	0.3	5.1
Southwest		24.3	30.6	19.5
Border	42.4	26.7	15.9	10.6
Southeast	32.3	39.2	40.1	26.1
Other		0.1	0.9	1.6
United States Total, thousands	757	4,442	9,828	18,872

Definitions of regions:
Northeast: New England, New York, New Jersey, Pennsylvania, Delaware, Maryland, West Virginia, District of Columbia.
East North Central: Ohio, Indiana, Illinois, Michigan, Wisconsin.
Pacific: Washington, Oregon, California, Alaska, Hawaii.
Southwest: Mississippi, Arkansas, Louisiana, Oklahoma, Texas.
Border: Virginia, Kentucky, Tennessee, Missouri.
Southeast: North Carolina, South Carolina, Georgia, Alabama, Florida.
SOURCE: Hart, 1960, and *U.S. Census of Population, 1960.*

as well as custom; elsewhere it is drawn by custom only.* Nevertheless, many light-colored persons of mixed ancestry have been, and are being, absorbed into the white population. At present there is little intermarriage between Negroes and whites. The marriage circles of the two groups are to all intents and purposes mutually exclusive. If the legal and social barriers to marriage remain, the American Negro population may stabilize in physical appearance somewhere near the midpoint between the Northwest European and West African.

Great Britain

In Europe, racial tensions are rare because its population has a relatively homogeneous composition. (The Nazi racist doctrine was a fabrication born from national and economic mo-

*In June, 1967 the Supreme Court ruled unanimously that states cannot outlaw marriages between whites and nonwhites.

tives.) The recent immigration of West Indians and Pakistanis into Britain provides an interesting case of confrontation on the home ground of a European nation.

The West Indies, especially densely populated Jamaica, Barbados, and Leeward Islands, have large numbers of Negroes. Because the small white minorities for a long time marked their upper-class status by a strong color bar, the West Indian Negro is of purer West African ancestry than the North American Negro. An East Indian element also has been added to the Negro, white, and mixed groups in the Windward Islands, Trinidad, Tobago, and Guyana.

Many West Indians, especially Jamaicans, have migrated since 1950 to Britain, where they now form a small but conspicuous minority. There is no legal discrimination against them, but they have been relegated to the lower levels of what remains of the old British social-class structure. Most of them have "working-class" jobs in London and other large cities. Racial tension exists (although the problem does

4. Race: Biological Facts and Social Attitudes

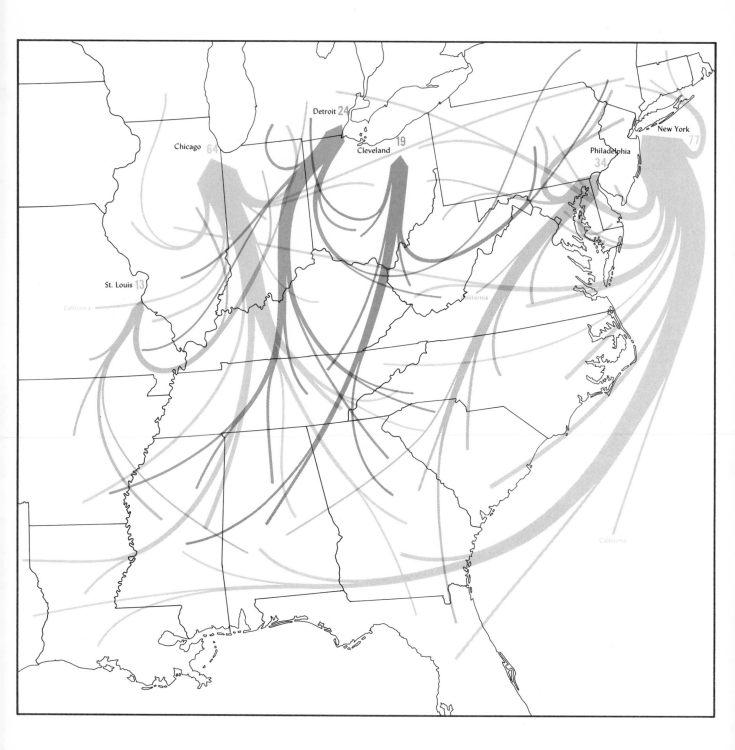

The flow lines join states of residence in 1955 to places of residence in 1960. Compiled from data in U.S. Bureau of the Census *U.S. Census of Population, 1960,* Subject Reports, *Mobility for Metropolitan Areas,* Washington, D.C., 1963.

Flow line widths show numbers changing residence 1955-1960

▬▬▬▬▬	More than 10,000
▬▬▬▬	5,000 — 9,999
▬▬▬	2,500 — 4,999
▬▬	1,000 — 2,499
▬	500 — 999

24　Thousands of migrants 1955-1960

not reach the scale of that in the United States or South Africa) and has led to some restrictions limiting the free influx of immigrants. An instructive sidelight on the nature of race relations and prejudice is that the Britons tend to show more bias against Pakistanis, who, like them, are physically Caucasoid but are Moslems and do not speak English, than against West Indians, who fit more easily into the British milieu because they are culturally Christians and speak English.

South Africa

The most acute race tensions, blindest prejudice, and most stringent color bar (*apartheid*) occur in South Africa. The whites, of Dutch and English origins, make up about one-fifth of the population, which totals over 17 million. The Negro Africans constitute more than two-thirds of the total population. They speak various Bantu languages, although many also know English or Afrikaans, the South African version of Dutch. The Cape Coloreds, descendants from the time when there was much mixing between settlers, or sailors, and the Hottentots, account for 7 percent of the population. Other groups that are recognized as socially and physically distinct include the Cape Malays and the Indians; the latter number about one-third of a million and are concentrated in Natal. The uneven distribution of these groups is shown on Figure 4–7.

The whites control South Africa, the Boers dominant in politics, the Britons in the economy. With a strong police force to back their power they have put into effect a system of Bantu segregation governing residence, circulation, education, marriage, and all other social associations. However, since the whites need the labor of the Bantu Africans, they employ them in large numbers for all lower-level production and service jobs.

The position of the Cape Colored population has deteriorated because new and old anti-Bantu measures have been applied to them without distinction. Until the 1950s the Cape Coloreds were treated as a special group in the political sphere as well as in social matters, as "befitted their status" halfway between the African and the European. Now the Boers seem to view them as being even "lower" than the Bantu because they are the fruit of what they consider illegal and sinful unions. Apparently, the Bantu also tend to reject the Cape Colored.

Some whites justify the policy of *apartheid* on the ground that their race is inherently superior. And even those whites who do not believe in their biological superiority maintain that integration of white and Bantu would lead to the destruction of both cultures and, in their place, to a much debased South African society.

The government recognizes its responsibility for improving the lot of the Bantu and spends considerable sums of money on their education and welfare, but always and only within the objectives of its segregation policy. To understand these attitudes one must, of course, keep in mind the vulnerable position of this small white world at the edge of black Africa. Still, one wonders whether all these repressive meas-

4. Race: Biological Facts and Social Attitudes

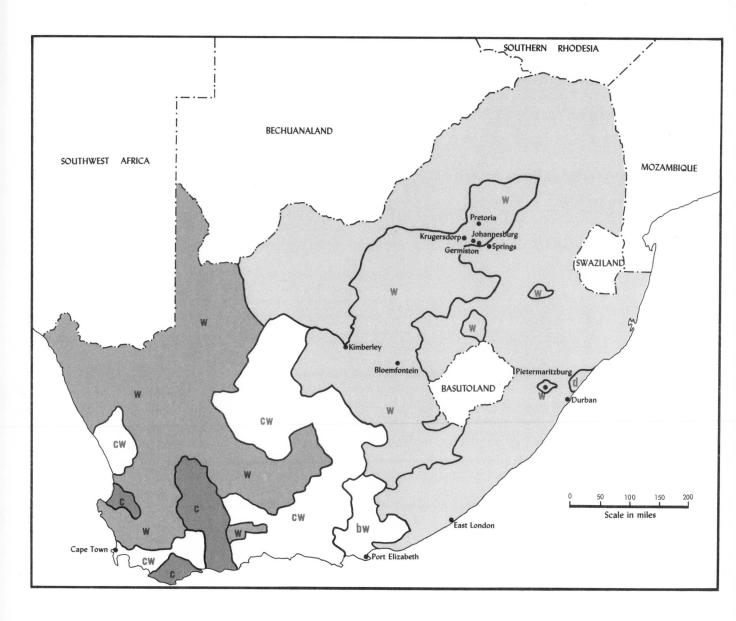

Figure 4–7. SOUTH AFRICA: ETHNIC GROUPS

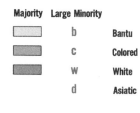

Majority	Large Minority	
	b	Bantu
	c	Colored
	w	White
	d	Asiatic

Figure 4–7. SOUTH AFRICA: ETHNIC GROUPS

White majorities, combined with Cape Colored minorities, appear only in small areas of Cape Province. In the east a crescent of almost completely Bantu areas surrounds the cores of Transvaal and Orange Free State, but the Bantu are a majority even in these cores. Bechuanaland (Botswana), Basutoland (Lesotho), and Swaziland are not part of the Republic of South Africa. After K. M. Buchanan, 1956, 764.

II. Cultural Diversity

ures do not merely postpone the day of a more just solution—if it is not too late for a solution.

Conclusion

Research in the biological nature of mankind belongs to the fields of genetics, anatomy, and physical anthropology. The geographer uses the findings because they throw light on the relations between race and place.

There is no biological justification for race prejudice. Nevertheless, race prejudice exists among many peoples, in some to such a degree that tension and fear are critical features of their society. To understand these situations one must switch from the biological to the sociocultural approach. The geographer can contribute to this line of investigation through his focus on place: Why does confrontation of "races" lead to discord in one area and not in others? And how do these conditions affect the character of countries?

Far too little is known as yet to give satisfactory answers to these questions. However, it is clear that racial intolerance is not inborn, but acquired. If bias is learned it also can be unlearned. Nevertheless, it is illusory to expect such changes to occur overnight. It has been said that to split the atom has proven easier than to eradicate race prejudice. Unless and until rational thought and desire for justice catch up with the findings of the biological sciences, racial discrimination will remain as proof of man's inhumanity to man.

Citations

Barnett, A. *The Human Species,* London, 1950.
Blumenbach, J. F. *The Anthropological Treatises of Johann Friedrich Blumenbach* (translator and ed. T. Bendyshe), London, 1865.
Buchanan, K. M. "The Union of South Africa," in: East, W. G., and Moodie, A. E. (eds.) *The Changing World,* London, 1956. [Map]
Coon, C. S., Garn, S. M., and Birdsell, J. B. *Races: A Study in the Problems of Race Formation in Man,* New York, 1950.
Hart, J. F. "The Changing Distribution of the American Negro," *Annals of the Association of American Geographers,* 50 (1960): 242–266.
Montagu, M. F. A. *Man's Most Dangerous Myth: The Fallacy of Race,* New York, 1942 (4th ed. Cleveland, 1964).
———. *An Introduction to Physical Anthropology,* Springfield, Ill., 1951.
Mourant, A. E., et al. *The ABO Blood Groups,* Oxford, 1958. [Map]
"The Human Species," *Scientific American,* 203 (September 1960).
UNESCO *The Race Question in Modern Science,* Paris, 1952.
Whitney, D. D. *Family Treasures,* New York, 1942.

Further Readings

Biasutti, R. *Le Razze e i populi della terra* (3d ed.) Turin, 1959.
Boyd, W. C. *Genetics and the Races of Man,* Boston, 1950.
———, and Asimov, I. *Races and Peoples,* New York, 1955.

Butzer, K. W. *Environment and Archaeology: An Introduction to Pleistocene Geography,* Chicago, 1964.

De Laubenfels, D. J. "Australoids, Negroids, and Negroes: a Suggested Explanation for Their Disjunct Distributions," *Annals of the Association of American Geographers,* 58 (1968): 42–50.

Dobzhansky, T. *Evolution, Genetics, and Man,* New York, 1955.

Dunn, L. C., and Dobzhansky, T. *Heredity, Race, and Society,* New York, 1952.

Gates, R. R. *Human Ancestry from a Genetical Point of View,* Cambridge, Mass., 1948.

Hooton, E. A. *Up from the Ape,* New York, 1958.

Howells, W. W. *Back of History,* New York, 1954.

———. *Mankind in the Making,* New York, 1959.

Kluckhohn, C. *Mirror for Man,* New York, 1949.

Korn, N., and Smith, N. R. (eds.) *Human Evolution,* 1954.

Kroeber, A. L. *Anthropology,* New York, 1948.

Montagu, M. F. A. *Man: His First Million Years,* New York, 1957.

Simpson, G. E., and Yinger, J. M. *Racial and Cultural Minorities,* New York, 1953.

Taylor, G. *Environment, Race, and Migration,* Toronto, 1937.

Tax, S. (ed.) *The Evolution of Man,* Chicago, 1960.

5. The Mosaic of Languages

Introduction

Language is a part of culture, a part of society's equipment for living. In this respect it is like social organization, government, and law. But language is more than just another segment of culture, because it also serves as the vehicle of communication between all components of society and as the main means of culture transmission from one generation to another. Furthermore, writing and reading also involve language, for systems of writing are symbolized language.

This chapter is concerned with the distribution of languages to show how the world varies in this respect; the relationships of different languages to illuminate the obscure subject of past migrations; bilingualism, a distinctive feature of some places; the use of language as a means of identifying culture groups; changes in the distribution of languages; and the relationships between languages and the physical earth.

There are thousands of languages and the study of their nature, relations, and meaning for the distinctiveness of cultures is complex. For this reason we must begin with some definitions. A *language* is a system of meaningful sounds produced by the human voice tract. To qualify as a distinct language, a tongue must have a core that is intelligible to all persons in a group, even though some may use variations. A *dialect* is a variant of a language, differing from other dialects in vocabulary, pronunciation, or grammar. Sometimes it is difficult to decide whether or not a tongue is a dialect or a completely separate language. In such matters national or local feeling may brush aside academic distinctions and demand recognition of a dialect as a separate language. The term *vernacular* is commonly used to denote the native language when another language, imposed on a people from outside, is the medium of education and government. A *dead language* is not acquired as a mother tongue, but was in the past. Some dead languages, such as Latin and Sanskrit, are learned today, not for general communication but for religious or scholarly reasons.

A *standard language* (sometimes called "official language") is a version that is recognized for education, government, and other public affairs. In a *script,* written symbols are used to express a language on paper or other substance. Often a standard written form of a language emerges. With the development of *literacy* (the ability to read and write), the written standard spreads widely and may lead to submersion of local or provincial variations. A *linguistic family* (or *linguistic stock*) is a group of languages that have a common origin. They resemble each other in systematic ways, usually through similar sounds or clusters of sounds, frequently with the same meaning and also sometimes through likeness in grammatical and vocabulary structure. Almost all *communi-*

cation comes through language or symbolized language, such as writing, smoke signals, drumbeats, and codes. The use of standard spoken and written versions of a language facilitates communication within a country. Communication is also possible between peoples who have different standard versions of the same language and usually also between those who speak dialects of the same language.

To sum up, we can use the following examples: English is a language spoken by some 300 million people in many parts of the world. Its standard versions differ in the United Kingdom, the United States, Canada, and Australia. Its dialects include Cockney, Brooklynese, American Southern speech, and Scottish. English, together with such languages as German, Swedish, Dutch, and Danish, belongs to the Germanic group which forms a subfamily of the Indo-European linguistic family.

World Distribution of Languages

The term linguistic family means that "a number of mutually unintelligible languages all represent divergent forms that can be shown historically to go back to a common original . . ." (Whatmough, 1957, 23). This is a *genetic* classification, for it shows relationships by origin and development. Of course one can classify languages in many other ways, for instance, by using the frequency of certain kinds of sounds. This aspect might interest the linguist, but it would be of little value from the historical and cultural point of view.

In countries with a long literary tradition, such as parts of Asia and Europe, the genetic associations of related languages are easier to observe than where the literary record goes back only a few decades. For example, Anglo-Saxon, Old High German, and Old Norse preceded the modern tongues of English, German, and Danish. From writings in these ancient languages we know that they had similar grammatical forms, sounds, and vocabularies. We can study the development of each into its

Children of Morotai Island, in the eastern part of Indonesia, are learning the common national language, *bahasa Indonesia,* which is quite different from their mother tongue.
[A Shell photograph]

modern equivalent in the voluminous literature written over the last thousand years.

Figure 5–1 (pp. 100–101) shows the location of the principal linguistic families and subfamilies. Table 5–1 (pp. 102–103) summarizes the distribution and importance of all individual languages spoken by more than 20 million persons. The world map of linguistic families and subfamilies has some shortcomings. Many different families and subfamilies of languages spoken by relatively small groups have been combined, for example, those of the American Indians and those in New Guinea. Moreover, the structure and relationships of numerous tongues in Africa and eastern Asia are far less known than those of the Indo-European languages. Further research by linguists may in time clarify the familial relationships of these languages. Thus, the map reflects the inadequacy of our present state of knowledge. In spite of these limitations, world distribution maps and detailed tables like Figure 5-1 and Table 5-1 contain enormous amounts of information which in textual form would cover scores or even hundreds of pages.

The Indo-European Linguistic Family

The study of linguistic affiliations can shed light on migrations and contacts between different human groups in prehistoric as well as historic times. The following discussion illustrates the way linguistic materials can supplement other data in attempts to re-create past human geography.

The Indo-European linguistic stock includes the principal languages of Europe and of areas colonized by Europeans, together with many tongues of southern and southwestern Asia (for Europe see Table 5-2, pp. 104–107 and Figure 5-2, p. 109). Member languages are spoken by about one-third of mankind. This family can be divided into two broad branches. The western one comprises the Greek, Romance (also called Italic), Celtic, Germanic (or Teutonic), Tokharian, and Anatolian languages; these last two, now extinct, were used in western Asia and Asia Minor, respectively. To the eastern branch belong the many Indo-Aryan languages, Iranian, Armenian, Illyrian (including Albanian), and the Balto-Slavic tongues.

In the nineteenth century, comparative and historical study of these languages and their predecessors established that all were descended from a cluster of related dialects spoken in prehistoric times. The speakers of these dialects left no documents to read or inscriptions to decipher; however, their language has been partly retrieved by linguistic methods. The reconstructed language, called Proto-Indo-European, should not be confused with the family after which it is named. From the study of words in Proto-Indo-European it is possible to infer the way of life of the peoples who spoke

it, and the approximate location of their homeland.

Since these ancient folk had words for the ox, sheep, pig, the plow, and cereals used for bread making, we may assume they were farmers and had connections with the Middle East, where this kind of agriculture originated. However, they had no words for tropical or Mediterranean animals such as the elephant, donkey, or camel, or for cultivated plants such as the vine and fig. They knew how to refine metal ores and make alloys, and how to fashion axes and other implements. They hunted the goose and duck, but did not know the lion and tiger. The conclusion that they resided in a temperate, not a tropical, climate is reinforced by the fact that they had words for winter and snow. From their knowledge of the beech, birch, pine, apple, and oak we can narrow down the location of their habitat to the western part of the Eurasian landmass. Almost all scholars agree that they lived in Europe north of the Alps–Black Sea line. From this area of general agreement opinions diverge: some advocate a Scandinavian homeland, others the extensive plains of north Germany and the Baltic lands, still others the Danubian basin. It seems best to think of the original distribution as covering a broad continuous area in east-central Europe. From here the speakers of the Proto-Indo-European language, or rather its various dialects, dispersed in several directions, broke up into divergent groups, and intermingled with others, leading in the course of thousands of years to the present linguistic mosaic (Myres, 1935, 184–193).

Our knowledge of the Indo-Europeans is not deduced solely from the study of languages. Archaeological finds and historical records of the societies which they penetrated or contacted provide us with clues about their migrations and the effects they had on other peoples. It is clear that from about 2000 B.C. the Indo-European speakers began to spread out in all directions. The Aryans supplanted the urban civilization of the Indus Valley. During the first half of the second millennium B.C., Babylonia was under alien, possibly Aryan, rule. In the

5. The Mosaic of Languages

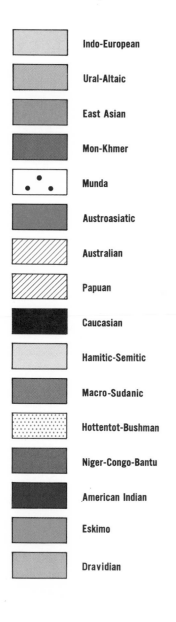

Figure 5–1. WORLD: PRINCIPAL LINGUISTIC FAMILIES AND SUBFAMILIES

Based in part on the maps in Meillet and Cohen, 1952.

- Indo-European
- Ural-Altaic
- East Asian
- Mon-Khmer
- Munda
- Austroasiatic
- Australian
- Papuan
- Caucasian
- Hamitic-Semitic
- Macro-Sudanic
- Hottentot-Bushman
- Niger-Congo-Bantu
- American Indian
- Eskimo
- Dravidian

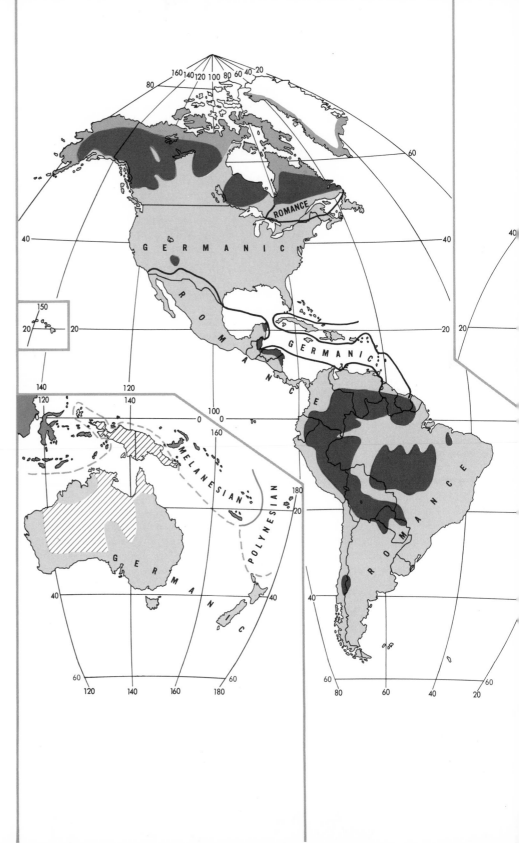

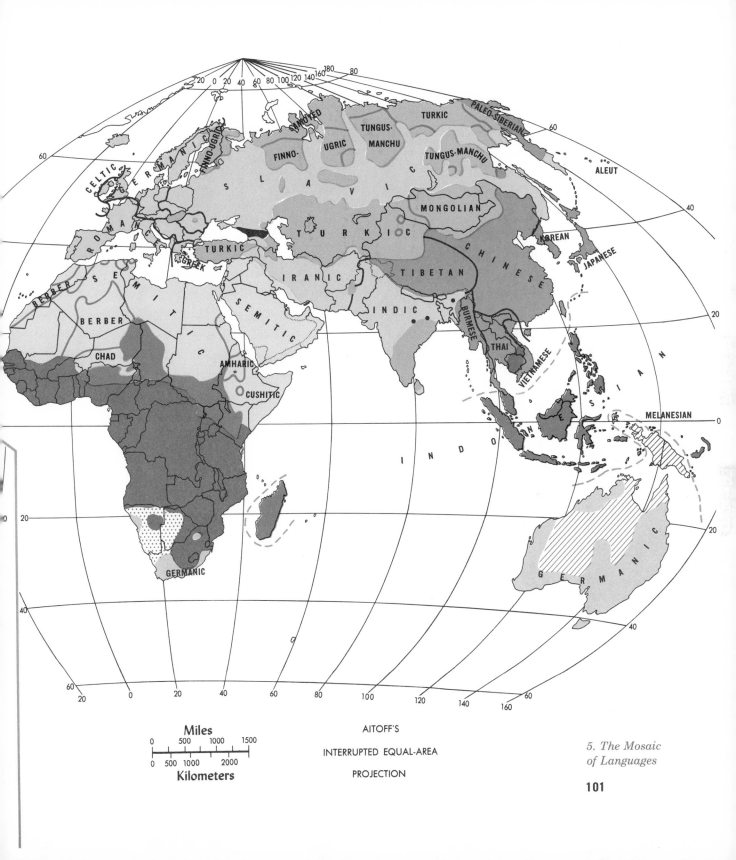

5. *The Mosaic
of Languages*

Table 5-1. The Principal Linguistic Families and Languages of the World

Linguistic family	Languages	Speakers, millions	Regions where standard language	Other regions	Remarks
Indo-European	English	300	United Kingdom, United States, much of (British) Commonwealth	Republic of Ireland	Worldwide lingua franca for diplomacy, commerce, and science
	Hindi	175	India, West Pakistan		Mother tongue in much of north India; lingua franca of Hinduism; Urdu dialect used by Moslems in much of India and Pakistan
	Spanish	190	Spain, all Latin American republics except Brazil and Haiti	Parts of north-western Africa	
	Russian	130	Russian Soviet Federated Socialist Republic	Others parts of Soviet Union	Official language of Soviet Union
	Bengali	95	East Pakistan, West Bengal (India)	Banaras and part of Bihar	55 million speakers in East Pakistan; 40 million in West Bengal
	Portuguese	90	Portugal, Brazil	Portuguese possessions	
	German	85	Germany, Austria, Luxembourg, Switzerland	Alsace and Lorraine	Area of German speech much contracted since 1944
	French	60	France, Belgium, Haiti, Canada, Switzerland	Parts of the French Union	Widely used as a lingua franca
	Italian	55	Italy, Switzerland	Corsica	A dialect in northwest Spain is Galician
	Ukrainian	45	Ukrainian S.S.R.	Nearby U.S.S.R.	Closely related to Russian
	Marathi	40	Maharashtra (India)	Nearby India	
	Polish	31	Poland	Nearby U.S.S.R.	Area much changed since 1944
	Punjabi	30	Punjab (India)	West Pakistan	
	Rajasthani	20	Rajasthan (India)		

Linguistic family	Languages	Speakers, millions	Regions where standard language	Other regions	Remarks
Sino-Tibetan	Chinese	550	China, Taiwan		The Mandarin dialect is standard
	Cantonese	20(?)		Southern China Southeast Asia Fuchien, Taiwan	In southern China many dialects are spoken; these three are the most important: others are Hakka, Shant'ou, and Tai-shan
	Fuchienese	25(?)			
	Wu	60(?)		Chechiang, Chiangsu	
Dravidian	Tamil	45	Madras (India)	Nearby parts of southern India	Also spoken by most Indians in Malaya and Burma
	Telegu	40	Andhra Pradesh (India)	Nearby parts of southern India	
	Kannada	20	Mysore (India)	Nearby parts of southern India	Also called Canarese
Japanese	Japanese	98	Japan	Pacific Islands	
Hamitic-Semitic	Arabic	115	Morocco, Algeria, Iraq, Syria, Tunisia, Libya, Sudan, Egypt, Jordan, Saudi Arabia, Yemen, Kuwait, Aden, Muscat and Oman, etc.	Western Sudan, east coast of Africa	The lingua franca of Islam in the west
Austronesian	Indonesian	100	Indonesia		The new official language of Indonesia, based on a Sumatran tongue
	Javanese	40		Java	The main vernacular on Java
Ural-Altaic	Korean	40	Korea (North and South)		
	Turkish	25	Turkey		Formerly more widespread
Niger-Congo-Bantu				Western, central, and southeast Africa	A large grouping with scores of languages and dialects

SOURCE: United Nations *Demographic Yearbook* and *Statistical Yearbook*, various years; Meillet and Cohen, 1952; official yearbooks of various countries.

Table 5–2. The Languages of Europe*

Linguistic family and subfamily	Language†	Speakers, millions	Regions where standard	Remarks
Indo-European Celtic	*Cornish*	None		Spoken in Cornwall until 1800s
	Welsh	0.7		Recent revival in Wales as a means of artistic expression
	Breton	0.9		Spoken in Brittany, but giving way to French
	Manx	None		Spoken in Man until the 1900s
	Modern Irish	0.03	Republic of Ireland	School language in Ireland
	Scottish Gaelic	0.08		In northwest Scotland, but dying out
Italic (Romance)	*Latin*	None		Language of Roman Empire; official language of Roman Catholic Church
	French	60	France, Belgium, Haiti, Switzerland, Canada	Parisian French is standard; many historic dialects
	Provençal	None		Written version of southern French dialects, not used anymore
	Catalan	5		Spoken in Catalonia, Valencia, the Balearics, and Roussillon (Fr.)
	Spanish	190	Spain, Latin America except Brazil and Haiti	Castilian is standard; many dialects in Spain and Americas
	Portuguese	90	Portugal, Brazil	Galician in northwestern Spain is a dialect
	Italian	55	Italy, Switzerland	Also in Corsica. Many dialects, which lose to Tuscan, the standard
	Rhaeto-Romanic	0.6	Grisons (Graubünden) in Switzerland	Also in northern Italy; three main dialects: Romansh, Ladin, Frioul

* Some minor languages in the European part of the U.S.S.R. are omitted.
† Dead languages are italicized.

Linguistic family and subfamily	Language†	Speakers, millions	Regions where standard	Remarks
	Romanian	18	Romania	Many words borrowed from Slavic; Zinzar is a dialect
	Sardinian	1		Spoken in Sardinia
Balto-Slavic	Lithuanian	2.5	Lithuanian S.S.R.	
	Lettish	1.5	Latvian S.S.R.	
	Russian	130	Russian Soviet Federated Socialist Republic	Official language of U.S.S.R. Includes 25 million elsewhere in U.S.S.R.
	Byelorussian	9	Byelorussian S.S.R.	
	Ukrainian	45	Ukrainian and Moldavian S.S.Rs.	Includes Ruthenian; also spoken in the Kuban
	Czechoslovakian	14	Czechoslovakia	Two main dialects: Czech and Slovak
	Polish	31	Poland	Area much changed since 1944
	Wendish	0.01		Close to Polish, spoken in Lusatia
	Slovenian	1.5	Slovenija (Yugoslavia)	
	Serbo-Croat	12	Serbia and Croatia (in Yugoslavia)	Serbian and Croatian use Cyrillic and Roman alphabets respectively
	Macedonian	1	Macedonia (Yugoslavia)	A dialect of Bulgarian
	Bulgarian	6	Bulgaria	
Germanic	Icelandic	0.1	Iceland	
	Danish	5	Denmark	A dialect is used in the Faeroe Islands
	Norwegian	4	Norway	Two main versions: Riksmål in southeast, Landsmål in southwest

Table 5–2. The Languages of Europe (continued)

Linguistic family and subfamily	Language†	Speakers, millions	Regions where standard	Remarks
	Swedish	8	Sweden	Also spoken in southwest Finland
	German	85	Germany, Austria, Luxembourg, Switzerland	High German is the standard; many dialects, including those of Alsace-Lorraine and Yiddish
	Plattdeutsch			Vernacular of the north German plain
	Dutch-Flemish	17	Netherlands, Belgium	Afrikaans, the language of the Boers in South Africa, is derived from Dutch
	Frisian	0.3		The language closest to English; vernaculars in north Netherlands, Oldenburg, and western Slesvig
	English	300	United Kingdom, United States, much of (British) Commonwealth	Also spoken in Ireland; used as a lingua franca for diplomacy, commerce, and science
Illyrian	Albanian	3	Albania	Also spoken in Kosmet district of Yugoslavia
Greek	Greek	9	Greece, Cyprus	Also spoken in western Turkey
Armenian	Armenian	3	Armenian S.S.R.	Also spoken in nearby Turkey; many dialects
Indo-Aryan	Romany	1(?)		The Gypsy language spoken in Russia, Balkans, England, etc.
Basque	Basque	0.5		Spoken in northern Spain and southwestern France; no known relatives
Ural-Altaic Uralic	Lapp	0.01		Spoken in northern Scandinavia and in Karelia

Linguistic family and subfamily	Language†	Speakers, millions	Regions where standard	Remarks
	Finnish	4.5	Finland	Suomi is standard
	Esthonian	1.5	Esthonian S.S.R.	
	Mordvinian	1.3		Mordvinian Autonomous S.S.R. and Middle Volga region
	Cheremissian	0.6		Mari A.S.S.R. and Upper Volga region
	Votiak	0.6		Udmurt A.S.S.R. and the Kama River region
	Zyrian	0.6		Komi A.S.S.R. and the Pechora River region
	Magyar	14	Hungary	Also spoken in central Romania and in Slovakia
Altaic	Kazan Tatar	5.5		Tatar and Bashkir A.S.S.R.
	Bashkirian	1.1		Bashkir A.S.S.R. and southern Urals region
	Chuvash	1.6		Chuvash A.S.S.R. and Middle Volga region
	Turkish	25	Turkey	Spoken in parts of the Balkans
	Azerbaijanian	3.3	Azerbaijan S.S.R.	Also spoken in nearby Caucasus
Caucasian	Georgian	3	Georgian S.S.R.	

SOURCE: United Nations *Demographic Yearbook* and *Statistical Yearbook*, various years; Meillet and Cohen, 1952; official yearbooks of various countries.

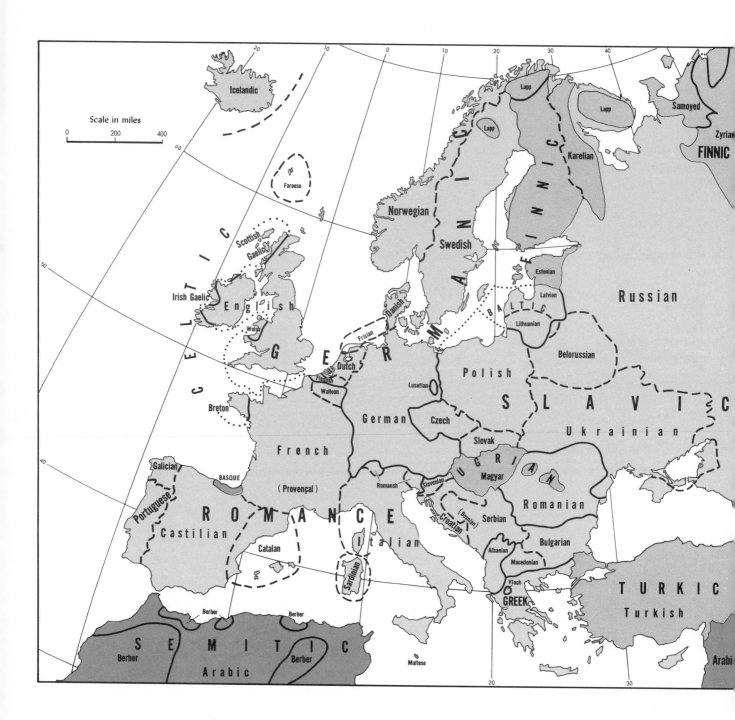

Figure 5–2. EUROPE: LANGUAGES

For the full distribution of the Uralian languages
see Figure 5–5.

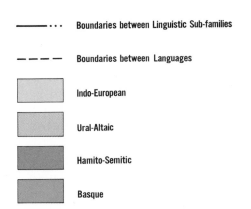

—— · · · Boundaries between Linguistic Sub-families

— — — Boundaries between Languages

[ ] Indo-European

[ ] Ural-Altaic

[ ] Hamito-Semitic

[ ] Basque

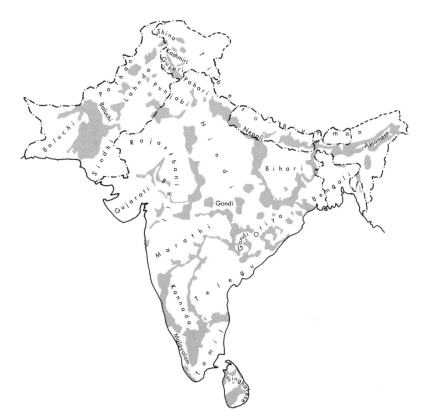

Figure 5–3. SOUTH ASIA: LINGUISTIC MIXING

Two or more languages are spoken in the areas
shown. In many of these regions the population is
bilingual. The principal languages are named.
Based on *Karta Narodov Indostana*, 1956.

same period the Hittites were pressing from
the northwest. Toward the end of the second
millennium the Mycenaeans built a trading
empire on the traditions of Minoan Crete. The
Persians under Cyrus and Darius stretched
their domain from the Aegean Sea to northern
India and as far south as the Sahara Desert. In
turn, the Phrygians destroyed the Hittites;
Dorians and other Greeks superseded the
Mycenaean civilization centered on the Aegean
and Crete. Peoples speaking Italic tongues sub-
jugated the prehistoric inhabitants of the
Italian peninsula. The Celts burst into Europe
south of the Danube and west as far as Britain
and Gaul. The Germanic peoples pressed behind the Celts and eventually overthrew them
and their Roman overlords; they also pushed
eastward toward the Vistula River. The Slavic
and Baltic folk, at first penned within the backwoods of east-central Europe, later supplanted
Celts, Germans, and Scythians in more open
lands.

What forces caused these migrations is a
matter of conjecture. Some scholars think that
an unfavorable change in climate brought about
the movements. Another view is that technological development, including the use of the
horse and the making of superior weapons, led
to population pressure and the urge to conquer
new lands, especially the richer ones to the
south.

Bilingualism

Usually we think of individuals as speaking one
language, their mother tongue. Maps of language distributions, such as Figures 5–1 and
5–2, strengthen the notion that people living

*5. The Mosaic
of Languages*

Table 5–3. Bilingualism in Selected Countries

Canada (1961)	Ability to speak	Mother tongue	Swaziland (1956)		Ability to speak
English	12,284,000	10,660,000	Afrikaans		727
English and French	2,231,000		English		2,494
			English and Afrikaans		3,854
French	3,489,000	5,123,000	Swazi		218,544
Neither English nor French	232,000		Swazi and English		11,230
			Other		220

Cyprus (1960)			Belgium	(1930)	(1947)
Greek only	387,328	442,138	French only	3,039,000	2,911,000
Turkish only	60,277	104,320	Flemish only	3,473,000	3,554,000
Other language only	19,216	27,108	German only	69,000	59,000
Greek and Turkish	33,582		French and Flemish	1,046,000	1,326,000
Greek, Turkish, and English	10,888		French and German	67,000	83,000
Greek and English	44,920		Flemish and German	9,000	23,000
Turkish and English	4,502		French, Flemish, and German	54,000	216,000
Others	12,853				

Scotland (1961)	Use of Gaelic
Gaelic only	1,079
Gaelic and English	75,508

Union of South Africa (1960)

	Europeans	Colored	Asiatics
Afrikaans	1,790,000	1,337,000	7,000
English	1,151,000	154,000	64,000
English and Afrikaans	44,800	14,000	1,300
German	32,654		
Netherlands (Dutch)	22,554		
Other	46,692	4,600	403,900

SOURCE: United Nations *Demographic Yearbook, 1963,* table 10, 321ff. For Belgian statistics: *Annuaire statistique de la Belgique, 1961,* Bruxelles, 49.

in each area use only the language shown. Actually, many millions also are fluent in a language additional to the one learned at home, because they need it to engage in commerce, a profession, or politics. Bilingualism is particularly necessary in countries where some other force than language has fused a nation, such as religion in India and Pakistan, insular habitat in Ceylon, historical circumstance in Belgium.

Worldwide statistics on bilingualism are at present not available; only in some countries

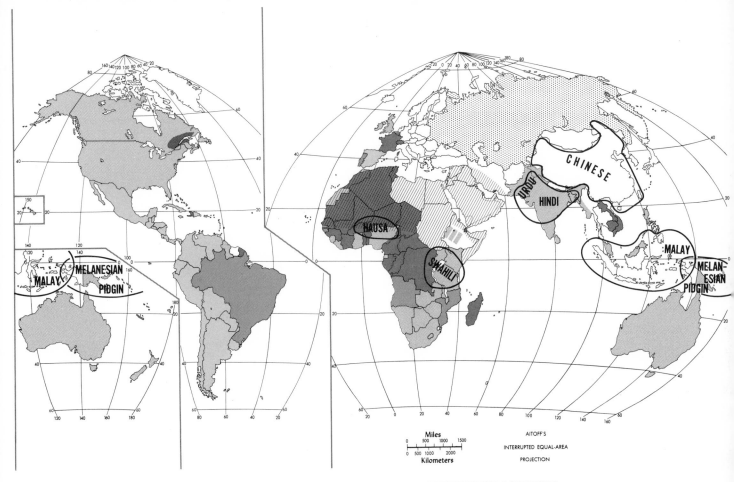

	Spanish
	French
	Russian
	English
	Portuguese
	Arabic

Figure 5–4. WORLD: INTERNATIONAL LANGUAGES

A few languages have achieved importance as media of communication among groups with diverse languages of their own. Those identified in the key at left are used in many parts of the world, often far from their original homeland. The languages named on the map have not spread as widely, but have an important function as regional lingua franca.

where more than one language is important have such data been collected. Table 5–3 is taken from these sources. Some examples of bilingualism are briefly discussed here.

India (Figure 5–3). In 1951 the Census of India collected information on "mother tongue" and "subsidiary language." Although the data are suspect, due to political influences at census time, they reveal a substantial degree of bilingualism, despite the prevailing low level of literacy. Bilingualism is most common in regions where there is much fragmentation in the distribution of mother tongues or where those speaking minor languages are isolated among a population that uses one of the major languages. In 1951 the state of Hyderabad

5. The Mosaic of Languages

(which has since been replaced by other states with different boundaries) had four principal languages: Telegu, Marathi, Urdu, and Kannada, also called Canarese. Of those who spoke one of the four principal languages as their mother tongue, only 14 percent had a subsidiary language. But of those who spoke a minor language as their mother tongue, more than half had a subsidiary language.

Belgium. In 1947 in Belgium 44 percent of the population spoke only Flemish, a slight decline since 1930; 36 percent spoke only French as against 38 percent in 1930. Those with both French and Flemish increased from 12 percent in 1930 to 16 percent in 1947. German, although only prevalent in a small eastern border section, is also recognized as a national language. While in 1930 only 1 percent of the population could speak all three languages, the percentage had risen to 3 in 1947. These small advances in tri- or bilingualism had no effect on the perennial strife between Belgium's language groups (see Chapter 7).

Cyprus. Two main cultural—and antagonistic—groups occupy Cyprus: Greek Cypriot and Turkish Cypriot. The numbers speaking each language and combination of languages are shown in Table 5–3. Recent events led to the island's independence from the British, who had ruled it for a number of decades. There followed an uneasy truce, marred by terrorist acts; eventually the United Nations took over supervision of the community relations between the two main factions. The Turks, as one might expect from their minority position, are more bilingual than the Greeks; many more Turks speak Greek than vice versa. And more Greeks speak English than Turkish.

A second kind of bilingualism involves a *lingua franca,* that is, a language used over a wide area as a means of communication between peoples of different speech. For instance, English is the most widely known lingua franca in India and in other parts of the (British) Commonwealth; besides, it has international importance in commerce, science, and diplomacy. Hindi, the lingua franca of Hinduism, is spoken by many millions in northern India who have not learned one of its dialects as their mother tongue. Although designated as the official

Figure 5–5. THE URALIAN LANGUAGES

This linguistic family is now dispersed over western Asia and eastern Europe. Present speakers have highly varied cultures from Finns and Magyars of central Europe to the reindeer-herding Lapps and Samoyeds. See also Figure 5–2. Based in part on a map in Meillet and Cohen, 1952.

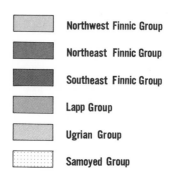

Northwest Finnic Group

Northeast Finnic Group

Southeast Finnic Group

Lapp Group

Ugrian Group

Samoyed Group

language of all India, it meets strong resistance in the south, where Dravidian speech prevails. Urdu, similar to Hindi, but with many words borrowed from Persian and Arabic, is somewhat of a lingua franca in West Pakistan and has been selected as its official language. In West Africa, Hausa is used for business purposes by perhaps as many as 40 million people who have varied mother tongues. In East Africa, Swahili is the lingua franca and provides a common means of communication for many groups in Kenya, Tanzania, and Uganda (Figure 5–4).

If a lingua franca is greatly changed and simplified, a "pidgin" comes into existence, "pidgin" being a Chinese version of the English word "business." In the southwestern Pacific in the nineteenth century a basic version of English developed called Beche-le-mar (Beach-la-mar). This language broke up into several variants of which the most important survivor is spoken around the coasts of New Guinea and in the Solomon Islands. Bazaar Malay, derived mainly from the vernacular of the coastal Malays of Sumatra, is the lingua franca of the island world of southeast Asia. Indians in the Pacific Northwest of the United States have Chinook Jargon, a mixture of Chinook, French,

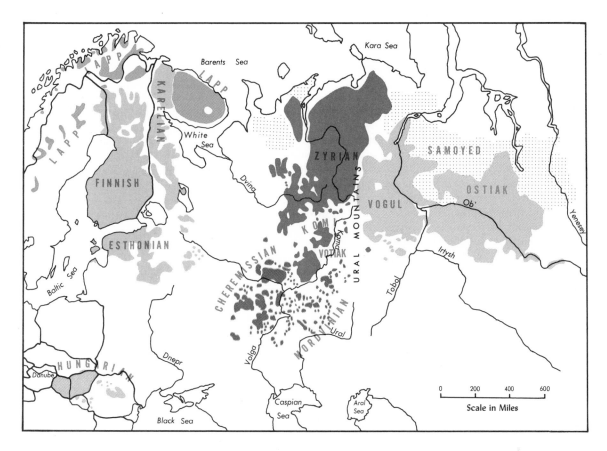

The map includes the following labels:

Kara Sea

Barents Sea

LAPP

LAPP

LAPP

KARELIAN

White Sea

Dvina

SAMOYED

ZYRIAN

FINNISH

OSTIAK

Ob'

VOGUL

URAL MOUNTAINS

ESTHONIAN

K O M I

Baltic Sea

CHEREMISSIAN

VOTIAK

Kama

Irtysh

Tobol

Yenesey

Ural

Dnepr

Volga

MORDVINIAN

HUNGARIAN

Danube

Caspian Sea

Aral Sea

Black Sea

0   200   400   600

Scale in Miles

and English. Tupi-Guarani is the "lingua geral," or general language, of many Indian tribes in Paraguay and Brazil.

Sometimes a pidgin becomes the chief language of a group or set of groups, each abandoning its own in favor of the one they all understand. An example is French Creole, which exists in many varieties, notably in Louisiana and Haiti, where slaves who had no common tongue converted the language of their masters to their own use. The versions of English in Jamaica, the Bahama Islands, and parts of Surinam serve a similar function.

Race and Language

The world distribution of languages corresponds, broadly, with that of human races. Most Caucasoids speak Indo-European languages, most Mongoloids Sinitic languages, most Negroids Niger-Congo-Bantu tongues. The correspondence is not surprising, for children inherit the physical features and also learn the language from their parents.

In the course of time as peoples migrated and mingled, the once coincident boundaries of race and language became blurred. Many Negroid peoples now speak Semitic and Hamitic tongues, formerly the sole possession of Caucasoids. Some groups transported into other cultural areas have taken over the local speech; examples are the Negroes who talk English in the United States, a version of French in Haiti, and Portuguese in Brazil. The official language of Liberia is English, which the returned slaves brought along to the state they founded in the early nineteenth century. Peoples speaking the individual tongues of the Uralic and Altaic family include Mongoloids in Asia and Caucasoids in Central Europe, such as the Magyars

5. The Mosaic of Languages

(Figure 5-5). Evidently, race and speech are innate, but the ability to speak a specific language is acquired.

Language and Culture

As language is the principal means of communicating culture, it can be useful to identify culture groups. Linguistic families are too broad to be employed for this purpose; for example, the Indo-European family does not form one cultural unit, as it comprises Indians, Pakistanis, Persians, Greeks, and Norwegians. Even linguistic subfamilies are not reliable guides to cultural entities. It is true that the entire Romance subfamily of the Indo-European stock has a common culture; however, the cultural likeness of the Italians, French, and Spanish arose not because they spoke related tongues but because their culture traits stemmed from the Roman (Latin) culture of classical times or because they were subject to similar influences of the Mediterranean environment. In examining the relationships between language and culture it is best, therefore, to consider each language separately. After all, mutual intelligibility is what counts in language as a means of communication. As Philip L. Wagner says:

Linguistic heterogeneity is one of the most obvious, most absolute, and most fixed of the categories of diversity that apply to human populations. The sharp discontinuities and relatively uniform blocs that characterize modern linguistic communities strongly influence human behavior, and particularly the association of people and their interaction. Political, social, and economic structures are often closely related with linguistic usage, and distributional patterns of these phenomena tend to coincide strikingly with linguistic areal patterns. (Wagner, 1958, 86)

It should be noted, however, that the identification of language with culture is far from complete: some Frenchmen speak German and many Irishmen speak English. Furthermore, the generalization often fails to apply to colonial areas where language transference has occurred. The peoples of France and Haiti both speak French, but the ties between them are less than the cultural ones between France and western

Europe and between Haiti and other Caribbean islands.

Usually differences in dialects are guideposts to determine subdivisions within cultures. In the United States most Southerners are easily recognized by their distinctive manner of speech. In Britain, the Scots use a dialect of English, unless they have consciously learned standard English; like the Southerners, the Scots are recognized as a cultural subgroup.

A new field known as *linguistic geography* has grown up in recent decades. It describes the character and extent of dialects and languages on the basis of data gathered from numerous personal interviews. By combining results of detailed studies concerning the occurrence of individual words, one can map dialect regions, and ultimately language regions (Figure 5-6).

There are vast differences in language structure, that is, in the vocabulary, the arrangement of words in grammatically significant sequences, the turns of phrase, and so on. Some linguists have put forward the hypothesis that logic and perception are functions of the language structure. Because of this, a certain people may view reality quite differently from another one. For instance, European languages have built into their structure a strong sense of defining actions according to their relative occurrence in time. Several East Asian languages appear less able to talk about the passage of time. Or, as another example, European languages contain many terms expressing opposite extremes, such as good—bad, strong—weak. Chinese, on the other hand, has few such pairs of opposites. It is possible, therefore, that the way a given people grasps reality reflects, in some measure, linguistically structured concepts of time, space, validity, and objectivity. Much more evidence needs to be gathered to make this suggestion an acceptable theory. But clearly, this line of thought opens new vistas on the relationship between language and culture.

Language and Society

The individual acquires, usually from his parents, the ability to speak a specific language as part of his cultural equipment. Since languages

Figure 5–6. THE DIALECTS OF THE
EASTERN UNITED STATES

Each of the major dialect regions shown
can be divided into a number of subareas.
After Kurath, 1949.

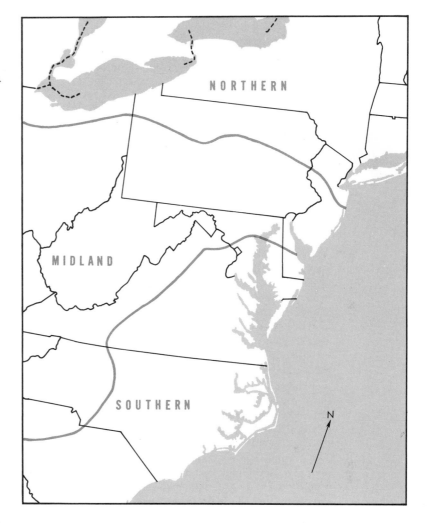

N O R T H E R N

M I D L A N D

S O U T H E R N

N

can also be learned later in life, a person can change his language. Most descendants of immigrant families to the United States lose their mother tongue after two generations. But for a whole society the process of change-over is slow, often taking centuries to complete. And while many people have in the course of time accepted a foreign language, others cling to their native tongue in spite of severe pressures.

If two peoples intermingle, it appears that the language of the "higher" culture eventually will be accepted by the other group. When the Romans pushed north of the Apennines into the plain of the Po River (Cisalpine Gaul) and northwestward into Gaul proper, their Latin, with local variants, replaced the Celtic dialects. Centuries later, Germanic-speaking tribes which swept into the western portions of the collapsing Roman Empire often took over the versions the Romanized Celts were using. During the Middle Ages, universal submission to the Catholic Church, which used Latin for all secular and religious purposes, helped to spread the Romance languages.

Arabic has been accepted throughout much of North Africa and in southwest Asia as far east as the Tigris-Euphrates Valley. In ancient times the peoples of this huge region spoke a

*5. The Mosaic
of Languages*

115

variety of Semitic and Hamitic languages; Arabic was then confined to the Arabian peninsula. Today Hamitic tongues remain only in small areas of northwest Africa and in southern sections of the Nile watershed. The change to Arabic came about during the Middle Ages, not only because it was the language of the conquerors and the ruling class, and thus of all governmental business, but also because it was the language of the Koran, the Holy Book of Islam. This trend toward acceptance was later reinforced when Arabic also became the vehicle of commerce over a wide region of the Old World.

A similar process is responsible for the present distribution of Indo-European and Dravidian languages in the Indian peninsula. In early times Dravidian languages were spoken over much of the subcontinent; they gave way, from the second millennium B.C. onwards, to the languages of the Aryan invaders from the northwest, who had a more complex culture and religion (Figure 5–7).

In our times we see the gradual decline of minor languages in lands where one language dominates. Welsh, Irish, and Scottish Gaelic have retreated before the advance of English, and Manx and Cornish have died out completely. Such developments are hastened today because government, business, school, radio, and television use the standard language of the majority. As literacy spreads, local dialects disappear. In Italy the standard version, which originated in middle Italy, replaces local dialects in north and south; in northern Germany, Low German (Plattdeutsch) persists only among the less-educated folk.

For a group to accept a new language there must be a willingness to change, prompted by religious, economic, or other social reasons. For example, in the sixteenth century the Welsh of the upper and middle classes realized that the recent political union of their country with England could profit them only if they learned to speak English; otherwise social positions would be closed to them because of language. Conversely, a ruling group often promotes its language by conducting all secular and religious business in its own language, to the exclusion of others.

Figure 5–7. SOUTH ASIA: LANGUAGES AND LINGUISTIC FAMILIES

This map is a generalization of the complex linguistic mosaic of the subcontinent. In many regions distinct languages are spoken by small groups not identified on the map. Many areas have mixed language patterns (see Figure 5–3). Based on *Karta Narodov Indostana,* 1956.

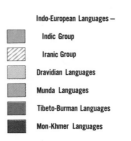

Indo-European Languages —

Indic Group

Iranic Group

Dravidian Languages

Munda Languages

Tibeto-Burman Languages

Mon-Khmer Languages

In certain circumstances, groups have retained their language in the face of competition from a dominant and linguistically alien society. What matters in such cases is the strength of the retentionist movement rather than the pressure exerted by the dominant culture.

Feelings of "loyalty to the group" seem to be the prime motive in resisting the imposition of another language. A community with strong attachment to its way of life will feel a threat to its language as a menace to its entire culture. Since most persons identify themselves with a group foremost through the common language, they feel any outside interference with it as a direct grievance. Thus, language becomes the central symbol around which opposition to foreign domination crystallizes.

Of the Celtic subfamily, Welsh and Modern Irish are likely to survive even though they have been declining for centuries. In the case of Welsh there is an underswell of "cultural nationalism," which aims to preserve the language for cultural purposes, such as in literature, music, and drama. Modern Irish, the official language of the Republic of Ireland, is taught in the schools and serves as the medium for conducting much government business. This

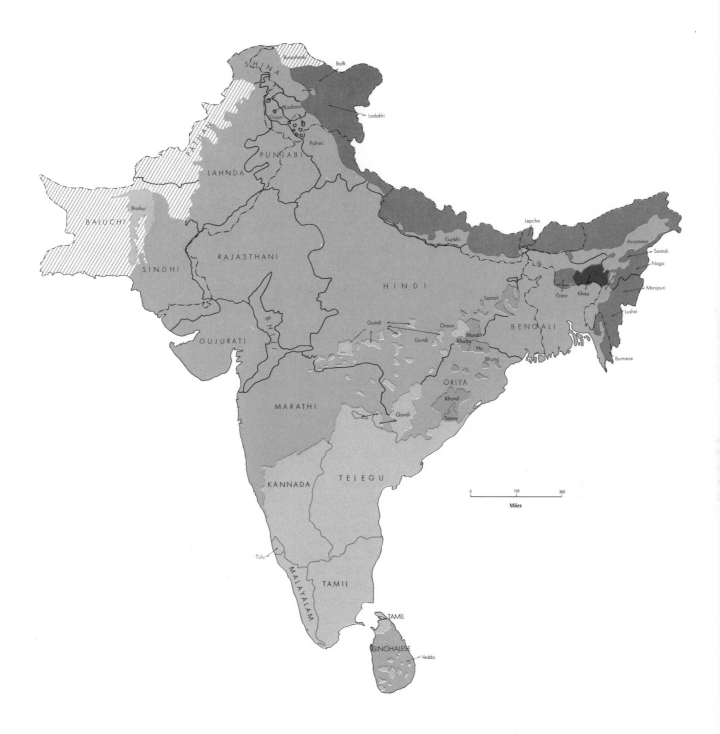

5. *The Mosaic
of Languages*

117

is, in part, a protest against the use of English, the tongue of the conquerors who exploited Ireland and gave up political control only after a long period of agitation and bloodshed.

In North America the French-speaking population of Quebec and nearby areas of Canada numbers 5.6 million, almost one-third of the total Canadian population. They have remained as an anomaly in an otherwise English-speaking Canada and United States, despite the fact that the French area has received no substantial influx of French speakers since the eighteenth century. The Roman Catholic religion and the French language are twin bonds that unite "*les Canadiens.*" Politics also worked in favor of retention. After the conquest of Quebec in the eighteenth century the French region was administered as Lower Canada. Discussions about the union of British possessions in North America were long and bitter. By the time of confederation and self-government (1867), the inhabitants of Lower Canada had become fully conscious of their linguistic distinctiveness and knew it gave them unity and power. Preservation of their language became a political issue which was resolved by giving French official status in Canada (see also Chapter 7).

A further example of language retention comes from Poland. The old kingdom of Poland, long an outpost of Western Christianity, disappeared at the end of the eighteenth century when Prussia, Austria-Hungary, and Russia divided it between them. During the nineteenth century the Polish language was outlawed and officially replaced by German and Russian. But many Poles, resenting foreign rule, kept their mother tongue. They succeeded in reasserting Polish nationality after World War I and again following World War II, during which there had been another German-Russian partition.

Political problems, associated with linguistic divisions, exist in other countries. In Ceylon, the Sinhalese claim supremacy, while the Tamil minority demands equality. In Italian Tyrol a German-speaking minority presses for recognition of its language and for local political autonomy. In northern Spain the Basques and in northeastern Spain the Catalans assert their

Figure 5–8. FRANCE: LANGUAGES

Based on sheet 70 of *Atlas de France,* 1959.

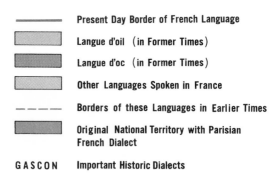

——————— Present Day Border of French Language

▨ Langue d'oil (in Former Times)

▨ Langue d'oc (in Former Times)

▨ Other Languages Spoken in France

– – – – – Borders of these Languages in Earlier Times

▨ Original National Territory with Parisian French Dialect

GASCON Important Historic Dialects

individuality by covert and occasionally overt action against the decrees of Castilian-speaking Madrid.

Both past and present support the notion that the languages of "higher" culture groups remain stable in the face of competition, frequently from much larger groups. For example, the numerous Chinese who settled among the Malay-speaking peoples of Southeast Asia have usually retained their language and customs because of their higher social and economic status. Similarly, Arabs who penetrated south of the dry belt of North Africa have kept their language though living among larger groups with other speech. Germans who, up to the end of World War II, lived in scattered communities all over central and eastern Europe, stuck to their language for many centuries, partly because they considered themselves on a higher cultural level than the peoples among whom they lived, and partly because they felt affinity with the increasingly coherent German nation.

Growth of the French Language

The development of the French language to its present condition and location (Figure 5–8) illustrates many of these points. At the time of Julius Caesar's conquest Celtic languages

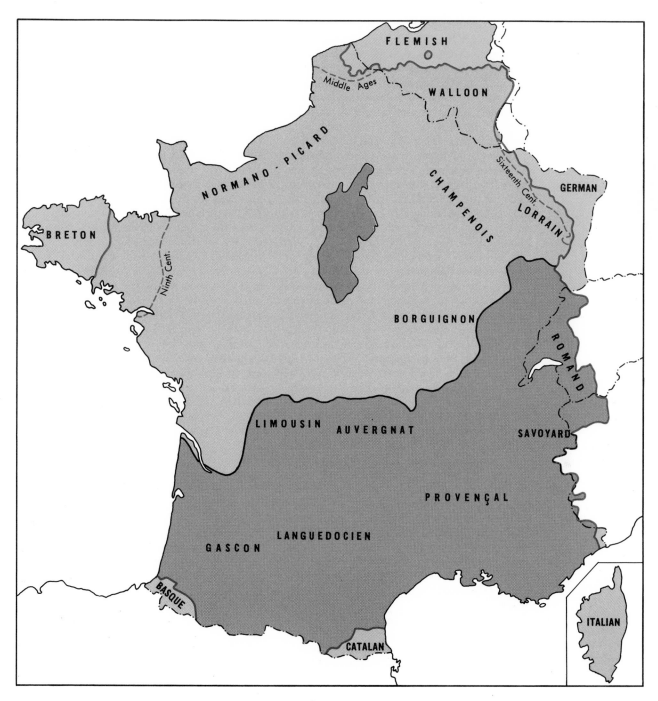

FLEMISH

WALLOON

Middle Ages

GERMAN

NORMANO - PICARD

CHAMPENOIS

LORRAIN

Sixteenth Cent.

BRETON

Ninth Cent.

BORGUIGNON

ROMAND

LIMOUSIN AUVERGNAT

SAVOYARD

PROVENÇAL

GASCON

LANGUEDOCIEN

BASQUE

CATALAN

ITALIAN

*5. The Mosaic
of Languages*

119

were spoken in most of Gaul (the ancient name for continental western Europe). By the fourth century A.D. Latin had replaced the old tongues; this was not the classical Latin some of us learn in school, but a vernacular called Romance. After Roman authority collapsed, Romance in Gaul developed local peculiarities, removing it further from classical Latin, and also distinguishing it from other changing local versions of Romance in Iberia and Italy. Within Gaul differences emerged between the north and the south, largely due to dialect alterations made by the Salian Franks who, though they entered Gaul speaking a Germanic dialect, accepted Romance later after conquering the country.

In the ninth century the Frankish Emperor Charlemagne attempted to reintroduce classical Latin as the official language. The attempt was short-lived, for by this time the dialects were far removed from classical Latin; moreover, after his death the empire collapsed. By the twelfth century the feudal rulers of the region around Paris were gaining political control of the emerging national state of France. The dialect of the capital region, Parisian French, became the court language and later the official written version. The Parisian dialect also had the advantage of standing midway between the dialects of the north and those of the south.

In southern France a literary language, Provençal—developed by strolling lyric poets (troubadours)—was briefly used, but receded before the growing influence of Paris. Today the term Provençal is sometimes applied to the southern dialects of France. Between the northern and southern dialects (named *langue d'oïl* and *langue d'oc* respectively, from the pronunciation of the word meaning "yes") there was a transitional zone where their features intermingled.

While the standard written version of Paris was accepted by the seventeenth century, it took much longer to develop a standard spoken version. In the nineteenth century, military service, universal schooling, and the newspaper helped to establish Parisian French as the standard, and now it is used almost exclusively except for those regions where another language is the mother tongue. The local *patois,*

distinct dialects deeply rooted in the Romance period, have virtually disappeared. These patois should not be confused with provincial ways of pronouncing Parisian French.

Standard French has also made inroads into areas of non-French languages, all on the periphery of France. Basque, spoken in the southwestern corner of the country, seems to have maintained its position in recent decades after having been much reduced in importance during the previous century. Catalan is the language of Roussillon, a province on the Mediterranean which France acquired from Spain in 1659. Italian has declined as the language of the Nice area (Nizza in Italian) taken from Savoy in 1860. Breton, once spoken over the entire Brittany Peninsula, has withdrawn to the western half. This Celtic language was brought into the region during the fifth and sixth centuries by settlers from southwestern Britain. Flemish in the north has also decreased and undergoes continual erosion. In Alsace and Lorraine, annexed in the seventeenth and eighteenth centuries, German vernaculars still are spoken, though reduced in area. German and French reacquisitions of these provinces resulted in alternating emphasis on the national language of whichever country held control. Figure 5–8 shows the retreat of the non-French languages.

As a result of French colonial rule, French is spoken by many educated people in northwestern Africa, in areas of western and central Africa, in Vietnam, and in some Pacific islands. In addition, because French culture held the dominant position during the eighteenth and nineteenth centuries, its language was adopted as a medium of international diplomacy and commerce. Although French still has significance in this regard, English now overshadows it.

Language and Physiography

The surface of the earth with all its variety of landforms and climates is like a tremendous stage for the drama of language change, migration, acceptance, and retention. How have these

The Wipp Valley in Austrian Tyrol, leading to the Brenner Pass on the
Austro-Italian border, in background. Beyond the pass lies South Tyrol,
settled long ago by German-speaking people, but annexed by Italy in 1918
to control the strategic Brenner route. In the foreground runs the old Roman road.
A later road and the new autobahn follow the right (western) slope
of the valley. [Courtesy of Tiroler Verkehrswerbung, Innsbruck]

physical features affected the mosaic of language? It might be thought that since language is a part of culture, and thus derives from man, there can be no relationship between language and physical environment. This may sound logical, but the truth is more complex. Friedrich Ratzel, pioneer in the study of migration and diffusion, pointed out that when any movement occurs the routes taken, and the places avoided, reflect the conditioning influences of the earth.

Easily accessible areas certainly favor rapid and wide dispersal of a language or group of related languages. Germanic languages prevail on the north European plain from Flanders to the Polish border, and formerly had many sizable outliers to the east. The subfamily of Indic tongues occupies the plains of the Indus and Ganges, but peters out at the Himalayas and the mountains of Burma, behind which different language families are ensconced. The mounted

5. The Mosaic
of Languages

121

nomads ranged over the huge arc of flat land from Mongolia to central Europe and brought their languages to present-day Hungary and to many regions further east. Similarly, islands close to others or to the mainland are readily accessible. This explains the spread of Malayo-Polynesian tongues far into the Pacific.

On the other hand, rough topography tends to turn aside the main streams of movement. Where migrants settled in coves and valleys, like the Scotch-Irish in the southern Appalachians, they remained cut off from the crosscurrents of American life and kept their distinctive dialect. The Slavic dialect area in Lusatia (Lausitz), south of Berlin, has survived since medieval times because marshy conditions isolated the folk and prevented their assimilation into the German people.

The mainland part of Southeast Asia in its language distribution shows a marked contrast between lowlands and uplands. Each lowland is the core of a state—Burma, Thailand, Cambodia, Laos, and Vietnam—and is relatively homogeneous in speech, though quite distinct from the next lowland. The highlands between them, however, are occupied by numerous tribal groups whose tongues, although usually related to one or the other of the lowland languages, are a veritable linguistic hodgepodge. In the same way, the hundred or more distinct languages of the Caucasus Mountains in the southern part of the Soviet Union, and the many linguistic families of New Guinea, are the products of isolation, not only separated from the main streams of language migrations but also from each other.

Language boundaries tend to correspond with physical features. The Pyrenees divide Spain from France; the Alpine zone is the complex meeting place of French, German, and Italian; the Pripet Marshes cut Byelorussian from Ukrainian; the swampy belt along the lower Danube lies between Bulgarian and Romanian.

With these and other examples, can we speak of cause and effect? Close inspection of the Pyrenees barrier and of the local distribution of languages reveals that the linguistic boundaries do not follow the mountain crests; in particular, Catalan and Basque occur on either side. The present line between the Czech and German languages runs along the highland rim of Bohemia, but in this case, the political border is responsible for the linguistic divide. Prior to 1945, German extended well within the highland rim; after 1945, forced migration pushed it back to coincide with the political boundary, located along the highland crest. In North America the course of the Rio Grande marks the boundary between the standard languages of the United States and Mexico. Nevertheless, many people whose families for generations have lived north of the river retain Mexican Spanish as their vernacular.

At first sight, then, the association of the earth's physical features with linguistic distributions might seem to be a matter of cause and effect. On further thought, it becomes clear that language areas, in common with other cultural diffusions, cannot be explained by reference to any one set of factors. They must be understood as the result of a complex interplay of historical forces and environmental conditions that affect individual lives and the groups of individuals that make up societies.

Citations

Atlas de France, Paris, 1959. [Map]

Ethnographic Institute of the Soviet Academy of Sciences *Karta Narodov Indostana* (Map of the People of India), Moscow, 1956. [Map]

Kurath, H. *A Word Geography of the Eastern United States,* Ann Arbor, Mich., 1949. [Map]

Meillet, A., and Cohen, M. *Les Langues du monde,* Paris, 1952. [Map]

Myres, J. N. L. *Prehistoric Man and Earliest Known Societies,* vol. 1 of Eyre, E. (ed.) *European Civilization, Its Origin and Development,* New York, 1935.

Wagner, P. L. "Remarks on the Geography of Language," *Geographical Review,* 48 (1958): 86–97.

Whatmough, J. *Language: A Modern Synthesis,* New York, 1957.

Further Readings

Allen, H. B. (ed.) *Applied English Linguistics,* New York, 1958. Part 3 of this book contains a series of discussions on the linguistic geography of the eastern and midwestern United States.

Atlas Linguistique de la France, Paris, 1902–1910.

Bloomfield, L. *Language,* New York, 1933.

Bottiglioni, L. "Linguistic Geography: Its Achievements, Methods and Orientations," *Word,* 10 (1954): 375–378.

Bruk, S. I., and Aperchenko, V. S. (eds.) *Atlas Narodov Mira* (Atlas of the People of the World), Moscow, 1964.

de Carvalho, C. M. D. "The Geography of Languages," in Wagner, P. L., and Mikesell, M. W. (eds.) *Readings in Cultural Geography,* Chicago, 1962, 75–93. Translated from *Boletim Geográfico,* 1 (1943): 45–62.

Dominian, L. *The Frontiers of Language and Nationality in Europe,* American Geographical Society Special Publication no. 3, New York, 1917.

Encyclopaedia Britannica, various articles on languages and linguistic families.

Hymes, D. *Language in Culture and Society,* New York, 1964.

Jones, E., and Griffiths, I. L. "A Linguistic Map of Wales, 1961," *Geographical Journal,* 129 (1963): 192–196.

Kiddle, L. B. "The Spanish Language as a Medium of Cultural Diffusion in the Age of Discovery," *American Speech,* 27 (1952): 241–256.

Kroeber, A. L. *Anthropology,* New York, 1948.

Kurath, H., and Bloch, B. *The Linguistic Atlas of New England,* Providence, R.I., 1939–1943.

Sapir, E. *Selected Writings in Language, Culture, and Personality* (ed. by D. Mandelbaum), New York, 1949.

Whorf, B. L. *Collected Papers on Metalinguistics,* New York, 1952.

6. Religions: Origins and Dispersals

Introduction

A society depends for its existence on a common ideology. The word *ideology* as used here does not connote a specific—and usually dogmatic—interpretation of all social phenomena as, for instance, when one speaks of "the Marxist ideology." Rather, we define it in a wider and more neutral sense as the set of beliefs, sentiments, and values that bind together the members of a group and thereby set them apart from other societies. It includes religious as well as secular thought patterns. Some authors speak of the value system, others of the ethos, the great traditions, or the major themes of a society.

To assert that each people has its ideology is easy; to pin down the specific character of each group is very difficult. It is hard enough to describe and understand the personality of one individual. How can we analyze and comprehend the character of a nation or, still broader, the ways of thought of an entire civilization? This question can be countered by another question: Can we afford to ignore the topic because full understanding is beyond our reach? We need to know what peoples are like, one's own included. The foreign affairs officer contemplating a potential international conflict, the politician seeking election, and the businessman exploring a foreign market all formulate some image of the people with whom they deal. Various social sciences study village communities, tribes, regional societies, and nations for the purpose of discovering what ideals and attitudes condition the behavior of each group. The results so far are often more impressionistic and speculative than verifiable, but the research holds promise for more exact achievement in the future.

Religion is among the foremost of ideologies. As a cultural universal it is open to worldwide inspection and comparison. The main religions each have their center of origin, routes of diffusion, and pattern of present distribution. Even the most secularized societies retain many traits rooted in religious tradition.

Like all other cultural universals, religion is difficult to define because it has so many facets in different cultures. In essence, it refers to man's belief in the supernatural, in what arouses in him a feeling of awe or piety, in what he considers sacred. Religion, therefore, comprises any form of faith from monotheism to ancestor worship and even magic insofar as it contains an element of reverence for the supernatural. In concrete situations it is hard to decide where the religious part of an ideology ends and the profane, the secular, begins. Confucianism is usually considered among the religions, although its founder actually taught the ethics of daily life. Among simple tribal folk, and even in some traditional societies, such as India, religion is an all-pervading force. On the other hand, in modern commercial-industrial societies religion has retreated to a more modest position. In the Communist countries the official ideology is atheistic, but religion still persists.

Influence of Religion on Way of Life

According to the German sociologist Max Weber, a religion produces a distinct attitude toward life, and this orientation affects the further development of the society in question. In a stimulating work, Weber demonstrated the effect of Protestant ethics on the development of capitalism in northwestern Europe (Weber, 1904). His thesis was a reaction to the Marxist contention that the methods of material production determine the social superstructure, including religion. Neither of the two positions represents a universally valid generalization. Most cultural situations show a mutual interaction between religion and social, political, and economic factors. At this point we will consider, with some illustrations, how religions have put their mark on human societies.

History and current international relations offer numerous examples of religion in politics, of which the division of India and of Ireland and the establishment of Israel are a few recent examples. Internal political differences, from party politics to minority problems, often have a religious undertone or overtone, as for instance the party system in West Germany or the Netherlands, and the position of the French Canadians.

Religion strongly influences social institutions, and thus law. In many countries marriage contracts require religious sanction. Islam permits polygyny (polygamy for men), Christianity insists on monogamy. Most high Hindu castes forbid remarriage of a widow. The caste system in India, whatever its origin, is closely associated with religion. Religious doctrine regarding the function of marriage may influence the size of the family, and thus population growth.

The major religions have carried with them the use of the language, script, and calendar of the homeland, or at least of the adopted homeland. Our modern economy strives to be so rational that one tends to overlook the religious factor in the daily round of making a living. However, in traditional peasant societies, religious practices closely tie in with food production, on which, after all, life literally depends. Rituals accompany the selection of propitious days for planting and sowing, and for the start of the fishing season. Most diet restrictions have religious significance and affect agriculture. Jews and Moslems consider the pig an unclean animal and exclude it from their livestock. In Hindu India the veneration of the cow prohibits the killing of cattle and the eating of beef. The huge cattle population may even hinder better land use.

In medieval Europe the Christian church took a strong stand against moneylending at interest (usury), and Islam did the same. This explains in part the role of the Jew as moneylender, since he was not bound by these rules. Another economic aspect of religion is related to the vast number of pilgrims who visit holy shrines. They inject large sums of money into means of transportation and into the local economy of such pilgrimage places as Jerusalem, Rome, Banaras in India, Mecca in Arabia, Lourdes in southern France, or Ste. Anne de Beaupré in Canada. The areal organization of religion has often led to the growth of settlements whose main function is religious administration or practice, such as the cathedral and abbey towns in Europe.

Ceremonial seasons (holidays, fast periods) also have their economic effects because of the reduction or ban on work, or the demand for goods, from clothing to fish. The search for aromatic gums and woods for incense stimulated commerce as, for instance, the ancient Egyptian trade with Somaliland for myrrh wood and the Chinese quest for sandalwood in Southeast Asia.

Elements of the physical environment play or have played a significant role in most religions: holy mountains and rivers (Mount Sinai, Mount Fuji, Mount Tabor, the Ganges and Jordan rivers), sacred caves, groves, and lakes. Some sanctuaries may be visited only on special occa-

Hindu temple in Tanjore, southern India, built in Dravidian
style characterized by pyramidal towers, horizontal mouldings, and
lavish figure sculpture. The shrine is part of an enclosed temple complex. In
the tenth and eleventh centuries Tanjore was the center of the Chola
Empire, which had widespread influence in Southeast Asia.
[Courtesy of Government of India Tourist Office]

sions and under strict ritual observances. Others
must be avoided by the ordinary mortal. Taboos
on the use of plants and animals are common
in primitive religions, and a number have survived in more advanced faiths. Some plants
are cult symbols of specific religions, such as
the lotus and bo tree in Buddhism, the oak and
spruce in ancient Germanic ritual (whence our
Christmas tree), the conifer in Shinto.

The Variety of Religions

Religion among primitive peoples consists in
the belief in some power, or powers, beyond
man to which he appeals for aid in hazardous
moments. These powers may be souls of the
departed, spirits living on mountains, in stones,
trees, or animals, or ghosts and any other forms
of disembodied beings. Belief and worship of

this kind is called *animism.* Somewhat different is the belief in *mana,* supernatural power which manifests itself in persons who have unusual and mysterious skill, or in things that have extraordinary, miraculous properties. These beliefs and related practices persist among many nonliterate peoples of today.

Interesting as these beliefs are, they are for our purpose of minor significance because as "ideology" they exist only at the tribal level. That is why, from a social point of view, they are often called "tribal religions." There is, of course, a continuum from "primitive" to "high" religions, as well as from tribal to universal religions. We must limit our overview to those religions that have large numbers of followers, or an important genetic relationship to these widespread beliefs.

The Main Religions

Buddhism, Christianity, and Islam are often called "universal" religions, because each aims at worldwide, supranational acceptance. They, as well as Judaism, are also exclusive in the sense that each holds its truth incompatible with that of the others (Kroeber, 1948, 406). All three missionize actively, in contrast to Judaism, a religion now more reserved for the ingroup, although bona fide voluntary converts are admitted. The enormous variety of creeds and practices in Hinduism indicates great religious tolerance, but this inclusiveness operates within the limits of the social system.

On the whole, there seems to be more interpenetration of faiths in South and East Asia than in the Middle East and Europe. Even Buddhism, although generally characterized as exclusive, shows more adaptability to other religious environments than do the three monotheistic religions. The most inclusive appears to be the Chinese tradition of religious thought and ritual, where ancestor worship, Taoism, and Confucian ethics mix in various blends with Buddhism and even Christianity.

How many people belong to each major faith is hard to say, and Table 6-1 is therefore

Table 6-1. Main Religions and Estimated Number of Adherents, 1967 (in millions)	
Christianity	975
Roman Catholic	600
Eastern Orthodox	145
Protestant	230
Islam	475
Hinduism	415
Confucianism	370
Buddhism	170
Shinto	68
Taoism	54
Judaism	13.7

only a rough approximation. Exact data, in the form of civil or religious census enumerations, are lacking for many countries. Church organizations have different ways of defining membership. Individuals make their own decisions in answering the question of religious faith in a civil census. In North America and Europe, for instance, where the population is preponderantly Christian by tradition, large numbers do not actively participate in any church affairs, and many declare they have no religion. The blend of religions in China makes one wonder how it is possible to arrive at meaningful separate figures for followers of the various creeds present. In Communist countries most people will at least outwardly conform to the atheist position of their governments.

Altogether, there are many reasons to use quantitative data with considerable caution. Available facts indicate that Christianity has the largest number of adherents, with Islam and Hinduism ranking next, the latter closely followed by Confucianism. However, if one recalls the intermingling of beliefs in China, it is probably more correct to give the Chinese amalgam second place, and Islam and Hinduism third and fourth. This ignores the effect of Marxist doctrine in China, which is hard to evaluate in the sphere of the traditional beliefs of 700 million people.

Cradlelands of the Main Religions

If we leave aside the native ancestor cults and moral codes of East Asia, it is striking in how small a section of earth the present main religions originated. Hinduism appeared in northwestern India, its offshoot Buddhism began in the north central part, Judaism and Christianity originated in Palestine, and Islam, partly based on the latter two, had its birth in western Arabia (Figure 6–1).

This area of origins coincides fairly well with the zone of ancient civilizations. Spatial correspondence by itself does not prove cause and effect, but enough is known of cultural evolution to accept some form of causal relationship, even if its exact nature escapes us. In the alluvial valleys of the Fertile Crescent and of the Indus, water control required group effort. Irrigation increased food production and made possible division of labor and the rise of cities. Religion changed from tribal rites to an elaborate system for the preservation of the state. Tribal customs were replaced by laws, backed up by religious sanction, to regulate the complex activities of the enlarged societies. These are some of the factors that lie at the root of the development of supratribal religions and the elaboration of ethical and social rules. One must keep in mind that southwestern Asia was the hub of migrations and trade routes, which led to exchange of ideas over wide areas. But all this—and much more could be added—at best indicates that the ground was prepared for the growth of the great religions. Why they grew as they did is a matter of historical interpretation.

Judaism

Among the Semitic tribes that wandered through the deserts of the Middle East some 3,800 years ago were the ancestors of the Jews. From their contacts with the peoples of the irrigated valleys they acquired ideas of more advanced agriculture, and also of religion. Abraham and his people set out from Ur, in southern Mesopotamia, reached Canaan (in Palestine), went to Egypt, and back again to Canaan. In Mesopotamia they may well have heard about the great king Hammurabi of Babylon (2067–2025 B.C.), who had received from the sun god the tablets with the laws of the kingdom. The idea of one god as sovereign over all other gods appears to have been widespread among ancient Semitic-speaking peoples. What came to distinguish the Hebrew religion was the commitment to the one and only God, who had chosen them in a solemn covenant to bear witness to this belief.

Moreover, Yahweh (Jehovah) demanded ethical virtue of his people. This exclusive monotheism, fostered by many rituals, together with ethical and civil laws welded the Jews into a distinct and closely knit religious community quite different from other Semitic peoples. Victories over their enemies and political unification of the tribes under a monarchy added to the feeling of national consciousness. But the pressures from the surrounding empires were too much for this small nation. The end of the ancient Jews as an independent people came in 586 B.C., when Babylonian conquerors destroyed Jerusalem and sent them into exile. Although the Jews were later allowed to return, they remained under control of different foreign masters. A revolt against the Romans led to their full dispersal in A.D. 70.

The civil and economic status of the scattered Jewish communities was fairly good in the Roman Empire before Christianity became the official religion. From then on, and all through the Middle Ages, the Jews in Europe suffered discrimination, expulsion, or massacre, depending on place and time. For instance, they were expelled from England in the thirteenth cen-

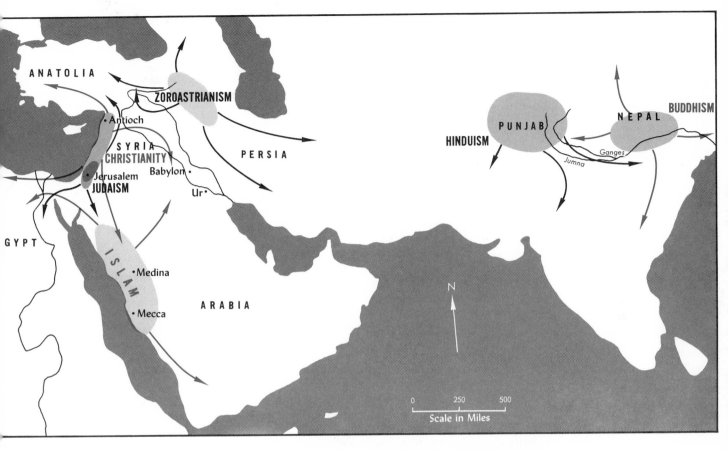

Figure 6-1. CRADLELANDS OF THE MAIN RELIGIONS

tury, and were only admitted again after the middle of the seventeenth century. Even where they were tolerated, exclusiveness on both sides kept Christians and Jews apart, particularly where the latter were gathered in ghettos. In the middle of the fourteenth century, when persecution in Germany was severe, the king of Poland offered refuge, and thus Judaism concentrated in that country, which then included much of the present Ukraine. The Rhine-Frankish dialect of the refugees, mixed with Hebrew and Slavic words, became known as Yiddish (from the German *jüdisch,* meaning Jewish).

Under the feudal system the Jews, as strangers, could not own land and were excluded from many occupations. The majority became traders and artisans, the rich ones bankers. In the prevailing agrarian society the Jews assumed the role of middlemen between the ruling landed nobility and the peasants. When and where native groups felt able to take over the position of middle class, but not strong enough to compete with the Jews, they strove to remove the "foreign" rivals.*

On the other hand, Jews had considerable liberty in the Middle Eastern and North

*At present there is an instructive parallel in the function and status of the Chinese in Southeast Asia.

6. Religions: Origins and Dispersals

129

African countries conquered by the Moslems, and especially in Moslem Spain, which became a center of revival for Jewish culture. After the Iberian Peninsula was cleared of Arab rule (1492), the Jews were expelled unless they accepted Christianity. Many of them—the so-called *Sephardim* of the Spanish-Jewish rite—fled to North Africa and to the Turkish empire around the eastern Mediterranean. A number moved to Holland and later to England, and from there to the colonies.

Emancipation began toward the end of the eighteenth century when Rationalism demanded religious tolerance. Moreover, the bourgeois society which had developed with capitalism matched the Jews in economic prowess. France was the first country to give explicitly equal rights to Jews, followed in the nineteenth century by most countries of West and Central Europe. For the mass of European Jewry, living in agrarian eastern Europe, emancipation had to wait, and in the meantime suppression continued, punctuated by pogroms (organized massacres). The treaties after World War I gave, on paper at least, equal rights and protection to all minorities in the postwar states of East and Central Europe, but actually much discrimination remained. The Communist revolution in Russia, although it outlawed anti-Semitism, ruined most Jews economically because it eliminated their role of entrepreneur.

Germany had in 1930 some 600,000 Jews, about 1 percent of its total population. Under Hitler's leadership they were persecuted in medieval fashion. Then, during World War II, the Nazis exterminated an estimated six million Jews, gathered from Germany, the occupied lands, and satellite states (Figure 6–2).

Against this European background we must view the Jewish immigration into the United States. Before 1800 there were only a few thousands in this country, and the Sephardim were the leaders. From about 1820 until 1870 the majority of Jewish immigrants came from Germany (the so-called *Ashkenazim*). At the latter date there were some 200,000 Jews in the United States. After that time, severe persecutions in Russia and other parts of eastern Europe led large numbers of Jews to seek

Figure 6–2. JEWISH POPULATIONS IN EUROPE AND THE MEDITERRANEAN, 1933 AND 1956

The changes in the location of the Jewish populations are startling, especially the sharp reductions in continental (mostly eastern and central) Europe, rapid growth in Israel, and slow growth in northwest Africa. Based on sheet 4/X of *Atlas of Israel,* 1956–1960.

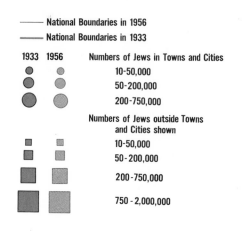

——— National Boundaries in 1956
——— National Boundaries in 1933

1933 1956   Numbers of Jews in Towns and Cities
             10-50,000
             50-200,000
             200-750,000

             Numbers of Jews outside Towns
             and Cities shown
             10-50,000
             50-200,000
             200-750,000
             750-2,000,000

refuge in this country, a movement which continued until World War I. Thereafter, the establishment of the quota system kept down the influx from eastern Europe. The Nazi terror brought, between 1936 and 1946, about 150,000 Jewish refugees to the United States, to whom another 100,000 survivors of concentration camps were added later. There now are over five million Jews in this country, for the greater part of east European origin. Not more than four million are members of synagogues.

Like any other religion, Judaism has its different sects or movements. In the nineteenth century, when emancipation took great strides in Western countries, many Jews accepted a reform which aimed at adapting Jewish rite to modern society. This included the abolition of many customs, while retaining the essence

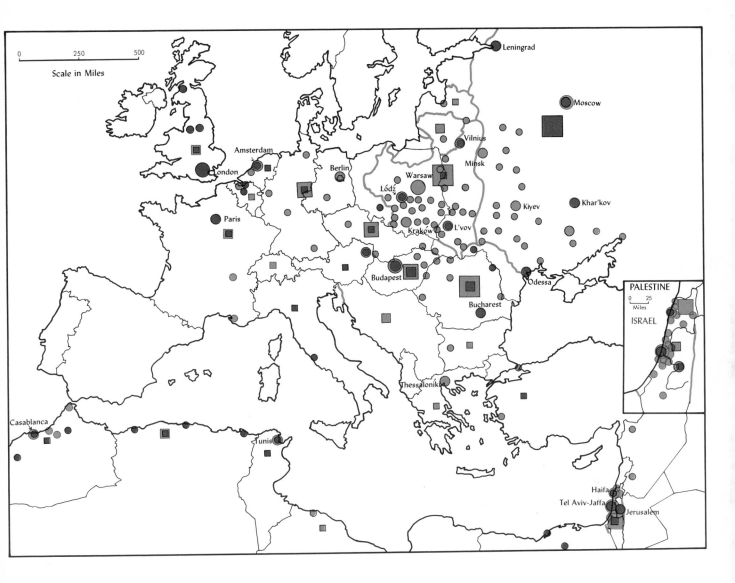

Scale in Miles
0   250   500

Leningrad
Moscow
Vilnius
Minsk
Khar'kov
Amsterdam
London
Berlin
Warsaw
Łódź
Kiyev
Paris
Kraków
L'vov
Budapest
Bucharest
Odessa
Thessaloniki
Casablanca
Tunis
Haifa
Tel Aviv-Jaffa
Jerusalem

PALESTINE
0   25
Miles
ISRAEL

of the religion, so that they could participate in the national life of a state like any other citizen. Other Jews, however, feared that emancipation would lead to assimilation and thus loss of identity. And then there were those who believed that anti-Semitism would always remain a threat to Judaism. These last two motivations led to a political Zionism. The founder of this movement originally advocated the establishment of a "Jews' State" in either Argentina, Uganda, or Palestine; but the last project gained favor and received invaluable support from the Balfour Declaration of 1917. After many vicissitudes the state of Israel was proclaimed in 1948, in the face of violent Arab opposition. The ingathering, which had been restricted before, could now begin. In the process, half a million Moslem natives of Palestine fled the country. At present there are more than two million Jews in Israel. Political Zion-

6. Religions: Origins and Dispersals

131

Table 6–2. Distribution of Jews*								
	1825		*1850*		*1930*		*1964*	
	Millions	*Percent*	*Millions*	*Percent*	*Millions*	*Percent*	*Millions*	*Percent*
Europe	2.7	83	3.9	78	10.0	63	3.9	30
Americas	0.01		0.4	8	4.7	30	6.6	50
Asia	0.3	9	0.4	8	0.7	4	2.3	17.5
Africa	0.2	7	0.3	6	0.5	3	0.3	2
Australia					0.03		0.07	0.5
TOTAL	3.2	100	5.0	100	15.93	100	13.17	100

* Based on various sources, of which Lestshinsky, 1930, 1931, is particularly useful for the years before 1930.

ism has also caused dissension in the Jewish world. Among the objections is the fear that outsiders may identify all Jews with the national state of Israel, thus jeopardizing the position of many who wish to be loyal nationals of their country of residence.

"The Wandering Jew" is an old expression, but still an apt one if one considers the great shifts of the last century (see Table 6–2). From the large concentration in Europe—chiefly its eastern part—there has been such a great migration across the Atlantic that now half of the world's Jews live in the Americas, and 42 percent in the United States alone. After the migrations and massacres, the absolute number of Jews in Europe is down to the level of 1850. The creation of Israel has raised the absolute as well as the relative figures for Asia above those of the nineteenth century. The spatial shifts have been accompanied by changes in the mode of life. In eastern Europe the Jew lived as a middleman between gentry and peasants, and thus usually in a village or small-town environment. In the western countries he moved toward the cities, particularly the large ones. Israel is, of course, the exception in that Jews also fill the rural occupations; but here too the cities are the centers of attraction.

II. Cultural Diversity

Christianity

The Beginning. Under the Roman oppression it seemed to the Jews that nothing could save them but the Messiah, who would restore the rule of God. They differed, however, on how this kingdom-on-earth might come about: by force of arms, or by spiritual regeneration. According to the early accounts, Jesus came from Galilee, on the margin of the old Judaic state, a district conquered only a few generations before his birth. His teachings contained many elements of Judaic thought, but instead of invoking the authority of old traditions, he explained the meaning of love for God and for one's fellowmen, and insisted on ethical thought and behavior as the road to the supreme kingdom. His mission might have remained a dissenter's movement within Palestine, one of the alternatives for salvation to a sorely tried people. What gave it appeal beyond the homeland was, first of all, the universal validity of the message, speaking to the downtrodden everywhere. Secondly, the denationalized, Greek-educated Paul gave the originally simple gospel the interpretation and organization by which it could effectively penetrate the Greco-Roman civilization. As the new religion spread it changed still further, absorbing from its new environment philosophical ideas, elements of mystic cults, and other popular beliefs. Even so, hostility and active persecution burdened its first three hundred years. The conversion of Emperor Constantine established Christianity as the state religion in the early fourth century and opened the way for militant proselytizing throughout the Roman Empire.

Eastern Christianity (Figure 6–3). In our preoccupation with the direct lineage of our culture we usually place the western part of the Roman Empire in historical focus, but leave the eastern part a blurred and receding image. Yet, in the era of early Christianity the countries around the eastern Mediterranean had the richer heritage of the ancient civilizations and the greater population. In comparison, the west European territories of Rome were mere conquest colonies, semicivilized and soon to be overrun by new bands of barbarians. As the West Roman Empire disintegrated and the "Dark Ages" spread over its former realm, the eastern part remained, in spite of all spiritual changes and material losses, the main center of Christian-Hellenistic culture.

There were, in the fourth century, three patriarchs (highest ranking prelates) of the church, namely, those of Rome, Antioch, and Alexandria, to whom the bishops of Jerusalem and Constantinople were soon added. Each had autonomy in his domain. When the seat of the empire was moved to Constantinople (A.D. 330), the see of the bishop of Rome stood like an outpost amidst a rising tide of barbarians. At the same time, the Roman bishop gained considerable independence from direct imperial control, while his eastern colleagues, particularly the patriarch of Constantinople, became heavily involved in the affairs and politics of the court. The bishop of Rome claimed primacy, based on Jesus' word to Peter, but the other patriarchs challenged his authority on many occasions. Differences in dogma ostensibly caused the conflicts, but underneath lay cultural distinctions and political considerations. After many disputes the estrangement between East and West led to the final schism of 1054.

The Eastern, or Orthodox, churches never developed the close-knit unity of the Roman Catholic Church. While the latter became a supranational organization under the authority of the Pope, the Orthodox churches remained territorial—later national—organizations, each with considerable autonomy. The Ecumenical Patriarch of Constantinople was—and is—recognized as the spiritual leader, but the final jurisdiction on the matters of doctrine lies with the prelates of all the churches, gathered in council. Because of this decentralization the Orthodox churches have always been closely identified with the respective countries. Each has strengthened the national feelings among its followers and has taken part in national politics, sometimes in opposition to the ruler, but more often as a tool in support of the government.

The great Slavic immigrations into the Balkan Peninsula started in the third century and lasted for some four hundred years. The conversion of the Slavs to Christianity became the task of the Byzantine Empire. Eventually the entire area from Serbia and Macedonia to Romania and Bulgaria became Orthodox, divided into various patriarchates. Eastern Christianity also spread to Russia in the tenth century, along the old trade routes across the Black Sea, and up the Dnepr River where Scandinavian chiefs held control. With the religion went a form of the Greek alphabet, but the Slavic languages came into use for liturgy and church service; this contrasted with the retention of Latin in Roman Catholicism and underscores again the national character of the Eastern churches.

The spread of Islam gravely affected Eastern Christianity. When the Osmanli (Ottoman) Turks took Constantinople in 1453 this spiritual center lost much of its significance. The rise of the Russian Empire made the patriarch of Moscow the most powerful among the prelates, a position he held until the Russian Revolution of 1917. The Soviets separated church and state and proceeded to liquidate religion. Although they abandoned this effort in 1939, there remain many restrictions on religious worship and education, and the church is a captive of the government. Much the same

6. Religions: Origins and Dispersals

situation, in various degrees of severity, now exists in the countries of Orthodox faith which came under Communist control after World War II: Romania, Bulgaria, and Yugoslavia. The largest Orthodox unit outside the Slavic countries is the independent Church of Greece, which still is the state church of the country. The immigration from eastern Europe has brought large numbers of Orthodox Christians into the United States. They are split into numerous groups according to national origin.

Although "The Holy Orthodox Catholic Apostolic Eastern Church," to use for once the official title, is by far the dominant one in influence and number, there are some other sects of Eastern Christianity outside this main body. Some of them deserve attention because of their historic or present role in world affairs.

Schismatic Sects of Eastern Christianity. In the fifth and sixth centuries, heated controversies on matters of doctrine drove several "heretical" groups out of the main church. Among them were the *Monophysites,* so called because they believed that the divine and human in Christ were of one (*monos*) nature (*physis*). To this group belonged the Christians of Egypt, of which small communities remain as the *Coptic* Church. Another survival of the Monophysites is the *Abyssinian* Church, saved from Islam by the protection of the mountains. Both groups, long isolated from the remainder of Christianity, have stagnated.

Another sect is that of the *Maronites* of Lebanon, who are roughly equal in number to the Moslems in that country. Since about A.D. 700 they have considered themselves an autonomous nation. At the time of the Crusades they made contacts with Rome and France. This led eventually to the bond of communion with the Roman Catholic Church, although the Maronites have retained the Eastern rite.

The *Nestorians,* named after a heretical bishop of the fifth century, widely diffused their form of Eastern Christianity. They were numerous in Mesopotamia in spite of Moslem rule until the ruthless Mongol invasions of the thirteenth and fourteenth centuries. Refugees reached the mountains of Kurdistan, where some communities still survive. In the seven

Figure 6–3. EASTERN CHRISTIANITY

This map shows the main autonomous churches of Eastern Orthodoxy and the Christian sects of the Middle East and India that remain from the time when Christianity was practiced widely in Asia.

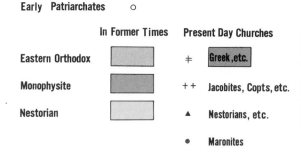

Early Patriarchates   o

	In Former Times		Present Day Churches
Eastern Orthodox		╪	Greek, etc.
Monophysite		+ +	Jacobites, Copts, etc.
Nestorian		▲	Nestorians, etc.
		●	Maronites

centuries before the Mongol devastation, the Nestorians had been very active as missionaries along the Asian trade routes. All along the caravan trails of inner Asia and into China there were Nestorian congregations, in such famous cities as Tashkent, Samarkand, Kashgar, and Peking. Their church language was Syriac, derived from the old Semitic Aramaic of Syria and Palestine, written in a script similar to the Hebrew alphabet. Although Nestorianism as a separate religion has disappeared in this realm, its function as medieval cultural intermediary between southwestern and eastern Asia was significant.

Equally important, and more lasting, was the missionary work of the Nestorians in India. According to Indian tradition, the disciple St. Thomas brought Christianity to Malabar, on the southwest coast. However, there is little doubt that Nestorians introduced Christianity in the sixth century. Hindu influence has added some non-Christian features. The main concentration of the so-called Syrian Christians is in the present Kerala state, where they form about one-fifth of the population.

The *Armenian* Church prides itself on being the oldest Christian state religion, dating back to A.D. 300 when St. Gregory converted the ruler of the Armenians. The situation of

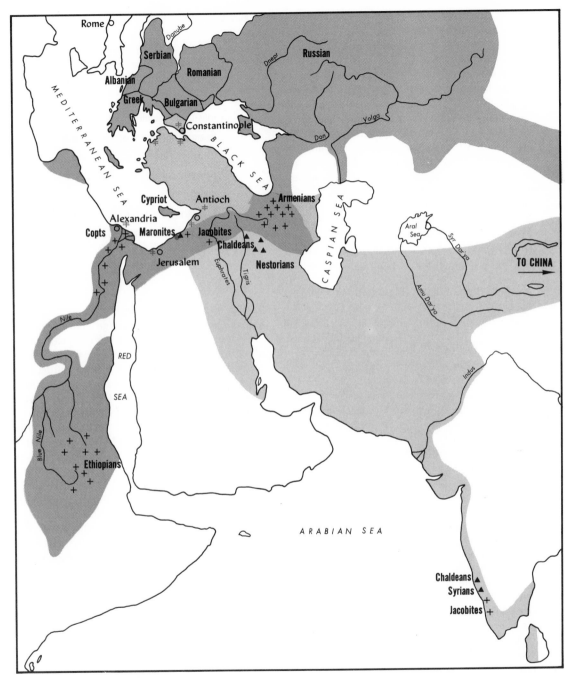

Rome ○

Serbian

Albanian

Greek

Bulgarian

MEDITERRANEAN SEA

Danube

Dnepr

Russian

Romanian

Volga

Don

BLACK SEA

Constantinople ○

Cypriot

Antioch ○

Alexandria ○

Copts

Maronites ▲

Jacobites

Chaldeans ▲ ▲

Nestorians ▲ ▲

Jerusalem

Armenians

CASPIAN SEA

Aral Sea

Syr Dar'ya

TO CHINA

Euphrates

Tigris

Amu Dar'ya

Nile

RED SEA

Blue Nile

Ethiopians

Indus

ARABIAN SEA

Chaldeans ▲

Syrians ▲

Jacobites

6. Religions: Origins and Dispersals

135

Armenia in the rugged mountains between the Byzantine and Persian empires enabled its people to retain a measure of autonomy, and their church reflects to this day the spirit of independence. Their stubborn resistance to foreign rule led to severe persecutions by the Turks, to massacres around 1900, and deportations in 1915. Their homeland lies partly in northeast Turkey, partly across the border in Soviet Russia. Numerous Armenians are scattered all over the world, usually engaged in trading, in which they excel. In this respect they show somewhat the same characteristics as the Jews in their wide dispersion and the Chinese in Southeast Asia—evidence, if needed, that not a specific race or a specific religion alone causes national traits, but the particular circumstances in which the group finds itself.

Western Christianity (Figure 6–4). During the great migrations and the decline of the West Roman Empire, Christianity maintained its foothold. The former prestige of the emperor now belonged to the Pope, who maintained a semblance of law and order through his ecclesiastical organization. In Italy, the Iberian Peninsula, and France the invaders soon joined the Roman Catholic Church (sixth century). Ireland had remained Christian during the invasions of Great Britain by pagan Anglo-Saxons. This "far western" Celtic-Christian culture waxed to a remarkable level in the early Middle Ages.

The conversion of the Germanic and West Slavic tribes beyond the Rhine-Danube frontier from approximately A.D. 600 onward took about four centuries. In this same period falls the conversion of the Magyars and of those South Slavic groups (Slovenes and Croats) who had settled on the east flank of the German and Italian territories. The expansion eastward included the Poles, whose pagan ruler, fearing the German-Catholic advance, decided to join them (966) rather than fight them and soon thereafter placed his kingdom under papal protection. East of Poland began the domain of Eastern Christianity. To the north lay Lithuania, which long remained a stronghold of paganism. It joined the Roman Catholic Church in 1386.

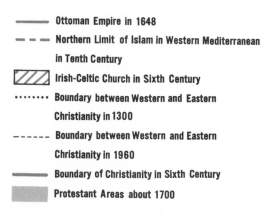

Figure 6–4. CHRISTIANITY AND ISLAM IN EUROPE

——— Ottoman Empire in 1648

– – – Northern Limit of Islam in Western Mediterranean in Tenth Century

///// Irish-Celtic Church in Sixth Century

······· Boundary between Western and Eastern Christianity in 1300

------ Boundary between Western and Eastern Christianity in 1960

——— Boundary of Christianity in Sixth Century

▓▓▓ Protestant Areas about 1700

The introduction of Christianity was accompanied by the Latin language and script, not only for church use but also as the medium for diplomatic intercourse and for the intelligentsia. Equally or more important was the diffusion of many other aspects of Mediterranean civilization among the newly settled peoples, from construction methods and agricultural practices to law and political organization. The monks, forming the veritable field army of the Church, had a large part in transmitting the culture.

While Christianity won northern Europe, it lost most of the Iberian Peninsula to Islam; Moslem rule lasted from 700 until almost 1500, when their last stronghold in the south fell. The momentum of the Christian counterattack led the Portuguese along the coast of Africa and eventually to India, enveloping the "Moor" domain. Spanish and Portuguese discoveries opened Middle and South America to Christianity. They also gained small, and often only temporary, victories among the civilizations of South and East Asia. Only in the pagan Philippines did the work of the Spanish missionaries create a largely Christian society.

In the nineteenth century the Catholic Church became quite active in newly opened-up Africa, and again in Southeast as well as East Asia. In view of current nationalism, often

II. Cultural Diversity

coupled to anti-Western attitudes, it is too early to say whether these recent gains will hold, and if so, in what form.

Protestantism. The religious strife of sixteenth-century Europe centered on the issue of authority versus private judgment on the meaning of the Scriptures. But the religious issue, in its formulation, acceptance, or rejection, was intricately bound to social, economic, and political currents and events. Demands and movements for church reform were common in all countries of Roman Catholic Europe from the twelfth century onward. The Reformation, however, succeeded only in a fairly well-

*6. Religions:
Origins and
Dispersals*

defined part of Europe, and has maintained itself in that area. It will be noted that the Protestant realm lies almost entirely beyond the Rhine-Danube boundaries of the former West Roman Empire (Figure 6–4). Were the imperial institutions on which the Church built its centralized control less firmly anchored in the new (post-sixth-century) Christian lands than in the old empire itself? The case of Poland (which remained Catholic) would seem to refute this suggestion. But Poland is a special case. It had its religious crisis and might have gone Protestant. Fear of German aggression, which at this time meant German-Lutheran aggression, strengthened the Catholic cause. A similar argument can be made for Ireland because of its antagonism to the English aggressors, although its ancient and deep-rooted Catholicism might be a sufficient ground in itself.

It has been suggested that the rise of the middle class in northwestern Europe, associated with capitalism (in the sense of private free enterprise) led to Protestantism. This leaves the question why the earlier development of capitalism in northern Italy and in France did not lead Protestantism to victory in those lands. If the answer is that in the latter countries the conservative forces were strong enough to suppress reformation movements (as indeed they were), we are back at the initial query why Protestantism succeeded in the north and not in the south. One notes frequently in history that a new idea is accepted and more fully developed on the periphery of a culture than in the center. Traditions, institutions, and vested interest groups have deeper roots in the core than on the frontier, where cultural patterns are less crystallized, more fluid, and thus more open to change. The success of the Reformation in northwestern Europe, beyond the old Roman Empire, conforms to this model.

It has also been argued that physical barriers contributed to, or even caused, the salvation of Protestantism from the onslaught of the Counter Reformation. The English Channel, the marshy delta lands of Holland, and the Swiss Alps gave indeed advantages to the defense, but they seem secondary to other factors.

Figure 6–5. UNITED STATES: RELIGIOUS AFFILIATIONS, 1950

Areas occupied by patterns or letters have at least 50 percent of all reported church memberships in the designated denomination. Data are by counties. Based on a map prepared by John Tremblay for Gaustad, 1962. By permission of the author.

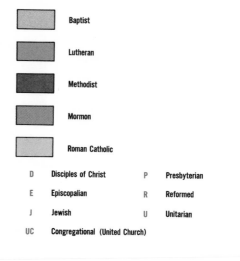

Baptist

Lutheran

Methodist

Mormon

Roman Catholic

D	Disciples of Christ	P	Presbyterian
E	Episcopalian	R	Reformed
J	Jewish	U	Unitarian
UC	Congregational (United Church)		

The break with Rome led to the establishment of national Protestant churches. The vernacular replaced Latin in the church services. There had been earlier translations of the Bible, but now that the Scriptures had become the essence of religious authority for the Protestant, new "approved" renditions were necessary. Every family read the Bible, which had a standardizing effect on the various dialects.

There were, of course, the various sects of Protestantism. Luther's creed prevailed in the German-speaking and Scandinavian countries and spread from Sweden into Finland and the Baltic states. Calvinism took root in the Netherlands, Scotland, parts of Switzerland, and among the English Puritans. The Church of England retained a more Catholic character, inherent in the history of that particular schism. Those who refused to conform split off in various dissenting groups, such as the Bap-

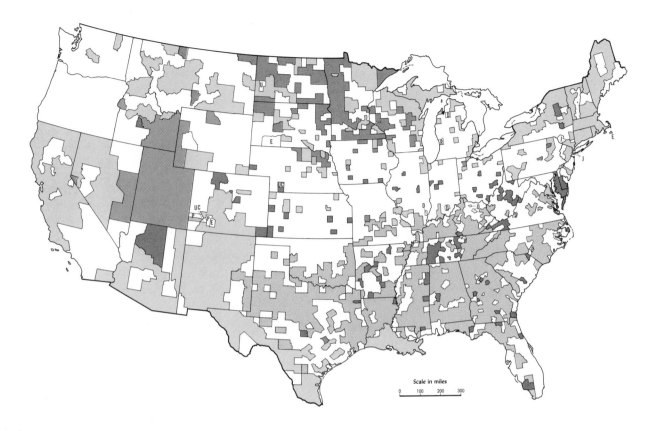

Scale in miles

0   100   200   300

tists, Congregationalists, Quakers, and, at a later time, the Methodists.

The insistence on personal salvation tended to favor strenuous morality, austerity, and diligence. Economic success was esteemed, if combined with righteousness. These values were strongly held by the Calvin-inspired groups in Holland, Scotland, England, and their brethren overseas in North America. Without opening again the question of which came first, religion or economic milieu, it can be said that the two together produced a remarkable breed of entrepreneurs in agriculture, commerce, and industry. The spirit of free inquiry—though not always observed—and the obsession with material progress stimulated the interest in science and technology which is still very typical of Protestant lands.

The migration overseas from Britain, the Netherlands, and other Northwest European countries to North America, South Africa, and later Australia and New Zealand gave all these colonies an essentially Protestant character. The only significant exception was the French settlement along the St. Lawrence River, the nucleus of the present French-Canadian Catholic community on the flank of the Anglo-Saxon Protestant realm. Protestant commercial enterprise among the peoples of Africa and Asia gave initially little attention to the spread of religion. Since the nineteenth century, however, there has been widespread missionary activity. As with similar Roman Catholic efforts, only the future can tell what will remain.

Religious Groups in the United States (Figure 6–5). In advanced urban-industrial countries religion has less direct impact on the mode of life than in the more traditional societies. The United States conforms to this general rule. But it would be a mistake to underestimate

6. Religions: Origins and Dispersals

139

Table 6–3. United States Church Membership, 1964

Protestant churches	68,300,000
Roman Catholic*	45,641,000
Jewish†	5,600,000
Eastern Orthodox churches	3,167,000
Old Catholic, Polish National Catholic, Armenian	491,000
Buddhist	110,000
TOTAL	123,309,000

*Roman Catholics 14 years and over number about 35,500,000.
†Includes Jews of Orthodox, Conservative, and Reform persuasion, whether or not related to a synagogue.
SOURCE: *Yearbook of the American Churches, 1966.*

religion as a factor. It is related to the economic level, social status, political alignment, and cultural interests. "Religious difference—as distinct from religious feeling *per se*—is a powerful and often highly emotional element in the mind of Americans that works to bind together or separate groups of people and thus to create areal resemblances or contrasts" (Zelinsky, 1961, 166).

The religious composition of the population reflects the origin of the immigrants (see Table 6–3). One should, however, beware of placing too much trust in the figures on church membership. The data for the various denominational groups are noncomparable, owing to the variety of definitions of what constitutes membership. For instance, the Roman Catholic Church counts all baptized persons, including infants, while most Protestant bodies count only persons who have attained full membership, that is, after confirmation at the age of 13 or older. Obviously, membership ranges from passive adherence to militant participation.

Fortunately for the national cohesion of the

United States, the large denominations are spread all over the country. Some groups are more urban, others more rural. Jews are almost entirely concentrated in cities, and Roman Catholics, Episcopalians, and Unitarians also tend to be urban. Baptists, in contrast, mainly reside in rural areas, and so do numerous small sects, such as Mennonites (including Amish), and various fundamentalist creeds of old Anglo-American stock. Locally, there are often striking departures from the national pattern, as, for example, rural Catholic groups in the Middle West and urban Baptists in California. A brief review of the areal distribution (Figure 6–5) follows, based on the work of Gaustad (1962).

Roman Catholics predominate along the Mexican border in Texas, New Mexico, and Arizona, partly as the legacy of the former Spanish-Mexican domain, partly the result of recent immigration from across the border. Louisiana shows its French heritage in the coastal region. The large Roman Catholic influx from Ireland and later from central and southern Europe has almost submerged the originally Protestant character of New England. Massachusetts, Rhode Island, and Connecticut have Catholic majorities. The entire manufacturing and mining belt westward as far as Wisconsin and Illinois is a zone of Catholic concentration. On the other hand, the South—with the exceptions noted—has very few Catholics, since it had little attraction for the European immigrant of the industrial era. Another part with few Catholics is the intermountain region centering on Utah, where the Church of the Latter-day Saints (Mormons) is without rival. In all but three counties of Utah, 90 percent or more of the church membership is Mormon. In Hawaii, with its racially as well as denominationally very mixed population, about one-fourth is Roman Catholic. It may be noted in passing that Buddhism in the United States has its strongest representation here, owing to the immigration from East Asia.

Eastern Christianity entered North America with the Russian settlement in Alaska and moved southward along the Pacific Coast. Its real growth came from the 1880s onward with the immigration from east and southeast Europe. Most of these immigrants were absorbed into the industrial areas of the Middle West.

Of the Protestants, the Baptists are mainly found in the South; Lutherans, in contrast, are chiefly in the Middle Western farm belt. Both groups are, like all others, well represented on the Pacific Coast, the true melting pot of modern America. Congregational churches are still strong in New England and scattered throughout the Middle West. Least regionally concentrated of the Protestant denominations are the Methodists, Presbyterians, and Episcopalians. Even so, Methodists are especially numerous in a band from the Middle Atlantic states through the southern part of the Middle West to the Rocky Mountains, and Episcopalians in their old core area from southern New England to Virginia.

In summary, there is a general zoning along east-west lines, with the exception of the Pacific Coast, where denominations are much intermixed. The South, apart from areas of Romance heritage, is a Protestant region, mainly of Baptists and Methodists. The central intermountain area, with its Church of the Latter-day Saints, is the most distinct religious region in the country. In the North, there is a great intermingling of religions, although here, too, some specific patterns can be observed, such as Jewish concentrations in the large cities, Lutheran and Catholic mixtures in the North Central states, and a strong, even dominant, Catholic element in the East.

The World of Islam

General Characteristics. Islam means "submission to God." It was about A.D. 600 that Mohammed began his mission. He lived in Mecca, the transfer point on the caravan routes from southern Arabia to Syria, and the site of many shrines of tribal deities. In his new religion he combined Arab beliefs and customs (such as the practice of polygyny and the veneration of stones) with elements of Judaic and Christian doctrines and ethics. The keystone of the creed was strict monotheism: "There is no God but Allah." Mohammed admitted that Allah had revealed Himself to previous prophets, among them Abraham, Moses, and Jesus, but insisted that he, Mohammed, had received the definitive truth. This divine and full truth was written down by the prophet—in Arabic—as he received it through successive revelations and was gathered in the Koran. This holy book contains not only religious doctrine and rules of worship, but many pronouncements on worldly matters. Since the Koran is divinely inspired from beginning to end, it is the unalterable fountainhead of Moslem law. Each Moslem must observe the "five pillars" of the faith: repeated saying of the basic creed, frequent prayers, a month of fasting between dawn and dusk, almsgiving, and pilgrimage to Mecca, "if able." Those who perform faithfully these tasks are brothers in the Moslem community, which knows no bars of color or caste.

There are, of course, many other rules in addition to the five pillars. Some were adopted because they were traditional among many peoples in the Middle East, such as circumcision and avoidance of the pig. Others were presumably borrowed from Judaism or Christianity, among them the prohibition of human and animal images, of usury, and of gambling. The use of alcohol also was forbidden. As in all other religions, some of these rules were at some periods and among some peoples not strictly observed, if at all. In contrast to the streaks of puritanism stands sexual latitude, which the Koran allows, or at least does not explicitly forbid. Even so, the great majority of Moslems have only one wife, and divorce—available to the husband at his will—is probably no more common than in Western countries. But most Western observers agree that in the world of Islam the esteem for women has generally remained at a low level. However, this may be due to socioeconomic, rather than religious, conditions.

Spread of Islam. The first city where Mohammed found acclaim was not his hometown of Mecca, but Medina, where he had fled in A.D. 622. (The year of the flight—*Hegira*—is the beginning of the Islamic calendar.) Religious

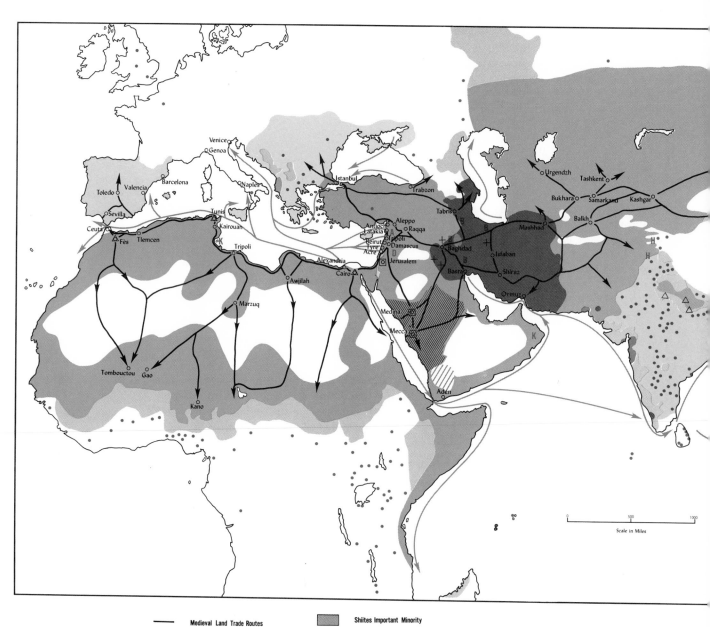

Medieval Land Trade Routes
Medieval Sea Trade Routes
△ Islamic Universities
□ Holy Places of Islam
+ Holy Places of Shiites
○ Principal Medieval Trade Centers

Sunnites Majority
Sunnites Important Minority
• Sunnites Scattered Minorities
Shiites Majority

Shiites Important Minority
Ismailites
Zaidites
Sunnites Majority and Wahhabites
K Kharijites
Areas Formerly Islamic or under Islamic Control
A Alawites
B Bahais
D Druzes
H Ahmadiyahs

*II. Cultural
Diversity*

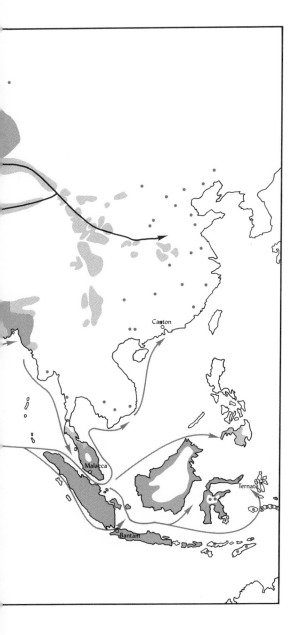

Figure 6–6. ISLAM

The main trade routes, as shown on the map, help to explain the diffusion of Islam. Based on many sources, but especially on *Les Mussulmans dans le monde,* 1952.

conversion required political control. At the time of his death (A.D. 632) all of Arabia was under Mohammed's rule. Then came an amazing burst of Arab-Moslem expansion: in less than one hundred years they conquered all lands from the Atlantic Ocean to the borders of India, including Spain, North Africa, Egypt, Syria, Mesopotamia, and Persia. In all these countries, except Persia, they overpowered a predominantly Christian population, interspersed with Jewish communities. Since Mohammed had recognized both Christians and Jews as followers of a sacred book, conversion "at sword's point" was not required of them. If they surrendered peaceably, but refused conversion, they were allowed to submit under treaty, which gave them protection as noncitizens on payment of a tax. This explains the survival of Christian and Jewish groups in Moslem countries. Nevertheless, economic and social discrimination were powerful factors in gradually converting the great mass of the population. Moreover, the confusion and dissension caused by doctrinal disputes among medieval Christians gave Islam many wedges for penetration. The simplicity of Islam's basic creed also facilitated absorption (Figure 6–6).

In the following centuries Islam expanded into India, Central Asia, Southeast Asia, the Sudan, and the fringes of East Africa. Moslem invaders from Central Asia ruled large territories in northern India from about the eleventh to the eighteenth century, and thus laid the foundation for the present West Pakistan. In East Bengal—the present East Pakistan—where Buddhist influence had lingered quite long and the population belonged to tribes or low castes, Islam was welcomed as an escape from socioreligious segregation which a then-resurgent Brahmanism would have imposed.

6. Religions: Origins and Dispersals

Islam was born in the desert, and the Koran reflects this environment. It is said that this helped its acceptance among peoples of the arid and semiarid belt stretching from North Africa to the heart of Asia. In support of this argument some writers point to the isohyet of 20 inches rainfall as coinciding with the main body of Islam. The territorial correlation is there, but only if we ignore more than half of the Moslems who live in humid climates of coastal East Africa and South and Southeast Asia. In view of the total distribution, we must reject the suggestion of a cause-and-effect relation between climate and the spread of Islam.

The more satisfactory answer lies in another direction, namely, the trade routes. The caravan trails led from the Middle East through Central Asia to North China (where there are still a good number of Moslems), as well as across the Sahara to the Sudan. The overseas routes led from Arabia down the east coast of Africa, or to India, and from there through the Straits of Malacca to Java and the Spice Islands, and even to China. The traders, according to the duty of every Moslem, were missionaries. Even so, the greatest zeal can accomplish little unless the circumstances are favorable. For instance, Arab-Moslem traders were in East Asia by the eighth century, but the real impact of Islam did not come in the Malay Archipelago until about 1300, when the Hindu-Buddhist superstructure had begun to disintegrate.

Since the Koran may not be translated from the original Arabic, this language is in ritual use wherever Moslems live. In the early expansion period the prestige of the Arabic language was such that it replaced the vernacular in several countries of the Middle East and North Africa (see Chapter 5). Outside the Arabic-speaking world the male youths learn by heart a number of ritual passages as required for worship. The ritual script is also Arabic; this has been adopted in a number of Moslem countries as the alphabet for their own written languages. When Turkey was secularized in the 1920s, the government replaced the Arabic alphabet by the Latin script; some other countries, including Indonesia and Malaya, have followed suit.

Diversity within Islam. As in other religions, the tenets of Islam have been subject to different interpretation or emphasis. In the early expansion over the Middle East, Hellenistic philosophy mixed with Arab faith. Scholarship flowered; Western Christianity in comparison looked like a rustic grade school. But in the twelfth century there came a strong reaction against legal and ethical judgments based on reason. Return to the orthodox faith, in the form as taught by Mohammed, became the guiding principle. What this meant can best be shown with one example. There is an Arabic description of the methods of Chinese printing, written in 1307, more than one hundred years before Gutenberg "invented" (read: learned of) the process. But Moslems were unwilling to use it. Printing one book might lead eventually to printing the Koran, a sacrilegious act. There may have been other reasons, but it was not until 1729 that the first attempt was made to print a book in the Islamic world. It led to riots and prohibition of the project. The first Moslem Arab press was established in 1825 in Cairo (Kroeber, 1948, 417–418, 495).

Education without printed books is difficult. Add to this a suspicion of all knowledge which comes from unbelievers and it becomes clear why orthodox Moslems long opposed modern— that is, Western—education. In India in the middle nineteenth century, Hindus accepted English education, but most Moslems continued to reject it for two generations. In Indonesia, Malaya, and among the Moslems of Mindanao in the Philippines, there was the same reluctance to learn from Westerners. Literacy rates are, to this very day, lower for these groups than for their Christian or Hindu neighbors.

Now that most countries of Islam are independent again and seek to modernize themselves, the conservative, quasi-medieval outlook forms a hindrance to progress. Various sects and movements are actively seeking ways in which a new interpretation of Islam can meet the challenge of today's world. Turkey has gone farthest in this respect; for instance, it has abolished Islamic law, using instead a legal system derived from western European countries.

Disputes have divided Islam into several

Lahore, West Pakistan: Moslems praying inside the great mosque, built by Moghul Emperor Aurangzeb in the seventeenth century. In this ritual position the faithful, turned toward Mecca (here westward), touch the floor with their foreheads, symbolizing complete submission to Allah.
[Courtesy of United Nations]

sects and subsects. The first and greatest split came over the succession. The *Sunnis,* or *Sunnites,* claimed that the caliphate (*caliph* means the head of the Moslem community as successor of the prophet) should be an elective office, but the *Shi'ahs* or *Shi'ites* insisted that it be held by the prophet's descendants. The schism, involving the crucial issue of religious authority, has led to diverse interpretations of doctrine. The Sunnites are now by far the larger body, comprising over 400 million people. The Shi'ites, numbering perhaps 50 mil-

lion, are mainly concentrated in Iran and adjacent parts of Iraq, with smaller groups in India, Syria, and Lebanon.

A strongly puritanical movement developed among the Sunni of Arabia in the early eighteenth century. The *Wahhabites,* as they are called, rejected all intrusions on pure monotheism—such as the adoration of saints—and stretched Mohammed's teachings on sobriety to ban the use of tobacco and coffee. Saudi Arabia, whose rulers are Wahhabites, enforces these regulations, as Western temporary resi-

6. Religions: Origins and Dispersals

145

dents (mainly of the petroleum companies) well know. Fortunately for Arabs and Westerners alike, air-conditioned cars and homes were beyond Mohammed's vision and its subsequent interpretations.

The Pan-Islam movement of the nineteenth century was an attempt to unite Islam, especially against Western aggression. It was doomed to fail, if for no other reason than the tide of nationalism. Even the conflict with Israel did not bring an outraged Moslem world to unity.

Hinduism

General Character. The complex of forms of belief and ritual behavior prevalent in India is not a religion in the same sense as the ones previously sketched. There is no founder, no church establishment, and no defined dogma. Hinduism ranges from crude superstition and practice to highly refined philosophy. Every generalization about Hinduism has, therefore, its exceptions. It is as difficult to comprehend as "Occidental culture": one knows in general what it means, but how can it comprise Lincoln, Nietzsche, and Einstein, monastic austerity as well as the antics of Madison Avenue? In the same way, we should perhaps see Hinduism as the manifestation of the Indian ethos, of a deep-rooted spiritual-cultural pattern that has spread from its core to the manifold peoples and tribes of the subcontinent, blending with the local beliefs and forming new offshoots in the course of time.

About 1500 B.C. Aryan tribes—seminomadic cattle herders and plow cultivators of Indo-European speech—invaded India from the northwest. As they came in contact with the people of the Indus Valley they must have taken over much of the culture of this more advanced indigenous society. After the tenth century B.C. the center of Aryan power shifted southeastward to the *doab* (interfluve) between the Jumna and Ganges rivers. It appears that by this time the Aryans had accepted female deities from Dravidian cults and had abandoned beef eating for the veneration of the cow. From the Jumna-Ganges doab, Hinduism, as elaborated and taught by a hereditary class of Brahman priests, spread eastward down the Ganges and southward into the peninsula, grafting itself onto other beliefs and institutions.

The reform movements of Buddhism and Jainism—both around 500 B.C.—gained the upper hand for a time, at least among the upper classes. But in the end Hinduism virtually absorbed them again, certainly in the homeland. In the meantime, from the beginning of the Christian era onward, Indian colonists had spread into Southeast Asia as far as Java, Celebes, and South Vietnam. Their culture, including Hinduism and later Buddhism, strongly influenced local societies. In mythology, folk culture, and vocabulary the heritage persists to this very day, even where it is submerged under the later spread of Islam. Bali, the small island east of Java, is the only area in Indonesia where Hinduism, interspersed with traces of Buddhism, is still the predominant religion.

The Caste System. Although there are different theories about the origin of the Indian caste system, its relationship to religion is evident and its impact on social organization is profound. There are innumerable caste groups, defined by various criteria. A Hindu is born into a caste, marries within his caste, worships and works according to the rules of his caste. The key word to the understanding of caste is ritual purity, with its converse, avoidance of pollution. Anything that has to do with destruction of life, or with decaying matter, is unclean. Thus the people who perform tasks which expose them to pollution are restricted in their contact with those of higher, purer caste groups. Workers with menial occupations—fishermen, butchers, garbage haulers, laundrymen, those who crush oilseeds—are necessarily of low caste.

The belief in caste order lies deeply anchored in the metaphysical concept of the universe. The all-embracing order, arranged in a hierarchy, gives all creatures their rank. Man stands at the top level, with the Brahman caste on the highest step. Above and beyond is the final release from earthly existence. Through reincarnation the soul moves into a being, high or low on the ladder, man or beast. At what level it is reborn depends on the conduct during the previous existence. This is *karma,* the law of the deed, establishing a strict cause-and-effect relationship between past behavior and present form of life, including caste level. The caste is thus a part of the universal, eternal order. The individual cannot escape it, but has the chance to move up in the next existence by earning merit in the present. He can do so in three ways: by following the path of duty (according to the usage of his caste); by devotion to the gods; or by pursuing knowledge. The third is the more sure and rapid route to promotion in the next life, but the most difficult because it requires the arts of asceticism and meditation.

The belief in a universal law of retribution gives a rational answer to the question why one is what he is. At the same time it provides little stimulus for material progress beyond the confines of the caste rules.

If the individual is virtually fixed in his caste group (for his present life), there is, fortunately, some mobility for the groups. They can collectively change their customs (for instance, by rejecting widow marriage, by observing certain food taboos, or by abandoning an occupation), which may result, after some generations of good behavior, in acceptance of their caste at a higher level.

The impact of Occidental culture, under British rule, as well as after independence, compels Hinduism to reconsider its character as a social force. Plantations, mines, factories, and construction projects bring workers together from various caste groups, using crowded means of transportation and common eating facilities. Neither can the schools and modern forms of mass entertainment observe the neat rules of segregation.

The lot of the *Harijans,* also called the scheduled or depressed castes, or untouchables, has improved greatly. Their members, numbering now about 65 million, had been excluded from the ordinary social and religious institutions, such as schools and temples. Gandhi championed their cause. Under the constitution of

1949 "untouchability" was outlawed and discrimination against Harijans made a punishable offense. In addition to the scheduled castes there are the 30 million people who belong to "scheduled tribes." Most of them are nominally Hindus (1.5 million were listed in 1961 as adhering to a tribal religion and 1.4 million as being Christian); but because they keep to themselves in remote habitats neither the caste rules of Hindu society nor the new legislation against discrimination really affect the tribal folk.

Relaxation of caste rules is more noticeable in the north than in the south, and mainly in the cities. Whether it will eventually result in the disappearance of the caste system is hard to foretell. The roots of this tradition are deep and its practice is interwoven with religion. Moreover, the beneficial side to caste must not be overlooked. It has the quality of a cooperative mutual-welfare society, an important feature in an economy where so many people live at bare existence level.

The Sikhs. Among the many offshoots of Hinduism, the religion of the Sikhs deserves mention because it has resulted in an areally distinct pattern. The confrontation with Islam led a number of Hindu thinkers to attempt syntheses of the two religions. One of them was Nanak, a Hindu native of the Punjab, who lived about A.D. 1500. He favored monotheism and attacked the veneration of idols and the caste system. Later, about 1700, his sect developed into a militant theocracy which waged war against the Moslem Moghul Empire. During this period the Sikhs developed a strong national consciousness. There are now some eight million of them. The British used them in their army and police forces, for which their long military tradition well suited them. Full beard and long hair, carefully wrapped in the turban, are among their distinguishing features. Their center is at Amritsar, where the Golden Temple enshrines the sacred book containing the wisdom of their early teachers. Their traditional hostility to Islam made the Sikhs join India at the time of partition. A number of their shrines now lie within the territory of

6. Religions:
Origins and
Dispersals

Pakistan. To meet Sikh grievances against their subordinate position among the Hindus of Punjab, a new state was created in 1966 (see Chapter 7).

Buddhism

Origin and Development. According to tradition, Gautama was born in the foothills of Nepal in the late sixth century B.C. and spent most of his life in the middle Ganges region. He became Buddha—the Enlightened One—when he perceived the path of salvation in the Four Noble Truths. The first is the recognition that life is full of sufferings; the second is perception of the cause of suffering, namely, craving, desire; the third is that pain ceases through cessation of desire; the fourth is knowledge of the means to stop suffering, including the right views and the right conduct: honesty, non-injury of any creature (*ahimsa*), forgiveness of enemies.

In essence it was not a religion, but a do-it-yourself psychotherapy. Ignorance was at the root of desire's evils; knowledge was the cure. Worship of deities, blood sacrifices, and caste division had no place in this moral road to salvation. Gautama retained, however, the concept of transmigration of the soul, although in somewhat modified form.

Many of the ethical precepts appealed to the common man, but the full program of self-salvation, with its emphasis on meditation, required a special environment. Monastic orders for men and women soon came into being. The monks became the missionaries of Buddhism. Monastic orders maintain their important position to this very day. Many lay folk spend at least one year as novice monks or nuns in the religious orders. In some countries a substantial fraction of the male population is in this way withdrawn from the economic production process. Since underemployment is common in underdeveloped countries, this is no serious problem, though the time may come when society will demand the release of this manpower.

Figure 6-7. BUDDHISM

Buddhism, although no longer prevailing in the land of its origin, has spread to other parts of Asia and has become the dominant religion in many countries. The map is based on a number of sources, but especially *Grosser historischer Weltatlas*, 1957, vol. 3, 183.

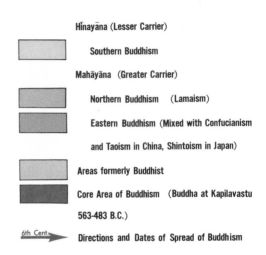

Hīnayāna (Lesser Carrier)

Southern Buddhism

Mahāyāna (Greater Carrier)

Northern Buddhism   (Lamaism)

Eastern Buddhism (Mixed with Confucianism and Taoism in China, Shintoism in Japan)

Areas formerly Buddhist

Core Area of Buddhism   (Buddha at Kapilavastu 563-483 B.C.)

6th Cent. Directions and Dates of Spread of Buddhism

In the course of centuries, the essentially simple doctrine has been greatly modified. The gods, as incarnations of Buddha, returned, revered in splendid pagodas. Among the various sects, two stand out as the main schismatic bodies. The *Hinayana,* or southern school—because it is chiefly found in Ceylon and Southeast Asia—emphasizes the road of salvation through the Four Noble Truths. This virtually requires becoming a monk. For this reason the southern branch has been called by its opponents Hinayana, meaning the Little or Lesser Vehicle, because only few can journey to redemption. The other branch is the *Mahayana,* the Greater Vehicle, which has its followers in East Asia. It opens the road to salvation to far greater numbers, because Buddha and many other deities are considered as saviors for all men of true devotion.

Expansion of Buddhism (Figure 6-7). Buddhism made slow headway in northern India

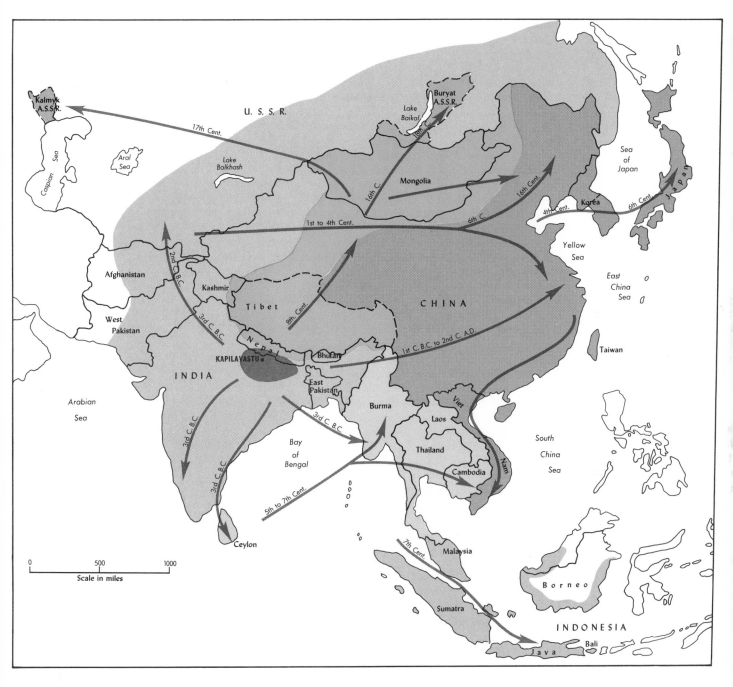

Kalmyk
A.S.S.R.

U. S. S. R.

Caspian Sea

Aral Sea

Lake Balkhash

Buryat
A.S.S.R.

Lake Baikal

17th Cent.

16th C.

18th C.

Mongolia

16th Cent

Sea
of
Japan

Afghanistan

Kashmir

2nd C. B.C.

3rd C. B.C.

1st to 4th Cent.

8th Cent.

6th C.

CHINA

4th Cent.

Korea

6th Cent.

Japan

West
Pakistan

Tibet

Yellow
Sea

East
China
Sea

Arabian Sea

INDIA

N e p a l

KAPILAVASTU

Bhutan

East Pakistan

1st C. B.C. to 2nd C. A.D.

Taiwan

3rd C. B.C.

Bay
of
Bengal

3rd C. B.C.

Burma

Laos

Viet

Thailand

Nam

Cambodia

South
China
Sea

3rd C. B.C.

5th to 7th Cent.

Ceylon

7th Cent.

Malaysia

B o r n e o

Sumatra

INDONESIA

Java

Bali

0   500   1000

Scale in miles

*6. Religions:
Origins and
Dispersals*

until the conversion of Emperor Asoka (third century B.C.). He became the patron of his new faith and supported its spread not only in his own domain but in other parts of India and in Ceylon. The Buddha figure as we know it from Indian sculptures was strongly influenced by Greek art, following Alexander's invasion of India. In the first century A.D. Buddhism came into China over the inner Asian trade routes, though it did not become popular there until the fifth century. Chinese missionaries brought the faith to Korea and Japan in the form of the Mahayana. This also radiated southward, with much of Chinese culture, into Tonking and Annam, the present Vietnam.

The peoples of Mongolia and Tibet also accepted the Mahayana form, but infused it with other ideas, some of them probably harking back to Nestorian Christianity. In Tibet, until the Chinese Communist regime took over, the head of the priestly hierarchy was the revered Dalai Lama. Monasteries owned much of the land, and monks formed close to one-fourth of the population before the Communist rule.

In the fifth to the seventh centuries Buddhism spread throughout Southeast Asia as far as Java. Hinayana was the dominant creed, with great centers of learning where Indian and Chinese scholars met. Later it lost to Islam its influence in Malaya and the nearby islands, but it has persisted in the greater part of the mainland. It is the state religion in Burma, Thailand, Laos, and Cambodia. In South Vietnam it has no official position, but claims 70 percent of the population. In recent years there have been clashes between Buddhists and Roman Catholics (one-fifth of the population of South Vietnam). The latter have a strong economic position, owing in part at least to their superior education.

While Buddhism was advancing abroad, it began—in the seventh century—to lose ground at home, mainly through reabsorption into the all-embracing Hinduism. By about 1200, Buddhism as a distinct creed had almost vanished from India proper. It has maintained itself among the Himalayan mountain folk and on the island of Ceylon.

East Asian Religions

Ancestor worship is a very ancient form of religion, once widespread. While elsewhere later religions largely replaced it, in East Asia it has blended with them. This has kept the family as the prime unit of social organization, especially in China.

The teachings of Confucius, who lived about the time of Gautama Buddha, were ethical precepts based on empirical knowledge. He stressed the reciprocal moral obligations between father and son, ruler and subject: each person must treat others as he wishes them to treat him. He compared the state to the family, acknowledging the ruler as a father to whom filial piety is due, but who must equally observe his obligations toward his sons.

Under the Han dynasty in 136 B.C., Confucianism became the state religion and the source of all education. This led to the examination system for all bureaucratic functions, founded on the Confucian notion that only qualified persons should rule. This system lasted until 1911.

At the same time as Confucius lived Lao-tse. He taught The Way (*Tao*), showing how man must strive to be in harmony with the universal order by communicating with nature, seeking simplicity, tranquillity, and spiritual freedom. Much of Chinese art reflects these attitudes. However, there also developed another kind of Taoism, which for some centuries—from the fifth onward—was a state cult. As a religion of the masses it degenerated, combining the veneration of many gods, from ancestors to emperors, with the use of magic charms and the arts of divination, all directed toward the search for a long life with material blessings.

Buddhism intermingled with these native ideas and practices to such an extent that one is justified to speak of a Chinese religious ideology. In its ideal form it blends Confucian moral precepts, such as the golden rule; Buddhist virtues, such as compassion; and Taoist values, such as simplicity. Even Christianity—before the Communists came into power—fitted into this eclectic thought pattern and made its ethical contributions. The total impression is one of deep concern with life on this earth. In this respect Chinese and Occidental cultures resemble each other, in contrast to the other-worldliness of the Indian ethos. The materialistic ideology of communism is not alien to the Chinese mind. The history of China suggests that the foreign ideas will be modified and absorbed, as happened to so many earlier imports, bringing change but not destruction of Chinese culture.

In Korea there prevails much the same kind of religious blend as found in China. In Japan the ancient native religion is Shinto, a mixture of nature and ancestor worship. For a time it was subservient to Buddhism, but in the nineteenth century the challenge of the Occident led to its revival. The ancient belief that the emperor was of divine descent was resurrected. Shintoism became the state religion, a powerful tool for welding the Japanese people together into a modern nation. After Japan's defeat in 1945, Shinto was disestablished as the state church and the doctrine of divine descent disavowed.

Other Ideologies

In the beginning of this chapter ideology was defined as a system of beliefs, sentiments, and values that is prevalent in a specific culture. We have reviewed the main religions as influential ideologies and observed the intertwining of religious and secular elements. In "modern" societies the role of religion is often overshadowed by other beliefs and feelings. The extreme case of a consciously secular ideology is that which dominates now in the Soviet Union and China. Fascism and national socialism were short-lived examples of specific nationalistic ideologies. In contrast to these exclusive creeds, communism has the character of a "universal" ideology, a pseudoreligion proclaiming its worldwide mission. Thus communism is intolerant of other ideologies. It has a doctrine, a hierarchy, and a proselytizing zeal. And again, similar to religions, interpretations of the teachings of the prophet multiply and schisms occur, as communism spreads to other countries and faces new conditions.

Citations

Atlas of Israel, Department of Surveys, Jerusalem, 1956–1960. [Map]

Documentation Française *Les Mussulmans dans le monde, Notes et études documentaires,* Paris, 1952. [Map]

Gaustad, E. S. *Historical Atlas of Religion in America,* New York, 1962.

Grosser historischer Weltatlas, 3 vols., München, 1957. [Map]

Kroeber, A. L. *Anthropology,* New York, 1948.

Lestshinsky, J. "Die Umsiedlung und Umschichtung des jüdischen Volkes im Laufe des letzten Jahrhunderts," *Weltwirtschaftliches Archiv,* 30 (1930), Heft 1: 123–156; 32 (1931), Heft 2: 563–599.

Weber, M. *The Protestant Ethic and the Spirit of Capitalism* (translated by T. Parsons), New York, 1930. Originally published in *Archiv für Sozialwissenschaft und Sozialpolitik,* 20–21 (1904–1905).

Zelinsky, W. "An Approach to the Religious Geography of the United States," *Annals of the Association of American Geographers,* 51 (1961): 139–167.

Further Readings

Atlas of Canada, Department of Mines and Surveys, Geographic Branch, Ottawa, 1957. Contains maps of the six leading denominations.

Braden, C. S. *The World's Religions,* New York and Nashville, Tenn., 1954.

Clark, A. H. "Old World Origins and Religious Adherence in Nova Scotia," *Geographical Review,* 50 (1960): 317–344.

Deffontaines, P. *Géographie et religions,* Paris, 1948.

Fickeler, P. "Fundamental Questions in the Geography of Religions," in Wagner, P. L., and Mikesell, M. W. (eds.) *Readings in Cultural Geography,* Chicago, 1962, 94–117. Originally published in *Erdkunde,* 1 (1947): 121–144.

Fleure, H. S. "The Geographical Distribution of the Major Religions," *Bulletin de la Société Royale de Géographie d'Egypte,* 24 (1951): 1–18.

Gibb, H. A. R. *Mohammedanism: An Historical Survey,* London, 1949.

Isaac, E. "Religion, Landscape, and Space," *Landscape,* 9 (1959–1960), no. 2: 14–18.

———. "The Act and the Covenant: The Impact of Religion on the Landscape," *Landscape,* 11 (1961–1962), no. 2: 12–17.

McEvedy, C. *The Penguin Atlas of Medieval History,* Harmondsworth, England, 1961.

Paullin, C. O. (ed.) *Atlas of the Historical Geography of the United States,* New York, 1932. For distributions of denominations, see 49–51 and plates 82–88.

Planhol, X. de *The World of Islam,* Ithaca, N.Y., 1959. First published as *Le Monde islamique: Essai de géographie religieuse,* Paris, 1957.

Rondot, P. *Les Chrétiens d'Orient,* Paris, 1952.

Schwartzberg, J. E. "The Distribution of Selected Castes in the North Indian Plain," *Geographical Review,* 55 (1965): 477–496.

Simoons, F. S. *Eat Not This Flesh: Food Avoidances in the Old World,* Madison, Wis., 1961.

Sopher, D. E. *The Geography of Religions,* Englewood Cliffs, N.J., 1967.

Tawney, R. H. *Religion and the Rise of Capitalism,* New York, 1926.

Toynbee, A. J. *A Study of History,* abridged ed. by D. C. Somervell, 2 vols., New York and London, 1947, 1957.

Van Der Meer, F. *Atlas of the Early Christian World,* London, 1958.

7. Ideologies and the Political Order

The State: Territory and People

The bond between a community and the territory it occupies is an elementary principle of life, observable among animals as well as man. Human groups have partitioned the earth into territorial units, from tribal lands to huge sovereign states. The principles guiding the political organization of earth space have varied in time and place. Empires and dynasties have gathered under their rule territories inhabited by different peoples; elsewhere and at other times likeness in culture has been the test for delimiting the state.

Any state to survive requires

... the conviction of integration in the minds of all groups in all areas . . . , a feeling, that is, of identification of themselves with the region as a whole and with its organization as a political state. This identification further must be accepted as stronger than any other forms of identification that might lead to conflict: such as identification with a lesser part of the state, a section or a locality; or identification in religious communities overlapping many states; or identification with people of the same language overlapping into another state. (Hartshorne, 1954, 192–193)

Homogeneity. The sovereign state creates a measure of political homogeneity over its territory, however varied the peoples and regions under its rule may be. The greater the homogeneity the greater will be the internal strength of the state. This homogeneity has two aspects:

uniformity and *coherence* (Hartshorne, 1954, 188–189).

Uniformity does not require that the beliefs, customs, rights, and obligations of all citizens be exactly the same. One has only to think of the many religions in the United States, or of the differences in local laws and taxes, to realize that a great deal of diversity in detail and for the parts can be combined with uniformity of general rules and standards for the whole. Even so, the sovereign state tends to strive for a high degree of uniformity in those matters that vitally affect its welfare.

Coherence, the second aspect of homogeneity, means a union of parts. The more and stronger the interrelations between the sectors and sections of a state, the greater the coherence. Barriers of the spirit (different languages, different religions, race prejudice) as well as barriers of nature (seas, mountains, deserts) may form obstacles to coherence. The state makes special efforts to remove such barriers. For instance, Indonesia developed a national language to counteract the linguistic regionalism, and Canada built its first transcontinental railway to bind together its far-flung provinces.

The National State. Currently we are in an era in which nationalism is almost universally regarded as the foremost concept for the organization of sovereign states. According to Hans Kohn, American historian, nationalism is a state of mind which considers the sovereign nation-state as the ideal form of political organization, and the nationality as the source of all creative cultural energy and of economic well-being (Kohn, 1944, 16). Nationalism claims the supreme loyalty of all members of the nation, organized in the state. National spirit, national independence, national economy, national product, international relations, United Nations, all recognize the idea of nationalism as the guiding principle of the state idea.

It is ironic that while modern technology and economy need integration of resources and markets by large territories, nationalism fragments the earth into numerous exclusive compartments. Inevitably such fragmentation calls forth counterforces that point toward forms of supranational organization.

What Is a Nation? "To be different from others and proud of one's own special features is an essential trait of every human group. No group greatly resents its example being followed, but none likes to follow another's lead. This basic character, inherent to human psychology and sociology, makes every unit of space inhabited by man essentially a human unit. The most stubborn facts are those of the spirit, not those of the physical world" (Gottmann, 1951, 164). This "pooled self-esteem" of the group, whether of a clan of mountaineers in their valley, of a section like "The South," or of a country like France, Gottmann compares with an *icon,* a symbolic image. He uses the word *iconography* to describe "the whole system of symbols in which a people believe." This is another term for what we would call the regional, or the national, ideology. To quote his statement further:

These symbols are many and varied. A national "iconography" in our sense encompasses the national flag, the proud memories of past history as well as the principles of the prevailing religion, the generally accepted rules of economics, the established social hierarchy, the heroes quoted in the schools, the classic authors. . . . For any group of people, the iconography is the common cherished heritage. (Gottmann, 1952, 516–517)

The French historian Ernest Renan said in 1882: "A nation is a large community, founded on the consciousness of voluntary sacrifices made for the common weal, and on the understanding that this unity of purpose is to continue in the future."

These statements may seem rather vague to one who wants definitions as precise as the formula of a chemical compound. He may well ask whether there is not a specific element which forms the essential cement, such as one language, one religion, or a physically well-defined habitat. However, inspection of the world's nations shows that, while such features—especially language—are important ingredients, they do not in themselves provide the necessary and sufficient bonds for national unity.

Problems of Heterogeneity. Ideally, the nation-state is a politically independent group of like-minded people who occupy their own territory. Its areal differences are merely regional variations on the major national theme, giving it the rich expression of diversity-in-unity. Reality often is far from this ideal. Internal friction often occurs. Before illustrating this by a number of case studies, it may help to distinguish some major forms of heterogeneity.

A *foreign national group* concentrated in one part of the country may gravely endanger the stability of the state, especially if the dissenting faction feels a unity with an adjacent nation. This neighbor may even claim the territory as an unredeemed part (*irredenta*) of its own domain. Examples of this kind abound in recent European history.

Some states are composites of *multiple nationalities* or *subnations.* Although these groups may adhere to the general state idea, their identification ranges from wholehearted support to reluctant participation. Switzerland, the Soviet Union, India, and Belgium are such composite states.

Tribal groups are not well integrated, if at all, with the state in whose territory they live. Tribes differ from nationalities or subnations in the small scope of their societies, which restricts identification with other tribes or with the body of the state's citizens. Tribes usually occupy lands beyond the ecumene of the state, as for instance those living in the tundra and

"The Wall" in northern Berlin, pointing up how ideological-political conflict cleaves in two the functional whole of a city. [Courtesy of German Tourist Information Office]

taiga of Canada and the Soviet Union, the Indian tribes of Central and South America, or the "hill tribes" of India and Southeast Asia.

Sectionalism is an aggravated form of regional consciousness. It does not arise from contrasts in language, religion, or other ethnic traits that usually separate subnations. Sectionalism refers to a strong sentiment of distinctiveness in a segment of the country where adherence to the ideology of the whole is restrained by tensions arising from divergent social and political norms. Sectional self-assertion may grow into the demand for autonomy or, if this is denied, the section may wish to secede to form its own national state. The American South has been at various points of this regionalism-sectionalism continuum.

In a *plural society* groups differing in culture and economic status live intermingled rather than in distinct territories. Such societal fragmentation occurs frequently in countries that were until recently under colonial rule, especially in eastern Africa and Southeast Asia.

Different forms of heterogeneity do not necessarily form clear-cut and separate categories. For instance, the concepts of tribe and subnation merge into one another; or, in a multinational state one group may assert its identity so vigorously that it acts like a foreign minority.

Nationalities and Nations in the European World

For such a small landmass, Europe has an astounding number of sovereign states. The diversity is even greater than the political map indicates, because within the borders of each country there are the old provinces, regions, *pays*, each with its memories of the past, its claims on the present, and its hopes for the fu-

7. Ideologies and the Political Order

155

ture. To grasp the broad pattern in this areal mosaic, one must see it in the historical perspective.

The Alpine ranges divide Europe into a Mediterranean part, which gave rise to the Greco-Roman civilization, and a northern part, which later received that culture. Even more important is the contrast between West and East, although no obvious barrier marks the divide. The West is maritime, the East continental. The former has its roots in the Latin culture of the West Roman Empire, the latter in the Hellenistic culture of Byzantium. From the east came the Asian invasions, sometimes penetrating deep into Europe, and always setting in motion the folk who were in the path of conquest. These migrations lost momentum as they moved westward or were successfully repulsed by the peoples on the Atlantic Seaboard. The result is that the eastern part of Europe has a far greater variety of peoples than its western counterpart.

The western people developed a lively maritime traffic, which eventually led to overseas colonies, world commerce, and a relatively prosperous economy. The East did not take part in this expansion and remained much longer a feudal agrarian, backward realm.

These differences also affected the degree of national unity attained in the parts of Europe. It is no accident that there are few national minorities in western Europe. First of all, there were not so many residues of foreign invasions. More important, the growth of the middle class fostered national unity and, in alliance with the kings, restricted the power of the local lords. There was mobility of people, exchange of ideas between city and country, and integration of the parts under strong central governments. Education spread among the middle class and eventually to the entire population, strengthening the national iconography.

Far different was the situation in the East. The feudal agrarian way of life favored self-sufficient regions and discouraged the free movement of persons. It kept the manifold peoples in the Russian and Turkish empires segregated from the ruling groups. The Habsburgs created a frontier empire—the later

Figure 7–1. EAST CENTRAL EUROPE (THE SHATTER BELT): BOUNDARIES AND STATES IN THE TWENTIETH CENTURY

Map A shows boundaries and states before and after World War I, Map B those before and after World War II.

Map A   1914-1920

————————	1914 Boundaries in existence in 1920
————————	1914 Boundaries not in existence in 1920
————————	New Boundaries 1920
POLAND	States formed after 1914-18 war

Map B   1920-1965

————————	1920 Boundaries in existence in 1965
————————	1920 Boundaries not in existence in 1965
————————	New Boundaries 1965
MOLDAVIAN S.S.R.	States formed after 1939-45

Austro-Hungarian Empire—in which Germans ruled a multitude of national groups. Oppression, discrimination, and denial of self-government hardened the personality of each individual community and locality. What little there was of a middle class consisted of foreign elements such as Germans, Jews, or Greeks. In such a plural society the middle class was a divisive rather than a unifying force.

Up to 1918 one could define fairly accurately the boundary between West and East. It would have run through the Gulf of Bothnia to Danzig (now Gdansk) on the Vistula and then overland to Trieste, and from there south through the Adriatic. To the west lay the Europe of integrated nation-states; to the east were the empires of Russia, Austria-Hungary, and Turkey, as well as the eastern fringes of the German

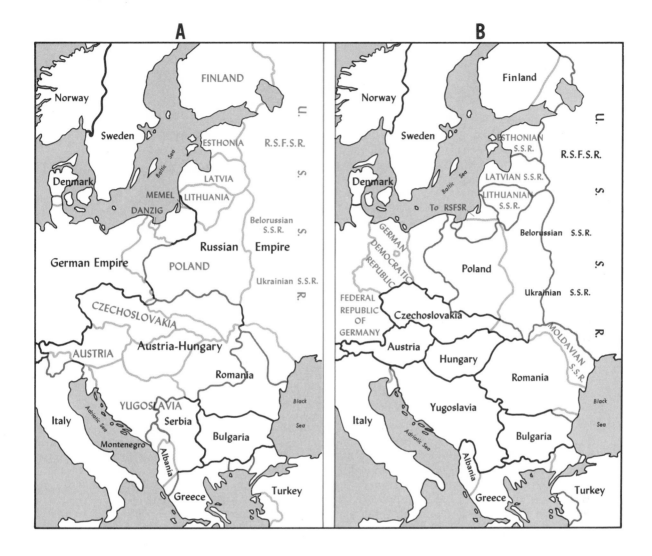

Empire, each composed of many nationalities (Figure 7–1). The war of 1914–1918 broke up the Austro-Hungarian monarchy, cut off parts of the German Empire, wiped out the remains of Turkish control over European peoples, and pushed back Russia's boundaries. As a result, a new zone appeared. The Danzig-Trieste line formed its western border, the Leningrad-Odessa line its eastern border. This in-between strip, often called the shatter belt, held a crazy quilt of national and social groups, a combination of multinational territories and plural societies.

It is true that Russia, now the Soviet Union, also contained many nationality groups within its boundaries—some 20 distinct territorial units within European Russia alone—but each of them was small when compared to the mass of the Russian nation. The main question was what policy the new state with its Communist ideology should pursue to integrate these minorities.

The problem in the shatter belt was much more complex. The new sovereign states were formed according to the principle of national self-determination. While in western Europe

7. Ideologies and the Political Order

157

the state and the nation had gradually evolved into the nation-state, in eastern Europe the new political units were superimposed on a jumble of jealously guarded sentiments which defied neat territorial demarcation. Thus, virtually every new state had to put up with some, if not many, national minorities. In several instances the new states had their eyes not only on including their own nationals but also on gaining valuable territory such as an outlet to the sea, a share in the river trade, or a mining district, regardless of the sentiments of the inhabitants. Such annexations compounded the national diversity. To protect the minorities in the new states, the various treaties contained clauses safeguarding their rights. Actually, though, few countries fully observed the rules once they had gained independence.

Besides suffering from internal friction, the countries of the shatter belt were poor; almost all of them lived by agriculture and were backward in organization, equipment, and marketing. The only exceptions were the industrial district of Upper Silesia, which Poland had won, and the Bohemian-Moravian section of Czechoslovakia. Independence had come to the shatter-belt states not through internal strength, but through the victory of western Europe and the United States over the central European empires, and through the collapse of Czarist Russia. Their survival depended on Germany and Russia remaining weak and on continued aid from Western countries. These conditions prevailed less and less during the interwar years. Germany struck first, but lost. The field lay open for the Soviet Union. It incorporated some borderlands into its domain, expanded its power over almost the entire shatter belt (and well into Germany), and imposed its ideology on the subjected peoples.

The hodgepodge of nationalities in eastern Europe has undergone significant changes as a result of World War II, leading to greater unity within each state. The Nazis virtually eliminated the Jews, and the liberated peoples expelled the Germans. In addition, there were mass transfers to "cleanse" the national territory of foreign minorities. Examples are the expulsion of Italians from the Adriatic coast of Yugoslavia; Slovaks from the Carpatho-

Figure 7–2. THE FEDERAL PEOPLE'S REPUBLIC OF YUGOSLAVIA

SLOVENIJA	**Republics**
VOJVODINA	**Autonomous Regions**
● Beograd ○ Pula	**Important Towns**
MAGYARS	**Linguistic Minorities**
▬▬▬▬	**Boundary between Roman Catholic and Eastern Orthodox Christians**
☽	**Adherents of Islam**
	Land over 5000 feet

Ukraine, which Russia had annexed; Finns from the Karelian Isthmus and some other areas lost to the Soviet Union; exchanges of national groups between Bulgaria and Romania and between Hungary and Czechoslovakia (Figure 19–3). At the cost of millions of personal tragedies there now exists in each state a far greater degree of national uniformity than before the war.

Yugoslavia, an Example of a Multinational State (Figure 7–2). Although the heterogeneity of Yugoslavia is now more the exception than the rule in eastern Europe, this country affords a good example of the problems facing a multinational state. The Dinaric Mountains form the core of the country. Only in the north, on the edge of the Pannonian (Hungarian) Basin, are there large arable plains along the Danube and its tributaries. The narrow Morava-Vardar route leads from the Danubian lands toward Greece and the Aegean Sea. The hilly west flank is Dalmatia, bordering the Adriatic. Although most people live in the plains, the mountains

have been the historical refuge areas in times of trouble. Montenegro never was effectively occupied by the Turks, and this region as well as the highlands further north were the center of resistance to the Germans in the last war.

Of Yugoslavia's 20 million population, almost nine-tenths speak a South (*yugo*) Slavic tongue. However, the location of the country led the western part in the Middle Ages to turn toward the Roman Catholic world, and the eastern part toward Eastern Christianity. Yugoslavia was formed after World War I by adding to Serbia (which had won independence from Turkey in the nineteenth century) the South Slavic territories of the Austro-Hungarian monarchy, the independent kingdom of Montenegro, and some border districts of Bulgaria. To weld together the variety of peoples, the Serbs insisted on a centralized state under their hegemony. The concept and its crude execution led to bitter conflicts with the other nationalities. After World War II the state was reconstituted as a federal republic on the Russian model. There are now six "People's Republics," an Autonomous Province (Vojvodina), and an Autonomous Region (Kosmet). The last two are within the Serbian Republic. Although Communist party control gives centralist direction, the cultural autonomy for the parts seems to work better than the enforced unity of prewar days.

In the Alpine foothills of the northwest live the Slovenes (10 percent of the population). They were for centuries linked to Austria and are economically the most advanced group in Yugoslavia. They are Roman Catholic and use the Latin script for their language, which in its standard form differs somewhat from the Serbo-Croatian that most Yugoslavs speak. Actually, the Slovene dialects merge eastward into the Croat dialects.

The Croats (25 percent of the population) share with the Slovenes the Roman Catholic religion and the Latin script, but have the same standard language as the Serbs. Proud of their central European heritage, the Croats refused to submit to the hegemony of the Serbs, in whom they saw rude mountaineers, tainted with "Eastern" ideas. The Croats live mainly in the plains of the Drava and Sava rivers and in the old province of Dalmatia along the Adriatic. They form at least one-fifth of the population of Bosnia-Hercegovina.

The Serbs (43 percent) are Orthodox in religion and use the Cyrillic script (identical to that of Russia, except for a few letters). In addition to Serbia itself, the Serbs form the majority of the population in the fertile Vojvodina north

of the Danube, and about two-fifths of the inhabitants of Bosnia-Hercegovina. The people of Montenegro (2.5 percent) are also Serbian, although their historical traditions make them into a somewhat separate group.

These three main Slavic groups account for 80 percent of the population. The fourth is the Macedonians (6 percent). Their homeland has been a cradle of conflict between Serbia, Bulgaria, and Greece, and now lies divided among all three. The Macedonian dialects are transitional between Serbian and Bulgarian. The predominant religion is Orthodox, although there are some Moslems. Traditions, more than any specific trait, keep alive a feeling of nationhood in spite of—or because of?—pressures from all sides. Macedonians fared badly under the old Serbian centralist government, when even the use of their speech in public was forbidden. Now they form one of the people's republics, and this has eased the tensions.

The remainder of the population consists of a number of minorities, each concentrated in some part of the country. Close to a million Albanians, mainly Moslems, live in the southwest, most of them in the autonomous Kosmet Region. Their language is not a Slavic one, but a vestige of the Illyrian languages spoken in the peninsula before the Slav invasions. To make things still more complicated, there are also Moslems of Serbo-Croat speech in Bosnia. In the Vojvodina are some 500,000 Magyars and some 50,000 German-speaking people, the remains of much larger colonies which existed here before the last war. To top it off, one must add Romanian settlements in the very northeast corner of Yugoslavia, Bulgarian ones along the east border, and a scattering of Jews throughout the country.

Here is indeed a mosaic of groups to which even the most conscientious territorial partitioner cannot do justice. There is little doubt that the present federal union is a more constructive solution than the former unitary state. Age-old rivalries and resentments do not disappear overnight, but there is now a basis for cooperation on the foot of equality, which may lead to a genuine unity-in-diversity.

II. Cultural Diversity

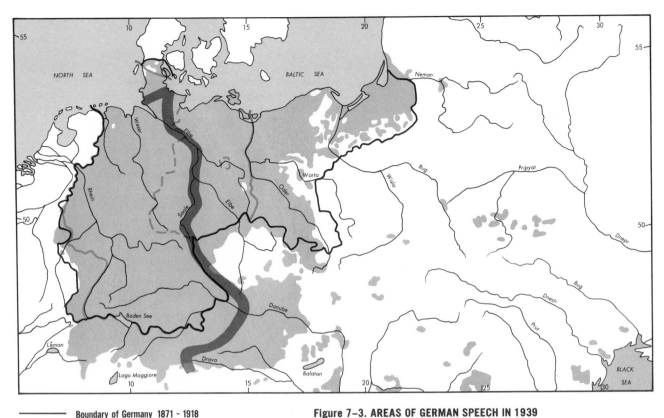

 Boundary of Germany 1871 - 1918

German Boundary after 1945

Boundary between East and West Germany after 1945

 Areas of German Speech, 1939

Eastern Boundary of German Speech ca. 800 A.D.

Figure 7–3. AREAS OF GERMAN SPEECH IN 1939 AND POLITICAL BOUNDARIES OF GERMANY FROM 1871 TO THE PRESENT

German Expansion and Contraction (Figure 7–3). Germany's location gave her inevitably a special role in the struggle between West and East. On the European plain beyond the Roman Empire lived Germanic tribes, and east of them were the Slavs. At the time of Charlemagne (A.D. 800) the boundary between the two ran from about where Lübeck is now, along the middle Elbe and its tributary the Saale to the Bohemian Forest. Shortly thereafter began the German push eastward (*Drang nach Osten*), a combination of crusade against the pagans, settlement by land-hungry peasants, and expansion of the German feudal system. The domain between the Elbe and the Oder became solidly German territory. Further advance straight eastward was hampered by marshes as well as increasing Polish resistance. Easier was the expansion northeast along the coast of Prussia, and southeast up the Oder into Silesia. In these two wings some Slavic groups remained, but the Germans soon outnumbered them. In addition,

7. Ideologies and the Political Order

161

the Germans had thrust eastward along the Danube, creating amidst the Slavs the frontier province of Austria (*Ostmark,* eastern march, *Oesterreich*). They also spilled across the mountain wall surrounding Bohemia-Moravia, gaining the majority in most of the mountain valleys, and establishing substantial communities in the cities of the basin itself.

Many Germans migrated beyond these territories, but they had to be content with more modest roles. German merchants and craftsmen formed an important urban element in many east European cities. German gentry owned large estates in the Baltic countries. German peasants were invited to set up agricultural colonies in Russian, Hungarian, and Romanian wastelands, or amidst the local peasantry to demonstrate better farming methods. Their different religion and socioeconomic status impeded assimilation. German expansionists of the nineteenth and twentieth centuries always considered these settlers in eastern Europe as planters of *Kultur* amidst the barbarians and as the advance guard of the future empire.

The defeat of Germany in World War II wiped out much of one thousand years of eastward expansion. The new Polish frontier was established along the lower Oder and its tributary the Neisse, although it has not yet been confirmed by treaty. Virtually all Germans had to leave the lands east of this line. The Czechoslovaks cleared the Germans out of their country. The remainder of Germany was divided into two republics, of which the Russians control the eastern one. Thus communism extends over Europe as far as the line Lübeck-Elbe-Saale–Bohemian Forest, roughly the same boundary as that in the ninth century between Germanic and Slavic tribes. Between 1944 and 1947 more than ten million ethnic Germans moved from eastern Europe to the remaining territories west of the Oder-Neisse boundary. There was a time when Germany was a buffer between east and west, the heart of a *Mitteleuropa* she hoped to rule someday. Now the buffer zone has shrunk to a line—the iron curtain.

Western Europe. Most sovereign states of

Figure 7–4. SWITZERLAND

The map shows the cantons which formed the original confederation of A.D. 1291 (Obwalden, Nidwalden, Schwyz, Uri). The map does not show the important linguistic and religious minorities present in the main towns.

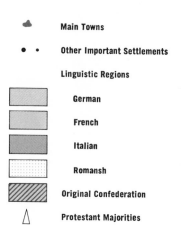

🔺	Main Towns
● ●	Other Important Settlements
	Linguistic Regions
	German
	French
	Italian
	Romansh
	Original Confederation
△	Protestant Majorities

western Europe long have had the advantage of substantial national uniformity and coherence. An important cultural division is that between the Romance and the Germanic parts. The two meet in a transition zone which merits closer inspection.

When Charlemagne's empire was partitioned between his three grandsons by the Treaty of Verdun (A.D. 843), one received what is now France without its eastern section, another what is now Germany east of the Rhine, and the third the lands between, stretching from the Low Countries to central Italy, including eastern France, Switzerland, and Germany west of the Rhine. This middle kingdom soon fell apart under pressures from both sides. But to this very day the belt shows up as a transitional zone, in Switzerland, through Alsace-Lorraine and Luxembourg to Belgium. Alsace, originally a German-speaking region, came more and more under French cultural influence. Yet the Alsatians in many ways are themselves, neither

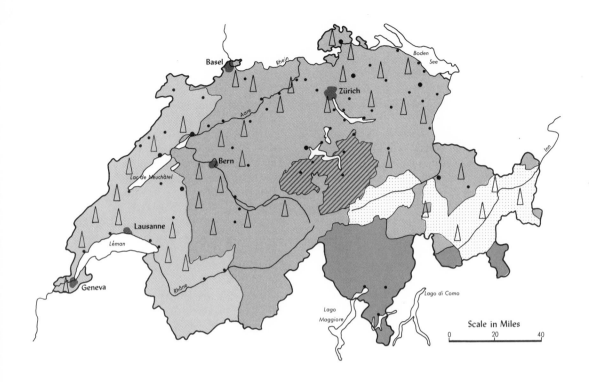

Basel
Rhein
Boden
See
Zürich
Aare
Bern
Lac de Neuchâtel
Lausanne
Léman
Inn
Geneva
Rhône
Lago di Como
Lago Maggiore

Scale in Miles
0   20   40

French nor German. The same can be said of Luxembourg, where both French and a German vernacular are spoken. Switzerland and Belgium deserve special attention because they show different aspects of the composite state.

Switzerland (Figure 7–4). The territory of this confederacy consists of three landform regions. On the border of France lie the parallel limestone ridges of the Jura. To the east extends the Swiss plateau, a fertile rolling land, which covers only one-third of the country, but contains 70 percent of the population. Over half of Switzerland is in the Alpine area, stretching from Lake Constance (Bodensee) in the northeast to Lake Geneva (Léman) in the southwest. Across this high watershed passed the medieval trade from north Europe to Italy. In the thirteenth century the main route shifted from the St. Bernard Pass to the St. Gotthard. The German emperors, eager to preserve this access route to Italy, freed the mountaineers on the northern approaches to the pass from feudal

control on condition that they would prevent neighboring lords from gaining possession of it. From this small nucleus of free peasants grew the present confederacy. All groups that entered the union—whatever their language—did so because they adhered to the democratic principles of the original cantons. They wanted no part in the dreams of empire their big neighbors cherished, nor did they wish to dominate their partners in the commonwealth.

Of Switzerland's six million population, 72 percent speak, as mother tongue, one of the several German dialects, but they share standard German as the literary language. French is the language of 21 percent, located along the western border. Another 6 percent, in the canton of Ticino, speak Italian, and 1 percent, in a part of the eastern canton of Graubünden (Grisons), speak Romansh, a relic of a Latin vernacular. All four languages have equality at the federal level. There is no uniformity in religion. About two-fifths of the population are

7. Ideologies and the Political Order

163

Catholics, and three-fifths are Protestants, mainly of the Reformed denomination. There is some concentration of each faith but also much interpenetration.

In spite of this diversity the Swiss have developed a strong national cohesion. Each cultural group, secure in its right to live according to its own traditions, shares with all others a common set of national values, evolved—not without trial and error—over six and a half centuries. The formula seems a good one for any composite state. It would be nice if countries were like human individuals. One could call in the doctor, who after making the right diagnosis would prescribe the Swiss cure, which the patient would faithfully follow until complete recovery. . . . Alas, allegory is not reality.

Belgium (Figure 7-5). The Kingdom of Belgium is an interesting case of changing relationships between two groups long united in one political entity. In the northern part the people speak Flemish. Its dialects merge with the Dutch across the border, and the standard language is identical with Dutch. In the south live the Walloons, French-speaking in dialect forms as well as in standard language. The line dividing the two language areas dates back to early medieval times. Originally, Flemish was spoken as far south as the Heights of Artois, near Calais in France, but here it has retreated under French pressure. Today the line starts on the French Channel coast at Dunkirk, curves south and east, and enters Belgium near Flemish Kortrijk (Courtrai). From this point it runs east through the rolling plain to the very south tip of the Netherlands near Maastricht. In Belgium this boundary has virtually not moved since early medieval times; only the capital city of Brussels (Brussel in Flemish, Bruxelles in French) has changed to an enclave of predominantly French speech.

It is far from clear why and how this boundary came to rest where it is. Apparently the invading Franks retained their Germanic speech in the north and gave it up in the south, where they intermingled with the Romanized Celts. The presence of sparsely settled, heavy forests at that time across the center of Belgium may have acted as a divider between the two groups.

Most of Belgium, together with the Netherlands, formed part of Lothair's middle kingdom (A.D. 843), later of the Burgundian domain, and then of the Habsburg Empire.

The wars of the Reformation split the Low Countries. Holland and associated provinces—now the Netherlands—gained their independence from Habsburg Spain as a Protestant nation. In the southern part—now Belgium—Spain with the help of the Jesuits firmly reestablished Catholicism. For more than three centuries Belgium was subject to foreign rule: Spanish, Austrian, and French. After the Napoleonic wars the Great Powers united Belgium with the Netherlands to form a barrier against France. However, the two peoples had grown too far apart, and the forced marriage ended in divorce in 1831.

Through the centuries, French cultural influence had gained ground, not only among the Walloons but also among the upper-class Flemings. Moreover, the Industrial Revolution mainly benefited the Walloons because the coal mines and associated industries were in the south. French was the language of the government, the army, the court, the universities. Not to speak French meant exclusion from all positions of leadership. The nationalistic spirit of the nineteenth century led the Flemings to insist on equality, which they finally and fully attained after World War I.

Since then, the Walloons have felt increasingly uncertain about their position in the kingdom. The rate of natural growth has been—and is—larger among the Flemings than the Walloons, so that now the former have the majority (55 percent). Other issues crystallize around the linguistic differences. In recent decades the Flemish north has developed economically faster than the south. The busy ports of Antwerp (Antwerpen) and Ghent (Gent) and the adjacent new coalfields in the Campine (Kempen) have stimulated industrial growth, while the south stagnates with exhausted mines and outmoded industrial plants. In addition there are sociopolitical conflicts. Although the entire population is nominally Catholic, the Flemings are, on the whole, militant members of the Church while the Walloons (like the

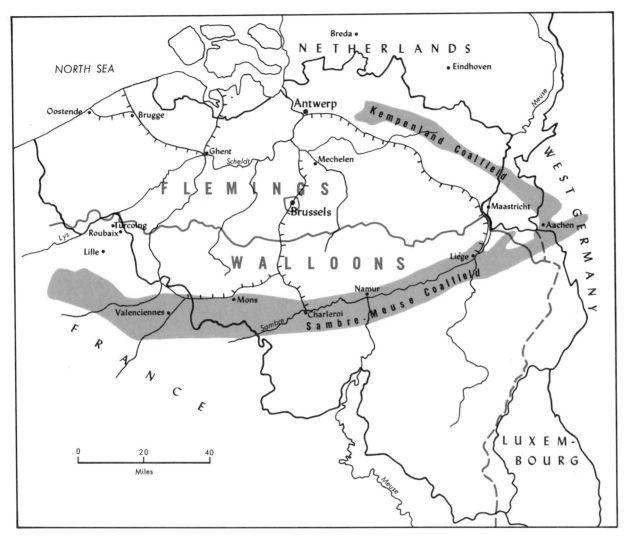

Figure 7–5. BELGIUM

Internal political problems derive mostly from the antagonisms between French-speaking Walloons and the Flemings.

National Boundaries
Principal Canals
French-Flemish Linguistic Boundary
French-German Linguistic Boundary
Coalfields

French) tend to be anticlerical. The Christian-Socialist party, the largest in the country, is essentially Flemish and strongly supported by the Catholic Church. The Socialist party, second in size, is mainly Walloon. The different political attitudes showed up sharply in the question whether Leopold III should come back as king after the recent war. The Flemings favored his return, the Walloons were against it. Although this problem was solved, other points of friction lead to ever sharper antagonisms.

7. Ideologies and the Political Order

165

We have here, then, the case of two groups who have lived together for many centuries without serious conflict, but who now face each other in a grave domestic crisis. The fact that both France and the Netherlands have scrupulously avoided involvement in the conflict has discouraged any serious thoughts of dissolving the state and joining the parts to neighboring countries. The past cannot be undone. Belgium is neither French nor Dutch. The solution must be found within the country itself, perhaps through a federation of the two parts with the boundary along the language line. What to do about preponderantly French-speaking Brussels is a delicate problem.

National Independence and Economic Interdependence. In the larger view, the trouble with modern Europe lies not in the internal minority problems, but in the fragmentation of space among the nation-states themselves. Broadly speaking, the nation-states represent areas of settlement of various tribes or nations, dating back to the Middle Ages; but the technology and economy are of the mid-twentieth century. Everywhere are disparities and tensions. The coking coal of the Ruhr is in Germany, the iron ore in France; the port of Trieste is Italian, but its hinterland is largely Yugoslav and Austrian; the Rhine and Scheldt rivers flow through several countries, but have their mouths in the Netherlands. Less obvious, but even more restricting, are the different social and economic systems that have grown up behind the national boundaries, each protecting in one way or another the nationals against competition from abroad.

Efforts to overcome the throttling effects of fragmentation have been made for over a century, for instance, by the internationalization of rivers. Action since World War II holds promise of far more significant advances in cooperation and integration. The war stimulated thought on how to create a better Europe, free from the old constraints and the fears of armed strife. Soon after the war these hopes combined with anxiety about a new tyranny which stood already on the Elbe and threatened to engulf western Europe. The United States, intent on creating a West European counterweight to Soviet pressures, gave a mighty impetus toward unification through the Marshall Plan (1947), which provided aid on condition that the European nations coordinate their reconstruction programs.

In the meantime Belgium, the Netherlands, and Luxembourg (Benelux) had been working toward economic union. A great step forward was the establishment of the European Coal and Steel Community, comprising France, Germany, Italy, and the three Benelux countries. The same six countries formed the Atomic Energy Community (Euratom) and then, most importantly, formed the European Economic Community (EEC) or Common Market (1957). The latter aimed at achieving a high degree of both economic and political unity. Great Britain, torn between its commitments to the Commonwealth and its connections with the Continent, passed up the initial chance to join in these endeavors, but later expressed definite interest. At the same time, it organized the European Free Trade Association (EFTA) with the Scandinavian countries, Austria, Switzerland, and Portugal—"The Outer Seven" as compared to the "Inner Six" of the EEC (Figure 7–6).

The Common Market countries form a powerful combination of human and material resources. They comprise 185 million people and are second only to the United States in industrial production. At its founding, the EEC member states had committed themselves to remove customs duties between each other, establish a common tariff for outsiders, and abolish obstacles to the free movement of persons, services, and capital. Various institutions and procedures were set up to carry out these aims.

While it is true that the Common Market countries have created several supranational bodies, it should be kept in mind that the structure is not a federation, or even a confederacy. It is a functional integration of independent sovereign states, endeavoring to combine their economic resources. Its long-range goal is a political union based on common values and aspirations. However, it is far from clear as yet how that goal will be reached, and the views

Figure 7–6. ECONOMIC COOPERATION IN EUROPE

This map shows the situation in 1967. All European countries (except Albania) belong either to the Organization for Economic Cooperation and Development (OECD) or to the Council for Mutual Economic Assistance (COMECON). Belgium, the Netherlands, and Luxembourg formed a customs union (Benelux) in 1944, but now, with France, the German Federal Republic, and Italy, are members of the European Economic Community (EEC), the European Coal and Steel Community (ECSC), and the European Atomic Energy Community (Euratom). Countries which belong neither to the EEC (Common Market) nor to the European Free Trade Association (EFTA) have developed special arrangements to maintain their trading links.

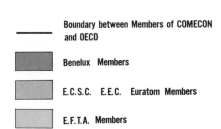

— Boundary between Members of COMECON and OECD

▨ Benelux Members

▨ E.C.S.C. E.E.C. Euratom Members

▨ E.F.T.A. Members

of the national leaders—even within one country—differ sharply on this point.

Some insist that the constituent national states must continue to provide the mainsprings of decision and action. Others press for the day when a common parliament will make the laws for all citizens of a United States of (West) Europe. Americans, used to their vast federation comprising persons from all corners of the globe, are apt to be puzzled by the doubts, delays, and crosscurrents present in western Europe. West Europeans want to ban the evils of narrow nationalism while keeping the treasures of their national heritage. It requires time to

solve this dilemma. In the meantime one must respect the accomplishments so far, an achievement which hardly would have seemed possible thirty years ago.

In eastern Europe the need for integration has led to the formation of the COMECON (Council for Mutual Economic Assistance), consisting of the Soviet Union, Poland, East Germany, Czechoslovakia, Hungary, Romania, and Bulgaria. Initially the Soviet Union tried to force the others into accepting a division of tasks in which each satellite country would continue to develop the specialty to which its economy had been geared theretofore. Such a

7. Ideologies and the Political Order

167

scheme would have been especially detrimental to the agrarian countries—Hungary, Romania, Bulgaria—which aspired to a more diversified economy. The determined opposition has led to more flexible forms of cooperation, which take into account the varied needs of all countries concerned.

It is too early to ascertain the outcome of the European drives toward integration, but one observation must be made. A political boundary is like a bundle of limits of legal, social, and economic systems. Now, within a bloc such as the Common Market, boundaries have lost, or are losing, several of these functions. On the other hand, where boundaries coincide with the line between opposing ideologies, they form greater barriers than ever. There is no better illustration of this than the ease with which the traveler moves from one EEC country to the next, in contrast to the wall and no-man's-land dividing East and West Germany.

"Les Canadiens." European settlement overseas has led generally to much larger territorial units than the cramped national compartments of the homeland, and to a blending of the various immigrant groups. All the more interesting is, therefore, the case of the French-speaking population of Canada, who call themselves *les Canadiens,* in contrast to the others, *les Anglais.*

When England acquired Canada from France in 1763, it brought under its rule some 65,000 French, who then formed the chief body of white settlers in that colony. About 1830, their number had grown to about 250,000, but de Tocqueville believed them to be "the wreck of an old people lost in the flood of a new nation." Many people, at least *les Anglais* in Canada as well as in the United States, must have agreed with him. Now the French Canadians number 5.6 million, close to one-third of the population of Canada, and they are as conscious as ever of their collective personality.

That they survive as a separate group is all the more remarkable because no mother country keeps alive the national ties, and no oppressive foreign rule welds the bonds of common suffering. The French Canadians share in language, religion, and tradition, but these traits might not have prevented their absorption into the English-speaking Canadian majority if they had not solidly occupied a territory which is their genuine homeland, the southern part of Quebec Province. Here they form four-fifths of the population. In addition, substantial numbers live in the adjacent parts of the Maritime Provinces (forming almost half of the population of New Brunswick), and in Ontario (where they make up one-tenth of the population).

Their core land lies along the St. Lawrence. As their numbers grew they spread up the Saguenay River to Lake St. John, and along the Ottawa River. South and east of the St. Lawrence they moved into the Eastern Townships, where they are now the dominant element. In the eighteenth century the English deported and dispersed a large part of the French settlers from New Brunswick and Nova Scotia ("Acadia"), but later *les Canadiens* moved in again. Scattered colonies were also established on the prairies. Many migrated to the United States, which has now close to two million people of French-Canadian stock.

In the seventeenth and first half of the eighteenth centuries the French government had encouraged farm settlement in the St. Lawrence Valley, chiefly through a quasi-manorial system whereby peasants (*habitants*) farmed the lands granted to noblemen. Most of the peasants as well as coastal fishermen had come from Normandy, Brittany, and other parts of northern France. Only Catholic French had been admitted. However, since France showed little interest in Quebec the provincial governor and the Church shared the responsibility for the welfare of the population.

When England took over Canada, many French aristocrats left the country, and the Church remained as the only source of leadership. The Quebec Act of 1774 guaranteed freedom of worship, language, and customs, the latter as embodied in the local civil law. Whatever feelings of loyalty toward France might have remained disappeared during the French Revolution, when the motherland turned against the Catholic Church. Quebec's freedom of religion attracted a number of Catholic refugee priests from France. The Church has maintained its strong position, not least through the educational system, which is managed by mixed committees of clergy and laity. The prominent and well-frequented churches, the processions and other religious festivals show the strong bond between *les Canadiens* and their faith.

The people have clung to the virtues of their peasant tradition. They are hardworking, sober-living, conservative folk. Until recently these French Canadians had a much higher reproduction rate than their English-speaking neighbors. They doubled their numbers every generation, which enabled them to keep pace with the natural growth-plus-immigration in the remainder of Canada. But the size of their families has been shrinking until now the birth rate equals that of Ontario.

Although in former times many sons sought new farmland (others became priests or teachers), most of them now find work in factories. In the past large numbers moved to the textile towns of New England, but in recent decades branch factories of various kinds have been established in Quebec, using the plentiful and disciplined local labor supply. The French Canadians have shown little interest in entrepreneur functions. Montreal's big business is mainly in the hands of English Canadians or Americans, who also own and manage many industries elsewhere in Quebec. Of the positions in the federal service, only 15 percent are filled by French Canadians, and that usually at the lower levels. Quite understandably, the French Canadians are unhappy at this state of affairs. Yet, their own culture is at least partly to blame for this. "To preserve language and faith, the French Canadian continues to receive an education that has been described as much better designed for life in the Kingdom of Heaven than in *La Province de Québec*. But if many of its leaders live in a world of backward-looking introspection, its young folk face a scientifically-oriented, technologically complex present. . . . And they are disturbed and confused, in that they have been taught to be suspicious of the very basis of the society and economy into which they must integrate themselves" (Clark, 1962, 34–35).

The devotion to their own *genre de vie* joins with dissatisfaction with their role in Canadian life. There is a strong sense of "perpetual injury and frustration," from the memories of English misdeeds in Acadia to the feeling that *les Anglais* set the national goals without regard for French-Canadian aspirations. Over and over the divergent outlooks have led to crisis. For example, in two world wars *les Canadiens* opposed conscription, because they were against involvement in "those English wars." At other times there has been friction because the French Canadians desired constitutional changes which would assure them a stronger position in the federation as a whole while safeguarding their own way of life. In recent years the federal government has taken positive steps to ease tensions. Also, the younger generation of French Canadians inclines toward a more progressive attitude than their elders.

Diversity in Postcolonial Asian and African States

The various European colonial territories in Asia, Africa, and tropical America often consisted of diverse principalities or tribal groups, each amalgam held together by the ruling power. Or, the colonial powers carved up a territory with a homogeneous culture, with slices going to each of them. Within a colony, economic development, administrative organization, and education brought about greater coherence of the composite parts. But these unifying efforts rarely added up to the creation of a nation, even though the educated elite, exposed to Western ideas, aspired to an independent nation-state. It is, therefore, not surprising that a large number of newly independent states show great regional diversity, face sectionalism, struggle with minorities, claim *irredente,* worry about their plural society, or have a combination of these problems.

For many of these heterogeneous countries a confederacy might be a better structure than a unitary state. However, the ruling group often fears that in a loose federation the centrifugal forces of subnationalism—or tribalism—would tear the state apart, and thus it prefers centralized control (for example, Indonesia). In other cases the diversity is so obvious that a federation or a confederacy is the only way to launch the new ship of state (as in Nigeria, Malaysia). Many of these new states are still in an experimental phase. Must these countries go through the painful stages like Europe, of tribalism, nationalism, and "Balkanization"? Or will they find a shortcut to supranational cooperation and political integration? From the many problem areas in the Caribbean, Africa, and Asia, we select two samples: the Indian subcontinent and Nigeria. Finally we discuss the special problems of plural societies, using the example of Malaysia.

The Indian Subcontinent (Figures 5–7 and 7–7). In an area as large as the Indian subcontinent and with such a long, tempestuous history one must expect a great variety of races, religions, languages, and social organizations. British rule tolerated particularism and even found it useful for maintaining its hold according to the old Roman maxim of "divide and conquer." On the other hand, it imposed on this land many institutions and a network of transportation which have greatly aided in forming the present large states.

The chief cause of internal conflict in recent times has been religion, but religion must be understood as involving here a far wider sphere than in Western nations. Being a Hindu (further subdivided by castes), Moslem, Sikh, Jain, Parsee, or Christian determines one's diet, dress, calendar, holidays, and, more important, education, social status, and economic activities; in short, religion dictates one's code and mode of life. In Indian politics, as well as in the census, the term "community" is often used to express the notion that more than creed distinguishes the various religious groupings.

The Partition of 1947. When independence loomed ahead, the leaders of the Moslem minority insisted on a territorial partition along communal lines. According to the census of 1941, the population of the entire British Indian Empire was 387 million, of whom 92 million (24 percent) were Moslems. However, only the western borderlands solidly adhered to Islam. In the Punjab there was a gradation from over 90 percent in the west to 30 percent in the east. Moslems also were concentrated in eastern Bengal, comprising about three-fourths of the local population. Throughout the remainder of India there were scattered groups of Moslems.

After long and bitter negotiations, a partition plan was finally agreed upon in 1947. It created a West Pakistan with 23 million Moslems (according to the 1941 census) and an East Pakistan with 30 million Moslems, leaving in India some 39 million brothers in the faith, and in Pakistan some 20 million Hindus. Large transfers took place, partly in panicky flight from bloody riots immediately following the partition, partly in more orderly fashion during subsequent years. As a result, West Pakistan is now 97 percent Moslem. In 1961 Hindus formed 18 percent of East Pakistan's population; a renewed exodus in the middle sixties must have reduced this proportion.

India's Linguistic Diversity. The sovereign Republic of India is about one-third the size of the United States and has a population of 495 million. Under British rule there were directly governed territories, the so-called provinces, and hundreds of princely states ranging in size from mere estates to big countries, all gathered under British suzerainty by treaties, but almost fully autonomous in domestic affairs. Following independence, this archaic structure was streamlined by mergers, a real step forward toward national unity and more efficient administration.

But nationalism can also be a divisive force if it imbues local peoples with a consciousness of their own distinct character. While the territorial reorganization was in progress, voices were raised in favor of a division according to linguistic units. There are over 150 languages in India—ignoring hundreds of dialects—but only a dozen are spoken by sufficiently large numbers (say, over five million) to be politically significant. A redivision along linguistic lines would disrupt many existing economic relationships, and worse, might seriously undermine the incipient Indian national unity. Neverthe-

Figure 7-7. SOUTH ASIA: POLITICAL DIVISIONS

Compare with Figure 5–7 and note the correspondence of languages and states within India and the lack of correspondence between linguistic and international boundaries. The letters refer to small administrative areas: N—Nagaland, M—Manipur, G—Goa, T—Tripura, HP—Himachal Pradesh. The status of Jammu and Kashmir and of the India-China boundary is in dispute. In 1966 the state of Punjab was split into two new states: Hariana, a Hindi-speaking part, and Punjabi Suba, a Punjabi-speaking part. The latter state now accommodates the Sikhs, who had long advocated their right to a separate state.

less, the persistent demands have compelled the government to accept the linguistic principle as the major criterion in the establishment of new states.

The state of Andhra has been cut out of the old province of Madras to give the Telugu-speaking people a unit separate from their Tamil neighbors. More recently the large Deccan state of Hyderabad was carved up and the Telegu-speaking section added to Andhra. The section of Hyderabad speaking Canarese was joined with areas of the same predominant language in the southern part of Bombay province, Mysore and Coorg, and is now the new state of Mysore. The proud Marathi of the northwestern Deccan now also have their own state, including the remainder of Hyderabad and a section of Bombay province. This has caused serious conflicts with the Gujarati-speaking group in Bombay city, who control the trade and dislike being dominated by the Marathi. The northern part of the former Bombay province has been incorporated into Gujarat state.

Although the Sikhs joined India at the time of the partition, they insist on their national individuality. In 1961 there were 7.8 million Sikhs in India, with 6.8 million concentrated in Punjab, where they constituted one-third of the state's population. In order to gain a more favorable position they agitated for a territorial revision, ostensibly to create a Punjabi-speaking state, but actually to make a unit in which Sikhs would have the majority. In 1966 the government of India gave in. The reduced new

7. Ideologies and the Political Order

171

Punjab state has 11.5 million inhabitants, of whom 6.1 million (53 percent) are Sikhs.

In view of this linguistic subnationalism, there is more need than ever for one language to serve as a means of nationwide communication. For this purpose Hindi, the main language of the north, spoken in various dialects by 135 million, has been chosen.* Putting the decision into effect requires a tremendous educational effort, the more so because Hindi has its own script—Devanagari—which differs greatly from most other regional alphabets. The resistance is especially strong in the south—beyond the line running from Goa northeast and east to a point midway between the Mahanadi and Godavari river deltas—where the population speaks Dravidian languages of an entirely different character from the Indo-Aryan languages of the north. Until now, English has remained the lingua franca among educated people, and the chief vehicle for affairs of government and higher education.

Among the other minorities, less militant but often important in local political issues and economic affairs, are the ten million Christians, mainly in the southwestern state of Kerala, and the almost two million Jains, another distinct Hindu sect, concentrated in Gujarat and Rajasthan. The latter sect includes a large number of traders and bankers, with considerable influence all through northern India. The Parsees, followers of the ancient Persian religion of Zoroaster, are a mere hundred thousand, but they have an economic position out of all proportion to their number. Most of them live in the Bombay area, among them many powerful industrialists and financiers, such as the Tata family.

Pakistan. The partition and continuing hostility between India and Pakistan has severed many bonds of interdependence that had grown during the previous era. The tragedy is

compounded by the politically awkward structure of Pakistan, consisting of two sections a thousand miles apart, two blocs that are entirely different save for the fact that they are inhabited by people of the same creed.

West Pakistan reminds one of the arid Middle East, East Pakistan of the humid tropics. The western section is the largest, but the dry climate restricts its use. Its core is the densely populated and fairly prosperous western Punjab, where cotton and wheat are produced under canal irrigation. To the north lies Kashmir, from where come most of the streams providing the lifeblood of West Pakistan. The Northwest Frontier is inherited from the British, with all its problems of tribal warfare, raids, and doubtful loyalties. To the south lies the arid Sind, where large-scale irrigation works by the British have created a zone of cotton and rice farming.

In contrast, East Pakistan is a water-soaked delta country, intensively cultivated. The average population density is over one thousand per square mile. There is always a food deficit, which is made up by rice imports from Sind. Jute is the great cash crop. When Calcutta, the metropolis, port, and jute-processing center, was assigned to India, East Pakistan was virtually decapitated. It now has built some jute mills of its own and developed a seaport at Chittagong, unfortunately at an offside location.

Associated with the different ways of life in east and west are cultural differences. The west speaks Punjabi, Sindhi, and other languages, with Urdu as the lingua franca; the east speaks Bengali. The peoples of West Pakistan, with a long tradition of militant Islamism, feel close bonds to other Moslems in the Middle East and have proud memories of their conquest of India under the Moghuls and earlier dynasties. The eastern folk, descendants mainly from converted lower-caste Hindus, have no such tradition. In fact, they have remained "Indian" in many ways. It is no wonder that the idea of Pakistan was born in western India, and that West Pakistan now supplies the driving force of the new state. The divergent interests and rivalries, compounded by controversies between

---

* To the number of Hindi-speakers one may add those who use it in its Urdu version (23.5 million). Furthermore, Bihari (17 million), Rajasthani (20 million), and a few minor languages are closely related to Hindi. Altogether, the persons speaking tongues of the Hindi group number about 195 million.

orthodox and progressive Moslems, have led to a welter of constitutional proposals, territorial-administrative schemes, and political experiments. A few dominant facts are clear, at least for the moment: Pakistan is an Islamic Republic (in spite of opposition by modernists) and consists of a federation of two large autonomous provinces, West and East Pakistan, each with its own legislature. The western section is clearly the carrier of the state-idea, the east a reluctant follower. Some observers predict that eventually East Pakistan may be reabsorbed into India.

The Kashmir Conflict. In the western part of the high mountains, reaching from the Karakorum across the Himalayas to the edge of the Punjab, lies the state of Jammu and Kashmir, as it was officially called in prepartition days. It was then ruled by a Hindu prince, but three-fourths of his subjects were Moslems. Its core land is the fertile upper Jhelum Valley, the "Vale of Kashmir." In the mountains to the north and west live Moslem mountain folk. The east toward Tibet is lightly inhabited by Mongoloid tribes, Tibetan in language and Moslem or Buddhist in religion. China, now in control of Tibet, claimed part of this area and has recently occupied it. In the southern portion of Jammu, Moslems formed only a small majority (53 percent in 1947) over Hindus and other communities, and now are less than half of the population in that area.

At the time of partition, the Maharajah, faced by communal riots and invasions of Moslem tribesmen, used his princely prerogative to join India, and India's claim to this area rests on this legal fact of accession. India sent troops, Pakistan counterattacked; but when finally a cease-fire line was established in 1949 India held most of the country. On India's side are most of the five million inhabitants and virtually all the agricultural lands. The Pakistanis argue that this area should have been joined with their state because it has a Moslem majority and is contiguous to West Pakistan. The Indians maintain that a great part of the Moslems do not want association with Pakistan. Only a free plebiscite—to which India had formerly agreed in principle—could prove this

contention. Meanwhile, India has pushed social and economic reforms in an attempt to gain friends and influence. In late 1965 the tension over Kashmir led to a new armed conflict, which ended under severe diplomatic pressure from the Soviet Union and the United States. No resolution of the dispute is in sight. An independent Kashmir, supposing that both parties would agree to this, seems hardly viable. A condominium of Pakistan and India could only work if both countries were on good terms, a condition that obviously does not exist. The cease-fire line may well become the new boundary.

The loss of Kashmir is far more important to Pakistan than its gain is to India. Kashmir forms the watershed of the western Punjab and thus controls—at least theoretically—West Pakistan's supplies for irrigation and hydroelectric power. In the past, all economic relations of Kashmir with the outside world have been through what is now Pakistan. To offset the traditional trade routes, India has been building transportation facilities to join with Kashmir.

Nigeria (Figure 7-8). The Federation of Nigeria is one of the larger countries of Africa, as large as the combined states of Texas, Louisiana, and Arkansas, with a population of almost 60 million. It extends from the Sudan savanna country and Lake Chad to the tropical rain forest and mangrove swamps of the Guinea Coast. It derives its name from the great river that enters the country in the northwest and forms the large delta on the eastern coast. The semiarid north has long been in contact with Mediterranean Africa, as evidenced by the intermingling of Caucasoid and Negroid races, the presence of Hamitic languages, and the more advanced forms of state organization. Islam arrived here in the thirteenth century over the trans-Saharan trade routes, and Moslem emirs reside in the large trade centers, such as Sokoto and Kano.

The forest lands to the south were the source of Negro slaves for the Sudanese raiders and traders and, from the sixteenth century onward, also for the Europeans who visited the coastal regions. In the nineteenth century the English gradually penetrated into this vast realm and made an end to the slave trade, but it was not before the beginning of the present century that they combined north and south under effective colonial rule. Among the southern pagan tribes, Christian missionaries were quite active. The emirs of the north, who retained much power under the system of indirect rule, excluded the missions and their schools. As a result there are far fewer Western-educated leaders in the north than in the south.

Since in Nigeria permanent white settlement was prohibited by law, it escaped the friction between native and white farmer which occurs in the eastern highlands of Africa. But a host of other rivalries arise from the multitude of native peoples. When, after World War II, the question of independence was raised, it was quite clear that the only hope for maintaining Nigeria as one country lay in a federative system. The independent Federation, proclaimed in 1960, consisted originally of three Regions, each having its leading nation, but also including many other groups. A fourth Region was formed later. In view of the medley of tongues, English is the official language for federal affairs as well as the lingua franca of the educated elite. Some leaders are of the opinion that optimum self-rule would require many more regions instead of four, but even such schemes would leave scores of smaller tribes under the rule of others.

The Northern Region comprises no less than four-fifths of the Federation's territory, and has a population of some 32 million. The north central part has a fairly dense population of Hausa (12 million). They are farmers and traders, belong mostly to Islam, and are ruled by Fulani emirs. The Fulani (6 million) speak a Hamitic language; part of them are nomadic herders. To the south, but still in the Northern Region, lies the thinly populated "Middle Belt." Here sleeping sickness is widespread. Wars and slave raids of past centuries have desolated the country. The hill sections served as refuge areas for Negroes who escaped Islamic rule or slavery. Only one-tenth of the inhabitants of this shatter belt belong to Islam, but all are under Moslem control. Many would like a

Figure 7–8. NIGERIA

These maps are based in part on the work of D. Greenberg, K. M. Buchanan, and J. C. Pugh.

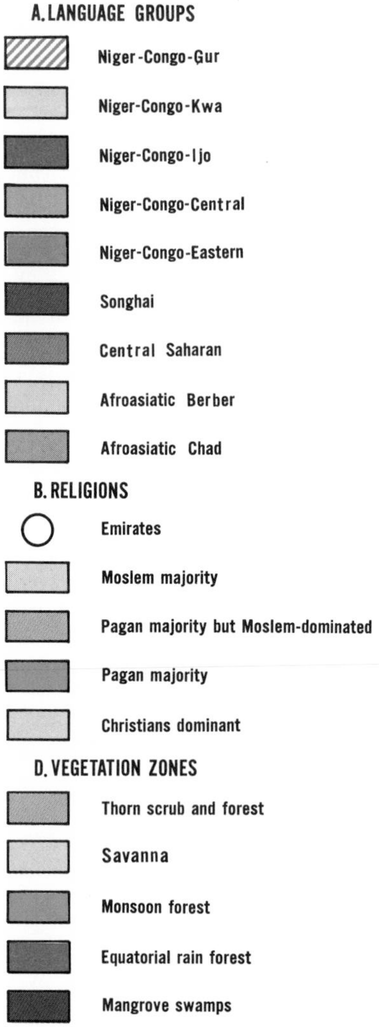

A. LANGUAGE GROUPS

Niger-Congo-Gur

Niger-Congo-Kwa

Niger-Congo-Ijo

Niger-Congo-Central

Niger-Congo-Eastern

Songhai

Central Saharan

Afroasiatic Berber

Afroasiatic Chad

B. RELIGIONS

Emirates

Moslem majority

Pagan majority but Moslem-dominated

Pagan majority

Christians dominant

D. VEGETATION ZONES

Thorn scrub and forest

Savanna

Monsoon forest

Equatorial rain forest

Mangrove swamps

separate, autonomous Region, but the ethnic fragmentation precludes such a structure.

The Western Region reaches inland from the coast and has 12 million inhabitants, almost all of whom belong to the mighty Yoruba nation. It is well-developed country with many cities,

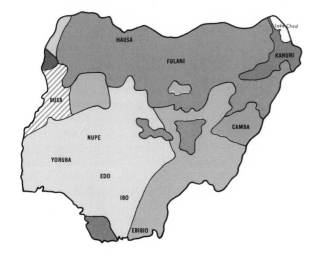

B. RELIGIONS

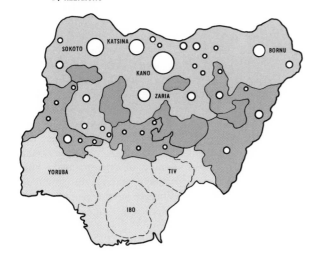

D. VEGETATION ZONES

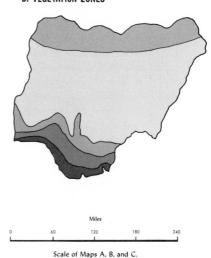

Miles

0   60   120   180   240

Scale of Maps A, B, and C.

among them Ibadan with over half a million inhabitants. Nearby is the old but modernized port city of Lagos, which has been set aside as the federal capital and as a sea link for the North, much to the dislike of the Yoruba, who form most of the city's population. Many of the Yoruba leaders, educated in Christian mission schools and in Europe, are quite progressive in outlook. They have an outlier in the Northern Region, where over half a million Yoruba, part of them Christian, live under Fulani rule.

The Eastern Region is quite small in size,

7. Ideologies and the Political Order

175

but has 13 million inhabitants. It is the land of the Ibo, who play a significant role in Nigerian politics through their Western-educated leaders. The Midwestern Region, with 3 million people, occupies part of the Niger Delta and an area to the west of it, centering on the old kingdom of Benin.

To this baffling ethnic variety one must add economic contrasts. The semiarid north is a land of grain, peanut, and cotton farming, and of nomadic herding. In east Nigeria the oil palm is still king, but the discovery of petroleum has opened up new vistas of industrialization. The Western Region is the richest part, with exports of cocoa, kola nuts, rubber, and timber. One must, of course, keep in mind that Nigeria's diversity reflects the large size of the country. If the Federation manages to survive the centrifugal forces, it may set an example for the integration of the dozen small-sized, independent states that now cover West Africa.

Problems of Plural Societies. When the Europeans landed on the coasts of East Africa and South Asia, they found there, besides the native peoples, a number of Arab, Indian, and Chinese traders. The initial phase of European dominion was chiefly the struggle to obtain a share in the commerce—if possible, the monopoly. In the nineteenth century, with the industrialization and urbanization of western Europe, came the mass demand for raw materials and foodstuffs, such as vegetable oils and fats, tin, and later rubber. In most colonies the native population, living in self-sufficient village communities, was unwilling or unable to furnish the wage-labor force for the plantations, mines, and port or railroad construction works. Moreover, there was no native middle class to perform the various services in the emerging urban centers, from shopkeeper to artisan and business clerk. Thus, laborers were imported from India or China. Many of them, after serving their contract term, started a petty business in town. Others came in the old tradition as traders and moneylenders, but now in larger numbers to profit from the expanding economy.

The new economic development thus re-flected itself fully in the occupations of the ethnic groups. The indigenous agrarian people formed the broad base of the social pyramid. The Europeans, who occupied the executive positions in government and private enterprise, were at the top. In the middle were the Chinese, Indians, and Arabs, partly as wage laborers, but increasingly as intermediaries between native mass and ruling group. In this way the normal economic competition between big and small business, capital and labor, agrarian producers and city folk combined here with the rivalry between ethnic, cultural, even racial groups. They all met in the marketplace, but culturally each group kept to itself, with its own values, its own standards of conduct. The hierarchy resembled a caste system, but without the metaphysical rationale and religious sanction of the Indian system.[*]

Inevitably there was friction, but as long as the colonial authority held the reins there could be no political struggle for power. All this changed when colonial rule withdrew. Now the plural society had to find a common set of values and a common purpose if the new state were to survive. The indigenous people felt that they were the masters of their land and that their culture patterns should prevail. However, a stiff-necked execution of this maxim would give the other groups the choice between assimilation to the native culture or exclusion, either through denial of citizenship or through expulsion. Removal of "foreign" groups would mean the loss of virtually all entrepreneurs, and that at a stage when economic development was crucial. Assimilation would be difficult if not impossible because the immigrants from China, India, and Arabia considered their own culture far superior to that of the native peoples.

The problem of the plural society in the

[*]The concept of the plural economy and society was developed by the Dutch economist J. H. Boeke. For a translation of one of his works, see Boeke, 1942. J. S. Furnivall, for years in the British civil service in Burma, adapted and spread the thesis of the plural society in wider circles through his publications (Furnivall, 1939 and 1941).

Sibu, Sarawak, exemplifies the plural economy of the country. The population of this commercial center on the Rejang River, some 80 miles from the sea, consists almost entirely of Chinese. The fronts of the "shop-houses" are closed at night with vertical boards. Note the sign for outboard motors, popular in this tropical-forest environment, where the canoe is the main means of transportation. [A Shell photograph]

modern state and the attempts to resolve it vary according to the local situation.* Indonesia has pursued a policy of rejecting foreign elements, without regard for the economic consequences. Its neighbor, the Federation of Malaya, which contains proportionally much larger minority groups, has faced the problem in a more constructive way. More recently it

*The racial segregation in the United States has produced some features similar to a plural society, but the status of the Negro does not result from the possession of a distinct ideology, which is the leading thought in this section. The case of the American Indian gives a closer parallel, but their number is too small to create a plural society.

has dared to expand and compound the challenge of a plural society by initiating the formation of the Federation of Malaysia. This instructive example is the subject of the following case study.

The Federation of Malaysia (Figure 7–9). After World War II, Britain resumed control over the Malay Peninsula and the offshore island and free port of Singapore, the two colonies of North Borneo and Sarawak (before the war under private British rule), and the protectorate over the Sultanate of Brunei. The Federation of Malaya became independent in 1957. Singapore was excluded from the Federation and became a "self-governing state,"

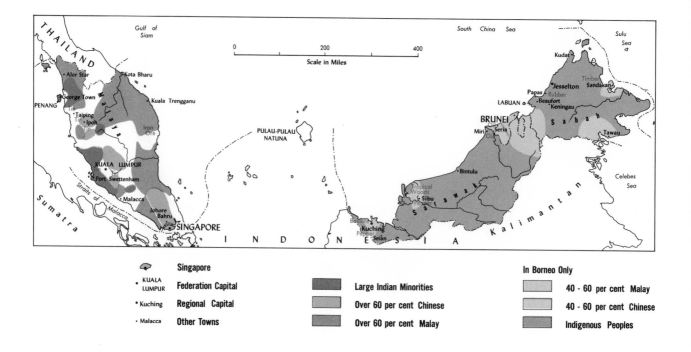

Figure 7–9. MALAYSIA

Singapore			
KUALA LUMPUR	Federation Capital		
Kuching	Regional Capital		
Malacca	Other Towns		

Large Indian Minorities
Over 60 per cent Chinese
Over 60 per cent Malay

In Borneo Only
40 - 60 per cent Malay
40 - 60 per cent Chinese
Indigenous Peoples

The proportions of ethnic groups are based on separate census data for
Malaya, Singapore, and the Borneo territories. The percentages employed to show
the various groups differ in Malaya and Borneo.

sharing the responsibility for its internal security with Britain and Malaya, and granting Britain the use of the naval base. In 1963 North Borneo (renamed Sabah) and Sarawak joined with Malaya and Singapore in the new Federation of Malaysia, but in 1965 Singapore was expelled.

It is only within the last sixty years that Malaya has been transformed from a collection of somnolent, backward sultanates, almost smothered in the tropical rain forest, to a well-organized and relatively advanced country, specializing in tin and rubber production. Singapore's fame is older. After Raffles established a free port here in 1819 it became the great entrepôt for the trade of Southeast Asia.

The plural society that resulted from the economic development is shown in Table 7–1. The Malays are Moslems. Most of them still live in agrarian villages, growing rice for food and rubber, on small plots, for cash. Their culture—like that of so many peoples of Southeast Asia—lacks the competitiveness which is so conspicuous in, for instance, Chinese culture. They show little interest in entrepreneurship. The well-educated prefer positions in government or in the professions, leaving business beyond the village sphere mainly to the immigrant groups.

In contrast to the easygoing Malays, the Chinese are industrious, persevering, and aggressive. Many have risen from coolie to big businessman, although, of course, the majority toil at menial tasks as tin miners, truck farmers, and factory hands. It is no exaggeration to say that the Chinese made possible the modern economic development of Malaya and Singapore. At the same time, their presence has largely created the problem of the plural society. The Chinese have remained Chinese, handing on their cultural heritage to the next generation through home training and school education.

The third main population element of Malaya comprises Tamils from southern India, who were recruited for labor on the large rubber plantations and on railroad and port-construction work, and smaller groups of Pakistanis, Sikhs, and Sinhalese. They, too, cling to their own cultures. The Tamils have developed a well-trained leadership group through their labor unions, which gives them greater weight in politics than their numbers might indicate.

With so many potential sources of friction, it is only through moderation and tolerance on the part of all communities that the Federation of Malaya has survived the first critical years. The Malays have the political power, even though they form only half of the population, because all adults may vote, while various tests for citizenship restrict the ballot of the Chinese.

Although the Chinese form 37 percent of the population, perhaps not more than one-fifth of them have the right to vote. Islam is the state religion, but other religions have freedom of worship. The language problem is a delicate one. The more extremist Malays have insisted that their language shall be the official one. The private Chinese schools have been brought under federal control—and receive federal subsidy—and now must teach Malay in addition to Chinese. But most Chinese consider Malay a peasant tongue unfit for a modern society, far less useful than English, which they would prefer as their second—and also as Malaya's official—language. Since the Malays have the political power, backed up if necessary by Malay army and police, they can force the issue, but so far their leaders have wisely abstained from such action. After all, the Chinese have virtual control over finance, commerce, and manufacturing and could wreck the economy if driven to despair.

Across the causeway from Malaya lies Singa-

		Percent of population*			
Political units	Population, thousands	Malays and other Moslems	Chinese	Indians	Indigenous peoples
Federation of Malaysia	8,210	46	36	10	7
Federation of Malaya	7,000	50	37	11	1
Sarawak	760	24	31	—	40
Sabah†	450	20	23	5	50
Brunei	80	50	23	—	26
Singapore	1,700	12	76	7	—

Table 7–1. Main Ethnic Groups in Federation of Malaysia, Brunei, and Singapore, 1962

* Other small groups, mainly Europeans, omitted.
† The census of Sabah reports by ethnic groups, regardless of religion; percentage of Moslems is, therefore, an estimate.

7. Ideologies and the Political Order

pore Island with its great port city, whose population is three-fourths Chinese. It needs Malaya's trade, and Malaya needs the port. But Singapore's Chinese added to those of Malaya would make them equal in number to the Malays and might further increase their economic hold on the country. That is why Singapore was initially excluded from the Federation of Malaya. However, there was the danger that Singapore, if left by itself, might fall under Communist control. From this dilemma came the plan to enlarge the Federation and draw in the Borneo territories as a counterweight to the inclusion of Singapore.

On Borneo the cultural pluralism has a somewhat different hue. As in Malaya and Singapore, the British held the top positions in administration and commerce. There were few plantations and thus no great influx of Indians. Instead of tin there is petroleum, by an irony of fate concentrated in the little sliver of territory that remains of the once mighty sultanate of Brunei. This tiny but rich state has been unwilling to join the Federation of Malaysia. Rubber, petroleum, pepper, coconuts, and timber are the chief exports of the Borneo territories. The three main ethnic groups are the indigenous pagan people (some converted to Christianity) of the interior, the coastal Malays and other Moslem peoples, and the Chinese, who are mainly town folk. Only a fraction of the Malays are actually descendants of settlers from the homeland in Sumatra; the majority stems from indigenous people who joined Islam and were assimilated into Malay culture.

The indigenous tribes are the Dayaks, Dusuns, and many others. Most of them live in longhouses and exist by primitive subsistence farming. Where given the opportunity, they show great ability for adjustment to modern life, perhaps more so than the "indolent" coastal Malays. Islam as well as Christianity continues to make converts and this, together with the penetration of new ideas from the secular world, erodes the traditional culture. In the three Borneo territories together the indigenous tribes constitute 46 percent of the total population, against 28 percent Malays and other Moslems and 26 percent Chinese. They need protection against economic exploitation by the Chinese and political oppression by the Malays. Although the Malays must have hoped they could line up the indigenous tribes in a common front against the Chinese, they have had little success so far because of their domineering posture. The competition for power between Malays and Chinese may strengthen the position of the indigenous groups, if their leaders know how to use it.

The Malaysian Federation—in spite of the term, actually a confederacy—is an experiment in political and economic integration, and as such deserves sympathetic consideration. At the same time, it has increased the heterogeneity of social groupings, cultural patterns, and historical traditions. Since it is an experiment, each group has insisted on safeguards for its own interests and institutions. For instance, Sarawak and Sabah have received assurances that their religious freedom (including Christian missionary activity) will be respected. Singapore kept a free hand in pursuing its socialist aims. Apparently its political stance exasperated the conservative government of Malaya, leading to the expulsion of Singapore from the Federation.

The Federation of Malaysia lies on the meeting ground of Chinese overseas expansion and Moslem Malay culture. In the larger view, the question is whether these two groups will subordinate their distinct ideologies to a common allegiance or will tear apart in a struggle for Chinese versus Malay supremacy.

Citations

Boeke, J. H. *The Structure of the Netherlands Indian Economy,* New York, 1942.

Clark, A. H. "Geographical Diversity and the Personality of Canada," in

McCaskill, M. (ed.) *Land and Livelihood, Geographical Essays in Honour of George Jobberns,* Christchurch, N.Z., 1962.

Furnivall, J. S. *Netherland India: A Study in Plural Economy,* London, 1939 and 1944.

———. *Progress and Welfare in Southeast Asia,* New York, 1941.

Gottmann, J. "Geography and International Relations," *World Politics,* 3 (1951): 153–173.

———. "The Political Partitioning of Our World: An Attempt at Analysis," *World Politics,* 4 (1952): 512–519.

Hartshorne, R. "Political Geography," in James, P. E., and Jones, C. F. (eds.) *American Geography: Inventory and Prospect,* Syracuse, N.Y., 1954.

Kohn, H. *The Idea of Nationalism,* New York, 1944.

Further Readings

Buchanan, K. "The Northern Region of Nigeria: The Geographical Background of Its Political Duality," *Geographical Review,* 43 (1953): 451–473.

Cahnman, W. J. "Frontiers between East and West Europe," *Geographical Review,* 39 (1949): 605–624.

Cohen, S. B. *Geography and Politics in a World Divided,* New York, 1963.

Dominian, L. *Frontiers of Language and Nationality in Europe,* New York, 1917.

East, W. G., and Moodie, A. E. (eds.) *The Changing World: Studies in Political Geography,* New York, 1956.

———, and Spate, O. H. K. (eds.) *The Changing Map of Asia,* New York, 1961.

Fisher, C. A. "The Malaysian Federation, Indonesia and the Philippines: A Study in Political Geography," *Geographical Journal,* 129 (1963): 311–328.

Gottmann, J. *La Politique des états el leur géographie,* Paris, 1952.

———. *A Geography of Europe,* New York, 1952, 3d ed. 1962.

Hamdan, G. "The Political Map of the New Africa," *Geographical Review,* 53 (1963): 418–439.

Harrison Church, R. J. *West Africa: A Study of the Environment and Man's Use of It,* New York, 1961.

———. *Environment and Policies in West Africa,* New York, 1963.

Johnson, J. H. "The Political Distinctiveness of Northern Ireland," *Geographical Review,* 52 (1962): 78–91.

Kimble, G. H. T. *Tropical Africa,* 2 vols., New York, 1960 (see especially vol. 2, "Society and Polity").

Kristof, L. K. D. "The Nature of Frontiers and Boundaries," *Annals of the Association of American Geographers,* 49 (1959): 269–282.

Mayfield, R. C. "A Geographic Study of the Kashmir Issue," *Geographical Review,* 45 (1955): 181–196.

Melamid, A. "The Geographical Distribution of Communities in Cyprus," *Geographical Review,* 46 (1956): 355–374.

Nystrom, J. W., and Maloff, P. *The Common Market: European Community in Action,* New York, 1962.

7. Ideologies and the Political Order

Pounds, N. J. G. *Divided Germany and Berlin,* Princeton, N.J., 1962.

——— . *Poland between East and West,* Princeton, N.J., 1964.

Prescott, J. R. V. "Nigeria's Regional Boundary Problems," *Geographical Review,* 49 (1959): 485–505.

Sabbagh, M. E. "Some Geographical Characteristics of a Plural Society: Apartheid in South Africa," *Geographical Review,* 58 (1968): 1–28.

Sauer, C. O. "The Personality of Mexico," *Geographical Review,* 31 (1941): 352–364.

Siegfried, A. *France: A Study in Nationality,* London, 1930.

Stanislawski, D. *The Individuality of Portugal: A Study in Historical-Political Geography,* Austin, Tex., 1959.

Stephenson, G. V. "Pakistan: Discontiguity and the Majority Problem," *Geographical Review,* 58 (1968): 195–213.

Wade, M. *The French Canadian Outlook,* New York, 1946.

Weigend, G. C. "Effects of Boundary Changes in the South Tyrol," *Geographical Review,* 40 (1950): 364–375.

Whittlesey, D. *The Earth and the State,* New York, 1939.

8. Culture Realms

Every individual is distinct and unique. But he is also willy-nilly a member of many groups, whether these actually exist as organizational units or are conceived by the social scientist as categories of generalization. In the previous chapters we have explored several of these generalizing rubrics—race, language, religion, and nationality—and have noted how each acts like a filter projecting a different mosaic on the map.

The question is now whether we can carry spatial generalization one step further by sorting the many diverse segments of the earth into a simple but meaningful framework of broad *culture realms*. The term culture realm signifies a large area that has fundamental unity in the composition, arrangement, and integration of significant traits, which distinguishes it from other culture realms. Since we have not yet discussed types of economy, forms of settlement, and patterns of population change—all parts of culture in a wider sense—we should perhaps use a more specific term, such as sociocultural realm, but the prefix would add cumber rather than clarity. This chapter is in the nature of a provisional synthesis. Subsequent parts of the book should demonstrate the merit of the tentative regional scheme.

Problems of Classification and Mapping

Any division of the earth into regions involves decisions regarding (1) criteria for defining the regions, (2) dateline of the presentation, (3) scale of the investigation, and (4) regional boundaries.

Criteria.   The geographer who wants to divide the earth into climatic regions selects what seem to him significant measures of universal occurrence (such as precipitation and temperature) and notes their spatial variation; he then makes a classification of climates, and maps their distribution. Can we use this method for dividing the world into culture realms? As we proceed it will become clear that the spatial configuration we are seeking cannot be exactly defined by selecting a few universal criteria. The traits or complexes that may be good indicators for one culture may be quite different from those characterizing another. The problem is analogous with that of defining nations: the essence of a nation cannot be found by combining a few cultural variables such as language and religion. A nation derives its distinct nature from a large number of features in their historically grown relationship. In the same way we must understand a culture realm in its totality—its *ensemble,* its *Gestalt*—as a historically evolved individual entity. While this comprehensive view would seem to leave the door wide open for an infinite number of personal judgments, in practice there is, as we shall see, considerable agreement on the main outlines of the various culture realms.

Dateline. Cultures are in constant change, and their realms expand and contract. Therefore, a map of culture realms is like a still from a movie, an image true only for a specific cross section through time. Although our primary concern is with the present, it would be a mistake to adopt a "current-affairs" attitude in delimiting the realms. For instance, the fact that the Soviet Union dominates the larger part of Central Europe does not make this area automatically a part of Russian culture. Political control and associated social and economic pressures are powerful levers toward cultural assimilation, but they require a long time span when applied against deep-rooted traditions. A good counterweight against arguments based on the current situation is the historical perspective gained from a knowledge of various culture realms some centuries ago.

Scale of Study. If one considers only a part of the earth, such as the Caribbean, West Europe, or the Middle East, one can make fine distinctions based on many culture traits and produce a map showing many culture areas. For instance, A. L. Kroeber in his study of native Indian cultures of North America distinguished 84 culture areas, grouped within ten broad categories (Kroeber, 1949). Such studies, then, are on a relatively large scale. However, since we aim at a generalized overview of the earth as a whole, our end product is necessarily on a small scale. Inevitably we must neglect details and ignore exceptions. Only the major lineaments will stand out for the very purpose of presenting a simplified, but all the more meaningful, image of the main culture realms.

Boundaries. Cultures grade one into another in a vast continuum. The Rio Grande is often quoted as a clear divide between Anglo-America and Latin America, but closer inspection shows even here a transition zone where elements from both realms mingle. Thus, the Rio Grande boundary is a political *line* drawn through a cultural frontier *zone*. Where different cultures have mixed over a long period, as for instance in the African Sudan, the intermediary belt may be quite wide. In such a case one can, of course, designate it as a separate unit, but this necessitates delineating two boundaries instead of one, and so compounds the problem. In some areas where a strong foreign influence is superimposed over the native culture pattern one can use the technique of presenting both cultures by their respective map symbols. Again, every meeting ground so marked increases the complexity of the map.

The problem is similar to that of the historian when he defines periods. In European history, where does he draw the line between "medieval" and "modern"? At the beginning of the Renaissance in Italy, at the time of the Great Discoveries, or at the Reformation? If the historian aims at a broad overview he may select an approximate date; if he wants a fuller understanding he may introduce transition periods ("Middle Ages gamma," "Modern Period alpha"), but then he faces the problem of what dates he shall now assign to the in-between eras. But the method of division is a minor matter compared to the agreement among historians that "medieval" and "modern" are significant historical concepts. In the same way for the geographer, the heart of the matter is the concept of different culture realms, not the exact location of their boundaries.

Various Proposals for Culture Realms

Several writers have proposed a division of the earth into culture realms. The concern of most anthropologists with preliterate peoples lessens the value of their classifications for our purpose. The interest of historians, if it includes culture realms, rarely reaches to the present. The work of sociologists is largely ethnocentric, that is, it deals mainly with social phenomena within

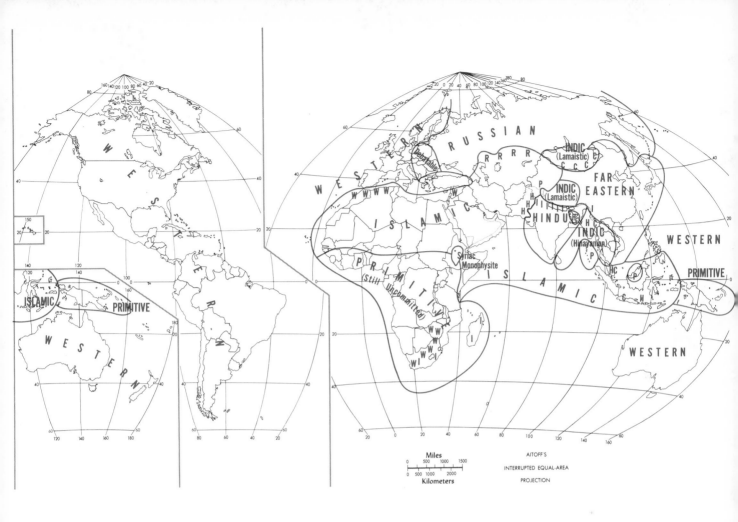

Figure 8–1. A. J. TOYNBEE: CIVILIZATIONS CURRENT IN A.D. 1952

Toynbee includes the whole Pacific Ocean, the Americas, and West Europe
in his "Western" civilization. Russian civilization is a distinct unit.
Intrusions from other civilizations are shown by initial letters (W—Western,
R—Russian, I—Islamic, H—Hindu, C—Chinese). P refers to "Primitive" remnants.
After Toynbee and Myers, 1959, vol. 12, 93.

their own culture sphere and is, therefore, centered on the Occidental culture. Several geographers have produced maps of culture realms. Before presenting our own design it will be useful to examine briefly some of the other proposals.

Toynbee's Civilizations. An important exception to the usual concern of historians is Arnold J. Toynbee's view of the current era. In his majestic *Study of History* he "presents a single continuous argument as to the nature and pattern of the historical experience of the human race since the first appearance of the species of societies called civilizations. . ." (Toynbee, 1947, ix). A small map in the atlas which accompanies the work depicts cartographically the extent of the present "civilizations" (Figure 8–1).

It should be noted that Toynbee does not examine all cultures, but only those on the higher level which show, or have shown, a high degree of creativity. He discusses each of these civilizations in its genesis, growth, and breakdown, as well as in its relation to other civilizations.

Toynbee distinguishes 26 civilizations, including five "arrested" and several "abortive" ones. Of this total, 16 are now dead, leaving 10 survivors. Among the latter he characterizes three as "arrested": Polynesian, Nomad, and Eskimo. According to him, each of the three poured its energy into a determined attempt to meet the "challenge" of a difficult physical environment and suffered the consequences of its overspecialized "response." There is no need to examine here the validity of the thesis. It suffices to note that he lists seven living civilizations: our own Western Society, or Western Christendom; Orthodox Christendom in southeastern Europe; its transformed offshoot in Russia; the Islamic Society; the Hindu Society; the main body of the Far Eastern Society in China; its offshoot in Japan.*

Culture Realms by Geographers. Geographers before and after Toynbee—and in the latter case not necessarily dependent on him—have devised systems of division, without much discussion of the rationale behind their scheme or reference to other authors. Sociocultural as well as economic features seem to be the criteria employed for most of their maps (Figure 8–2).

Virtually all distinguish, under whatever name: East Asia (or "Orient"); South Asia ("Hindu" or "Indic"); North Africa together with Southwest Asia ("Islamic," "Dry World," "Orient" in the German literature); and Europe-North Asia ("Western World," "Occident"), usually divided into a western and an eastern part. A few American publications combine the cultures of East and South Asia into one realm, and call this the Oriental world.

There is general agreement that the Americas belong to the Western world. Most authors make a distinction between Anglo (*Germanisch* in German) and Latin (Ibero) America. Australia and New Zealand are usually included in the Occidental realm, but in some cases are part of a "Pacific" culture area. Since none of the geographers limit their categories to "civilizations" in Toynbee's sense, they recognize a special culture realm in Central Africa—an area which Toynbee calls "primitive, still uncommitted"—and some also distinguish Arctic, Central Asian, and Melanesian cultures.

Map of Culture Realms. The consensus of various geographers on the major culture realms suggests the basic validity of their schemes. While agreeing with the broad alignments, the writers of this book have their preferences regarding details and propose, therefore, the following classification (Figure 8–3).

We distinguish two groups of culture realms. One consists of four major realms (comparable to Toynbee's civilizations), the other of two minor realms. This division ignores some waning cultures—American Indian, Melanesian, Polynesian, and Arctic—already so deeply affected by others that their inclusion as distinct realms seems not justified in a broad survey.* Here follows the list of the six culture realms, with alternate names in parentheses:

A. Major Realms (Civilizations)
   I. Occidental (Western; European)
   II. Main Islamic (North African–Southwest Asian; Arab-Persian)
   III. Indic (Indian; Hindu)
   IV. East Asian (Sinitic)

* At various points of the discourse and also on Map 4 in the atlas there are references to an Indic Hinayanian Buddhist civilization, or Southern Buddhism.

* On Figure 8–3 a "Southern Pacific" (Melanesian-Polynesian) culture realm is shown because it can be identified more clearly than survivals of Arctic and American Indian culture areas.

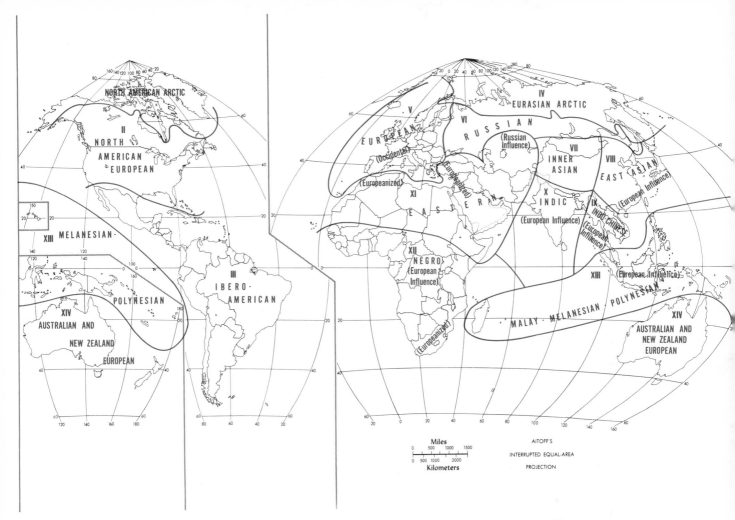

Figure 8–2. F. JAEGER: CULTURE REALMS

North American Arctic and Eurasian Arctic are called "natural regions";
Inner Asian, Eastern ("Orientalisch"), and Australian and New Zealand
European, "natural and cultural regions"; the rest "cultural regions."

From Jaeger, 1943, map 4.

B. Minor Realms
   V. Southeast Asian
   VI. Meso-African (Negro-African)

Each of these realms can be subdivided further. The widespread Occident may serve as an
example. Its European cradleland can be divided into (1) Maritime Europe and (2) Continental Europe. Maritime Europe can be split
into a Mediterranean Europe and b Northwestern Europe. Each of them has its overseas
expansion wing or wings: a^1 Latin America; b^1
Anglo-America; b^2 South Africa, and b^3 Australia and New Zealand. Continental Europe
comprises c Central Europe (the shatter belt),
and d Russia, with its continental expansion,
d^1 into Asia.

*8. Culture
Realms*

187

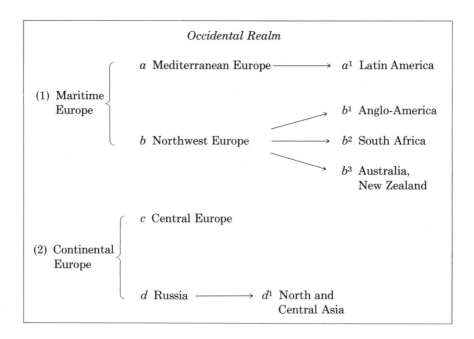

Occidental Realm

```
                              a  Mediterranean Europe ──────────→  a¹ Latin America
          (1) Maritime  {
              Europe                                            ──→  b¹ Anglo-America

                              b  Northwest Europe ──────────────→  b² South Africa

                                                              ──→  b³ Australia,
                                                                      New Zealand

                              c  Central Europe
          (2) Continental  {
              Europe

                              d  Russia ────────→  d¹ North and
                                                       Central Asia
```

Culture Realms in the Fifteenth Century

To provide historical perspective on the present scene it is useful to survey briefly the extent of the main cultures before the European eruptive expansion (Figure 8–4). Even before 1500 the areas of civilization formed a continuum, surrounded by a periphery of simpler, if not primitive, ways of life. In the Old World the belt of civilizations stretched through the middle latitudes from the Atlantic to the Pacific Ocean. Each civilization—Occidental, Islamic, Indic, and Chinese—had its nucleus which was spatially distinct or even far distant from the other centers, but their margins touched and often interpenetrated each other. This zone of civilizations formed the cultural ecumene—not all of the inhabited Old World, but its creative, dynamic core.

The native American civilizations were, of course, remote from those of Eurasia, but within the Americas they, too, were linked together by marginal zones. Deserts, mountains, and tropical rain forest separated the belt of culture hearths from other favorable but as yet only primitively used habitats. These barriers and the relative youth of Indian civilizations may explain why such vast areas in the Americas remained peripheral in culture until the Europeans arrived.

In the other continents the peripheral, low-level cultures characteristically occupied lands either far distant from the cultural ecumene, or those climatically handicapped. Thus, preliterate tribes lived in most of Africa, Eurasia's taiga and tundra, parts of Southeast Asia, all of Australia, New Zealand, and other islands in the Pacific. To be sure, most of them had received in the course of time a number of culture traits from more advanced peoples, but these were mainly in the material sphere, such as domesticated plants and animals, iron tools, or the wheel: and some areas (south tip of Africa, Australia, and Tasmania) had received very little.

The civilizations of the cultural ecumene all had their elaborate ethical or religious ideologies; calendars and written languages, and thus historical records; territorial organization in states; a well-developed agriculture and high level of craftsmanship; division of labor, long-

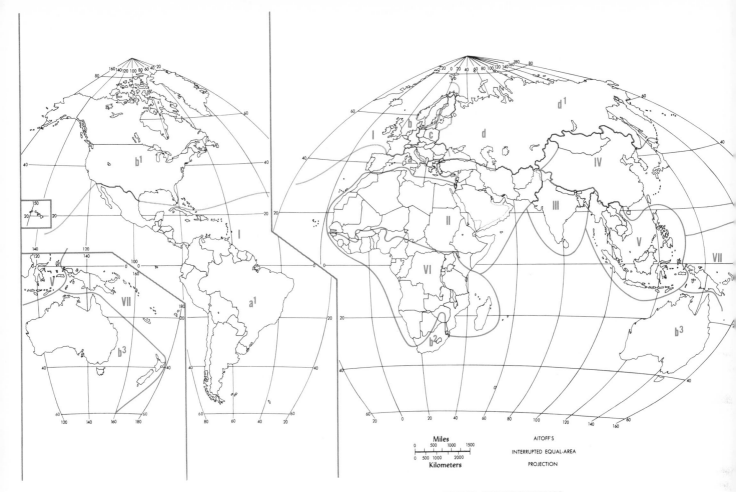

Figure 8-3. J. O. M. BROEK: CULTURE REALMS

This map was originally designed in 1950. Only the Occidental culture realm has been divided into subregions. A similar procedure could also be applied to the other realms.

A. **Major Realms**
  I. **Occidental**
    1. **Maritime European**
      a. **Mediterranean European**
        a^1 **Latin American**
      b. **Northwestern European**
        b^1 **Anglo-American**
        b^2 **South African**
        b^3 **Australia - New Zealand**
    2. **Continental European**
      c. **Central European**
      d. **Russian**
  II. **Main Islamic**
  III. **Indic**
  IV. **East Asian**
B. **Minor Realms**
  V. **Southeast Asian**
  VI. **Meso-African**
  VII. **Southern Pacific**

8. Culture Realms

189

distance trade, and cities; and relatively advanced means for controlling the physical environment, such as the use of water and wind for energy production.

In the late fifteenth century the Occidental realm occupied a modest area in the western peninsula of Eurasia. There was a lively trade among the countries on the seaboards of Mediterranean, North, and Baltic seas, and the Portuguese were groping their way down the west African coast. Five hundred years earlier Norsemen had already crossed the Atlantic by way of Iceland and Greenland, and had reached Newfoundland, but their accounts had not become part of general European knowledge. Central Europe was—and remained for centuries—the arena of struggles between continental empires. On its eastern margin the grand duchy of Muscovy was emerging as an offshoot of Byzantine culture, but not as yet assimilated to Europe.

The core lands of the Islamic, Indic, and Chinese realms were in 1500 much the same as now. The Moslem Turks controlled most of the Balkan Peninsula and would continue to threaten Christendom until the end of the seventeenth century, but their conquests in Europe always remained marginal to the central zone of Islam. In most of Southeast Asia, Indic cultural influence prevailed, at least until about 1300. By 1500, though, Islam had superimposed itself upon Hinduism and Buddhism in the island world. Meso-Africa, while in contact with the Arab world in the Sudan and on the east coast, had remained for the greater part beyond the purview of the civilized world.

In the fifteenth century the various Eurasian civilizations appeared as distinct, self-sufficient units, although they were aware of each other's existence through the accounts of sailors, missionaries, ambassadors, and other travelers by land and sea. The Iberian sea voyages and the rediscovery of America marked the beginning of a new era, in which the whole earth was to become an interlocked unit. Whatever the future judgment on European civilization may be, its linking together all parts of the earth will be acknowledged as one of the great achievements in the history of mankind.

Figure 8–4. CULTURE REALMS ABOUT A.D. 1450

Based in part on the work of Hettner, 1929, and Bobek, 1959.

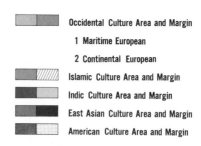

Occidental Culture Area and Margin
1 Maritime European
2 Continental European
Islamic Culture Area and Margin
Indic Culture Area and Margin
East Asian Culture Area and Margin
American Culture Area and Margin

The Occidental Culture Realm

Spread of Occidental Culture. The expansion of European civilization during the last four centuries took three forms: settlement, colonial rule, and cultural diffusion.

Europeans spread overland and overseas into northern Asia, the Americas, South Africa, Australia, and New Zealand. These settlements were in the mid-latitude climates and to some extent in the tropical highland zones. Equally important, they were in areas of weak, peripheral cultures. Nowhere did European settlement displace native peoples in the core areas of other civilizations.

Europeans controlled trade, investment, and strategic colonies by superimposing their administration and business management on peripheral cultures (tropical Africa, Southeast Asia, and America) and on large parts of non-Occidental civilizations (Peru, Mexico, India, Middle East, and to some extent China).

In addition, the Occident even without settlement or political control has affected the entire earth through cultural diffusion. The products of Western technology have dispersed much faster and farther than Western value

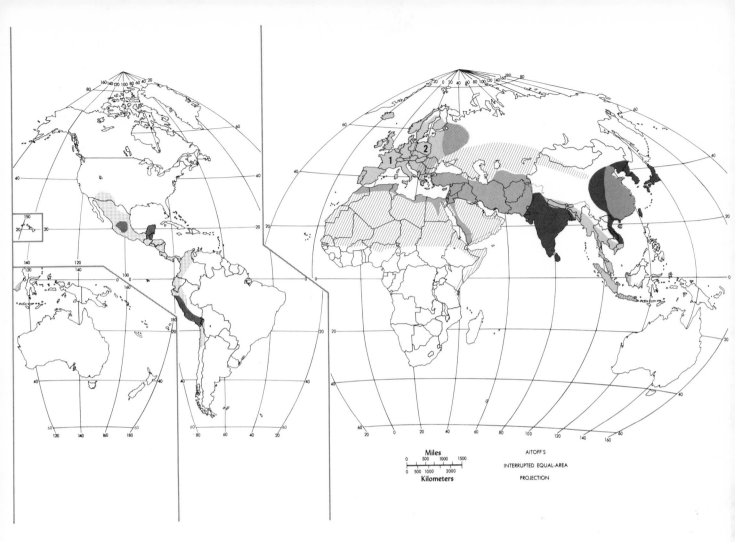

Miles
0   500   1000   1500
0   500 1000   2000
Kilometers

AITOFF'S
INTERRUPTED EQUAL-AREA
PROJECTION

systems and institutions. Can a non-Western society accept the former and reject the latter as if the parts of a culture had no connection? The answer is not a simple yes or no. Adoption of Occidental forms of technology and economy will inevitably affect other sectors of life, but the new ideas must be fitted into the indigenous cultural heritage.

Thus, we must not look upon non-Occidental civilizations as obsolescent vehicles, ready to be replaced by a uniform and worldwide standard model of Western design. Instead, they appear as living entities with capacity for adaptation to new circumstances. To be sure, civilizations develop and decay, but none of the present major cultures show clear signs of a swift demise, in spite of what prophets of doom may say. The underlying thought of this chapter, and indeed much of this book, is that different culture realms will continue to exist side by side, though in ever closer association.

Mediterranean Europe and Latin America. In the late Middle Ages Mediterranean Europe was still the nucleus of Occidental culture. The merchants of Genoa and Venice had built commercial empires extending over the entire midland sea. They, together with Italian geographers and navigators, laid the basis for the later oceanic voyages of Portugal and Spain.

8. Culture Realms

191

Cerro de Pasco, Peru, one of the world's highest towns (13,970 feet), grew
with the mining of the fabulous silver ores, after 1630. Now gold, vanadium, and
other metals are extracted in the vicinity. The plaza with monument and surrounding buildings reflects Spanish colonial culture, but the population (about 30,000) is
mainly Indian and Mestizo. [Standard Oil Company (N.J.)]

The Spanish conquest of Middle and South America destroyed the superstructure of the Indian civilizations from Mexico to Peru, but not the Indians, although it severely reduced their numbers. Spanish institutions were imposed wherever feasible on the indigenous population. Viceroys administered the colonies by order of the absolute monarch and with the help of the army. The Catholic Church converted the Indians and held a close rein on the spiritual life of the entire population. Members of the elite received large land grants, including feudal rights over the Indian inhabitants. Thus army, church, and landed aristocracy became the ruling triad in Spanish America, separated economically and socially from the mass of the population.

The Portuguese colonization in Brazil was in many ways similar to the Spanish system. However, their domain lacked the magnets of the highland civilizations with their precious metals which drew the Spanish into the interior at an early date. The Portuguese showed more interest in cultivating export crops. This explains why their settlements remained for a long time in the coastal areas.

Diversity of habitats, peoples, and governments makes Latin America less a unit than the name might indicate. Within the zone of pre-Columbian civilizations the Indian way of life, including language, social organization, and communal landholding, has survived to a large extent, at least at the village level. English, Dutch, and French incursions into the Caribbean area and the Guianas left their mark in speech, political institutions, style of life, and racial composition. Plantation agriculture on the islands as well as the tropical mainland resulted in large concentrations of Negroes. On the other hand, in the so-called temperate climates of Argentina, Uruguay, the southern part of Brazil, and Chile, the population is in great majority of European stock. The permissive attitude of Latins toward intermarriage with nonwhites has led to considerable race mixing. The *Mestizo,* blend of European and Indian, is the predominant type in Mexico and southward into Colombia and Venezuela. In the Antilles and Brazil intermarriage with Negroes has produced the widespread *mulatto* type.

Politically fragmented Hispanic America stands in sharp contrast to the two huge units of Anglo-America. The revolt against Spain in the early nineteenth century involved only the Spanish colonial elite. In each population cluster the leading group took over the authority of the Spanish Crown and assumed control over the outlying areas as far as it could maintain effective power. Brazil preserved its unity principally because the Portuguese royal family moved to Brazil during the Napoleonic Wars.

In Europe the many states reflect the mosaic of nations, but this is not true in Spanish America. Here the cultural tradition of the elite in one country is much the same as that in the other countries. The cleavage between classes within each country exceeds that between members of the same class in different countries. The spatial variety in culture and economy is thus often more one of regionalism or sectionalism than of nationalism.

The democratic spirit of the French and American revolutions hardly touched Latin America, or did so only recently and in isolated instances. The bulk of the population remains in virtual bondage, illiterate, poor, and only partly assimilated in the national entity. A wealthy minority of landed aristocracy still governs most countries, allied with the army, and sets the tone in values, customs, and institutions.

Northwestern Europe and Its Overseas Wings. From A.D. 1600 onward northwestern Europe became the veritable dynamo of the Occident. Its inhabitants overtook the Iberians in exploration, trade, and colonization, developed modern capitalism, strengthened the middle class, extended democratic institutions, and turned rational thought into modern science and technology. The diffusion of Occidental culture over the world since 1600 was largely the spread of ideas and things which originated in Northwest Europe. In the vanguard were France, the Netherlands, and Britain, but Scandinavians, Germans, and Swiss also participated in the overseas ventures or were di-

8. Culture Realms

Figure 8–5. THE WESTERN HEMISPHERE

Contrary to popular notions, this hemisphere includes not only the Anglo-American and Latin American culture regions, but also the Solomon Islands, Fiji, New Zealand, Iceland. a corner of Siberia and a large part of Antarctica.

rectly affected by the economic and social development generated by the new overseas frontier.

Until World War I northwestern Europe was the main seat of political and economic power. The outcome of World War II made it the chief arena of struggle between the new superpowers of the United States and the Soviet Union. The remarkable reconstruction after that war demonstrated the vitality of the nations of Northwest Europe. The European Economic Community, by including Italy as a member—and

probably to admit later other Mediterranean countries, Great Britain, and Scandinavia—affirms the idea of the fundamental unity of Maritime Europe. If a political union were to result, it would add a third superpower to the present two. Such a Maritime Europe would re-create in enlarged form the ancient West Roman realm.*

Anglo-America. The term Anglo-America must, of course, not be taken too literally. The remaining indigenous peoples from the Arctic to the Rio Grande, the French Canadians, and the national origins of most of the English-speaking inhabitants suggest plurality rather than monolithic unity. Yet, the term is apt if one considers that the English language and institutions have molded the predominant culture pattern.

Even the most astute observer in 1750 could hardly have foreseen this "Anglo-America," stretching from Atlantic to Pacific, and divided into only two sovereign states. At that time there was only a narrow band of English colonies—which had incorporated the Dutch and Swedish settlements—between the ocean and the Appalachians. Enveloping it in a large arc lay the French empire controlling the St. Lawrence and Great Lakes drainage basin as well as the Ohio-Mississippi valleys. In the far west, Spanish rule extended across the Rio Grande and Colorado rivers into the southern plains and California. Yet, within half a century the French were to give up all claims and the British were to recede to Canada. Annexation of Spanish territories came later, not because of their strength—to the contrary, they were a tenuous and neglected extension of the Spanish-Mexican frontier—but because their distant location beyond arid lands and mountains separated them from the advancing Anglo-Saxons.

Unlike Latin America, North America had no native civilizations whose riches attracted Europeans into the interior. But this also meant that there was no large and settled Indian population to subdue, exploit, and assimilate, Nor was there, as in Latin America, the voice of the

*For other characteristics see relevant sections of Chapters 6 and 7.

Catholic Church, demanding conversion of the heathens as an essential task of the conquest. The virtual elimination of the Indians made the greater part of Anglo-America a white man's country, where the settlers themselves had to perform all tasks from the most menial to the most exalted.

The important exception was the subtropical South, where the planters of cash crops came to rely on imported labor from Africa. Here a different way of life developed, with strictly observed caste rules dividing the free whites and the slave Negroes. The "cancer of slavery" eventually was removed, though one hundred years thereafter the place of the Negro in American society, whether in South or North, was still at issue.

The vast domain of the United States with its rich resources and its common market offered great economic opportunities. Moreover, its location between two oceans afforded protection against outside interference during the formative years. These were the necessary conditions that gave rise to paramount world power in the first half of the twentieth century. But the ultimate causes lay in the kind of society that grew up in the new habitat. The immigrants, while turning their backs on Europe, brought along their aspirations for a new freedom as conceived by visionaries in their homeland. In America, on new ground, released from the fetters of tradition, the incipient modern ideas received fresh meaning and expression: "industrialism as a technology, capitalism as a way of organizing it, and democracy as a way of running both" (Lerner, 1957, 39).

In Canada, with the exception of Quebec, the British tradition remains, of course, stronger than in the United States, but the differences are minor compared to the overall similarity between the two Anglo-American subcultures. Canada suffers from two handicaps. One is the division between the English and French, which is far from resolved. The other is the contrast between the narrow strip of effective settlement and the vast wilderness that reaches south to Lake Superior and thus cuts the ecumene in two. Fur trappers, loggers, and miners by their scattered and often ephemeral occupancy created a typical frontier economy, but farm settlement has not followed, as would have happened in more genial climates. At the same time, Occidental intrusions have deeply disturbed the native way of life. Thus, most of Canada lies on the periphery of Occidental culture, an indefinite area between the old which is going and the new which is reluctant to take hold. Alaska has much the same character, though its role in relation to the United States' ecumene is far less important than that of the Canadian Northlands in relation to inhabited Canada.

Other Transoceanic Offspring from Northwest Europe. Australia offers interesting similarities and contrasts to Canada. Here too a narrow populated zone is joined to a vast and virtually uninhabited domain. While Canadians can take some comfort in the thought that beyond its Arctic borders the wilderness continues into the northern regions of the Soviet Union, Australians know that beyond their dry wastelands lie the well-populated Asian countries. And while Canada's location makes it an integral part of the North Atlantic community, Australia's situation destines it to remain a distant and isolated outlier of Occidental culture. Even within the inhabited part, occupancy is patchy and rural settlement thin because of the large size of the farm units. Over two-thirds of the 12 million people live in cities, and half of the population is concentrated in five of them.

Development of Australia's tropical north is of serious concern: little has been accomplished so far in spite of considerable efforts. Environmental restrictions on agriculture, as well as the distance from markets and from the amenities of the ecumene, are inhibiting factors. The fact that this tropical fringe has been left to the Australian aborigines over thousands of years, although certainly known to Indonesian sailors, indicates its inhospitable nature.

If Canada and Australia carry burdens of empty empire, the offshoot of Occidental culture in South Africa faces point-blank, on its borders and in its midst, the rising consciousness of Negro-Africans. Unlike the situation in the United States, the ten million Bantu Negroes form the majority of population and are, for the greater part, unassimilated to the dominating Occidental culture. The antagonisms are compounded by the presence of other racial groups, such as Indians and Malays, and by the split between the Afrikaners (Boers) and the English. Nowhere else does Western civilization face such a challenge to its very existence as in this outpost.

In comparison to Australia and South Africa, conditions in New Zealand are almost idyllic. In a genial climate, its immigrants have created an egalitarian and somewhat more comfortable new England. The indigenous Maori, who since the 1880s have been treated quite well, form only a 6 percent minority. Remoteness—at the very opposite side of the earth from what the older New Zealanders still regard as "home"—is the greatest drawback of this South Pacific outlier of West European civilization.

Continental Europe and Its Eastward Expansion
(Figure 8–6). Inland from Maritime Europe lies the shatter belt of Central Europe. Essentially continental in character, it did not participate in the great adventure of oceanic discovery and expansion, nor in the subsequent economic upsurge of northwestern Europe. It has been the meeting ground of Slavic and Germanic peoples, of Eastern and Western Christendom. It is a transition zone which deserves recognition because it is neither western nor eastern (Russian) Europe. Since its composite character has already been discussed in Chapter 7, we may turn to Russia to conclude our overview of the Occidental culture realm.

Toynbee classifies Russia as a separate civilization, for he considers Russia a successor to Byzantine-Eastern Christianity, in his view something quite different from Western Christianity. Perhaps his emphasis on religion has made him minimize other features which justify the inclusion of Russia as part—a distinct part—of Occidental civilization.*

The Muscovy of 1500 was still on the fringe

of Western culture, a semibarbarous state in spite of its Orthodox Christianity and its linguistic affiliations to other Slavic peoples further west. But in the following century the process of acculturation to western Europe began, and by 1700 it gained momentum when Czar Peter made a purposeful drive for westernization.

The Communist ideology drew its inspiration from West European ideas, even though it perverted their ideals. Again, one is reminded of the thesis that innovations often find a better home on the periphery of a culture than in its center. In Russia, untouched by Reformation and French Revolution and virtually without the vested interests and liberal traditions of a middle class, a new type of industrial society replaced at one swoop the semifeudal system. By the nature of its totalitarian regime and doctrine, Russian communism is committed to creating a homogeneous society for its multinational population. Harmless diversions such as folk dancing are encouraged, and religions such as Islam are tolerated as long as they do not lead people to "backward nationalism." Nothing must interfere with the progress toward what the Communist party elite sees as the ideal of modernity.

The original Muscovy grew up in the forests on the margin of the Tartar Empire, which controlled the steppe to the south. Russia's initial expansion across the Urals followed the narrow belt of open woods and prairies between the subarctic forests to the north and the deserts to the south. Here the advance was rapid, not only because the environment was favorable, but also because the sparse indigenous population, loosely organized in many tribes, offered little resistance. Through this zone was built, at the very end of the nineteenth century, the Trans-Siberian Railway, the spinal cord of Russian Asia.

The conquest of Central Asia came in the latter third of the nineteenth century, much later than that of Siberia. The Soviet government has made intensive efforts to integrate the Turkic Moslems, and to modernize their traditional dual economy of oasis agriculture and nomadic herding.

---

* On the relation of Russia to the West see also Kroeber, 1962, 32–33 and 47–54.

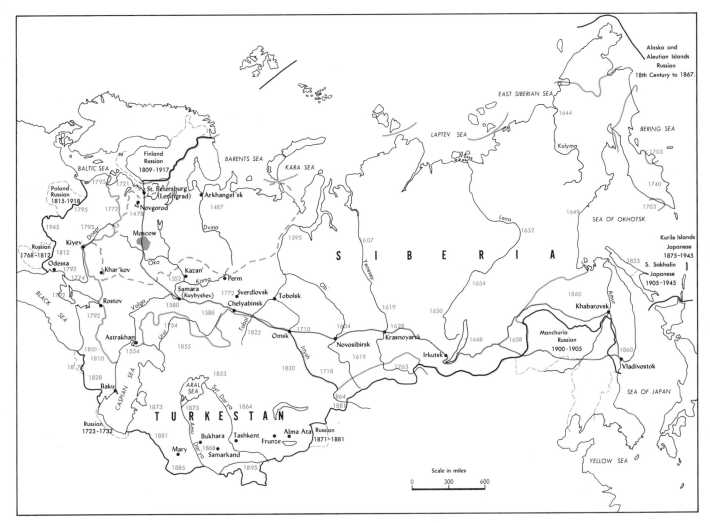

Figure 8–6. THE EXPANSION OF RUSSIA

The dominions of the czars were extended rapidly in
the seventeenth century across the wastelands of
Siberia to the shores of the Pacific Ocean. Expansion
southward into Asia proved more difficult as the
Russians encountered the Islamic and Chinese societies.

Map legend:

- Muscovy in A.D. 1300
- Muscovite Empire at the Death of Ivan the Great 1505
- Russian Empire at the Death of Peter the Great 1725
- U.S.S.R. 1965
- Other Boundaries
- Trans-Siberian Railway 1891-1901

Between the heartlands of Russia and China lies a wide belt which is peripheral to both cultures. This zone, from the borders of Manchuria to Sinkiang (Chinese Turkestan) is not a cultural unit, being sparsely occupied by peoples of widely divergent languages and traditions. The political boundary between the Soviet Union and the People's Republic of China marks the respective spheres of influence—at least in their overt forms—but the line must be understood as the current divide in an unstable power equilibrium. It has shifted widely during recent centuries and may do so again in the future.

The Main Islamic Realm

To find a fitting name for this realm is somewhat of a problem. In German it is called the *Orient,* a term formerly also used in English but now commonly reserved for East Asia. Everyone stretches "The Middle East" to suit his convenience, but extending it as far west as Morocco and east to West Pakistan overstrains its elasticity. The same goes for the French *Levant* ("rising"; land of the rising sun), which essentially refers to the lands around the eastern Mediterranean.

Although the Islamic realm includes less than one-half of all Moslems, the prevalence of Islam over this vast area is its chief cultural feature, a sort of common denominator that suggests the name (Figure 6–6).

North Africa and Southwest Asia have arid to semiarid climates. Everywhere there is the contrast between the pastoral nomad and the oasis dweller, between the steppe and the sown. The time is long past when the Middle East comprised the hearths of civilization, but its location always has given it strategic significance either as a bridge or a barrier between different cultures.

Within the local horizons of Central Europe, the Ottoman sultanate remained the great threat to Christendom until its defeat near Vienna in 1683. At about the same time, the Moslem Moghul Empire reached its greatest ex-

tent in India. However, in the broader view, the European expansion overseas and overland had already outflanked Islam. By 1500 the Portuguese had entered the Indian Ocean and begun to disrupt the Arab trade routes. From 1600 onward, the Russian Cossacks moved eastward into the Asian interior, reaching the Pacific in 1638. Subsequent West European colonial conquests pushed the rule of Islam back to its core lands in Southwest Asia and North Africa. Even this inner domain of Islam was, for the greater part, swallowed up by the British, French, and Russian empires in the nineteenth and early twentieth centuries, leaving only Afghanistan, Iran, an amputated Turkey, and Arabia as nominally independent buffer states. This historic reminder serves to point up the rapid retreat of Western rule in the middle of the present century when all lands of Islam, with the exception of those in Communist Russia and China, became independent again.

Under the influence of Occidental ideas the traditional authority of family, clan, and tribe is breaking down. Instead, the nation-state claims the full loyalty of its citizens as individuals. Loyalty implies identification with the goals of the new state, but these goals are as yet often far from clear. In all these lands there is an ancient contrast between the poor and debt-ridden peasants in the countryside and the rich landlords and merchants in the cities. Economic development demands from the upper strata sacrifices they are loath to make and the pursuit of productive work most of them disdain. Thus, social and political instability is characteristic for the entire zone from Morocco to Pakistan.

In addition there are deep cleavages between the various countries. Turkey and Iran, both non-Arabic and once the seats of great empires, are antagonistic to the Arabs. West Pakistan, the other major non-Arab unit, has always been more involved in the affairs of the Indian subcontinent than in the Middle East. The North African countries of Morocco, Algeria, and Tunisia have been much influenced by European rule. And the Arab countries of the Middle East still feud among themselves in spite of the ideal of Pan-Arab unity.

Kano, northern Nigeria, lies in the zone where Islamic and Meso-African
cultures have met for many centuries. The city (population about
170,000), long a focus of caravan routes through Sahara and Sudan, now
is an important entrepôt served by roads and railroads. The Moslem Hausa,
of Negroid stock with Caucasoid infusions, form the main population group.
The buildings, of unique architecture, have mud walls. [A Shell photograph]

8. Culture
Realms

199

In view of this diversity it may seem idle to insist on the fundamental strands of internal unity—the preponderance of Islam, the Arab-Persian roots of culture, and the similarities in mode of life. If this uniformity seems contrived, one may turn the argument to the question whether a more meaningful classification is feasible by dividing this realm among its neighbors. If this proves invalid it reaffirms our view that, for both positive and negative reasons, the area is a distinct cultural entity.

In Africa the southern boundary of the realm runs through the zone where Islam impinges upon the tribal religions of Meso-Africa. For many centuries Caucasoid peoples, speaking Hamitic or Semitic languages, have penetrated into the Sudan and the highlands and coastal areas of East Africa. The limit, as shown in Figure 8–3, coincides fairly well with the boundary between the grass and thornbush steppe to the north, and the wooded savanna to the south. To be sure, the coastal strip of East Africa, southward as far as Beira in Mozambique, has many Arabs and Arabic culture traits as a result of long trade contacts with southern Arabia, but on the whole this area may properly be regarded as part of the Meso-African realm.

While elsewhere the boundaries of the Islamic domain meet with cultures that are equal or superior in strength, in Africa there is the opportunity to extend its influence. Infiltration from the north is an old theme here, which may intensify now that European colonial rule has withdrawn.

The Indic Realm

Mountain walls and ocean shores make the Indian subcontinent a distinct physical unit. However, the northwestern section has always been in close communication with Central Asia and the Middle East and shares many aspects of life and landscape with these regions. This justifies the exclusion of West Pakistan from the Indic culture realm. Even with this restriction there remain such diversities and incongruities that it may seem rash to assert its individuality. Yet there is truth, however evasive, in this concept.

Religion is doubtless a major force in Indic culture. The deep concern with the fate of the individual soul has cast its spell over Indian life, for which the ultimate rewards are not in this world, but in a better birth in a subsequent incarnation. Monks and other holy men are highly esteemed because they present the ideal conduct through their retreat from life's ignoble struggle.

The individual-spiritual ends are pursued within and through the social organs of family, village community, and caste. There is a rift between these primary groupings and the political organization of the state. In the absence of an enduring tradition of imperial government, political rule has been largely of a personal nature, often despotic and always fleeting. Foreign conquerors, entering the subcontinent from Persia or inner Asia, built the larger and more lasting empires, but their successive domains fell apart again as their power waned. At the same time, the weakness of the political and administrative systems prevented the state from interfering substantially with the established social order.

In view of these considerations, it is no wonder that India's impact on other parts of the world has been chiefly of a spiritual nature. Its religions, especially Buddhism, have profoundly influenced the cultures of Central, East, and Southeast Asia. Campaigns of conquest outside India have been rare, and the number of settlers in overseas colonies has been small, if one excludes Indian workers who were recruited for manual labor overseas during the last century.

Because of its religion, East Pakistan, which in other respects is an integral part of the Indic culture realm, has been torn off politically and linked with distant West Pakistan. Ceylon, because of its island nature always somewhat different from the mainland, has resumed its separate course since British rule ended.

The problems of present-day India are in many ways similar to those of other underdeveloped countries. It has the advantage of a long tradition of civilization, and of political unity, frail as it may be, over a vast area. In the entire realm the dense and still rapidly growing population, mainly agrarian and living on the edge of hunger, makes the problem of economic growth especially urgent as well as difficult to solve. If India is to go modern it must change its social order and reinterpret its ideology. But its tradition, together with the legacy of British political thought, militates against ruthless regimentation of the individual. India seems to prefer gradual advance rather than great leaps forward. One must hope its pace is fast enough to escape the clutches of poverty.

The East Asian Culture Realm

Essentially this is the area of Chinese, or Sinitic, civilization with its variants in Korea and Japan. Although China's physical frame lacks the clear-cut boundaries of the Indian subcontinent, the vast deserts, high plateaus, and rugged mountains of Central Asia have shielded China, more than any other major culture realm, from outside contacts. To be sure, in its formative stage Chinese civilization received much from southwestern Asia, for which the string of inner Asian oases served as relay points; but from then on, its development has been essentially a native growth. By the end of the Han dynasty (206 B.C.–A.D. 214) imperial China covered much the same area as China Proper today. The enduring unity of the country for 2,000 years manifests the fundamental homogeneity and stability of its social order and political institutions. Invasions by pastoral nomads were frequent, but the foreigners ruled "through a state organization originally created by the Chinese and . . . operated through an officialdom which has usually been overwhelmingly Chinese" (Latourette, 1951, 68). And commonly the conquerors adopted the Chinese way of life.

Feelings of cultural superiority create ethnocentric attitudes. Just as the Greeks distinguished between themselves and the barbarians, so the Chinese divided the world into the Middle Country—their own—and the Outside Countries, whose inhabitants were beyond the pale of civilization. This self-satisfaction suffered rude shocks when the Occident at last forced its way into East Asia in the nineteenth century, but now there is good reason to believe that a new version of the old chauvinism is emerging.

The Chinese ethos stands in stark contrast to that of India. Whereas the latter is metaphysical, Chinese thought stays close to concrete reality. Rather than religion it emphasizes human relations. Thus the maxims on the organization of society, from family to state, take precedence over the claims of otherworldly religions. Temporal power had divine sanction (the emperor was considered a manifestation of Heaven), but there was never any doubt that the state came first, with religion as its servant. Not the priesthood but the civil service bureaucracy, selected by examinations and promoted by merit ratings, supervised the social order.

It is still too early to tell how much the Communist revolution will actually transform the foundations of Chinese society. The traditional social structure was already crumbling under the impact of the Occident. It is idle to speculate whether timely reforms by a strong and democratically minded government could have prevented the Communist victory. Only one thing seems certain: the Chinese, while adopting Western things and thoughts, will mold them in their own image, as they have done before with foreign intrusions. If they succeed in their modernization, China may again rise as one of the great powers, and, in Chinese eyes, be again the Middle Kingdom, the pivot of the earth.

Pride in the homeland explains to a large degree the posture of the ten million or more Chinese in Southeast Asia. Most of them have been reluctant to conform to the local ways of life, which they consider inferior to Chinese culture, although China's humiliations in the nineteenth century made many falter in their loyalty. China's rise in stature under the Communist regime gives many, even those who loathe communism, new pride in the motherland and confirms their belief in China. At the same time, it makes the possibility of their assimilation into the local societies more remote than ever.

Japan and Korea. While Chinese influence in Japan and Korea has been substantial, these two countries must not be considered as mere transplants of Sinitic civilization. Many Japanese words show ancient relationships with Polynesian languages, and the grammar indicates links with the Altaic (North Asian) linguistic family. Much later, in the fourth century A.D., the impact of horse-riding pastoral nomads from northeastern Asia brought about unification of the tribes in southern Japan (the Yamato empire). Direct contacts with China began after A.D. 500. The Japanese incorporated many Chinese words into their vocabulary, modeled their writing system after the Chinese example, and borrowed many other customs and institutions.

In all these culture transfers, Korea by its very position and shape served as the bridge between mainland and islands. It received from northern Asia and China, handed on to Japan, and had its own culture molded in the process. All through Japanese history there appear the alternating themes of continental and maritime influences and interests. In Korea the present split between North and South is a sharp reminder of its traditional position as an embattled zone of passage.

The Japanese islands became the home of a tightly organized nation, able to surmount the shock of exposure to Occidental civilization. It purposefully imitated the ways of the intruders, even to building a vast, though short-lived, empire along the rim of the western Pacific. The energetic reconstruction of the economy and the disciplined acceptance of reforms after the war give additional evidence of Japan's social stability. It is unlikely that it will ever again dominate East Asia, but its ability to fuse Asian and Occidental strains assures it of a special position in the Far East.

The Southeast Asian Culture Realm

In contrast to the previously discussed realms, Southeast Asia is not a unit with its own culturally distinct character. Instead, it is an area of transit and transition where different cultures meet and mingle. Its personality is defined in a negative way, in that it is neither East Asian nor Indic, neither Islamic nor Occidental, and yet contains elements of all.

Southeast Asia comprises the Asian mainland east of India and south of China, as well as the entire archipelago. The predominant race is South Mongoloid, and thus more related to the peoples of East than of South Asia. Some ancient customs, such as building houses on stilts, suggest a primeval unity, but this unity has been virtually obliterated by the heavy overlays of subsequent foreign intrusions. The cultural impact of India has been strong over most of the area, as evidenced by religion and the arts. Commercial and political relations existed with China, but the Chinese made no attempt to civilize the barbarians of the Southern Seas (Nan Yang). Only Tonking-Annam (Vietnam), for centuries a vassal state on China's southern frontier, was strongly affected by Chinese culture, but without losing its identity. Islam replaced Hinduism and Buddhism in the Malay Peninsula and Archipelago, but had not advanced much beyond the limits of Indic influence at the time the Europeans arrived. Thus the pagan population of the Philippines was Christianized and in the course of years became the carrier of that peculiar hybrid culture in which indigenous traits mingle with those from Spain and the United States (Figures 8–7 and 8–8).

The chief nations on the mainland are separated from each other not only by highlands with unassimilated tribes, but also by memories of bitter strife and by the different experiences during the centuries of European hegemony. Malaysia, the Philippines, and Indonesia together may be considered as a distinct subunit because of their linguistic affinity. However, most of their languages are mutually incomprehensible. More important, each of these countries has been subject to very different impacts,

Figure 8–7. SOUTHEAST ASIA: LANGUAGES

Based on a map in Broek, 1944. By permission of the *Geographical Review*.

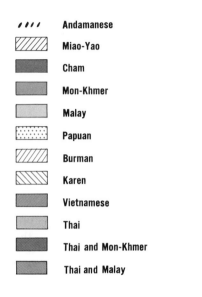

Andamanese
Miao-Yao
Cham
Mon-Khmer
Malay
Papuan
Burman
Karen
Vietnamese
Thai
Thai and Mon-Khmer
Thai and Malay

Figure 8–8. SOUTHEAST ASIA: RELIGIONS

Based on a map in Broek, 1944. By permission of the *Geographical Review*.

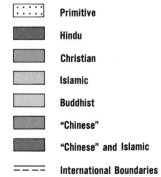

Primitive
Hindu
Christian
Islamic
Buddhist
"Chinese"
"Chinese" and Islamic
International Boundaries

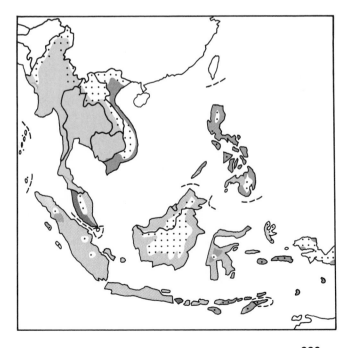

of which British, American, and Dutch rule were only the last in a succession of foreign influences.

All the countries of Southeast Asia for at least the last 2,000 years have been culturally a low-pressure area. As such, they have been recipients rather than donors of culture. It would be rash to project past performance into the future and declare Southeast Asia a permanent cultural ward of other civilizations. (What Roman could have foreseen the future role of northwestern Europe?) Nevertheless, now that Occidental rule has receded, India and China may well return to their former roles as dynamic culture centers and thus confront this vast area with new challenges. Southeast Asia's strategic position between the Indian and Pacific oceans, and between the landmasses of Asia and Australia, its sparsely populated sectors, and its rich resources combine to make it of special interest to many outsiders. In the face of these external relations and potential pressures, the glaring weakness of this realm is its ethnic and political fragmentation—a kind of Asian Balkans. It needs greater unity for defense and for internal development. Even its leaders as yet only dimly perceive this long-range self-interest amidst the diversity of memories and aspirations.

The Meso-African Culture Realm

There are many scattered survivals of peripheral cultures—such as those of the American Indians, Melanesians, Polynesians, and Arctic peoples—but Negro Africa is different not only because it is such a large unit, but also because it has preserved its identity to a much larger degree than the others. The Western-educated elite prefers to be called African rather than Negro. This self-designation ignores the fact that the northern and southern parts of the continent are occupied by, or shared with, quite unlike societies which are part of the Islamic and Occidental realms, respectively.

For a culture realm it is preferable to avoid the term "Negro" with its racial connotations. One could call it Central or Middle Africa, but these terms have already other (admittedly vague) geographic meanings. We propose, therefore, "Meso-Africa" as a fresh term, not burdened by political, physiographic, or racial meanings.

Physical barriers hampering communication between Meso-Africa and other regions are largely responsible for the cultural retardation of the area. Even so, during the course of the last five thousand years or more a number of traits filtered in. The great desert, in spite of its barren width, provided the main passageway for diffusion from north to south, especially in the east where the Nile Valley connects the Mediterranean with the interior.

Hamitic pastoral nomads penetrated into the grasslands of the Sudan and also moved southward over the savanna corridor of the eastern highlands into South Africa. Besides livestock, they doubtless introduced other materials and traits derived from northern Africa. The east coast received impulses from southern Arabia, India, and even the Malay Archipelago. Sailing ships used the monsoons to travel west in one season and return eastward with the reversal of the winds. Arab contacts with Africa's coast may reach back two thousand years, and became frequent after the seventh century A.D. Islam is strong in the coastal towns, and Swahili, the lingua franca of eastern Africa, contains many Arab words. The peoples and cultures of Madagascar show so clearly the imprint of Malay settlers (dating back perhaps 1,500 years) that one must assume they also frequented the coast of the mainland. The widespread occurrence of crops from the Malay Archipelago in tropical Africa supports this view.

In contrast, the west coast of Africa was exposed to foreign influences much later when the Portuguese extended their voyages southward. Until the middle of the nineteenth century, however, the impact of the European was limited to some coastal areas, chiefly along the Guinea Coast. Good harbors were few, and the rivers that tumbled over the highland escarpment were a hindrance rather than a help in entering the interior. Tropical rain forest and diseases also discouraged exploration. Thus, the greater part of Meso-Africa remained a blank on the map until only a century ago.

The economic basis of traditional Meso-African culture consisted of crop farming on shifting fields with the hoe as main tool, and the raising of cattle, sheep, and goats in regions free from the tsetse fly (see Chapter 10). Although a number of crops and animals were received from outside the realm, it appears that the upper Niger country was the center of autochthonous domestication of several African plants. West Africa—more specifically the Cameroons—also seems to have been the original home of the Bantu peoples, who spread east and southward some 2,000 years ago, first settling the savannas and open woodlands, and later pushing into the tropical rain forest. In their expansion they either absorbed or obliterated the primitive hunters and gatherers, of whom only scattered remnants survive in the Congo forest and in the Kalahari Desert.

In common with other peripheral cultures, Meso-Africans had no form of higher religion and no written languages. In some respects, however, their level was above that of other primitive cultures, owing to the trickle of impulses from civilizations to north and east. The density of population, considerably higher than among the Indians of tropical America, reflects the greater diversity of means available to cope with the habitat. Among other more advanced traits were the art of iron smelting, the relatively well-developed (though despotic) tribal organization, a feeling for law, and a fairly keen interest in the acquisition of property.

European exploration of "Dark Africa" was swiftly followed by its partition. Since then, as in all other colonial countries, there has been humiliation and exploitation of the native peoples, but also much constructive effort. The scourge of slave raiding and trading, already an old one by the time that the Europeans began to participate, was abolished, and tribal warfare was suppressed. Occidental forms of religion, law, education, medicine, production, and trade

were introduced. These intrusions deeply affected the traditional ways of life. Thus, when European rule withdrew from Meso-Africa after the middle of the twentieth century it left behind a multitude of societies, too much disturbed to return to their native folkways, but not enough transformed to possess a new social order.

The change from primitive tribe to modern society, which took some 2,000 years in other parts of the world, could hardly have been accomplished here in one hundred years, even though the pace of change has quickened. The crucial issue now is whether the native-born, Western-educated elite has the competence to lead the mass of conservative and illiterate tribal folk toward the professed goals of a better life. Closely related is the problem how to create new territorial frameworks for socially coherent and economically viable states instead of the colonial conglomerates and strategic slices and slivers.

Resident groups of non-African descent can materially assist in future economic development, unless social and political pressures isolate or even expel them. Among these groups are the white farmers in the eastern highlands from Kenya to Rhodesia, the mixed-bloods in Angola and Mozambique, and the Indians in the coastal areas of East Africa. They occupy managerial, administrative, technical, and commercial positions which the Meso-African is not yet prepared to fill, but at the same time their special position economically and racially makes them an easy target for discrimination.

All these fateful issues suggest that independence is the beginning of a time of troubles, whose end and outcome cannot be foreseen. Nor will the decisions lie solely within Meso-Africa. Its economic resources and political weakness inevitably attract influences from abroad, whether these take the form of welcome "foreign aid" or suspect "neocolonialism." Although the legacy of West European culture is at present the dominant force in the process of change, one cannot be certain whether Meso-Africa will pattern itself in this mold or turn to other culture realms for its inspiration.

Citations

Jaeger, F. "Anthropogeographische Gliederung der Erde nach der Kultur-landschaft," *Petermann's Geographische Mitteilungen,* 89 (1943). [Map]

Kroeber, A. L. *Cultural and Natural Areas of Native North America,* University of California Publications in American Archaeology and Ethnology, no. 38, Berkeley, Calif., 1939.

————. *A Roster of Civilizations and Culture,* Viking Fund Publications in Anthropology, no. 33, New York, 1962.

Latourette, K. M. *A Short History of the Far East,* rev. ed., New York, 1951.

Lerner, M. *America as a Civilization,* New York, 1957.

Toynbee, A. J. *A Study of History,* abridged ed. by Somervell, D. C., 2 vols., New York and London, 1947, 1957.

————, and Myers, E. D. *A Study of History,* vol. 12, *Atlas and Gazetteer,* London, 1959.

Further Readings

Augelli, J. P. "The Rimland-Mainland Concept of Culture Areas in Middle America," *Annals of the Association of American Geographers,* 52 (1962): 119–129.

Bacon, E. "A Preliminary Attempt to Determine the Culture Areas of Asia," *Southwestern Journal of Anthropology,* 2 (1946): 117–132.

Banse, E. "Die geographische Gliederung der Erdoberfläche," *Petermann's Geographische Mitteilungen,* 58 (1912), no. 1. [Map]

Bobek, H. "The Main Stages of Socioeconomic Evolution from a Geographical Point of View," in Wagner, P. L., and Mikesell, M. W. *Readings in Cultural Geography,* Chicago, 1962, 218–247. Originally published in *Die Erde: Zeitschrift der Gesellschaft für Erdkunde zu Berlin,* 90 (1959): 259–298.

Broek, J. O. M. "Diversity and Unity in Southeast Asia," *Geographical Review,* 34 (1944): 175–195.

Fisher, C. A. *Southeast Asia: A Social, Economic and Political Geography,* London and New York, 1964.

Hettner, A. *Der Gang der Kultur über die Erde,* Leipzig and Berlin, 1929.

Jackson, W. A. D. *Russo-Chinese Borderlands: Zone of Peaceful Contact or Potential Conflict?,* New York, 1962.

James, P. E. *Latin America,* 3d ed., New York, 1959.

————. *One World Divided,* New York, 1964.

Jones, S. B. "Views of the Political World," *Geographical Review,* 45 (1955): 309–326.

Kolb, A. "Die Geographie und die Kulturerdteile," in *Hermann von Wissmann Festschrift,* Tübingen, 1962, 42–49.

Kroeber, A. L. "Culture Groupings in Southeast Asia," *Southwestern Journal of Anthropology,* 3 (1947): 175–195.

Maull, O. *Das politische Erdbild der Gegenwart,* Leipzig and Berlin, 1931.

McNeill, W. H. *The Rise of the West: A History of the Human Community,* Chicago, 1963.

Miller, E. J. Wilson "The Ozark Culture Region as Revealed by Traditional Materials," *Annals of the Association of American Geographers,* 58 (1968): 51–77.

Murdock, G. P. *Africa: Its Peoples and Their Cultural History,* New York, 1959.

Russell, R. J., and Kniffen, F. B. *Culture Worlds,* New York, 1951, abridged ed., 1961.

Schmitthenner, H. *Lebensräume im Kampf der Kulturen,* 2d ed., Heidelberg, 1951.

Siegfried, A. *America at Mid Century,* New York, 1955.

Spencer, J. E. *Asia East by South: A Cultural Geography,* New York, 1954.

Unstead, J. F. *A World Survey from the Human Aspect,* 5th ed., London, 1961.

Wanklyn, H. G. *The Eastern Marchlands of Europe,* London, 1941.

Wertheim, W. F. *East-West Parallels: Sociological Approaches to Modern Asia,* Chicago, 1965.

Part III. Patterns of Livelihood

Part II presented the social and cultural variety of mankind. We now turn to the analysis of economic differentiation and integration, confident that the reader will not think of "economic systems" and "economic man" in the abstract, but of forms of economy practiced by real peoples in concrete places. The point gains meaning when we consider economic development. There is no standard remedy for economic stagnation; its treatment demands measures that fit the cultural matrix of a given society.

In line with this thought we will discuss economic activities within the framework of a threefold division of societies: tribal, traditional, and modern. The first portion of Chapter 9 presents this idea. The remainder of the chapter and the one following examine the economic life of tribal societies. Chapters 11 and 12 discuss agriculture in traditional and modern societies. A review of the plantation is placed between tribal and traditional agriculture because this enterprise appears typically as a Western intrusion in other societies. Large-scale manufacturing, so characteristic for the Occidental world, forms the theme of Chapter 13. Part III concludes with an inquiry into the nature of underdeveloped countries and ways to raise their levels of living.

Part-opening photograph: The port of Rotterdam. [A Shell photograph]

9. Forms of Economy: Tribal Gathering, Hunting, and Herding

The contrast between rich and poor peoples presents the most striking feature in the manifold diversity of mankind. To understand these disparities requires knowledge of the different forms of economy. The word economy, as used here, refers to the system of techniques, tools, resources, and organization by which a society makes its living.

A Threefold Division of Societies

To bring order into the infinite variety of economic pursuits requires that they be classified in some broad categories. Since we view economic activity in the context of sociocultural differentiation, it follows that the primary division must be according to the kind of society; each is then further subdivided into dominant forms of economy.

The marked differences in level of living between the so-called developed and underdeveloped countries suggest a basic division into industrial-commercial societies and all others. But the "others," comprising most of the earth's population, range from bands of primitive food collectors to ancient and quite sophisticated cultures. Evidently, we must make some further distinction. At the risk of oversimplification, we propose a threefold division of societies and label them *modern, traditional,* and *tribal,*

the latter two as subdivisions of the economically underdeveloped world. These primary categories suggest the general social, economic, and political framework in which people gain their livelihood (Figure 9–1).

Tribal societies are small in scale; they base their social relations on kinship or village community. Their simple technology affords little or no margin beyond production for immediate consumption. They rarely save for capital equipment or specialize beyond dividing the labor between the sexes. The insecurity of life, the effort and uncertainty of making a living demand solidarity of the group. Mutual aid is common, especially in sharing a fortuitous food surplus. Work and gift exchanges are the mechanisms of redistributing wealth—such as it is—and cementing social relations. Rules of custom prescribe these rights and obligations. To claim the exclusive enjoyment of the fruits of one's labor is to make oneself an outcast. Here lies a severe barrier to economic advance. Nevertheless, the tribal societies are in the process of change. Purposeful production for the external market is now an important element in several areas, although it is still peripheral to the subsistence economy. Processing and long-distance trade are largely in the hands of foreign merchants, not inhibited by the social customs of the indigenous community. Urban centers, where present, are foreign creations.

At the other extreme are the *modern societies.*

They intensively use science and technology as developed in the Occidental world over the last two hundred years. Output per worker is high, allowing a comfortable level of living as well as substantial savings for new investments. Differentiation and integration characterize industry and services as well as regions and countries. Agriculture employs only a small portion of the labor force. Personal competence and achievement rather than inherited social position usually determine financial awards. There is scope for considerable mobility on the vertical scale of status. The private entrepreneur—unless the state has taken over his function—plays a large role in organizing and directing the production.

The *traditional societies* occupy the middle of the spectrum. Some of them are hardly beyond the tribal phase, others are approaching the modern one. China exemplifies the difficulty of classifying countries in a period of rapid change. An Oriental state that proclaims itself to be the model of the Marxist revolution seems hardly to belong in the category of traditional countries. However, its current efforts gain meaning exactly because they strive to transform a traditional society.

The traditional society is prescientific, that is to say, based on attitudes toward knowledge and technology prevailing before Western science created a new concept of nature and of man's power to manipulate it. Agriculture is the mainstay of the economy. Productive power depends largely on the muscles of man and beast, supplemented by water and wind, although increasingly joined by modern forms of energy. The peasant provides first and foremost for his household or his village, but normally he has a surplus which serves to support the small fraction of the population that lives in towns and cities. The status of the individual is largely determined by his birth into a specific family, clan, or caste. Wealth rests mainly on owning land, which in turn gives political power and access to top positions in government. The landlords reside in urban centers and spend their profits either on conspicuous consumption or investment in more land, rather than in industrial or commercial ventures. Often they consider such enterprises below their dignity and leave them

to the other classes or even to foreign entrepreneurs. Thus the middle class is apt to be small. The illiterate peasants are an inert mass, living in ignorance and grinding poverty. For people

---

Table 9–1. Forms of Land Use

A. *Tribal societies*

1. Gathering, hunting, and/or fishing
   a. Nonspecialized foraging
   b. Specialized hunting and fishing

2. Reindeer herding

3. Shifting cultivation

4. Cattle herding

5. Tillage of permanent fields

B. *Traditional societies*

1. Intensive cultivation, with plow or hand tools

2. Extensive plow cultivation, supplementary large livestock

3. Pastoral nomadism

C. *Modern societies*

1. Mixed crop and livestock farming

2. Dairy farming

3. Crop farming
   a. Mediterranean agriculture
   b. Specialized horticulture
   c. Grain farming
   d. Cotton farming

4. Livestock ranching

5. Plantation farming

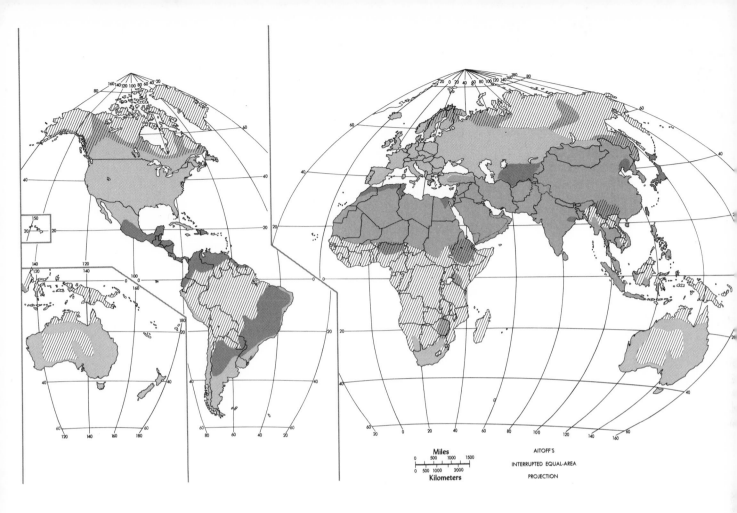

Figure 9–1. WORLD: TRIBAL, TRADITIONAL, AND MODERN SOCIETIES

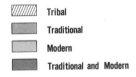

Tribal	
Traditional	
Modern	
Traditional and Modern	

The threefold division, although tentative, provides a broad perspective
on types of economy. The boundary lines are actually zones of contact.
Significant areas of mixture are shown; in some cases they indicate
two kinds of society living side by side, in others a blending of old
and new forms of societal organization.

whose existence leaves no margin for error, new
ways of doing things—even if not taboo—are a
gamble, where failure means starvation. Such
economic and social conditions result in a well-
nigh static economy, which maintains a precarious balance between production and population.

Forms of Economy

We turn first to the ways in which man earns a
living directly from the land, leaving to later
discussion manufacturing and service industries.
Within each type of society there are various

9. Forms of
Economy:
Tribal
Gathering,
Hunting, and
Herding

213

forms of land use, which tend to be localized in different regions (Table 9–1). Thus we can speak of, say, a winter-wheat region, an area where the predominant form of agrarian economy is the production of winter wheat. It does not mean that all people in the area are engaged in this activity, or that only winter wheat grows here, or that the entire production of winter wheat is concentrated in this area. Instead of distinguishing agricultural regions by commodity it is often more significant to note the methods of production (e.g., irrigation, plow, or hoe tillage), or the purpose (subsistence or commercial).

Some tribal societies still live by gathering, hunting, and/or fishing; not much above this level are the nomadic reindeer herders of Eurasia's northern fringe. Most tribal societies practice a simple kind of agriculture, either on temporary clearings or on permanent plots. The predominant agrarian occupations in the traditional societies range from intensive tillage with irrigation to nomadic herding.

Modern societies too have great agricultural diversity, from intensive market gardening near urban agglomerations to livestock ranching or grain farming in sparsely settled regions. The plantation is an intrusion of Western large-scale commercial-agrarian enterprise into other culture realms. The retreat of Western control diminishes the scope of the plantation and changes its character. For these reasons we will discuss the plantation in association with the tribal and traditional societies.

Tribal Gathering, Hunting, and/or Fishing

Man has lived as a predatory creature for almost all his existence. The beginnings of agriculture date back only some ten thousand years. In the relatively short time span since then, man has changed over almost completely to crop growing. Now only scattered survivals remain of what once was the universal way of life (Figure 9–2). True, food gathering and hunting are still practiced in other societies. Many subsistence farmers supplement their diet by foraging; even our most modern fishing methods are merely

Figure 9–2. WORLD: GATHERERS, HUNTERS, AND FISHERS, ABOUT A.D. 1500

In the Americas, nonagricultural types of economy prevailed over far wider areas than in the Old World, and many of them were specialized forms of hunting and/or fishing.

Distribution about A.D. 1500

Unspecialized Gatherers (with Subsidiary Hunting and/or Fishing)

Specialized Hunters and Fishers

Hunters and Fishers with some Cultivation

Hunters and Fishers with Herding (Mostly Reindeer)

Paiute — Unspecialized Gatherers (Mentioned in Text)

Pacific Coast Fishers — Specialized Hunters and Fishers (Mentioned in Text)

gigantic means of gathering. But these forms of acquisition are but adjuncts to well-established ways of purposeful production.

Insignificant as the remnants of gathering and hunting societies may seem, we cannot ignore them. They afford us glimpses of what man's life once was like everywhere. More important, primitive man greatly affected his biologic environment. Almost certainly what looks to us like a pristine wilderness man has changed at one time or another.

Nonspecialized Foraging. Relics of the oldest way of life occur now only in a few marginal locations: in the recesses of the tropical rain forest, in some of the tropical scrub forests, and in some deserts. For a few groups the present habitat may be the ground where their ancestors lived for ages. For most, however, it is a rather recent refuge from the pressure of more advanced peoples, an impoverished way of life compared to that in their former, more richly

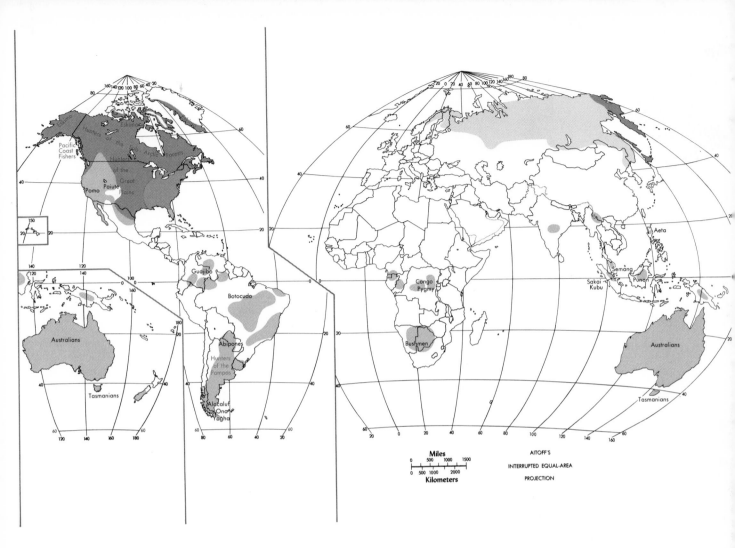

endowed habitat. We know this for certain of various Indian tribes in North America; there is no reason to think such displacements have not occurred elsewhere.

Among the groups that live, or lived until recently, by general foraging are the Indian tribes in the western part of the United States (such as the Paiute and Pomo), in central South America (the Guajibo, Abipones, and Botocudo), and in the extreme south end of that continent (the Yaghan, Ona, and Alacaluf). In Africa they include Pygmy (Negrillo) bands in the Congo, and Bushmen in the Kalahari. In Southeast Asia, scattered through the forests, live the Negrito Semang (Malaya) and Aeta (the Philippines), the Australoid Sakai (Sumatra and

Malaya) and Kubu (Sumatra), and also some Mongoloid groups such as the Punan of Borneo. Before the white man came, all of Australia and adjacent Tasmania were sparsely occupied by nonagricultural peoples, of whom now only a fraction survive in the least hospitable parts of the continent.

In Africa and Asia most gatherers belong to another race than that of the now predominant peoples. This difference—or rather cultural differences associated with contrasts in race—may partly explain why they still cling to their ancient ways. This argument, however, cannot be used in the case of the pre-Columbian American Indians. Here one might point to the environment as unfavorable to agriculture: the dryness

9. Forms of Economy: Tribal Gathering, Hunting, and Herding

215

Jivaro Indians, upper Amazon Basin, Ecuador. The Jivaros practice some shifting cultivation, but do much hunting with long blowpipes and darts tipped with curare—a paralyzing poison extracted from a plant root. They are probably best known for their custom of shrinking the heads of slain enemies. [A Shell photograph]

rabbits, ground squirrels, and field mice. Even so, the Californian Indians might have changed to crop growing had they lived closer to the agricultural cores in Meso-America. Isolation certainly is the main reason for the backward economy of the natives at the south tip of South America, and in Australia and Tasmania.

These people often are called "primitive." This refers to their economic organization and technology, not to their individual abilities. A gatherer's life can be quite complicated, requiring much forethought and many skills. There is no evidence that his intelligence is less than that of economically more advanced peoples. His mind is often intensely occupied with matters we consider unimportant. For instance, the Australian aborigines have an elaborate kinship system and mythology.

Almost everywhere there is a division of labor according to the sexes. Women gather the vegetable supplies for food and fiber, prepare the meals, and store the surplus; men do the hunting and fishing. A pointed stick is the usual tool to dig up roots and tubers as well as little delicacies such as beetles and grubs. The women also prepare skins, cloth from bark, fiber nets, and similar equipment. The "Digger Indians" of California developed basket weaving into a fine art, so that they could use the baskets even for cooking. They boiled the water for their acorn-meal gruel by dropping hot stones into the baskets.

The tools and methods for hunting and fishing show a great variety and often remarkable ingenuity. Most peoples have, or had, bow and arrow except the Australians, who developed the throwing stick into the returning boomerang. Blowguns with or without poison darts are widely used, and so are snares, traps, and nets.

The dog is the only domestic animal. The common explanation for its domestication presents the early wild dog as a camp follower that was tamed, bred in captivity, then used for hunting purposes. However, the more primitive gatherers and hunters do not use the dog for hunting. Because our own culture is so utility-minded we assume all peoples at all times had the same motivation. It may well be that the

of the western United States or the bleak environment of Patagonia and Tierra del Fuego. But this simple answer fails to explain why Pueblo Indians raised crops in a desert, while other Indians did not do so in the intermontane basins to the north.

In the case of California, perhaps the return on gathering and hunting afforded such a good living (always relative, of course) that the additional effort needed for crop growing made the latter unattractive. Abundant acorns provided the staple food, supplemented by grass seeds, bulbs, berries, and other wild fruits. Shellfish were easily available along the coast, huge flocks of ducks and geese came to the marshes in fall, and there was always open season to hunt deer, domestication of the dog—and later of other small animals—started with young ones being adopted as pets.

Gathering and hunting imply mobility. But it does not necessarily mean that the bands are on the move all the time. Campsites near streams or water holes are occupied by the women and children as long as they provide a good base for foraging in the surrounding countryside, while the men on longer forays search for game. Each family or band needs a large territory to sustain itself throughout the seasons. In general, population density remains therefore quite low, about one person per 5 to 10 square miles. But this refers to present conditions where these primitive folk eke out a living in submarginal lands. In the past wherever there were more genial environments, as in California, the density may have been considerably higher.

Specialized Hunting and Fishing.

Until a century ago these forms of economy were widespread in the Americas. Now they survive only —and precariously at that—in areas not occupied by people of Occidental culture.

Pacific Coast Fishers. Along the Pacific Coast from southern Alaska to Oregon only vestiges remain of the once flourishing Indian fishing economy. Here at the foot of the heavily forested coastal mountains and on the island chains that dot the glacier-sculpted sounds, the Indians lived in villages at the water's edge. The men went out in sturdy boats to exploit the sea and its shores. By far the most important resource was the salmon, caught in rivers as well as in the salty inlets. Seals and sea lions, dolphins and porpoises also were hunted. Some Indians even went out into the open sea to harpoon whales. The women gathered berries, roots, and seeds in the forest clearings, and the men occasionaly made hunting trips on land. But all this was decidedly secondary to the fishing activities.

Hunters of the Grasslands. The hunters of the Great Plains have vanished completely. They followed the American buffalo, or bison, their prime resource for meat, skins, and sinews; they also caught antelope, deer, coyote, jackrabbit, and prairie dog (actually a kind of squirrel). The acquisition of the horse from the Spaniards, some four hundred years ago, revolutionized the way of life. Before that time the Indians had lived mainly on the humid prairies by means of hunting and rudimental agriculture. They rarely ventured out to hunt on the dry, high plains. The horse gave mobility and changed the Great Plains from a submarginal region into a rich hunting domain. Bison hunting provided a relatively affluent livelihood; some agricultural peoples abandoned farming entirely in favor of the hunt. But this era lasted at most only a century. With the coming of the whites, the rifle supplanted bow and arrow, rapidly depleting the bison. In their struggle with the white man, the Indian hunters on horseback became swift cavalry brigades. But their defeat and expulsion were inevitable.

A similar economy in a similar environment existed in the Pampas, the great grasslands of Argentina and Uruguay. Here the main game animals were the rhea, or American ostrich, and the guanaco, a species of the American camel related to the llama and the alpaca. Here too hunting was done traditionally on foot. The main weapon was not the bow and arrow, but the bola, a throwing device consisting of round stones attached to a bundle of leather thongs, which entangled the legs or strangled the prey. After the Spaniards came, the story of the Pampas virtually duplicated what happened on the Great Plains. Adoption of the horse by the Indians brought a drastic change to their economy. Later the Indians struggled fiercely with the whites, but in the end were defeated and displaced.

Hunters of the American Subarctic Forests. Only in the polar and subpolar areas, where the impress of Occidental culture is as yet weak, have hunting and fishing economies survived. However, they are undergoing drastic transformation, as will be shown in some detail for the Eskimo.

South of the Arctic tundra lies the wide zone of subarctic forest. The recent retreat of the land ice has left behind an undulating surface. Streams wind through chains of lakes, and bogs fill the shallow hollows. Snow covers the entire region during the long winter, quite heavy in

9. Forms of Economy: Tribal Gathering, Hunting, and Herding

the more humid coastal areas, but lighter in the inland parts. This is the home of many browsing and gnawing animals, such as caribou, moose, deer, porcupine, beaver, otter, and mink.

The Indians move from place to place every few weeks in pursuit of game. They have developed means of transportation well fitted to this environment. In winter they use the snowshoe, which enables them to walk with ease on top of the snow. In this manner they can even approach the dangerous moose, whose movements are slowed by breaking through the snow at every step. Their few belongings, including the skin tent, they carry on a toboggan, a sled without runners which glides over the snow without sinking into it. In summer the Indians travel by canoe, a frame of spruce covered with birch bark. It rides high on the water, which often is shallow and filled with rocks. The canoe, being so light, can easily be carried around rapids or across portages from one stream to the next. The Indians hunt in summer from the canoe by driving the moose into deep water where it is almost helpless. During the short summer they pick berries and dig roots.

The Eskimo. Everyone learns in school about the Eskimo, but the stereotyped treatment masks regional variations and ignores the great changes taking place in their way of life, especially since World War II. Altogether there are some 70,000 Eskimo living under four flags: 32,000 in Greenland, 12,000 in Canada, 23,000 in Alaska, and 1,000 across Bering Strait in Soviet Chukchi Peninsula (Hughes, 1965).

The popular image of the Eskimo is mainly derived from their traditional way of life in the Canadian Arctic. Here the seal is the main source of food, clothing, implements, fuel, and light. During the winter the people live in igloos, houses built of snow blocks on the sea ice; they catch the seal by harpooning it when it comes up to the breathing holes in the ice. Hunters travel over the ice by dog-drawn sleds. In summer they hunt the seal and other sea mammals by boat, the light, skin-covered kayak. In spring many Eskimo groups move to the tundra, where they catch freshwater fish and birds and collect eggs. When the caribou were plentiful, hunters intercepted them in their annual migrations.

The Eskimo of Greenland have more open water than do their cousins in the central part of the Arctic, and thus depend more on the kayak than the sled. The warming of waters in the Labrador Sea since the early twentieth century has caused seals to move farther north; at the same time cod and other fish have come northward, providing southern Greenland with a new resource base. Alaska presents another regional variation on the general theme. Because of unstable ice conditions along the north coast, winter settlement on the sea ice is rare. For the western Alaskan groups the main game are, or were, the sea lion, fur seal, and especially the walrus. Since the walrus and sea lion do not keep breathing holes open in the ice, they frequent the edge of the open sea.

In Greenland the first European contacts came with the Norse settlements from the eleventh to the fifteenth centuries, but the impact on the indigenous economy was relatively small. For the last two hundred years Greenland has been under Danish influence and rule. In the present century the government has used an integrated approach to the problems of social and economic change: While protecting the Eskimo against the disruptive influences of the outside world, it provided them with churches, schools, and health clinics, and encouraged shifts to more productive forms of economy. In the southern part of the island, fishing with the aid of motorboats is becoming the predominant activity. Here also the Danes introduced raising livestock, mainly sheep. Seasonal migrations are decreasing. Though the Greenlanders have lived in small permanent settlements a long time, they now move more and more to the larger villages. In the north the sea mammal–based economy continues. When the large United States air base was built at Thule in 1954, Eskimo of that area were shifted to another location to minimize external influences. Even so, new ideas seeping in cause the social order to disintegrate.

In the Canadian Arctic, the government only recently has begun concerted efforts to help the Eskimo adapt to new circumstances. Here as elsewhere the rifle has replaced the harpoon and the bow and arrow as a much more efficient weapon, a weapon that has depleted the game resources. The caribou herds in Canada have declined catastrophically. The Eskimo considered the Arctic fox a worthless scavenger until the fur trader asked for its pelt. Fur trapping introduced an exchange economy, but proved a fluctuating source of income, which in recent years has dwindled in significance. The commercial concern that virtually monopolized the fur trade closely bound the Eskimo fur trappers—as well as the forest Indians to the south of them—to its policy. The rifle, the steel trap, and cash have led to breaking up old patterns of collective hunting and sharing.

After World War II the construction of military facilities, especially of the Distant Early Warning (DEW) Line of radar stations, and smaller posts at every 25 miles (roughly following the 68th parallel, from Alaska to Baffin Island) had strong repercussions on native life. Many Eskimo took jobs as unskilled construction workers. Formerly the Canadian Eskimo had no villages of the size and permanence known in western Greenland and on the Bering Sea coast. Later small settlements grew up around trading posts and mission stations. Now there are new ones at the defense installations. The shantytowns with crowded and poorly ventilated hovels of discarded construction materials show the lack of a wood-building tradition. Tuberculosis and other respiratory diseases, common among all Eskimo, are here particularly severe. The government's heightened interest in these indigenous peoples resulted in a more deliberate welfare policy. It introduced rational game management, fish canning, and reindeer herding—the last not an unqualified success.

Seal hunting and whaling during the nineteenth century brought the Eskimo of the Aleutians and coastal Alaska into close contact with outsiders, and thus with alcohol, tuberculosis, and other diseases. By the end of the century the harpoon gun and rifle had seriously depleted whale, walrus, seal, and caribou. Reindeer herding, introduced in the 1890s, failed in the long run. The reindeer joined the wild caribou or were eaten by wolves. In some areas the herds grew too large and overgrazed the pastures. The caribou, however, now again are increasing.

As in Canada, the Eskimo have become involved in a money economy. First it was the pelt trade, then wage labor in fish canneries and mines and on defense installations. The Eskimo now tend to concentrate in larger settlements along the coast. Health problems are severe, abetted by poor nutrition, for no well-balanced diet has replaced the former high consumption of animal protein. American policy in recent decades has tried to improve conditions through education and various welfare measures. While the Danes rather consistently have aimed at economic stability of Eskimo communities, American policy, besides being more haphazard, has been directed more toward assisting the individual in his adaptation to new conditions.

The Eskimo are forced to adjust to fundamental shifts in the ecological setting as well as in the technical, social, and psychological environment. But, as one observer remarked, "the difficulty is that they are adapting not to the Arctic but to a Temperate Zone way of living. The new people with their new standards have nearly overwhelmed the Eskimos, not in numbers but in wishes and wants" (Margaret Lantis, 1957, 126, as quoted by Hughes, 1965).

Only a thousand Eskimo live across Bering Strait in Soviet territory, their economy based on reindeer herding and sea-mammal hunting. The Russian policy resembles the Danish in its concern for the welfare of the ethnic group as a whole, but differs in that it deliberately organized collective enterprises on the Soviet model.

Reindeer Herders of Northern Eurasia

In contrast to North America the indigenous peoples of the Eurasian tundra do not depend on sea mammals. Their main resource is the reindeer, the domesticated variety of the caribou. In winter the herds feed in the taiga, the subpolar forest, while in summer they pasture on the mosses, lichens, and grassy meadows of the tundra. The people gain a supplementary food supply from fishing and hunting, also by gathering tree bark, roots, and berries in the taiga.

Perhaps the reindeer was domesticated in the

9. Forms of Economy: Tribal Gathering, Hunting, and Herding

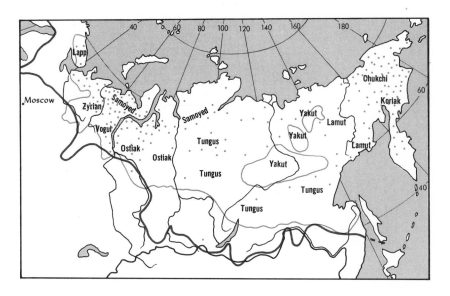

Figure 9-3. NORTHERN EURASIA: REINDEER HERDING

In the last century reindeer herding has, on the whole, receded northward under pressure of more intensive forms of land use. The Yakut enclaves are areas of cattle and horse rearing.

Lake Baikal region of southern Siberia in imitation of the pastoral nomads to the south. Some writers claim its separate domestication among the Lapps, after contact with the husbandry of European peoples. But it is also possible that prehistoric hunters of the north European plain formed some symbiosis with the reindeer, leading to its domestication. The use of the reindeer differs among the various tribes. Milking is practiced mainly by the Tungus and the Lapps. Most tribes use the animal for drawing the sledge, but the Tungus ride and pack it. The Chukchi and Koryak consider their large half-wild herds mainly as a meat reserve on the hoof. All over the region, dogs are used to guard the herds (Figure 9-3).

The only exception to reindeer herding in the Arctic are the Yakuts, Turkic-speaking breeders of cattle and horses, who came from the south and pushed their way of life into the forest lands of the Lena Basin beyond the Polar Circle. They protect their animals against the severe winter cold by barn feeding.

Like the American Arctic, its Eurasian counterpart has significantly changed in recent times. The Russian Cossacks who invaded this domain in the early seventeenth century exacted tribute in furs. In the nineteenth century Russian farm colonists moved into the southern fringes of the taiga and along the Lena even farther north, to its confluence with the Aldan. Mining and lumber enterprises, port and defense installations, as well as political exiles and prisoners from European Russia all contributed to cultural and economic changes in the Russian northlands. Russia's more northward location, compared to the United States and Canada's ecumene, makes integration of the polar and subpolar zone imperative. Exactly how the native peoples of this belt have fared under this

III. Patterns of Livelihood

expansion as compared to those in North America is hard to judge without more objective information than that available in the Soviet literature.

Primitive Man's Impact on the Earth

At first thought it might seem that the technology of primitive man was too weak to make any permanent impact on his habitat. He lived off the bounty of the land, one might argue, and nature quickly replaced the little he took. In recent years, however, this image of early man living in idyllic harmony with his physical milieu has been challenged. While one small band of hunters and gatherers may hardly disturb the habitat, the cumulative effect of occupance over hundreds of thousands of years must have been considerable. One of early man's great achievements was to make fire. At first he used it to warm himself and to make plant foods more palatable. He must have observed how animals fled before forest fires caused by lightning or by an unattended campfire. He learned to use fire himself to drive game past hunters or to stampede it over a cliff. Some hunters may have taken a further step: burning to increase the expanse of grazing grounds for the favorite game, herbivores. This must have led to systematic burnings which in the course of time surpassed fire drives in causing deforestation. Fire killed trees, or at least sufficient trees to let ample sunshine penetrate to the forest floor. Repeated firing prevented seedling trees from growing to maturity while grass seeds, buried in the ground, bided their time for the next life cycle. In this way man changed extensive areas from forest to grassland. Some trees withstand heat better than others, or grow much faster and may thereby survive the next fire. Also, the seedlings of some species tolerate glaring sunlight and dried-out topsoil while others need shade and moisture. In this manner fire acts as a selector, causing change in the composition of the forest, or resulting in a grassland with scattered trees of a few or only one species.

In lands with year-round precipitation the forest—though it may be a forest changed in composition—is likely to reestablish itself, but in regions with sparse moisture, or with a pronounced dry season, the forest vegetation is much more vulnerable. A large part of the world's grasslands, in tropics as well as in middle latitudes, may well be a form of man-induced vegetation. It is a well-known fact that the extensive grassy uplands of the Middle West, devoid of woody vegetation when the white man arrived, now grow trees wherever desired.

Another result of early man's predatory activities was the extermination of game animals. According to some scientists, climatic changes during the glacial and interglacial periods caused certain species, such as the American forms of elephant, camel, horse, and sloth, to disappear from the western deserts and steppes of what is now the United States. But there are indications that man was at least a strong contributing factor. In New Zealand the moa, a gigantic herbivorous running bird, became the prey of the early nonagricultural Polynesians who held the land from perhaps the ninth to the fourteenth century A.D.* Since they were few in number and had only simple tools they used fire to hunt the moa and in the process changed much forest into grassland (Cumberland, 1962). In Europe too several game animals vanished in recent prehistoric times, when climatic change could hardly have been the cause. Primitive man modified his environment in other ways too. Boat and raft travel must have spread rodents, insects, parasites, and plants from mainland to offshore islands. Destruction of vegetation on sloping surfaces may have sped up the natural processes of erosion.

Man's role in changing the face of the earth is not merely a modern creation. Although present techniques enable us to bring about spectacular changes, for better or for worse, we cannot ignore how primitive man over the ages altered his habitat.

* Although the Polynesians practiced agriculture, the first arrivals in New Zealand must have reached this land accidentally. This would explain why they carried no plant materials. Or, what little there remained after a long voyage bore no fruit in the unaccustomed climate and soil.

9. Forms of Economy: Tribal Gathering, Hunting, and Herding

Citations

Cumberland, K. B. "Moas and Men: New Zealand about A.D. 1250," *Geographical Review,* 52 (1962): 151–173.

Hughes, C. C. "Under Four Flags: Recent Culture Change among the Eskimos," *Current Anthropology,* 6 (1965): 3–54.

Mirow, N. T. "Notes on the Domestication of Reindeer," *American Anthropologist,* 47 (1945): 393–408. [Map]

Further Readings

Curtis, E. S. *The Kwakiutl,* New York, 1919.

Hahn, E. "Die Wirtschaftsformen der Erde," *Petermann's Geographische Mitteilungen,* 38 (1892): 8–12 and map in back pocket.

Haines, F. "Where Did the Plains Indians Get Their Horses?", *American Anthropologist,* 40 (1938): 112–117.

———. "The Northward Spread of Horses among the Plains Indians," *American Anthropologist,* 40 (1938): 429–437.

Herskovits, M. J. *Economic Anthropology,* New York, 1952.

Kroeber, A. L. *Cultural and Natural Areas of Native North America,* University of California Publications in American Archaeology and Ethnology, no. 38, Berkeley, Calif., 1939.

Lewis, O. *The Effects of White Contact upon Blackfoot Culture, with Special Reference to the Fur Trade,* American Ethnological Society, Monograph no. 6 (1942).

Métraux, A. "The Botocudo," *Handbook of South American Indians,* Washington, D.C., 1947, vol. 1, 531–540.

Oakley, K. P. "On Man's Use of Fire, with Comments on Tool-making and Hunting," in *Social Life of Early Man,* Viking Fund Publications in Anthropology, 31 (1961): 176–193.

Sahlins, M. D. "On the Sociology of Primitive Exchange," in Gluckman, M., and Eggan, F. (eds.) *The Relevance of Models for Social Anthropology,* New York, 1965.

Sauer, C. O. "A Geographic Sketch of Early Man in America," *Geographical Review,* 34 (1944): 529–573.

———. "The Agency of Man on the Earth," in Thomas, W. L. (ed.) *Man's Role in Changing the Face of the Earth,* Chicago, 1956, 49–69.

———. "Sedentary and Mobile Bents in Early Societies," *Social Life of Early Man,* Viking Fund Publications in Anthropology, 31 (1961): 256–266.

Sonnenfeld, J. "An Arctic Reindeer Industry: Growth and Decline," *Geographical Review,* 49 (1959): 76–94.

———. "Changes in Eskimo Hunting Technology: An Introduction to Implement Geography," *Annals of the Association of American Geographers,* 50 (1960): 172–186.

Stefansson, V. *The Friendly Arctic,* New York, 1943.

Stewart, O. C. "Fire as the First Great Force Employed by Man," in Thomas,

W. L. (ed.) *Man's Role in Changing the Face of the Earth,* Chicago, 1956, 115–133.

Wagner, P. L. "On Classifying Economies," in Ginsburg, N. (ed.) *Essays on Geography and Economic Development,* University of Chicago, Department of Geography, Research Paper no. 62, Chicago, 1960.

——— . *The Human Use of the Earth,* New York, 1960.

Whittlesey, D. S. "Major Agricultural Regions of the Earth," *Annals of the Association of American Geographers,* 26 (1936): 199–240.

10. Agriculture in Tribal Societies, and the Plantation

Multiple Origins of Agriculture

All available evidence points to the Middle East and Nuclear America (Mexico to Peru) as the earliest sites of agriculture. But this does not preclude the possibility that plant and animal domestication in another part of the world may prove to be of even greater antiquity. Carl O. Sauer has proposed that the earliest farmers lived in Southeast Asia (Sauer, 1952). According to him, they were planters rather than seed growers, that is to say, they planted stem cuttings, parts of rootstocks, or pieces of tubers to reproduce the desirable qualities of the parent plant, such as yam, taro, banana, breadfruit, and sugarcane. In Sauer's view the planting of seeds developed later on the margins of the lands where cuttings were used: in North China, the Middle East, including the lower Indus and Nile valleys, and Ethiopia. In the Americas, he believes, there was a similar sequence of planting of cuttings (cassava, squash, sweet potato, white potato), followed by planting of seeds (maize). This highly stimulating hypothesis needs much more evidence than is now available before it can be accepted as a true reconstruction of agricultural beginnings.

No doubt several areas contributed to the present assemblage of crops and animals (Figures 3–1 and 3–2). Most of these areas are tropi-cal or subtropical with considerable differences in relief, offering a great variety of environmental niches for plants. Here early man could select from a wide diversity what best suited his needs. From these early centers the man-altered crops and animals spread to other lands as far as conditions allowed. Especially the European colonization of the Americas and Australia resulted in a rapid transfer of agricultural plants and animals. Today one can hardly imagine the Americas without cattle, horses, sheep, wheat, barley, rice, and other small grains, or Asia and Europe without maize and various kinds of potatoes. Rubber, cinchona (quinine), and cacao were introduced into tropical Asia and Africa, which now are the main producers. In turn, coffee from the Old World is now a major commodity of America.

Shifting Cultivation

Probably man first tilled the land on forest clearings which, when the fertility was creamed off, he abandoned for fresh patches. Shifting cultivation was once quite common over wide parts of the earth. The Roman Tacitus observed of the Germanic tribes: "They change their plow-lands yearly, and still there is ground to spare. The fact is that their soil is fertile and plentiful, but they refuse to give it the labor it deserves. They plant no orchards, fence off no meadows, water no gardens; the only levy on the earth is the grain crop." The Europeans of the seventeeth century noted that the Indians along the Atlantic Seaboard of North America cultivated temporary clearings.

Today shifting cultivation, though surviving in remote corners of Europe and East Asia, is found mainly among the less advanced peoples of tropical lands (Figure 10–1). It has been estimated that some 200 million people, occupying 14 million square miles (one-fourth of the land surface) live chiefly by this form of land use (Food and Agriculture Organization, 1957, 5). The broadest definition of shifting cultivation is: "any continuing agricultural system in which impermanent clearings are cropped for shorter periods in years than they are fallowed." (Conklin, 1961, 27). Other terms for shifting cultivation are: bush-fallow, slash-and-burn agriculture, forest-field rotation, or land rotation. They all stress some salient aspect of this form of land use, although it is not always a universal trait (burning is not practiced everywhere; "rotation" and "fallow" are not strictly correct where the land is abandoned without plan). Each language has its own term for the cleared plot. Some of them are now widely used in the literature, as for instance *swidden* (from early English for a burned-over field), *milpa* (Middle America), *roça* (Brazil), *chitemene* (Central Africa), *ladang* (Indonesia), and *caiñgin* (Philippines).

Shifting cultivation is usually not associated with moving of the residence (Figure 10–2). Each village holds its territory in communal ownership. A villager has the use-right on the cleared land he has under cultivation. He may build a temporary shelter near his plot if it is far from the village. The whole settlement may be moved to a new and more convenient site only when the clearings are quite distant. More commonly, a group may split off from the parent village and start anew in virgin territory.

The cultivation cycle runs about as follows: After the men by common consent have selected a site for a swidden, they clear the forest in the dry season with ax or machete. Depending on tools and vegetation cover, they girdle or actually fell the big trees and slash the smaller woody growth. Cutting down a scrub or grass cover requires, of course, less work. At the beginning of the rainy season they burn the trees and the trash. Each family receives a part of the clearing for its own use. The women do most of the planting, but the men usually participate. Cuttings and seeds are planted by dibble or hoe in the soft top layer of forest earth and wood ash. Draft animals and plow, even if known, have no place in the labor amidst the tree stumps. Usually each plot carries many kinds of plants, often growing in tiers, each being cared for individually and harvested at the proper time. Although to the Western observer the swidden looks like chaos, it is actually a quite rational form of intercropping. The dense plant cover, not arranged in rows, protects the soil from erosion, and the association and succession of various crops retard soil exhaustion.

The crop complex differs according to the environmental situation, dietary habits, and other cultural factors. Maize is the staple grain in America, millets and sorghums in Africa, and rice in Southeast Asia, but all of them occur in all continents. Rice is of the so-called upland or "dry" variety, which does not need flooding. It is often grown as the single crop on swiddens in Southeast Asia and West Africa. Also important are various root crops and tubers such as yam, sweet potato, manioc (cassava), and taro. The banana and a multitude of vegetables, among them beans and peas, squash, melon, and eggplant, are quite common.

The time span the land is cultivated depends on the fertility of the soil and on the kind of crops grown. In some areas the plot is used only one year, but more common is two to three years. Besides loss of fertility, there is the problem of keeping back the forest growth which invades the clearing from every side. The abandoned plot is left to regenerate under natural vegetation succession. Light-loving grasses are the first to occupy the clearing, but they disappear as the shade increases. After some ten to twenty years a good forest of second-growth trees has reestablished itself, and the land can be cleared again to start the new cycle. Many tribes

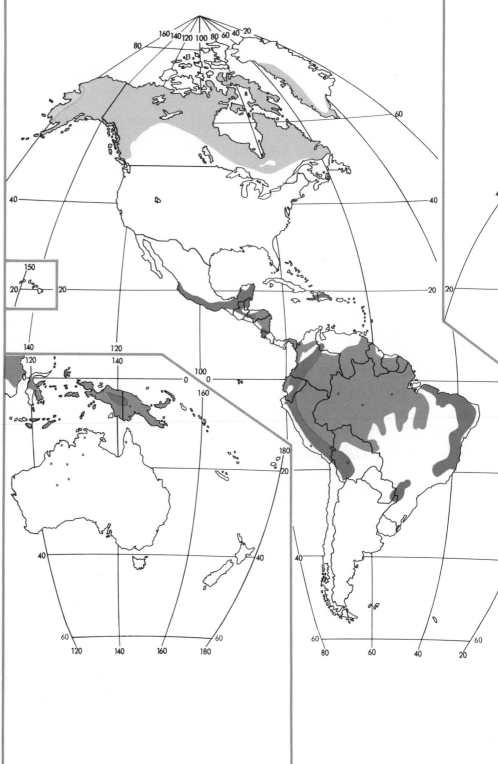

Figure 10–1. WORLD: FORMS OF LAND
USE IN TRIBAL SOCIETIES

Gathering, Hunting,
and/or Fishing

North Eurasian Herding
(Mostly Reindeer)

Swiddens (Shifting
Cultivation)

Tillage of Permanent Fields
(in Some Areas together with
Cattle Herding)

Meso–African Herding
(Mostly Cattle)

Miles

0   500   1000   1500

0   500 1000   2000
Kilometers

AITOFF'S

INTERRUPTED EQUAL-AREA

PROJECTION

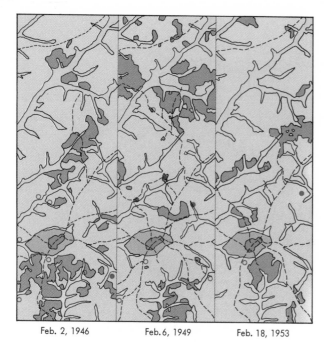

Feb. 2, 1946   Feb. 6, 1949   Feb. 18, 1953

Figure 10–2. SHIFTING AGRICULTURE AT FOKOLE, LIBERIA

The village of Fokole has about 1,000 inhabitants, most of whom engage in shifting agriculture. Dry or upland rice is the main crop. About 6 acres of land are in fallow for each acre in crop. Notice that by 1953 the farmers had returned to cultivate land that was used in 1946 but fallow in 1949. The area covered by the map accounts for only part of the land used by the people of Fokole. Based on maps prepared by P. W. Porter from air photographs taken on the dates shown.

▨ Land in Crop	◗ Village of Fokole
▨ Land in Fallow	• Half-Town (10-20 Huts)
▨ Swamp	
▨ Forest	○ Farmstead or Small Half-Town (Under 10 Huts)
----- Trail	

that practice shifting cultivation have in addition to the swiddens small permanent gardens within or near the village. Here grow coconut and other palms and fruit trees, as well as various vegetables and spices. Gathering forest products and hunting add sources of sustenance. In the African savanna* shifting cultivation occurs in association with livestock herding (p. 231).

Several intensive studies provide data on the economics of input and output of shifting cultivation in tropical America, Africa, and Asia, but it is hard to generalize them because of the diverse conditions of culture and habitat. H. C. Conklin's investigation of the Hanunoo in Mindoro, the Philippines, yielded fairly exact comparative data on labor expenditure for a new clearing in a climax forest and a new one in a secondary forest (Table 10–1). Although the two swiddens show great differences in amount of time spent on felling (a much harder job in

the older forest), guarding, and weeding, the total number of man-hours per hectare (2.47 acres)—adequate to feed a family of six—runs about the same, around 3,000. To obtain the labor expenditure per person one must divide the 3,000 hours between the family workers. Data such as these show that the labor requirements of shifting cultivation are low.

The system can function only if each village owns a sizable territory. Taking the Hanunoo data of 0.4 acre for one person's yearly food supply and assuming a fallow period of twelve years, the total area needed to feed one person is 5.2 acres. If all land were arable, a village of 200 inhabitants would need 1,040 acres, resulting in a density of 127 persons per square mile. Actually, perhaps no more than one-fourth can be used for swiddens, so that the total village area must comprise 4,160 acres or 6½ square miles. This would mean a density of 32 per square mile. Data from other areas of shifting cultivation would indicate that the density is frequently below this figure.

The usual explanation of the prevalence of

*Savanna is a vegetation cover consisting of scrub or grass with scattered trees.

shifting cultivation in the wet tropics stresses low soil fertility. Indeed, the top layer of the soil, unless rejuvenated by silt-carrying floodwaters or volcanic ash, tends to be poor in plant nutrients because physical, chemical, and organic processes intensify under constant heat and moisture conditions. The natural forest maintains a stable equilibrium with the other components—climate, soil, fauna—of the ecosystem. The shifting cultivator disrupts the closed system. His crops catch the transient availability of nutrients available in the topsoil. Inevitably, after fertility declines, the cultivator must move on to greener patches. But this presents only one side of the argument. The other is the level of technology. The tribes of Tacitus' Germania were shifting cultivators—and contrary to his opinion often on very poor, leached, gray podzols—but in time, by changing their techniques, they became tillers of permanent fields. Without denying the severe challenge of the tropical environment we need to emphasize equally man's ability to overcome such handicaps. The relatively small areas of shifting cultivation in tropical Asia suggest that its inhabitants have developed or borrowed more effective techniques to deal with their habitat than similarly located people in Africa, and particularly than those in tropical South America.

These considerations gain urgency because living conditions in many areas of shifting cultivation are deteriorating rapidly. As long as the population was sparse and wants were few this system of farming was well adjusted to the habi-

Table 10–1. Hanunoo Labor Expenditure		
	Man-hours per hectare of new swidden	
Activity	Climax forest	Secondary growth (woody)
Site selection	6+	3+
Slashing	60	100+
Felling	350+	150
Firebreaking, firing, and reburning	189+	142+
Planting	465	445
Guarding	400+	200+
Weeding	300	600
Harvesting, storing, and cleaning	610	610
Nongrain cultivation and harvesting	500+	500+
TOTAL	3,180+	2,975+

SOURCE: Conklin, 1957, 150. By permission of the Food and Agriculture Organization, Rome.

10. Agriculture in Tribal Societies, and the Plantation

Southeast Nigeria: An Ibo woman harvesting cassava (manioc) in a swidden. The flour from the starchy roots is popularly known as tapioca. The cassava plant is a native of tropical South America. [A Shell photograph]

tat. However, in the last fifty years or so, the pressure on the land has increased at an accelerating rate. First of all, colonial rule and other forms of impact from the Occident have led to a rapid growth of population. Second, more and more shifting cultivators plant part of their swiddens to commercial crops. For instance, in Indonesia a ladang, instead of being abandoned to natural vegetation, would be planted with rubber seedlings. In Africa it might be oil palms, in Polynesia coconuts, in America coffee. Such tree crops occupy the land a long time, and consequently remove it from the food-producing rotation cycle. Although theoretically one might argue that the sale of these cash crops diminishes the need for homegrown foodstuffs, in practice it does not work that way. Food production by shifting cultivation is not merely a farming method; it is the way of life, closely linked with religious values and community rituals. Every critical stage—selecting the site, clearing, planting, and harvesting—needs com-

munal action, but also the approval or appeasement of the spirits. Thus shifting cultivation continues, but more land must be cleared to provide food for more people, while the total area available has shrunk because of commercial crops. This leads to shorter fallow periods, with the result that the soil fails to regenerate completely. To counter the lowered soil fertility the agriculturists clear larger areas than formerly, which further increases the pressure on the land. Frequent fires result in grass cover and a sod hard to break with simple tools. Such grasslands in effect also must be subtracted from the arable land. In Africa, however, the use of grass savanna for swiddens is not uncommon. Perhaps the African hoe is a better tool to deal with the sod.

External forces also restrict the area available for temporary clearings. Formerly colonial governments often granted European planters land rights in "unused" village territories, unaware of how these lands functioned in the native's agricultural cycle. Modern resource management looks with disfavor on the destruction of forest, because of its economic value as well as its merit in preventing soil erosion.

There is no simple solution to these problems. One may expect that the growing pressure will gradually force people to more intensive methods of farming, as has happened in the past, but this will be a very slow process, and more painful than is acceptable in our modern age. Everywhere government agencies, often with aid from advanced countries, are searching for new farming methods to replace shifting cultivation. The schemes must take into account the specific features of each habitat as well as the habits of the people.

Livestock Herding in Africa

The tropical rain forest is inimical to grazing animals. The inhabitants of the Amazon Basin, the Guinea Coast, the Congo Basin, and the interior of Borneo have only small domestic animals, such as poultry, ducks, and pigs. But most tribal societies live in lands that have only seasonal rainfall, where the natural vegetation consists of open deciduous forest, but more often of savanna. Although the grasses are usually not very nutritious, they provide extensive grazing for cattle, sheep, and goats. The integration of crops and livestock, which seems so obvious to us as a means to maintain soil fertility, hardly exists in indigenous farming. This separation of livestock and cropping is particularly marked in Meso-Africa, where vast areas of savanna surround the tropical rain forest.

In Africa the blood-sucking tsetse fly largely determines the distribution of livestock (Figure 10–3). Certain of the various species carry the single-celled organism known as trypanosome, which when passed into the blood of man causes sleeping sickness, and into the blood of domestic animals, the so-called nagana disease. The tsetse fly flourishes in the shady but warm environment of tree and scrub cover, forming discontinuous "fly belts" within Africa south of the Sahara. The tsetse fly is doubtless an important factor in the retardation of this realm. Owing to modern drugs, sleeping sickness has ceased to be a main cause of death, but the nagana disease still wastes the cattle. For this reason alone mixed farming cannot be the substitute for shifting cultivation in many parts of Meso-Africa.

Livestock husbandry and crop farming, even where they exist side by side, are often practiced by ethnically different groups. The pastoralists, although the minority, dominate the cultivators. They attach great social, even mystical, value to their stock. The more cattle a man has, regardless of its quality, the higher is his status. The animals are not sold for beef and produce very little milk. They are like a bank account, a means of acquiring wives, who in turn will bear girls who can be married in exchange for more cattle. This value system has affected many cultivator tribes: The men tend the cattle on the natural pastures while the women work the fields. Because of the low carrying capacity of the grasslands (25 or more acres are needed for one head of cattle) the herds have to move over wide areas. Even so, most pastures in the tsetse-free areas are grossly overstocked, causing severe soil erosion. The tsetse fly is being pushed

Figure 10–3. AFRICA: REGIONS INFESTED WITH THE TSETSE FLY

Based on a map in Stamp, 1964, 160.

back by elimination of scrubland, but the new expanses of grassland are quickly filled with more half-wild cattle instead of serving to produce food crops.

Agriculture on Permanent Fields

In the tropics there are, in addition to shifting cultivation, three forms of cropping on permanent fields: (1) intensive subsistence tillage, mainly in the more advanced "traditional" societies (Chapter 11), but some in tribal societies, (2) small-scale cash-crop production, and (3) large-scale plantation farming. In this section

10. Agriculture in Tribal Societies, and the Plantation

231

we will examine these forms of land use insofar as they are employed in tribal societies.

In Southeast Asia shifting cultivation appears as a marginal and shrinking form of land use, mainly among the forest dwellers in the highlands of the Indochinese Peninsula, in Borneo, and in islands farther east. There are several well-documented cases of the change-over from swiddens to permanent fields, as for instance in the nineteenth century in Cebu, the Philippines, and the hill lands of Java, and more recently among the Toradja in central Celebes, the island now called Sulawesi. In the highlands of East Africa the dense population around Lake Victoria and on the slopes of Kilimanjaro has developed an intensive system of permanent garden cultivation, with plantains (green cooking bananas), sweet potatoes, cassava, and maize as food crops and cotton or coffee for cash. Some groups even practice stable feeding of livestock and manuring of fields in addition to crop rotation. In the wetter parts of the low savanna lands of the Sudan, especially among the Hausa of Nigeria, permanent fields are expanding with the aid of various government experimental schemes. In dry Senegal and Mauretania crops are planted as the annual floods recede from the river and lakeshores, among them rice, millet, sorghum, and beans, with peanuts as the big cash crop.

In Latin America the term tribal societies refers to Indian groups who have retained their ancient ways of life. Although milpa agriculture is common—and not only among the Indians—the Andes of Peru and Bolivia stand out as an area of permanent fields, a legacy of the civilization that once occupied this area. Land utilization is not so intensive as it once was, but in the intermontane basins and valleys, lying well below the cold plateau surface, one can still see carefully terraced plots rising from the valley bottoms in 20 to 50 or more tiers against seemingly unscalable mountain slopes. The higher terraces are not more than 10 feet wide and rise 10 feet above the lower one. Skillfully built rock walls retain the earth layer on each terrace. The lower layer of earth, coarse stones and clay, is covered by a 3-foot top layer of fine soil, carried up by human labor. These "hanging gardens"

are irrigated from ditches, fed by highland streams. The land in the valley or basin depends for irrigation on the local river, carefully canalized between stone walls. In this system, the enormous amount of labor input stands in no monetary relation to the produce. It can only be understood as a way of life of people to whom the land is almost sacred.

The temperatures at different altitudes cause a marked vertical zonation of the crops. Below 6,000 feet cassava is the main food crop, between 6,000 and 11,000 feet maize and barley prevail, and from 11,000 to 12,000 feet, the potato. Higher still, on the semiarid and cold *altiplano,* from 12,000 to 15,000 feet in elevation, Indians graze their cattle, sheep, llamas, and alpacas on coarse grasses and thorny shrubs.

Cash-crop Farming

Although the tribal societies live primarily by subsistence agriculture, to an increasing extent they produce commodities for the market. In some cases colonial governments and foreign enterprises have pressured them into doing this; in other cases they have imitated on their own initiative and in their own way the examples of plantation agriculture. Most of these cash crops do not fit into the regular swidden practice. Many are perennial bushes or trees. Their production by native smallholders means the expansion of sedentary field—or "orchard"—agriculture. The need for transportation tends to limit production to areas near the coast and navigable rivers and along the few tentacles of railroads and highways that penetrate the interior.

In Southeast Asia the main commodity is rubber from the *Hevea braziliensis,* in the 1890s introduced as a plantation crop, but soon planted by native people on abandoned ladangs. The coconut palm of Southeast Asia and the South Pacific, highly valued since ancient times for its many food and household uses, is now also widely grown for export of copra (dried coconut meat).

Within Africa there are many "islands" of

More than half of Bolivia's Indians live at high altitudes in the Andes. Since ancient times llamas, well adapted to the mountain environment, have served as beasts of burden. [Courtesy of United Nations]

native commercial production, even though their total surface is small compared to the huge area used for shifting cultivation. The Atlantic side of Africa has a far larger share of the export agriculture than the opposite side, reflecting greater proximity to the traditional European market. Senegal and Gambia produce vast amounts of peanuts while Ghana and the Western Region of Nigeria specialize in cacao, all grown by native smallholders. The same is true for the coffee and cacao of the Ivory Coast, the peanuts and coffee in northern Nigeria, and the oil palm in southeastern Nigeria. However, in the former Belgian Congo, plantations organized by Europeans grow most of the oil palms.

In the 1950s the Belgian colonial government initiated a new system to encourage the Congolese to improve their farming methods. Peasants who enrolled in the scheme were taught how to plant food and cash crops in rotation on permanent fields. A government agency bought up the cash crops such as cotton, coffee, and palm oil to eliminate the profits of middlemen and to provide a stable market. The plan appeared to work well; its continued success under present conditions is uncertain. In the eastern highlands of Africa, smallholders raise coffee and cotton, especially north and west of Lake Victoria.

Although tropical America is an important producer of agricultural commodities for the world market, the share of the Indian tribal societies is virtually nil. This lies in the peculiar nature of the socioeconomic stratification in Latin America. The Indian who has retained his bonds with his ancestral community—and only he is identified as Indian—is a subsistence cultivator. Insofar as he works outside his village he is a wage earner, a tenant, or a debt-bonded sharecropper. One can, of course, point to small amounts of surplus production that leave the Indian village for the mining center or nearby town, such as corn, wheat, coffee, bananas, and vegetables, or the sheep and alpaca wool that is sent down from the central Andes to the coast, even for export. But on the whole the tribal Indians are commercially inert.

The Plantation

It is one thing to speak of "the plantation," but quite another to define it. Everyone agrees that it is a large-scale commercial-agricultural enterprise, but few would consent to the obverse and call every large farm a plantation, such as the big wheat farms in Montana and Kansas, the huge orchards in California, the sugar-beet farms in Colorado or northern France, and the various collectives in the Soviet Union. Some writers distinguish the plantation by its location in the tropics or subtropics—in other words, they use a climatic definition. In this line of thought the large citrus farm in Florida is a plantation, but the complex of vegetable farms under central management in New Jersey is not. Others have sought the answer in the kind of crops grown, or in the use of cheap native or imported labor. Still others have pointed out that the typical plantation combines cultivation with processing of the product, giving it the character of an agricultural-industrial business. The lack of agreement has led to the counsel of despair that the word plantation should be banned from any serious discussion of agricultural production systems.

However, the term is so widely used that it cannot be ignored. The fault of all definitions so far mentioned is that they fail to include the sociocultural component present in all typical plantations. The plantation is essentially a phenomenon occurring when one culture realm intrudes into another. This view has been most clearly expressed by Edgar T. Thompson, who gave the following definition:

The plantation . . . is a large landed estate, located in an area of open resources (i.e., land-rich and labor-poor), in which social relations between diverse racial and social groups are based upon authority, involving the subordination of resident laborers to a planter for the purpose of producing an agricultural staple which is sold in a world market. (Thompson, 1935, 5)

Thompson called the plantation a "frontier institution." This is true if one admits two different interpretations of the frontier concept. In the United States the Southern plantation was a way of organizing production on land that had been virtually denuded of its indigenous tribal societies, and was, therefore, on the frontier of expanding white settlement. Here most plantations have gone with the wind of change. The other interpretation of the plantation as a frontier institution emphasizes its role as the wedge of a foreign economy into other, less advanced, societies. This, rather than migration and settlement, has been the "frontier" nature of the plantation in Asia and Africa. In the last four hundred years the plantation has been almost exclusively a form of Occidental expansion into other, non-Occidental, realms, the main exceptions being Japanese enterprises in Taiwan and western Pacific islands and the Chinese concerns in Malaysia and Indonesia. Plantations have been established not only among tribal societies, but also in countries of traditional society such as India, Ceylon, and Java.

The Plantation in Latin America. By conquest Spain and Portugal foisted onto the southern part of the New World a system of large land-ownership, often including seignorial rights over the labor of the resident Indians. Many of the early Spanish *haciendas* and *estancias de ganado* (cattle ranches) had little direct commercial purpose, but were landed estates that served the prestige and comfort of the new aristocracy. The *caballero*—the Spanish landowner on horseback—and the *peon*—the servile Indian worker—symbolized the dualism of the socioeconomic structure. Even today, in the backcountry at least, the hacienda is more a way of life for the owner and his family than a business.

The Portuguese were on the whole more interested in obtaining direct profits from their land than the Spaniards. Europe had no market for the strange American plants, so sugarcane was brought over from the Old World to provide a cash crop. The Indians did not know how to cultivate the cane, nor had they any tradition of private landownership and commercial production. Thus, the plantation came into being, with capital and management provided by the Portuguese entrepreneur, labor by the Indians (soon to be complemented and then replaced by Negro slaves), on land taken from the Indian communities and granted by the king. Subsequently other crops were added, such as cotton, tobacco, cacao, coffee, and, much later, bananas. English, Dutch, and French invaded the Iberians' domain and took over or created new plantations in the Caribbean and the Guianas.

Toward the end of the nineteenth century, western Europe and the United States had far surpassed Latin America in commercial-industrial development. The latter was looked upon as a source of raw materials, vegetable as well as mineral. This led to a new cultural intrusion, especially of entrepreneurs from the United States. They furnished capital and management, but used local land and wage labor to produce the needed staple goods, such as bananas and sugar. This stratification of cultures—Indian, traditional Latin, and modern industrial-commercial—occurs over large parts of Middle and South America. It is least so in Argentina, Uruguay, southern Brazil, and Chile; here the Indian element is virtually absent and the modern way of life dominates the cities, leaving the countryside as the refuge of the traditional

economy. But in rural areas too, significant social and economic changes are taking place with the result that the large-scale agricultural enterprises are more like farms than plantations.

In Mexico, land tenure has changed so much in the last fifty years that little is left of the old *latifundium* system (from Latin *latus,* broad, and *fundus,* estate). Before 1910 a small minority of landed aristocrats owned most of the land, which was worked by Indian sharecroppers or debt-bonded tenants. There were sugar and coffee plantations, but most of the private holdings were used for cattle grazing. In the second half of the nineteenth century Spanish-Mexican landowners in northern Yucatan developed a veritable plantation district, replacing maize and livestock by henequen, an agave plant yielding hard fiber.

In the Mexican Revolution of 1910–1920 and by subsequent reforms, estate lands over 750 acres were expropriated, reassigned to adjacent Indian *pueblos* (towns) as *ejidos* (common lands), and then parceled out for the use of individual families.. These measures eliminated the old landed aristocracy and raised the morale of the peasants, but they also caused a decline in productivity of the land, because the small farms produced less efficiently than the former large-scale enterprises.

The henequen plantations of Yucatan have been transformed, too, but have retained some of the old features. Most Spanish-Mexican landowners still have their allotment of 750 acres, and, highly important, also the fiber-processing plant. Maya Indians now cultivate former sections of the hacienda, and bring their bundles of henequen leaves to the *desfibradora* for processing. The former functional unity of landownership and agricultural management has been replaced by a probably unique compromise: an association of communal and private land tenure, both producing the cash crop, which is processed by the private producer. It seems to work, although it should be added that the yields in the *ejido* sector are lower than those obtained on the private hacienda fields.

Puerto Rico offers a good example of the Spanish agrarian system incisively modified by planned evolution rather than revolution. Before 1940 large absentee corporations, mostly

American-owned, used the best lands for sugarcane production, and less favorable areas for livestock. The land reform restricted ownership by corporations to 500 acres and gave the excess to Puerto Rican farmers in private ownership. The companies still operate sugar refineries, but buy most of the cane from the small planters. In contrast, Cuba follows the Communist model of eliminating private enterprise and substituting large-scale state-run farms for the former latifundia. It is too early to evaluate the effect on Cuba's economy, but the term "collective" is now more appropriate than "plantation."

Between these transformations in the north and south of Latin America there remains a vast area where the plantation survives—either as the traditional hacienda with peonage or as the modern estate with wage labor. Among them are the plantations on several of the Caribbean islands raising sugar or bananas, those in the coastal lowlands (*tierra caliente*) of Central America growing bananas, sugarcane, or cotton, and others in the highlands (*tierra templada*) producing coffee. Estates along the dry Peruvian coast raise sugar and cotton under irrigation. The northeastern coastal region of Brazil has sugar and cacao plantations, but the industry is only a shadow of its golden age in the sixteenth and seventeenth centuries when sugar was king. A plantation boom in coffee started in the 1850s in the southern hill lands of Rio de Janeiro state and then moved to the large expanse of *terra roxa* in the state of São Paulo, which still is the main coffee region. As so often with commercial crop production in Brazil, the coffee *fazenda* was, and partly still is, a migratory, speculative enterprise. When the virgin soil is exhausted the planter moves on to new lands.

Plantations in Asia and Africa. The Spaniards transplanted their colonial land tenure from Mexico to the Philippines, more specifically to the lowlands of Luzon and the Visayan Islands, where they gained effective control. The incentive for production of staple commodities was small; apart from raising some sugar, tobacco, and abaca (Manila hemp), the haciendas, including large church holdings, remained at subsistence level until late in the nineteenth century.

In India and the present Indonesia events took a different turn. For ages the spices from these lands had reached Europe by means of various intermediary traders. The discovery of the sea route to the "East Indies" enabled the Europeans to gain control of this trade. There was no need, as in America, to superimpose a new production system on the native forms of economy. Forced deliveries were often demanded, but the actual production of crops was left to the local people. The picture changed in the nineteenth century. Two major events diminished the earning power of the American plantations: The abolition of slavery disturbed the labor supply, and the newly won independence of Latin American countries resulted in unstable governments. In Europe and North America the spreading industrialization demanded more as well as new raw materials, and the growing urban population needed or desired tropical fats, sugar, tobacco, coffee, and tea. Investors as well as entrepreneurs began to look for places more promising than tropical America. In South and Southeast Asia colonial governments were expanding and strengthening their rule. The crowded peasants of India, Java, and China offered a large reservoir of docile and industrious labor. The opening of the Suez Canal in 1869 greatly diminished the handicap of larger distance from Europe than the "West Indies." From then on the trickle of investment in tropical Asia swelled to a stream. Grown on plantations, cane sugar became a major export commodity of Java and the Philippines, and tea of Assam and Ceylon. Cinchona and *Hevea brasiliensis,* both American plants, were introduced into Southeast Asia, which soon gained virtually a monopoly on the production of quinine and rubber. Coconut and oil palm, sisal, abaca, tobacco, and kapok also became important plantation products.

American rule in the Philippines, faced with the Spanish legacy of a severe land tenure problem, discouraged the formation of new large holdings. Moreover, the announced intention to prepare the islands for independence made American investors reluctant to put money into long-term business ventures. Nevertheless, on a considerable number of existing large landholdings in Luzon, Panay, and Negros, sugar production was intensified. Building upon the Spanish tradition, the plantation consists of a number of tenant farms, each producing sugar cane under the direction of the central management, and food crops for family use. The tenants bring the cane to the owner's mill (*central*) for processing.

When the Dutch in Indonesia and the British in Malaya and India began to develop plantations in the mid-nineteenth century, they had to choose between locating in densely populated areas where labor was abundant but land scarce, or in sparsely populated sections where large tracts were available but labor was absent. In most cases they took the latter alternative and imported the necessary labor. In this manner evolved the tea plantations in the hills of Assam, of southern India, and of Ceylon. Similarly, the lowlands of the western Malay Peninsula became the site for numerous rubber plantations, using Indians as laborers (Figure 10–4). The Dutch developed a virtually empty wilderness on the northern east coast of Sumatra into a prosperous estate region, with the aid of Chinese and, later, Javanese labor, as well as the participation of British, American, and other foreign capital. Here tobacco, rubber, oil palm, and sisal grow in the lowlands, and tea at higher elevations. In densely populated Java the available ground lay in the highlands, which drew cinchona and tea estates. The sugar plantations, however, needed space in the irrigated plains. A complex system of rotation was worked out by which the plantation used the peasant's rice lands and labor for one crop of cane, followed by several years of peasant rice farming. Growing population pressure as well as national sentiment militated against this arrangement, which was not revived after World War II.

The late "opening up" of Africa retarded establishment of plantations in this continent. True, the Portuguese at an early date developed plantations on the little islands of Príncipe and São Tomé, in the Gulf of Guinea, and the Arabs in the early nineteenth century planted large orchards of cloves on Zanzibar Island. But else-

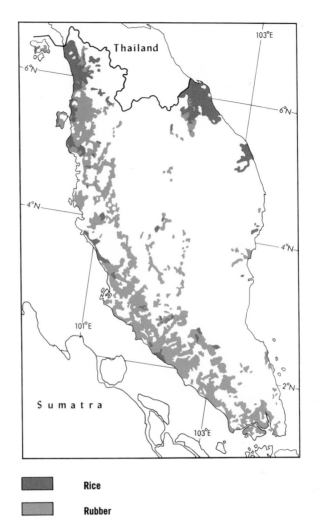

Figure 10–4. MALAYA: RUBBER- AND RICE-PRODUCING AREAS

Since Malaya some fifty years ago was very sparsely populated, much land was available for rubber planting, first by estates, later also by smallholders. The rice-growing areas indicate the main concentrations of Malay semisubsistence agriculture. Most of the remainder of the Federation of Malaya is dense forest, on mountains and in swamps. Based on a map published by the Superintendent of Maps, Federation of Malaya.

10. Agriculture in Tribal Societies, and the Plantation

237

where the European large-scale agrarian enterprise dates only from the end of the nineteenth century or later.

The eastern highlands, because of their temperate climate, areas of volcanic soil, and sparse population, attracted European settlers, who acquired medium- to large-size landholdings. Although most are regular farms, run by the settler, his family, and some servants, there are also a number of sisal and tea plantations, worked with a large labor force under white management. The sugar plantations in the lowlands of Natal (Republic of South Africa) have also long used Indian labor. On the Atlantic side there are coffee and oil-palm plantations from Cameroon to Congo and Angola. The inaccessibility of Africa's interior has remained a hindrance to the spread of plantations. They are either close to the coast or along the few railroads that penetrate inland.

Prospects of the Plantation. The prospects of the plantation, defined as a cultural intrusion or a "frontier" institution, look dim. The desire for national independence, including freedom from foreign economic interference, tends to restrict or even eliminate the role of the plantation. The reforms in several Latin American countries and the taking over of foreign plantations in Cuba and Indonesia are cases in point. Moreover, since economic development involves the further diffusion of Occidental production methods, the plantation is likely to lose its distinct character amidst other large-scale commercial-agricultural enterprises.

In retrospect it is easy to detect the faults of the plantation, especially in the acquisition of land, treatment of labor, or political interference. But such criticisms must be balanced, or at least supplemented, by recognizing the beneficial effects of the system. In many areas it was the plantation that led to the building of roads, railroads, and ports. The modern plantation also supports schools and hospitals, either directly or indirectly through taxes. Introduction of new crops by the plantation has frequently led to their adoption by the local subsistence cultivator, thus broadening his economic base. Efficient, often highly scientific, methods of cultivation and processing demonstrate, however unintentionally, to the native population standards of production which they must emulate in striving for economic progress. And last but not least, in many underdeveloped countries plantation products provide much of the foreign exchange needed to purchase manufactured articles, especially producer goods, for the further development of the country.

Citations

Conklin, H. C. *Hanunoo Agriculture: A Report of an Integral System of Shifting Cultivation in the Philippines,* Food and Agriculture Organization, Forestry Development Paper no. 12, Rome, 1957.

———. "The Study of Shifting Agriculture," *Current Anthropology,* 2 (1961): 27–61 (with extensive bibliography).

Food and Agriculture Organization "Shifting Agriculture," *Unasylva,* 2 (1957).

Sauer, C. O. *Agricultural Origins and Dispersals,* The American Geographical Society, New York, 1952.

Stamp, L. D. *Africa: A Study in Tropical Development,* New York, 1964. [Map]

Thompson, E. T. *The Plantation,* Chicago, 1935.

Further Readings

Domestication of Plants and Animals

Ames, O. *Economic Annuals and Human Cultures,* Botanical Museum, Harvard University, Cambridge, Mass., 1939.

Anderson, E. *Plants, Man, and Life,* Boston, 1952.

Burkill, I. H. "Habits of Man and the Origins of the Cultivated Plants of the Old World," *Proceedings of the Linnean Society of London,* 164 (1951–1952): 12–42. Reprinted in Wagner, P. L., and Mikesell, M. W. (eds.) *Readings in Cultural Geography,* Chicago, 1962, 248–281.

Candolle, A. de *Origin of Cultivated Plants* (translated from the French edition of 1855), New York, 1885.

Cutler, H. "Food Sources in the New World," *Agricultural History,* 28 (1954): 43–49. Reprinted in Wagner, P. L., and Mikesell, M. W. (eds.) *Readings in Cultural Geography,* Chicago, 1962, 282–289.

Epstein, H. "Domestication Features in Animals as Functions of Human Society," *Agricultural History,* 29 (1955): 137–146. Reprinted in Wagner, P. L., and Mikesell, M. W. (eds.) *Readings in Cultural Geography,* Chicago, 1962, 290–301.

Hahn, E. *Die Haustiere und ihre Beziehungen zur Wirtschaft des Menschen,* Leipzig, 1896.

Harris, D. R. "New Light on Plant Domestication and the Origins of Agriculture: A Review," *Geographical Review,* 57 (1967): 90–107.

Vavilov, N. I. "The Origin, Variation, Immunity and Breeding of Cultivated Plants" (translated from the Russian), *Chronica Botanica,* 13 (1951): 1–366.

Shifting Cultivation

Bartlett, H. H. "Fire, Primitive Agriculture, and Grazing in the Tropics," in Thomas, W. L. (ed.) *Man's Role in Changing the Face of the Earth,* Chicago, 1956, 692–720.

Cook, O. F. "Milpa Agriculture: A Primitive Agricultural System," *Annual Report of the Smithsonian Institution for 1919,* Washington, D.C., 1921, 307–326.

Deshler, W. "Cattle in Africa: Distribution, Types, Problems," *Geographical Review,* 53 (1963): 59–78.

Forde, C. D. *Habitat, Economy, and Society,* 2d ed., London, 1952.

Freeman, J. D. *Iban Agriculture,* Colonial Research Studies, no. 18, London, 1955.

Gourou, P. "The Quality of Land Use of Tropical Cultivators," in Thomas, W. L. (ed.) *Man's Role in Changing the Face of the Earth,* Chicago, 1956, 336–349.

Murdock, G. P. "Staple Subsistence Crops in Africa," *Geographical Review,* 50 (1960): 523–540.

Ormeling, F. J. *The Timor Problem,* Groningen, the Netherlands, and Djakarta, Indonesia, 1957.

Pelzer, J. K. *Pioneer Settlement in the Asiatic Tropics,* American Geographical Society, Special Publication no. 29, New York, 1945.

Schlippe, P. de *Shifting Agriculture in Africa: The Zande System of Agriculture,* London, 1955.

Watters, R. F. "The Nature of Shifting Cultivation," *Pacific Viewpoint,* 1 (1960): 59–99.

Tillage on Permanent Fields and Cash-crop Farming

Barrau, J. *Polynesian and Micronesian Subsistence Agriculture,* South Pacific Commission, Noumea, 1956.

Brass, L. J. "Stone Age Agriculture in New Guinea," *Geographical Review,* 34 (1944): 555–569.

Buchanan, K. M. "Recent Developments in Nigerian Peasant Farming," *Malayan Journal of Tropical Geography,* 2 (1954): 17–34.

Hance, W. A., et al. "Source Areas of Export Production in Tropical Africa," *Geographical Review,* 51 (1961): 487–499.

Highsmith, R. M. (ed.) *Case Studies in World Geography,* Englewood Cliffs, N.J., 1961.

Jarrett, H. R. "The Present Setting of the Oil Palm Industry: with Special Reference to West Africa," *Journal of Tropical Geography,* 11 (1958): 59–69.

Spencer, J. E., and Hale, G. A. "The Origin, Nature, and Distribution of Agricultural Terracing," *Pacific Viewpoint,* 2 (1961): 1–40.

Swanson, E. "Terrace Agriculture in the Central Andes," *Davidson Journal of Anthropology,* 1 (1955): 123–132.

Ward, R. G. "Cash Cropping and the Fijian Village," *Geographical Journal,* 130 (1964): 484–506.

Plantations

Allen, G. C., and Donnithorne, A. G. *Western Enterprise in Indonesia and Malaya,* London and New York, 1957.

Broek, J. O. M. "The Economic Development of the Outer Provinces of the Netherlands Indies," *Geographical Review,* 30 (1940): 190–196.

Chardon, R. E. *Geographic Aspects of Plantation Agriculture in Yucatan,* National Academy of Sciences—National Research Council Publication no. 876, Washington, D.C., 1961.

———. "Hacienda and Ejido in Yucatan: The Example of Santa Ana Cuca," *Annals of the Association of American Geographers,* 53 (1963): 174–193.

James, P. E. *Latin America,* 3d ed., New York, 1959.

Pan American Union, *Plantation Systems of the New World,* Social Science Monographs, no. 7, Washington, D.C., 1959.

Prunty, M., Jr. "The Renaissance of the Southern Plantation," *Geographical Review,* 45 (1955): 459–491.

Thompson, E. T. "The Climatic Theory of the Plantation," *Agricultural History,* 15 (1941): 49–60.

Waibel, L. *Probleme der Landwirtschaftsgeographie,* Breslau, 1933.

———. "The Tropical Plantation System," *Scientific Monthly,* 52 (1941): 156–160.

———. "The Climatic Theory of the Plantation: A Critique," *Geographical Review,* 32 (1942): 307–310.

Withington, W. A.: "Changes and Trends in Patterns of North Sumatra's Estate Agriculture, 1938–1959," *Tijdschrift voor Economische en Sociale Geografie,* 55 (1964): 8–13.

11. Land Use in Traditional Societies

Land utilization in the Islamic, South Asian, and East Asian civilizations ranges from highly intensive crop tillage on well-watered alluvial plains to nomadic herding in arid regions. While advanced in technology and organization compared to tribal economies, the societies occupying Asia's rimlands and North Africa are backward when contrasted with the level of productivity which most of the Occident has attained in recent centuries. There are, of course, no clear and firm lines dividing the types of economy. Some traditional societies are catching up with the West; on the other hand, some parts of the Occidental world still cling to ancestral ways of making a living.

Low Productivity per Worker

The most striking feature of the Middle East and the monsoon lands of Asia is the high density of agricultural population. Everywhere farms are small, from 2 to 5 acres, rarely over 10. Moreover, the holding is often fragmented into several parcels scattered around the village. Draft animals and plow, even if available, cannot be used effectively on the smaller plots. Much labor, therefore, is performed with hand tools. The yields, even where fairly high per acre—an exception rather than the rule—are distressingly scant when measured against the input of labor. This small productivity per worker is the root cause of the low level of living. The amount of food the average farmer produces sustains his family and one to two additional nonfarming people at the bare subsistence level. In contrast, the American farm family produces enough food to support lavishly twenty families. To put it in another way, in the traditional societies over two-thirds of the labor force are engaged in agriculture. Although all are needed at the critical phases of production, such as planting and harvesting, there is little work at other times. Thus, the villages hide much unemployment; under near static economic conditions the outlets for more productive employment outside agriculture are small.

Intensive Crop Tillage

Although agriculture appears to have started in the uplands of the Middle East where grain cultivation depended on rainfall, it reached its early climax in the river lands of Mesopotamia, Egypt, western India, and northern China (Chapter 3). In these arid and semiarid regions evolved techniques of water control and plowing, organization of labor, and forms of land use which spread widely into other parts of Asia and North Africa.

A different form of agriculture originated in moist tropical Asia, based on the propagation of tubers by vegetative reproduction and, above all, the growing of rice on flooded fields. Wet rice or *sawah** cultivation is one of the truly great inventions of agriculture. Its origin lies in Bengal or one of the other floodplains of mainland Southeast Asia. In vital contrast to the tropical swidden, the sawah is a permanent field not subject to erosion, which can be relied upon to yield good harvests generation after generation. In the course of prehistory the practice of wet-rice cultivation moved north and west, where it met and mingled with the Middle Eastern system in its spread to east and south. Out of the encounter have come various "crossbreeds" of agriculture: planting of rice, followed by a wheat crop; the use of hoe or spade on small plots side by side with plowing on larger fields; and the raising of root crops on hilly ground next to grain cultivation on level surfaces (Figure 11–1).

Crop rotation and manuring of fields are widely practiced. Irrigated lands are leveled and diked, in some areas rising in tiers of terraces above the valley floor. Or man-made levees protect the lowlands against river floods. Canals and ditches (often with ingenious devices to lift water), wells, dams, and reservoirs serve to irrigate the fields. Intercropping—that is, raising two or more crops simultaneously on the same field—is a common technique. In like manner, the flooded rice fields may be stocked with fish to provide a double harvest. Where climate permits, two or even three successive crops are raised in one year. Though all these tasks require a tremendous labor input, the produce supports in turn a large agrarian population. Like the chicken and the egg, it is hard to say whether increasing population forced more intensive production, or the development of more productive techniques led to the survival of more people. However this may be, the need for food prohibits the detour of plant foods via large livestock to produce meat and dairy products, so common in Occidental society. Only land not suitable for crops, or the

Sawah is the Malay-Indonesian word for a field capable of being flooded for the cultivation of rice. Another term is paddy field, derived from the Malay-Indonesian *padi,* meaning unhusked rice.

Figure 11–1. AFRICA AND ASIA: FORMS OF LAND USE IN TRADITIONAL SOCIETIES

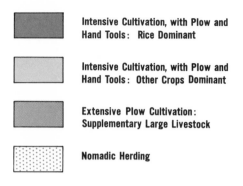

Intensive Cultivation, with Plow and Hand Tools: Rice Dominant

Intensive Cultivation, with Plow and Hand Tools: Other Crops Dominant

Extensive Plow Cultivation: Supplementary Large Livestock

Nomadic Herding

stubble on harvested fields, is left for grazing cattle, water buffalo, donkeys, or camels—used mainly as draft or pack animals. Milk is not part of the traditional diet in East and Southeast Asia, and has only a modest place in India and the Middle East. Fowl and pig serve as scavengers around the village and are eaten, unless religious taboos prohibit the pig's presence. Fish provide an important source of animal protein, but simple boats and gear keep down the catch. Lack of good preservation methods restricts marketing to coastal areas. Japan is the outstanding exception to this general statement.

Toward the dry interior, land use becomes less intensive, except for oasis culture, and often consists of dry farming of one crop, before giving way to pastoral nomadism. Along the Mediterranean Sea, agriculture shows greater resemblance to its south European counterpart, with many fruit and olive orchards and vineyards. In Southeast Asia the mingling of cultures has caused a mosaic of land use from shifting cultivation to terrace farming.

Main Crops

Rice, a highly nutritious grain, needs a hot growing season and a great deal of water. It requires much labor to care for the seedlings in

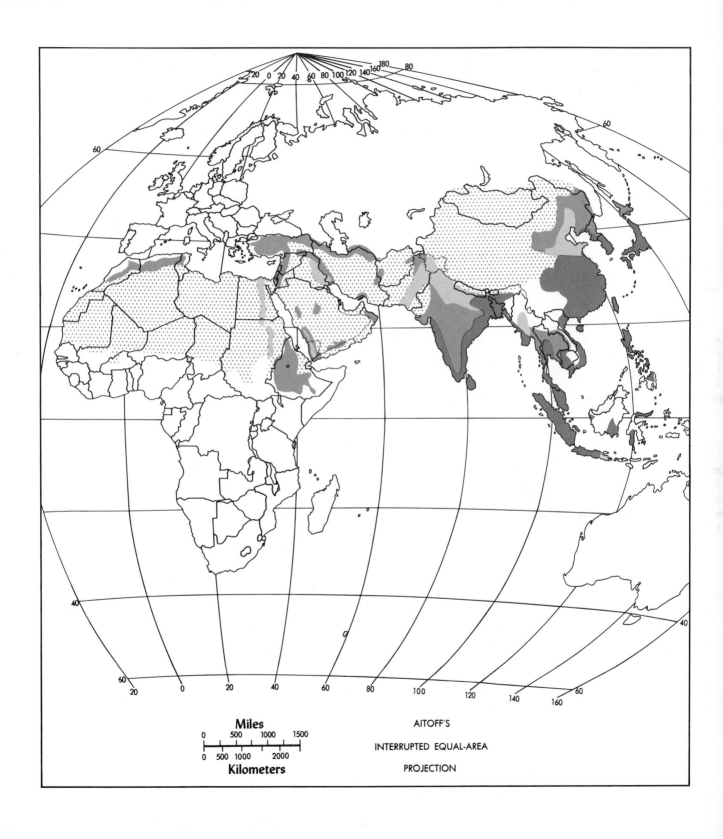

Miles
0   500   1000   1500

0   500   1000   2000
Kilometers

AITOFF'S

INTERRUPTED EQUAL-AREA

PROJECTION

the nursery bed, to transplant them to the prepared field, to regulate the flooding of the field and its draining when the grain ripens, and to harvest the crop. Water is the critical element. Fortunately the Asian "wet" monsoon brings rain in the warm season. This provides water for one rice crop and in a few areas even for two. More commonly, if the growing season is long enough, a "dry" crop follows the rice harvest on the drained sawah. Paddy fields must be level. Terracing hillsides requires a tremendous amount of labor. And the soil must not be so porous that it lets the water drain off underground. All this means that only a part of the arable land is suitable for rice. The remainder grows "dry" or "upland" crops, either annuals like maize, tubers, and leafy vegetables, or perennials such as fruit, nut, and rubber trees, or tea and coffee bushes.

The other major grain, wheat, though irrigated in some dry climates, is mainly raised in lands of moderate rainfall. It does not do well in moist and hot climates. Moreover, it meets in these areas the cultural preference for rice. However, wheat often is the second field crop (after another "dry" crop or rice), sown in the fall and harvested in spring. In cold-winter climates it is sown in spring and harvested in the summer. Though wheat does not need large amounts of moisture, some other grains such as barley, millet, and sorghum resist drought better. These crops, therefore, characterize lands of low and uncertain rainfall where irrigation is not feasible. The following brief survey of some major regions will help to obtain a more concrete picture.

Land Use in East Asia

Intensity of land use reaches its peak in the humid lowlands of China, Japan, and Korea. The laborious care bestowed on each plot, even each plant, is like that of the painstaking gardener. As Marco Polo said of China as early as the thirteenth century, "no spot on earth is allowed to lie idle that can possibly be cultivated."

China. Before the Communist regime collectivized agriculture in mainland China, the average farm comprised 2 to 3 acres, and consisted of some six plots scattered around the village. Although the need for land of different quality (e.g., for dry crops and for wet rice) justified some dispersal, the excessive fragmentation resulted from land-tenure customs, as well as from land hunger, which made each bit of land, however poorly located, desirable. In the classical Chinese tradition, landownership gave higher prestige than wealth gained in trade or manufacturing. Before the Communist revolution the wealthier families and clans left the working of the soil to tenants, who comprised perhaps as much as 60 percent of all farmers.

Much of China is too mountainous or dry for growing crops. Estimates for cultivated land run from 10 to 15 percent of the total area. (For India and Pakistan this percentage is 29, for Japan 16, the United States 14). Pasture occupies 20 percent, mainly in the semiarid western and northern sections, and forest only 8 percent, partly because of destruction of the tree cover on hillslopes, followed by soil erosion.

In China Proper, the agrarian way of life as well as the landscape differ sharply in north and south, the division running approximately along the Chin Ling Mountains and the Hwai River. In the North the growing season ranges from five to eight months, the precipitation (mainly in summer) from 16 inches in the northwest to 30 inches in the southeast. The rainfall varies from year to year, exposing the region to severe drought as well as to the devastating floods of the Huang Ho. The longer growing season of the South extends to the full year on the southeastern coast, and its longer rainy period measures from 40 to 60 inches, in some areas even over 80 inches. The North has, however, the advantage of a larger cultivable plain, since the South, though it includes the Yangtze Valley, is for the larger part a hilly or even mountainous land.

Farming has adjusted itself to these contrasting ecological conditions. The North grows mainly wheat, kaoliang (a sorghum), cotton, soybean, and millet, while in the South the dominant crop is rice. The nonirrigable lands in the South produce sweet potatoes, yams and other tubers, maize, peanuts, citrus fruits, tea, and tung (valuable for its oil), also, though less than formerly, mulberry trees to feed silkworms. In the North, oxen are widely used to draw plow and cart; in the South the water buffalo pulls the plow, but often the peasant works his small plot by hand tools. Much of the traditional transportation in the South is by boat over the numerous rivers, canals, and lakes. The Yangtze region forms the transition zone between North and South. Its preferred food crop is rice, but wheat is grown as the second crop on the drained paddy fields.

The peasant who favored the revolution because he longed for an unencumbered farm of his own was led in three stages to living in a commune. The first step, formation of *mutual-aid teams,* brought together a few farm families to pool labor, field animals, and tools, but not the land. Next came the *cooperative,* which managed the land as a unit. The final step established the *commune,* comprising scores of villages and 20,000 or more people, in which everyone became a wage earner, with no other possessions than a few personal belongings.

The reforms released large numbers of farm workers who were forced into labor battalions to build dams for new irrigation and hydro-electric projects, construct dikes for flood control, reforest hillsides, or work in new factories. Since China has little capital, but an abundance of labor, humans are exploited to the last twitching muscle to produce capital goods. Besides land reforms, the new Chinese government has intensified agricultural research, the fight against crop damage by insects, rodents, and diseases, and the production of commercial fertilizers.

Though changes brought about by the Communist revolution cannot as yet be evaluated, there can be little doubt that Chinese farming needed reform. Yields per acre, while fairly good when compared with those of countries like India and Java, took inordinate amounts of labor, mainly by debt-burdened tenants who paid exorbitant rents to landlords. The trend in modern agriculture is toward larger units that make possible more efficient employment of labor. Such field consolidation, however, is less advantageous in much of southern China because of the terrain and because transplanting rice is best done by hand. It may have been more successful in the plains of northern China, especially in Manchuria, which because of its recent settlement had already a more commercial-agricultural structure and larger farms.

Japan. The simple fact that only one-third of the labor force is employed in agriculture underscores the repeated assertion that Japan does not fit the stereotype of the traditional Asian society. But even "modern" Japan is quite Oriental in its way of farming. The average operating unit comprises only 2½ acres, and over half of the cropland is used for wet-rice cultivation. The "gardening" form of agriculture, so typical for China, extends into Japan.

The climate of Japan favors agriculture. Although the northern island of Hokkaido has only 120 to 150 days of growing season, the very southern end of Kyushu rarely has frost. Precipitation is adequate for agriculture in all parts, ranging from 40 inches in interior basins to 125 inches in some coastal districts. The mountainous terrain, however, severely restricts the arable land. Only 16 percent of the surface is cultivated (with very little room for expansion) and 4 percent is in pasture.

The year-round warm and moist climate along the south coasts of Kyushu and Shikoku islands permits the harvesting of two successive rice crops per year. From here on north to about the latitude of Sendai in northern Honshu two varieties of rice are interplanted, one maturing several weeks in advance of the other. Or, the drained rice fields are planted in fall to wheat, barley, or vegetables. But many low-lying rice lands remain fallow after the harvest because they are too waterlogged for raising other crops. The upper level of the lowlands is hard to irrigate, and is therefore devoted to dry crops, such as sweet potatoes, grains, and vegetables. On the lower hillslopes tea is an important crop. Mulberry trees, once so vital to Japan's silk industry but now of minor importance, are being replaced more and more by orchards,

11. Land Use in Traditional Societies

from oranges in the warmest sections to apples on the mountainsides.

The northern island of Hokkaido, not settled by Japanese farmers until the latter half of the nineteenth century, remains in many ways still a frontier. In spite of the rather short growing season, the Japanese have succeeded in producing rice here, but the cash crops are typically those of a northern climate: sugar beets, white potatoes, beans, and apples. There is also a substantial dairy industry, with cornfields, pastures, and silos reflecting the influence of American advisers in the nineteenth century. Farms are about 10 acres, considerably larger than those in the homeland.

Modern Japanese agriculture developed in response to the industrialization of the country. The growing market sales provided cash for buying commercial fertilizer and better seed and planting stock. But until the end of World War II only one-third of the farmers owned any land at all. Land rents were high, farming folk poor. Land reform, initiated by the American occupation authorities, transformed the peasants into a class of landowning farmers. Nearly 80 percent now are full owners, and 18 percent part owners. Yields per acre increased with intensive use of commercial fertilizers, insecticides, and high-grade seeds; together with better techniques, including the introduction of small tractors, they have raised considerably the productivity per man-hour. Since the small farms support a family of five or six persons, there is much underemployment. The government strives to broaden other opportunities for employment so that the farm population may be further reduced by one-fourth. In spite of all improvements, supplying food for Japan's population of 100 million remains a serious problem (see Chapter 18).

South Asia

This realm, stretching from the mountain arc in the north to the island of Ceylon in the south, is less than half the size of the United States, but contains 600 million people, over two-thirds of them tillers of the soil. Again, as in East Asia, the amount of labor applied to each acre of arable land is prodigious, but crop yields are well below those of China, not to speak of Japan. It is no wonder that the peasants of South Asia are among the poorest.

The tillable land lies mainly in the vast alluvium-filled trough at the foot of the mountains, drained by Indus, Ganges, and Brahmaputra, and in the coastal plains and river deltas on the east coast. The dissected plateau of the peninsula offers only pockets and ribbons of arable land. The length of the growing season presents no problem, since in the lowlands killing frosts occur only in the very northwestern corner. The moisture supply is the critical factor. South Asia's seasonal rhythm of rainfall depends largely on the monsoons.

Most of South Asia has a pronounced division into dry and wet seasons. The duration of each and the amount of rain vary regionally as well as annually. While the Sind and the Thar Desert in West Pakistan remain virtually rainless the year-round, the Assam hills in the northeast receive a deluge of 400 inches (average) during the six months of their rainy season. The monsoon-exposed west rim of the peninsular upland and the southwestern highlands of Ceylon measure an average annual total of 100 to 200 inches, all of it coming in June to October. But these wet places are exceptions to the generally scant and uncertain moisture in the areas where most Indians live. Best off are the lower Ganges plain and the delta it shares with the Brahmaputra, in Bihar and Bengal, the latter now divided between India and East Pakistan. Here, where the mean annual rainfall of over 60 inches is ample for agriculture, including wet-rice cultivation, the population reaches its greatest density. The upper Ganges plain, the upper Punjab, and the northeastern part of the peninsular upland receive between 40 and 60 inches, which seems adequate until one remembers the high rate of evaporation and the annual variability of precipitation. The remainder of the subcontinent, apart from the mountains, has less than 40 inches; it comprises most of peninsular India and of the fertile Punjab. Although on the

**Figure 11–2. A VILLAGE IN HIMACHAL
PRADESH, INDIA**

Shakrori, a small village of about 350 inhabitants,
lies in the foothills of the Himalaya Mountains on
the bank of the Sutlej River. The main crops are
wheat, rice, and corn. Irrigation water is drawn
from the river. The three main groups living in the
village are Brahmans, Rajputs, and Lohars (black-
smiths). Other castes represented are Sood (traders),
Chamar (scheduled caste), and Kumhar (potters).
Based on a sketch in *Census of India*, 1963,
vol. 20, part 6.

▨ Pasture	— Field Boundaries
▨ Grove	— Streams
▨ Housing	┉ Irrigation Channel
— Motorable Road	+ Temple
--- Mule Road	○ Playground
— Footpath	○ Water Mill

wetter margins some hardy crops succeed on
natural moisture, more intensive land use and
dependable harvests must rely on irrigation
(Figure 11–2).

Land classified as "arable" amounts to 490
million acres, of which actually some 310 million acres (0.6 acre per person) are used each
year. The remainder lies fallow, or is hardly
ever planted, because of unfavorable soil or
drainage conditions or lack of water. The 310
million acres of cropland comprise 29 percent of
the total land surface of the subcontinent. Only
a small fraction is double-cropped. Rice is grown
on one-fourth of the crop area, various sorghums and millets on almost one-third, wheat
on one-tenth; cotton and oilseeds each occupy
about 6 percent of the cropland.

Rice, though produced wherever the water
supply is adequate, is mainly concentrated in
the lower Ganges plain and the delta lands from
Bengal southward along the east coast, as well

as in the narrow western coastal zone. In the
Ganges-Brahmaputra delta, jute, the main export crop of the region, occupies part of the
flooded lands.

Wheat, an important crop in the north, is
planted as a second crop after rice or on dry
fields; in the arid west it is grown under irrigation. The semiarid western sector as well as
the interior of the peninsula produce dry crops
such as millets and sorghums. The poor can
rarely afford rice, though they may live in rice-
growing regions; instead they eat millet and
sorghum. Only in Punjab and west thereof is
wheat the staple grain. Various kinds of peas,
beans, and tubers add to the diet.

Fats and oils are mainly derived from oilseed
plants such as sesame, castor, flax (linseed),
rape, and peanuts, which are widely grown
under dry cultivation. Some of them, especially
peanuts, make a substantial item for export.
Cotton, most of it yielding a short, coarse fiber,

*11. Land Use
in
Traditional
Societies*

is an important cash crop in the western Deccan, and in Gujarat, Punjab, and Sind; in the arid sections it must, of course, have irrigation.

The number of livestock in South Asia is huge; for India alone it is estimated there are over 175 million cattle, 50 million water buffalo, 40 million sheep, 60 million goats, and 1.3 million horses. Hindus eat no beef, and many Indian Moslems avoid it, although their religion permits it. Apart from the beef taboo, many Indians are vegetarians. Animals thus contribute mainly milk to the diet, largely in the form of ghee (clarified butter), but the yield per animal and the average consumption per person are sadly low. Since livestock feed on nonarable or fallow land, supplemented by grain straw, they are generally undernourished. Cattle dung, so badly needed to restore soil fertility, is mainly used for fuel. Oxen and buffalo serve chiefly as draft animals for cart and plow.

Though there are serious deficiencies in animal protein, the people exploit the surrounding seas very little. Their fishing vessels have very limited range; their methods and facilities for preserving the catch are inadequate. The average annual consumption of fish per capita is less than 5 pounds, except in Ceylon, where it is close to 20, but even this is very little when compared with the 70 pounds in Burma. In many other ways Ceylon presents a less gloomy picture than the mainland. It has less pressure on the land—as suggested by the fact that only half of the labor force is employed in agriculture—and there is room for expanding food production. Within India and Pakistan there are, of course, also regional differences in economic level. Especially the Punjab, now divided between India and West Pakistan, stands out as a relatively prosperous region, thanks to the vast system of canal irrigation the British developed.

New irrigation facilities are the best way to bring more land under cultivation, enlarge the double-cropped area, and raise the yield per acre. Since the possibilities of diverting normal river flow into irrigation canals have been virtually exhausted, the present projects in India and Pakistan call for high dams and large reservoirs to store floodwaters for use in the dry season and, where feasible, to generate electricity (Figure 11–3). Also coming into use more and more are tube wells with electric pumps to tap the groundwater.

Modern technology, however, will accomplish little unless accompanied by reconstruction of the traditional agrarian way of life. Farm units —5 acres on the average—are too small and fragmented for efficient production; tenancy, coupled with exorbitant rents, makes farming a hopeless struggle; thousands of villages are without roads to local markets; peasants lack cash to buy commercial fertilizer for exhausted soils; malnutrition and disease sap both energy and initiative; ignorance, tradition, or mere caution makes any innovation suspect. And there is, of course, the ever-increasing population which threatens to devour all gains in production.

In the face of these difficulties the many and multiple government efforts to revitalize the agrarian economy deserve respect and appreciation. The aim is improvement through individual and village initiative rather than forcing change by revolutionary measures. One may heartily agree with the philosophy and yet wonder whether the rate of progress is fast enough to avoid a disastrous food crisis.

Southeast Asia

The lands east of India and south of China have been subjected to many foreign influences. The impact has been slight in the less accessible parts, such as the interior highlands of the mainland and the eastern islands of the archipelago. The simple agriculture of these tribal societies has been discussed in Chapter 10. Here we turn to the more advanced peoples; although included among the traditional societies, they are in many ways marginal to the classical ones of China, India, and the Middle East.

The climate, though tropical, is not uniform over the whole area. There are, of course, the differences in temperature between lowlands and uplands; but more important are those of rainfall. Along the equator, including Malaya,

Figure 11–3. INDIA: IRRIGATION PROJECTS

Based on a map in *Focus,* September, 1963, published by the American Geographical Society.

▉	Major Irrigated Areas
▲	River and Irrigation Projects Recently Completed or Under Construction
1,000,000	Additional Irrigated Land in Acres

Sumatra, West Java, Borneo, and the southern Philippines, rain comes in all months, amounting to at least 80 inches per year. The remainder of the region has a dry season which restricts but does not preclude agriculture. As elsewhere in the humid tropics, the percolating rainwater tends to leach plant nutrients from the topsoil. All the more important are, therefore, the river valleys and deltas which receive fresh silt in the flood season. In the Philippines and Indonesia volcanic eruptions have rejuvenated the soil in many areas. This may partly explain why Borneo—which has no volcanoes—supports far fewer people than Java or Sumatra. But historical circumstance must not be overlooked. The Red River delta of Tongkin (northern Vietnam) has supported for many centuries a dense population, thanks to its intense water management and crop tillage in Chinese fashion, whereas the southern delta of the Mekong is still part of an agricultural frontier. Java, although its density was probably always higher than that of adjacent islands, had only some

five million people in 1815; the intensification of land use under Dutch rule made it possible to sustain ten times that number by 1940.

Apart from a few heavy population concentrations, Southeast Asia as a whole is like a frontier settlement compared to crowded China and India. Each country has ample land to expand farming if it can invest in irrigation, drainage, machines, fertilizer, and so on. The present modest level of living results from low productivity per worker, not lack of natural endowment.

As in all traditional societies, subsistence farming remains the primary way of making a living in Southeast Asia. The percentage of population so engaged is in general even higher than in East and South Asia, except for the more urban and commercial economy of Malaya. Farming units range from 2 to 3 acres in the densely populated sections and are 5 acres or more elsewhere. The main food crop is wet rice, wherever it can be grown, but it is rare to find it as well tended as in China or Japan.

11. Land Use in Traditional Societies

249

Flooded rice fields (sawahs) in terraces fill the valley of the Tjitarum
southeast of Bandung in the volcanic Priangan Highlands of West Java.
Dry fields lie among the woods on the upper slopes.
[Koninklijk Instituut voor de Tropen, Amsterdam]

The contrast is most striking in the delta lands of the Irawaddy (Burma), Menam Chao Phraya (Thailand), and Mekong (the old Cochin-China in South Vietnam). Here the farmers grow only one crop of rice in the rainy season, and leave the land fallow until the next year. Yields are low: 1,200 to 1,500 pounds per acre, compared to 2,400 pounds in China and 4,200 pounds in Japan. But the large areas under rice monoculture and the relatively sparse population make these three regions the chief exporters of rice, at least under peaceful conditions. Although farming may be called "intensive" in terms of labor applied in raising the crop— certainly so by Western standards—it is a far cry from the "gardening" methods of East Asia.

However, in well-settled parts of the Philippines (central Luzon, Cebu), in Java and Bali, and in most of the Vietnam lowlands, the use of land is more expert. Even in these areas two successive crops of rice are uncommon. A dry crop usually follows the rice crop on the drained sawah, such as maize, sweet potato, cassava, peanut (all American domesticates), yam, or soybean, and various leafy vegetables. Land that cannot be flooded also produces these same dry crops as well as perennials, among them bananas, coconuts, citrus, and other fruit trees.

In some areas rice is a minor crop, either because there is not enough water to flood wide areas (e.g., the dry zone in interior Burma) or because the soils are too permeable to hold the water on the surface (e.g., on limestone islands like Cebu and Madura). In eastern Java both factors, combined with intensive use of all available land, result in a preponderance of dry-field crops over rice.

Many farmers produce a small food surplus that is sold to the cities, or even abroad. Coconuts especially have long found a ready market. More recently, maize has become a significant export of Thailand. The expansion of cassava cultivation is a mixed blessing. It gives a fair yield on poor soils where other crops fail. If sold to processing plants for industrial purposes, it provides welcome cash. However, dependence on cassava as the main food leads to malnutrition, because it provides only starch. The growing acreage in Java reflects an increasing need for food, any food, rather than a welcome diversification.

In addition to the subsistence crops—and whatever surplus they provide for sale—there is widespread cultivation of crops specifically for the market. Commercial production occurs mainly in regions with relatively abundant land, where the smallholder can devote some acreage entirely to cash crops as an adjunct to subsistence farming. For instance, local farmers may have a coconut, kapok, or abaca (Manila hemp) planting, a coffee, tea, or pepper garden, and a cassava or maize field. Fifty years ago they began to imitate the Western estates in planting *Hevea* rubber trees, and now they produce two-thirds of Southeast Asia's rubber. Their product, on the whole of lower quality than that of estates, obtains a lower price, but this is easily accepted since the family does much of the work and puts in little capital. In the Federation of Malaya, the largest natural-rubber producer in the world, 46 percent comes from smallholders; in Indonesia, second in rank, 70 percent, mainly from Sumatra and Borneo. Thailand's rubber plantings are in the wet peninsular part, all on small holdings. Until the rubber boom of the early 1900s, Malaya—the peninsular part of the Malaysian Federation—was a sparsely inhabited country with very little commercial agriculture. There was ample room for rubber planting. This explains why rubber now occupies almost two-thirds of the cultivated area (Figure 10–4). This stands in marked contrast to other Southeast Asian countries, where rubber and other cash crops occupy only a small fraction of the land. In Malaya the position of large-scale plantations, controlling one-third of the planted area, also is exceptionally strong. In contrast, on Java—often considered an outstanding case of plantation economy in prewar times—only 6 percent of the cultivated area was in 1940 under estate management; for prewar Indonesia as a whole the proportion was about 4 percent. However, this relatively small area contributed over half of the value of all agricultural exports. As mentioned before, plantation agriculture in Indonesia has declined since World War II. In recent years the government has taken over almost all that remains of the large-scale enterprises.

Although the population pressure in Southeast Asia is less acute than in adjacent realms, the rapidly growing numbers, as well as the desire for economic uplift, demand far-reaching reforms. The nature and urgency of the problems vary from country to country. Thailand provides a good example of projects accomplished or planned to expand the arable land. Because the central plain of Thailand does not receive sufficient rainfall to flood paddy fields, additional water from the Menam Chao Phraya is needed to ensure a good harvest. But the irregular summer flow in some years does not flood the plain adequately, while in other years its volume drowns the crop—unless it is a variety that adapts to high water by growing 10 or more feet of stem, the so-called floating rice.

Since about 1900 Thailand has carried out various works to control and distribute the floodwaters. After World War II new projects have been undertaken aiming at overall development of the Chao Phraya River. The major diversion dam is at Chainat, at the head of the delta; it benefits one million acres of rice land. On the Ping River, which enters the plain at Yanhee in the west, a high dam has been built to form a large reservoir. This project opens up new land below the dam which could not be used before for rice because of excessive flooding; also, it will provide part of the Bangkok plain with irrigation for a second rice crop. Altogether some 650,000 acres will profit from the Ping River project when it is completed.

The giant Mekong River, which runs through the eastern part of the Indochinese Peninsula, can be harnessed for the benefit of several countries. Various agencies of the United Nations and a number of countries have joined in a multipurpose development scheme. The main river as well as several of its tributaries have a rich potential for generating electricity and for irrigating millions of acres. Moreover, floods could be controlled. Transportation, now hampered by rapids, could use the Mekong deep into the interior. Cheap electricity would be particularly useful to produce low-cost fertilizer. Work is now in progress to dam several minor Thailand tributaries of the main stream.

Egypt and Sudan

Herodotus said, "Egypt is an acquired country, the gift of the river." Apart from some oases in the western desert, all cultivated land lies as a ribbon along the Nile and in its triangular delta below Cairo. The gift of the river has more complex origins than Herodotus knew. The White Nile has its sources in the rainy equatorial region. In the southern Sudan its flow, together with that of some tributaries, spreads out over a vast, low plain through reed- and grass-covered channels and marshes. This region, El Sudd, acts as a regulator so that the flow downstream is quite even. Other sources of Egypt's water supply are the Blue Nile and

the Atbara, both rising in the Ethiopian highlands. Here rains come only in summer. The floods carry along masses of red silt and arrive in Egypt late in June, reaching their maximum in October, then subsiding quickly. The volume of both White and Blue Nile decreases markedly downstream because of high evaporation in the desert climate (Figure 11–4).

The earliest cultivators planted their seeds in the muddy soil as soon as the floodwaters began to recede. About 4000 B.C. basin irrigation was introduced, which prevailed for almost 6,000 years. It consisted of trapping the floodwaters by building low dikes around tracts varying in size from 5,000 to 50,000 acres and letting it stand on the ground for a month or two. Then in October or November the peasant planted wheat, barley, and other crops. After the harvest in April he left the land fallow to await the next flooding. Thus his entire rhythm of life was attuned to the seasonal ups and downs of the river.

About 1820 the Egyptians started to build dams in the river so that water for irrigation would be available beyond the flood season. This so-called "perennial irrigation" did not work well until modern hydraulic technology was introduced about 1890. British engineers built dams with navigation locks and sluice gates in the river at the head of the delta near Cairo, at Aswan some 500 miles upstream, and at some other spots in between. The high floods pass through the sluice gates, but barrages catch the tail of the flood in October and November to use it for irrigation in the low-water period. At Aswan the river flows through a granite outcrop, causing the first of a series (counted upstream) of rapids or cataracts. This dam was completed in 1902, but heightened at later dates. The backed-up Nile waters form a lake of 150 miles in length reaching into Sudan. In 1960, with Russian aid, the Egyptians began to construct a new high dam a few miles upstream from Aswan. This huge project will have a far larger capacity to hold water than the old Aswan barrage. It will add 2 million acres of irrigated land to the 6 million now available in Egypt.

Perennial irrigation has greatly increased

Figure 11-4. NILE VALLEY: IRRIGATION

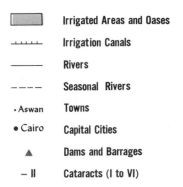

▨	Irrigated Areas and Oases
⊦⊦⊦⊦	Irrigation Canals
——	Rivers
– – – –	Seasonal Rivers
• Aswan	Towns
● Cairo	Capital Cities
▲	Dams and Barrages
– II	Cataracts (I to VI)

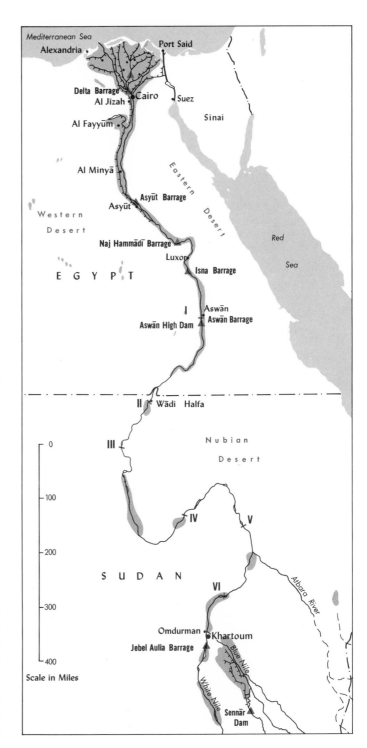

production by permitting year-round cultivation with a dependable water supply. It has, however, eliminated from the fields the silt deposits that formerly rejuvenated the land year after year. Crop rotation and chemical fertilizer are now required to maintain the high yields for which Egypt is justly famous. Two or three crops are raised from the same piece of soil. The big commodity, cotton of the long-staple variety, came to the fore when American production lagged during the Civil War. Although it occupies only one-fifth of the cultivated area, it accounts for at least two-thirds of Egypt's export income. Besides the traditional grain crops of wheat, barley, and millet the *fellahin* raise much maize and rice, the latter mainly in the delta. Although modern production methods are more and more common on the larger farms, most peasants still use the sickle, threshing board, and archaic wooden plow drawn by ox or water buffalo.

Until the land reforms of recent years, Egypt suffered under a feudal landholding system. Six percent of the landowners, most of them living in the cities, held two-thirds of the land. The great majority of the agricultural workers owned less than ½ acre, if any land at all, and worked parcels of the estates as debt-ridden sharecroppers. Since 1961 agricultural holdings have been restricted to 100 feddans (104 acres) per individual, and redistribution of the land is in progress. This opens the way for relieving the fellah's hopeless misery. Newly created agricultural cooperatives help to compensate for the lack of capital and experience of the new smallholder.

Because of the large area under cotton (and in spite of high crop yields per acre), Egypt does not produce enough food for its 30 million inhabitants. The density of population in inhabited Egypt is now 2,100 per square mile; the density per acre of irrigated land is 5. The promotion of small holdings, while beneficial in many respects, may reduce the production efficiency common to large enterprises. Moreover, Egypt has a fast-growing population. The additional land to be irrigated from the new high Aswan dam will barely suffice to feed the expected population increment of the next 20 years (see Chapter 18).

While the Sudan was a British-Egyptian condominium, a highly successful irrigation project was undertaken in Gezira, the triangular area between the White and Blue Niles, south of their junction at Khartoum. Climate and soil favor the production of long-staple cotton under irrigation. Plans to use the Blue Nile, however, had to consider that Egypt needs all of its flow during the low stage. A dam at Sennar, completed in 1925, created a reservoir that provides water for Gezira as well as releases it gradually down to Egypt as its needs increase.

From Sennar an elaborate canal system leads the water to well over a million acres of land west of the Blue Nile. Of particular interest is the cooperative nature of the project. Tenants work holdings of about 30 acres; they grow cotton, but also food and fodder crops in carefully prescribed rotation. A specially created local board administers the district, gins the cotton, and sends it to market. The government is responsible for the irrigation. The three partners split proceeds of the cotton crop, the tenants and the government each receiving 40 percent, and the Gezira Board 20 percent. This scheme for economic development has been quite successful in raising the level of prosperity. Works to expand the irrigated area are now under way.

Pastoral Nomadism

In spite of the persistent popular notion, nomadic herding of livestock is not an evolutionary economic stage preceding sedentary farming. It appears to be an ecologically conditioned offshoot from early Middle Eastern agriculture—grain growing and livestock herding as separate yet intertwined activities. The biblical story of the brothers Cain, "tiller of the soil," and Abel, "keeper of sheep," reflects the ancient agricultural dichotomy. Those who left the sown land for the steppe became pastoral nomads, wandering in search of pasture and water for their flocks. Yet even the full nomad cannot quite divorce himself from the farmer. He needs flour and dates, tea or coffee, which he obtains in exchange for skins, leather, wool, or cheese. Nomadic herding is a land-extensive form, somewhat similar to the land rotation among shifting cultivators. Since fodder and water must be obtained throughout the year, the herders move seasonally from one grazing ground to another (Figure 11–1).

Nomadic herding has, of course, some traits in common with ranching, especially in the early days of the "cattle kingdom" on the American Great Plains when the herds moved freely over vast areas of unfenced land. But nomadic herding differs fundamentally in that it is a traditional subsistence mode of life for the entire family or clan, while ranching is an Occidental commercial-agricultural enterprise, centered on the ranch establishment.

Forms of Pastoral Nomadism. The theme of pastoral nomadism has almost endless variations. In eastern Africa we have already met the herder-on-foot, either as full or part-time cattleman. In the steppes and deserts of North Africa and Asia, many nomads use horses or camels as trained auxiliaries to guide and guard sheep, goats, and cattle, as well as for travel and transportation of the family. But others use the horse mainly for rounding up cattle, and employ oxcarts for transportation. This fully nomadic existence contrasts with that of the seminomad, who has instead of a tent a house,

Nomads in Chad, north central Africa. On the savanna cattle-raising tribes migrate with their herds to fresh pastures as the summer rains move across the land. The physique of the people reflects the long-time mingling of Negroid and Caucasoid peoples in the Sudan. [Koninklijk Instituut voor de Tropen, Amsterdam]

owns land in an oasis, and only moves for one season with his family to an encampment on fresh pastures. Or, one may distinguish between nomadic groups by radius of movement: some groups oscillate only some 20 to 50 miles between regular summer and winter pastures; others cover a much longer circuit with many encampments along the way. The type of en-vironment—mountains or plains, cool or hot summers, cold or mild winters, grass or scrub vegetation—conditions the time, direction, and duration of the trek, the kind of animals reared, and the relations to sedentary folk. It is generally true that among full nomads there is no private landownership. A clan or federation of clans considers its grazing lands common prop-

11. Land Use in Traditional Societies

erty. Individual wealth depends on the number of livestock one owns. But here again, there are many exceptions to the rule, especially where land is scarce. For instance, it is not uncommon for a nomadic group to have well-demarcated plots for each family herd in the narrow valley of its winter encampment, while all members of the group freely use the wide summer pastures.

Distinct from pastoral nomadism is *transhumance;* this term refers to the seasonal movement of livestock, accompanied by a few shepherds only. It is quite common in countries where sedentary agriculture is well established, such as in the European highlands and in the western United States. It is also characteristic where former pastoral nomads have become sedentary keepers of livestock.

Horse- and Camel-riding Nomads.

The horse and dromedary transformed the pastoral nomad from a plodding shepherd into a swift-moving aggressive warrior. As mentioned earlier, the horse was probably domesticated in the open woodlands or steppes of southern Russia or Central Asia and was used—apart from food— to draw the light chariot before it became a riding and pack animal. (Not until the horse collar was invented in the ninth century A.D. could the horse pull heavy loads.) Horse riding may date back to 1800 B.C. in Central Asia; 600 years later it had spread throughout the Middle East.

Although the two-humped or Bactrian camel had been domesticated earlier (3000–2500 B.C.?), this slow pack and draft animal could not compete with the horse as a means of travel. The one-humped camel, or dromedary, probably domesticated in southern Arabia before 1000 B.C., provided the desert dweller with a fast-moving mount, one that could endure drought much better than the horse. The dromedary spread gradually through all desert regions, although it appeared in North Africa only in Roman times.

Apart from their value as riding and pack animals, camels and horses have other uses. Various Asian nomads milk the mares, to make *kumyss,* a fermented beverage. Also, they eat

horsemeat, which the Arabs do not. Arabs consider the camel a working beast and the horse a nonutilitarian showpiece of the rich—at least until the advent of the Lincoln and Rolls-Royce. Many nomadic groups also milk camels, eat their flesh, manufacture their hide and hair into rugs and clothing, and use the dung as fuel.

The mobility that horse and dromedary gave the nomads overshadowed the domestic qualities. The impact the swift and ruthless marauder made on sedentary peoples lives on in their legends from centaur to Hun. These roughriders over and over invaded and ruled large parts of the rimlands of Eurasia. The so-called Aryans and many other peoples from inner Asia down to the Moghuls thrust into India. The Manchus were but the last of the many nomadic tribes, including Tartars and Mongols, that entered China in spite of the wall; Mongols, Arabs, and Turks penetrated deep into Europe. Some scholars seek to explain these human eruptions by severe drought conditions which prevailed at certain periods. The evidence is doubtful, and it seems wiser to consider additional factors—social, economic, and political. After all, the steppe and the sown existed side by side for thousands of years in a highly unstable association. A new technique of irrigation would expand agriculture into the desert, but withdrawal of imperial border guards might tempt the nomads to regain former pasturelands.

The caravan trade was another and equally important feature of the dry lands of the Old World. It linked by land the advanced countries of the Middle East, China, and India with each other as well as with their sources of raw materials. This long-distance transportation inevitably had to cross deserts and steppes occupied by nomads, be it Sahara or Sind, Tarim or Gobi. The nomads offered little in trade goods, but controlled the terrain. For long-distance journeys the merchants therefore usually made arrangements with a nomad chief who provided the camels and the escort of drivers, guides, and guards. As on the sea, commerce invited piracy. Safe passage depended on skill as well as luck. For greater security the long-distance caravans were quite large, like ships traveling in convoy, consisting of hundreds and even thousands of laden camels. To transport salt from the mines at Taoudenni, in the central Sahara, to Timbuktu (Tombouctou), caravans used over 10,000 beasts. Because the caravans needed pasture and water, they timed their journeys according to the best season for both.

Decline of Nomadism. The domain of the pastoral nomad has shrunk substantially in the last hundred years. The spread of farming, with or without irrigation, more and more restricts the wide open spaces, and even where they still exist, closed frontiers deny access to former pasture grounds. The railroad, truck, and plane have severely reduced the income from caravan trade, transport, camel breeding, and pillage. In many countries government policy aims at settling the nomads, either as farmers or as livestock ranchers, so that they may be absorbed in the nation-state. Others have been attracted to work full or part time in the petroleum fields of Iraq, Arabia, and the Sahara. In Russian Central Asia, where once Kirgiz, Kazakh, and many other nomadic peoples roamed the steppe, the traditional way of life is virtually gone. Instead, the indigenous people now work on collective ranches and farms, in mines, and manufacturing industries. In Saudi Arabia, fixation of the nomad is the declared policy of the Wahhabite government. Of Saudi Arabia's estimated population of 7 million perhaps no more than 300,000 are fully nomadic, living mainly along the Persian Gulf. Syria, which had some 350,000 pure nomads in the 1920s, now has fewer than half that many. The countries along the northern border of the Sahara show the same trend.

Outer Mongolia. The Mongolian People's Republic is still largely the domain of pastoral nomads, who are estimated to comprise three-fourths of the population. The southeastern part of the country lies in the flat to rolling Gobi Desert and adjacent steppe, but the north and west are mountain country with forested ridges and grassy valley floors. Only a strong physique can endure the hardships of drought, cold winter, and hot summer under primitive living conditions. The Mongols have long been known as a tough lot, whether as shepherds or warriors. This was the homeland of Genghis Khan and his grandson Kublai Khan, who ruled much of Asia in the twelfth and thirteenth centuries.

In winter the Mongol nomads stay in the lower parts of the valleys, which afford some protection against the icy blasts. In summer many groups move with their animals to the high valleys and mountain slopes, but others wander down to the steppe in late summer after the rains have revived the cover of short bunch-grass—unless a severe drought parches the land. Usually several related families band together, setting up their *yourts*—tents made of black felt —in small encampments between moves. Apart from the very rich, who may count their livestock in thousands, the average family possesses some 50 sheep, half as many goats, and some heads of cattle, horses, and camels. Sheep are the prized animals, providing wool for felt making, skins for clothing, mutton and milk (in sour form the main beverage, or made into cheese and butter) for food, plus dung for fuel.

Dairy products from the other animals, and flour and tea bought from traders, supplement the diet. Wool and hides form the main exports. The number of livestock in Outer Mongolia is estimated at 25 million, of which over 13 million are sheep, 6 million goats, 2 million cattle, 2.3 million horses, and 850,000 camels.

Russians have introduced improvements in livestock rearing, such as more hay production and better shelters. These help to cut down the heavy loss of animals in winter. Communist pressure abolished most Lamaistic Buddhist monasteries; their vast herds have been handed over to collectives. Many poor shepherds have been drawn into these enterprises. Expansion of dry farming is making inroads on the pastures of the nomad, but most of the land is too dry for crop growing. It is likely that nomadic herding will maintain itself for a long time in this northern outpost.

11. Land Use in Traditional Societies

Citation

Government of India, "A Village Survey of Shakrori," *Census of India, 1961,* 20:6, Simla, Himachal Pradesh, 1963. [Map]

Further Readings

Ackerman, E. A. *Japan's Natural Resources and Their Relation to Japan's Economic Future,* Chicago, 1953.

Adams, R. M. *Land behind Baghdad: A History of Settlement on the Diyala Plains,* Chicago, 1965.

Ahmad, N. *An Economic Geography of East Pakistan,* New York, 1958.

Andrus, J. R., and Mohammed, A. F. *The Economy of Pakistan,* London and Stanford, Calif., 1958.

Awad, M. "The Assimilation of Nomads in Egypt," *Geographical Review,* 44 (1954): 240–252.

Beardsley, R. K., Hall, J. W., and Ward, R. E. *Village Japan,* Chicago, 1959.

Boeke, J. H. *Economics and Economic Policy of Plural Societies, as Exemplified by Indonesia,* International Secretariat, Institute of Pacific Relations, New York, 1953.

Bonné, A. *State and Economics in the Middle East: A Society in Transition,* London, 1955.

Buck, J. L. *Land Utilization in China,* 3 vols., Nanking, 1937.

Chi Ch'ao-ting, *Key Economic Areas in Chinese History,* London and New York, 1936.

Clarke, J. I. "Studies of Semi-nomadism in North Africa," *Economic Geography,* 35 (1959): 95–108.

Coon, C. S. *Caravan: The Story of the Middle East,* New York, 1951.

Credner, W. *Siam: Das Land der Tai,* Stuttgart, 1935.

Cressey, G. B. *Land of the 500 Million,* New York, 1955. [China]

Davies, D. H. "Observations on Land Use in Iraq," *Economic Geography,* 33 (1957): 122–134.

Davies, H. R. J. "Nomadism in the Sudan," *Tijdschrift voor Economische en Sociale Geografie,* 57 (1966): 193–202.

De Planhol, X. *De la plaine pamphylienne aux lacs pisidiens: Nomadisme et vie paysanne,* Paris, 1958.

Eyre, J. "Mountain Land Use in Northern Japan," *Geographical Review,* 52 (1962): 236–252.

Farmer, B. H. *Pioneer Peasant Colonization in Ceylon: A Study in Asian Agrarian Problems,* London, 1957.

Fisher, W. B. *The Middle East: A Physical, Social, and Regional Geography,* 4th ed., London, 1961.

Fryer, D. W. *World Economic Development,* New York, 1964.

Gautier, E. F. *Sahara: The Great Desert,* translated by D. F. Mayhew, London, 1935.

Glacken, C. J. *The Great Loochoo: A Study of Okinawan Village Life,* Berkeley, Calif., 1955.

Hance, W. A. "The Gezira: An Example in Development," *Geographical Review,* 44 (1954): 253–270.

Helburn, N. "A Stereotype of Agriculture in Semiarid Turkey," *Geographical Review,* 45 (1955): 375–384.

Ho, R. "Mixed-farming and Multiple-cropping in Malaya," *Journal of Tropical Geography,* 15 (1961): 46–65.

Hsieh Chiao-min, *Taiwan—Ilha Formosa: A Geography in Perspective,* Washington, D.C., 1964.

Humlum, J. *La Géographie de l'Afghanistan: Etude d'un pays aride,* Copenhagen, 1959.

International Bank for Reconstruction and Development. Several surveys of development and economic prospects in Asia and Africa.

Jin-Bee, Ooi, "The Rubber Industry of the Federation of Malaya," *Journal of Tropical Geography,* 15 (1961): 46–65.

Kanitkar, N. V. *Dry Farming in India,* Indian Council of Agricultural Research, 2d ed., New Delhi, 1960.

King, F. H. *Farmers of Forty Centuries,* 2d ed., New York, 1927. [China]

Ladejinski, W. "Agrarian Revolution in Japan," *Foreign Affairs,* 38 (1959): 95–109.

Lambton, A. K. S. *Landlord and Peasant in Persia: A Study of Land Tenure and Land Revenue Administration,* London, 1953.

McCune, S. *Korea's Heritage: A Regional and Social Geography,* Tokyo, 1956.

Mikesell, M. W. *Northern Morocco: A Cultural Geography,* University of California Publications in Geography no. 14, Berkeley, 1961.

Murphey, R. "The Decline of North Africa since the Roman Occupation: Climatic or Human?," *Annals of the Association of American Geographers,* 41 (1951): 116–132.

Myrdal, J. *Report from a Chinese Village,* translated by M. Michael, New York, 1965. Describes the impact of the social and political revolution on a village in northern Shensi.

Pelzer, K. J. *Pioneer Settlement in the Asiatic Tropics,* American Geographical Society, Special Publication no. 29, New York, 1945.

Pendleton, R. L. *Thailand: Aspects of Landscape and Life,* New York, 1962.

Purcell, V. W. *The Chinese in Southeast Asia,* London, 1951.

Shen Tsung-han, *Agricultural Resources of China,* Ithaca, N.Y. 1951.

Simoons, F. J. *Northwest Ethiopia,* Madison, Wis., 1960.

Spate, O. H. K. *India and Pakistan: A General and Regional Geography,* London and New York, 1957.

Spencer, J. E., and Horvath, R. J. "How Does an Agricultural Region Originate?," *Annals of the Association of American Geographers,* 53 (1963): 74–92.

Stamp, L. D. *A History of Landuse in Arid Regions,* Paris, 1961.

Tannous, A. I. "Land Reform: Key to the Development and Stability of the Arab World," *Middle East Journal,* 5 (1951): 1–20.

Tawney, R. H. *Land and Labour in China,* London, 1932.

Thompson, J. H. "Urban Agriculture in Southern Japan," *Economic Geography,* 33 (1957): 224–237.

Trewartha, G. T. *Japan: A Physical, Cultural, and Regional Geography,* 2d ed., Madison, Wis., 1965.

UNESCO, "Nomads and Nomadism in the Arid Zone," *International Science Journal,* 11 (1959): 481–585. A symposium of eleven authors.

UNESCO, "Problems of the Arid Zone," Proceedings of the Paris Symposium, in *Arid Zone Research,* vols. 18–19 (1962–1963).

Whittlesey, D. S. "Major Agricultural Regions of the Earth," *Annals of the Association of American Geographers,* 26 (1936): 199–240.

Wickizer, V. D., and Bennett, M. K. *The Rice Economy of Monsoon Asia,* Stanford, Calif., 1941.

12. Agriculture in Modern Societies

General Observations

In modern societies, agriculture has changed from a way of life into a specialized industry closely integrated with other commercial and industrial activities. Like other forms of business, it applies science and technology to achieve high productivity per worker (Figure 12-1).

Formerly the farmer himself processed and marketed most of his produce. As much as possible he supplied the needs of his own household from the farm. His wife made bread from wheat or rye harvested from their own land, and wove cloth from thread spun from home-grown wool. Today others perform these tasks, while the farmer concentrates on raising whatever brings the most profit in the market.

Now that the output per worker has greatly increased, only a fraction of the national labor force is needed for farming. In Anglo-America, northwestern Europe, Australia, and New Zealand persons engaged in farming constitute less than 20 percent of all employed—in the United Kingdom only 4 percent, in the United States 8 percent (Figure 12-2). As one goes east and south in Europe the percentages rise, indicating less complete change-over to the modern economy, but still they are low compared to those of traditional agrarian societies.

One should keep in mind, however, that workers outside farming have taken over many tasks formerly done on the farm. According to the 1960 U.S. Census of Population, 2.8 million people comprised the working "rural farm" population; another 1.5 million were engaged on farms, but lived in towns or "rural nonfarm" residences. But no less than 3.4 million processed or manufactured and 1.5 million transported and dealt wholesale in agricultural products. In addition 1.7 million served in food stores. Thus, in 1960 there were 10.9 million persons—about 17 percent of the United States employed labor force—directly or indirectly associated with the production, processing, and distribution of farm products.

The rise of industrial-commercial agriculture in the Western world has not completely obliterated traditional ways. Many vestiges of old forms remain. Some regions have few machines; others retain a feudal-like land-tenure system. Elsewhere farmers are still intent on supplying the local market. Furthermore, since continuous innovation characterizes modern society, new and improved farming methods constantly develop, but take time to spread from their points of origin to other areas. As an example, we have shown already in Figure 2-2 the diffusion of new varieties of hybrid corn from the first centers of production in Iowa in the 1920s.

Rapid and forceful changes create stresses that governments hopefully try to ameliorate. As agriculture seeks to adjust to new technological and commercial patterns, many Western countries subsidize farmers in one way or another. In the United States the "farm problem," including the disposal of surplus commodities, looms large in internal politics. Western Europe finds it difficult to integrate farming into the Common Market. Since farmers, as a carry-over from the traditional way of life, still hold much political power, other elements in society often pay them subsidies in the form of taxes or higher prices.

Mechanization and commercialization of modern agriculture favor the large over the small farm. The former obtains capital more easily and gains significant economies by the scale of its operations. There is, however, an optimum size for the efficient management of farm units, varying according to product, technology, and ecological conditions. The small, semisubsistence family farm is fading away, but farming as a capital-intensive family business seems not in danger of being replaced by corporate giants.

Land Tenure

Much as agriculture in the modern world differs from the olden days, the ties between farmer and land remain. Thus, the rules controlling ownership of land and the rights of its use are as important as ever. In some countries outdated laws and customs still prevail, in others they have gradually been adapted to new circumstances, while elsewhere revolutionary land reforms have at one stroke abolished the old order. The four main types of land tenure existing today are: (1) communal tenure, (2) latifundium or estate, (3) freehold ownership, and (4) tenancy (Fryer, 1965, 83–118).

Communal tenure, in a variety of forms, was once widespread among simple agrarian societies. The land was considered to be common property of the community. Each member had the right to work a parcel of land and enjoy its produce for private use. Redistribution of farm plots after a number of years was not uncommon. This system has tended to give way to private ownership of land, be it as free-

hold of small farmers or as large holdings of powerful individuals who in one way or another usurped the rights to former communally held lands.

Old though communal tenure is, variations of it have been adopted in some revolutionary situations during this century: for example, in Mexico the *ejido,* in Israel the *kibbutz,* in eastern Europe and the Soviet Union the *kolkhoz* or collective, in China the *kung-she* or commune. Whether these methods of farm organization can succeed in economically advanced countries is open to question, though in Israel the *kibbutz* seems to be a flourishing institution. In the Soviet Union agriculture has been the least successful branch of the economy, partly because of too much central and regional bureaucratic control, partly because rewards are lacking for better performance. Some socialist countries, such as Poland and Yugoslavia, have largely rejected collective farms and have injected the personal-profit motive into the system, either by reinstating individual ownership of farms or by adding personal inducements to the remaining collective operations.

The *latifundium* (from the Latin meaning "large estate") also has ancient as well as modern manifestations. Latifundia have existed for centuries throughout the Mediterranean, Middle East, South Asia, and Latin America. The landed aristocracy, basing wealth and power on the control of vast estates, has proved to be long-lived. Even in countries undergoing land reforms they often survived, though in reduced circumstances. In many regions, owners do not operate the latifundia themselves, but let out their lands in small plots to the local population, who pay rent in labor or harvest.

While the large estate sometimes disappears in a violent popular revolution, replaced by small farms operated by the formerly landless peasantry, it is somewhat paradoxical that a country with a soviet political system sets up another form of latifundium in its agricultural frontier regions. In the Soviet Union, virgin lands recently put to the plow in the steppes of Kazakhstan have been divided into large

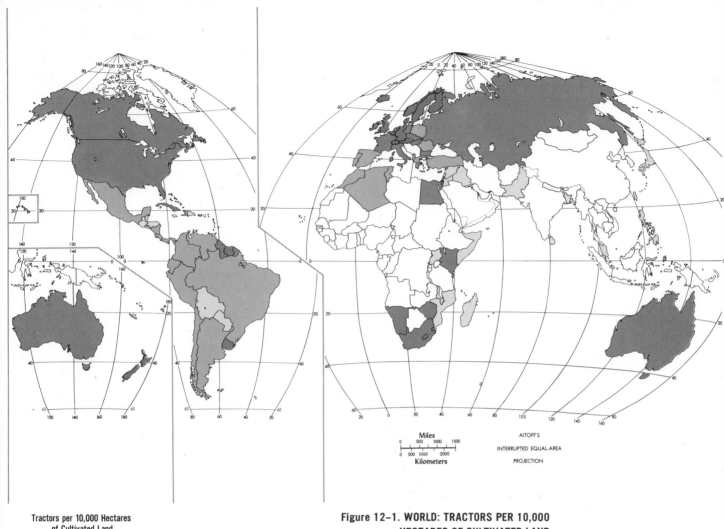

**Figure 12–1. WORLD: TRACTORS PER 10,000
HECTARES OF CULTIVATED LAND**

Among the countries with modern farming those that combine
intensive land use with mechanization have the highest number
of tractors per unit of cultivated land. In the underdeveloped
countries mechanization is mainly associated with production
of commercial field crops, such as wheat and cotton.

state farms with their managers and laborers operating under central-government control. In present-day China, state farms are numerous in northern Manchuria and on the drier western margins of the agricultural frontier. State farms in the Soviet Union and other Communist countries tend to produce less than their proponents would wish.

In countries where the capitalistic system of private enterprise operates, the number of

*12. Agriculture
in Modern
Societies*

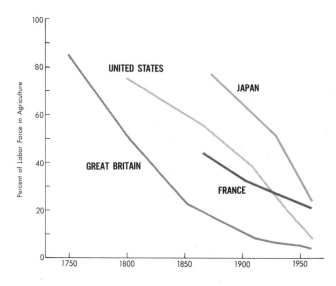

Figure 12–2. PERCENTAGE OF LABOR FORCE IN AGRICULTURE IN SELECTED COUNTRIES

farms with corporate structure increases. Many corporate crop and livestock farms in western Europe and North America lead in technological and organizational development. Such farms operate purely from the profit motive, and provide the incentives for personal performance that collective and state farms usually lack. The plantation, discussed in Chapter 10, is a variant of the latifundium.

The *freehold* (especially fee-simple or absolute) ownership of a farm is greatly prized among many peoples. Most freehold farms in continental western Europe are small, the average size less than 50 acres. Division of freeholds has often led to uneconomic fragmentation of farm units. Owner-occupied farms are larger in the British Isles, and especially in North America, Australia, and New Zealand. In the Midwest of the United States the freehold farm provided a livelihood for millions of immigrants who came to North America in the latter part of the nineteenth century.

Farm tenancy is the legal condition under which a farmer pays the owner for farming the land. Tenancy of many different kinds flourishes in the traditional society, where often

it seems to block increased economic efficiency. Sharecropping, an arrangement by which the tenant pays the owner with part of the crop, is common in all continents, but especially in Asia and Latin America. Sharecropping marks backward regions even in otherwise modernized lands, such as parts of the southeastern United States. The system is inefficient because it does not give the tenant increased income from improvements he has made. The owner, like the slum landlord in cities, acts as rent collector, not as an improver of the land and its use.

In many modern situations, however, the position of tenancy differs considerably from this. Tenants pay cash for the use of their farms, hold legal contracts that guarantee their rights, receive compensation for improvements they make, and are protected from landlord exploitation. Such legal safeguards in Britain explain why among modernized countries it has the highest rate of farm tenancy. With proper measures tenancy can be efficient and profitable for both tenant and owner.

Types of Agriculture

Types of farming differ according to what crops and animals the farmer raises and with the purpose of production. In Europe there are two very old traditions of farming: in the Mediterranean region, growing field and orchard crops tends to be distinct from raising livestock; in Europe north of the Alps, mixed or general farming, featuring integrated production of crops and animals, is the basic type. From these two have evolved various specialized forms (Figure 12–3).

Mixed (Crop and Livestock) Farming. The essential feature of mixed farming lies in cultivating crops partly for sale and partly for fodder to feed farm animals that are sold for meat. Although operators of mixed farms use a wide range of crop and livestock associations, all practice crop rotation—that is, a succession of different crops in a specified order on the

Farms in the Northeast Polder of the Zuider Zee reclamation project, the Netherlands. Since 1942, when the 120,000 acres of this area were pumped dry, carefully planned land development and colonization have created a landscape of medium-sized family farms, with modern prefabricated homes and barns, snugly nestled within their tree shelters, neat and geometrical as a Mondrian abstraction. [Aerofilms, Ltd.]

*12. Agriculture
in Modern
Societies*

Figure 12–3. WORLD: FORMS OF LAND USE IN MODERN SOCIETIES

Intensive Crop Farming

Crops and Livestock Farming

Dairy Farming

Livestock Ranching

Plantation Farming

Extensive Crop Farming: Supplementary Livestock Husbandry

Subsistence and Local Market Type

Commercial Type

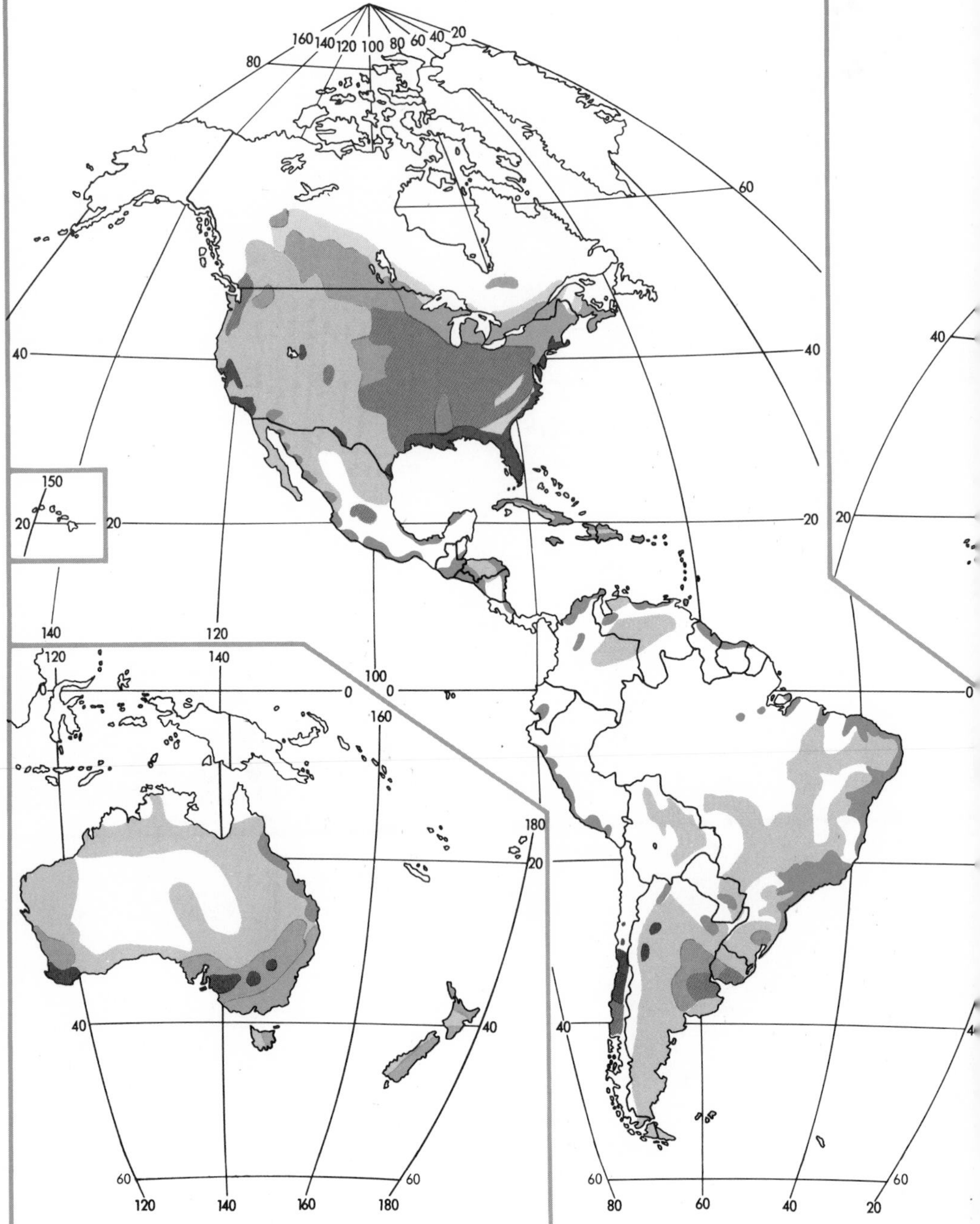

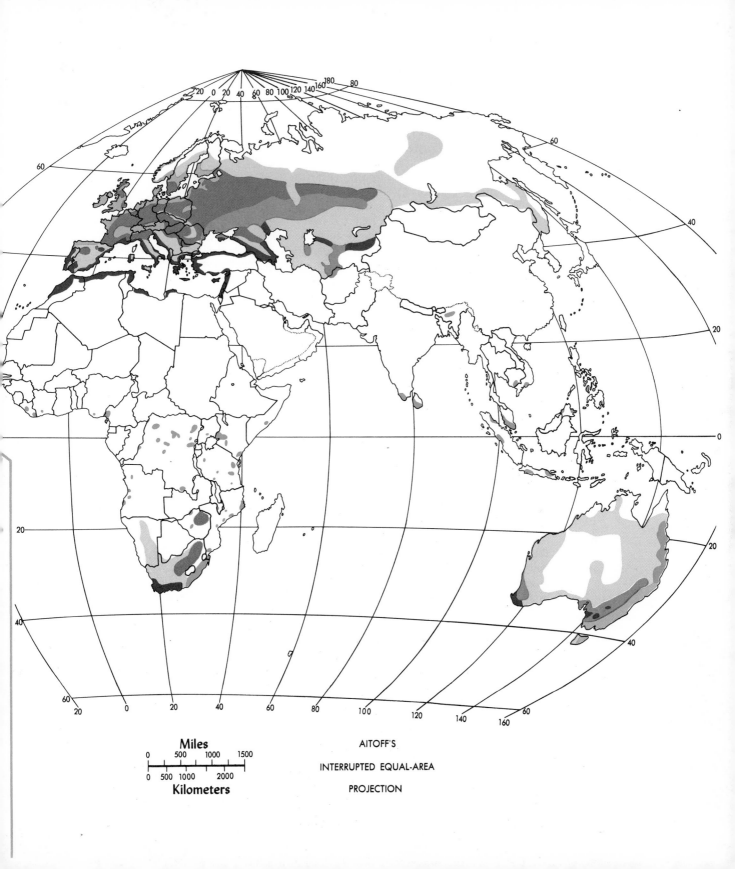

Miles
0   500   1000   1500

0   500   1000   2000
Kilometers

AITOFF'S

INTERRUPTED EQUAL-AREA

PROJECTION

same field. In eighteenth century Europe the introduction of roots and legumes in the cropping cycle made it possible to eliminate the age-old fallowing of land. The higher yield in fodder crops enabled the farmer to keep more livestock, which in turn increased the manure so necessary for maintaining soil fertility. Great progress occurred in the nineteenth century, when rotation practices were scientifically tested and chemical fertilizers developed.

In essence, rotation crops are selected from three groups of plants: (1) row crops such as corn, potatoes, beets, turnips, and other roots, (2) close-growing grains like wheat, rye, oats, and barley, and (3) sod-forming or rest crops, among them clover, soybeans, and alfalfa (lucerne). A simple rotation cycle would be, for instance, corn—oats—clover, grown in succession over three years on the same field. A farm using this plan would be divided into three fields, each planted to a different crop. Thus, each year the farmer would produce the desired variety of fodder and grain, and at the same time protect his land resource. Actually most rotation systems involve more crops and stretch over more years, depending on quality of land, market value of crop and livestock products, and also on the farmer's attitude. A sound rotation system will not aim at the highest immediate returns, but at satisfactory yields which at the same time maintain soil fertility.

In Europe mixed farming occupies a broad zone between the intensive crop cultivation of the Mediterranean lands to the south and the dairy-farming regions to the north. In the Soviet Union mixed farming borders in the south on the grain zone of the Ukraine. In the United States it occupies the core of the eastern part, fringed by dairy farming to the north, specialized-crop farming to the east and south, and grain farming and stock ranching to the west. America's heartland of mixed farming lies in the Corn Belt, a wedgelike zone reaching from central Ohio westward to southern Minnesota and central Nebraska. In Canada the Ontario Peninsula also belongs to this type. In the Old South, monoculture of tobacco and cotton has given way to a mixed form of agriculture. Traditional cash crops still have a

Figure 12–4. WORLD: SELECTED CROPS AND FARM ANIMALS; PROBABLE REGIONS OF DOMESTICATION AND PRESENT MAIN AREAS OF PRODUCTION

Shown on the map are areas of production for domestic use as well as for export; for instance, India and China produce very large quantities of crops and animals which never enter into international trade. Although the areas of domestication of most plants and animals are not known with certainty, it is quite clear that many of them have spread far from their regions of origin.

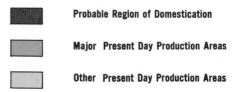

Probable Region of Domestication

Major Present Day Production Areas

Other Present Day Production Areas

place, but now blend in rotation systems with other land use, especially improved pastures. For example, the Alabama "black belt," once the type area for Southern plantation farming, has become a highly productive beef-cattle region. In the southern hemisphere mixed farming is much less developed, and quickly shades over into other forms, principally stock rearing and grain farming.

The distribution of mixed farming relates only in a general way to environmental conditions: flat to rolling plains, deep soils, adequate moisture and heat during the growing season. Each of these factors, however, influences the choice of the particular crops and animals assembled in each specific region. Hot moist summers as in the United States and southeastern Europe allow concentration on corn, while the cool summers of northwestern Europe force reliance on other cereals, potatoes, and root crops. In mild climates pasture can be used the year-round, but in cold climates shelter and stall feeding are necessary. Oats adapt better to cool rainy summers than wheat; some barley varieties can be raised in very short summers;

WHEAT

MAIZE (CORN)

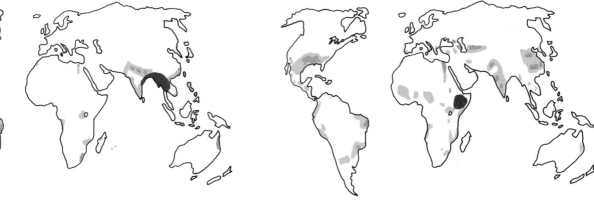

SUGAR CANE

COTTON

SHEEP

SWINE

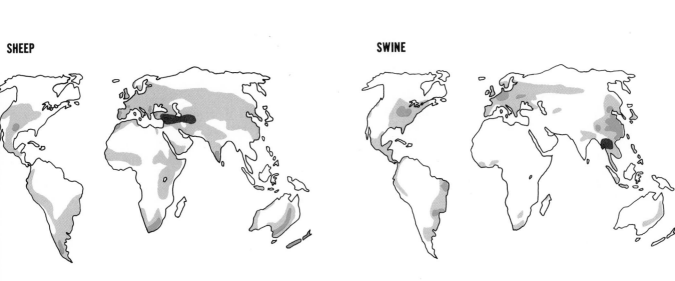

others grow in semiarid conditions. Tilled land gives way to permanent pasture on rough surfaces or where the water table is high. On poor sandy soils rye yields better than wheat.

But food habits too must be considered. The West European eats mainly wheat bread, the Central and East European, rye. Potatoes have a much larger place in the diet of Europe than of Anglo-America. High consumption of meat in the United States leads farmers to put a greater proportion of their land in fodder crops than do the European farmers, who grow more food crops.

Each subtype of mixed farming covers large areas in the United States, but in Europe the mosaic is on a microscale. Here farmers have worked out over the ages fine adjustments to the variety of ecological conditions. Moreover, transportation in much of Europe was formerly poor and expensive, which promoted local production of as many different foodstuffs as possible. Today protective tariffs still help to maintain a degree of local diversification unjustified by production costs.

Dairy Farming. Milk and milk products have been part of the Occidental diet for a very long time, but their production on specialized farms is of rather recent date. Dairy farming expanded in response to growing demands from cities for milk, cream, butter, and cheese. Advances in the technologies of preservation and transportation aided its development.

Because fluid milk is bulky and perishable, it must be produced within reasonable distance from consumption centers. Therefore, every urban agglomeration has dairy farms in its vicinity, even though its dominant regional type of agriculture may differ. An instructive case is that of dairying in southern California, which grows apace with rapid urbanization.

Dairy farming as the regionally dominant form occupies two large areas, one in Anglo-America, the other in Europe. Smaller areas exist elsewhere, but only a few (Alpine region, New Zealand) can be shown in Figure 12–3.

The localization of the main dairy belt in the United States illustrates more clearly than in Europe, with its fragmented political structure

and regional traditions, the interplay of economic and environmental factors. The American dairy zone lies mainly on the north flank of the vast urban market. Rainy, short, and even cool summers, while adverse to the ripening of corn, favor grass. Also, rough topography and poor, often stony, soils serve better for pasture than cropland. Thus, while mixed farming tends to occupy the more favorable lands south of the urban zone, dairying has developed as the main agricultural activity to the north. Within the dairy belt the eastern part specializes in fluid milk, which brings a premium price in this highly urbanized section (Figure 12–5). But the western part, especially Wisconsin and Minnesota, produces far more milk than cities can buy. The surplus is converted into less perishable form. Butter, cheese, and other manufactured products have high value per weight and allow transportation over great distances. Canada, apart from the "fluid milksheds" around the cities, exports cheese, butter, and condensed milk to Britain.

Although natural or improved pastures and hay meadows occupy much land, fodder crops also are quite important. Severe and long winters necessitate stall feeding. If the cool summer does not allow corn to ripen, it is cut green for silage; or other small grains and root crops are grown instead of corn. Moreover, stall feeding brings higher yields per cow than grazing. Many dairy enterprises resemble crop and livestock farms, except that they concentrate on an output of milk rather than meat. They often gain additional income by selling calves, hogs (fed on skimmed milk and whey), and also old cows, poultry, and eggs. The larger enterprises, to a great extent mechanized, have low production costs; in contrast, many small farms hold an economically marginal position. Tenancy is low, because the owner-operator has greater incentive to devote care and demanding labor to the animals.

Agricultural regions as shown on small-scale maps are always gross simplifications. This is particularly true for the zone in Europe commonly designated as the dairy belt. A large-scale view of any section of this belt would show how intermingled it is with districts of

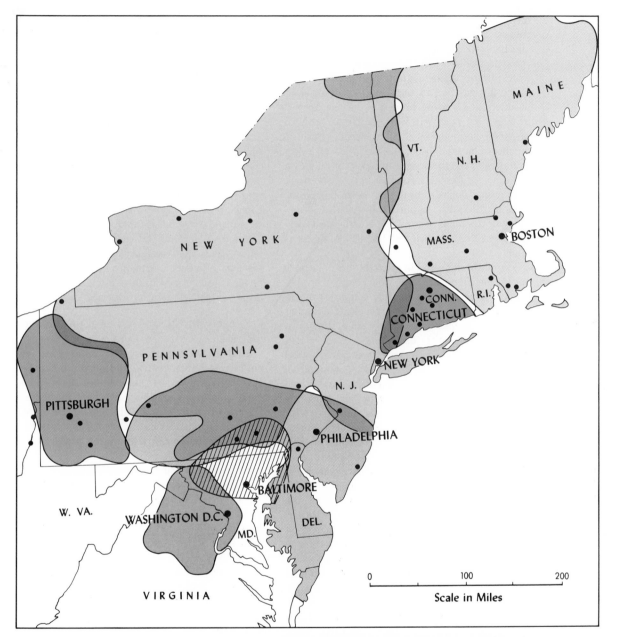

Figure 12–5. UNITED STATES: MAJOR MILKSHEDS IN THE NORTHEAST

Seven milksheds are shown, six of them supplying large metropolitan areas (Boston, New York, Philadelphia, Baltimore, Washington, D.C., and Pittsburgh), and one serving the cluster of cities in western Connecticut. In areas where the main markets are close together, there is considerable overlap of the milksheds as in southern Pennsylvania. The smaller dots are medium-sized cities which compete with the larger cities for milk supply. Based on a map in Gottmann, 1961, 230.

12. Agriculture in Modern Societies

271

mixed farming, specialized horticulture, and transitional forms hard to place in one class or another. West European agriculture went through a crisis in the late nineteenth century, when imports of cheap grain from overseas compelled farmers to find more specialized forms of production. Dairying proved to be the answer in much of northern Europe. Urban growth provided ever-increasing markets. Besides, much of the land because of either cool rainy summers or rough topography or a combination of both, was better suited for raising livestock than crops. Thus dairying became an important —often the most important—agricultural activity in the lands around the North and Baltic seas as well as in interior highlands like Switzerland.

Denmark pioneered in modern dairy methods and farmers' cooperatives, now common to this branch of agriculture. In that country pasture grazing is quite secondary to the feeding of cultivated crops, especially barley, but also lucerne and clover hay, fodder beets, and turnips. In addition the cows receive imported corn and high-protein oil cakes. A cooperative creamery collects the milk and makes it into butter and cheese. The farmer buys back the skimmed milk to feed his pigs, together with barley and imported concentrates. A cooperative bacon factory buys the fattened hogs. This example shows the complexity of production. Such farms are, in essence, intensive converters that change plants into milk and meat.

In the Netherlands many polders* along the North Sea have a water table too high to permit crop cultivation. Thus, grazing on permanent pastures is more common there than in Denmark. Holland's bacon production for export is minor, but condensed and powdered milk and cheese are important trade commodities. In the mountains of Switzerland and adjoining countries the dairy cattle are moved late in spring from the valleys to higher pastures (*alps*). The attendants make the milk into cheese. For the winter they bring the cows down to the stables and feed them hay and other fodder

*A polder is a dike-enclosed area with a controlled groundwater level.

crops grown in the valleys. Condensed milk and milk chocolate are well-known Swiss exports. Other industrial countries in Europe have their own dairy districts, but may import part of their butter and cheese. This is especially true for Great Britain in spite of the fact that much of its land surface is in dairy farms.

The flourishing dairy industry of New Zealand contributes almost one-third to the total export value of the country. The main concentration lies in the North Island, where mild winters and adequate moisture provide year-round grazing on fine improved pastures. Efficient production on large enterprises and rigid quality standards make it possible for New Zealand butter and cheese to overcome high labor costs and freight charges to distant markets. British Commonwealth preferential tariffs greatly aided in developing the dairy industry in this remote location (Figure 12–6).

Crop Farming. *Mediterranean Agriculture,* as practiced in southern Europe and along the coastal strip of Southwest Asia, differs considerably from that in central and northern Europe. Livestock has far less importance here; moreover, crop cultivation and livestock husbandry are usually separate or only loosely associated activities. Unless irrigation is available, summer drought severely restricts animal pastures and summer crops.

Since ancient times cereals—mainly wheat—have been grown in the moist winter season. Drought-resistant vines and trees, above all the grape and olive, occupy much of the remaining farmland. The small water volume available in summer restricts irrigation. It is, however, a necessity for citrus fruits, introduced to this area from their more humid homelands in eastern Asia. Livestock browse on deforested, often badly eroded, uplands during the summer, and graze in winter on whatever lowland pastures can be found.

Agriculture in these lands is gradually becoming integrated with the modern commercial economy, though many vestiges of the past remain. Almost everywhere the semifeudal latifundia (with absentee ownership and share tenants) sharply contrast with the small semi-

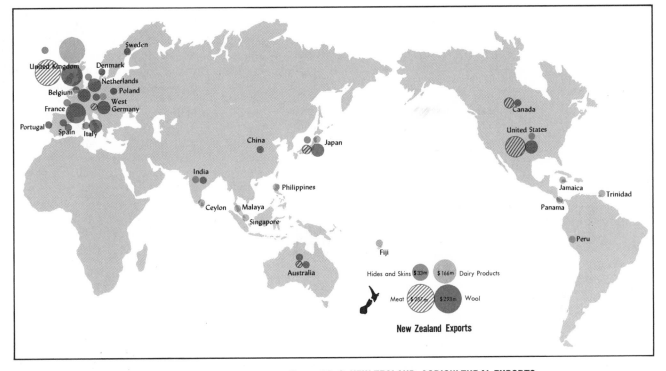

New Zealand Exports

Hides and Skins $33m $166m Dairy Products

Meat $257m $293m Wool

Value of Exports from New Zealand:

Millions of U.S. Dollars

○	1 - 4	◯	25 - 49
○	5 - 9	◯	50 - 99
○	10 - 24	◯	100 - 199

Figure 12–6. NEW ZEALAND: AGRICULTURAL EXPORTS

The map shows the principal destinations of four categories of exports from New Zealand for the period July 1962 to June 1963, inclusive. Their total value was U.S.$729 million; all other exports from New Zealand amounted to U.S.$123 million. Data from United Nations *Commodity Trade Statistics 1963,* Statistical Papers, Series D. vol. 13.

subsistence peasant plots. Compared to northern Europe a larger proportion of the population depends on agriculture, and their productivity is low. Even on the large wheat estates of southern Italy and the Spanish plateaus production methods remain inefficient and yields poor.

Raising grapes for wine is widespread. A few districts have become famous for their specialty, among them Malaga wine, Andalusian sherry from Spain, and port from northern Portugal.

Some parts of Greece and Turkey are well known for currants and raisins. Here as in southern Italy tobacco is an important cash crop. The irrigated coastal fringes of southern Spain are veritable garden spots (*huertas*), where rice fields alternate with almond and citrus orchards, or vegetable plots. Northern Sicily and southern Italy, too, produce citrus fruits. Israel has made the desert bloom, using modern cultivation methods to produce a variety of fruits and early vegetables. The French

12. Agriculture in Modern Societies

and Italian *rivieras,* protected by mountains, long have been noted for their diversity of production, including that of flowers, partly for the extraction of perfumes and partly for seeds. Much of Mediterranean agriculture is in the nature of gardening. Hand labor results in intricate patterns of interculture, especially in favored plains and basins. A three-storied use of land is not uncommon, with grapevines festooned between olive trees, and vegetables covering the ground.

The olive tree occupies vast areas unfit for other crops because its long roots tap moisture from deep below the surface and it does fairly well on poor, stony soils. The main product is the oil, used in place of butter and lard, so common to Europe beyond the Alps. Scarcity of pasture discourages cattle husbandry, although a few oxen may be kept for work purposes. Donkeys and mules serve for riding or carrying heavy burdens. Goats and sheep provide milk that is made into cheese, but sheep are chiefly kept for wool. Large flocks under the care of a few shepherds move seasonally from winter to summer pastures and back again (*transhumance*).

The broad fertile plain of the Po River in northern Italy, although within the Mediterranean region, forms a transition to the types of land use in transalpine Europe. Its winters are too cool for olives and other subtropical trees; summers are hot, but with more rain than in lands to the south. Water from rivers that come down from the Alps floods rice fields in the western and central plain. Unirrigated lands are widely used to produce corn. The lower plain grows mainly sugar beets and hemp. Irrigated meadows and fodder crops support large herds of dairy and beef cattle; milk is manufactured into well-known Italian cheeses. While the natural environment, so different from southern Italy, explains in part the agricultural features of the Po plain, the progressive character of its farming owes much to the stimulus of the large industrial centers in this region.

Specialized Horticulture. Although medieval central and northern Europe had vineyards and market gardens to supply nobles, churchmen, and merchants with wines, fruits, and vegetables, horticulture as a regional dominant is a modern phenomenon, closely related to the increasing city population with its rising living standards and to the technology of conservation and transportation. The United States with an affluent market of continental size and a great variety of climatic conditions strikingly demonstrates this interplay of various factors. Although most cities have "truck farms"* in their vicinity, they buy the bulk of their fruits and vegetables from specialized, often quite remote districts. Each horticultural area has developed its own organizations and services for harvesting, processing, and marketing, thus uniting agricultural, industrial, and commercial functions into an efficient regional complex.

The three Pacific Coast states produce over half of all fruits and nuts and one-third of all vegetables sold in the United States. Washington and Oregon have their apple districts on the inner flanks of the Cascades, and walnuts and hops in the Willamette Valley. But California by far exceeds them in output and versatility of production. Old World specialty crops each have found their ecological niche in climates ranging from cool, foggy summers like those of northwest Europe to blazing desert skies like Egypt's. California has a long growing season, soils of great variety, and water for irrigation almost everywhere. The southern part, including the Imperial Valley, grows citrus fruits, olives, and dates, as well as vegetables, the Salinas Valley head lettuce, the foggy headlands along the coast lima beans, the valleys around San Francisco Bay wine grapes, the San Joaquin Valley raisin grapes. Many areas of the state produce apricots, peaches, plums, walnuts, and almonds, and also abundant vegetables of many kinds.

Harvesting this diversity of crops requires a large labor force. Unskilled migrant workers have been used—and often abused—for a long time: Chinese and Japanese in the nineteenth

---

*The term "truck farming," used in the United States since the eighteenth century, derives from the French "troquer," meaning "to exchange."

century, Filipinos and "Okies" before World War II, more recently Puerto Ricans and Mexicans—the latter on special entry permits. Even so, high labor costs compel farmers to mechanize operations wherever possible, especially on large holdings, many owned by corporations. These large farms often switch from one crop to another, depending on the estimated consumer demand and the prices for particular items. This type of industrial-commercial agriculture is a far cry from the more traditional horticulture of Mediterranean Europe.

Specialized horticulture occurs in a number of districts along the Atlantic and Gulf coasts to supply adjacent city markets or to use favorable climate or soil. Cigar tobacco is a specialty of the Connecticut Valley; truck crops prevail on the seaboards from New Jersey to Virginia, tobacco farther south. Citrus fruits and early vegetables characterize Florida's horticulture, sugarcane the western Gulf Coast, citrus fruits and vegetables the Texas coastal region. Soils, particularly where sandy, require large amounts of commercial fertilizer. Even though the climate is humid, irrigation is applied with increasing frequency to ensure good quality and heavy yields. More inland lie the peach orchards of South Carolina and Georgia and the apple orchards of the Shenandoah and other Appalachian valleys. In the north the frosts of late spring or early fall may easily hurt fruits. Vineyards and orchards in the Great Lakes states therefore seek shores where large bodies of water temper the climate.

Although Europe north of the Alps grows great quantities of vegetables and fruits, political fragmentation has discouraged the large-scale regional specialization so evident in the United States. Small market gardens are almost everywhere. Each farmer produces with intense hand labor as many crops as he can coax from the land. Much fruit still comes from orchards that are part of general or dairy farms. It is uneven in quality for lack of proper care. However, this is more true for eastern than western Europe, where affluent city people pay premium prices for high-grade products. Here, too, much trade flows across international boundaries from specialized horticultural districts to urban agglomerations; for instance, from the Netherlands to the Ruhr district. Near the great cities, greenhouses cover extensive areas, producing table grapes, tomatoes, and other fruits and vegetables that need protection against inclement weather. Some districts concentrate on flowers, seeds, or bulbs; others produce hops. Probably the best known horticultural specialty of western Europe is the wine-producing vineyard. Some districts because of climate, soil, and traditional skill have become famous for their red or white premium wines, among them the region near Bordeaux in southwest France, Burgundy and Champagne in the northeast, also the Rhine and Moselle valleys of adjacent Germany.

Grain Farming. While the cultivation of grains is obviously a major element in most types of farming, only in some regions is the land almost exclusively devoted to cereals. This commercial specialization came to the fore when growing urban populations of the Occidental world required ever more bread grains. The pioneer farmer in the Middle West, Australia, and Argentina responded by making wheat his cash crop. Scarcity of labor as well as the nature of grain cultivation encouraged use of machinery. As more intensive forms of agriculture occupied the humid lands closer to the markets, specialized grain farming found itself largely restricted to the subhumid lands in more remote locations. The lower yields per acre were countered by increase in farm size, demanding in turn more mechanization of the production. Thus, grain farms are on the average the largest of all crop-growing enterprises and the most mechanized.

Climatic risk presents an ever-present danger. The mean annual precipitation in most wheat regions is between 10 and 25 inches, but varies greatly from year to year. When grain prices are high, the farmer expands beyond the safe climatic limits until a series of crop failures beats him back. In the United States the lessons of droughts and dust storms have been taken to heart, but in the Soviet Union the plowing up of the "virgin lands" on the dry margins of Turkestan suggests that each country has to learn its own lesson the hard way.

12. Agriculture in Modern Societies

A combine crew moves across a Nebraska wheat field. These harvesters rent
their services to farmers, beginning in the middle of May in Texas and ending
up by the close of September at the Canadian border. On a seasonal circuit a
crew operating four combines will travel about 3,600 miles and harvest 22,500
acres. [Courtesy of U.S. Department of Agriculture]

In North America grain farming predominates in three distinct areas. The spring-wheat
region extends from the plains of western Minnesota west and northwest to Montana and
Alberta. Because of the severe winters, seeding
must wait until spring; harvest comes in August
and September. Flax—for linseed oil—is a subsidiary crop. The steeply rolling dry loess soils
of the Palouse country of southeast Washington
also specialize on wheat, mainly spring sown.
Kansas and sections of surrounding states grow
winter wheat because the milder winter allows
sowing in the fall with harvest in early summer.

In the Southwest the very high summer temperatures favor sorghum rather than wheat.

In Europe much wheat is grown in France,
Spain, Italy, and Hungary, but specialized grain
farming as the regional dominant is more characteristic of the steppe soils of the eastern
Ukraine, southern Siberia, and, in recent years,
the Kazakh and Uzbek republics (Figure
12–7).

In the mid-latitudes of the southern hemisphere lie the grain belts of Australia and
Argentina. They differ, however, from their
counterparts in the northern hemisphere be-

cause their grain cropping is more commonly associated with livestock grazing. In Australia wheat is by far the main crop inland from the Great Dividing Range, stretching as a crescent from southern Queensland through New South Wales and Victoria into South Australia. A smaller zone lies in the southwest corner of the continent. Many wheat farmers use part of their large properties for sheep pasture.

In Argentina the dense railroad net connecting farmland with nearby seaports greatly aids export agriculture on the fertile Pampa soils. However, the full potential of the region has not been attained because of the latifundium (*estancia*) system. The association of grain and livestock usually consists in growing alfalfa as feed for beef cattle, followed by wheat, or by corn in the moister northeastern part. Since most of the corn is not needed for local fodder, it is exported, as is most of the beef and wheat.

Cotton Farming. A generation ago the American Cotton Belt was an acceptable regional generalization. At the time cotton was by far the ranking cash crop in the Old South. Sharecroppers worked parcels of plantation holdings with hoe and mule-drawn plow; at harvesttime entire families moved between the rows to pick the cotton bolls. The sharecropper lacked the motivation, the knowledge, and the means to break the vicious routine of cotton growing. Monoculture exhausted the land. Production per worker as well as per acre remained low, and poverty was the inevitable lot of most of the population, Negro tenant as well as poor white. The Old South has greatly changed in recent years. The scourge of the boll weevil in the 1920s, the depression of the 1930s, and subsequent government restrictions on cotton growing, together with mechanization, all brought about diversification in agriculture. Although cotton is still an important crop, it now shares the land with pastures and fodder crops for beef cattle, and with soybeans, peanuts, vegetables, and fruits. New crops, better methods of tillage, and wide use of fertilizers have restored soils and stopped erosion. Scarred slopes have been planted to new forest, yielding timber, pulp, resins, and turpentine. The use of machines, including the mechanical cotton picker, compelled the consolidation of small tenant farms. The released manpower has moved to industrial jobs, mainly in northern cities.

The only part of the Old South where cotton is still king lies in the rich river-bottom lands of Arkansas and Mississippi. Form of enterprise and traditional social structure justify including this area among the world's plantation regions. Cotton growing invaded the fertile prairie soils of eastern Texas in the 1880s, and has since expanded into the subhumid lands: northward into Oklahoma and westward as far as the San Joaquin Valley of California. Today the Southwest, together with the Mississippi floodplains, is the main cotton producer. The drier climate discourages the boll weevil, and the flat plains, divided into large farms, favor mechanized operation. Over the greater part of this region irrigation is necessary. The shift of cotton to better lands and controlled water supply have substantially raised the average yield per acre. Although the area under cotton has shrunk in the last forty years from 43 to 11 million acres, production has dropped only from 15 to 11 million bales. In other words, while formerly 3 acres of cotton were needed to obtain one bale (500 pounds gross), now 1 acre suffices. As with other government crop-control programs, the policy of stemming overproduction through acreage reduction has been largely thwarted by higher output per acre.

The only other leading cotton producer among the industrial countries is the Soviet Union. (Among the less advanced countries important producers are mainland China, India, Brazil, Mexico, Egypt, Pakistan, and Sudan.) Despite the rather short growing season, some cotton is raised in the Ukraine and near the Caucasus Mountains; but the main area lies in the irrigated river plains east and south of the Aral Sea in Soviet Asia. Almost the entire crop is raised on state farms and collectives.

Livestock Ranching. Like nomadic herding, ranching depends on extensive livestock grazing, but here the similarity ends. Ranching is a specialized commercial offshoot from European agriculture—either from Mediterranean or from mixed farming—with the operator living in a permanent residence on privately owned property. Although ranching mainly occupies dry lands with short grass or shrub vegetation, it also occurs on more humid grasslands remote from large markets, as in New Zealand and the southern parts of Africa and South America.

Europeans occupied most of the mid-latitude grasslands in the course of the nineteenth century. Initially, lack of transportation prohibited production of beef or mutton; only hides, wool, and tallow had value for export. Herds of livestock grazed on the open range under the care of cowboys, *gauchos,* or *vaqueros.* Overstocking the range was common; herds were exposed to droughts or blizzards. In most countries the clash between advancing farmer and rancher ended in the latter's retreat to sections unsuitable for crop production. The range changed into the ranch, with barbed-wire fenced pastures, provision for water, and where necessary, animal shelter. Fencing not only regulated grazing, but also protected the herd against interbreeding with poor strains. Better means of transportation have made hides and tallow minor products as compared to meat. Nevertheless, livestock ranching remains, on the whole, a marginal agricultural activity. It competes with increasing difficulty against the ever more efficient production in regions of intensive livestock husbandry. The latter areas support also, by far, the larger number of animals, a fact sometimes overlooked because livestock ranching takes in such vast expanses of land.

The drier the climate, the sparser the vegetation and the lower the carrying capacity of the land—that is, the number of animals that can be supported per unit of pasture. In Nebraska, on the humid edge of the Great Plains, the carrying capacity averages one cow per 5 acres, while in Nevada this ratio is one to at least 75 acres. Most cattle ranches in the United States own over 2,500 acres and many have more than 10,000 acres. In Australia the holdings are even larger. Ownership by corporations is not uncommon, especially by those operating packing and other processing plants. But size alone is inadequate to judge the character of the operations. In Canada and the northern United States the livestock must be sheltered and fed during the harsh winter, and even in summer many ranchers provide supplementary feed. They either grow this on their own irrigated fields, or buy it from nearby irrigation districts, particularly alfalfa and tops of sugar beets as well as the beet pulp from the sugar-beet factories. In such favorable areas the ranch has virtually become a mixed-farming enterprise. Elsewhere herdsmen take the livestock in summer to mountain pastures in the public domain, and return it in the fall to more sheltered locations. Moreover, the western rancher does not attempt to fatten his cattle, but sends it to the Middle West to gain weight on corn and other farm crops.

In Australia only 15 percent of the surface receives more than 30 inches of rain annually, and over 60 percent is classified as arid or semiarid. High variability of precipitation from year to year exposes agriculture to the risks of severe droughts. These conditions, together with sparse population and remote location, favor sheep raising in large parts of the country. The main concentration is in New South Wales and Victoria. The rough terrain of the Great Dividing Range, though having a relatively moist climate, is more suitable to pastoral activity than crop raising. Here many farmers specialize on merino breeding and fattening of lambs, while others rear beef cattle.

The zone adjoining the highlands on the west has a mean annual rainfall of 15 to 30 inches. Here lies the wheat and sheep zone mentioned before. The sheep are chiefly kept for wool. A purely pastoral economy prevails where the erratic rainfall averages less than 15 inches. The vegetation grades from shrub steppe to desert scrub. The critical factor in determining the carrying capacity is the amount of fodder available during the drought period. Less than 20 acres pasture per sheep leads to overgrazing. Stations, as ranches are called here, necessarily cover wide areas, averaging some 20,000 acres. Although the land itself is cheap, substantial investments are required for fencing the "paddocks" (pastures) and supplying adequate water. On the other hand, supplementary feeding is rare, and the mild weather obviates the

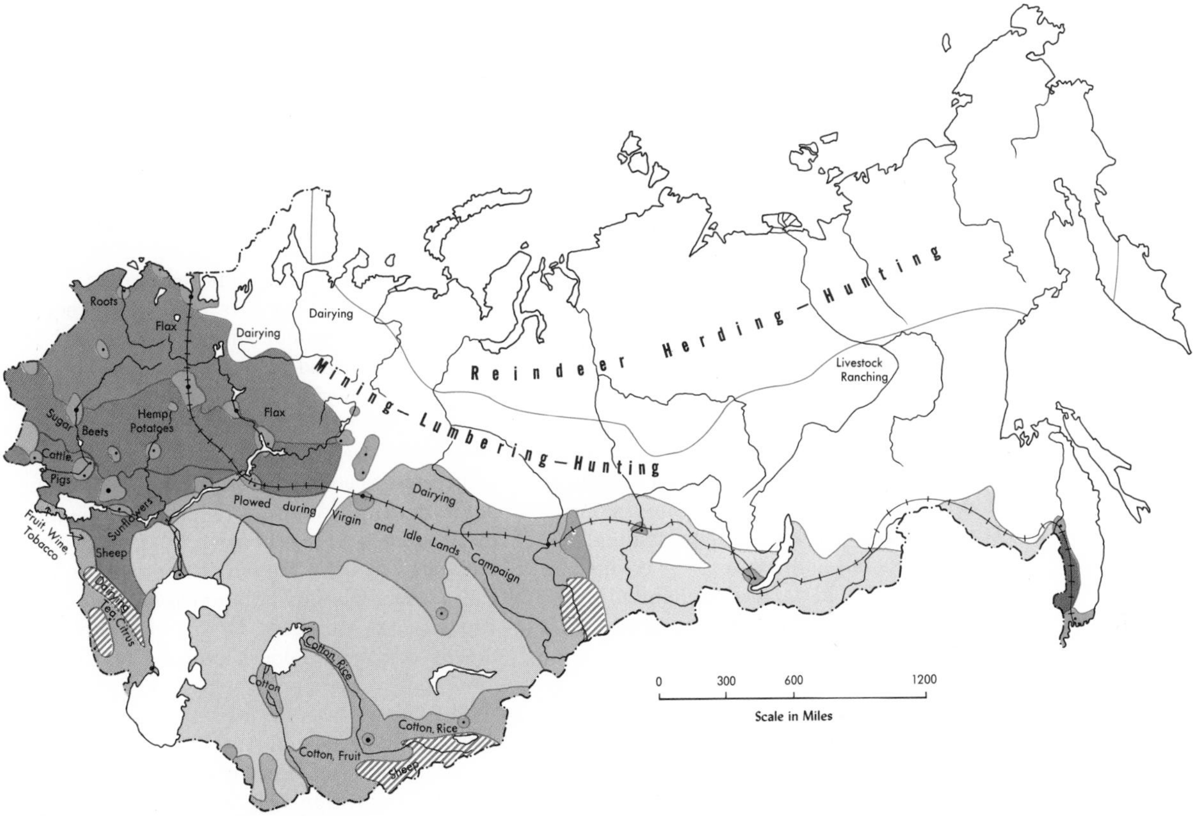
Roots
Flax
Dairying
Dairying
Mining—Lumbering—Hunting
Reindeer Herding—Hunting
Livestock Ranching
Hemp, Potatoes
Flax
Sugar Beets
Cattle
Pigs
Sunflowers
Fruit, Wine, Tobacco
Sheep
Dairying, Tea, Citrus
Plowed during Virgin and Idle Lands Campaign
Dairying
Cotton, Rice
Cotton
Cotton, Rice
Cotton, Fruit
Sheep
0 300 600 1200
Scale in Miles
Mixed Farming (Dairying, Pigs, Rye, Potatoes, and Hay)
Mixed Farming (Maize, Wheat, and Beef Cattle)
Cereals, Industrial Crops, and Livestock
Spring Wheat Region
Sheep Herding
Mountain Herding
Intensive Horticulture
Scattered Grain and Livestock Production
Maize, Rice, Soybeans, and Potatoes
Market Gardening and Dairying
Principal Cities
Trans-Siberian Railway

Figure 12–7. SOVIET UNION: LAND-USE REGIONS

Within the broad regional types, production specialties are shown by name. After Cherdantsev, 1958.

need for shelter. In this interior region wool provides the exclusive source of income.

While sheep prevail in the southern dry lands of Australia, temperatures are too high for them in the north. Beef cattle predominate there and are sent to market by driving them from station to station to the railheads in eastern Queensland.

Ranching is also quite important in New Zealand, with emphasis on sheep in the cooler South Island. Irrigation water from the western mountains supplements the moderate rainfall to maintain the rich improved pastures. In addition to wool, lamb provides an important export commodity for the British market.

In Argentina and Uruguay the general farming of the humid pampas shades off into livestock ranching on the drier margins. In Patagonia wool sheep are the principal animals. A mixture of savanna and scrub forest covers the interior of Brazil. This sparsely inhabited country is mainly used for cattle grazing. The gauchos (herders) live a seminomadic life around the widely scattered ranch headquarters. The thin scrub cattle are slaughtered for hides, tallow, and the production of salt beef (the poor man's meat), or driven long distances to farms to be fattened before being sent to the city slaughterhouse. The very south corner of Brazil, bordering on Uruguay and Argentina, enjoys a more humid temperate climate with a much better grass stand than the interior. Although this region seems well suited for mixed farming, it has so far remained chiefly the domain of large pastoral estates, where gauchos round up the cattle and sheep that graze on the prairies.

Trends in Modern Agriculture

The vast and rapid changes in twentieth-century Occidental farming have significance not only in themselves but also as forerunners of a transformation that sooner or later will confront other societies. These modifications, virtually amounting to a new agricultural revolution, are most clearly seen in the United States.

The farm becomes an industrial enterprise requiring large investment of capital and competent management. Mechanical power replaces manual labor wherever feasible. Integrated machines shake trees, sort fruits, test and pick radishes and cotton, process and pack head lettuce. Airplanes broadcast seed, spray pest- and weed-killing chemicals, spread fertilizer, and frighten away birds. In dairying all except the cow becomes a fully automated industry.

Mechanization permits, but also requires, mass output of standardized commodities. Production, controlled at every step, ensures high yields of the desired quality. Even in normally humid climates overhead irrigation provides crops with water in the right amount at the right time. Seeds and breeds are created to meet environmental conditions, mechanical handling, or consumers' preferences. In the Old South, for instance, the introduction of improved subtropical grasses has greatly increased the carrying capacity of pastures. Here, too, new cattle breeds adapted to local climates and diseases have replaced the poor "piny" cattle of former times. New wheat strains are constantly being developed to withstand disease, to ripen in short summers, or to facilitate machine harvesting.

Industrialization of agriculture leads to larger-sized enterprises, either by consolidation of adjacent small farms or by integration of widely scattered holdings. It is not uncommon for a cattleman, grain farmer, or horticulturist to own or rent land in different parts of the country as a hedge against climatic risk or as a means to use his machinery the year-round. In addition to this horizontal combination there is increasing vertical integration, forging closer links between farm and market. Besides corporate structure, the expanding practice of contract farming relates orchards to processing plants, hatcheries and dairies to supermarket chains.

Efficient production leads not only to consolidation and integration, but also to abandonment of poor land. Thus, fewer farmers produce more and better commodities on fewer farms occupying less area. Land taken out of production is put into forest or used for public and private recreation. New types of farming re-

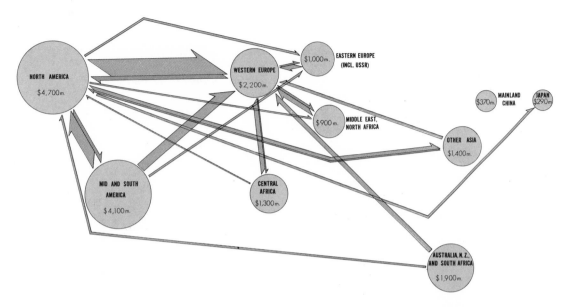

Figure 12–8. WORLD REGIONS: TRADE IN FOOD PRODUCTS

The circles on this diagram are proportional to the total exports of foods, beverages, and tobacco from each of ten regions. The arrows joining the circles show the direction and value of trade in these commodities. Only those regions which import or export more than a quarter of a billion dollars' worth from or to another region are joined. SOURCE: United Nations *Monthly Bulletin of Statistics,* March 1965, table 3.

Amount of Trade in Food, etc.
in Millions of U.S. Dollars
(Imports and Exports Calculated
Separately)

250
500
1,000
2,000

place old ones: dairy farming and beef-cattle rearing expand in the South, and diversified agriculture invades the Great Plains.

The modern farmer is a businessman. He may reside on his farm or in town, or live "out of a suitcase" while supervising operations on one of his holdings. He follows market trends closely, consults agricultural experts, and reads journals reporting the results of the latest research in agronomy and farm management. While this sketch represents only a minority of farmers today, it promises to be true for nearly all before the end of the century.

The same general trends can be observed in western Europe. Although this region needs imports, especially of animal fodder, the impressive postwar gains in agricultural output

demonstrate what can be accomplished in an area where land use was already at a high level of intensity. The tremendous productivity of American farming has presented the paradox of an embarrassing plenty at home while much of the world goes hungry. Without entering into a discussion of how to deal with this perplexing problem, it is quite clear that in the near future the world's staggering population surge will require all the surplus food the United States, Canada, and a few other nations can spare. At the same time the underdeveloped countries must make every effort to boost their own production. The American and West European experience, though by no means a perfect model, suggests ways and means toward greater abundance for everyone.

12. Agriculture in Modern Societies

Citations

Cherdantsev, N. S. *Ekonomicheskaya Geografiya SSSR,* Moscow, 1958. [Map]

Fryer, D. W. *World Economic Development,* New York, 1965.

Gottmann, J. *Megalopolis: The Urbanized Northeastern Seaboard of the United States,* New York, 1961. [Map]

Further Readings

Alexander, J. W. "International Trade: Selected Types of World Regions," *Economic Geography,* 36 (1960): 95–115.

———. *Economic Geography,* Englewood Cliffs, N.J., 1963.

Baker, O. E. "Agricultural Regions of North America," *Economic Geography,* 7 (1931): 109–153; 8 (1932): 325–377.

Black, J. D. *The Rural Economy of New England: A Regional Study,* Cambridge, Mass., 1950.

Calef, W. *Private Grazing and Public Lands: Studies of the Local Management of the Taylor Grazing Act,* Chicago, 1960.

Chisholm, M. *Rural Settlement and Land Use: An Essay in Location,* London, 1961.

Cumberland, K. B. "The Agricultural Regions of New Zealand," *Geographical Journal,* 112 (1949): 43–46.

Curry, L. "Climate and Economic Life: A New Approach, with Examples from the United States," *Geographical Review,* 42 (1952): 367–383.

Dana, S. T. *Forest and Range Policy: Its Development in the United States,* New York, 1956.

Dickinson, R. E. *Germany: General and Regional Geography,* 2d ed., London and New York, 1961.

Dovring, F. *Land and Labor in Europe, 1900–1950: A Comparative Survey of Recent Agrarian History,* The Hague, 1956.

Dumont, R. *Types of Rural Economy,* New York, 1957.

Durand, L., Jr. "The Major Milksheds of the Northeastern Quarter of the United States," *Economic Geography,* 40 (1964): 9–33.

Freeman, T. W. "Farming in Irish Life," *Geographical Journal,* 110 (1948): 38–59.

Fried, M. H. "Land Tenure, Geography and Ecology in the Contact of Cultures," *American Journal of Economics and Sociology,* 11 (1952): 391–412. Reprinted in Wagner, P. L., and Mikesell, M. W. (eds.) *Readings in Cultural Geography,* Chicago, 1962, 302–317.

Gibson, L. E. "Characteristics of a Regional Margin of the Corn and Dairy Belts," *Annals of the Association of American Geographers,* 38 (1948): 244–270.

Gottmann, J. *A Geography of Europe,* 3d ed., New York, 1962.

Griffin, P. F., and Chatham, R. L. "Population: A Challenge to California's Changing Citrus Industry," *Economic Geography,* 34 (1958): 272–276.

Hambidge, G. (ed.) *Climate and Man,* 1941 Yearbook of Agriculture, House Document no. 27, 77th Congress, 1st Session, Government Printing Office, Washington, D.C., 1941.

Harris, C. D. "Agricultural Production in the United States: The Past Fifty Years and the Next," *Geographical Review,* 47 (1957): 175–193.

Haystead, L., and Fite, G. *The Agricultural Regions of the United States,* Norman, Okla., 1955.

Henderson, D. A. " 'Corn Belt' Cattle Feeding in Eastern Colorado's Irrigated Valleys," *Economic Geography,* 30 (1954): 364–372.

Hewes, L., and Schmieding, A. C. "Risk in the Central Great Plains: Geographical Patterns of Wheat Failure in Nebraska, 1931–1952," *Geographical Review,* 46 (1956): 375–387.

Higbee, E. C. *The American Oasis: The Land and Its Uses,* New York, 1957.

———. *Farms and Farmers in an Urban Age,* New York, 1963.

Highsmith, R. M., Jr. (ed.) *Case Studies in World Geography: Occupance and Economy Types,* Englewood Cliffs, N.J., 1961.

Jackson, W. A. D. "The Virgin and Idle Lands of Western Siberia and Northern Kazakhstan: A Geographical Appraisal," *Geographical Review,* 46 (1956): 1–19.

James, P. E. *Latin America,* 3d ed., New York, 1959.

Kollmorgen, W. M., and Jenks, G. F. "Suitcase Farming in Sully County, South Dakota," *Annals of the Association of American Geographers,* 48 (1958): 27–40.

——— and ———. "Sidewalk Farming in Toole County, Montana, and Traill County, North Dakota," *Annals of the Association of American Geographers,* 48 (1958): 209–231.

Large, D. C. "Cotton in the San Joaquin Valley: A Study of Government in Agriculture," *Geographical Review,* 47 (1957): 365–380.

Lewis, R. A. "The Irrigation Potential of Soviet Central Asia," *Annals of the Association of American Geographers,* 52 (1962): 99–114.

Lewthwaite, G. R. "Wisconsin and the Waikato: A Comparison of Dairy Farming in the United States and New Zealand," *Annals of the Association of American Geographers,* 54 (1964): 59–87.

Mather, E. C., and Hart, J. F. "The Geography of Manure," *Land Economics,* 32 (1956): 25–38.

McNee, R. B. "Rural Development in the Italian South: A Geographic Case Study," *Annals of the Association of American Geographers,* 45 (1955): 127–151.

Mead, W. R. *Farming in Finland,* London, 1953.

———. *An Economic Geography of the Scandinavian States and Finland,* London, 1958.

Meinig, D. W. *On the Margins of the Good Earth: The South Australian Wheat Frontier, 1869–1884,* Chicago, 1963.

Olmstead, C. W. "American Orchard and Vineyard Regions," *Economic Geography,* 32 (1956): 187–236.

Prunty, M. C., Jr. "Recent Quantitative Changes in the Cotton Regions of the Southeastern States," *Economic Geography,* 27 (1951): 189–208.

Schwartz, H. *Russia's Soviet Economy,* 2d ed., Englewood Cliffs, N.J., 1954.

Shimkin, D. B. "Economic Regionalization in the Soviet Union," *Geographical Review,* 42 (1952): 591–614.

Simpson, E. S. "Milk Production in England and Wales: A Study in the Influence of Collective Marketing," *Geographical Review,* 49 (1959): 95–111.

Stamp, L. D. *The Land of Britain: Its Use and Misuse,* 2d ed., London, 1950.

Thoman, R. S. *The Geography of Economic Activity: An Introductory World Survey,* New York, 1962.

—— and Patton, D. J. *Focus on Geographical Activity: A Collection of Original Studies,* New York, 1964.

Van Royen, W. *Atlas of the World's Resources,* vol. 1: *The Agricultural Resources of the World,* Englewood Cliffs, N.J., 1954.

Van Veen, J. *Dredge, Drain, Reclaim: The Art of a Nation,* 4th ed., The Hague, 1955. [The Netherlands]

Wadham, S. M., and Wilson, R. K. *Land Utilization in Australia,* 4th ed., Melbourne, 1964.

Wallace, W. H. "Railway Traffic and Agriculture in New Zealand," *Economic Geography,* 34 (1958): 168–184.

Weaver, J. C. "Changing Patterns of Cropland Use in the Middle West," *Economic Geography,* 30 (1954): 1–47.

Webb, W. P. *The Great Plains,* Boston, 1931; New York, 1959.

Yates, P. L. *Food, Land and Manpower in Western Europe,* London, 1960.

Zimmermann, E. W. *World Resources and Industries,* 2d ed., New York, 1951.

13. Industrial Nations and Regions

Industrialization may be viewed as a process of diffusion from the cradlelands of modern technology into other parts of the world. In the most advanced nations manufacturing and all that goes with it has completely permeated society, while in the least developed countries it is, as yet, merely a foreign intrusion amid the ancient way of life. Most countries lie somewhere between these two extremes. Useful indicators of the degree to which industrialization has spread include: industrial workers as a proportion of the labor force (Figure 14–3), use of energy per capita (Figure 14–4), transportation systems (Figure 3–12), and income or product per capita (Figure 14–2). Supporting evidence can be gleaned from the extent of education at all levels, and the degree to which urbanization prevails along the full range of town and city sizes. In all these indexes the heavily industrialized countries score high.

The geography of manufacturing is quite complex. Industry comprises many branches, each with its own combination of technique, organization, supply, and market factors. New industries are free to choose appropriate sites, but older ones often still occupy their original locations, selected under conditions far different from today. Many governments allow industry considerable freedom of decision where to locate, except in matters of defense. Other governments, such as the Soviet Union, plan the entire economy, including industrial locations

and the types and sizes of the manufacturing plants. The kinds of industries a nation has reflect its level of income, technological knowhow, and degree of contact with other peoples—in short, the nature of its culture.

To discuss the geography of manufacturing, we begin with an inquiry into the factors that influence decisions about plant location, and illustrate them by the example of the iron and steel industry in the United States. Then comes an overview of the main industrial regions, followed by a closer look at one region, South Wales.

Factors of Industrial Location

Why is each specific plant located where it is? This question has many possible answers. For example, one could discuss the decisions made at the board meetings of industrial companies, the wishes of individual executives, the actions of legislatures, the dictates of economic ministries. No doubt by studying these one can gain insight into the factors determining location of industry.

Another approach would be to consider the origins of the raw materials a particular industry needs and the destination of its products, using the transportation system as the key to analyze plant location.

Yet another point of view stresses the technology of the nation and the markets available for industrial products—in other words, the kind of society in which the industry is present. Compare, for example, manufacturing locations in the early phases of industrialization with those in a fully developed industrial-commercial situation. Early in the Industrial Revolution the production of basic metals and textiles was the main concern. Plant locations were usually tied to a specific advantage, whether a coalfield for power supply, a mine for raw materials, or a port for transportation. Such factories were self-contained, and had easily recognizable connections with a few raw materials, power sources, and markets. These characteristics we find today in countries in the initial stage of developing a modern manufacturing industry.

In an advanced economy, a multitude of different industries provide for the needs and wants of the consumer in great variety. Industries relate not only to raw materials, power, and markets, but also to each other in complex ways. The automobile that runs off the assembly line at Gorki, Detroit, Paris, or Coventry represents a final product of many different components made in many different plants, each of which depends in turn on other factories for its supplies. In this situation proximity to certain industrial plants often presents the principal factor that influences industrial location (Figure 13–1). This cumulative process of location through interaction and interdependence is often called agglomeration, or aggregation (Weber, 1929; Ullman, 1956).

Market. As an industrial location factor, the market increases in importance with the degree of economic development and the growth of wealth in a society (Harris, 1954). In countries like India the masses of population do not enter into a monetary economy to any degree; big-scale population-oriented consumer industries, therefore, are largely missing. Market influences can be thought of in three ways. First, many industries need to be close to the consumers of their products. People like to eat

Figure 13–1. MICHIGAN: MANUFACTURING EMPLOYMENT, 1960, BY COUNTIES

The northern boundary of the main American manufacturing belt runs east and west through central Michigan. Based on data in U.S. Bureau of the Census, *Census of Population, 1960.*

Number Employed in Manufacturing	Places with 2,500 or more inhabitants	Remainder in County
250 - 1,000		
1,000 - 5,000		
5,000 - 10,000		
10,000 - 25,000		
25,000 - 50,000		
229,000		

bread fresh from the bakery; thus, bread factories tend to locate in population centers. Much of the printing industry in the United States is also oriented to local markets. This is especially true for newspaper and job printing, the latter done in thousands of relatively small plants throughout the country (Figure 13–2).

Second, many industries prefer to be located in or near the largest single metropolitan area in any country. From this prestige location, whether New York, Paris, or Tokyo, they supply the metropolitan market and also, by using the fine network of transportation facilities that converge on the metropolis, serve other regions. New York, the largest single concentration of manufacturing in the United States, has a great share of the apparel and publishing industries.

Third, industries that provide other industrial plants with components for manufacturing tend to locate near their market. This is the process of agglomeration already noted.

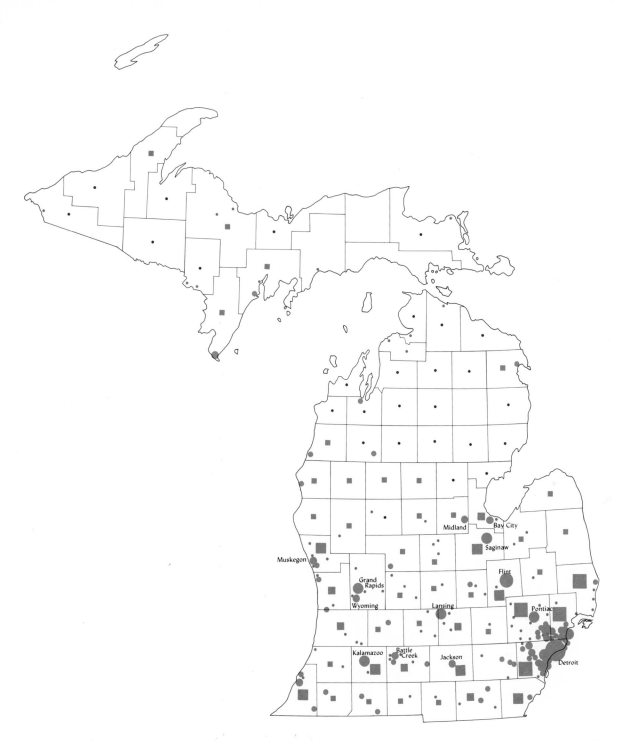

Labor. Sometimes industries locate in particular places to take advantage of known qualities in the local labor force. Many important textile districts have their origin in factories established in poor farming areas to draw upon the cheap labor available. A substantial part of the United States textile industry moved earlier in this century from the high-priced labor of New England to the low-priced labor of the Southeast. The garment industry established itself in New York in the nineteenth century not only because of the market, but because of the available cheap immigrant labor.

Second, industries may locate in a region where the inhabitants possess a particular tradition of skills. The Lyon district in southeastern France once was the center of European silk weaving. When synthetic fibers came to the fore, it was feared that Lyon's textile industry would collapse. In fact, the district remains a leading textile center because the local expertise of entrepreneurs and operatives attracted the new fiber industries. In the United States the electronic-computer industry concentrates in areas where it can recruit highly skilled personnel from universities. Its main focal points are in New York, New England, and southern California, with a subsidiary area in Minneapolis–St. Paul.

Third, government policies concerned with employment often affect industrial location. Regions depressed by technological change (coal-mining areas of Appalachia) or loss of market (shipbuilding in Britain) present social and political problems hardly attractive to new industries. In such cases, the people unable to help themselves need government assistance for the retraining of workers, tax allowances, low-interest loans, and other inducements to new enterprises. Such schemes sometimes are initiated to integrate low-income rural areas with the industrial economy. Most notable of these government-sponsored projects was the development of the Tennessee Valley in the 1930s. In recent years "Appalachia" has received substantial government aid. In western Europe, too, governments have taken steps to spur the development of backward areas such as southern Italy, southern Belgium, and

Figure 13–2. MICHIGAN: EMPLOYMENT IN THE PRINTING AND AUTOMOTIVE INDUSTRIES, 1960, BY COUNTIES

These two maps show the contrast between a service industry located according to the distribution of population, and a manufacturing industry located according to the forces of industrial agglomeration. The shades within the circles show the percentages of employees in the printing and automotive industries. The frequency diagrams indicate that most counties have a small proportion of their work force in printing, but that a few counties have high percentages in the automotive industry and many have very low percentages or none. Based on data in U.S. Bureau of the Census, *Census of Population, 1960.*

Per cent in Printing, Publishing, and Allied Products

O   less than 0.5
◐   0.5 - 1.5
◉   1.5 - 3.0

Key for Map A and B
Number of Employees in All Industries

O   1 - 5,000
O   5,000 - 10,000
O   10,000 - 25,000
O   25,000 - 50,000
O   50,000 - 100,000
O   100,000 - 250,000
O   over 250,000

Per cent in Motor Vehicles and Motor Vehicle Equipment

O   less than 0.5
●   0.5 - 5.0
●   5.0 - 10.0
◉   10.0 - 25.0
●   25.0 - 50.0

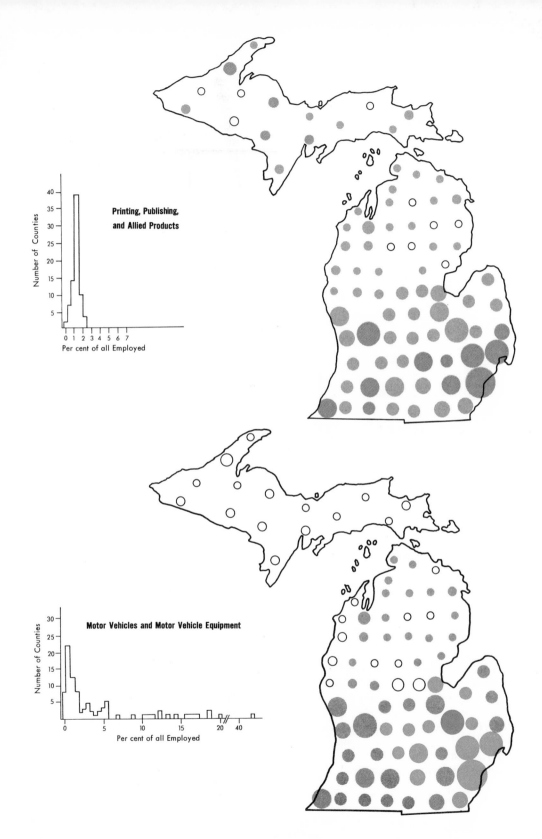

Printing, Publishing,
and Allied Products

Per cent of all Employed

Number of Counties

Motor Vehicles and Motor Vehicle Equipment

Per cent of all Employed

Number of Counties

289

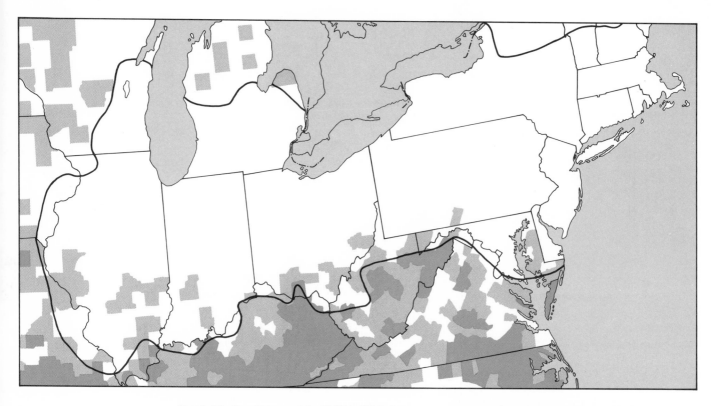

Percent of Families with Incomes below $3,000 in 1959 By County

☐ under 35 percent

▨ 35 - 50 percent

▓ over 50 percent

— Industrial Region Boundary

Figure 13–3. NORTHEASTERN UNITED STATES: FAMILY INCOME BELOW $3,000, 1959

Many counties immediately to the south of the main North American industrial region, especially in Kentucky and West Virginia, have income levels well below those of the manufacturing belt. Based on the map *Families with incomes under $3,000 in 1959, by Counties of the United States,* prepared by the Geography Division, U.S. Bureau of the Census, Washington, D.C., 1960.

western France (Figures 13–3 and 13–4). The case of South Wales, as an example of British "development areas," will be discussed later.

Power. The use of large amounts of energy is, of course, the essential feature of modern manufacturing. As a determinant of location, however, power has declined in significance.

In the early stages of industrialization, factories located mainly where power was available. At first the waterwheel was the most widely used producer of mechanical energy. This explains why many New England industries originally located where they did, and some still maintain their initial sites. A variant of the waterwheel was the windmill, used for

III. Patterns of Livelihood

Figure 13-4. WESTERN EUROPE: INCOME PER CAPITA, 1962

This map shows per capita income, a different criterion than that used for Figure 13-3. All currencies were converted to United States dollars. No adjustments were made for differences in the purchasing power of the national currencies. After *Chase Manhattan Bank*, 1964, with permission.

Per Capita Income in U.S. Dollars

(By County, Province, or Equivalent Division)

Below 800

800 - 1000

Above 1000

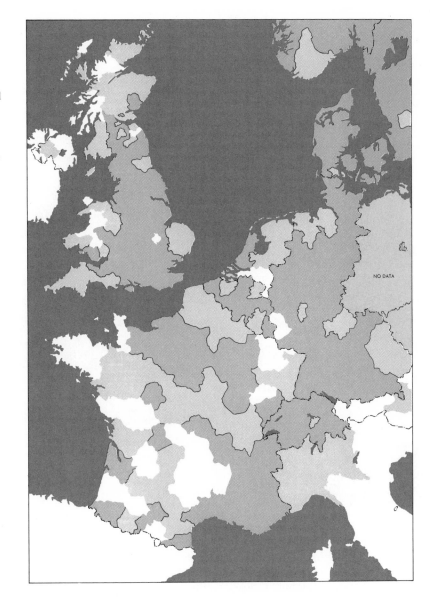

pumping as well as milling. In the seventeenth and eighteenth centuries over a thousand windmills powered the industries of Amsterdam along the Zaan, just north of the port.

When coal supplanted waterpower, the new "mills" located on or close to coalfields, unless they could receive coal cheaply by river, canal, or sea. As steam-powered railroad nets developed, coal could be sent over greater distances to other locations, thereby spreading the impact of manufacturing.

Coal performed a different function in iron and steel making. Here it was used in the form of coke to smelt the iron ore in blast furnaces. Because of the large amounts of coke needed for this process, proximity to the source of

13. Industrial Nations and Regions

In the eighteenth century, at the start of the Industrial Revolution, the new machines were driven by waterpower. The picture shows an old water mill in upland Yorkshire, a row of workers' cottages, and the owner's house. A steam engine, powered by coal, came later and led to expansion of the factory. Stone walls enclose the open fields in this region. [Aerofilms, Ltd.]

metallurgical coal was commonly the decisive locational factor.

Steam engines have been outdated as direct suppliers of industrial power. But they still provide the principal means of converting fuels like coal, oil, and natural gas into electricity, now the chief power source for industry. Electricity is transported much more easily than mechanical steam power. However, it loses considerable voltage over long distances, and thus places some restrictions on industrial location. With the growth of transmission networks and strategically placed power stations, most regions of developed countries have access to electricity in industrial quantities. The first objective of newly industrializing countries is to create an electrical power network.

For most industries, energy is now only a small fraction of the production cost. They can, therefore, locate according to market, labor, raw materials, or other conditions. Nevertheless, certain industries need very large amounts of power to refine metals or produce chemicals. They tend to locate near sources of abundant energy, mainly the big hydroelectric power stations. In turn they attract clusters of fabricating plants. In this way many once remote uplands have received a share of modern industry, among them the Alpine and Scandinavian highlands in Europe, upland Canada, and various mountain regions in the United States.

Raw Materials. Metallic ores and similar raw materials (salt, sulphur) are very bulky. Rather than transporting them over long distances the ores are concentrated, if at all feasible, near their source to rid them of the weight that would have to be removed anyway at the end of the haul. Thus, raw materials having a high weight-loss ratio tend to be processed where they are won.

The United States copper industry illustrates this principle. Many American copper ores contain only 1 percent copper. Initial concentration is done at the mines in Montana, Utah, Arizona, and New Mexico. It removes about 97 tons of waste material for every 100 tons of ore. The next stage, smelting, eliminates almost all the remaining impurities. Since relatively little weight is lost in the reduction of concentrate to "blister copper," the copper smelters are not bound to the mineheads. Nevertheless, most of them are in the mining areas. The smelters in Tacoma, Washington, and in the New York City area rely upon imported concentrates. The last stage is refining the blister copper, during which small amounts of valuable impurities (gold, silver, zinc) are removed. This occurs at places where much electrical power is available, or near the area where the copper will be used. This explains why half of the copper refining capacity is located on the eastern seaboard, mainly in New Jersey.

A similar case concerns the low-grade iron ore of the Lake Superior region. In northern Minnesota, iron ore with only about 30 percent iron content, known as taconite, is refined near the mines into high-grade iron-ore pellets with about 65 percent iron content. These can then be shipped economically via the Great Lakes system of waterways to the iron and steel centers in the heart of the American industrial belt.

Transportation. In essence, locating a factory resolves itself in the question how best to overcome distance separating markets, raw materials, power, labor, and other elements of the production process. Means of transportation and communication are therefore the vital organs of the modern economy, whether tankers, trains, trucking fleets, transmission and pipelines, or telephones (Ullman, 1956). For this reason economists, geographers, and others have singled out transportation to develop a general theory of industrial location. It is useful in two ways: as a generalized explanation of the many forces that determine industrial location; and as a set of hypotheses that can be applied when investigating single places. A German economist in the early twentieth century, A. Weber, first refined such a theory (Weber, 1929). While he recognized the importance of areal variation in labor costs and the attractive force of industrial agglomeration, he assumed that basically weight and distance of materials determined transportation costs and that these costs were the decisive factors of industrial location.

Transportation costs include (1) terminal costs incurred on entering or leaving a particular system, (2) increasing costs with greater distance carried, but (3) decreasing rates per mile for longer hauls (Figure 13–5). Costs vary, of course, for different transportation systems. At present (and the diverse carriers change their relative costs over time) trucks have the lowest terminal costs and ships the highest. Rates per mile are cheapest for short hauls by trucks,

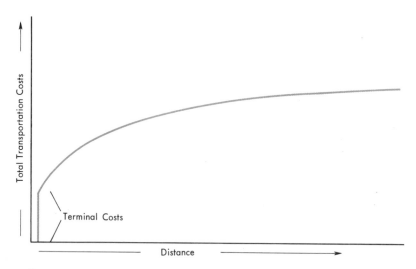

Figure 13-5. DISTANCE AND TRANSPORTATION COSTS

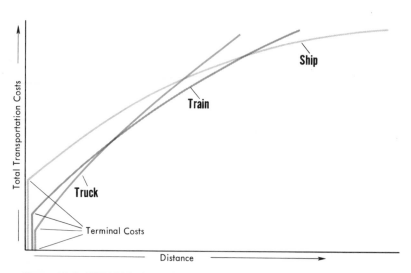

Figure 13-6. DISTANCE AND COSTS FOR DIFFERENT TRANSPORTATION SYSTEMS

for medium distances by train, and for long distances by ship or barge (Figure 13–6) (Alonso, 1964, 79–106).

In a simple problem of location (Figure 13–7) involving only one kind of carrier we can see that the total transportation costs are at a minimum at either end of the haul; in other words, the optimum plant location in this respect is at the source of materials or at the market. Production would locate at A or C, other things being equal, but not at B (or any other point between A and C) because new terminal costs will be added and the cost per mile will be higher since two 500-mile hauls are more expensive than one of 1,000 miles.

However, suppose that A to B is over water and B to C over land (Figure 13–8). Given the present-day transportation technology, B now becomes a necessary transshipment point: Thus there are now no extra costs of locating the industrial plant at B. This simple fact helps to explain why so many industries are located at ports. A multitude of examples illustrate this condition. Grain is shipped by Great Lakes freighter from the west to Buffalo, where it is milled at lake side; the flour is distributed by rail. Raw materials for the production of iron and steel are assembled at Sparrow's Point, Maryland; steel products are sent away by rail and coastal carrier. In northwestern Europe many large oil refineries lie at tidewater, where supertankers can unload petroleum from the Middle East and from the Gulf-Caribbean oil fields; the refined products are distributed by coastal tanker, pipeline, rail tank car, and truck.

This generalizing approach also offers valuable insights when applied to weight-reducing industries (e.g., ore processing) where costs differ widely between transporting raw materials and partly finished or finished products. Other industries yield goods that gain weight during the manufacturing process, having used ubiquitous materials like water and air in their production (e.g., the soft-drinks industry).

Personal Factors. In spite of all purely economic generalizations there remains a personal element in the location and success of a new enterprise. Family traditions or the preference stated by the wife of the chairman may be the deciding factor in choosing the place. Or the skill of an entrepreneur may build an industrial empire where others failed. The Ruhr region in western Germany, with many advantages for industrial development since the mid-nineteenth century—coal and other raw materials, a fine water-transportation system, and a large supply of experienced labor—also has benefited from the managerial élan of industrial wizards like Krupp and Thyssen who helped bring the Ruhr to its industrial dominance (Pounds, 1952).

Legacy of the Past. Many industrial plants are located where they are because of decisions made in the past under conditions that no longer have relevance. We have seen how many waterpower sites lost their hold on industry with the introduction of the steam engine, and how in turn electricity freed many industries to seek any convenient site. Yet a number of industries have remained at formerly favored sites. With the ubiquity of electricity and better transportation many industries are "footloose" in the sense that they are not tied to any specific locations. Old sites may therefore be just as good as others. This "historical momentum" or "geographical inertia," as it is variously called, gives the world's industrial regions a complexity that can only be understood by reference to the past.

The United States Iron and Steel Industry

Modern society relies on steel as the basic material for industrial goods, consumer items, and construction. In the United States about two-thirds of a million workers or 1 percent of the labor force are employed in the steel industry. Since this country leads the world in industrial power, it has the largest iron and steel industry, with a total capacity of about 150 million tons annually. It fully uses this capacity, however, only for a few short periods during a single year; thus its annual production usually is about 100 million tons. Total output

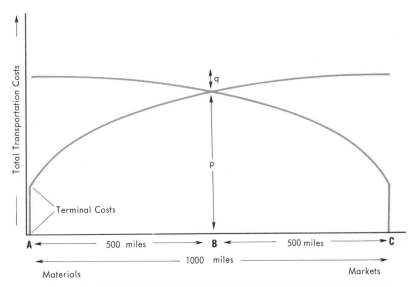

Figure 13–7. TRANSPORTATION COSTS AT AND BETWEEN TWO DIFFERENT LOCATIONS

Total costs of an industrial plant using location A or C are only $p + q$, but at B are twice p.

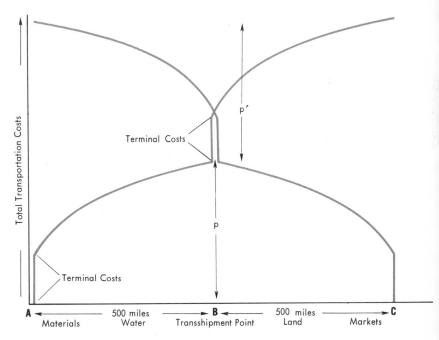

Figure 13–8. TRANSPORTATION COSTS TO AND FROM A TRANSSHIPMENT POINT

Total costs for locations A, B, and C are the same; for A and C, $p + p'$; for B, $p + p$.

rises more slowly than world production, with the result that the American share of world steel production is gradually declining.

The main production centers lie in three clusters: (1) along the rivers that run through or connect with the Pennsylvania and West Virginia parts of the Appalachian coalfield; (2) on the southern shores of the Great Lakes; and (3) on the Middle Atlantic Seaboard. Important centers in each of these groups are Pittsburgh and Youngstown; Chicago-Gary, Detroit, Cleveland, and Buffalo; and Baltimore and Philadelphia (Figure 13–9).

The purpose of the iron and steel industry is to remove impurities from iron ores and scrap iron and to produce steel, which is purified iron with a small proportion of carbon in it. This requires large amounts of investment capital and huge quantities of raw materials including iron ore, coal, limestone, scrap iron, hot air, oxygen, and cold water. It needs ample tracts of land for plants and stockpiles, transportation facilities with big capacities for assembling materials, and a great deal of managerial and operative labor.

The technology is complex. Most steelworks produce pig iron in blast furnaces. These furnaces are very expensive to build and operate, but once lit, and with proper materials and management, they can turn out pig iron on a continuous basis. Many modern blast furnaces are 120 feet high and over 30 feet in diameter. Machines charge the furnaces, usually automatically, with iron ore, limestone, and metallurgical coke. The key feature of the process is that the enormous heat created in the furnace is recycled to produce a hot-air blast. The operation produces pig iron which has a high carbon content. The physical and chemical reactions in the furnace have removed most other impurities. Modern substitutes for the blast furnace, though some have advantages under special conditions, offer no real competition.

Pig iron needs further refining. This is done by four different methods: (1) in Bessemer converters (first used in the 1850s), in which a hot-air blast directed through molten pig iron rapidly burns out the carbon; (2) in LD converters (called after the towns of Linz and Donawitz where they were developed in the 1940s), which blow oxygen and lime into the charge of molten pig iron; (3) in open-hearth furnaces (first developed by Gilchrist and Thomas in the 1860s), in which hot air and gas further treat the molten iron and slowly remove impurities; (4) in electric-arc furnaces, which are particularly good at producing high-quality ferroalloys.

Each of these processes has advantages and disadvantages for different types of iron ores. For example, many iron ores contain small percentages of phosphorus, which must be removed from the pig iron before steel of reasonable quality can be made. The Gilchrist-Thomas process utilizes limestone linings in its furnaces; during the refining stage the phosphorus combines with the lime. In this way phosphoric ores like those of Lorraine became usable for steelmaking; it also made some ores with low phosphorus content, like those of the Mesabi Range in Minnesota, easier to handle in the steel-producing stage. Some converters, especially the LD process, can include quite large amounts of scrap iron in addition to pig iron. At the present time fast converters of Bessemer and LD types tend to replace the slower open-hearth furnaces; the latter, however, retain the advantage of allowing fine quality control.

The largest areas of modern plants are not occupied by blast and steel furnaces, but by rolling mills, pipe mills, and similar installations that form raw steel into a series of primary shapes. The continuous-strip mill, often ½ mile long, produces sheet steel for various purposes from automobile bodies to cans. With the growth of consumer industries requiring such materials, many iron and steel centers throughout the industrialized world have set up strip mills.

The enormous expense of building these installations prevents quick shifts to new methods; also it tends toward maintaining plants that were constructed to use raw materials which since have been exhausted or replaced by better sources. Thus the iron and steel industry more than any other is likely to persist at outdated locations.

The first ironworks in the United States

Figure 13–9. EASTERN UNITED STATES: PRODUCTION CAPACITY OF THE STEEL INDUSTRY, 1959

There are also large steel plants at Pueblo, Colorado; Geneva, Utah; and Fontana, California; and smaller plants at Seattle, Portland, San Francisco, and Los Angeles. After a map in Alexandersson, 1961.

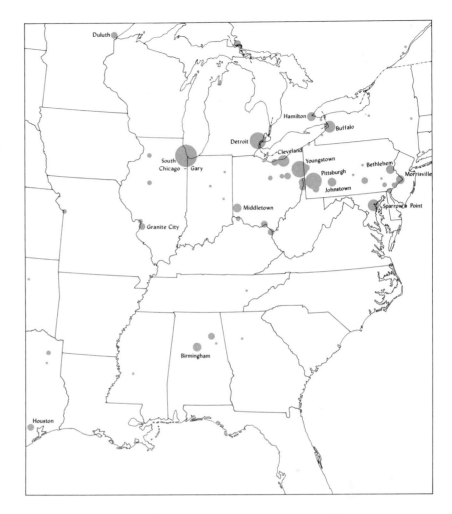

Steel Capacity

·	Under 0.5 Million Tons
●	500,000 - 1,000,000
●	1,000,000 - 2,000,000
●	3,000,000 - 5,000,000
●	5,000,000 - 10,000,000
●	10,000,000 - 20,000,000
●	20,000,000 or more

were small operations near the coast of the Middle Atlantic states. Local hardwood trees provided the charcoal used for smelting iron ore from small pockets. In the early nineteenth century larger blast furnaces were set up in eastern Pennsylvania, near supplies of anthracite valuable for smelting. After the Civil War and the discovery of great seams of high-quality metallurgical coal in western Pennsylvania, a large industry developed around Pittsburgh. At this time most of the ores still came from the east, but toward the end of the century vast newly discovered bodies of iron ore were tapped, especially along the Mesabi Range of northern Minnesota. Boats transported the ore from Lake Superior to the south shore of Lake Erie, whence the railroads carried it to Pittsburgh. The open-hearth method had then come into general use and provided the best method of refining the Mesabi ores with their relatively high-iron and low-phosphorus content.

By the first decade of the twentieth century Pittsburgh and nearby production centers like Youngstown, Ohio, and towns along the Ohio River completely dominated the industry. Coal still determined the location, for it required more coal than ore to make a ton of steel. Materials could still be assembled at lowest cost

13. Industrial Nations and Regions

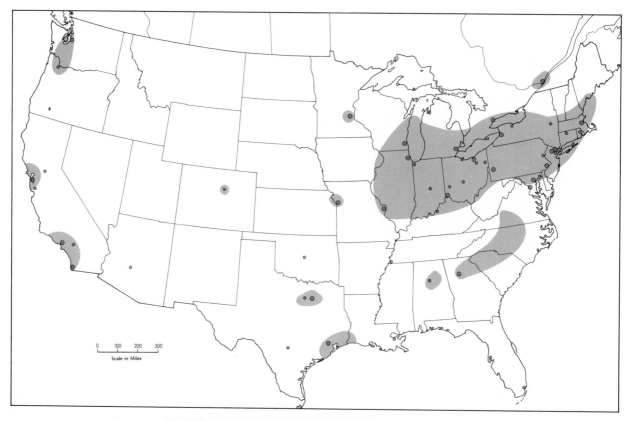

Figure 13–10. ANGLO-AMERICA: INDUSTRIAL REGIONS

in western Pennsylvania. Furthermore, investment in plants already there militated against development of new projects in different locations (Rodgers, 1952).

Gradually other locational influences made themselves felt. The Midwest, the most rapidly growing part of the industrial region, had become a huge market for steel. Improvements in technology had reduced somewhat the amounts of coal necessary in the refining process. The Lake Superior mining district increased its lead in iron-ore output. These factors led to the building of new iron and steel plants in the Midwest at the southern end of Lake Michigan and on the south shore of Lake Erie.

These two regions in time surpassed Pittsburgh in capacity and production (Hartshorne, 1928).

By the 1930s and even more after World War II, the advantages for steel production began to move back toward the east coast, and to some degree, to extend to the west coast. Overseas iron-ore fields in Cuba, Chile, and later in Canada, Venezuela, and West Africa were delivering high-quality ores at cheap prices to tidewater locations on the east coast. This caused the building of large integrated iron and steel plants at Sparrow's Point near Baltimore and at Morrisville near Philadelphia. Coal comes to these locations by rail and water from West Virginia via Norfolk. In California shipbuilding created a new market during World War II. After the war, consumer industries developed, giving rise to the use of scrap and imported ores, mostly refined by a direct process. In Texas the steel industry is expanding also to serve the local market. It uses local ores and hydrocarbon fuels provided by the gas and oil industries.

It is clear from this overview that the location of the United States iron and steel industry reflects a historical process. The fact that the industry has been established at different locations at different times shows the impact of changing technology, markets, sources of fuels, and raw materials. Other industrial countries which have experienced analogous changes show a similar diversity of location.

Main Industrial Regions

Industrial plants, although each may manufacture a different product, tend to cluster (de Geer, 1927). Thus, even within the most industrialized countries some regions stand out by their industrial aggregation compared to others, where the economy, though quite mechanized, does not primarily depend on manufacturing. The following section outlines the major industrial regions.

Anglo-America's Chief Manufacturing Belt. Over two-thirds of all persons employed in manufacturing in the United States, and about the same proportion in Canada, live in the industrial heart of Anglo-America (Figures 13–10 and 13–11).

Foremost among the subregions within this vast area is the *New York metropolitan region* with over 50,000 large and small industrial plants. On Manhattan Island the clothing, food, publishing, and printing industries hold particular importance. Refining of petroleum and metals, shipbuilding, and meat-packing concentrate in New Jersey. The industries of Long Island show more diversity, among which the making of instruments deserves special mention.

What are New York's advantages for manufacturing? It offers the greatest single market for all kinds of consumer goods, from telephones and bread to women's clothing and office equipment. Its large pool of skilled and unskilled workers results chiefly from its position as the principal port of entry. On its excellent harbor converge extensive networks of rail, highway, water, and air transportation. New York is headquarters of the managerial class and the organization man; it is the center of international finance and business.

Two great industrial wings spread to either side of New York, their economic life intimately bound with the city. *New England* is the country's oldest manufacturing district, its past and present importance resting on textiles, shoes, fabricated metal goods, and electrical and other machinery (Figure 13–12). In early days machines were brought over from England and set up in factories at many small waterpower sites. These old mill sites lost their locational advantage to the coast when steam power based on shipped-in coal came into general use. In western New England, especially in the valley of the Connecticut River, industrial towns concentrate on metal fabrication and produce items ranging from guns to kitchen utensils.

The *Middle Atlantic states* include the industrial complexes of Philadelphia and Baltimore. Manufactures run the gamut from iron and steel to food and canning factories. The older iron and steel plants near Bethlehem originally used local raw materials, but now their coal comes from western Pennsylvania and West Virginia, and the iron ore from Canada and South America. Like New York, this Middle Atlantic agglomeration of industrial cities controls a large market, and has a series of fine ports that connect with other parts of the country by road and rail.

In *central New York State* numerous industrial cities lie between Albany on the Hudson River and Buffalo on Lake Erie. The towns in the Mohawk Valley fabricate a wide variety of metals, machines, and instruments. These valley cities, among them Rochester and Syracuse, developed along the Erie Canal (1825), which was dug through the only low-level connection between the east coast and the interior; in 1857 the first railway to the west was built along this same route. The Buffalo area manufactures

Figure 13–11. ANGLO-AMERICA: LABOR FORCE IN MANUFACTURING, BY COUNTIES

The areas of the circles are proportional to manufacturing employment by county; colors represent proportions of total employed labor force in manufacturing. Based on data in *U.S. Census of Population, 1960,* and *Census of Canada, 1961.*

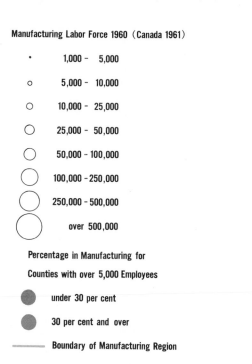

Manufacturing Labor Force 1960 (Canada 1961)

- ·   1,000 – 5,000
- ○   5,000 – 10,000
- ○   10,000 – 25,000
- ○   25,000 – 50,000
- ○   50,000 – 100,000
- ○   100,000 – 250,000
- ○   250,000 – 500,000
- ○   over 500,000

Percentage in Manufacturing for Counties with over 5,000 Employees

- ●   under 30 per cent
- ●   30 per cent and over
- ⎯⎯⎯   Boundary of Manufacturing Region

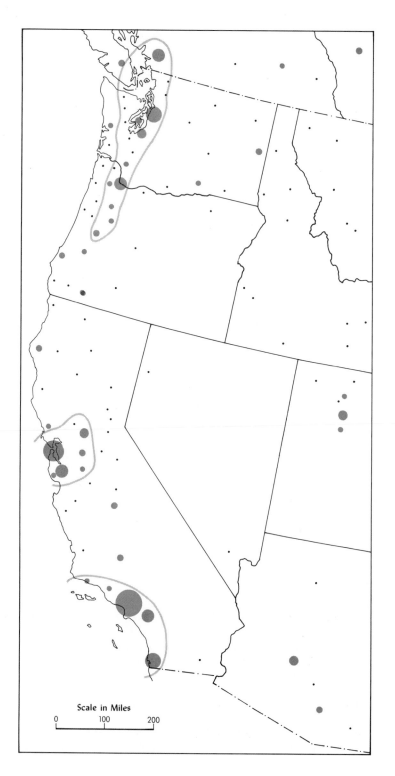

Scale in Miles
0   100   200

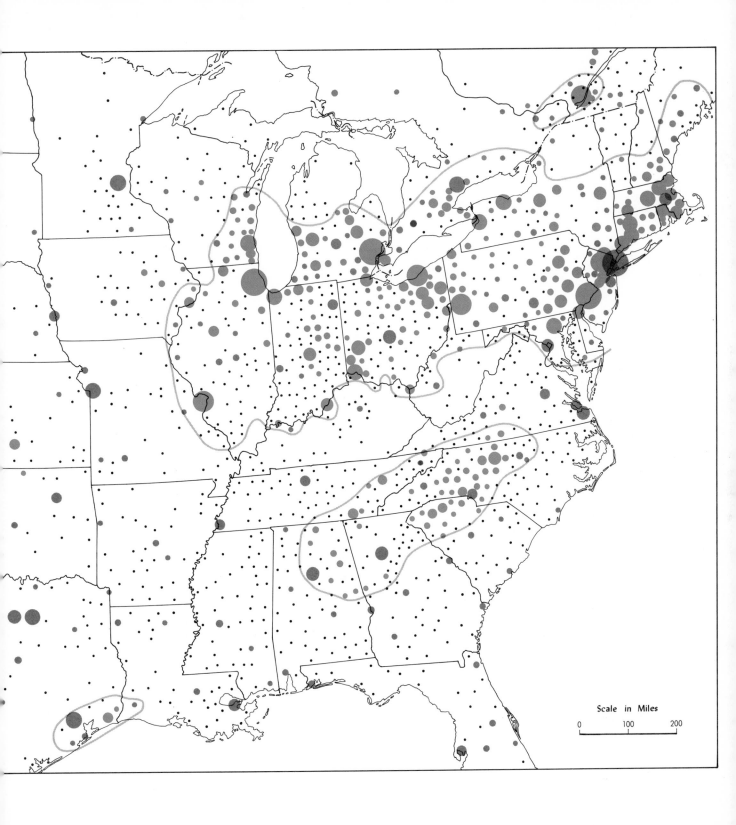

Scale in Miles

0   100   200

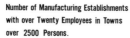

Number of Manufacturing Establishments
with over Twenty Employees in Towns
over 2500 Persons.

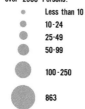

Less than 10

10-24

25-49

50-99

100-250

863

Figure 13–12. MASSACHUSETTS: INDUSTRIAL ESTABLISHMENTS, 1958

The map shows the number of manufacturing establishments with more than 20 employees in all towns with 2,500 or more inhabitants. In 1958 there were 4,377 such establishments in the state, and a further 7,132 establishments with fewer than 20 employees each. SOURCE: *U.S. Census of Manufacturing*, 1958.

III. Patterns
of
Livelihood

302

steel, flour, and, owing to the Niagara Falls power, an array of heavy chemicals.

The *Middle West* includes large industrial cities like Pittsburgh, Cleveland, Detroit, and Chicago, many more of the size of Akron and Peoria, and a host of smaller manufacturing towns. Between the Appalachian coalfields and the shores of Lake Erie lies a band of heavy industry based on steel production, with Pittsburgh and Cleveland as its poles. The automotive industry dominates Detroit and nearby Michigan cities. The Chicago district, which swings around the southern end of Lake Michigan, is a big producer of steel and machinery, but also has important food industries. A constellation of cities in southwestern Ohio and adjacent Indiana turns out, among other things, machine tools and a variety of machinery, office equipment, and paper. On or beyond the margin of the main industrial belt lie Peoria and Rock Island–Davenport–Moline, which make farm equipment, the diversified manufacturing complex of St. Louis, and the Appalachian towns of the Kanawha and Ohio river valleys, with their large chemical and metal plants.

The *Ontario Peninsula* contains a large proportion of Canada's industrial assemblage. A series of industrial cities extends from Toronto to Hamilton and on to Windsor. This Canadian manufacturing region, smaller in scale though similar to the industrial Midwest, creates a variety of products.

Other Industrial Districts of Anglo-America. Textile, furniture, and tobacco dominate the industrial towns in the southeastern United States. In addition to the raw materials cotton, timber, and tobacco, the South also has the advantages of a large labor supply and of lower wage rates and overhead costs.

In the Southwest, industrial cities along or near the Gulf Coast of Texas, such as Beaumont, Dallas, Fort Worth, and Houston, are less numerous, though larger than those in the Southeast. Foremost are aerospace, petrochemical, flour-milling, and meat-packing industries.

In the West food-processing and aerospace industries dominate the important manufacturing regions of San Francisco and Los Angeles.

These and smaller centers, such as San Diego and cities of the Puget Sound, benefit from the fast-developing local market propelled by the population influx.

Lastly, there are some important industrial cities in more isolated locations: Montreal on the St. Lawrence River, largest single manufacturing city in Canada; Denver, an important aerospace center; and Minneapolis–St. Paul (the Twin Cities) with a diversified structure.

Western and Central Europe. The content and intensity of Europe's industrial regions differ from those of North America. An imaginary line connecting Londonderry in Northern Ireland with Bergen (Norway), Stockholm, Warsaw, Budapest, Rome, Barcelona, Bilbao (Spain), and back to Londonderry takes in the broad industrial region of western and central Europe. Within this we can identify a number of industrial concentrations (Figure 13–13).

British Isles. Most manufacturing cities in Great Britain lie in the center and south (Figure 13–14). This zone contains: London, largest single manufacturing center of Europe with a great variety of industries; South Wales (see below); the Black Country and the west Midlands, noted for machines and metals of all kinds; the textile areas of Lancashire and the West Riding of Yorkshire; metallurgical centers like Sheffield; and the Merseyside region with engineering and chemical plants. Industrial districts elsewhere in the British Isles take in the Scottish Lowlands, of which Glasgow is the leading metropolis; the metal and engineering settlements of northeastern England; and the Belfast area of Northern Ireland.

Continental Western Europe. In western Europe the most concentrated and diversified industrial area on earth spreads from northern France across Belgium and the southern Netherlands into West Germany (Figure 13–15). The highest density falls within the circle from Amsterdam to Boulogne (France), Cambrai, Köln (Cologne), Hamm (Ruhr), and back to Amsterdam. On its south and east side lie the heavy industries related to the coalfields, above all the Ruhr district with its blast furnaces, steel mills, and machine and chemical plants.

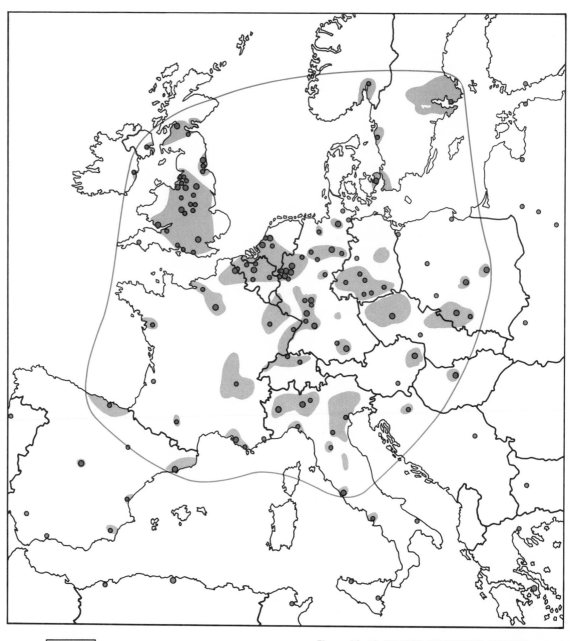

Industrial Areas

● Urban Centers over 1.0 Million Population

● Urban Centers 0.5 to 1.0 Million Population

Figure 13–13. EUROPE: INDUSTRIAL REGIONS

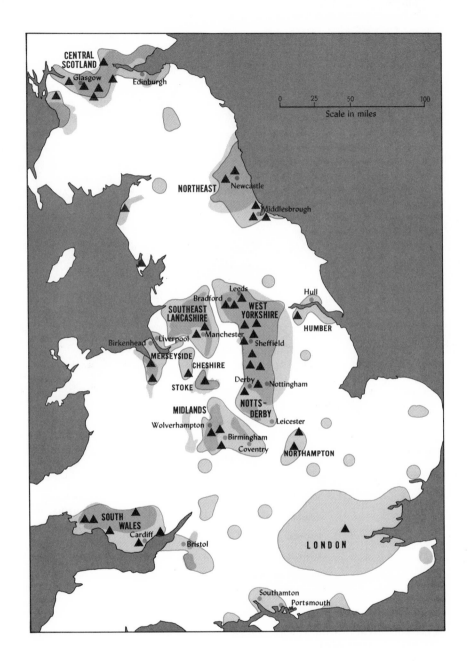

Figure 13–14. GREAT BRITAIN: INDUSTRIAL DISTRICTS

Major Industrial Districts

Industrial Centers

Iron and Steel Production

Coalfields

Scale in miles

0   25   50   100

CENTRAL SCOTLAND

Glasgow   Edinburgh

NORTHEAST   Newcastle

Middlesbrough

Leeds

Bradford

SOUTHEAST LANCASHIRE   WEST YORKSHIRE

Hull

Birkenhead   Liverpool   Manchester   Sheffield

HUMBER

MERSEYSIDE

CHESHIRE

STOKE   Derby   Nottingham

NOTTS-DERBY

MIDLANDS

Wolverhampton   Leicester

Birmingham

Coventry   NORTHAMPTON

SOUTH WALES

Cardiff

Bristol

LONDON

Southamton

Portsmouth

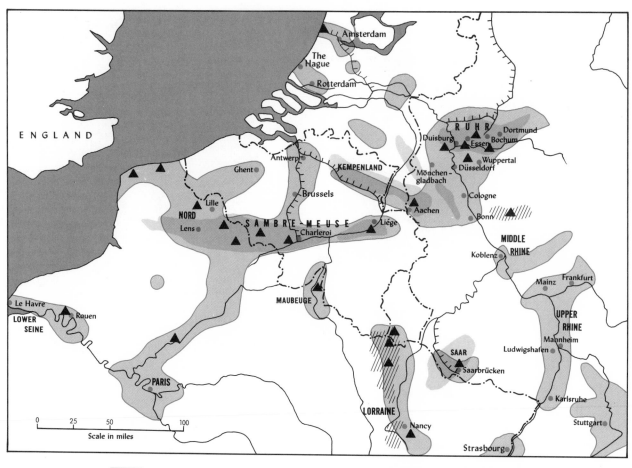

Major Industrial Districts	
Industrial Centers	
Ironfields	
Coalfields	
Iron and Steel Production	

Figure 13–15. CONTINENTAL WESTERN EUROPE:
INDUSTRIAL DISTRICTS

On its west side are the port cities of Antwerp, Rotterdam, and Amsterdam, connected with their hinterland by the Rhine and canals, and by railroads and superhighways. These port cities process imported raw materials from foodstuffs to fertilizer, refine petroleum and metals, build ships and engines. Between coast and coal mines lie many other industrial centers such as Lille, Brussels, and Eindhoven, producing textiles, drugs, machinery, and electronic equipment.

Other important industrial districts are close by. The Paris metropolitan region, nerve center and biggest single market of France, has the usual industries that are connected with large agglomerations in highly industrialized coun-

At Duisburg-Ruhrort, where the Ruhr flows into the Rhine, lies the largest inland port of Europe. Barges, loaded with iron ore, petroleum, grains, lumber, and other raw materials, come up the Rhine and return with coal, steel, chemicals, and other industrial products. Much traffic also moves up and down the Rhine above the port, or by canals to north Germany. [Courtesy of German Information Center]

tries, but it emphasizes engineering, clothing, and printing. From Lorraine across into Luxembourg and through the Saar district of West Germany, heavy industries exploit the local iron ore and adjacent coal supplies, with good transportation connections to other parts of western Europe. The upper Rhine Basin includes a series of large industrial cities, among them Frankfurt am Main, Strasbourg, Mannheim-Ludwigshafen, and Stuttgart, all manufacturing a wide variety of goods. Switzerland has built up an enviable reputation for craftsman-

ship, whether in making precision instruments, pharmaceutical items, or huge turbines. The larger cities lie on the central plateau, smaller ones—famous for their watches—in the Swiss Jura.

These industrial regions of northwestern Europe, including England, possess distinct advantages. They have capital for industrial expansion, substantial resources of coal, iron ore, chemicals, and newly discovered natural gas and oil—also a superb location for river and sea communications. Moreover, the population has

Figure 13–16.
SOVIET UNION:
INDUSTRIAL REGIONS

Industrial Areas

Industrial Centers
◉ Over 1 Million Population
• Under 1 Million Population

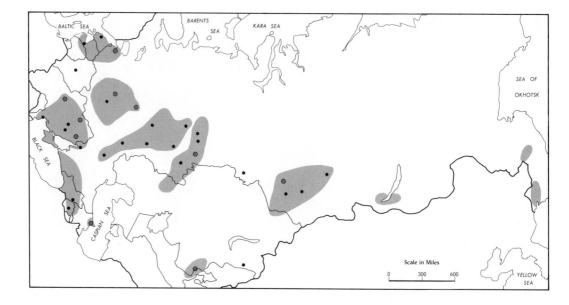

a tradition of technical skill and economic organization that has built up vast markets at home and overseas.

Other Industrial Districts. Outside this core, other regions of Europe contain smaller industrial concentrations, many of them highly significant in relation to the individual countries. Central Sweden has a varied industrial base, its steel industry being noted for high quality products. In northern Italy many industrial cities—Milan and Turin the largest—make especially textiles, machinery, and automobiles. In central Europe a series of industrial cities extends from the borders of East and West Germany to Bohemia in Czechoslovakia. Their raw materials include potash and lignite. Of their many industrial products, textiles, machinery, and precision instruments are best known. Major industrial centers are Berlin, Prague, and Leipzig. Upper Silesia, Poland's equivalent of the Ruhr, takes in the cities of Katowice, Zabrze, and Bytom, and concentrates on heavy industries like iron and steel, chemicals, and engineering products. Lastly, many industrial cities of Europe lie outside the districts outlined above. Some of these are Barce-

lona, Spain; Lyon, France; and most capital cities in Scandinavia and eastern Europe.

The Soviet Union. Industrial regions in the Soviet Union are easier to define than those in western Europe. The reason is the industrial expansion that began on a large scale in the 1920s, and produced mainly basic materials like metals rather than consumer goods (Figure 13–16). This means that raw materials more than the market determine where industries locate. The principal exception to this is the *Moscow region,* which has one-fourth of the Soviet Union's industrial output (Figure 13–17). Moscow's central location and the presence of the government have favored the growth of a wide variety of industries, among them textiles, machines, motor vehicles, and electrical equipment. Leningrad's remoteness from raw materials is partly countered by its accessibility as a port. Shipbuilding and the fabrication of metals and precision instruments are important.

The Soviet Union's main center of heavy industry is in the *Ukraine,* based on a large population, massive resources of coal, iron and manganese ores, waterpower, and an industrial

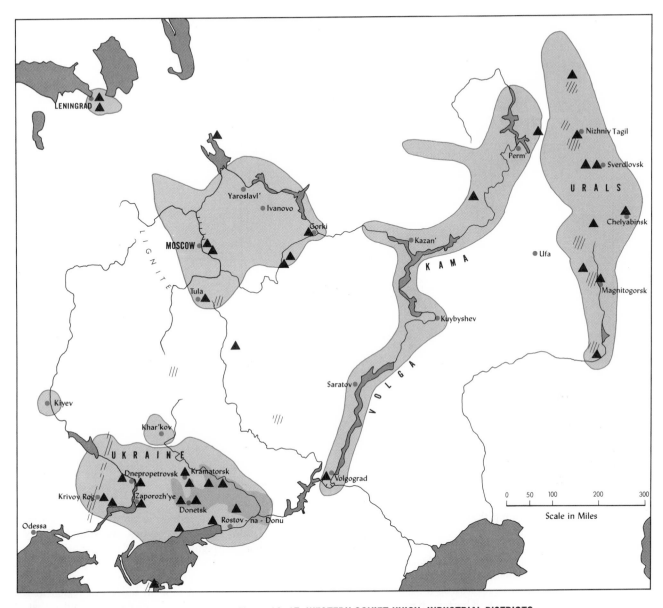

Figure 13–17. WESTERN SOVIET UNION: INDUSTRIAL DISTRICTS

Legend:
- Major Industrial Districts
- Industrial Centers
- Ironfields
- Coalfields
- Iron and Steel Production

Map labels:
LENINGRAD
Yaroslavl'
Ivanovo
Gorki
MOSCOW
Tula
LIGNITE
Kiyev
Khar'kov
UKRAINE
Dnepropetrovsk
Kramatorsk
Krivoy Rog
Zaporozh'ye
Donetsk
Rostov - na - Donu
Odessa
Saratov
VOLGA
Volgograd
Kazan'
KAMA
Kuybyshev
Perm'
Ufa
URALS
Nizhniy Tagil
Sverdlovsk
Chelyabinsk
Magnitogorsk

Scale in Miles
0   50   100   200   300

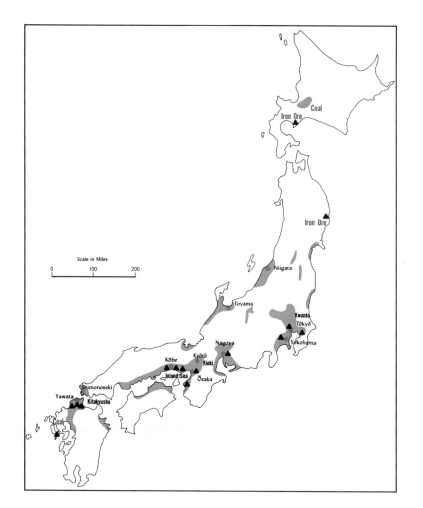

Figure 13–18. JAPAN: INDUSTRIAL DISTRICTS

The main industrial areas are the Kwanto Plain, the Kinki Plain, the shores of the Inland Sea, and Kitakyushu.

- Industrial Areas
- Industrial Cities
- ▲ Iron and Steel Production

buildup that began late in the nineteenth century. Its principal concentrations are in (1) the Donets Basin with its large coalfield (Donbas), (2) the bend of the Dnepr River with important metals and metalworking industries, and (3) the four large cities on the margins of these districts —Rostov, Kharkov, Kiev, and Odessa, with diversified manufacturing.

The *Ural Mountains,* containing a variety of metal ores equal to any on earth, early attracted smelting and fabricating works. The great expansion came during World War II, when the Axis forces occupied the Ukraine and threatened Moscow and Leningrad. New resources such as the Volga-Urals oil field and even the distant Karaganda coal basin added fresh im-

petus to the industrial growth of the southern Urals. The largest cities, Sverdlovsk, Chelyabinsk, Magnitogorsk, and Nizhny Tagil, emphasize the production of metals, fabricated metal goods, and machinery.

The existence of an industrial region in the *Kuznetsk Basin* of Siberia, 1,400 miles east of the Urals, illustrates the impact of Soviet planning on the location of industry. The area has enormous resources, especially in coal, iron ore, and potential hydroelectric power. It produces iron, steel, and machinery; also it processes food from the farms on the agricultural frontier of Central Asia. The Kuznetsk Basin (Kuzbas) was planned in the 1930s as the powerhouse for Central Asia and received much impetus for rapid expansion from migrations eastward from European Russia during and after World War II.

To the east and south of this frontier, industries are also developing, based on local minerals, hydroelectric power, agricultural resources, and increasing populations. Cities that have a strong industrial component are Irkutsk, Khabarovsk, Vladivostok, Tashkent, and Samarkand.

East and South Asia. Since Japan's pace of industrialization quickened in the 1950s, that country has become one of the world's important industrial powers. Its manufacturing forms a belt from Tokyo southwestward on the main island of Honshu and on the two smaller islands of Kyushu and Shikoku. Tokyo, together with Yokohama, has a great variety of establishments; Osaka and Kobe put more emphasis on heavy industries. Nagoya is a textile center. The coalfields of northern Kyushu have most of the iron and steel production (Figure 13–18).

Someday China may develop an enormous industrial capacity commensurate with its vast population. As yet its only full-fledged industrial region is Manchuria, based on the iron and steel industry the Japanese began during their occupation earlier in this century. Plans for a "great leap forward," promoted by the Chinese Communist government in the 1950s, envisaged widespread development of basic industries, particularly metals. This failed and appears to have given way to large-scale industrial plants gathered around a few cities such as Peking, Shanghai, Tientsin, Chungking, Chengtu, Wuhan, and Sian (Figure 13–19).

India shows some similarity to China in having also one main area of heavy industry and a number of cities with various kinds of lighter manufacturing. The abundant coal, iron, manganese, and waterpower of the Chota Nagpur plateau, 150 miles west of the Ganges Delta, supports now several large iron and steel plants, of which the one at Jamshedpur is the biggest. With metal-fabricating, cement, and fertilizer plants, this region is, on a modest scale as yet, the "Ruhr" of India. Important industrial cities outside this area are Calcutta and Bombay in

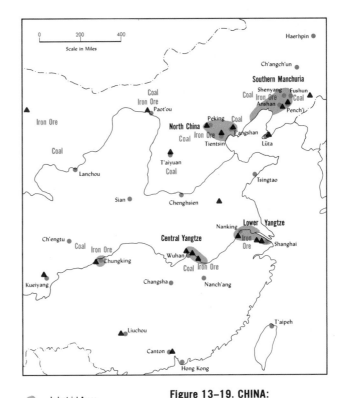

Figure 13–19. CHINA: INDUSTRIAL DISTRICTS

- Industrial Areas
- Industrial Cities
- Iron and Steel Production

northern India, and Madras and Bangalore in the south (Figure 13–20).

Other Industrial Centers. In some modern countries with but relatively small populations, incipient industrial regions are evident, as in Australia and South Africa. Some of the Latin American countries—especially Brazil, Argentina, and Mexico—have begun to industrialize, mainly within or near their metropolitan centers.

An Industrial Region: South Wales

Several early developed coalfields, once among the foremost producers of fuel, iron, and steel, have fallen on hard times when they have failed

13. Industrial Nations and Regions

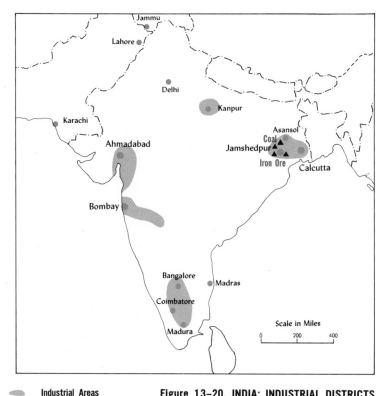

Figure 13–20. INDIA: INDUSTRIAL DISTRICTS

- Industrial Areas
- Industrial Cities
- ▲ Iron and Steel Production

a higher carbon content; in the past it powered the boilers of most of the world's steamships, but now it is mainly used for metallurgical processes. The almost pure-carbon anthracite of the northwest serves for cement making and central heating. In the "north crop," where the valleys run through gently sloping coal seams, mining has been relatively easy; along the "south crop" mining poses a greater problem, for the seams run into the ground at a steep angle (Figure 13–21A).

The Rise of Industry. The sea has cut into the western end of the coalfield in Swansea Bay and Carmarthen Bay; here mining took place before the Industrial Revolution, and the coal was shipped across the sea to Bristol and other places. During the eighteenth century metal industries, especially ironworking, gathered in the valleys and along the coast. Canals were dug to provide cheap transportation from pit to port. In the nineteenth century railways joined the mines to newly built harbor docks. Markets for Welsh coal expanded with the rise in metal production, factories run by steam, railway and steamship traffic, and domestic use. By the 1880s production had risen to 25 million tons annually. The landscape had changed to an intensely industrial scene, with pitheads, railways, slag heaps, and tiers of dark row houses.

The mines and factories were manned by a population that had increased rapidly since the eighteenth century. Many migrated to the coalfield from other parts of Wales, from nearby English counties, and even from overseas. In spite of unhealthy living conditions this population had a very high natural increase. The immigrants changed the population from a Welsh-speaking community with local origins to an English-speaking group who, nevertheless, became closely identified with Welsh nationality. The greatest increase in population came in the last half of the nineteenth century; for example, between 1851 and 1921 Rhondda's population rose from 2,000 to 163,000, and that of Cardiff from 18,000 to 200,000.

Regression. During World War I Wales lost its export markets for coal. Other disasters fol-

to adjust to new conditions. The Sambre-Meuse region, the industrial area of western Pennsylvania and eastern Ohio, and South Wales belong to this group. South Wales is a good example of a rather successful reconstruction after a period of severe depression (Figure 13–21).

A series of short valleys runs southward through the southern edge of the Welsh uplands and dissects the oval-shaped coalfield. Its varied layers of rock, including the coal strata, lie like a pile of broken plates. The field is about 55 miles long and, taking in the coastal towns, up to 35 miles wide. It is famous for its high-quality coals. In the southeast medium-quality coal is mined for gas making and for steam raising in locomotives and at electrical power plants. The center of the field contains coal with

Figure 13–21. SOUTH WALES

A. The Coalfield. Most of the coal has been mined in the narrow valleys of the eastern half of the field.

o o **Ports**
● **Principal Coal Mines**
— **Coalfield Boundary**
▨ **Land over 1,000 feet**

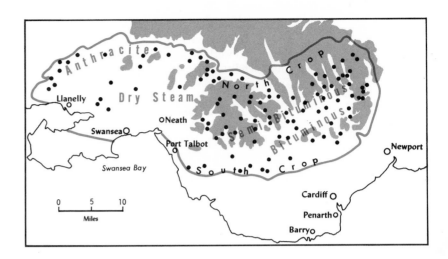

B. Metal Industries. Metal manufacturing has migrated from the coal valleys toward the coast.

o **Iron and Steel Production, Eighteenth and Nineteenth Centuries**
● ● **Iron and Steel Production, Twentieth Century**
o **Old Plate Mills**
● **Large New Steel Plate Mills**
△ **Copper Smelting**

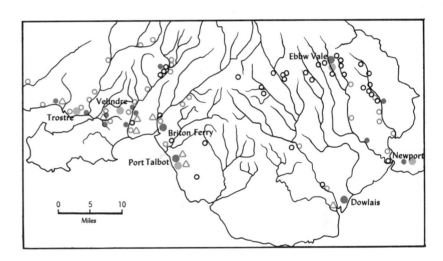

C. Industrial Reconstruction, 1934–1959. The largest groupings of new factories are on the coastal plain.

Number of New Manufacturing Establishments
· 1 - 4
● 5 - 9
● 10 - 19
● 20 - 30
● 50
● 80
▨ "Trading Estates"

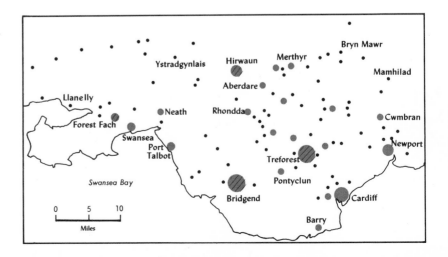

lowed: ships changed their power from Welsh coal to oil; free trade broke down in the 1920s; the general world depression of the 1930s aggravated conditions. In 1913 coal production was 57 million tons, two-thirds of which was exported. Since then it has declined until it now appears to have stabilized at 20 to 25 million tons annually. The number of miners has dropped from 270,000 in 1913 to fewer than 100,000 in recent years. The basic-metals industry of the region was hit severely. Life in the coalfield communities became hard. Mine-owners, unable to rationalize production methods or plan long-term investments, faced frequent strikes, or they used lockouts. Miners by the tens of thousands moved to coastal ports, sought work in other industrial regions, or migrated overseas. Many who remained were unemployed.

Industrial Reconstruction. The national government took the lead, as early as 1934, to halt the decline. It encouraged new industries and the refurbishing of old ones. For instance, the government assisted in rebuilding the old metalworks at Ebbw Vale into a large integrated iron and steel plant. A number of "trading estates" (industrial parks with many small to medium-sized factories) were set up and attracted scores of industrial operations making a wide variety of products. At the same time steps were taken to increase wages, rehabilitate housing, and improve social services. After World War II the coal industry was placed under public ownership. Uneconomic pits along the north crop of the field were closed; new deep shafts were sunk along the south crop. Thus, the focus of coal production shifted to an arc stretching eastward from Neath. This new industrial variety has helped to reduce unemployment to well below 10 percent of the work force. Between 1945 and 1960, 120,000 new jobs were created. Out-migration is now a mere trickle (Figure 13–21C).

Present Industrial Pattern. Metals, the foremost industry of South Wales, run the full range from iron and steel production to aluminum and copper refining (Figure 13–21B). In the western section Swansea and Neath are the chief towns. The port city of Swansea lies close to a supply of high-quality coal; the town and its environs provide a reservoir of skillful workers. The port has oil, chemical engineering, and metallurgical works, and lies between the steel rolling plants and the plating factories. Coated with tin to make tinplate, steel sheeting serves to make cans, car radiators, oil barrels, and other containers for materials that need protection from corrosion. The tin-plating industry has been modernized: a few large plants now do the work formerly carried on in scores of small mills. The steelworks at Port Talbot, much expanded since 1945 and now one of the largest in Europe, provide sheet steel. Other metal industries include refining nickel, titanium, copper, and duralumin.

The eastern half of South Wales is dominated by the coastal cities of Cardiff and Newport, with iron and steel production and many metal fabricating plants. There are also large populations in those coal valleys where modern offspring of the once important iron industry remain, such as at Ebbw Vale.

The Cardiff urban area grew from a small market town in 1800 to become, recently, the national capital of Wales. Its rise paralleled the growth of coal mining and manufacturing in South Wales; it has become an important industrial center with various metal fabrication plants.

Economic renewal and social improvement have changed the way of life in South Wales. Work is now farther from home than formerly. Instead of a walk down the valley side to the pithead, many now take a bus or go by car or cycle to a plant some miles away. Most of the new industries have not been built in the coal valleys, but at locations where the valleys enter the coastal plain. Thus, the population continues its long-term shift from the valleys to the coast.

The occupations in which people are engaged now represent the diversity to be expected for a balanced industrial region. Coal miners, numbering about 90,000, and workers in metal industries, some 120,000, make up only two-fifths of the labor force. One-fifth are employed in light manufacturing, the remaining two-fifths in service occupations from retailing to the professions.

Citations

Alexandersson, G. "Changes in the Location Pattern of the Anglo-American Steel Industry: 1948–1959," *Economic Geography,* 37 (1961): 95–114.

Alonso, W. "Location Theory," in Friedman, J., and Alonso, W. (eds.) *Regional Development and Planning,* Cambridge, Mass., 1964.

Chase Manhattan Bank, *Purchasing Power Map of Europe,* New York, 1964. [Map]

Davies, M. *Wales in Maps,* Cardiff, 1958. [Map]

De Geer, S. "The American Manufacturing Belt," *Geografiska Annaler,* 9 (1927): 233–359.

Harris, C. D. "The Market as a Factor in the Localization of Industry in the United States," *Annals of the Association of American Geographers,* 44 (1954): 315–348.

Hartshorne, R. "Location Factors in the Iron and Steel Industry," *Economic Geography,* 4 (1928): 241–252.

Pounds, N. J. G. *The Ruhr: A Study in Historical and Economic Geography,* Bloomington, Ind., 1952.

Rodgers, A. "Industrial Inertia: A Major Factor in the Location of the Steel Industry of the United States," *Geographical Review,* 42 (1952): 56–66.

Ullman, E. L. "The Role of Transportation and the Bases of Interaction," in Thomas, W. L. (ed.) *Man's Role in Changing the Face of the Earth,* Chicago, 1956, 862–880.

————. "Regional Development and the Geography of Concentration," *Papers and Proceedings of the Regional Science Association,* 4 (1958): 179–198.

[Weber, A.] Friedrich, C. J. (ed.) *Alfred Weber's Theory of the Location of Industry,* Chicago, 1929.

Further Readings

Alderfer, E. B., and Michl, H. E. *Economics of American Industry,* 2d ed., New York, 1950.

Alexander, J. W. *Economic Geography,* Englewood Cliffs, N.J., 1963.

Alexandersson, G. *The Industrial Structure of American Cities,* Lincoln, Neb., 1956.

Allen, G. C. *Japan's Economic Expansion,* London and Fairlawn, N.J., 1965.

Brush, J. E. "The Iron and Steel Industry in India," *Geographical Review,* 42 (1952): 37–55.

Estall, R. C., and Buchanan, R. O. *Industrial Activity and Economic Geography: A Study of the Forces behind the Geographical Location of Productive Activity in Manufacturing Industry,* New York, 1961.

Fleming, D. K. "Coastal Steelworks in the Common Market Countries," *Geographical Review,* 57 (1967): 48–72.

Fryer, D. W. *World Economic Development,* New York, 1965.

Fuchs, V. R. *Changes in the Location of Manufacturing in the United States since 1929,* New Haven, Conn., 1962.

Harris, C. D. "Geography of Manufacturing," in James, P. E., and Jones, C. F. (eds.) *American Geography: Inventory and Prospect,* Syracuse, N.Y., 1954, 292–308.

Isard, W. *Location and the Space-Economy,* New York, 1956.

Lewis, E. D. *The Rhondda Valleys: A Study in Industrial Development, 1800 to the Present Day,* London, 1959.

Li Choh-ming (ed.) *Industrial Development in Communist China,* New York, 1964.

Logan, M. I. "Locational Behavior of Manufacturing Firms in Urban Areas," *Annals of the Association of American Geographers,* 56 (1966): 451–466.

Lonsdale, R. E., and Thompson, J. H. "A Map of the U.S.S.R.'s Manufacturing," *Economic Geography,* 36 (1960): 36–52.

Manners, G. *The Geography of Energy,* London, 1964.

McCarty, H. H. *The Geographical Basis of American Economic Life,* New York, 1940.

———— et al. *The Measurement of Association in Industrial Geography,* Iowa City, Iowa, 1956.

Monkhouse, F. J. *The Belgian Kempenland,* Liverpool, 1949.

Ovdiyenko, I. Kh. "The New Geography of Industry of China," *Soviet Geography: Review and Translation,* 1 (1960): 63–78.

Patton, D. J. "General Cargo Hinterlands of New York, Philadelphia, Baltimore, and New Orleans," *Annals of the Association of American Geographers,* 48 (1958): 436–455.

Pounds, N. J. G. "Historical Geography of the Iron and Steel Industry of France," *Annals of the Association of American Geographers,* 47 (1957): 3–14.

————. "The Spread of Mining in the Coal Basin of Upper Silesia and Northern Moravia," *Annals of the Association of American Geographers,* 48 (1958): 149–163.

Shimkin, D. "Economic Regionalization in the Soviet Union," *Geographical Review,* 42 (1952): 591–614.

Smith, W. *Geography and the Location of Industry: An Inaugural Lecture, November 1, 1951,* Liverpool, 1952.

————. *An Economic Geography of Great Britain,* 2d ed., London, 1953.

Thomas, T. M. "Wales: Land of Mines and Quarries," *Geographical Review,* 46 (1956): 59–81.

Thompson, J. H., and Miyazaki, M. "A Map of Japan's Manufacturing," *Geographical Review,* 49 (1959): 1–17.

Ullman, E. L. "Amenities as a Factor in Regional Growth," *Geographical Review,* 44 (1954): 119–132.

————. *American Commodity Flow: A Geographic Interpretation of Rail and Water Traffic Based on Principles of Spatial Interchange,* Seattle, Wash., 1957.

Zimmermann, E. W. *World Resources and Industries,* 2d ed., New York, 1951.

14. Economic Development

At several points we have discussed instances of technical breakthrough, such as harnessing plant and animal energy—bringing about the agricultural revolution—and using mineral fuel, which heralded the mechanical revolution. Some societies quickly adopted new energy sources, others were slow to accept, or even remained ignorant of them. As a result there always have been "haves" and "have-nots."

There is, however, a difference between the present and olden times. Nations have become more aware of their own condition compared to that of others, and strive consciously to improve their well-being. This has changed the fact of inequality into the problem of development. This chapter surveys the areal differentiation in levels of living, examines their relationships with other spatial variables, and discusses the ways and means of economic progress.

The Rich and the Poor

The Role of Energy. Energy is the capability to do work. The geographer James Fairgrieve observed that "in its widest sense on its material side history is the story of Man's increasing control over energy." The story, as unfolded so far, divides into two main periods: before and after the Industrial Revolution.

Until two centuries ago man relied mainly on muscle strength, his own and that of domestic animals. To some extent he used fire to release energy from wood. With wind and water he propelled sailing ships and mills. All these forms of power, from plants that sustain animal life to air and water, depend ultimately on current receipts of solar heat and light.

The second part of the story opens with the advances of science and technology in Europe that made possible massive uses of new power sources: coal, petroleum, and natural gas. These are stored-up supplies of solar energy that in one way or another had escaped the normal cycle of life and decay. They gave a tremendous boost to man's capacity to produce, transport, and communicate. These fossil fuels, virtually nonrenewable, eventually will be exhausted. By that time advances in knowledge, with fair certainty, will provide other sources of energy.

The central concern of preindustrial societies was to grow enough food and fodder to furnish energy for man and beast so that they could work to replace what had been consumed. It was a virtually closed, self-perpetuating food-cycle economy, operating at a low level of input and output. Physical drudgery was rewarded with inevitable scarcity. Admittedly this exaggerates the picture. Civilizations could not have risen without some surplus beyond hand-to-mouth existence. But as long as animate energy provided the chief source of power, surpluses remained necessarily small, gained by squeezing the population masses, whether humbler citizens, slaves, or colonies.

In contrast, modern inanimate sources of energy produce a surplus more easily and much larger in relation to the input of human work. Man directs and manages the forces rather than furnishing the energy himself. Increasingly complex and versatile resource-converting techniques transform inorganic and organic substances into goods to satisfy human wants. Space-adjusting techniques, from telephone to elevator, shorten effective distance and permit intensified use of space (Ackerman, 1958). Information storage and retrieval complement the human brain. Such an economy vastly enhances the productivity per worker. It promises abundance not only of food, but of all kinds of commodities that may support the good life for everyone. Agriculture, once the main occupation, now employs only a small fraction of the labor force; sources of wealth other than land gain the upper hand.

The Meaning of "Underdeveloped."   The Western world of a generation ago referred to peoples with less advanced economies in simple blunt words: primitive, backward, colonial. New terms have replaced the old, terms ranging from undeveloped, underdeveloped, and less developed, to emergent and developing. At least the switch in terminology indicates greater courtesy, at best more understanding, even though clumsily expressed. The people so designated may not share these judgments. American Indians and Appalachian mountain folk do not necessarily consider themselves underdeveloped. They live another kind of life because their values differ from the standards prevailing elsewhere in the United States. What is true for these groups applies with even greater force to peoples beyond the realm of Occidental culture. Though many of them profess desire for material progress, they may cherish some of their values above all, and settle for less money and more bliss. Success or failure of development cannot be measured by material wealth alone.

Another warning concerns the use of the words "emerging" and "developing." If these euphemistic terms suggest that all poor nations are now in the process of catching up with the rich, nothing is further from the truth. In many countries economic development, if any, proceeds at a snail's pace when compared to the continuing advances of others. Thus, the range between top and bottom of the scale widens instead of narrows.

When speaking of developed and underdeveloped countries, one has in mind political

entities formed by sovereign states and territories. These units indeed we will consider in the following pages. One can, of course, also make a close-up of each country to inspect regional differences in levels of living. Even the rich United States has its poverty pockets, the United Kingdom its depressed areas, France its *zones critiques*. In turn, states classified as underdeveloped may have their places of plenty. Brazil shows great internal contrasts between the advanced southern portion and the underdeveloped, even undeveloped, remainder (Figure 14–1).

The Symptoms of Underdevelopment.   Before considering causes and cures, we must note the symptoms that characterize an underdeveloped economy. To classify all countries into categories according to their economic level requires worldwide statistical data. Unfortunately, essential facts are scarce for many underdeveloped countries, and even those reported for advanced countries are open to different interpretations. Most Communist countries restrict publication of vital figures; their system of accounting makes comparison with other countries difficult. Nevertheless, the data available permit an approximate classification. The following list suggests various criteria by which to judge the level of economic development. Lack of data prevents the use of several of these factors, but this is less serious than it might seem. Rather than being an independent variable, each factor presents one aspect of the interlocked economic structure. Thus, the known values of some measures provide clues to the others.

Measures of Economic Levels:
1. Income, or national product per capita
2. Occupational structure of the labor force
3. Consumption of (commercial) power per capita
4. Productivity per worker
5. Degree of commercialization of agriculture
6. Consumption of metals per capita
7. Means of transport and communication
8. Domestic savings (or investment capital) as proportion of total income
9. Percentage of family income spent on food

Economic structure affects social conditions and vice versa. If there is not enough surplus to pay for education, the people remain illiterate, and the prevailing ignorance bears upon the productivity of labor and many other economic aspects. Other social characteristics of underdeveloped countries are poor housing, poor health and sanitation, and inadequate diet. Birth rates usually are high, and so are death rates, unless checked by external aid. Most of the population is rural. The number of business and professional men, civil servants, and technicians is small. Where an indigenous people lack this middle class, foreigners often perform the services, thus giving rise to a dual or plural society.

Three Major Criteria. To judge the level of economic development we will use the three yardsticks at the top of the list of measures (see p. 318).

1. Gross domestic product is essentially the aggregate production of all resident producers. It differs from the gross national product, which also includes net income received from abroad. These measures can be refined in various ways: for instance, by allowing for capital consumption and depreciation, yielding the net product. Instead of using production data, one can also consider the distributive shares as they show up in income. National income, then, represents by and large the sum of incomes accruing within a year to the normal residents of the country.

The most commonly used criteria are the gross domestic product (GDP) and gross national product (GNP), because production statistics are more readily available than those on income. The product per capita is obtained by dividing the total product by the number of inhabitants. For the purpose of worldwide comparison, these values are expressed in the currency of a single country, usually United States dollars. This raises further questions, not only of the correct conversion rate, but also of adjustments to account for different purchasing power of the monetary unit. One should, therefore, treat with caution the figures on national income, national product, and domestic product, and not attach too great significance to small differences between countries. Figure

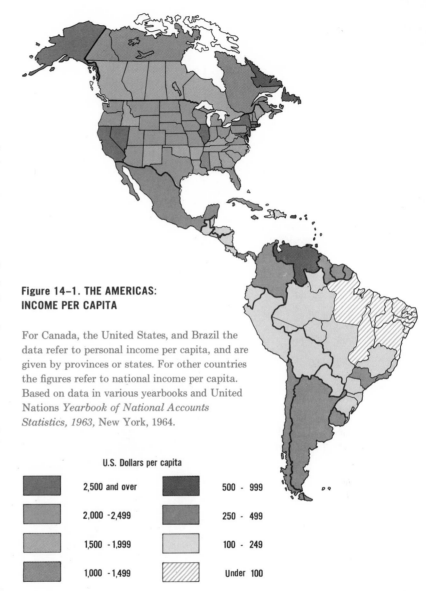

Figure 14–1. THE AMERICAS: INCOME PER CAPITA

For Canada, the United States, and Brazil the data refer to personal income per capita, and are given by provinces or states. For other countries the figures refer to national income per capita. Based on data in various yearbooks and United Nations *Yearbook of National Accounts Statistics, 1963,* New York, 1964.

U.S. Dollars per capita

2,500 and over	500 - 999
2,000 - 2,499	250 - 499
1,500 - 1,999	100 - 249
1,000 - 1,499	Under 100

14–2 presents the world distribution of gross domestic product per capita.*

* For explanation of the fundamental concepts and definitions of terms, see United Nations *Yearbook of National Accounts Statistics,* 1957– ; shorter definitions appear in the United Nations *Statistical Yearbook* at the end of the relevant tables.

14. Economic Development

Figure 14–2. WORLD: GROSS DOMESTIC PRODUCT PER CAPITA

Note the strong relationship between preindustrial agricultural economy and low product per capita. All currencies are expressed in United States dollars, but exchange rates are modified to take into account differences in purchasing power. Data for countries of the Communist bloc and certain Asian and African countries are estimates. Data from United Nations *Yearbook of National Accounts Statistics, 1963,* New York, 1964, table 3B.

U.S. Dollars per Capita

- Over 1000
- 500 -1000
- 250 - 500
- 100 - 250
- Under 100
- Over One-third of G.D.P. Originates in Agricultural Sector

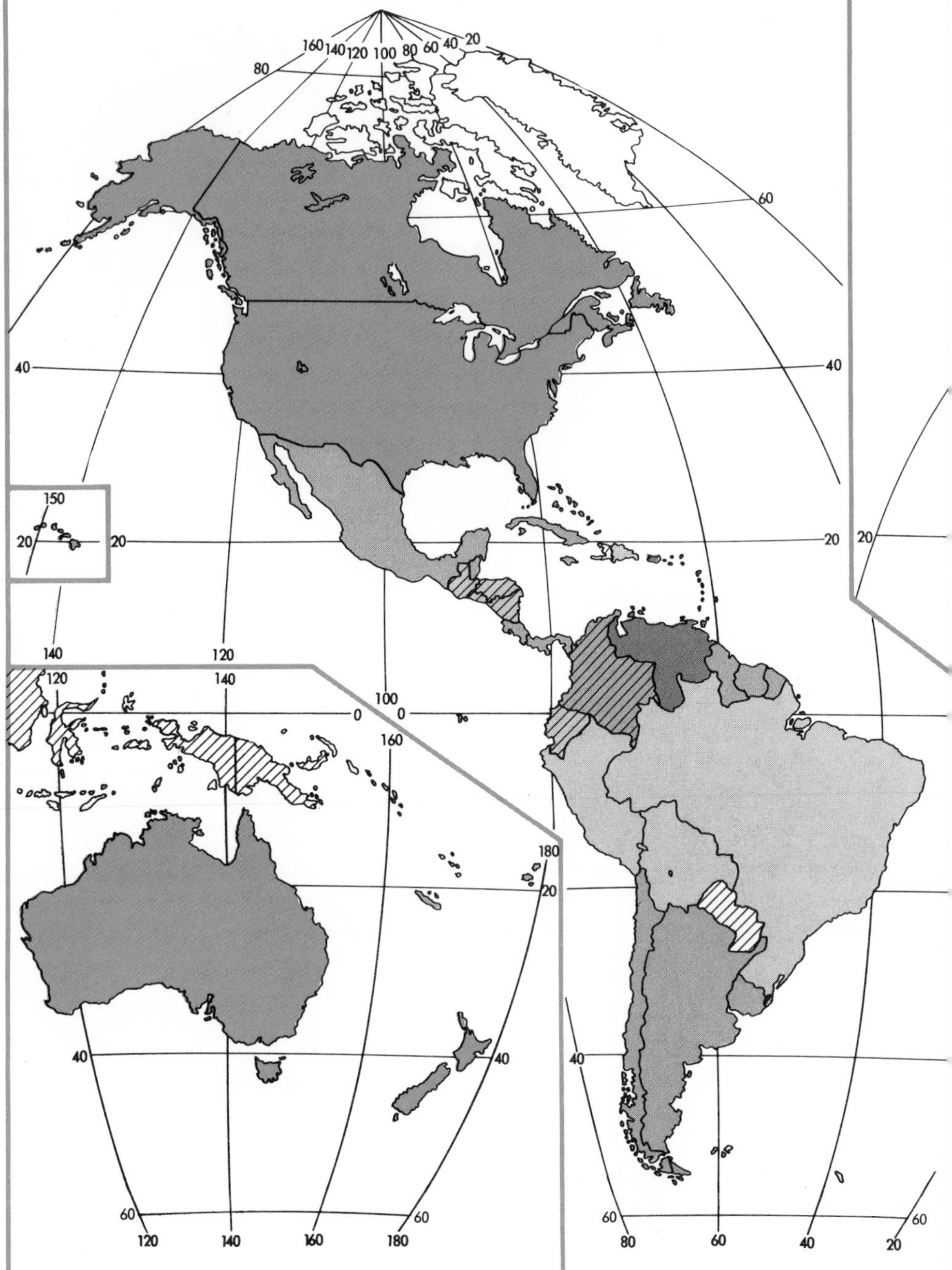

Miles

0   500   1000   1500
0 500 1000   2000
Kilometers

AITOFF'S

INTERRUPTED EQUAL-AREA

PROJECTION

*14. Economic
Development*

321

Figure 14-3. PERCENTAGES OF WORKING POPULATION IN AGRICULTURE, MANUFACTURING, AND SERVICES IN SELECTED COUNTRIES.

This triangular coordinate graph repays careful study. The total working population of each country has been allotted to three categories: agriculture (including fishing and forestry), manufacturing (including mining and construction), and services (including transportation and utilities). For example, the position of the dot for the United States results from 52 percent in services, 40 percent in manufacturing, and 8 percent in agriculture. Data from United Nations *Statistical Yearbook, 1964*, New York, 1965, table 9.

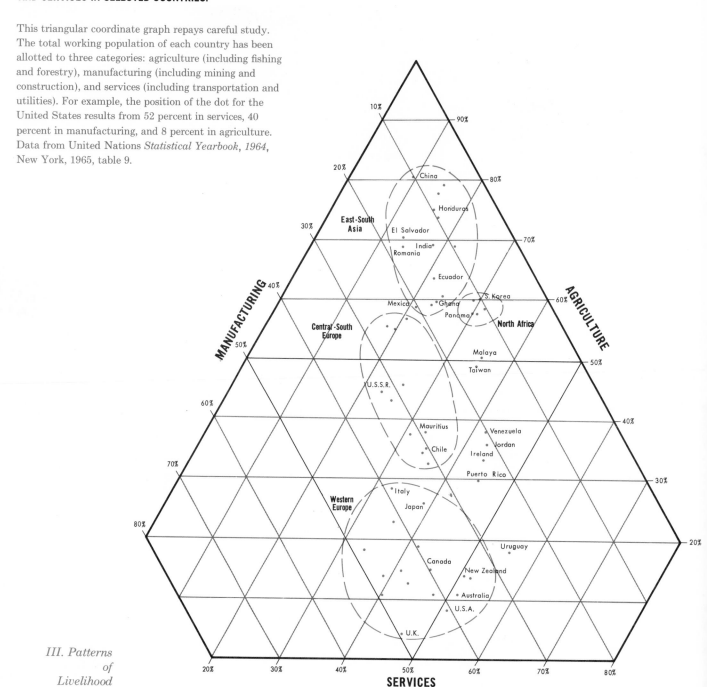

2. Another valuable yardstick to measure the economy is the proportion of the labor force employed in agriculture and related primary occupations (Figure 14-3), or conversely, those in secondary and tertiary forms of economic activity. As noted earlier, it is in the nature of underdeveloped countries that agricultural production demands the service of most of the labor force. In many of these countries over three-fourths of the workers are so engaged. One should remember, however, that this agricultural activity involves more than cultivating fields and tending animals. These workers also process the output, often transport and market it, build their homes, and make their tools. Employment in agriculture, therefore, has a different meaning here from that in advanced societies. For this very reason the measure significantly indicates the degree of labor division and thereby shows the general character of the economy.

3. The third important criterion is the per capita use of commercial energy (Figure 14-4). Excluded from the data are noncommercial sources, such as windmills on farms, wood and agricultural wastes for domestic heating and cooking, and the muscle power of man and animal. The resulting figures underestimate total energy use, especially in underdeveloped countries, but bring out all the more sharply the contrasts between preindustrial and industrial modes of life. Furthermore, the little commercial energy employed in underdeveloped countries usually is concentrated in urban areas; so the per capita consumption for the majority of people is even more meager than the reported average.

When comparing advanced countries, a point to bear in mind is that differences in temperature affect the share of energy used for heating. This may explain minor differences between countries in cold and mild climates. Apart from such reservations, the commercial power consumption per head indicates fairly well the level of economic activity.

The Pattern of Economic Development. To gain an overview one may consolidate the distributional patterns formed by specific criteria into one generalized map (Figure 14-5). This involves some arbitrary decisions where countries fall into different categories for specific measures—but these cases are not many. They could be minimized by setting up more classes, but this would defeat the purpose of this presentation. The map divides the countries of the world into three main classes: (1) advanced, (2) intermediate, and (3) underdeveloped, with the latter subdivided into (a) an upper and (b) a lower group.

1. The advanced class comprises the core of Europe and the overseas extensions of Occidental culture in Anglo-America, Australia, and New Zealand. Israel shows up as an outlier in the Middle East. All rank high in per capita GDP, use of commercial energy, and the degree of labor diversification. In this class, however, Ireland, East Germany, Czechoslovakia, and Italy occupy rather marginal positions. The advanced countries total about 520 million in population, almost 16 percent of the world's inhabitants.

2. The countries at the intermediate level in Eurasia are the Soviet Union, Japan, and those at the fringes of industrial-commercial Europe. In Latin America they include the three most southern countries and a few in and around the Caribbean. In Africa only the Republic of South Africa qualifies. Altogether it is a more heterogeneous group than category (1), approaching in various aspects modern ways of life. Some are well advanced in mechanized industry, but still devote a rather high proportion of their labor force to agriculture, and live on a modest income per capita (southern and eastern Europe, the Soviet Union, and Japan). Others (Venezuela, Cuba, Panama) rank but slightly above underdeveloped countries. The population of the intermediate class adds up to almost 500 million, close to 15 percent of the world total.

3. The remaining 70 percent of the earth's inhabitants live in countries we may call underdeveloped. Broadly speaking, they form the lands of "traditional" and "tribal" societies. Their great range of conditions warrants making a distinction between an upper and a lower group, although the lack of reliable data makes this a hazardous undertaking. The so-called Balkan countries in southeastern Europe certainly are in the forefront of the underdeveloped countries and can be properly termed "emerging." One might even argue they belong in class (2) together with the Iberian countries.

Many East and South Asian states would be in the lower (3b) group if rated only by their GDP per capita, but other indexes bring them into the upper group. North Africa and much of the Middle East, as well as the greater part of tropical America, rank in the upper group. Some countries in Southeast Asia can also be placed in (3a), though on the whole they are not much above the generally low level of this realm.

The map of levels of economic development (Figure 14–5) should be compared with that of culture realms (Figure 8–3). On the whole, Occidental culture areas rank high in economic development, especially the core of modern evolution. Then follow the East Asian, Indic, and Islamic realms (with Japan, as so often, a major exception). Southeast Asia and Meso-Africa for the most part trail the others.

Causes of Economic Stagnation. It is easier to recognize symptoms of underdevelopment than to understand causes. Yet all too commonly the casual observer, his conviction inversely related to his knowledge, points to a single mainspring as the force that determines advance or stagnation.

1. Some people consider racial differences adequate for explaining variety in economic levels. After what has been said in Chapter 4, there is no need to stress again that scientific evidence does not prove some biological groupings inferior or superior. However, we must recognize that beliefs and social attitudes toward race contribute to economic differentiation. Many groups or whole societies are deprived from access to the means of advancement because their "race" marks them as not belonging to the privileged ingroup. In turn, less advanced societies may reject ideas from a group that differs racially from their own, for fear of losing their identity.

2. Environmentalist doctrine proclaims that man is a product of his biophysical environ-

Figure 14–4. WORLD: ENERGY CONSUMPTION PER CAPITA

Consumption of energy from coal, lignite, petroleum products, natural gas, hydroelectricity, and nuclear electricity has been converted into kilograms of coal equivalent. SOURCE: United Nations *Statistical Yearbook, 1964,* New York, 1965, table 131.

Kilograms per Capita

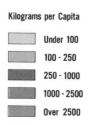

Under 100

100 - 250

250 - 1000

1000 - 2500

Over 2500

ment. As with racism, one must reject such single-minded explanations. This does not mean one can dismiss the factors of "natural environment" as irrelevant to economic development. Quite to the contrary, there is great need for further study of the direct influence of climate on man (a study now being made in environmental health research) and of the manifold and subtle forms of interplay between society and habitat. Only by examining specific situations can we escape the fog of meaningless generalities about man-nature relationships.

Aside from climate and related features there are the highly important mineral resources that supply raw materials and energy for the industrial economy. To possess abundant natural assets of this kind obviously is an advantage, but the fact is that no country can claim self-sufficiency in this respect. The more advanced the economy, the more energy and raw materials it needs, and the more it depends on foreign sources. Nevertheless, an underdeveloped country can derive great benefit from selling raw materials and investing the profits in enterprises that push the economy upward, such as education, land reform, or public utilities.

But proper use of the profits depends on

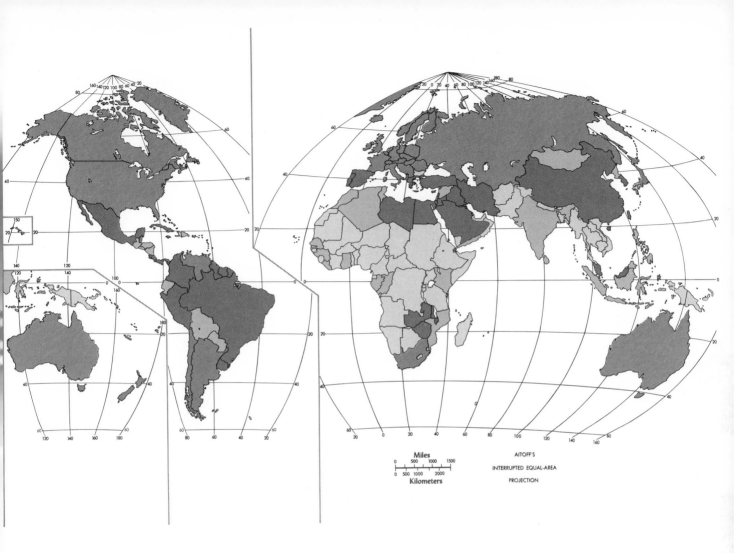

Miles
0   500   1000   1500

Kilometers
0 500 1000   2000

AITOFF'S

INTERRUPTED EQUAL-AREA

PROJECTION

many other factors. To make a comparative study of Venezuela, Saudi Arabia, Kuwait, Iraq, and Brunei—all countries with large incomes from petroleum—would give an instructive picture of the variant role natural resources play in economic development. It is also worth noting that some countries without substantial mineral wealth have achieved much in the modern world; witness Denmark, the Netherlands, and Switzerland. Evidently mineral resources can be a great asset, but are not by

themselves the touchstone to success in the modern world.

Instead of seeking the ultimate cause of stagnation in some internal condition, one can look for it among external influences. Two of these outside forces deserve inspection.

3. Many underdeveloped countries blame their poverty on that favorite scapegoat—colonial rule. One must agree, rapacious exploitation by powerful foreigners often has actually diminished, if not destroyed, native

14. Economic Development

wealth, morale, even a whole way of life. Though Occidental civilization carries the more recent guilt of such behavior, peoples of other cultures and other times, from Babylonian and Aztec armies to Arab slave traders and Chinese merchants, also have abused their power. However, a less emotional approach reveals a more positive side to many encounters between different peoples. In many ways the Romans exploited their colonial domain beyond the Alps, yet they enriched it by introducing the barbarians to the institutions and equipment of the Mediterranean civilization. In other words, colonial rule can be and often is an agent for culture transmission. It causes internal change in the colony, and thereby paves the way toward a more advanced economy.

4. Isolation from main avenues of traffic tends to have a retarding influence. Backwoods are backward. On several occasions we have noted the effect of marginal as well as central location. Shifts in trade routes and innovations in transportation change the pattern of accessibility. One might conclude that in the modern world there are no remote places anymore. But isolation always has been a relative condition, and so it is today. All places are accessible, but some are more so than others. However, favorable situation alone does not provide the magic key that opens the door to progress. Japan comes to mind, a country in a rather marginal location when it began its rise to industrial prominence.

Isolation may also result from a country's self-imposed wish to avoid foreign contacts. Seclusion has been a significant theme in periods of East Asian and Russian history. It crops up in other areas too, though less consistently and in different forms. Harsh foreign domination may lead to intense distrust of outsiders and their ideas; or a blind devotion to a national or religious ideology may also isolate a people. Attempts at autarchy (economic self-sufficiency), either combined with an ideology or strictly as an economic policy, tend to separate a country from others. While there is merit in the desire to protect a way of life, barring the door to outside influences very likely leads to stagnation.

Figure 14–5. WORLD: LEVELS OF ECONOMIC DEVELOPMENT

Advanced

Intermediate

Underdeveloped, Upper Group

Underdeveloped, Lower Group

The lesson to be learned from this brief review of various alleged causes for economic underdevelopment is at first sight a negative one: no single factor, whether race, resources, foreign domination, or relative location, can be the ultimate and universal cause of stagnation—or of progress. By freeing ourselves from these dogmatic assertions, we gain a vantage point that permits a broader view of the complex reality of rich and poor countries. Today's problems of overcoming the limitations of physical environment are not so much technological as economic and political. But in turn, economic handicaps and political hurdles form part of the wider field of sociocultural forces.

Paths Toward Economic Progress

The Idea of Progress. Yearning for the good life must be as old as Homo sapiens. Philosophers of ancient civilizations in China, India, and the Mediterranean world created visionary models of the ideal society. The spiritual ferment in West European thought expressed itself in numerous social designs, from Sir Thomas More's *Utopia* onward. But the ideal commonwealth usually was envisaged as a static state of moral paradise. The idea of progress, especially material progress of the entire national economy, came to the fore in eighteenth-century France and Britain. It found its most influential expression in Adam Smith's treatise on *The Wealth of Nations* (1776).

The Western notion of progress spread

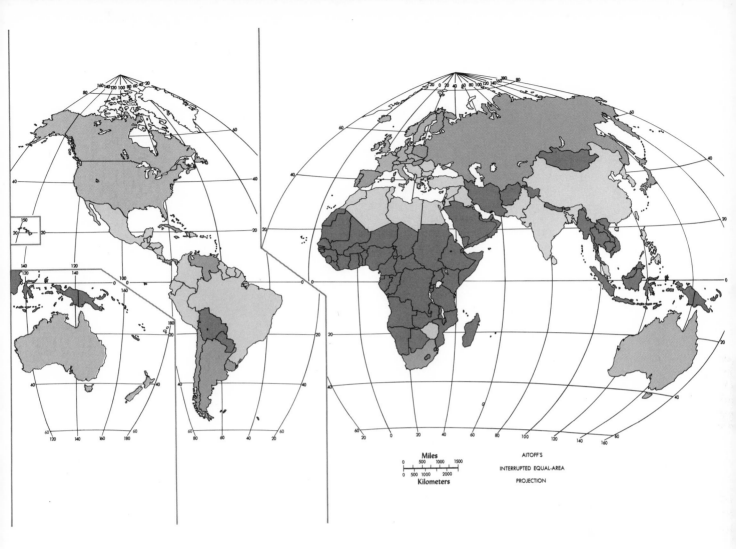

Miles
0   500   1000   1500

Kilometers
0   500 1000   2000

AITOFF'S

INTERRUPTED EQUAL-AREA

PROJECTION

around the world. All peoples, or certainly their leaders, now desire economic development. But it cannot be attained by merely importing the mechanical trappings. First and foremost, social and political transformation must break "the cake of custom" that stifles the traditional and, even more, the tribal societies. New attitudes that permit and even encourage innovations must replace value systems hostile to change. Institutions from family to school and church need to drop old tasks and assume new responsibilities. But the will to change is not enough. What is needed is the power to carry out the will. Whether by evolution or revolution, by capitalist or Communist methods or a mixture of both, the forces of reform must control the national economy before real progress becomes possible.

Assuming that the will and the power to change are there, how does one break the vicious circle of poverty and stagnation? In essence the recipe is simple: Instead of producing merely to replace consumed goods and services, all possible resources must be devoted to efforts that promote growth. As noted before, low labor productivity is the universal hallmark of underdeveloped countries. Raising the worker's productivity requires a more advanced technology, or as economists put it, more capital goods. How can this capital be obtained? It must either be imported or squeezed from domestic sources.

14. Economic Development

327

Rajasthan, western India: Old and new methods of cultivation. The ragged and undersized grain crop in the foreground contrasts sharply with the tall and grain-rich field in the background, which has benefited from chemical fertilizers. India could greatly increase her food production by improving farming methods. [Courtesy of Press Information Bureau, Government of India]

External Sources of Capital. In colonial countries the government of the metropolitan power or its private citizens provided most of the capital goods. They spent large sums on railroads, ports, other public works, agricultural experiment stations, hospitals, and to a lesser extent, on schools and public health. While it is true that part of the money came from profits made in the colony and was spent primarily for the benefit of the foreign investors, nevertheless it created in the favored areas the rudimental underpinnings—the "infrastructure"—for a modernized economy.

This form of capital import largely ended when colonialism collapsed. Unstable political conditions and restrictive economic measures in many newly independent countries have discouraged the private investor. Governments of affluent countries to some extent have restored the flow of capital through outright financial grants, development loans, and investments. However, strategic rather than economic considerations often have determined the direction of the flow, its volume, and use. Since World War II the United States has sent out some $100 billion in foreign aid—including military assistance—to underdeveloped countries. This does not include the $13 billion cost of the Marshall Plan, which served so successfully to rehabilitate Europe. At present this country's annual foreign-aid budget is about $3 billion, less than ½ percent of its GNP. Advanced countries of the British Commonwealth, and France also, provide substantial amounts (relative to their national incomes), mainly to former dependencies. In addition, the Soviet Union, Japan, and West Germany have granted or loaned funds. Though the International Bank for Reconstruction and Development is but a relatively modest source for loans, its role in intergovernmental cooperation and its sound advice on developmental policies give it a respected position. Some foreign-aid programs have succeeded quite well—for instance, that for Taiwan—some only moderately. In other cases, many millions of dollars miraculously have vanished without leaving a trace.

It is generally acknowledged that sound development is better served by trade than aid. In fact, less-developed areas do pay for most imports of capital goods by exporting raw materials such as coffee, rubber, palm oil, metal ores, or petroleum. But it is in the nature of underdeveloped economies that these surpluses are small in proportion to the population.* Moreover, colonial investments concentrated on one or a few commodities that a dependency seemed best able to produce, resulting in a very lopsided export package. To rely on a single export commodity is always hazardous, and even more so today because of the competition with synthetic rubber, fibers, drugs, dyes, and the many substitutes for metals and woods available in industrial countries. To make matters worse, prices for basic foodstuffs and raw materials have suffered a relative decline when compared to the prices for services and manufactured goods. Thus, an agricultural and mining country gets fewer machines and less structural steel than twenty years ago for the same volume of exports.

Internal Sources of Capital. The conclusion is inescapable that the underdeveloped country must find the greater part of needed capital within itself. It must save part of its current production to invest in growth-promoting activities, techniques, and equipment. How this can be done depends on the given situation in each state. To achieve this is much more difficult in a full-blown subsistence-farming economy than in one that has already a substantial commercial component. And it is harder in a country with great population pressure than in one with a more favorable ratio between population and material resources.

As noted earlier, agrarian communities at near-subsistence level have much hidden unemployment. This surplus labor must be siphoned off and led into productive work. If there is inadequate capital to provide them jobs, they can be put to work with shovels and baskets to create capital, such as roads, dikes, and dams. As services and industries expand, they provide the farmer with a growing domestic market. With the cash received—or with credit on anticipated sales—he can buy better seeds, tools, fertilizers, and insecticides; in short, increase his own productivity. As the agricultural population shrinks, little plots can be consolidated into larger farms, thus further increasing the productivity of labor. Countries blessed with reserves of arable land, like those in most of Latin America, Meso-Africa, and Southeast Asia, should use them to create relatively large commercial farms instead of permitting the spread of small homesteads which merely extend the poverty of subsistence.

Many other factors contribute to a higher productivity per worker, though in the end most depend on access to capital goods. Highly important among them is education in the broadest sense of the word. It must prepare workers to use new techniques, and above all, it must open their minds to new ideas (Figures 14-6 and 14-7).

*Exceptions are mainly the large petroleum exports of some very small states.

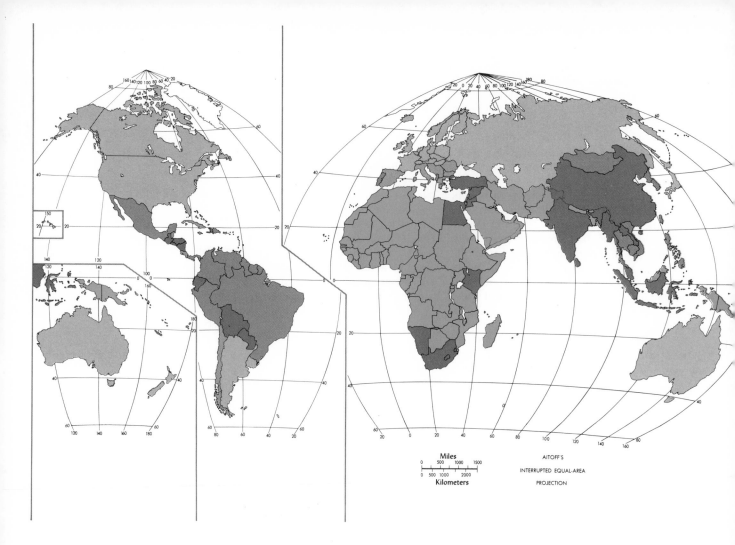

Percentage Illiterate

	Under 10
	10 - 25
	25 - 50
	50 - 75
	Over 75

Figure 14–6. WORLD: ILLITERACY

Percentage of population aged fifteen and over who cannot read *and* write. Illiteracy and economic underdevelopment are highly correlated.
SOURCE: United Nations *Statistical Yearbook, 1964,* New York, 1965, table 187.

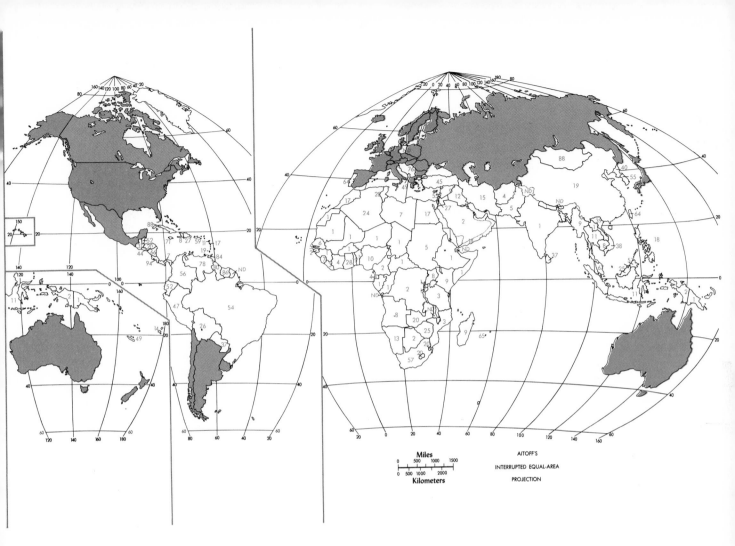

Figure 14–7. WORLD: DAILY NEWSPAPERS, NUMBER OF COPIES PER 1,000 INHABITANTS

In the underdeveloped parts of the world there is higher newspaper circulation in Latin America than in Meso-Africa and South and East Asia. In different countries the size of a daily newspaper may range from a single sheet to 50 or more pages.
SOURCE: United Nations *Statistical Yearbook, 1964,* New York, 1965, table 191.

14. Economic Development

The Role of the Entrepreneur. Many writers stress the significance of the entrepreneur, the man who organizes and directs business, who is willing to risk new ventures to make larger profits. As technical and commercial innovator he is considered the dynamic element in the market-oriented economy. Many agrarian societies, especially in Southeast Asia and Meso-Africa, lack business leadership of this type. Outsiders have filled the entrepreneurial positions in the incipient capitalist order: Westerners and, mainly at the lower levels, immigrants from the Middle East, India, and China. However, a society will not advance very far if it does not fill the slots of manager, merchant, and banker from its own ranks. Unfortunately, an energetic and imaginative class of entrepreneurs cannot be trained overnight. Such skill grows slowly in response to changing social values and economic institutions.

The Marxist doctrine considers it immoral and illegitimate to own private property and capital. Communist countries replace the market mechanism by allocating capital according to the national budget or plan. Clearly, where the government acts as manager of the "one-firm state," it allows no place for the entrepreneur class. By insisting on doctrinal policies, the Soviet Union and other self-styled socialist republics have committed serious errors and have increased the cost of economic development, especially if one considers the human cost. This criticism does not imply that a policy of complete *laissez faire* is best for underdeveloped countries. Even the most advanced states mix free market with government manipulation. Each country seeking progress must decide what combination of private and government enterprise best suits its own situation.

Many underdeveloped countries give the state far-reaching control over the economy, partly because they face a shortage of native entrepreneurs, and partly because they believe that the Communist conscious effort at self-improvement is highly successful. Yet, the signal progress made in countries like Puerto Rico, Taiwan, and the Federation of Malaya indicates that private enterprise is an effective partner in economic and social betterment.

Rostow's Stages of Economic Growth. The economic historian W. W. Rostow, with an eye to national variations in economic levels, offers a generalized description of the stages of economic growth by comparing the historical record of different countries for different times. To pull together the discussion in this chapter, it is useful to summarize his argument. He calls it "an economic historian's way of generalizing the sweep of modern history" (Rostow, 1960, 1).

Rostow identifies five stages of economic growth. The first is that of *the traditional society.* Here change is slow because of limited access to modern science and technology. Most people are farmers; the upper classes spend whatever capital is developed on monuments, wars, palaces, and high living. A landowning aristocracy holds the political power.

To change the traditional society requires a radical transformation; a national view must supplant local loyalties. Farming has to surrender its primacy to manufacturing, transportation, and the provision of services. Capital must be used to create the infrastructure of the industrial-commercial society: transportation, public utilities, and a school system. Specialized knowledge and expertise should replace parentage and family as the criteria for personal value and prestige. Not all these need occur together or simultaneously to prepare the traditional society to move into the first phase of economic growth.

The second stage embodies *the preconditions for take-off.* This stage first developed in western Europe during the seventeenth and eighteenth centuries, when science spurred production, world markets expanded, and international economic competition increased. Great Britain entered this stage ahead of the others, favored by internal and external geographic conditions and by a sympathetic social, political, and economic milieu. In modern times the impetus often comes from outside. China and India, for example, were shaken out of their traditional ways by contacts with Western societies already on the road toward economic growth. Rostow thinks that the key change in this stage arrives when a population becomes convinced that economic growth is essential to

School in Qatar, oil-rich sheikdom on the Persian Gulf. Wiping out illiteracy is a fundamental need in all underdeveloped countries. This grade school obviously is for the sons of upper-class Arabs. Arabic is written and read from right to left. [A Shell photograph]

attaining certain goals: personal advancement, social welfare, national power, a higher level of living.

The distinctive feature of Rostow's thesis is *the stage of take-off*—"the great watershed in the life of modern societies," as he calls it. Resistance to change is overcome, and economic growth becomes the normal situation. Take-off does not occur in all sectors of the economy, but in a number of vital industries, probably

14. Economic Development

including steel production and transportation. Farmers accept commercialization and innovation. "One can approximately allocate the take-off of Britain to the two decades after 1783; France and the United States to the several decades preceding 1860; Germany, the third quarter of the nineteenth century; Japan, the fourth quarter of the nineteenth century; Russia and Canada, the quarter century or so preceding 1914; while during the 1950's India and China have, in quite different ways, launched their respective take-offs" (Rostow, 1960, 9).

The *drive to maturity* follows take-off, and may last half a century or more: During this time economic growth extends to all branches of the expanding economy. Growth comes to the more technologically complicated industries; for example, in the twentieth century away from iron, steel, and coal, toward machine tools and electronics. An economy can produce almost anything it chooses, for during the drive to maturity it develops a wide range of technical and entrepreneurial skills. Britain completed this drive to maturity by 1850, the United States, Germany, and France soon after the opening of the twentieth century, but the Soviet Union only recently.

Then follows *the stage of high mass consumption,* "where in time, the leading sectors shift towards durable consumers' goods and services: a phase from which Americans are beginning to emerge; whose not unequivocal joys western Europe and Japan are beginning energetically to probe, and with which Soviet society is engaged in an uneasy flirtation." Rostow wrote this at the end of the 1950s; since then West Europeans have produced and bought masses of cars, refrigerators, washing machines, television sets, suburban houses, and apartments. Some of these products are also being bought in increasing numbers by people in Japan and in eastern and central Europe. In some modernized countries, like, for example, Sweden, substantial resources are devoted to social welfare; in others, especially the United States and the Soviet Union, enormous sums are being spent on defense and the exploration of space.

Beyond mass consumption of durable goods lies the possibility that a new stage may develop, characterized by heavy investment in new towns, city reconstruction, higher education, and the arts.

Rostow cautions us against mistaking his argument as an exposition of economic laws. There is nothing automatic about the process. He shows how each stage varies from country to country, depending on resources available, the number of the population, and the kind of society present.

The Widening Gap. "The revolution of rising expectations" has touched all countries. Some are well on the way toward an affluent life, some are at the take-off, others just beginning to feel the stirrings of change. If it were true that advanced nations had reached a plateau where they would rest a long time, one could expect the others to catch up eventually, after a shorter or longer climb. But all evidence suggests that modern economy and technology carry a highly dynamic potential for further growth—barring all-out nuclear war or other major catastrophes. At the opposite extreme poor countries, especially heavily populated ones, face enormous difficulties, even in getting under way for the long journey upward. They may even slip back before they start.

Gunnar Myrdal, the Swedish social scientist, stresses the mechanism of circular causation. He points out that a change normally "does not call forth contradicting forces but, instead, supporting changes, which move the system in the same direction but much further. Because of such circular causation a social process tends to become cumulative and often gathers speed at an accelerated rate" (Myrdal, 1957, 13). For example, private capital for new plants is much easier to obtain for an area that already has proven its worth for manufacturing than for one where modern industry is a pioneering venture. Or, entrepreneurs of advanced countries know how to take advantage of new opportunities, while the less resourceful native businessmen of a less-developed country may have to retreat in the face of stiff competition. Expressed in familiar terms, the rich get richer and the poor get poorer. Even as the poor inch forward they see the distance widen between them and the rich, who move ahead at a fast clip.

In Myrdal's view the increasing inequalities

between nations result from "the cumulative tendency inherent in the unhampered play of the market forces." The theoretical solution might be the presence of "a world state which could interfere in the interest of equality of opportunity." The reader who is aware of the stubborn problems that depress areas within national states—in spite of all government proddings and a constant gentle rain of favors—may well be skeptical of this answer. Myrdal realizes that there exists at present no basis of "mutual human solidarity" on which a world state necessarily must rest. In his opinion the best hope lies in expanding intergovernmental organizations that initiate and strengthen international economic integration and promote equality. These "are ideals which no country and, indeed,

no responsible human being can ever afford to give up." To which he adds wryly: "If for no other reason, we need them to console our international conscience" (Myrdal, 1957, 64–66).

Among obstacles to advancement, one looms perhaps larger than any other: the rapidly increasing population. A nation may show commendable growth of its domestic product, but if this gain merely equals that in population, no economic progress results. Underdeveloped countries in particular suffer under the burden of accelerated population increase—another instance of circular causation ("the rich get richer, and the poor get children . . ."). The topic of population growth in its areal differentiation and the accompanying problems receive special attention in Part V of this volume.

Citations

Ackerman, E. A. *Geography as a Fundamental Research Discipline,* University of Chicago, Department of Geography, Research Paper no. 53, Chicago, 1958.
Fairgrieve, J. *Geography and World Power,* London, 1915.
Myrdal, G. *Rich Lands and Poor,* New York, 1957.
Rostow, W. W. *The Stages of Economic Growth,* London and New York, 1960.

Further Readings

Boulding, K. E. *The Meaning of the 20th Century,* New York, 1964.
Brown, H. *The Challenge of Man's Future,* New York, 1954.
Buchanan, N. S., and Ellis, H. S. *Approaches to Economic Development,* New York, 1955.
Clark, C. *The Conditions of Economic Progress,* 3d ed., London, 1957.
Cottrell, W. F. *Energy and Society,* New York, 1955.
Dean, V. M. *The Nature of the Non-western World,* New York, 1962.
Dewhurst, J. F., et al. *Europe's Needs and Resources,* New York, 1961.
Ginsburg, N. S. "Natural Resources and Economic Development," *Annals of the Association of American Geographers,* 47 (1957): 196–212.
——— (ed.) *Essays on Geography and Economic Development,* University of Chicago, Department of Geography Research Paper no. 62, Chicago, 1960.
——— . *Atlas of Economic Development,* Chicago, 1961.
Gourou, P. *The Tropical World,* translated by E. D. Laborde, 2d ed., New York, 1962.
Hance, W. A. *African Economic Development,* New York, 1958.
Hartshorne, R. "The Role of the State in Economic Growth: Contents of the

State Area," in Aitken H. G. J. (ed.) *The State and Economic Growth,* New York, 1959, 287–324.

Hauser, P. M. "Demographic Indicators of Economic Development," *Economic Development and Cultural Change,* 7 (1959): 98–116.

Heilbroner, R. L. *The Great Ascent,* New York, 1963.

Kamarck, A. M. *The Economics of African Development,* New York, 1967.

Lee, D. H. K. *Climate and Economic Development in the Tropics,* New York, 1957.

Malenbaum, W. "India and China: Contrasts in Development," *American Economic Review,* 49 (1959): 284–309.

Mountjoy, A. B. *Industrialization and Under-developed Countries,* London, 1963.

Murphey, R. "Economic Conflicts in South Asia," *Conflict Resolution,* 4 (1960): 83–95.

Staley, E. *The Future of Underdeveloped Countries,* rev. ed., New York, 1961.

Ward, B. *The Rich Nations and the Poor Nations,* New York, 1962.

Part IV. Settlements

The word settlement indicates to the geographer all man-made facilities resulting from the process of settling, including the establishments that shelter people and their possessions, the roads that connect, and the fences that part them. The functions and forms of settlement express cultural differences.

Buildings and property lines remain long after the people who made them. Thus the study of settlements has a strong historical component: it views the present as an amalgam of old and recent forms, reflecting different phases of social organization and technical skill, or even a succession of cultures.

But settlement geography also relates immediately to the future, because it points up shortcomings of our present environment. The needs of a society in rapid transition strain the shell of wood, brick, steel, concrete, and asphalt that former generations have left behind. Changes in technology, economy, and social organization demand modification in the nature and arrangement of buildings, roads, and open spaces. Every citizen has a direct stake in creating surroundings that promote the quality of life.

Geographers usually classify settlements into rural and urban, but recognize that the distinction often blurs, particularly in modern societies. Chapter 15 deals with strictly agrarian occupance forms. Chapter 16 discusses the nature of cities in different culture realms and their distribution in different eras and regions. Chapter 17 analyzes the metropolis, the environment of modern man, full of baffling problems.

IV. Settlements   Batak village, Sumatra. [A Shell photograph]

15. Farm and Village

The medieval burgher was well aware of the political, social, and economic institutions and activities that set him apart from the folk beyond the city gates. The view from the ramparts simply confirmed what he knew about the proper functions of town and country in the scheme of things: here the towers of cathedral and city hall, the market square with its guild houses, the busy streets lined by the homes of merchant and craftsman; across the moat the open fields, the river meadows, and woodlots, with villages here and there or a sprinkling of single farmsteads.

Today the resident of that same city, or of an American one, observes also how his way of life differs from that of the farmer, but the differences are in degree, not sharp contrast. Means of transportation and communication have diffused an essentially urban culture all over the land. The once marked division between opposing landscapes, too, has blurred into a broad transition zone. On the urban fringe what looks like a rural scene actually is the dispersed habitat of people who work in the city or perform urban tasks in their rustic residence. In other words, the countryside surrounding the city now serves urban functions, though forms like farmsteads, lanes, fields, and woodlots still may reflect its former use. Such an area with city-directed activities has become urban in spite of its deceptively rural appearance.

This chapter on "Farm and Village" concerns rural settlement proper—that is, occupance patterns that primary production, principally agriculture, creates. The first portion draws attention to the various geographic aspects of rural occupance. The following sections illustrate some of the problems of settlement study by sampling western Europe, eastern North America, East Asia, and Southeast Asia.

Geographic Approaches to Rural Settlements

Distribution. The first thing the geographer wants to know about agrarian settlements is their distribution. As noted earlier (Figure 1–5), distribution has three aspects: (1) dispersion, (2) density, and (3) pattern. Dispersed living on isolated farmsteads is typical for North America and other European-colonized lands, but the village predominates in many parts of the world.

Upon closer inspection, the village reveals various degrees of dispersion. In some the buildings are grouped together forming a "compact" village;* others have a dense core surrounded by a looser sprawl of buildings—the "nucleated" village; still others appear as a swarm of buildings without a core—the "agglomerated" village. Many areas have only one characteristic form

---

* The communal longhouse can be considered an extreme form of compactness, a village under one roof in which each family occupies a one-room unit.

What to Observe in Rural Settlements

A. *Duration of occupance*

1. Movable shelters, tents
2. Permanent buildings, periodically used
3. Permanent buildings used throughout the year

B. *Distribution of settlements*

1. Dispersion
   a. Longhouse
   b. Compact village or hamlet
   c. Nucleated village
   d. Agglomerated village
   e. Single farmstead
2. Density
   Frequency of occurrence per unit area of:
   a. Villages or hamlets
   b. Single farmsteads
3. Pattern
   The spatial arrangement of settlement units in relation to:
   a. Some physical feature, e.g., river, ridge, spring line, beach ridge, sunny side of valley
   b. Some cultural feature, e.g., road, canal, levee, geometric land survey

C. *Relation of settlement unit to field system*
1. Homestead type
2. Separation of home and farmland

D. *Village plan*
   The closeup view of the village, revealing its layout, e.g., grid, circular, or star shape, linear (shoestring, double row), and irregular patterns

E. *Structure of farmstead*
   The closeup view of residence, associated buildings, and other facilities:
1. Plan: multiple units or all facilities under one roof
2. Construction materials, e.g., wood, brick, adobe, stone, thatch
3. Construction on the ground, or on stilts
4. Floor plan and roof shape
5. Architectural features, e.g., mode of construction, style, decorative motifs
6. Fence types, e.g., hedge, wall, ditch, rail, post, stone, wire

---

of dispersion; others combine two forms, e.g., Utah, with the old order of Mormon village settlement and later spread of isolated farms. In such cases we must describe the settlement as a mixture of two types.

The density of settlement results mainly from the degree of intensity of land use. The widely scattered farmsteads in Montana differ from the relatively close-spaced ones in New Jersey, and contrast decidedly with those in Java's countryside where one encounters a village every half mile or so.

Settlement pattern denotes the arrangement of the units according to natural or man-made features or designs, such as streams, spring lines, ridges, canals, and roads. Where a central authority determines division of land and layout of roads before allowing settlement, a geometric pattern results. The Romans established a regular system of land division (*centuriation*) in several parts of their empire (Figure 15–3). The United States Land Survey from 1785 onward divided the unoccupied lands of the western territories into a grid system. The Dutch lay out their newly reclaimed lands in meticulous detail before permitting the farmers to move in.

Any settlement plan, however well designed for the needs of the time, becomes inadequate under changing conditions of land use. This leads to a new settlement pattern that may only faintly show the imposed divisions of former times. In the United States changes in the technology of farming and transportation have in many instances altered the original lattice pattern of the Land Survey.

A West-African house type. This model village, near Tamala, northeastern Ghana, follows the building tradition of the large Dagomba tribe that inhabits this area. [A Shell photograph]

Field Systems. To understand rural settlements we need to analyze the spatial relationships between dwellings and farmland. In the United States the typical farmstead stands on the farm property, commonly a single tract of land. An entirely different situation prevails in some parts of Europe and over much of Asia and Africa, where village residence is the rule. Each farmer has property in the surrounding area, sometimes as one holding, but usually scattered in plots and strips. This manner of settlement reveals quite ancient forms of social organization. On large-scale agricultural enterprises, whether plantations or collective farms, the labor force often lives in compact settlements.

Structure of Village and Farmstead.

There remains one more aspect of the study of rural settlements: the closeup (large-scale) view of village or single farmstead to discover its ground plan, typical construction materials, architectural style, and other features of cultural significance. Villages in different parts of the world display a fascinating variety of traditional forms. For instance, a circle of beehive-shaped huts around the cattle corral (*kraal*) is a common type in East Africa. Some districts in China and Japan have the grid pattern. Linear villages string along Europe's river dikes or lie along roads, often with an open space in the middle. Other villages, however, have irregular shapes, with narrow lanes winding between dwellings and walled compounds or barnyards.

No less interesting are the buildings themselves, whether grouped in a village or constituting the isolated farmstead. Few people note the variety of American farmsteads, though regional contrasts exist and are worthy of attention. In Europe farmstead types are highly localized; on a day's drive one may discover several forms. In some areas the dwelling, with a characteristic floor plan, stands apart from the barn, stable, and other buildings, similar to American practice. Elsewhere the house, animal shelter, storage space, and workshop are under one roof.

It may be a two- or even three-storied building, take the shape of a T, an L, a U, or the units may fully enclose a courtyard with only a broad gateway giving access to the inner sanctum. Often such a courtyard has as its centerpiece a large manure pile, the mark of the skillful farmer.

Beyond the Occidental culture realm the villages and house types, although exotic in form, represent merely other solutions to the universal problem of constructing establishments that best serve social and economic needs in a specific physical environment (Figure 15–1).

After observation come the much more diffi-

cult tasks of analysis and explanation. As with most cultural phenomena, cause-and-effect relationships in settlement patterns are complex; the simple explanation that points toward one single force is always suspect. "Occupance patterns sum up . . . the nature of man's rapport with the earth. . . ." (Kniffen, 1965, 552). It follows that any explanation must consider both physical and cultural factors. The examples of rural settlements to be discussed in this chapter amply demonstrate how involved such a study can be.

Western Europe

The Germanic peoples that lived in England, France, the Low Countries, and Germany during the early Middle Ages practiced a simple kind of mixed farming. Most of these lands were covered with broadleaf deciduous forests, alternating with conifer stands on sandy soils and mountain slopes. Thus, agriculture was essentially an adaptation to forest environment. Crop growing predominated on fertile, well-drained, easily tilled soils, already cleared by earlier inhabitants, such as the gently rolling loess lands that stretch through northern France, the southern Low Countries, and central Germany. Stock raising held first place in marshy river bottoms and coastlands, as well as on cool, rainy uplands. In the fertile areas the villages were of substantial size, surrounded by a broad expanse of cropland; in the pastoral areas they were small, often no more than hamlets with a modest-sized "home field" or "infield" for crops and a wide "outfield" for grazing.

Ancient Forms in Lower Saxony.

In location and character Lower Saxony—northwestern Germany and the eastern Netherlands—occupied a position somewhat between the arable and pastoral types. Glacial moraines and sandy outwash plains, covered with forests, alternated with vast moors. Ribbons of alluvial river land cut through the plain. A sparse population lived in the forest clearings. Dwellings, perhaps no more than a dozen, stood in an irregular and

Figure 15–1. INDIA: A VILLAGE IN PUNJAB

The thousand inhabitants of Kunran village belong to several castes. Most numerous are the Sikh Jat (76 households), Ramdasia (27 households), and Mazhbi Sikh (12 households). Other castes represented include Tarkhan (carpenter), Bazigar (acrobat), Jhiwar (water carrier), Sunar (goldsmith), Nai (barber), and Bania (shopkeeper). Among the villagers are 30 Moslems, including those of Mirasi (drummer) and Teli (oil presser) castes. The map is based on a sketch in Census of India, vol. 13, part 6, 1963.

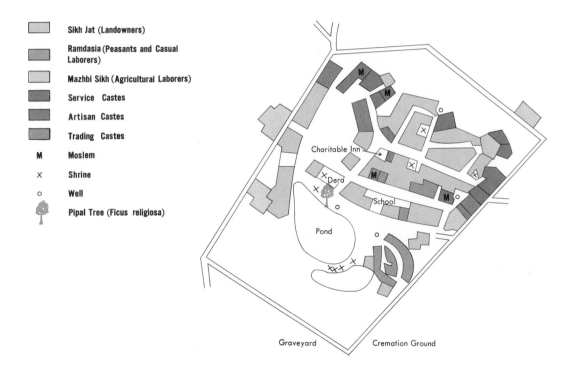

Sikh Jat (Landowners)

Ramdasia (Peasants and Casual Laborers)

Mazhbi Sikh (Agricultural Laborers)

Service Castes

Artisan Castes

Trading Castes

M   Moslem

×   Shrine

○   Well

Pipal Tree (Ficus religiosa)

Charitable Inn

Dera

School

Pond

Graveyard

Cremation Ground

loose cluster, sometimes around a central green (Figure 15–2). Each house sheltered a family, its harvest and livestock, although in later times the space became compartmentalized for the different uses. The cropland (*esch*) lay nearby on higher, well-drained land. Whether this cropland consisted of one or more fields cannot be answered in general terms. Condi-

tions varied in time and space. Under the one-field system the arable land was cropped year in, year out with rye. More commonly, from the ninth or tenth century onward, the cropland was divided into two or three fields. Each full member of the community held equal shares in each field, laid out in one or more long strips to facilitate plowing. (The English measure of

15. Farm and Village

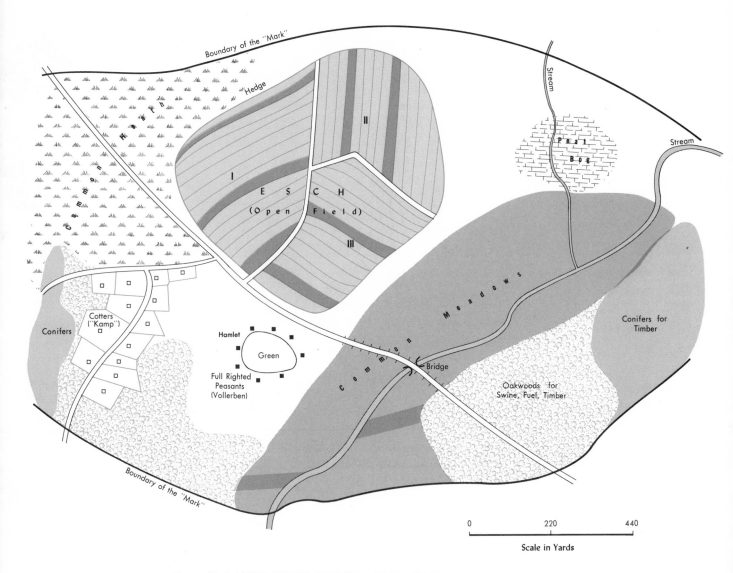

Figure 15–2. LOWER SAXONY: OPEN FIELD (ESCH) VILLAGE

This generalized diagram portrays the situation in the Middle Ages. The
darker strips in the three fields of the *esch* belong to one full-righted
peasant. The common meadows often were, at least in part, subdivided into
privately owned lots, of which two are shown in the sketch .The entire
land area belonging to the community was called the *mark*.

IV. Settlements

the furlong, 220 yards, was derived from the length of a furrow under a similar practice.) In the three-field system the usual rotation consisted of a spring sowing of barley or oats, a fall sowing of rye or wheat, and then a year of fallow.

Livestock raising was an important activity. Most communities used the meadows along small streams for pasture and for winning hay as precious winter fodder, either in common or in private parcels. All villagers shared the surrounding forest for pasture, timber, and fuel. Modern research indicates that heathland, so typical in the nineteenth century landscape, was not widespread in the early Middle Ages. It appears that heather, a woody scrub, gained dominance as the forest deteriorated from overgrazing and burning. With the change from woodland to heath came a shift from cattle to sheep, since the latter were better browsers.

Because the size and fertility of cropland on these leached sandy soils depended heavily on the availability of manure, the number of livestock a village could maintain was of crucial importance, quite apart from their value for meat, milk, wool, and hides. Stubble grazing after the harvest provided the field with animal waste. It is not clear when night stabling of animals became common practice. Sods cut in the forest were brought to the barn, and subsequently, enriched with manure, spread over the fields. This cutting of sod brought the surface closer to the groundwater level and further encouraged the growth of heather instead of trees. The practice of using heath sod to mix with manure in order to increase the organic content of the soil continued in this area from late medieval times until the last century. In the process the arable land was raised, so that now the *esch* often appears as a gently rising mound in the landscape.

This form of agriculture demanded that all community members cooperate. Farmers owning individual strips in each arable field had to agree on the rotation scheme, the proper time for plowing, sowing, and harvesting. They aided each other in harvesting and in repairing the fence enclosing the large field. Only a few tracks led to the *esch,* and almost every strip required passage across another man's property.

Village inhabitants with full community rights (in German, *Vollerben*) and those without (called cottagers or cotters) might be permitted to clear a forest patch of their own and build a home. In this way a number of new, dispersed farmsteads, each located on its compact enclosed property (called *kamp*), gradually spread around the *esch* village.

The feudal system made little impact in Lower Saxony. In other parts of western Europe the nobility often acquired property rights over village lands and reduced the peasants to servile status. This form of feudal agricultural unit was known as the manor. Village and manor might coincide, or there might be two or more manors in one village. The lord had his own home farm, the *demesne* (cf., "domain"), which he worked with hired or serf labor. On this demesne stood his manor house or hall. The arrangement and use of arable fields, pastures, and woods, however, was much the same as in communities of free farmers.

In the seventeenth and eighteenth centuries better rotation systems were introduced, including clovers and a variety of root crops, which made the fallow field unnecessary. These advances, first introduced on large estates in Holland and England, eventually also reached Lower Saxony. In the last hundred years the agrarian landscape of Lower Saxony has greatly changed. Chemical fertilizer enabled the farmers to convert heathlands into productive pastures and arable land. Faced by the competition of cheap American grains, they switched to fodder crops, dairy cattle, poultry, and hogs to feed the growing cities. More efficient production demanded consolidation of scattered small holdings into larger units. In many communities this has been carried out by voluntary exchange. It has encouraged residence on the farm instead of in the village. Yet, in spite of all the changes, remnants of the old order remain and give the region a character singularly its own.

Linear Villages (Figure 15–3). A very different settlement form developed from about A.D. 1200 onward in reclaimed marshlands along sea and river. In decided contrast to the scattered strip system of the *esch,* the land of each farmer stretched from the dike, where his home and other buildings stood, into the marsh as one long narrow lot. This type can be observed over much of the Netherlands and northern Germany; the village consists of a long row of houses along the dike road. Much the same arrangement characterizes settlement in the mountain valleys of central Germany: The farmsteads lie along the road on the valley floor, and the holdings run from the meadows along the river, via cropland on cleared higher ground, into the forest that covers the steep slopes (*Waldhufendorf*).

German Settlements East of the Elbe. German expansion eastward across the Elbe and Saale rivers into Slavic lands began around A.D. 900 and gained full momentum toward A.D. 1200. The Slavs practiced a simple agriculture, depending mainly on cattle raising. The farmsteads of a village were closely grouped around a roughly circular open space which served as an enclosure for the livestock. Around the village lay the arable land. The Germans moving into these territories often retained the original village layout, but added new arable land according to the strip system. One can still observe many of these *Rundling* (round-shaped) villages in central Germany (Figure 15–3).

Where the Germans settled unoccupied lands, they usually built the new colonies according to a carefully planned design. Often it was a regularized pattern of the clustered village and open-field system so familiar from the homeland. Other designs were the *Strassendorf* (*street village*) with farmsteads on both sides of a road, and the *Angerdorf,* farmsteads around an almond-shaped common (*Anger*) with the church and a pond. The arable land surrounding the village was usually divided into three blocks, each with individual holdings distributed in long narrow strips (Figure 15–3).

The nobles who participated in the conquest of the Slavic lands received grants commensurate to their status and service. They expanded their holdings when peasants in distress

Figure 15–3. EUROPE: RURAL SETTLEMENT TYPES

These diagrams are on the scale of approximately 1:10,000, except for the centuriation sample, which is about 1:33,000. Houses would usually face the road or stream.

- Gardens
- Arable
- Meadow
- Heath
- Woods

abandoned their land or offered it in return for protection. In this way many feudal estates grew up between the villages of free farmers. As expanding West European cities needed bread grains, the landed gentry of northern Germany converted their lands into large cereals-producing enterprises, using their serfs for labor. Although hereditary serfdom was abolished early in the nineteenth century, estates remained the dominant form of landownership in eastern Germany until the end of World War II, when the (East) German Democratic Republic and Poland broke up the large holdings. A similar development of large estates occurred in England during the fifteenth century, but here the impetus was the profits to be made from sheep raising. The gentry, by legal means or simple theft, acquired peasant lands and replaced the open-field system by consolidated enclosed fields and pastures, worked by tenants living in hamlets or on dispersed farmsteads.

We have purposely emphasized the village type of settlement in Europe, because it contrasts so sharply with that of the United States and Canada. It should be understood, however, that the dispersed form of rural settlement is present in many parts of Europe. Especially in modern times the trend has been toward locating farmsteads on the property instead of in the village. Numerous factors have contributed to

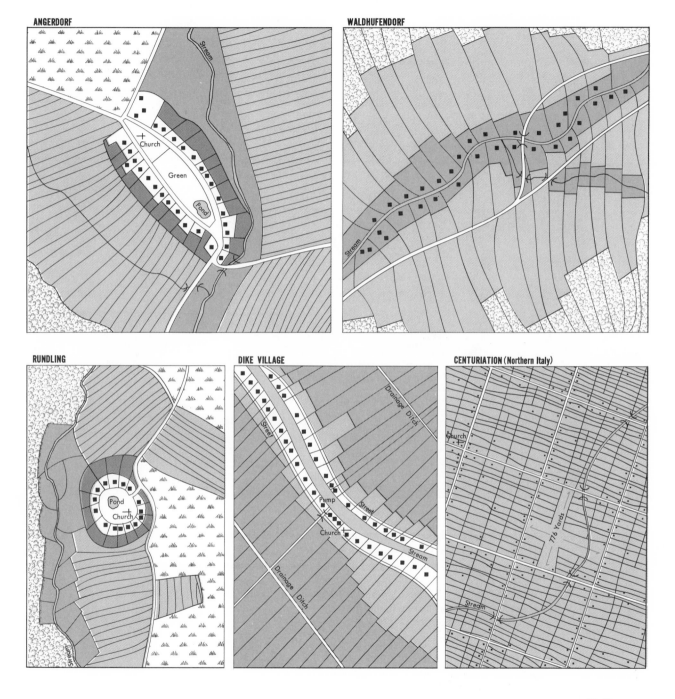

ANGERDORF

Stream

Church

Green

Pond

WALDHUFENDORF

Stream

RUNDLING

Pond
Church

Stream

DIKE VILLAGE

Street

Drainage Ditch

Pump
Street

Church

Stream

Drainage Ditch

CENTURIATION (Northern Italy)

Church

776 Yards

Stream

*15. Farm
and Village*

349

Laxton, England. The medieval open fields of this village escaped enclosure, and are now preserved as a historic monument. Although the old narrow strips have been consolidated to create more workable plots, and some of the old common lands are hedged, the layout of the fields and the typically straggling English village are clearly visible. The light patch in center background is the South Field. Between it and the village runs a stream (left to right), bordered by meadows. The East Field lies in the left foreground. [Aerofilms, Ltd.]

this, such as the removal of feudal restrictions, loosening of community bonds, allocation of communal village lands to private owners, consolidation of holdings, and the urge for efficient farm management.

Anglo-America

Early European colonists to America brought along notions of farming, land tenure, field patterns, and housing as practiced in their homelands. Although the climate and vegetation of the Atlantic Seaboard on the whole were remarkably similar to western Europe's, the challenge of organizing the new territory was an entirely different one. Inevitably it led to modifications of the traditional ways and to a distinct American imprint on the landscape.

Four separate settlement patterns evolved along the Atlantic Seaboard: (1) the French in Acadia (Nova Scotia) and along the St. Lawrence River; (2) the English in New England; (3) the ethnically mixed Middle Atlantic states from lower New York to southeastern Pennsylvania; (4) the English South from Maryland to Georgia. The occupance forms of these four source areas spread inland, some to a limited extent, such as the New England village; others eventually as far as the Pacific coast.

Even in the early years these four main settlement patterns were not sharply separated. Later, the flow of pioneers through the Appalachian valleys and across the ranges caused a still further meeting and mingling of traits. The dry and treeless plains of the interior presented the farmer from the eastern woodlands with new problems requiring different modes of settlement. The Land Ordinance of 1785 and the Homestead Act of 1862 also profoundly affected the layout of farms. Changes in agricultural practices and in building materials, as well as in construction methods, further modified the original occupance patterns. Nevertheless, their impact on the land, especially in the east, is clear; modern settlement forms can only be understood as descendants from the ancestral practices.

French Long-lot Farms. In the seventeenth century the kings of France, to stimulate colonization along the St. Lawrence River, awarded land grants with feudal privileges (*seigneuries*) to French noblemen and to the Church. Each tract had frontage of a mile or more on the river or its tributaries—they were virtually the only transportation routes then—and stretched inland several miles, a few even as far as 90 miles. The seigneurs parceled out their properties in parallel strips for settlement by peasants (*habitants*), in such a manner that each would have

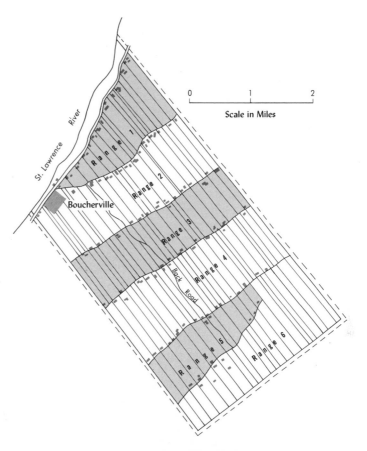

Figure 15–4. QUEBEC: LONG LOTS IN THE SEIGNEURY OF BOUCHERVILLE

Beyond the first range of lots, parallel roads were the starting lines for new ranges of lots as settlement proceeded. A road at right angles to the river, called the "back road," linked the successive ranges with the river. From Tomkins and Hills, 1962.

access to the river. Equal inheritance rights among the sons, in the French tradition, led in a few generations to subdivision of each farm. Roads at right angles to the river were built to reach the inland properties. In this fashion developed the long-lot farms that still characterize the zone between Montreal and Quebec (Figure 15–4). Instead of the manor village so typical for

15. Farm and Village

351

large parts of feudal France (and initially promoted by officials in Lower Canada), each settler built his farmstead on his land strip close to river or road. The resulting pattern resembles beads on a string. The same type of parallel strips with water frontage was used for French farms in Louisiana and the few agricultural settlements founded along the Great Lakes (Detroit) and the Mississippi (Kaskaskia).

New England. The account of life in the early village communities is a familiar part of American history. To explain this compact form of agricultural settlement, scholars emphasize different factors. Some see the New England village as an obvious transfer of the rural parish of the home country, though without the lord of the manor; others stress the need for defense against the Indians. A third group points to the social organization of the close-knit religious groups as the main reason why early colonists built their dwellings in clusters (Brown, 1948; Scofield, 1938; Trewartha, 1946). The fact that early colonists outside New England rarely settled in villages—in spite of European background, Indian danger, and government pressure—lends credence to the argument that the rural New Englander of the seventeenth century consciously chose the compact settlement as best suited to fulfill his religious, educational, and other social needs.

Early agrarian colonies in New England were group efforts in land development. The Crown had granted extensive lands to trading companies, which in turn gave out tracts ("towns" or "townships") of 4 to 10 miles square to groups of men called "proprietors," for the purpose of establishing a "plantation," that is, a planting or colony of immigrants.

Each settler received a home lot in the village, ranging from ½ acre in some places to 5 acres in others, but also varying within each village according to the owner's status. These lots accommodated at least the farmstead, including a kitchen garden, while the larger ones afforded space for an arable field. The degree of village compactness depended, of course, on the size of the home lots. Its center was the green, or common, flanked by the meetinghouse or

Figure 15–5. AMERICAN SETTLEMENT FORMS (SEE NEXT PAGES)

A. United States: Land Survey Systems

B. Springfield, Mass., 1640

C. Kaskaskia, Illinois

D. 1785 Plat: Geographer's Line

E. Mormon Village

F. West-Central Illinois

church, the burying ground, the school, and the homes of distinguished residents.

Around the village were the fields, pastures, and woodlands. The planting grounds usually were laid out in two or three blocks, in locations best suited for crops. Every family received several strips in each block to ensure an equitable share in the different types of land. A fence around the large planting fields kept out animals and relieved the individual farmer from the need to enclose his property. The woodlands and pastures were held in common by all original settlers, though the hay meadows often were divided into private parcels.

From the beginning there was an uneasy balance between the social advantages of village life and the economic disadvantages of scattered farm plots (Trewartha, 1946). Population growth in the village usually meant clearing new fields far from the center, further impairing the efficiency of the farm operations. The receding danger of Indian attacks encouraged the establishment of isolated farmsteads. Often before occupance, the farm tracts were designed in long narrow strips at right angles to a road. The new colonists tended to locate their farmsteads along such a road, resulting in a strung-out row settlement reminiscent of the European *Strassendorf* (Figure 15–5B). Where there was little planning the farmsteads lay dispersed throughout the town area. Although church

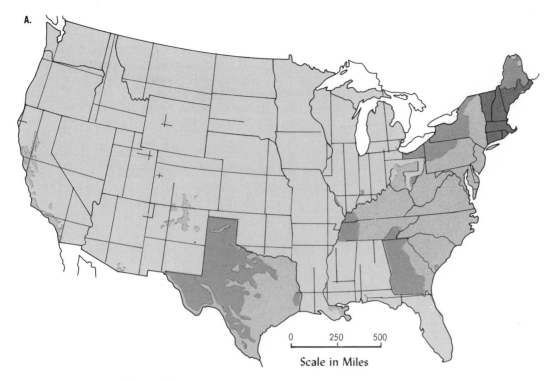

A.

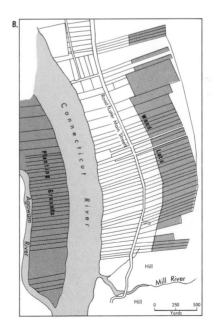

B.

A. United States: Land Survey Systems.
From Marschner, 1959, 20.

Federal Rectangular Survey

Areas Covered by Township
and Range Systems

Principal Meridians and Base Lines

Other Land Division Systems

Unregulated

Independent Rectangular Divisions
(States and Land Companies)

New England Towns

B. Springfield, Massachusetts, 1640.
From Reps, 1965, 121.

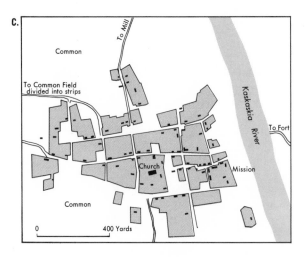

C. Kaskaskia, Illinois.
Eighteenth-century French settlement in the
Mississippi Valley. The fields adjacent to the village
were laid out in strips. From Reps, 1965, 74.

D. 1785 Plat: Geographer's Line.
Following the enactment of the Northwest
Ordinance of 1785, Thomas Hutchins (the Geographer
to the United States) began the survey of the
"Seven Ranges" at the point where the Ohio River
intersected the boundary of Pennsylvania.
Based on a map in Paullin, 1932, plate 41.

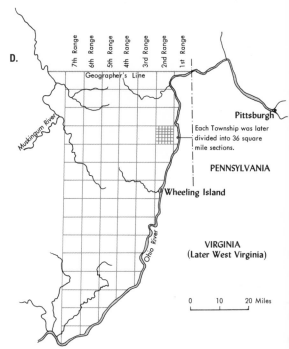

E. Mormon Village.
Escalante, Utah, like all Mormon villages, was laid
out in square blocks, each divided in four home lots.
The map shows the settlement in the 1960s. Houses
are black, barns are red dots. The shaded area is
wooded. Based on United States Geological Survey
1:24,000 Topographic Sheet, Escalante, Utah.

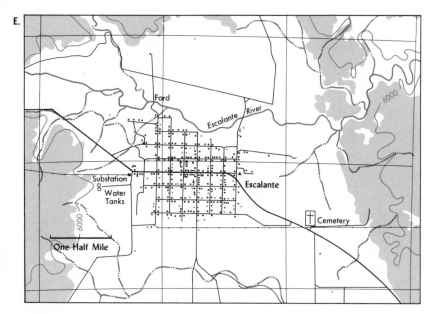

F. West-Central Illinois.

This set of four diagrams illustrates the basic system of the Federal Rectangular Survey, from Base Line and Principal Meridian, to Township and Range, and Section and Quarter Section.

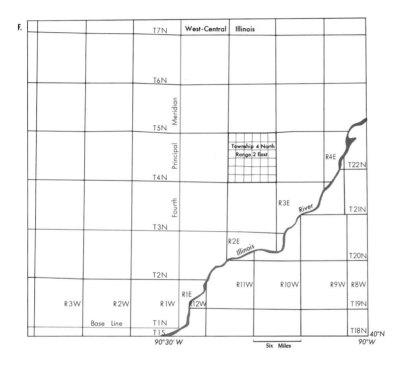

and school lots were provided near the center of each township section, they no longer formed the village nucleus, and the traditional common was omitted. The landscape of modern New England still reflects the difference between the layout of the old seventeenth-century villages, even where they have changed into urban centers, and the later settlements on individual farms (Scofield, 1933).

Mormon Villages (Figure 15–5E). The manner in which the Church of the Latter-day Saints

Figure 15–6. THE SOUTHERN PLANTATION after Prunty, 1955.

A. HOPETON PLANTATION, GEORGIA, IN 1827

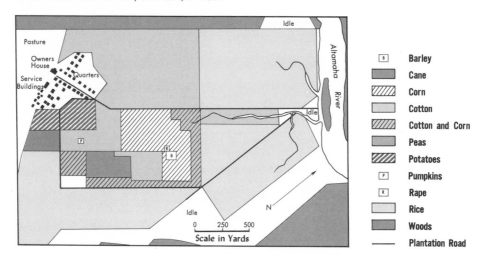

B	Barley
	Cane
	Corn
	Cotton
	Cotton and Corn
	Peas
	Potatoes
P	Pumpkins
R	Rape
	Rice
	Woods
——	Plantation Road

B. NEOPLANTATION TYPE, 1950s

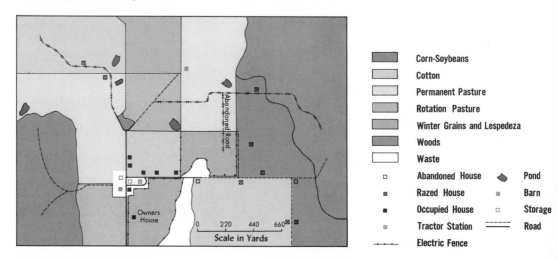

	Corn-Soybeans
	Cotton
	Permanent Pasture
	Rotation Pasture
	Winter Grains and Lespedeza
	Woods
	Waste

□	Abandoned House	◤	Pond
⊠	Razed House	▪	Barn
■	Occupied House	▫	Storage
▨	Tractor Station	-----	Road
	Electric Fence		

occupied Utah in the middle of the nineteenth century well illustrates the relation between community organization and village settlement. Already in Missouri and Illinois the Mormons had centered in villages. The church leaders carefully planned the Utah settlement so as to assure a form of colonization that would best serve the material and spiritual needs of their people. The design of Salt Lake City became the model for all Mormon agrarian colonies. Each village was arranged into square blocks, each about 4 acres in size, providing four home plots large enough to accommodate the various farm buildings, a kitchen garden, and an orchard. Sites were reserved for churches and schools. Irrigation ditches and shade trees lined the wide streets. Each villager had several fields in the surrounding farmland, rectangular where feasible, a small one nearby, larger ones farther out, to equalize the distance to the fields. In time, as the economy changed from subsistence to commercial farming and the society became more individualistic, the fragmentation of holdings proved a serious drawback to efficient agriculture. Many farmers now have moved out of the old villages onto their land, but they still must contend with scattered fields, often too small for modern techniques.

The Middle Colonies.

Colonization in the Middle Atlantic area differed markedly from that in New England. Although public officials and private landowners always allowed, often encouraged, and sometimes even demanded compact rural settlement, the village was the exception rather than the rule. Two reasons are usually advanced for the early prevalence of dispersed occupance. First, land development in this area from the beginning had a more pronounced commercial character. Vast tracts awarded to land companies or individuals were sold to settlers in compact freeholds. Second, the colonists came singly or in small family groups from many countries. They lacked, therefore, the homogeneity so characteristic of early New England: Dutch and Walloons along the Hudson, Swedes on the Delaware, Scotch-Irish and Germans in southeastern Pennsylvania, and English settlements all over. The im-

migrants found land prices low enough to set up good-sized farms of 100 to 300 acres. Under these circumstances, residence on the farm was the obvious choice.

The South.

Early colonists in Virginia lived initially in fortified villages established by the Virginia Company. After 1624, when this area became a Crown Colony, settlers had the opportunity to acquire private holdings, to which they moved their residence. Although some religious groups formed compact clusters and the trustees of the charity colonies in Georgia insisted on village organization for their semi-military frontier settlements, the dispersed pattern of occupance soon prevailed in the South.

Production of commercial export crops dominated Southern farming. Tobacco was the main crop in Virginia and North Carolina, spreading slowly inland toward the fall line. Rice and indigo became important in South Carolina and Georgia. Overseas markets made it necessary to site the holdings along the rivers. As long as labor—mostly European indentured workers—was scarce, the farms remained relatively modest in size, but the importation of large numbers of Negro slaves from around 1700 onward allowed many to develop into the classic Southern plantation (Figure 15-6A).

The comfortable planter's home—only rarely of the size and opulence depicted in modern novels and movies—usually was near the river and the wharf. Around it were grouped the slave houses, commonly in a compact rectangle, also the various service buildings, including sheds for tools and food storage, barns for draft animals, smokehouses, bakehouses, and salt houses, weaving and spinning quarters, a cotton gin or rice mill, and a blacksmith shop. Virtually all the plantation wants were satisfied by and within the establishment, obviating the need for local market towns. The plantation buildings formed a cluster, but were quite different in function and structure from compact village settlements elsewhere. Around the plantation center lay large fields, suitable for efficient employment and supervision of the labor gangs. Prunty, whose study of the Southern plantation we follow here, found that "in general, half or slightly more of the cropland was devoted to specialty staple crops and the remainder to plantation foodstuffs and feeds for livestock" (Prunty, 1955, 465).

Abolition of slavery led to an entirely new occupance pattern. The plantation owner divided his holdings into subunits of 30 to 40 acres, to be worked by sharecroppers or tenants. Instead of the agglomeration of dwellings around the plantation headquarters, the house sites now became dispersed, with each operator living on the land he worked.*

Since the 1940s a new occupance form has evolved on many old plantation holdings and apparently is still gaining ground (Figure 15–6B). Its main cause is farm mechanization. Because the poor sharecropper or tenant cannot afford to buy machinery, the control over cultivating power passes to the landowner. And because small plots are inefficient to cultivate and, especially, to harvest, mechanization makes it necessary to consolidate the fields. "The functional focus of the neoplantation† is the tractor station . . . which also shelters harvesting, cultivating, and accessory machinery, spare parts, repair tools, and fuel. . . . The tractor station is always located close to the manager's or owner's residence, a locational factor suggesting the intimate interrelationship of centralized management and cultivating power" (Prunty 1955, 485).

The new technique greatly reduces the labor force. These changes reflect themselves in the transformation of the rural settlement pattern. Houses have decreased in number. The remaining ones, often relocated to make room for large fields, now lie mainly in rows along all-weather roads, or even form loosely agglomerated settlements reminiscent of the antebellum plantation cluster. Prunty foresees still more nucleation of "neoplantation settlement" in years to come, because amenities sufficiently attractive to agri-

* For details concerning this change, see Prunty, *op. cit.*

† For an explanation of this term see Prunty, *op. cit.* According to our definition of the plantation (p. 234) we would speak of "large-scale farm" rather than "neoplantation."

cultural workers can be provided economically only by grouping the homes in a compact village.

Far outnumbering the plantations in the Old South were, of course, the small holdings. Their owners mostly produced grain and livestock for their own use, with at best a little tobacco as cash crop. At first they lived between the riverine plantation belts, and then moved gradually into the piedmont and beyond into the Appalachian ridge and valley country. Here they met and mingled with the southward thrust of Germans and Scotch-Irish from Pennsylvania. The folkways of the Appalachian region still give evidence of these origins and diffusions.

Systems of Land Division (Figure 15–5A). During colonial times in New England and through much of the Middle Atlantic and the South, parcels of land were defined by "metes and bounds": starting and ending at a given point, the boundaries were described by direction and distance of each segment between two points, often natural features, such as conspicuous trees, rocks, or river shores. As settlement increased and moved into the interior the lack of a fixed policy for land allocation and registry led to uncertainty of titles and frequent boundary litigations.

Following independence, the original states ceded to the federal government all claims to land north of the Ohio and east of the Mississippi. Thomas Jefferson, as chairman of a congressional committee charged with the task of devising a uniform method of land division for the Northwest Territory, proposed that it be divided into square blocks of 10 by 10 miles, each "hundred" to be subdivided into lots of 1 square mile. Jefferson may have been inspired by the Roman system of land division in square blocks (each called a *centuria*), but it is an established fact that the committee possessed information on the rectangular system used in Holland for reclaimed land.

When Congress in 1785 passed the Land Ordinance, it accepted the proposal of grid lines to be laid out on the cardinal points of the compass, but it substituted for the "hundreds" a system more like that of New England: 6- by

6-mile townships, divided into 36 sections of 1 square mile each. That year a line was surveyed westward from a point of origin where the Ohio River intersects the western boundary of Pennsylvania (Figure 15–5D). From this line surveyors laid out the first "Seven Ranges" of townships. As surveying extended farther into Ohio, the procedure was gradually modified; by the time the Indiana border was crossed it had become the form used later for all lands to the west. The primary operation was to survey a "base line" and a "principal meridian," the intersection of which served as the point of origin for dividing and numbering townships and sections (Figure 15–5F). As time went on, new base lines and meridians were set up until the Pacific coast was reached.

Parts of the west that the Spanish, French, and British had settled during the colonial era retained their metes and bounds divisions, as for example southern California, New Mexico, and a number of places along the Mississippi. With the coming of the federal system these areas became embedded in the rectangular surveys. Texas remained completely outside the federal system, although vast areas were surveyed in rectilineal fashion (Figure 15–5A). Rectangular divisions were also adopted in those parts of eastern states surveyed and settled after the United States had adopted the township and range method, as, for example, in northwestern Pennsylvania, western New York, northern Maine, and western Georgia (Marschner, 1959, 17–20).

American House Types. In Europe geographers have devoted much attention to the typology of folk housing, because the traditional home is still one of the most distinctive features of each agrarian landscape, and provides significant clues to cultural dispersals. By comparison, North America appears as a land of relatively recent Occidental settlement, with mobility of inhabitants and mixture of habits, and with spreading standardization modified only by fleeting fashions. For these reasons American geographers, on the whole, pay little attention to regional differences in rural house types. There are, nevertheless, significant ex-

ceptions. Kniffen in particular has vigorously advanced the view that the study of American rural dwellings is a fundamental and rewarding segment of geographic inquiry, not only in itself, but also because it sheds light on other cultural origins and continuities. The following paragraphs present in outline some of his findings on folk housing in the eastern part of the country (Kniffen, 1965; Kniffen and Glassie, 1966).

The four source areas of rural settlement patterns on the Atlantic Seaboard (p. 351) also show distinct house types. The early French used two modes of wood construction. In one they made walls of close-set upright posts or square timbers, either sunk in the ground or placed on sills, filling the spaces between with clay, mortar, or other materials. Kniffen sees this as "a method of construction which was very old and largely vestigial in western Europe [and which] experienced a brief rejuvenation in timber-rich colonial America." The other mode, which soon became the dominant one (where not replaced by stone) consisted of placing horizontal logs above each other—not, however, notched at the corners like the American log house, but slotted or tenoned into vertical posts on the corners and often also into intermediate ones. This method, still used in Quebec and neighboring areas of the United States, "permits the utilization of short logs and at the same time puts no restrictions on the size of the building" (Kniffen and Glassie, 1966, 51).

In New England, frame construction dominated. Initially settlers followed the European tradition of building a heavy frame of vertical, horizontal, and diagonal timbers and filling the interstices with various materials ("half-timbering"), but soon they used the abundant available wood to cover the frame with horizontal sidings or clapboards (weatherboarding). This evolved into a two-room deep, two-story high, rectangular building with gabled roof and one chimney in the middle, or two at the ends, with modifications according to the architectural fashion of the day. Only after 1850 did so-called balloon framing (using lighter timbers nailed together) prevail. The log cabin, if built at all, was viewed as a provisional shelter to be re-

15. Farm and Village

359

placed as soon as possible by a frame house. From New England the frame house spread westward toward the Great Lakes and beyond, its particular form "at any specific point on the westward trek [following] the principle of Dominance of Contemporary Fashion" prevalent in New England at the time of migration (Kniffen, 1965, 558, 560). The New England barn, a frame structure with a pitched roof and walls of upright boards, was taken westward almost unchanged.

The Middle Atlantic area, centering on southeastern Pennsylvania, made some important contributions of its own. One of these was the house of horizontal logs notched at the corners. The log cabin is commonly thought to be derived from the Swedish settlements on the Delaware in the 1630s. However, there is evidence that the English settlers did not adopt the Swedish log construction. It was the later-arriving Germans who built the prototype of the American log cabin, soon to be taken over by the Scotch-Irish (Kniffen and Glassie, 1966, 56–59). In origin it was a one-room house with a chimney at the end. The nature of notched log construction put limitations on enlarging the dwelling. It required either putting a story on top or extending the size by adding a second log room at the chimney end of the first cabin, resulting in a central-chimney house. Another and more common procedure was to build two separate log cabins with gable facing gable, and to roof over the intervening space, like a breezeway. This produced the so-called "dogtrot" or "two-pens-and-a-passage" house. With increasing affluence these log houses were sided with weatherboards; others—on the whole, later—were constructed as frame houses and enlarged with porches and other appendages. But all reveal their ancestral origin: gables to the side, a depth of only one room, a length of at least two rooms, and usually a height of two stories. This narrow "I" house, as Kniffen calls it, spread from Pennsylvania into the Appalachian valleys and through the entire upland South. It also diffused westward into Ohio, central Indiana, and southern Illinois, forming a distinct contrast to the New England type found in the northern parts of these states.

The original barn of the Pennsylvania "Dutch" (actually Germans), also built of logs, often resembled the dogtrot house. The planked floor between the two pens—right behind the wide doorway—served for threshing. Kniffen considers this structure the forerunner of the great Pennsylvania forebay barn.

Finally, there is the housing tradition of the tidewater South, extending from lower Chesapeake Bay all along the coast to the Mississippi. Although half-timbering was common in the early days, frame construction soon became the mode. The basic form was that of the English cottage: one room deep, two rooms in length, usually 1½ stories high, with a steep roof and exterior end chimneys. Later it became common to add a front porch and a rear shed for a kitchen, with its own chimney. In the last third of the eighteenth century "the cottage was raised as much as a full story on brick foundations or piers" (Kniffen, 1965, 565).

Village and House Types in East Asia

China. Since early times the characteristic Chinese landscape has presented a clear contrast between the city, seat of the district or provincial administration, and the countryside with its close-knit agrarian villages. Dispersed farmsteads do occur, but mainly in dissected uplands where arable land is scarce and fragmented. The larger villages often have a rough grid plan, in former times surrounded by a mud wall. But many villages consist of a double row of houses stretched along a road or levee (Figure 15–7). The house is usually constructed by raising four corner posts as roof supports and by filling in the walls with tamped earth, sun-dried adobe, or half-fired bricks (Spencer, 1947). This very old building method may have originated in the Middle East. It is well suited to the dry alluvial plains of north China where timber is scarce. The Chinese carried this tradition into the subtropical regions they colonized, but there they also adopted the indigenous way of using bamboo wattle and plaster for walls. In northern China the mud walls are left bare, blending land and building in an all-pervading yellow. In central China an outer layer of mud plaster is often

Figure 15–7. CHINA: RURAL SETTLEMENT IN CHIANGSU

The area shown is north of the Yangtze River, where the main crops are wheat and rice. The rows of houses are on dikes built up above low-lying land. Based on an aerial photograph in Buck, 1937.

——— Streams and Channels

▨ Houses

☐ Fields for Cropping

applied, while in south China and Szechwan whitewashing is common. The gray tile or thatched roof slopes down on both sides of a straight ridgepole. The curved tile roof seems to be a rather late modification, possibly developed in the south. The door is always placed in one of the walls parallel to the ridgeline. The more affluent farmer builds his home on an earth platform or a raised foundation with wooden floor, but the peasant usually is satisfied with a dirt-packed floor.

The Chinese, who highly prize privacy in family life, traditionally arrange the components of their homestead around a central courtyard. But many peasants must do with less than that, from a single-storied rectangular to an L- or U-shaped dwelling.

Japan. In Japan most lowland farmers live in hamlets or small villages, but in northern Honshu and especially Hokkaido, where farms are larger, dispersed farmsteads are common. The latter also prevail in mountainous regions (Trewartha, 1945, 151–192). The villages may be fairly compact and arranged according to a grid of streets and lanes. In the alluvial lowlands they stand on slight elevations amid the paddy fields. Since the dry sites are frequently old beach ridges, natural levees, volcano margins, or terrace benches, many villages string out in linear form. No general description, however, can do justice to the regional variety of settlement patterns.

A particularly interesting type prevails in the plains of the Kinki district of southern Japan between Kyoto, Nara, and Osaka (Hall, 1931, 1932). The rural population lives in small villages spaced no more than ⅔ mile apart. The distinctive feature is the rectangular arrangement of the settlements, which probably was derived from an old Chinese field system. Each village was laid out in checkerboard fashion and surrounded by a rectangular wall or hedge and moat (Figure 15–8). Although changed conditions have caused walls and many moats to disappear, the ancient design still pervades the landscape. Within the village each farmstead stands as a secluded unit; the dwelling and various service sheds face an inner yard. "One sees only continuous lines of walls and closed gates on either side of the narrow street. One receives a peculiar impression of deadness in such settlements, broken only by the voices which can be heard beyond the walls or by a fleeting glance of some individual disappearing through a neighbor's gate" (Hall, 1931, 102).

The light construction of the Japanese house reveals its tropical origin. The use of stilts instead of a continuous foundation gives a clue

15. Farm and Village

361

Figure 15–8. JAPAN: RURAL SETTLEMENT IN THE YAMATO BASIN

Based on a map in Hall, 1931.

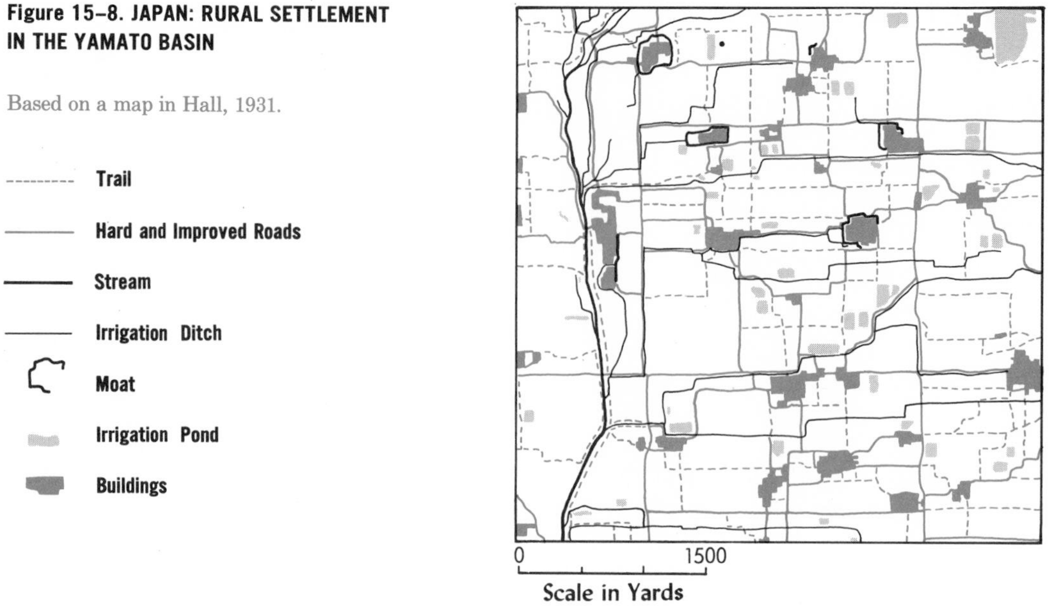

- - - - - - - -   **Trail**

—————   **Hard and Improved Roads**

—————   **Stream**

—————   **Irrigation Ditch**

   Moat

   Irrigation Pond

   Buildings

0   1500

Scale in Yards

to ancient cultural ties with Southeast Asia. While admirably suited to the long hot and humid summer, the traditional home provides little comfort during the winter season, which is quite marked in southern Honshu and downright cold in the northern parts of the country. Four corner posts resting on stones support the steep-pitched thatched or tiled gable roof. There is no chimney. The floor, on stilts, is 1 to 3 feet above the ground. The walls, well under the overhanging eaves, are essentially screens between vertical posts, and are made of mud plaster except on the sunny side of the house; there they are light wooden sliding panels with set-in translucent paper or glass panes. Instead of painting the exterior wood surfaces, the Japanese prefer to let them weather to natural grayish tints.

The farmhouse, usually of one story, contains three or more rooms in a rectangular floor plan, with the kitchen under a separate roof at a slightly lower elevation. Movable partitions and absence of special furniture make for versatile use of room space. Charcoal braziers take the place of stoves and fireplaces. The uncluttered interior with its rectilinear lines expresses the artistic quality as well as the economy and simplicity of Japanese traditional life.

The Stilt House in Southeast Asia

Houses built above the ground on piles or posts occur in widely separated parts of the world, but nowhere do they characterize such a vast area as in Southeast Asia. They extend from Assam and lower Burma in the west to the Philippines and Moluccas in the east, suggesting an ancient unity in a culture realm which in so many other ways is highly diverse (Chapter 8). Most writers try to explain this mode of construction by pointing out some utilitarian motive. For instance, pile dwellings built out into lake or sea facilitate fishing, while giving protection against human or animal intruders. On land the space under the house can shelter livestock and fuel wood or provide a shady, pleasant work place. Most often, the stilt house is considered an adaptation to the humid, warm climate and wet ground. None of these reasons explains, however, its present widespread occurrence, which includes well-drained land, sub-humid areas, and cool mountains. As so often with culture traits, the reason for building on stilts no longer is a rational one, but has become a deeply ingrained custom. The origin lies probably among the Neolithic peoples of mainland

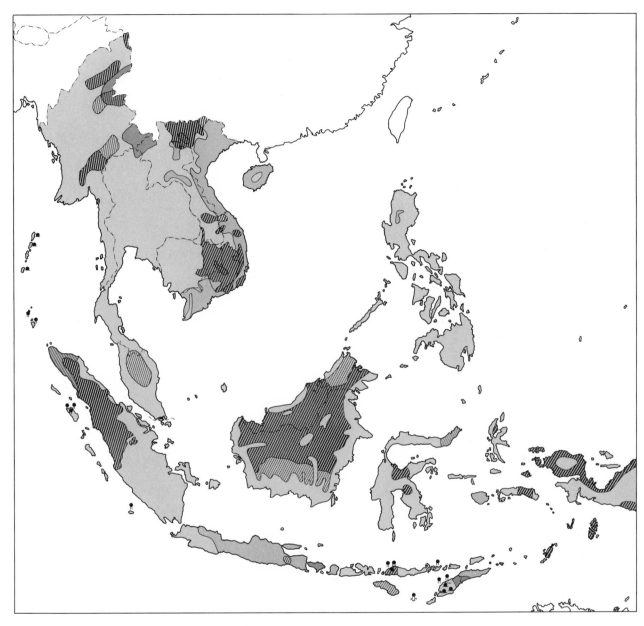

Symbol	Legend
♀	Round Houses on Stilts
●	Round Houses on the Ground
	Houses on Stilts
	Houses on the Ground
	Houses on Stilts and on the Ground
	Communal Dwelling Houses
	Communal and Single Family Houses
	Communal Dwelling Houses used in Former Times

**Figure 15–9. SOUTHEAST ASIA:
HOUSE TYPES**

*15. Farm
and Village*

Southeast Asia, including what is now southern China. Around 2000 B.C., if not earlier, they moved east into the island world and north along the coast of China toward Japan. In the archipelago these peoples are usually identified as Malaysians or Indonesians.

In Southeast Asia the dwellings are often more primitive than in Japan. The floors are usually much higher, from 5 to 15 feet above the ground. The walls consist of split and plaited bamboo or other fibers, rarely of plaster or wood. Palm thatch usually covers the steep roof. Although the one-family house now prevails, communal longhouses in remote parts throughout the mainland and archipelago point toward a common ancestral tradition of clan life under one roof (Figure 15–9).

There are some areas in Southeast Asia, however, where houses are built on the ground. Under the influence of Chinese culture the Tonkinese long ago took over their neighbor's building tradition, along with many other customs. From Tonkin they carried it southward along the coast to the Mekong delta. The Jav-anese, too, build their houses usually on the ground, though they also use short supports to keep the floor a foot or so from the earth. It is not clear whether this custom results from Indian contacts or from the growing scarcity of timber on this densely populated island. Granaries, for good practical reasons, are always built on stilts.

Building on the ground also occurs in some remote areas—for instance, on Timor and nearby islands. In a few places the inhabitants construct round instead of rectangular houses, either on poles or on the ground. All these are in peripheral locations, suggesting vestiges of an older culture stratum, perhaps of the Australoid peoples present before the Malaysian migrations (Figure 15–9).

Like settlement forms in other parts of the world, the house types of Southeast Asia pose many intriguing questions. The geographer finds these features significant because their diffusion and present distribution help to explain the character of places.

Citations

Brown, R. H. *Historical Geography of the United States,* New York, 1946.

Buck, J. L. *Land Utilization in China,* Nanking, 1937. [Map]

Hall, R. B. "Some Rural Settlement Forms in Japan," *Geographical Review,* 21 (1931): 93–123.

————. "The Yamato Basin, Japan," *Annals of the Association of American Geographers,* 22 (1932): 211–230.

India, Census of "Kunran: A Village in Sangru District of Punjab," *Village Survey Monographs of Punjab,* no. 36, Census of India, 1961, vol. 13, part 6, Chandigarh, 1963.

Kniffen, F. "Folk Housing: Key to Diffusion," *Annals of the Association of American Geographers,* 55 (1965): 549–577.

———— and Glassie, H. "Building in Wood in the Eastern United States: A Time-Place Perspective," *Geographical Review,* 56 (1966): 40–66.

Marschner, F. J. *Land Use and Its Patterns in the United States,* U.S. Department of Agriculture Handbook no. 153, Washington, D.C., 1959. [Map]

Paullin, C. O., Wright, J. K. (ed.) *Atlas of the Historical Geography of the United States,* Washington, D.C., 1932. [Map]

Prunty, M., Jr. "The Renaissance of the Southern Plantation," *Geographical Review,* 45 (1955): 459–491. [Map]

Reps, J. W. *The Making of Urban America,* Princeton, N.J., 1965. [Map]

Scofield, E. "The Origin of Settlement Patterns in Rural New England," *Geographical Review,* 23 (1933): 652–663.

Spencer, J. E. "The Houses of the Chinese," *Geographical Review,* 37 (1947): 254–273.

Tomkins, G. S., and Hills, T. L. *A Regional Geography of North America,* Toronto, 1962. [Map]

Trewartha, G. T. *Japan: A Physical, Cultural and Regional Geography,* Madison, Wis., 1945.

———. "Types of Rural Settlement in Colonial America," *Geographical Review,* 36 (1946): 568–596.

Further Readings

Ahlmann, H. W. "The Geographical Study of Settlements," *Geographical Review,* 18 (1928): 93–128.

Ahmad, E. "Rural Settlement Types in the Uttar Pradesh (United Provinces of Agra and Oudh)," *Annals of the Association of American Geographers,* 42 (1952): 223–246.

Aurousseau, M. "The Arrangement of Rural Populations," *Geographical Review,* 10 (1920): 223–240.

Bonham-Carter, V. *The English Village,* Harmondsworth, England, 1952.

Brooke, C. "The Rural Village in the Ethiopian Highlands," *Geographical Review,* 49 (1959): 58–75.

Darby, H. C. "The Clearing of Woodland in Europe," in Thomas, W. L. (ed.) *Man's Role in Changing the Face of the Earth,* Chicago, 1956, 183–216.

Demangeon, A. "The Origins and Causes of Settlement Types," in Wagner, P. L., and Mikesell, M. W. (eds.) *Readings in Cultural Geography,* Chicago, 1962, 506–516, translated from "La Géographie de l'habitat rurale," *Annales de Géographie,* 36 (1927): 1–23, 97–114.

Derruau, M. "A l'origine du 'rang' canadien," *Cahiers de Géographie de Québec,* N.S. 1 (1956): 39–47.

De Young, J. E. *Village Life in Modern Thailand,* Berkeley, Calif., and Los Angeles, Calif., 1955.

Dickinson, R. E. "Rural Settlements in the German Lands," *Annals of the Association of American Geographers,* 39 (1949): 239–263.

———. "Dispersed Settlement in Southern Italy," *Erdkunde,* 10 (1956): 282–297.

Evans, E. E. "The Ecology of Peasant Life in Western Europe," in Thomas, W. L. (ed.) *Man's Role in Changing the Face of the Earth,* Chicago, 1956, 217–239.

Garnett, A. "Insolation, Topography, and Settlement in the Alps," *Geographical Review,* 25 (1935): 601–617.

Goldthwait, J. W. "A Town That has Gone Downhill," *Geographical Review,* 17 (1927): 527–552.

Hickey, G. C. *Village in Vietnam,* New Haven, Conn., 1964.

Houston, J. M. *A Social Geography of Europe,* London, 1953.

Johnson, H. B. "Rational and Ecological Aspects of the Quarter Section: An Example from Minnesota," *Geographical Review,* 47 (1957): 330–348.

15. Farm and Village

Johnson, J. H. "Studies of Irish Rural Settlement," *Geographical Review,* 48 (1958): 554–565.

Kallbrunner, H. "Farms and Villages: The European Pattern," *Landscape,* 6 (1957) no. 3: 13–17.

Karan, P. P. "Land Utilization and Agriculture in an Indian Village," *Land Economics,* 33 (1957): 55–64.

Kniffen, F. "Louisiana House Types," *Annals of the Association of American Geographers,* 26 (1936): 179–193.

————. "The American Covered Bridge," *Geographical Review,* 41 (1951): 114–123.

Krenzlin, A. "Dorf, Feld und Wirtschaft im Gebiet der grossen Täler und Platten östlich der Elbe," *Forschungen zur deutschen Landeskunde,* 70 (1952).

Lee, D. H. K. "Thoughts on Housing for the Humid Tropics," *Geographical Review,* 41 (1951): 124–147.

Lewis, O. *Village Life in Northern India,* Urbana, Ill., 1958.

Loeb, E. M., and Broek, J. O. M. "Social Organization and the Long House in Southeast Asia," *American Anthropologist,* 49 (1947): 414–425.

Mather, E. C., and Hart, J. F. "Fences and Farms," *Geographical Review,* 44 (1954): 201–223.

Meitzen, A. *Siedlung und Agrarwesen der Westgermanen und Ostgermanen, der Kelten, Römer, Finnen und Slawen,* 3 vols. and atlas, Berlin, 1895.

National Academy of Sciences—National Research Council, *Rural Settlement Patterns in the United States, as illustrated on 100 Topographic Quadrangle Maps,* Publication no. 380, Washington, D.C., 1956.

Pattison, W. D. *Beginnings of the American Rectangular Land Survey System, 1784–1800,* University of Chicago, Department of Geography Research Paper no. 50, Chicago, 1957.

Pfeifer, G. "The Quality of Peasant Living in Central Europe," in Thomas, W. L., Jr. (ed.), *Man's Role in Changing the Face of the Earth,* Chicago, 1956, 240–277.

Schwartz, G. *Allgemeine Siedlungsgeographie,* Berlin, 1959.

Spate, O. H. K. "The Burmese Village," *Geographical Review,* 35 (1945): 523–543.

————. "The Indian Village," *Geography,* 37 (1952): 142–152.

Spencer, J. E. "The Development of Agricultural Villages in Southern Utah," *Agricultural History,* 14 (1940): 181–189.

Stone, K. H. "Swedish Fringes of Settlement," *Annals of the Association of American Geographers,* 52 (1962): 373–393.

Trewartha, G. T. "The Unincorporated Hamlet," *Annals of the Association of American Geographers,* 33 (1943): 32–81.

————. "Some Regional Characteristics of American Farmsteads," *Annals of the Association of American Geographers,* 38 (1948): 169–225.

Unger, L. "Rural Settlement in the Campania," *Geographical Review,* 43 (1953): 506–524.

Zelinsky, W. "The New England Connecting Barn," *Geographical Review,* 48 (1958): 540–553.

16. Towns and Cities

The present city stands in marked contrast to the settlements men have lived in through ages past. The physical and social complexity of the modern metropolis almost defies analysis. Virtually no one seems engaged in providing the few biological necessities of life. Everyone appears but a small cog in an intricate machine. To classify city workers, census bureaus use detailed lists of jobs that sometimes run to thousands of items. Most city people earn a living by continually interchanging goods, skills, and thoughts. Moreover, the modern citizen in performing his own role and in utilizing the labor of others need not be tied to any one part of town, nor to any particular town. He may reside in one place, work in another, attend school, relax, or vacation in still others.

A large part of the earth's inhabitants live in settlements ranging from the small market town to the great metropolis. Over one-quarter of the human population dwells in cities and towns, and this proportion increases as men forsake traditional rural ways and nations modernize their means of production. In many countries more than half of the people reside in such urban places (Figure 16–1).

This chapter describes towns and cities from a geographical point of view—as distinctive kinds of places which share some general and almost universal characteristics through time and space, but also possess individual, unique features that change through the ages and vary from culture to culture. First we note how con-

cepts of site and situation relate to growth of towns and cities; then we trace the spread of cities from their origin and discuss differences that developed between various culture realms. After this historical section we analyze the city from different viewpoints: numbers of inhabitants, internal physical features, functional structure, and spatial distribution. In the next chapter we consider trends in modern urban agglomerations, especially how the metropolitan region is emerging as the dominant type of areal organization in modern society.

Site and Situation

Site plays a considerable part in shaping the growth of urban places. A small island in the Seine River near the center of modern Paris marks the site of the original settlement, a defensive refuge in time of trouble, and a bridge point during peaceful conditions. The most distinctive feature of the site of Athens is a steep-sided, flat-topped hill near its center, first chosen for its defensive qualities, and later used for a group of temples. Venice also was originally built for defense, on a waterlogged group of islands at the end of the Adriatic Sea, a place of refuge from mainland marauders to the west. Today Venice, half in and half out of the sea, a city of historic associations, attracts so many visitors that its principal business has become tourism. Town builders have selected sites of many kinds: islands, hills, gaps between hills, flatland next to deep water, springs—all with qualities to exploit with advantage.

Though all cities have sites, the key to their character and growth is not so much site as situation, or relative location. Paris lay at a focal point of land- and water-transportation routes; it was also near the center of the emerging nation-state of France. Athens grew because it was the chief town of an important city-state, and in addition, possessed strategic location relative to the seaways of the eastern Mediterranean. Venice flourished as a result of its position at the head of the Adriatic Sea, the deepest penetration of the Mediterranean into the landmass of Europe, where land routes converged from west, north, and east.

As towns grow, they often acquire new functions which may alter their entire character. In the recent past, industrialization has reshaped many places. Many towns and cities retain a distinct core from former times, when functions and life differed. Often civic pride cherishes such historic areas, like Boston Common, the "old town" of many European cities, the Renaissance center of Warsaw, the ruins of ancient Rome. A case study of an American city will illustrate more fully the concepts of site and situation.

Site and Situation of Pittsburgh (Figure 16–2).

French and British colonial powers in the middle eighteenth century both perceived that a small point of land between the Allegheny and Monongahela rivers, where they join to become the Ohio, had great strategic value. They were engaged at the time in imperial rivalry for the North American interior. To protect their fur traders who worked in the Ohio frontier, the French built Fort Duquesne at the confluence of the two rivers. The site was easy to defend, and its relative location proved to be superb for strategic as well as economic purposes because rivers were the main highways in those days.

France lost its North American possessions in the war of 1756–1763 to the British, who themselves set up Fort Pitt on the same site the French had used. Mostly because of its situ-

Figure 16–1. WORLD: URBAN PERCENTAGES OF NATIONAL POPULATIONS

Based on national definitions of "urban population." These vary greatly between countries: They include, for example, localities with more than 5,000 inhabitants in Ghana, municipalities with more than 10,000 inhabitants in Greece, places with over 1,000 inhabitants in Australia, and incorporated places with more than 2,500 inhabitants in the United States. Many of the data are from United Nations *Demographic Yearbook, 1963,* New York, 1964, table 5.

Per Cent of Population Urban

75 and over

50 - 75

25 - 50

Under 25

ation astride the head of the Ohio River, the one important water route from Pennsylvania to the west, the town of Pittsburgh began to grow as the Middle West became settled in the nineteenth century. The population rose from 2,000 in 1800 to 140,000 in 1870.

Pittsburgh's greatest fame came with the establishment of the iron and steel industry in and around the city during the second half of the nineteenth century. By this time the discovery and exploitation of coal resources in the Appalachian Plateau were in full swing. Pittsburgh's location—on the waterway system that drained much of the coalfield near the center of the developing manufacturing belt—meant it was the best place for assembling the raw materials of iron and steel production, a place as good as any other for distributing steel to market. By the first decade of the twentieth century Pittsburgh led by far in iron and steel production. The 1920 population of its metropolitan area had grown to 1,750,000.

Though Pittsburgh's situation was close to

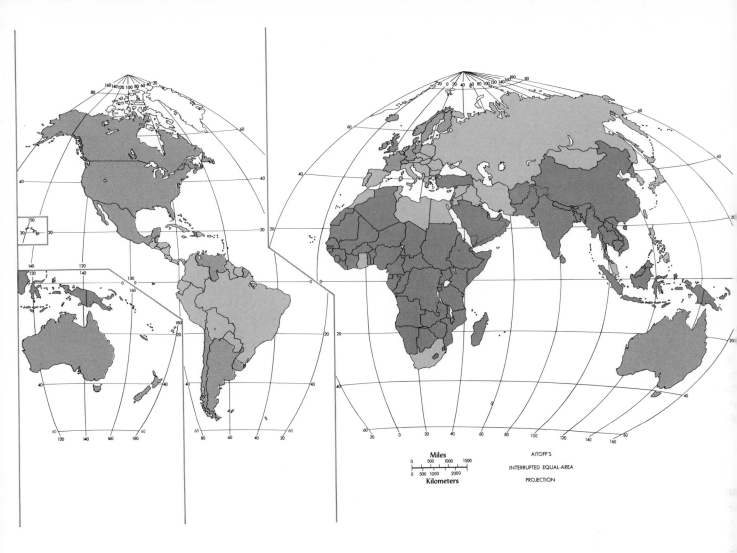

Miles
0   500   1000   1500
0   500 1000   2000
Kilometers

AITOFF'S

INTERRUPTED EQUAL-AREA

PROJECTION

ideal for a great industrial city, its site proved a handicap. Steel mills and blast furnaces need large areas of flatland at water level. Pittsburgh, limited by steep-sided valleys, had little such land. The narrow ledges along the rivers became crowded with mills. The business district centered on the place now known as "the golden triangle," just upstream from the site of the forts. As the city spread along the valleys and onto the plateau, riverboats and railroads—still the principal means of transportation—found it increasingly difficult to link the various parts of the industrial metropolis. The valleys trapped

the fumes from the iron and steel plants; often the low-lying city center was lost in a pall of smoke. Not until the 1950s, when strict smoke-abatement ordinances were enforced, did the smog disappear.

Today with many competitors in steel production, and steel no longer commanding the heights of the national economy, Pittsburgh nevertheless retains a vital locational advantage—its central position in the United States manufacturing belt. The rough terrain is more amenable to mid-twentieth-century living. Widespread use of cars and trucks enables the

16. Towns and Cities

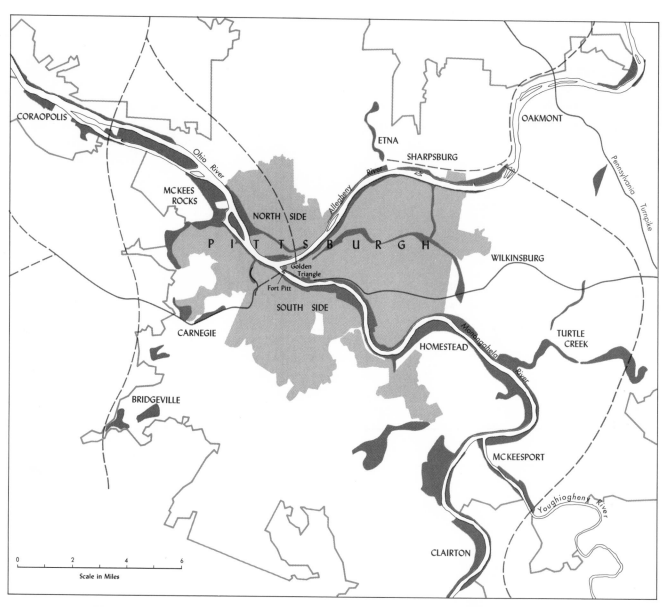

Figure 16–2. PITTSBURGH, PENNSYLVANIA

The rivers are slightly over 700 feet above sea level. Iron and steel plants crowd the narrow valleys. The land away from the rivers is dissected plateau country, mostly 300 to 500 feet above water level. Low density residential housing has spread beyond the limits of the urbanized area.

Main Industrial and Railway Zones
City of Pittsburgh
Boundary of Urbanized Area
Limited Access Highways
Proposed Limited Access Highways

IV. Settlements

metropolis to extend many miles in all directions over valleys and plateaus. The tourist appreciates the dramatic site of the central core with its reconstructed "golden triangle." Moreover, industrial and business services of all kinds find Pittsburgh a convenient location. Although the production of industrial materials remains basic to the city's economy, diversification is the trend, a development in which accessibility from the populous northeast of the United States plays a key role.

The Origin and Spread of Cities

Cities as we know them came into existence at a particular place and time: the Middle East during the fourth millennium B.C. Since then, urban ways have spread to many other regions. Urbanism, or civilization—from the Latin *civilis,* "citizen"—is not built anew with each generation, or with each city. It has developed throughout long periods of time. Modern man inherits some city ways of doing things from ages past. Historical events like the Industrial Revolution add to this wealth of experience that, never discarded, becomes modified to accommodate the new.

Man's control over his food supply through development of agriculture has been discussed in Chapter 3. In the Middle East lie the Old World beginnings of seed farming and animal herding; of irrigation on floodplains—especially along the Tigris and Euphrates; also of more efficient storage facilities and of metalworking to fashion better arms and tools. New institutions and organizations were established to meet the ever-growing complexities of life.

The First Cities. About 3500 B.C. in lower Mesopotamia, small farm villages became towns with sizable populations (Figure 16–3). They provided services and goods other than food. Economic relations between urban place and country brought into being a new kind of areal organization. A network of trade developed between towns and with more distant regions.

These urban features did not necessarily orig-

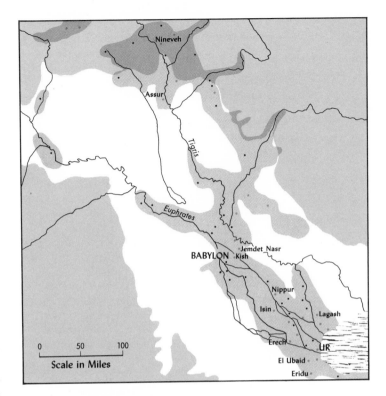

Urban Places by 3,000 B.C.

Urban Places by 2,000 B.C.

Approximate Extent of Cultivated Land

Land Over 1,000 Feet

Figure 16–3. MESOPOTAMIA: ANCIENT CITIES

Many of these places had been agricultural villages long before they became cities.

inate in the cities. Rather, it appears that cities emerged from joining distinct traits that had evolved in isolation from each other. This is why some writers refer to "the urban implosion," a centripetal coming together of traits within a container (Mumford, 1961, 34). The situation of the Middle East favored this proc-

16. Towns and Cities

ess. As Sjoberg puts it: "The region was a cross-roads that facilitated repeated contacts among peoples of divergent cultures for thousands of years. The resulting mixture of alien and indigenous crafts and skills must have made its own contribution to the evolution of the first true cities out of the villages of lower Mesopotamia" (Sjoberg, 1965, 56). Of course, the earliest cities, like Ur, Erech, and Lagash, could not have emerged without a surplus of food above the needs of the farmers. This surplus, however, was only a necessary condition for urban life, not the cause of it.

The Sumerian townspeople soon developed methods of writing and record keeping, and invented systems of measuring and reckoning. A class of writers and clerks sprang up. Trade, especially in woods and metals, increased. Craftsmen and merchants rose in importance. Armies were formed to guard traders, farms, and granaries, as well as to protect the city against capture and sack. A corporation of priests ran the irrigation systems. Eventually a class of lawyers became necessary to apportion and secure land rights and water rights by legal means. One of the distinctive features of the early cities is that they show this division of labor.

Each activity of the city had its own location, its own buildings, its own corps of workers, resulting in internal differentiation as to the place for temple, palace, fortress, granary, market, and metalworking. Although individual towns of Sumer varied in complexity, they shared many similarities. The Mesopotamian plain had a common culture, including language, religion, economy, social organization, and technology. The individual cities were, however, independent. The accepted political norm for a city-state consisted of a town with its surrounding farm and wasteland.*

At the end of the third millennium B.C., many towns based on the Mesopotamian model appeared around the eastern Mediterranean, first at Ugarit and Byblos, later at Tyre and Sidon, and on the island of Crete at Knossos and Phaistos. Cities evolved in the Indus Valley

about 2500 B.C., and also in China, where An-yang was built soon after 2000 B.C. in the Huang Ho Valley. Scholars argue whether the city of these eastern regions was invented independently; the preponderance of evidence implies diffusion from Mesopotamia, with unique cultural contributions from the regions concerned.

Still later, cities grew up around the Mediterranean, throughout Persia and Central Asia, and in the Ganges Valley of northern India. Many of these places show direct influence from the Middle East and eastern Mediterranean. In Egypt cities were few. They served as administrative centers, and failed to develop the variety of functions found in Sumeria. Most were occupied for relatively short periods, reflecting the character of Egypt's court civilization.

Cities in Classical Times.   The spread of cities westward in the Mediterranean and to Europe is associated with the seafaring Phoenicians and Greeks. They appear in historic records as traders and colonizers who formed a link between the barbarians of Europe and the civilizations of the Middle East. By the second half of the first millennium B.C. the Greeks had achieved a dominant position, first by the skillful use of seapower to monopolize trade and promote colonization, then by actual military victory over the Middle Eastern empires. Under Alexander the Great the Greeks conquered the Middle East and carried Hellenistic culture into Central Asia and far into the Indian subcontinent.

In the west, the Romans inherited Greek culture and also an urbanized Mediterranean basin. They in turn carried the city way of life inland, especially northward into Europe, where they built many military towns and long-distance trading centers. Furthermore, throughout their empire they set up administrative headquarters, which in the course of time also provided urban services to local populations.

Of the hundreds of cities large and small that the Romans built, the greatest was Rome itself. Its population varied from time to time, but during the second century of the Christian Era it probably had as many as half a million. The empire had few large cities in the west, mostly

* "Political" derives from the Greek *polis,* "city."

Dubrovnik, on the Adriatic, flourished for centuries as a trade link between Latin and Balkan countries, and is now the tourist center of the Dalmatian coast. Its main street (diagonally across center of photo) was until the thirteenth century a marshy channel that separated Latin Ragusa (right) from Slav Dubrovnik (left). The double walls and towers date from the fourteenth to the sixteenth centuries. [Courtesy of Yugoslav Information Service]

port towns around the Mediterranean. There were many in the east, however, including Athens, Alexandria, Antioch, Constantinople, Ctesiphon, and Seleucia.

Cities of Medieval Europe. After imperial Roman authority collapsed in the western part of the empire, administrative and long-distance trading functions ceased or became less impor-tant, and city life declined. Thereafter the Arabs attacked from the south, the Vikings from the north, and nomadic horsemen from the eastern steppes. Despite these disruptions of peace and trade, many cities survived. Residences of lords and kings and the palaces of the ecclesiastical hierarchy occupied the sites of former Roman authority, and helped to preserve the thread of city life. At times this thread was thin, and where it broke, rural life resumed dominance.

From the ninth century onward trade gradually revived and towns awakened. Paralleling this came a long period of land colonization, the turning back of the Islamic threat, and the containment or absorption of the Vikings and mounted nomads. The city reappeared as a flourishing institution in southern Europe, notably at Venice, Genoa, and other merchant towns of northern Italy. A similar development took place around the shores of the "narrow seas" between England and the Low Countries, where seamen and artisans combined to increase trade and manufacturing. Cities like Ghent, Bruges, Antwerp, and London soon rivaled Italian towns in size. In late medieval Europe a hundred or more cities existed, mostly concentrated in several regions. Capitals like Paris, seaports and river ports like Bristol and Köln and towns on land routes like Salzburg, Augsburg, and Nürnberg also became large.

Thus, cities again dotted Europe, although the number in any one region varied greatly and the proportion of total population living in them remained low. Their character reflected their diverse functions, whether commercial, religious, or administrative. In general, commerce was the prime force in the zone between the North Sea and Italy, but other factors marked towns in more peripheral regions. The cities differed according to whether "they grew in the heart of Europe or were planted instruments in the fringes. . . . Thus while the famed cathedrals and churches rise above so many of the cities of the continent, their massive, richly decorated towers not only marking the heart of the settlement but testifying to the wealth gained through commerce, above the towns of the outer fringes built during the process of conquest appear the harsher, cruder castles, softened by age and assimilated by association, but still preserving, where they remain intact, their aspects of military control and domination" (Carter, 1965, 14–15).

Medieval towns became partially independent political entities amid the rural feudal society, which opposed these new institutions. The city represented the main political force to modify the existing social order, usually in alliance with the king, whose powers waxed as those of the feudal nobility waned. City charters granted by royal decree gave a measure of self-government to towns. This alliance between town and crown greatly stimulated the development of modern western society. As Murphey has argued in a perceptive article that compares the city in Europe with that in China as a center of change: "The cities of western Europe have been, at least since the high Middle Ages, centers of intellectual ferment; of economic change; and thus, in time, of opposition to the central authority. They became rebels in nearly every aspect of their institutional life. It was trade (and to a somewhat lesser extent specialized manufacturing) which made them strong enough to maintain their challenge to the established order" (Murphey, 1954, 350).

Developments in Other Cultural Regions. Wherever the city remained strongly associated with the countryside, as in lands outside western Europe, it did not tend to become a stronghold for political radicals. More often than not it was dedicated to maintaining the *status quo*. This was especially true in China, as Murphey points out: "In China, while the peasant and the countryside were in some respects like the West, the cities' role was fundamentally different. Chinese cities were administrative centers. With few exceptions this function dominated their lives whatever their other bases in trade and manufacturing. Their remarkably consistent, uniform plan, square or rectangular walls surrounding a great cross with gates at each of the four arms, suggests their common administrative creation and their continued expression of this function" (Murphey, 1954, 353).

In the eastern Mediterranean the city continued its importance during the "Dark Ages" of western Europe. The Byzantine Empire, with Constantinople its chief city, preserved the ancient heritage. The Arabs in North Africa and the Middle East had inherited the classical civilization, and adopted the city as a dominant settlement form. They made Cairo, Alexandria, and Baghdad great centers of Arab culture. A little later they gave rebirth to city life in

Seville, Cordoba, Tunis, and Palermo in the western Mediterranean. Arab civilization kept its strong position until the Turks won control of much of this realm at the end of the Middle Ages. Before that time few cities of Christendom—among them Paris, and trade cities like Venice—rivaled Arab cities in size and complexity.

In India under the Buddhist kings and emperors of the last centuries before the Christian Era, the need for administrative centers stimulated the growth of cities in the Ganges Valley. Social and commercial functions were relatively minor; some of them may have been introduced as a result of Alexander's conquests. City life became increasingly complicated during the later Middle Ages, when Islam dominated many parts of India.

In Central Asia the cities along the great trade routes remained avowedly commercial. Despite the turmoil of invasion, plunder, and cultural clash, the towns along the roads between China and the West possessed remarkable resilience. Samarkand, Bukhara, Tashkent, and other towns at times grew rich and opulent.

Trading towns also developed along the sea route that connected South and East Asia with the Arab world, and ultimately with Europe and the Mediterranean. Wherever the ships stopped along the western coasts of India, on the Arabian littoral, and at the eastern entrances to the Indian Ocean, urban settlements came to life. Thus, even before the modern era, cities formed an important element in the fabric of settlement throughout much of Europe, North Africa, the Middle East, Central Asia, India, and China. But in all these regions, the rural population heavily outnumbered the town dwellers. Yet, because of its regional administrative power, commerce, and defensive advantage, the city not only had become firmly entrenched, but had an importance far in excess of its share of population.

Urbanization in Pre-Columbian America. In the Americas before the European invasions, settlements existed that had some features similar to those of Old World cities—particularly in Yucatan, Guatemala, and central Mexico. Since evidence that they were based on Old World models is lacking, we must assume an independent development.

After a late start, the archeological record is gradually being filled in. The physical remains of the Mayan civilization show many ceremonial temples and other structures surrounded by quite densely settled farming areas. While there was some division of labor among masons, metalworkers, scribes, and priests, the closely packed towns so characteristic of Old World urbanism do not appear; instead, loose aggregations possess both rural and urban features.

In central Mexico a similar development took place, perhaps derived from Mayan examples. Near modern Mexico City, the site of Teotihuacan reveals a very large settlement capable of containing at least 100,000 people. The city (if we may call it that) was much spread out and had a basic grid street pattern and many ceremonial buildings. No doubt many of its inhabitants were full-time or, more probably, part-time farmers.

Cities in the Modern Era

When Europeans left their homelands in the modern era for commerce, settlement, and empire in other parts of the world, they built towns where there were none, or converted the settlements of other peoples to their own uses, primarily trade and defense. In the Orient a European fort overlooked the trading town, often a coastal port. Some Asian, African, and American towns have a long European tradition added to that of indigenous groups. Around the eastern and western exits from the Indian Ocean and along the coasts of India the Arab element was strong. The older parts of towns, from Mombasa and Dar-es-Salaam to Goa and Malacca, show their variegated past; temples, mosques and churches, palaces and castles, markets, bazaars, and business quarters give a cosmopolitan air.

As European political control became firmer in Asian and African areas, many towns took on an administrative function. This was especially true in the subcontinent of India, where the apparatus of British imperial rule attached military and administrative quarters to the already mixed heritage of cities. In other cases, the imperial purpose was better served by founding new cities to perform manifold colonial functions, among them Calcutta at the head of the Bay of Bengal, Saigon in southern Vietnam, and Batavia, now Djakarta, the capital of Indonesia. In the New World the cities that the Spanish and Portuguese built developed strong administrative functions, reflecting the centralized nature of imperial rule. In North America the main towns of the colonial era were all ports—Charleston, Baltimore, Philadelphia, New York, Boston, Salem, Quebec, and Montreal—and the administrative element was less evident than in the Spanish cities, except in the case of Quebec.

Overseas enterprise brought rapid growth to many port cities in Europe, like Seville, Lisbon, Bordeaux, Bristol, Liverpool, London, and Amsterdam. These cities became particularly large where they combined port and capital functions. Their only rivals were inland capitals of centralized states. The biggest were London and Paris, each with over half a million inhabitants by the end of the seventeenth century. Madrid, chosen in the sixteenth century as the capital of Spain because of its central location, grew within a few decades from a small town to a large city. In central and eastern Europe the disparity between capitals and other towns was also marked, partly because the lesser towns had little long-distance trade. Moscow, Kiev, and Prague were unequaled in size within their regions. In all these cases we see the development of national "primate cities," to use the term Mark Jefferson introduced (Jefferson 1939).

The importance of the big cities should not make us overlook local centers and humbler market towns. The small town in Europe and its overseas extensions, especially in North America, represents a vital link in the settlement hierarchy between rural places and greater cities. As the European and North American economy became more commercialized, and the mass of the population wealthier, small towns increased in numbers, and their functional bases became more secure.

The Industrial City. Machine-driven large-scale manufacturing added a new dimension to urban life in the Occidental world. The process set in at different times in different countries. In Britain industrial centers like Birmingham, Manchester, and Sheffield had already become sizable towns by the early nineteenth century. In continental Europe and the eastern United States manufacturing towns mushroomed in the second half of the nineteenth century.

At that time coal was king, commanding the location of industry. Towns on or near coalfields became surrounded by mine shafts, slag heaps, mills, factories, railroads, and—amid these—row upon row of grimy workers' houses. As these towns merged they formed industrial agglomerations like those on the coalfields of central and northern England, Sambre-Meuse, and the Ruhr. These districts lacked the marked nuclear form so characteristic of the historic city. Instead, they presented a haphazard conglomeration of industrial, commercial, and residential units, enclosing surviving fragments of the former rural landscape.

In some instances, already existing large towns—most notably the great capitals—added an industrial component to their functions. They became the largest markets of their countries and the nodes of their transportation systems. Capitals such as London, Paris, Brussels, and Moscow became the largest single industrial cities as well. In North America a similar process saw manufacturing concentrate in the biggest cities, including the ports of New York, Philadelphia, and Montreal, and also on the coalfields and transportation points to the west, among them Pittsburgh and Chicago.

Outside Europe and North America, industrial cities developed mainly with Western capital. In Asia a number of port towns that had been expanded by European maritime connections now added manufacturing industries, using local materials and labor. Shanghai, Bombay, and Calcutta were the largest of these. In Japan the growth of industry was a native endeavor, although inspired by Western example.

The southern port cities—Yokohama-Tokyo and Kobe-Osaka—became centers for diversified industry, while the coal mines of Kyushu attracted iron and steelmaking.

The Service Center. An ever-increasing complexity of organization in commerce, banking, transportation, communication, and government services accompanied industrialization. At the same time living standards were rising. The mass of citizenry became a market for the goods and services the city provided. The genius of the modern city is that it offers in enormous quantities a massive range of products from foods and cars to government services and entertainment. In earlier times most people had to be content with the bare necessities of life, while only a privileged few had the right to enjoy, or could afford, luxuries. In the modern city the ordinary individual avails himself of many services—the "tertiary" sector of the economy. These services now rival manufacturing as employers of city people; in some countries they contribute a greater share of the national wealth. In the United States such services utilized 56 percent of the work force in 1960—well above the figure of 48 percent for 1940 and more than twice the proportion (26 percent) in 1900.

On the whole, apart from small market towns in purely rural areas, the services are provided mainly for urban populations. Small towns look to larger towns for certain needs; these in turn depend on bigger cities for specialized services. This hierarchy is a marked feature of the urban structure in modernized countries. Quantity and variety of goods and services increase as one proceeds up through different size levels.

Four Facets of Contemporary Cities

Numbers of Inhabitants. In our statistically minded age, lists of the world's great cities, with population numbers attached, attract much interest (see Table 17–1). Often signs along the highways announce a town's name and population. In most encyclopedias the first piece of information given about a place is its number of inhabitants.

Different terms suggest in a general way the size of places: hamlet (from the old Germanic *ham* for a group of buildings) and village (from Latin *villa,* meaning a place in the country) are used for rural settlements. Town (from Germanic *tun,* an enclosed area) usually connotes a smaller urban place than city (via French from Latin *civitas*). Metropolis (literally, mother city, from the Greek *meter* and *polis*) suggests an important central city, and megalopolis (the Greek *megale* meaning great) is a good label for the modern giant-city complex. But there is no general agreement on the size limits that mark town from city and city from metropolis.

Regardless of whether an urban place is a town or a large city, how shall its population be calculated? Who will be included and who left out? The answers to these questions have ramifications beyond the simple counting of heads: in city planning, in providing various services, redrawing boundaries, or including or excluding individual towns from certain political status.

What is "New York"? And what is its population? According to the 1960 census the population of Manhattan Island, heart of the city, was 1.7 million. The rest of the "core area," as defined by the Regional Plan Association of New York, includes the Bronx, Kings and Queens counties, all part of New York City, plus Hudson County and Newark in New Jersey, adding up to a further 6.9 million. There were 4.3 million more in the inner suburban and industrial areas of Richmond County (Staten Island), Nassau County on Long Island, part of Westchester County, plus four New Jersey counties. Grouped around these were another 3.2 million in thirteen counties in New York, New Jersey, and Connecticut. Thus, the New York urban region in 1960 covered some 22 counties and comprised 16.1 million people.

The U.S. Bureau of the Census defines the New York–Northeastern New Jersey *Urbanized Area* (the thickly settled area) as having 14.1 million inhabitants in 1960; the New York *Standard Metropolitan Statistical Area* (S.M.S.A.), including nine counties, as having 10.7 million; and the New York–Northeastern

New Jersey *Standard Consolidated Area* as having 14.7 million. For definitions of these census terms see page 393.

Obviously there are many ways of defining a city. At one extreme is Manhattan Island, nerve center of the city region and a great employer of people. At the other extreme and beyond the definitions given above, New York forms but a part of the urbanized seaboard of the northeast United States. Which definition to use must be a matter of informed choice depending on one's aims.

For comparing urban places within a single country one can use a standard definition based on groupings of local government units that conform to certain criteria. The U.S. Bureau of the Census defines "urbanized area" as a contiguous built-up area with a certain population density. The S.M.S.A. concept has less use for comparative purposes, partly because it is based on the county, which rarely coincides with the built-up areas, and partly because it was found necessary to use townships instead of counties in New England, where the urban mesh is closer than in other parts of the country.

Comparisons between different nations become more difficult, because their statistical areas and governmental units are organized on another basis. The character of urban and rural settlement varies greatly. Density criteria used in the United States may not apply at all to other lands.

The difficulty in defining the population of an individual town makes it impossible to determine accurately what percent of a country's population is urban unless the criteria for definition are explicitly stated. Most countries have a legal definition as to what constitutes an urban place. These definitions, however, differ considerably. England considers as "urban" all places with the governmental status of boroughs and urban districts, regardless of population size. In Japan all municipalities with over 30,000 are "urban." In the United States the census defines as "urban" all incorporated places with 2,500 or more inhabitants. All populations in unincorporated territory and in incorporated places below 2,500 are classed as "rural." Figure 16–1 is based on such statistics with varying national definitions of "urban."

It would have been possible to make a map showing the proportion of national populations living in settlements above a specific size level (for example, 2,000), but this would also have its drawbacks. Many countries have large agricultural villages with thousands of inhabitants, while in many modernized countries places numbering as few as 100 could properly be called urban.

Far from all countries have accurate population counts. Some have not even taken a census as yet, and in others the results are defective. Moreover, with many countries rapidly urbanizing, and with high internal migrations in others, a population census quickly gets out of date. Information published by administrative units often does not reflect the actual extent of urban places. This holds true not only for large cities which straddle many political units, but also for small urban centers that may not have independent political existence.

In most countries the process of political boundary change is very slow, and lags far behind changes in settlement pattern. In England, for example, the rural population grows at a greater rate than the urban population, despite a continuous drop in farm population. Many English "rural districts" on the outskirts of cities have 50,000 or more inhabitants at quite high densities.

Countries vary in the relative proportions of how many people live in towns of different size classes. In modernized countries towns grow in a large majority of size classes. If we disregard the problems of boundary definition, we note that in the United States since 1900 the population proportion living in different size classes above 5,000 has increased, but the proportion in settlements less than 5,000 has decreased. According to the 1960 census, cities with over 100,000 inhabitants represent 28 percent of the population; 63 percent live in the S.M.S.As. In England and Wales, where even greater proportions live in cities, over half of the people are in urban areas with more than 100,000 inhabitants.

Near the other extreme in distribution is a country like India. Here four-fifths of the people live in places with less than 5,000. A further 10 percent reside in centers with between 5,000

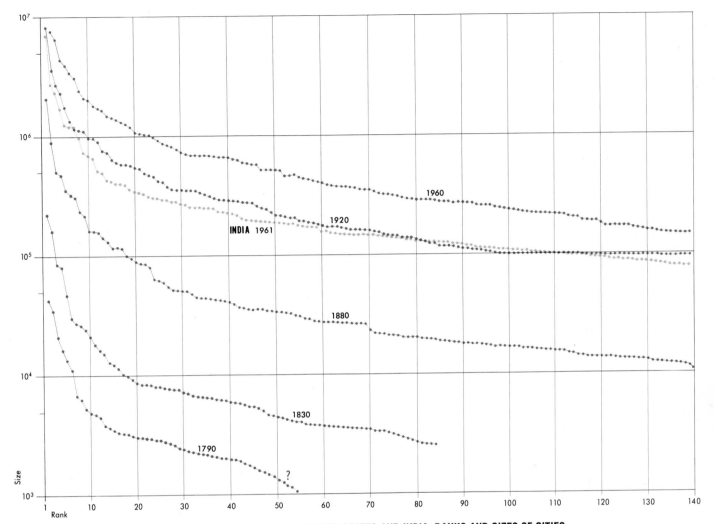

Figure 16–4. UNITED STATES AND INDIA: RANKS AND SIZES OF CITIES

On this graph the 140 largest cities of the United States (1790 to 1960)
and the 140 largest cities of India (1961) are ranked by population size
and plotted by semilogarithmic scale. Data for the United States
supplied by J. R. Borchert and F. Lukermann. Data for India from
Census of India, 1961, Paper 1 of 1962. *Final Population Totals.*

and 20,000, but many of these settlements can
be called rural, since most of the inhabitants are
farmers. Compared with advanced countries
India has few medium-sized towns. About 8
percent live in cities with over 100,000 population.

Similar differences between highly urbanized
and newly urbanizing countries become evident
if towns are ranked by size and plotted on a
graph. Figure 16–4 compares the United States
and India in this respect. The deeper curve of
the Indian line indicates the relative lack of

middle-sized cities. The changing depth of the United States curve since 1790, during the process of modernization and urbanization, illustrates the same point.

Internal Structure of Towns. Each city is an individual place with its own site and situation, its own population, its own history of development and change, and its own activities. All this expresses itself in the internal physical structure, comprising the road and street pattern and the location, as well as the nature, of different kinds of facilities: retail stores, wholesale warehouses, industrial plants, offices, residences, railroads, airports, parks. While each place may be unique in itself, it possesses, nevertheless, certain broad elements that repeat themselves from town to town.

The most distinctive feature common to small towns—many of them "market towns," or in modern terminology, "central places"—is the central business district where most of the citizens work, providing services for country and town dwellers. The closely packed shops and offices, mutually interdependent, offer economy of movement to the served and servers alike. The amount of floor space is increased by greater area of buildings in relation to the lot size than in other parts of town.

The larger the town, the more complex its internal structure. After studying many European and American cases, Dickinson made a basic division into four zones. The *central zone* is "the hub of the city and includes the older town and its pre-modern extensions." Roads and railways converge on it, causing traffic congestion. Competition for land leads to a heavily built-up condition that gradually invades the area around the zone. "It includes the retail, wholesale, administrative, commercial, and business districts; markets, hotels, residential enclaves for both the elite and the poor; and large public buildings that cater for the community as a whole" (Dickinson, 1964, 163). Buildings in the central zone quickly become obsolete, at times necessitating reconstruction and rearrangement of uses. Detailed study reveals that the population constantly is changing. On working days people fill the zone, but at night and on the weekend it becomes almost empty except for hotel and entertainment areas.

The *middle zone* was built mostly in the late nineteenth and early twentieth centuries. Row houses, tenements, and frame houses contain dense populations. Mixed with housing are small industrial plants, shopping areas, schools, churches, wasteland, and derelict buildings. The main lines of land and water transportation are flanked by industrial districts. The middle zone, then, is actually a conglomerate of diverse forms of land use. It contains many blighted neighborhoods, and it houses most of the low-income groups. These so called "gray areas" present a major problem in urban reconstruction.

The *outer zone* was first settled by wealthy people in the late nineteenth century. Since World War I, the spread of mass transportation has built it up fully. Wider-spaced houses keep these residential areas at a lower density than in the inner zone. Parks, shopping areas, and newer industrial plants interrupt the housing areas.

The *urban fringe,* the cutting edge of suburbanization beyond the outer zone, spreads out into the countryside along the highways and commuter rail lines. Often the tracts of new housing congregate around older villages or market towns. Between the newly built-up areas open land and woodland intervene.

Differences exist, of course, within this general scheme for the western city. In the United States, for example, most cities have a basic grid plan with straight streets intersecting each other at right angles. Some old highways, once outside the town, now cut across the grid and converge at the center. Railways also come to the center, often paralleling the radial roads, thus forming the main industrial axis lines. The American city usually exceeds its European counterpart in sheer areal size and extended suburban fringe.

On the European continent, cities show many distinctive features. The old medieval town, often with narrow and winding streets, is contained inside a ring road (French, *boulevard,* related to bulwark; German, *Ringstrasse*)

Edinburgh, the capital of Scotland. A lake bed, now drained and occupied by railway stations and tracks, separates the Georgian "New Town," laid out on the gridiron plan in the late eighteenth century, from the picturesque old city, tightly built on a narrow ridge (diagonally across right background) between Holyrood palace (left background) and the Castle (off to the right of picture). Famous Princes Street, the elegant promenade facing the ravine and the medieval city, forms the inner edge of the New Town. Salisbury Crag rises in the distance. [Aerofilms and Aero Pictorial Ltd.]

marking the line of old fortifications, now dismantled (Figure 16-5). Beyond this lies the city created in the nineteenth and twentieth centuries. Railways built their stations on the very edge of the old town. Industrial areas developed along these and existing roads from town. The ring roads and the later transportation net give to the whole a "radial-concentric pattern" (Dickinson, 1964, 168).

Since few British towns had walls, they lack

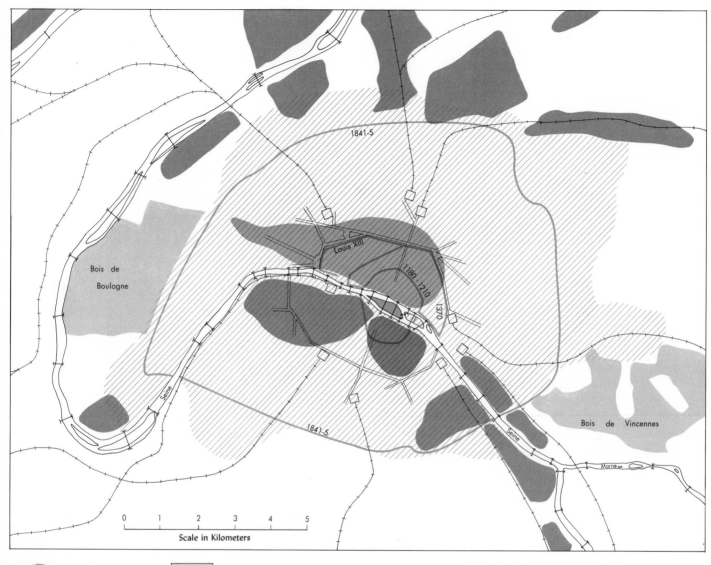

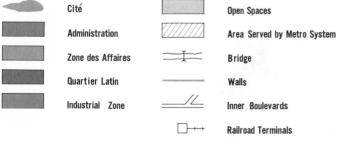

	Cité		Open Spaces
	Administration		Area Served by Metro System
	Zone des Affaires		Bridge
	Quartier Latin		Walls
	Industrial Zone		Inner Boulevards
			Railroad Terminals

Figure 16–5. PARIS: CENTRAL AREA

The modern metropolis extends far beyond the border of the map. See also Figure 17–7.

the well-defined structure so typical of many continental cities. In the modern age expanding cities in Britain engulf the dense net of towns and villages from the past. Many urbanized areas have multiple nuclei (see Chapter 18).

In Europe, the private car only recently has become a nearly universal possession, so that the widely spread suburbs of the American type have not yet arrived. They may never come. Governmental planning agencies generally control strictly the expansion within an already heavy mesh of settlement.

Cities in other cultural regions often differ radically from their Western counterparts. Other values and other ways of life give towns other roles. In Asia and Africa—and to a lesser extent in Latin America—city populations remain poor, and the masses lack permanent, well-paying jobs. Transportation systems are often too expensive to install, and where built are too expensive to use. The general density of population greatly exceeds that in the West. The poor quarters consist of shacks huddled together at the city outskirts. The middle class lives more toward the center. Markets, spread through residential areas, replace the distinctive shopping districts so typical for the West.

In the colonial era, Europeans directed their business, military, and governmental operations from the main towns. The newly independent national states have inherited these capitals and large cities, complete with central business districts, government quarters, military cantonments, and "civil lines" where Europeans lived. The Occidental urban frame is not always in harmony with the local culture. The vast inflow from the countryside increases tensions between the indigenous rural tradition and the necessary discipline of modern city life. Eventually these strains will ease and the cities will reflect more truly the national culture.

Urban Functions. The idea that the city performs certain functions is the essence of its definition. The things done in a city relate it to the surrounding area and to other urban settlements in the same web. Saying "this city does this (or that)" reduces the complex of activities, buildings, and people with all their interrela-

tionships, to a single term. Pittsburgh is a "steel town," Minneapolis the "mill city," Antwerp a port, Peking the capital of China. The term "market town," although rather more inclusive in its connotation, indicates the same directness of purpose.

The central place provides services for the surrounding country (tributary area or hinterland). Specialized occupations supply wider regions. A town may manufacture goods or offer services for a whole nation. Some cities proudly announce that they are the "such and such" capital. Washington is the nation's capital; Chicago the railroad hub; Detroit the center of the automotive industry; Hibbing, Minnesota, the iron-ore capital.

Many geographers have proposed classifications of cities by functions. Some concentrate on single activities that appear to dominate and that distinguish one town from another. Aurousseau divided urban places into six classes: administration, defense, culture, production, communication (including transportation and distribution), and recreation. He subdivided each class: for example, defense towns into fortress and garrison towns, and naval bases (Aurousseau, 1921).

Harris made a more refined functional classification of American cities, using various statistical criteria to define such types as manufacturing, wholesale, retail, transportation, and diversified. He then placed each city, according to its employment structure, in its proper functional category (Harris, 1943).

The idea that single city functions are responsible for the life of the community derives from the analogy that cities are organs of the national body, each performing its own distinctive task. This kind of notion became fashionable in the social sciences some decades ago, when many social scientists used analogies from the biological sciences to describe and explain the phenomena in which they were interested. At present the trend is to use concepts from physics. Cities are thought of as centers of gravity, exerting attraction on people and things in the surrounding field. In reality, of course, cities do not actually "do" anything, though writers today constantly use simple functional

16. Towns and Cities

terms to describe them. The danger of labeling cities by single function is that it obscures the fact that most of them have a multifunctional character.

Some recent classifications try to take into account both multiplicity and specialization of activities (Nelson, 1955; Webb, 1959). From these discussions two basic urban types emerge. One of these is the town which to a high degree maintains its association with a particular piece of local territory. It funnels to its hinterland goods and services from the outside world, and also collects and sends out regional products. Whether large or small, this is the typical central place or market town.

The other urban type is that which offers some special services or goods. Such a town can usually be identified by the large proportion of its work force engaged in a certain activity. For example, a small town may concentrate on mining, on being a railroad division point, or on manufacturing, perhaps with a single plant dominating urban employment. Large towns may also specialize, particularly as manufacturing centers. Other cities show high concentration of the labor force in insurance, public administration, or higher education. In fact, most cities have a specialized activity plus the general function of central place. Such towns are quite common in the great industrial belts of Europe and North America. Specialized functions develop strongly during the process of modernization when the settlement fabric becomes linked by efficient transportation systems. Figure 16–6 shows town types in the state of Minnesota: circle sizes indicate the degree of specialization; symbols, the type of specialization.

Spatial Arrangement. The above statement that central places serve their surrounding areas needs closer inspection, because it points up some general principles that affect the nature and spacing of urban settlements. The theoretical concept of a spatial hierarchy of central places, formulated by Walter Christaller in 1933, has since been developed further in a multitude of studies, especially in Sweden and the United States (Figure 16–7).

People tend to spend as little time and effort

Figure 16–6. MINNESOTA: FUNCTIONS OF SMALL URBAN CENTERS

The symbols represent different kinds of specialization. The main distinction is between relatively unspecialized towns with some concentration on wholesale and retail trade in the south and west of the state, and the specialized mining and manufacturing towns in the north and east. The cities of Minneapolis, St. Paul, and Duluth are not shown. Based on employment in 12 industrial categories for towns between 2,500 and 50,000 population as recorded in the *U.S. Census of Population, 1950*. The method of calculation is explained in Webb, 1959.

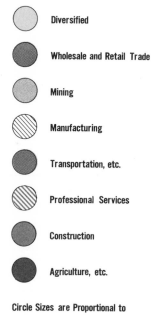

Diversified

Wholesale and Retail Trade

Mining

Manufacturing

Transportation, etc.

Professional Services

Construction

Agriculture, etc.

Circle Sizes are Proportional to Degree of Functional Specialization

as possible in using urban services. Therefore, they usually obtain what they need from the nearest center. Naturally their wants, and the time and distance they will travel to satisfy

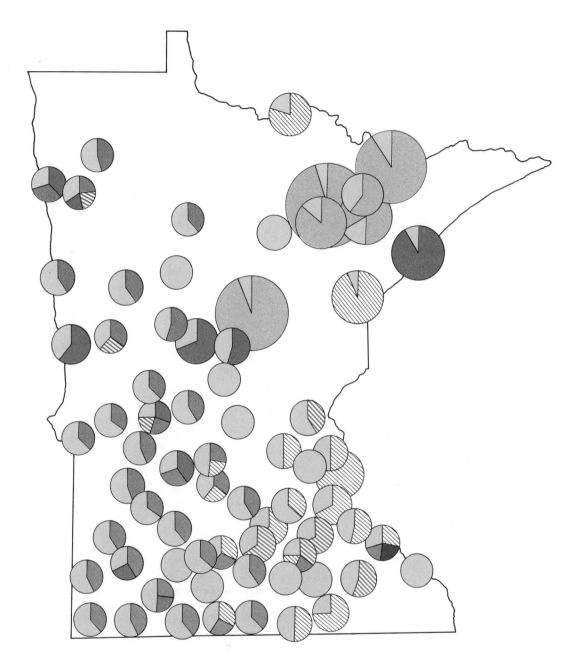

them, vary widely. One expects to find a grocery and drugstore in every neighborhood, but travels willingly a long distance to seek help from a medical specialist.

Each service, we can presume, needs a min-imum number of customers to maintain itself. This minimum level is called the threshold. For services of common daily need and convenience, such as food stores and gasoline stations, the thresholds are low; for more specialized services,

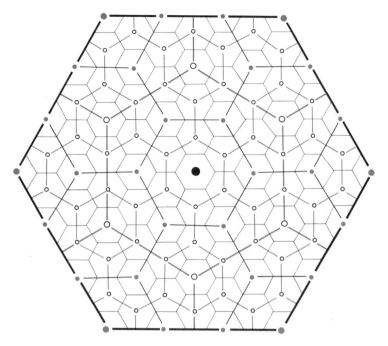

Figure 16–7. CENTRAL PLACE SYSTEM

The basis of the system is the small market town, represented by the small open circles. Six of these surround each higher order center, and so on successively up to the regional capital, represented by a black dot. After Christaller, 1933.

like a hospital, a stock brokerage, or a junior college, they are considerably higher.

If only thresholds mattered, services of various kinds might lie widely scattered, each in the center of its customer circle. But this is not so for a number of reasons. First, services must be accessible, and thus located on roads, railways, and other means of transportation. Second, transients as well as residents use the services, reinforcing the factor of accessibility. Third, mutual advantage draws services together, because each unit benefits from the customers attracted by the diversity and interdependence of what is offered in one locale. As a result, services agglomerate at specific locations, forming clusters of different sizes. The smallest

centers are closely spaced, and have only a few facilities with very low thresholds. Larger centers are farther apart, and offer services with higher thresholds, as well as greater numbers of those at the lower end of the scale. In this way a hierarchy of service centers emerges. "Centers of each higher order group perform all the functions of lower order centers plus a group of central functions that differentiates them from and sets them above the lower order. A consequence is a 'nesting' pattern of lower order trade areas within the trade area of higher order centers, plus a hierarchy of routes joining the centers" (Berry and Pred, 1961, 4).

Many regions have been studied in order to discover whether or not an urban hierarchy exists. Most work has been done on small towns, where issues involved are clearer, and where urban functions are mostly those that provide services to the immediate surroundings. However, the same notions of spatial arrangement also apply to big cities and large regions. The centrality of Paris and Madrid relative to their respective national territories was obviously an important factor in their growth. Chicago's *raison d'être* and its rise to urban dominance in the United States interior are a response to its central location, which made it the main rail and air hub of the country.

The way centrality influences the size and distribution of cities varies according to the density of population and the technical and economic level of a society. For instance, many eastern areas in the United States were settled when riverboat and horse-drawn wagon provided the only means of transportation, apart from foot travel. The railroads added new lines of long-distance transportation, but horse and buggy continued to serve in the interstices. Most of the Midwest and the Great Plains were settled during this stage of technology. Central places had to be relatively close together so farmers could journey to town and home again the same day. Figure 16–8 shows a part of the Canadian prairie province of Saskatchewan that was settled during the railroad and horse-wagon era. Rails crossed the land at regular intervals, so that no farming district in those days was more than a day's journey away, under

Figure 16–8. SOUTHWESTERN SASKATCHEWAN: CENTRAL PLACE SYSTEM

The "provincial city" is Moose Jaw; the "city" is Swift Current. The dashed lines indicate partial service function. Based on Royal Commission on Agriculture and Rural Life, 1957, and on a map in Lukermann, 1961.

Level in Hierarchy	Population (Range)	Services (Range)
● Provincial City	24,355	
○ City	7,458	156
◕ Greater Town	670-1,938	37-78
○ Town	218-728	13-45
• Village	60-388	8-29
○ Hamlet	3-196	2-13

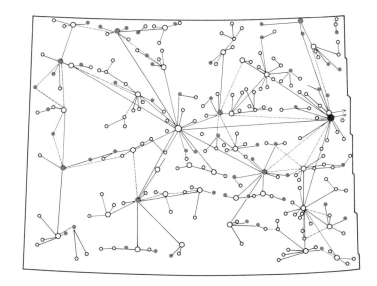

normal weather conditions. Service centers of different sizes, strung along the railways, still form an areal hierarchy of towns.

Few regions have a pattern as regular as that on the prairies. The heavily populated manufacturing areas of eastern North America and western Europe show a very different picture. Factors such as sources of power, raw materials, and sale of specialized goods over a widespread market determine location of industries. Manufacturing towns, therefore, do not adhere to the principles that govern the central-place hierarchy. Neither do resort, mining, and garrison towns, or any other urban places related to particular advantages of site. Nevertheless, they usually include the functions of central places by serving their own populations rather than those outside.

It becomes clear, then, that the main limitation of the central-place model lies in conceiving space as devoid of geographical content. The lay of the land, climatic differences, distribution of population, location of old cities, and lines of transportation—all these and other variables of real, "filled" space are omitted. The central-place model clarifies thought by the sheer logic of its design. It provides a means to understand a part of reality; however, it is not in itself the end of geographic inquiry.

Transportation and communication are the vital forces in developing and operating a network of central places. Within our time automobiles and trucks have increased the efficiency of road transportation, while telephone, radio, and television have vastly expanded electronic communications. These radical changes have upset the balance of area and distance of the former central-place hierarchy. Many small service centers cannot compete with larger towns that offer greater variety and quantity of service. Relics of once thriving small villages and hamlets dot the North American Midwest. In contrast, many small towns and villages of southern New England have been revitalized by closer contact with the expanding orbit of the Atlantic Seaboard Megalopolis.

Thus, late-twentieth-century man with his greatly increased mobility has altered spatial relationships forged between settlements of a different transportation age. Some central places waste away, but others come to life. More tenuous relationships replace the old

16. Towns and Cities

strong associations between a particular piece of rural territory and one specific town. "In the United States, and in other areas where economic integration has advanced far, the urban places do not provide services to their tributary areas exclusively. Tributary areas overlap. . . . The modern urban place acts as a funnel through which pass the products of many other urban places" (Webb, 1959, 58). How far this process of disassociation between towns and their immediate hinterlands will go, time alone can tell.

Citations

Aurousseau, M. "The Distribution of Population: A Constructive Problem," *Geographical Review,* 11 (1921): 563–593.

Berry, B. J. L., and Pred, A. *Central Place Studies: A Bibliography of Theory and Applications,* Regional Science Research Institute, Bibliography Series no. 1, Philadelphia, 1961.

Carter, J. *The Towns of Wales,* Cardiff, 1965.

Christaller, W. *Die zentralen Orte in Süddeutschland,* Jena, 1933. English translation by C. Baskin, New York, 1966.

Dickinson, R. E. *City and Region: A Geographical Interpretation,* London, 1964.

Harris, C. D. "A Functional Classification of Cities in the United States," *Geographical Review,* 33 (1943): 86–99.

Jefferson, M. "The Law of the Primate City," *Geographical Review,* 29 (1939): 226–232.

Lukermann, F. "The Role of Theory in Geographical Enquiry," *Professional Geographer,* 13, 2 (1961): 1–6. [Map]

Mumford, L. *The City in History,* New York, 1961.

Murphey, R. "The City as a Center of Change: Western Europe and China," *Annals of the Association of American Geographers,* 44 (1954): 349–362.

Nelson, H. J. "A Service Classification of American Cities," *Economic Geography,* 31 (1955): 189–210.

Royal Commission on Agriculture and Rural Life, *Service Centers,* Report no. 12, Regina, 1957. [Map]

Sjoberg, G. *The Pre-industrial City, Past and Present,* New York, 1960.

———. "The Origin and Evolution of Cities," *Scientific American,* 213 (September, 1965): 54–63.

Webb, J. W. "Basic Concepts in the Analysis of Small Urban Centers in Minnesota," *Annals of the Association of American Geographers,* 49 (1959): 55–72.

Further Readings

Adams, R. M. *The Evolution of Urban Society: Early Mesopotamia and Prehispanic Mexico,* Chicago, 1966.

Bartholomew, H. *Land Uses in American Cities,* Cambridge, Mass., 1955.

Berry, B. J. L., and Garrison, W. L. "A Note on Central Place Theory and the Range of a Good," *Economic Geography,* 34 (1958): 304–311.

———— and ————. "Functional Bases of the Central Place Hierarchy," *Economic Geography,* 34 (1958): 145–154.

Borchert, J. R., and Adams, R. B. *Trade Centers and Trade Areas of the Upper Midwest,* Upper Midwest Economic Study, Urban Report no. 3, Minneapolis, 1963.

Braidwood, R. J., and Willey, G. (eds.) *Courses toward Urban Life,* Viking Fund Publications in Anthropology, no. 32, Chicago, 1962.

Brush, J. E., and Bracey, H. E. "Rural Service Centers in Southwestern Wisconsin and Southern England," *Geographical Review,* 45 (1955): 559–569.

Carruthers, W. I. "A Classification of Service Centres in England and Wales," *Geographical Journal,* 123 (1957): 371–385.

"Cities," *Scientific American,* 213 (September, 1965).

Cornish, V. *The Great Capitals,* London, 1922.

Dickinson, R. E. *The West European City: A Geographical Interpretation,* London, 1951.

Frankfort, H. *The Birth of Civilization in the Near East,* Bloomington, Ind., 1954.

Gallion, A. B., and Eisner, S. *The Urban Pattern: City Planning and Design,* Princeton, N.J., 1963.

Ganshof, F. L. *Étude sur le développement des villes entre Loire et Rhin au moyen âge,* Brussels, 1943.

George, P. *La Ville: Le fait urbain à travers le monde,* Paris, 1952.

Gottmann, J. "Why the Skyscraper?" *Geographical Review,* 56 (1966): 190–212.

Green, C. M. *The Rise of Urban America,* London, 1966.

Green, F. H. W. "Urban Hinterlands in England and Wales: An Analysis of Bus Services," *Geographical Journal,* 116 (1950): 64–81.

Green H. L. "Hinterland Boundaries of New York City and Boston in Southern New England," *Economic Geography,* 31 (1955): 283–300.

Gutkind, E. A. *Revolution in Environment,* London, 1946.

Harris, C. D., and Ullman, E. L. "The Nature of Cities," *Annals of the American Academy of Political and Social Science,* 242 (1945): 7–17.

Hauser, P. M., and Schnore, L. F. (eds.) *The Study of Urbanization,* New York, 1965.

Hiorns, F. *Town Building in History: An Outline Review of Conditions, Influences, Ideas, and Methods Affecting "Planned" Towns through Five Thousand Years,* New York, 1956.

Houston, J. M. *A Social Geography of Europe,* London, 1953.

International Geographical Union, *Symposium of Urban Geography,* Lund, Sweden, 1960.

Isard, W. *Location and Space-Economy: A General Theory Relating to Industrial Location, Market Areas, Land Use, Trade and Urban Structure,* New York, 1956.

Jones, E. *Towns and Cities,* New York, 1966.

Mayer, H. M., and Kohn, C. F. (eds.) *Readings in Urban Geography,* Chicago, 1959.

Morrill, R. L. "The Development and Spatial Distribution of Towns in

Sweden: A Historical Predictive Approach," *Annals of the Association of American Geographers,* 53 (1963): 1–14.

Moser, C. A., and Scott, W. *British Towns: A Study of Their Social and Economic Differences,* Edinburgh, 1961.

Mumford, L. "The Natural History of Urbanization" in Thomas, W. L. (ed.) *Man's Role in Changing the Face of the Earth,* Chicago, 1956, 385–400.

Philbrick, A. K. "Principles of Areal Functional Organization in Regional Human Geography," *Economic Geography,* 33 (1957): 299–336.

Pirenne, H. *Medieval Cities,* New York, 1925. Also in paperback edition.

Pred, A. *The External Relations of Cities during "Industrial Revolution," with a Case Study of Göteborg, Sweden, 1868–1890,* University of Chicago, Department of Geography, Research Paper no. 76, Chicago, 1962.

Price, E. T. "The Central Courthouse Square in the American County Seat," *Geographical Review,* 58 (1968): 29–60.

Smailes, A. E. *A Geography of Towns,* London, 1953.

Stanislawski, D. "The Origin and Spread of the Grid-Pattern Town," *Geographical Review,* 36 (1946): 105–120.

––––––. "Early Spanish Townplanning in the New World," *Geographical Review,* 37 (1947): 94–105.

Stewart, C. T. "The Size and Spacing of Cities," *Geographical Review,* 48 (1958): 222–245.

Ullman, E. L. "Trade Centers and Tributary Areas of the Philippines," *Geographical Review,* 50 (1960): 203–218.

Weber, A. F. *The Growth of Cities in the Nineteenth Century: A Study in Statistics,* New York, 1899; Ithaca, New York, 1963.

Woolley, L. *The Beginnings of Civilization (History of Mankind: Cultural and Scientific Development,* vol. 1, part 2), New York, 1965.

Wycherley, R. E. *How the Greeks Built Cities,* London, 1962.

17. Emerging Urban Patterns

Twentieth-century cities have literally exploded into the countryside. In Western lands the metropolis dominates life; the old cultural patterns that separated town and country have collapsed. In much of heavily populated Europe and North America metropolitan life spreads over a wide area that might be called "metroland."

Some argue that metroland comes about because people flee from the machine-age city in search of a better way of life. The suburban dormitory, with its acres of low- and middle-priced housing and its road and rail links to city workplaces, is the twentieth century's contribution to mass settlement in the modernized Western world. Many people move beyond the suburbs to the "real country," bringing old villages and small towns, as well as farming areas, into the orbit of large cities. Jobs, stores, and schools follow, creating a diffused urbanism in which the various components of the city are separated by discontinuities, such as lakes, woods, and fields.

The Distribution of Large Metropolises

Among the first to perceive the new scale of modern cities was Patrick Geddes. In discussing British cities Geddes referred to southern Lancashire as "another vast province almost covered with house-groups, swiftly spreading into one, and already connected up at many points . . . the city-region of which Liverpool is the seaport and Manchester the market, now with its canal port also; while Oldham and many other factory towns, more accurately called 'factory districts,' are the workshops" (Geddes, 1915). Such a broad urban region with multiple nuclei Geddes called a *conurbation*. He envisaged seven such regions in the British Isles, and looking abroad, identified similar clusterings in Paris, the Ruhr, the northeastern seaboard of the United States, and Chicago.

Official governmental definitions usually claim areas smaller in extent than the facts warrant. The main statistical unit used for large cities in the United States is the Standard Metropolitan Statistical Area (S.M.S.A., see page 393), based on counties. However, counties are sometimes too large or their boundaries too arbitrary to provide an adequate basis for defining the regions of smaller cities. At the other end of the size scale, the city region of New York, which obviously takes in parts of New Jersey and Connecticut, has an S.M.S.A. that excludes nearby Jersey City and Newark, but includes Rockland and Westchester counties—farther from the center, but in New York State.

In England, the official definitions of the "conurbations"—a term the census now uses—enclose only continuous built-up areas, much smaller than Geddes's far-ranging "city regions and town aggregates." Between 1951 and 1961 the London city region, defined in moderately

Högdalen, one of the new suburbs of Stockholm, Sweden. This complex has a high density of dwellings, ranging from four-layer blocks to high-rise apartment buildings. Parks, playgrounds, and wide courtyards within the settlement, together with the surrounding forest, balance the built-up space. A shopping center is near the railroad station (left center). [Courtesy of Swedish Information Service]

broad terms as including populations within 30 miles from the center, increased from 11.6 to 12.4 million people. In contrast, the area officially classed as the London conurbation actually declined from 8.3 to 8.1 million over the same period.

The International Urban Research Group at Berkeley, California, developed a definition of urban aggregates suitable for application in most countries (see page 393). Figure 17–1 shows the world pattern of large metropolitan areas and is based on data modified from I.U.R. calculations. Table 17–1 lists all city regions with over two million inhabitants, plus moderately large cities separated by no more than 100 miles distance. At the present time 50 miles seems the limit of intensive influence of major urban centers. Map and table show that the main groups of adjacent metropolitan areas are in North America, Europe, and Japan.

Some Definitions of Metropolitan Areas

Urbanized Area (1960)

As defined by the U.S. Bureau of the Census in 1960, an "urbanized area" consists of a central city with at least 50,000 inhabitants in 1960, with contiguous urban fringes as follows:

Incorporated places with 2,500 or more inhabitants

Other incorporated places with at least 100 closely settled dwellings

Unincorporated areas with over 1,000 persons per square mile

Other unincorporated areas which eliminate enclaves, close indentations, or link exclaves nearer than 1½ miles to the urbanized area

In New England, New Jersey, and Pennsylvania towns and townships classified as urban (over 25,000 population, or over 2,500 population at more than 1,500 per square mile)

Standard Metropolitan Statistical Area (1960)

The U.S. Bureau of the Census defines an S.M.S.A. as a county or contiguous group of counties including a central city of 50,000 or more population (or two adjacent cities with a combined population of 50,000 or more). Two or more adjacent counties, each with a central city of 50,000 or more, combine into a single S.M.S.A. unless the cities are not integrated economically and socially. Other counties may be added if they meet the following conditions:

1. Seventy-five percent of the labor force is nonagricultural.
2. Half the population live in minor civil divisions with at least 150 persons per square mile.
3. The counties are (*a*) contiguous to the central city county or to each other; *or,* (*b*) have a nonagricultural working population of 10,000 or more, or have a non-agricultural working population at least 10 percent of that of the central county or counties; *or,* (*c*) are the residence of at least 10,000 nonagricultural workers or of at least 10 percent of the working population of the central county or counties.
4. Fifteen percent or more of the county's workers are employed in the central city county or the county has at least a quarter of its workers living in the central county or counties.

In New England, towns and cities are the basic units instead of counties. Similar criteria to those above are used in determining whether or not towns and cities should be added to the central city or cities.

Standard Consolidated Area (1960)

This category was created in recognition of the massive size of the New York and Chicago city regions. The New York–Northeastern New Jersey S.C.A. includes four S.M.S.A.s and two heavily populated New Jersey counties that are not part of any S.M.S.A. The Chicago–Northwestern Indiana S.C.A. includes the Chicago and Gary-Hammond–East Chicago S.M.S.As.

Metropolitan Area, International Definition (1959)

The basis of this definition (International Urban Research, 1959) was the 1950 definition of the Standard Metropolitan Area by the U.S. Bureau of the Census. Metropolitan regions of the world were defined as urban areas with at least 100,000 population, with over 50,000 in a central city. Administrative areas outside the central city were included if contiguous to the central city or to other areas that also met one of the following conditions:

Two-thirds of the employed population in nonagricultural occupations *or,*

Population density at least half of that of the central city, or at least twice that of the next ring of administrative areas at a greater distance from the central city

17. Emerging Urban Patterns

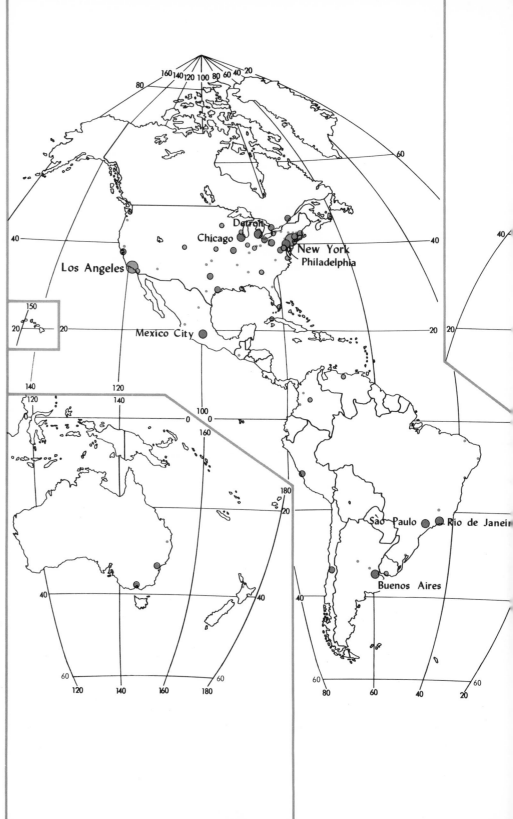

**Figure 17–1. WORLD:
METROPOLITAN POPULATIONS**

All city regions with over 500,000
population are shown. Those with over
four million inhabitants are named.
In many instances populations of
adjacent cities have been combined;
for example, western Connecticut;
Randstad Holland; Ruhr-Rhine.

·	0.5–1.0	Million
○	1 – 2	Million
●	2 – 4	Million
●	4 – 8	Million
●	Over 8	Million

IV. Settlements

Randstad
Ruhr-Rhine
Manchester
London
Paris

Moscow

Peking
Tientsin

Tokyo – Yokohama
Osaka – Kobe
Shanghai

Cairo

Bombay

Calcutta

Miles
0   500 1000   1500

0   500 1000   2000
Kilometers

AITOFF'S

INTERRUPTED EQUAL-AREA

PROJECTION

*17. Emerging
Urban
Patterns*

Table 17–1. City Regions with over Two Million Inhabitants and Their Neighbors with over Half a Million Inhabitants

City region	Population, millions	Associated cities*
Africa		
Cairo	4.6	Alexandria
Asia		
Tokyo-Yokohama	15.0	Shizuoka-Shimizu, Nagoya, Gifu-Ichinomiya, Osaka-Kobe, Kyoto
Shanghai	10.0	Soochow
Osaka-Kobe	8.5	See Tokyo-Yokohama
Calcutta	6.2	Howrah
Peking	5.0	Tientsin
Bombay	4.7	Poona
Hong Kong	3.5	
Seoul	3.4	
Tientsin	3.2	Peking
Shenyang (Mukden)	3.2	Fushun
Delhi	3.1	
Manila	3.0	
Chungching	2.9	
Madras	2.5	
Djakarta	2.5	
Bangkok	2.4	
Kuangchou	2.4	
Harbin	2.2	
Teheran	2.2	
Nanking	2.0	
Kyoto	2.0	See Tokyo-Yokohama
Kitakyushu	2.0	Shimonoseki, Hiroshima-Kure, Fukuoka
Saigon-Cholon	2.0	

City region	Population, millions	Associated cities*
Berlin(E.-W.)	4.3	Hamburg, Hannover, Bremen, Braunschweig, Magdeburg, Halle, Leipzig, Dresden, Karl-Marx-Stadt, Prague
Randstad Holland‡	4.0	See Inner Ruhr
Manchester	3.7	See London
Leningrad	3.5	
Silesia§	3.4	Kraków
Birmingham	2.6	See London
Madrid	2.5	
Hamburg	2.4	See Berlin
Rome	2.4	Turin, Genoa
Milan	2.2	Turin, Genoa
Athens	2.0	
West Riding	2.0	See London
Glasgow	2.0	See London
North America		
New York	16.5	Megalopolis¶
Los Angeles	7.6	San Diego
Chicago	7.0	Milwaukee, Gary
Philadelphia	4.8	See New York
Detroit	4.3	Toledo, Cleveland, Akron, Youngstown, Pittsburgh
San Francisco	3.6	Sacramento
Boston	3.2	See New York
Montreal	2.6	Ottawa
Pittsburgh	2.4	See Detroit
Washington	2.4	See New York
St. Louis	2.2	

City region	Population, millions	Associated cities*	City region	Population, millions	Associated cities*
Europe (including the Soviet Union)			Toronto	2.0	Hamilton, Buffalo, Rochester, Syracuse
London	12.7	Birmingham, Coventry, Stoke, Nottingham, Manchester, Merseyside, West Riding, Teesside, Tyneside, Edinburgh, Clydeside, Bristol, South Wales, Portsmouth-Southampton	*Middle America*		
			Mexico City	5.5	
Moscow	9.0		*South America*		
Paris	7.7		Buenos Aires	8.1	
Inner Ruhr	6.1	Rhine-Ruhr cities,† Mainz, Frankfurt am Main, Mannheim-Ludwigshafen, Karlsruhe, Stuttgart, Nürnberg, München, Randstad Holland,‡ Liège, Ghent, Brussels, Lille, Antwerp, Charleroi	Rio de Janeiro	4.7	
			São Paulo	4.6	
			Oceania		
			Sydney	2.5	
			Melbourne	2.1	

* An "associated city" is within 100 miles of another city in the same cluster, and at least one "associated city" is within 100 miles of the main city region.

† Rhine-Ruhr cities—Inner Ruhr, Düsseldorf, Wuppertal, Krefeld, Mönchen-Gladbach, Köln (Cologne), Bonn.

‡ Randstad Holland—Rotterdam, Amsterdam, Haarlem, 's Gravenhage (The Hague), Utrecht.

§ Silesia—Includes Katowice, Zabrze, Bytom, Gliwice, Chorzow, Sosnowiec.

¶ Megalopolis—Boston-Lowell, Worcester, Providence, Lawrence, Springfield-Holyoke-Chicopee, Hartford, New Haven, Bridgeport, Albany-Schenectady-Troy, Allentown-Bethlehem-Easton, Scranton-Wilkes-Barre, New York-Northeastern New Jersey, Philadelphia, Baltimore, Washington.

Based, in part, on recent statistics for metropolitan definitions in International Urban Research, 1959.

17. Emerging Urban Patterns

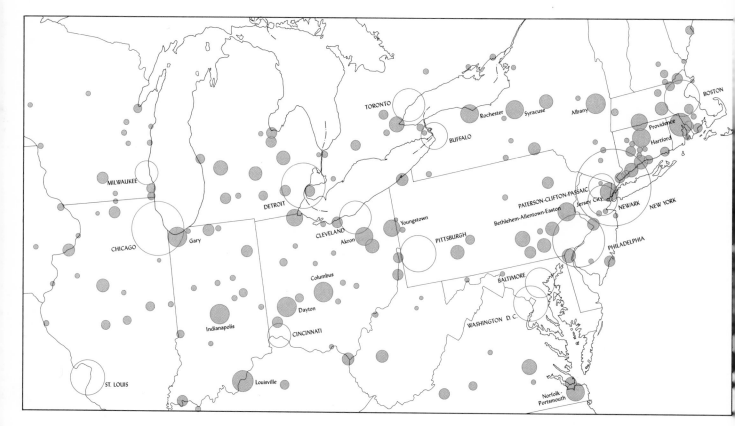

**Figure 17–2. EASTERN NORTH AMERICA:
LARGE AND MEDIUM-SIZED CITIES**

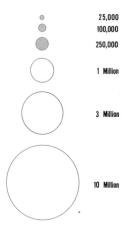

●	25,000
●	100,000
●	250,000
○	1 Million
○	3 Million
○	10 Million

North America. Many city groupings are co-alescing to form regional clusters, centered around two or more large cities. In North America, the peripheral expansion of large cities has been phenomenal since World War II. The urbanized northeastern Atlantic Seaboard—"Megalopolis"*—is the largest aggregation of city

*To Jean Gottmann the term has two meanings: first, a general connotation of "great city" (used earlier by Geddes and Mumford); second, as "the great *city of ideas* that predetermines and commands the material world in which we live, and this greater city of ideas [is] called Megalopolis" (Gottmann, 1961, 772).

Figure 17-3. SANTA CLARA VALLEY, CALIFORNIA: SETTLEMENT CHANGES

This valley lies directly south of San Francisco Bay. In 1875 it was entirely agricultural with San Jose as the local metropolis. By 1939 the northwestern part of the valley included some suburban outliers of San Francisco. In the 1960s the northern section had become part of the urbanized Bay Region. Based on materials in Broek, 1932, and White, 1965.

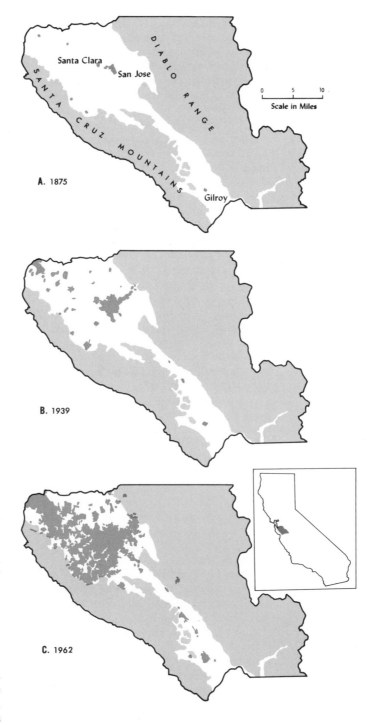

regions in the world. Between 1950 and 1960 its population increased by 18 percent; by 1965 it contained 35 million people. To the west another group of growing city regions extends from Pittsburgh to Cleveland and on to Detroit and the car-manufacturing towns of Michigan; these have about 14 million inhabitants. Still farther west begins the Chicago-Milwaukee complex with 10 million inhabitants, now extending around the south end of Lake Michigan. Megalopolis and these Midwestern city regions, with others like those of southwestern Ohio (2.5 million) and upstate New York–Toronto (3.5 million), may well fuse together before the end of the twentieth century (Figure 17-2).

In the western United States are two large and rapidly growing city regions. The more phenomenal is in southern California, largely a twentieth-century creation, with its main center at Los Angeles, but extending south to San Diego. Between 1950 and 1960 this widely spread urban belt increased in population by almost two-thirds, and by 1965 had 12 million inhabitants. The San Francisco Bay group grew almost as fast, with close to 6 million by 1965 (Figure 17-3). A third but smaller concentration extends along Puget Sound from Vancouver, British Columbia, to Tacoma, Washington.

Europe. Urbanized Europe differs in several respects from urbanized North America. The long-distance interaction of people, goods, and services, so common in North America, is less apparent in Europe. The greater age of the European city has given it a more distinct personality, which one hesitates to disregard by identifying multicity agglomerations. Furthermore, many large cities are adjacent to international boundaries: to join these may imply bonds that do not actually exist.

With these reservations in mind, we can outline groupings of large cities in Europe (Figure 17–4). London, with over 12 million inhabitants living in or near it, is the largest single metropolis of the continent. Heavily settled land stretches in all directions, especially along the coasts and toward the northwest, where Birmingham lies only a 100 miles away. Not far north of Birmingham, industrial agglomerations are but a short distance from each other: Stoke, Manchester, West Riding, Middlesbrough, Merseyside, Tyneside, Edinburgh, and Glasgow. In America such city regions would be brought under one heading, but in Britain we recognize five: London and the south-coast cities, Bristol and south Wales, central Scotland, Tyne-Tees, and a lenticular-shaped area running north from the Midlands and including Lancashire and Yorkshire.

Across the English Channel and the North Sea a great complex of cities stretches from the coastal and tidal river ports to the upper Rhine Basin and Bavaria. The international borders of France, the Benelux countries, and West Germany run between many cities in the northern part of this grouping. As economic integration proceeds and nationalism slowly declines, linkages increase between these cities. With urbanized Britain added, this dynamic and diversified region becomes comparable to the North American Megalopolis.

In the Low Countries the main city regions lie close together. Largest in the Netherlands are Rotterdam, Amsterdam, and The Hague, with short distances to many other towns including Utrecht. By the end of this century the urbanized region of the western Netherlands, already called *Randstad* (ring-city), will form one interconnected system with individual towns separated from each other by carefully preserved greenbelts. A similar development typifies Belgium, where Brussels, Antwerp,

Figure 17–4. WESTERN AND CENTRAL EUROPE: LARGE AND MEDIUM-SIZED CITIES

For the sake of cartographic clarity, cities of medium size below 65,000 population have been omitted. The sizes of dots and circles are not comparable to those of Figure 17–2.

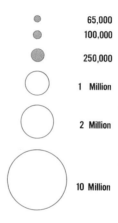

•	65,000
•	100,000
●	250,000
○	1 Million
○	2 Million
○	10 Million

Ghent, and Liège are the main foci of urbanization. These urbanized sections, unlike their Netherlands' counterparts, extend across the borders into France to join with Lille and nearby industrial towns, and into Germany to link up with Aachen and the Ruhr-Rhine cities.

The Ruhr-Rhine complex of cities, with 11 million people, is unique in that it has so many nuclei. No part dominates, although Düsseldorf is the "headquarters" city, Essen the center for heavy industry, and Köln (Cologne) a metropolis with diversified industry. The Rhine and its tributaries connect these expanding cities with others, including Frankfurt am Main, Mannheim-Ludwigshafen, Karlsruhe, Stuttgart, and the Saar, with München (Munich) and Nürnberg (Nuremberg) beyond.

The Paris conurbation, expanding northwestward along the Seine River, lies some distance from the other major cities of France, and might therefore appear isolated. However, a network of road, water, and rail routes connects

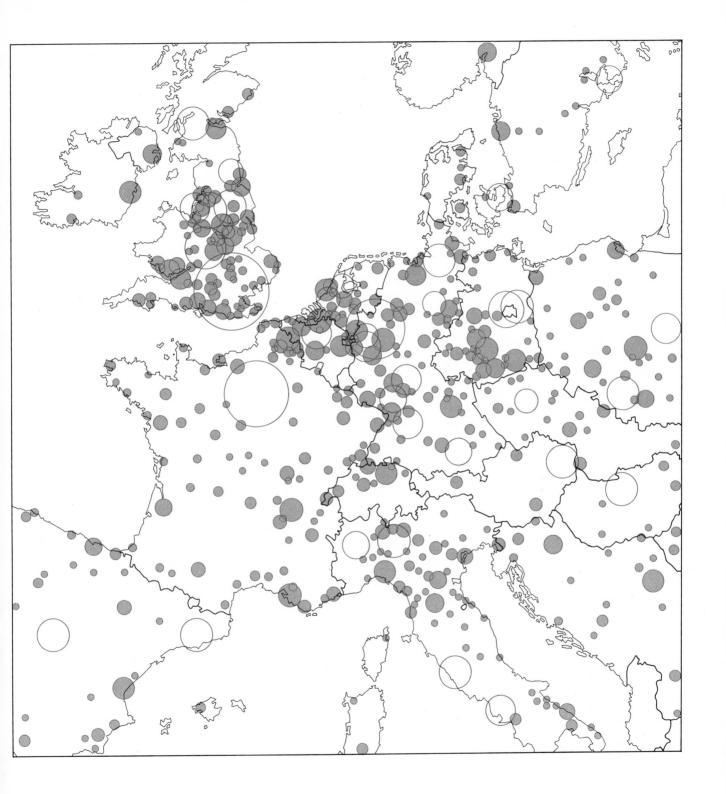

it with the urbanized peripheral regions of the country.

The borders between West Germany, East Germany, and Czechoslovakia intervene between groups of city regions that reach from Hamburg in the northwest, through Hannover, Magdeburg, and Berlin in central Germany, to Dresden and Leipzig in Saxony, and to Praha (Prague) in Bohemia. This varied group grows more slowly than the cities along the axis of the Rhine, mostly because the industrial metropolises of East Germany share in the population stagnation of that country.

In Upper Silesia the coalfield-industrial towns form a closely knit complex without any dominant center. Elsewhere in Europe city regions are comparatively isolated. While Madrid, Athens, and Barcelona each have their share of satellite towns, in none of these has an urbanized region developed. In northern Italy, however, Turin and Milan are the main centers of a growing urbanized area that includes many small and medium-sized towns.

Japan. Outside North America and Europe, groupings of city regions are rare, although some very large individual cities have grown rapidly in recent decades. The main exception to this is Japan, where northern Kyushu and the densely populated southern half of Honshu include a number of closely connected thriving centers. In the last two decades industrialization and commercialization have swelled in-migration from the country and smaller towns. The largest conurbations, Tokyo-Yokohama and Osaka-Kobe, are joined by high-speed rail service. The industrial centers at the strait where Honshu and Kyushu come together form another growth point.

Soviet Union. Groupings of city regions are conspicuously absent in the Soviet Union. Like all great cities, Moscow and Leningrad have their satellite settlements. Elsewhere, except for the Donets industrial region, there are no urban areas with many more than a million inhabitants. One reason for this is the large size of the populated territory of the Soviet Union. Another has to do with government policy: Successive groups of national planners have consciously tried to develop the Soviet economy on a regional basis. Thus, while many cities number between 100,000 and 1 million, there are no dominant groupings among them. Furthermore, many sectors of the Soviet economy remain only partly developed. Surprisingly many people still work in agriculture; if farming had been modernized, they long since would have swelled the number of city dwellers. By restricting service and consumer industries, the Soviet authorities provided an effective brake to the growth of metropolises and, incidentally, to the wealth and diversity that go with them.

Other Regions. Elsewhere in the underdeveloped and partly developed regions of the world, industrialization lies like a thin veneer over rural ways of life. Large cities are few, mostly associated with administration and other governmental functions, or they result from Western-oriented trading operations. When they are the main trading ports, their population includes a high proportion of their country's industry. They lack, nevertheless, the broad range of metropolitan activities and the diversity of occupations associated with great cities in North America and Europe.

The Qualities and Problems of Metropolitan Life

The Individual and the System. It is paradoxical that great cities, where increasing numbers live and newcomers arrive each day, are said to lack the graces of life, or even strangle the more valuable aspects of civilization. A national commission set up in the 1930s to investigate conditions in Britain's industrial cities reported "a vast—and many would add alarming—growth of population in London and Southeastern England largely at the expense of the rest of the country." London had absorbed, between 1931 and 1939, one-third of the national population growth. The results were "overcrowding, an increase in land values, the absorption of open spaces, smoke and noise and desolation, traffic congestion and long daily journeys, damage to health and national income from loss of vitality and waste of working hours in sickness and travelling, and the burdens of palliative services" (Barlow, 1940).

In a contemporary work Lewis Mumford added to the catalog of woes (Mumford, 1938). A polemical but scholarly writer on the quality of city life, Mumford has recently repeated his criticisms. He sees parallels between the modern city and ancient Rome. "They have come back today: the arena, the tall tenement, the mass contests and exhibitions, the football matches, the international beauty contests, the striptease made ubiquitous by advertisement, the constant titillation of the senses by sex, liquor and violence—all in true Roman style. So too, the multiplication of bathrooms and the over-expenditure on broadly paved motor roads, and above all, the massive collective concentration on glib ephemeralities of all kinds performed with supreme technical audacity . . ." (Mumford 1961, 242).

Many share these pessimistic views about metropolitan life, feeling that only a reorientation of values can save the modern city from becoming a repository of incurable ills. The opposite can also be argued. Life in great cities may have its problems, but increasing numbers vote for it; few suffer inhibitions about living in a metropolis of a developed country. The very large Western cities attract with completeness, variety, and range of choices. They are the centers of affairs. If there is much to spend money on, wages and salaries are higher than in smaller places. Hall, in his perceptive book about planning the London region, argues that the variety of life in a great city can satisfy everyone (Hall, 1963, 38). Even Mumford had to admit: "At present the world-cities . . . contain many of the best elements of man's heritage" (Mumford, 1938, 230). No one gives total criticism or approbation of city life. Though all applaud the diversity of the metropolis, many agree with Mumford that modern elements in its way of life too often lack "the human scale."

The modern metropolis offers an experience unique in human history. Most of its citizens share more or less in its many facets, though each leads his individual life. Whereas a village or small town presents personal associations near at hand, uncomplicated by spatial discontinuities, the city has become a phenomenon of quite a different scale. A city dweller has diffuse spatial associations; in the course of a single day he may meet and speak to a hundred people—many of them strangers or mere acquaintances—travel many miles from one part of the city region to another, and develop a feeling of rootlessness that persists after he returns home from work.

It is useful to think of a large city as a functioning whole, a system with interlocking parts, a complex with a "nodal" unity. Actually, most city folk conduct their daily business and even live through their entire lives without ever acquiring this holistic sense of their urban environment. They consider a city region a series of places—neighborhoods, districts, areas—some known intimately, others only in passing, many not at all.

To the knowledgeable, residents identify themselves by where they live, whether in a new suburb marked only by a real-estate signboard, in an area of recent housing around an older settlement, or in the city center. Naturally, they have the closest place associations with those buildings, streets, and organizations that have become familiar over a length of time. The difficult living conditions in slum districts are mitigated by numerous close contacts with relatives and longtime friends. In spite of these community sentiments, the handling of public affairs is usually left to the distant city authorities. Yet the city neighborhood offers the average citizen an opportunity to participate directly in city government. John Dewey took a strong stand in this matter: "Unless local community life can be restored, the public cannot adequately resolve its most urgent problem: to find and identify itself. Democracy must begin at home and its home is the neighbourly community" (as quoted in Dickinson, 1964, 573).

Metropolitan Problems and Planning. The individual living in a metropolis faces daily problems he is powerless to solve. The distance between his work and his home demands time and energy. Participation in city life creates tensions. The repair of decaying buildings, disposal of wastes, abatement of smoke and noise, these and other matters are beyond the powers of the individual.

The responsibility falls to local, regional, and national governments to keep up and improve the cities, and to engage professional city and regional planners who understand future as well as present needs. Citizens acting individually or in groups also attempt to bring changes for the better. Many countries grant power to local and other levels of government to shape the physical and, to a certain extent, the social nature of cities. This century has seen the rapid growth of interest in urban matters. Despite this, modern society still seems ill equipped to cope with the city's burgeoning problems. So far, theoretical discussions and many practical plans provide no agreed formula for urban design.

Though countries vary in the degree of government control, all modern ones already show the effects of planning on population distribution, transportation systems, patterns of land use, and in reconstruction of urban areas.

In the United States the federal government has linked major cities with superhighways, and created new road systems within the cities themselves. These changes inevitably affect the use of adjacent land. The federal government also has sponsored or supported schemes of "urban renewal"—physical reconstruction in and around the city center within national guidelines. However, there never has been a clear mandate for the large-scale rectification of land use within the cities. Little comprehensive planning has been done on a regional basis. The American genius excels in wholesale attack on a specific problem or a related group of problems, but fails to coordinate the different programs. Many argue that this is only proper, that too much government control would destroy what they think is a laissez-faire political and social system. They admit that problems exist but maintain that individuals or groups should gradually solve them. Others insist that the political system is mixed—laissez-faire *and* planned—and that both public and private elements should work at, even compete in, shaping the environment.

Concerning the cities of the United States eastern seaboard, Gottmann writes: "Laissez-faire or interference? The present period, with its great momentum of change, has had to ask [the question] again to cope with the remarkable concentration of population and activities in Megalopolis, where cities have been breaking out of old bounds. But the purpose . . . here is not to defend labor against employers, nor to call public authorities to limit the freedom of action of private business. For quite some time governments have been exerting their rights to interfere in these areas. Rather it is a call for the reform of the governmental structure, with a view toward securing better coordination and more far-sighted policies in a period of rapid change" (Gottmann, 1961, 744).

In western Europe both local and national governments have been granted wider powers to deal with the problems of large conurbations. In Britain, for example, no land can be developed or building altered unless the proposed change conforms to detailed zoning ordinances (development plans) laboriously worked out between planning agencies of local and national governments. Under this system the government holds considerable control of land use. Town planning in western Europe gives attention to detail unmatched in the United States: streets and roads are architecturally tidy, advertising is muted, new development minutely regulated. Until recently, though, the big problems associated with metropolitan aggregations were attacked only in piecemeal fashion. Now at last, rapidly compounding problems are being met by comprehensive programs for redistributing population, locating industry, and coordinating and improving transportation systems (see p. 412). The basic political problem in European as in American planning is to achieve a balance between governmental control and private action.

Metropolitan Migrations. Individual mobility characterizes metropolitan life. Migrants from other countries, from rural areas, from small towns and different city regions, commuters between residence and work, all combine to create a society on the move. Foreign settlers always have been attracted to large cities.

Though fewer enter the United States than formerly, most locate in such places. The large majority from Europe enter via the east coast ports. In 1960 over 80 percent of the almost ten million foreign-born residents of the United States lived in metropolitan areas, over one-fourth in New York. Less than 2 percent resided on farms. Of the two million emigrating to the United States between 1955 and 1960, three-fourths settled in cities, one-eighth in smaller towns, and one-eighth on farms or in nonfarm rural residence.

Immigrants in Europe also tend to concentrate in cities. In France, Algerians and others go to Paris and Marseille. In West Germany the mass of Italian, Greek, Turkish, and other immigrant workers locate in industrial centers like the Ruhr, Frankfurt am Main, and Köln. In Britain during the 1950s the influx of West Indians, Pakistanis, and Indians went especially to London and Birmingham.

In both North America and western Europe most migrants to cities come from small towns. Rural migrants also make up a sizable number; however, as the years pass this group forms a decreasing proportion of the population. Migration between city regions provides another important component. With the increasing affluence and ease of transportation, large cities continually exchange some of their populations. In the United States between 1955 and 1960, almost seven million of the residents of S.M.S.As. numbering over 250,000 moved to another large S.M.S.A. Of course, with each pair of cities exchanging people, one of them has a net gain—as from eastern to western cities (see Chapter 19). Proper interest in net migration should not make us forget the gross migration volume, which involves far more people (Figure 17–5).

Most people reside a good part of their lives in one city region, though they may move to another location, perhaps in the same neighborhood, but very often from central areas to the suburbs. Such moves may occur more than once as family income rises and more expensive housing becomes possible. In contrast, other groups are drawn toward the city center. Many of these are single people who work there, or retired and elderly folk. Others are minority groups who for reasons of poverty or discrimination cannot follow the mass exodus to more spacious suburban living.

The ebb and flow of residential migrations, coupled with expanding nonresidential land uses, lead inexorably to depopulation of the old city core. This area of population loss expands, and eventually engulfs old suburbs built decades before. Near the heart of the city some islands of minority groups increase, and new housing schemes may bring population gains to small areas; but these only tend to emphasize the more general decrease. In London the region of depopulation spread from its seventeenth-century heart to an area covering 4 square miles in the 1890s, 82 square miles in the 1920s, and 360 square miles in the 1950s. The same process is at work in other European and American cities. Peak populations pass outward from the old city, each peak lower in density per unit area as its distance from the center increases.

In response to the suburban trend, many jobs have moved out into newly built-up areas. Shopping facilities, office blocks, medical clinics, educational institutions, and industrial plants often draw their employees and clientele from locations well outside the old city. These developments add crosstown streams to the traffic focusing on the center.

Commuting: The Daily Journey to Work. Jobs follow but slowly the outward flow of population to the residential suburbs. The old city center, sometimes refurbished with new buildings and facilities, remains the chief employer. The journey to work even early in this century had become a common aspect of metropolitan life. Today hundreds of thousands travel each morning into lower Manhattan, central London, and inner Paris—and leave in the late afternoon. The daily tide comes and goes by commuter trains above and below ground level, by bus systems, by fleets of private cars, and in some countries by bicycle.

In America, and to a growing extent in Europe, the private car provides the main means of personal transportation, permitting further diffusion of residence out in the suburban periphery. In North America new highways run to, through, and around most cities.

The new freeways, built on the assumption that Americans like to go to work by car (some assert that this journey is the modern citizen's last resort of individualism), seem a massive rescue operation to maintain vital links between the more and more widely spaced home and job locations.

The new roads are good and wide, and travel is usually fast. Unfortunately, they do not lead to the car commuters' destinations—shops, offices, factories—packed closely together downtown where parking space is scarce. Freeways and parking lots are essentially noncentral land uses: They are means to an end, which is the mix of jobs and facilities in the core. The new freeways bring more cars downtown, but at the expense of traffic congestion and space-eating parking lots.

Car commuting in the United States has brought the decline of public mass transportation systems. Only in New York, Chicago, and Philadelphia do subway and rail bring most workers to their jobs. A few other cities, including Boston and Baltimore, have managed to maintain important rail systems. Now the federal government is assisting metropolitan areas to rebuild mass-transit facilities, in some cases from a very small base. Of these, the most revolutionary is that of the San Francisco Bay Area Rapid Transit District (BARTD). To be completed by 1971, this is the first new mass-transit system to be developed in the United States since before 1920. High-speed computer-controlled trains will run on 75 miles of track. Relatively long distances between stations in outlying areas of the Bay Region remind one of suburban railways; short distances between the stations in city centers recall local transit.

While getting commuters to use old or new public facilities may be an exercise in practical persuasion, the problem of traffic congestion at the core remains. American and European experiments to bar private cars from main shopping streets have met with mixed results. More radical proposals involve taxing cars that use central areas, or banning them entirely from wide sections many square miles in extent.

"Quarters." Since ancient times cities have contained quarters and ghettos where minority

Figure 17–5. UNITED STATES: INTERMETROPOLITAN MIGRATION, 1955–1960

The map shows three aspects of migration for Standard Metropolitan Statistical Areas of the United States with over 250,000 inhabitants in 1960: (1) number of residents in 1960 who lived in a different S.M.S.As. in 1955; (2) percentage of 1960 population (aged 5 and over) who lived in other S.M.S.As. in 1955; (3) intermetropolitan flows of more than 10,000 persons between 1955 and 1960.

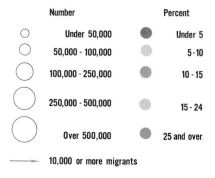

1960 Population (Aged 5 years and over) Resident in other S. M. S. As. in 1955

Number	Percent
Under 50,000	Under 5
50,000 - 100,000	5 - 10
100,000 - 250,000	10 - 15
250,000 - 500,000	15 - 24
Over 500,000	25 and over.

→ 10,000 or more migrants

populations live. Some minorities, especially in quarters of Middle Eastern and Oriental cities, performed particular functions as traders, metalworkers, soldiers, etc. In modern Western cities, ghettos and their distinctive populations sometimes pose social and political problems for whole nations.

Metropolitan segregation has complex origins. Some groups feel a strong cohesion that sets them apart from the main body of citizens. A different language, a distinctive skill or occupation, a religion, a common country of origin, these and other forces bind such peoples together for mutual benefit. On the other hand, some live together because they are rejected by the majority and subject to discrimination.

Such groups in large cities are usually poor, being recent immigrants or victims of prejudice.

They occupy old tenements and run-down housing abandoned by the majority. The presence of foreigners and minorities gives the very largest urban centers—New York, London, Paris—a cosmopolitan atmosphere. In London the residential areas around the business and fashionable shopping and office areas (the "City" and "West End") house many immigrant groups segregated from the main mass of Londoners, and at least partly separated from each other.

In New York the Negro population is concentrated heavily in Harlem on Manhattan Island; in Chicago on the south side of the Loop; in Los Angeles in the Watts district and other areas. New York has successively absorbed different immigration groups, among them Irish, Italians, Puerto Ricans, Jews, and Negroes. In turn, each has been segregated socially and residentially, then as assimilation developed has moved from its inner quarter outward to disperse into other housing areas. Negroes find their acceptance much slower than that of other groups. It will be a long time before the Negro ghettos of large American cities disappear (Morrill, 1965).

Since about 1955 southern Europeans, especially Italians, have poured into the large industrial cities of continental western Europe, mostly West Germany. In some cases housing

17. Emerging
Urban
Patterns

projects accommodate the groups. In contrast to the American situation, few of these migrant workers intend to settle permanently in the countries where they have come to work.

The "gray zone" is that belt around the center of the Occidental city occupied by immigrant and minority groups and by transitory populations. Some of these districts have very dense settlement, with acre after acre of multi-storied tenements. When the old buildings are torn down, nonresidential land uses often replace them, such as business structures and new inner-city highway networks. Industry and services of many kinds favor locations around the central core: warehousing, trucking, parking, printing, and certain kinds of retailing. Older nonresidential enterprises such as railroad terminals, classification yards, and factories interrupt the zones of residential land use.

Many living in this transitional zone of "social deterioration" (as it was classed by Park, Burgess, and Mackenzie, 1925) are long-term residents. Also living close to the city core are many transients, including young single women who stay for a few weeks to a few years, working in offices, banks, or other business.

The large metropolitan university in American cities forms a distinctive human and physical complex. Founded in the nineteenth century on the then outskirts of the city, it now has become hemmed in by the built-up city. Often students in great numbers occupy the slum or near-slum residential areas surrounding the universities. Some American campuses draw close to 50,000 people daily—students, faculty, and office staff—and their traffic patterns rival those of a medium-sized city. Some universities provide special housing for the students, but in many big cities the majority room nearby, have apartments, or are commuters. Faculty members sometimes appropriate the better residential areas near the university, or join the flight to the suburbs.

Urban Renewal in the United States. The fabric of cities needs constant repair. Completion of some single great renewal project does not mean that all is finished, but that efforts must shift to another area. Time moves on, buildings deteriorate, slums expand, business and industrial areas become outdated, streets need widening or replacement.

Many American cities (and European ones too) let things slide during the 1930s and 1940s. By the 1950s they faced a crisis which only massive expenditure of public funds could solve. The federal government stepped in and formed the Urban Renewal Administration.

Beginning about 1950, enormous sums have been spent on lifting the once familiar face of "downtown" and the gray zone around it. Projects have cleared areas by the square mile, especially in the older sections of eastern cities like New York, Philadelphia, Boston, and Washington. Block on block of slums have fallen; in their stead rise massive apartment houses. New skyscraper offices replace outworn buildings on the margins of the business districts. After the dust settles and the newly minted parts of the city appear, it becomes clear that even the largest rebuilding programs are no panacea for metropolitan ills. Relocating slum tenants in a relatively short time is exceedingly difficult, and has been less than successful in many cases. Other people find no adequate replacements for jobs they held in torn-down buildings.

Social dislocation, critics claim, vitiates much of the urban renewal program. It is said that instead of creating so many hundred or thousand housing units, adequate enough in themselves, efforts should concentrate on creating a community spirit. According to many experts, the vital theme of urban renewal should be to plan or reconstruct neighborhoods.

As renewal projects in specific locations are put into action, other areas deteriorate. In some cities the amount of inadequate housing increases during the time span of renovation programs. To be effective, physically and socially, renewal must be a continuous process, metropolitan in its scope (Glazer, 1965, 204).

Suburbanization. Each new suburb, flung farther and farther from the center of the city region, has its distinctive flavor. Around most

Singapore builds many apartment houses for its low-income groups. These modern, airy "flats" are a great improvement over the crowded slums behind the waterfront. Architects, bowing to the custom of drying the washing on long poles, provide metal holders next to the windows. [A Shell photograph]

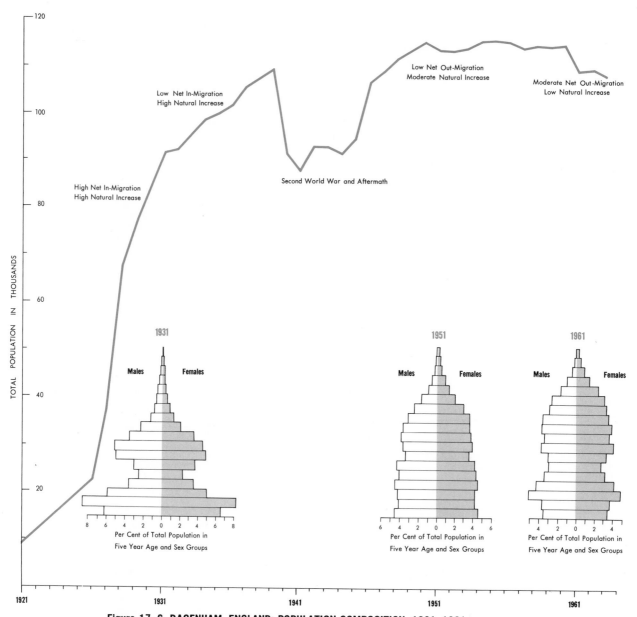

Figure 17–6. DAGENHAM, ENGLAND: POPULATION COMPOSITION, 1931–1961

The population of this industrial-residential suburb in east London rose sharply in the late 1920s and early 1930s. After the interruption caused by World War II and its aftermath, a peak population was reached in 1955, when a slow decline began. The age and sex diagrams show a change from a population of young adults and children (1931) to one with a large proportion in middle age (1961). Data are from census reports and annual statistical reviews published by the General Register Office, London.

Figure 17–7. GROWTH AXES FOR THE PARIS REGION

The salient features of the "master plan" for the Paris region, proposed in 1965, are large new urban zones as a counter to the monolithic nature of metropolitan Paris; new cities in these urban zones; the reconstruction and development of urban centers in Paris; and the guiding of growth along axes toward the sea parallel to the Seine River. Based on a map in Ambassade de France, 1965.

▬	New Urban Zones
▬	Existing Urban Complex
▬	Forests
● ·	New Cities
–	Urban Centers to be Renovated

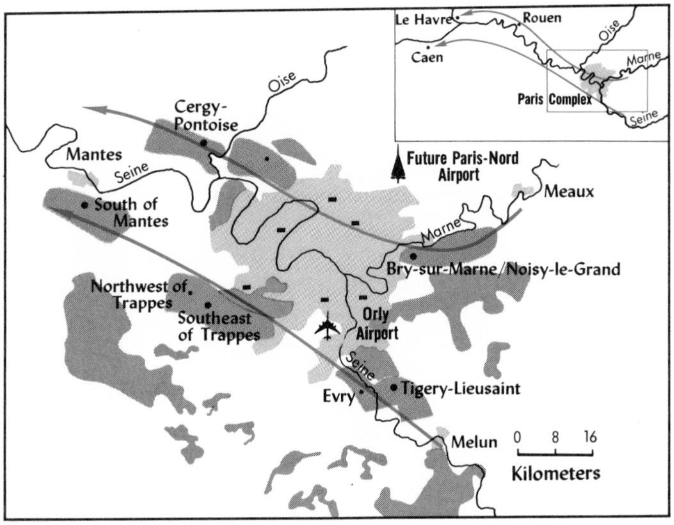

American cities the new suburb cuts into sparsely occupied territory. At first there are few schools, churches, and other social services, and only a makeshift shopping and business area. With not many jobs nearby, the working population mostly commutes daily from their dormitory to the central city. As time passes, families earn higher incomes, acquire a second car, and develop new interests. Enterprising groups emerge to diversify the economic livelihood of the place, and a sense of community impresses itself on the population.

In the initial stage the population grows rapidly. When house construction ends, growth remains high since the new suburbanites are mostly young married adults—there are many births and few deaths. The numerous children require large expenses for education. But as the suburbs age, the schools are half used, even empty. Children grow up, leave for college, take jobs elsewhere, marry, and settle in newer communities: "eventually out-migration begins as the now grown children of the original immigrants leave; as the population grows older, the death rate increases and the number of births drops; depopulation begins when the net out-migration becomes greater than the declining natural increase; a new dimension may be added when deaths exceed births and natural decrease is added to net out-migration" (Webb, 1963, 142). Figure 17–6 shows part of this sequence of events at Dagenham, an industrial-residential suburb to the east of the center of London.

For various reasons many large companies in the United States construct entire suburbs, each development usually within a limited price range. This, plus the general desire to live with one's own kind, tends to segregate suburban populations into districts indentifiable by income levels. Restrictive covenants to property titles and outside-the-law bars to minority groups make many suburbs white reservations. In 1960 in the Twin Cities area of Minneapolis–St. Paul, only 2,500 of the total of 27,500 "nonwhite" inhabitants—Indians and Negroes—lived outside the two central cities. At that date in 20 suburbs with over 440,000 inhabitants, only 1,360 were not white.

In western Europe governments regulate to

17. Emerging Urban Patterns

411

a far larger extent the building of new suburbs, rapidly providing schools, sewer lines, social services, and utilities. Suburbs develop in an already densely settled rural and small-town landscape. Income segregation is less apparent. Many suburbs are extensions of older heterogeneous settlements, and begin life already with a sense of place.

The Outer Fringe. Today personal mobility makes it possible to live in pleasant country miles beyond the built-up edge of the city. Those who can afford it may have a country home as well as an apartment or town house. The "stockbroker belts" around major financial capitals may be more than 50 miles from the city center.

At such distances the land area per person can be very large: the amount increases geometrically in successive concentric belts of city-oriented settlement. With increased efficiency and speed of transportation, people of middle income find formerly exclusive "exurbanite" zones within their means for settlement. As a result, quite far from some of the largest North American and west European cities, there are many growing, but discontinuous and disconnected, residential settlements with commuting populations.

Greenbelts, Growth Points, and New Towns. In the two decades since the end of World War II, the idea of comprehensive city planning has advanced far in western Europe. In 1945 the countries—victors and vanquished alike—were in a parlous state, their economies in disarray, cities in ruins, populations dislocated. A surge in planning accompanied postwar recovery. Far-reaching plans emerged for London, Paris, the Ruhr-Rhine, and Holland's Randstad (Figure 17–7). These plans provide for the preservation of greenbelts, controlled expansion of suburbs, slum clearance and house building, and the redistribution of central-city inhabitants into new towns and new growth points. The impetus for these policies came from various sources.

Britain has already put into practice a number of new concepts. London had become too

Figure 17–8. SOUTHEAST ENGLAND: PLANNED POPULATION REDISTRIBUTION

The map shows the existing program of planned population migrations to "new towns" and "expanded towns." The zone between the outer limit of the greenbelt and the main built-up area of London is almost all part of the greenbelt, and is not available for any extensive building. The proposed program provides for large new cities and expanded cities, many of them far from central London.

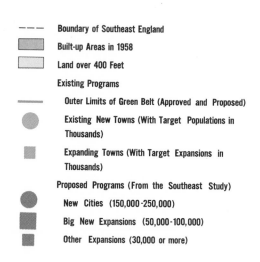

- - - Boundary of Southeast England

Built-up Areas in 1958

Land over 400 Feet

Existing Programs

Outer Limits of Green Belt (Approved and Proposed)

Existing New Towns (With Target Populations in Thousands)

Expanding Towns (With Target Expansions in Thousands)

Proposed Programs (From the Southeast Study)

New Cities (150,000-250,000)

Big New Expansions (50,000-100,000)

Other Expansions (30,000 or more)

crowded, its suburbs formless, its center congested, its quality of life deteriorated. During World War II plans were made for the peace to come. Among many prescriptions for the country's ills was the Greater London Plan (1944), which accepted the conclusions of the Barlow report (see above, page 402). The plan proposed that suburban house construction be restricted, that a greenbelt of open country be maintained around the built-up area, and that a number of new towns be placed beyond the greenbelt some 20 to 35 miles from the center of London. Each new town would be self-contained, having its own manufacturing industries and being peopled by families from central London. They were to be on the "garden city" model, advocated in the nineteenth and early

Existing New Towns
Proposed New Towns

Miles
0   50   100

Scale in Miles
0   10   20   30   40

Peterborough
11
1
Norwich
10
Northampton
9
7
Ipswich
10
3
10
10
Bedford
10
7
6
Bletchley
Luton 140 Stevenage
13
Welwyn 50 Stanstead 10
Garden City
80 28 Harlow
Hatfield 130
Hemel
Hempstead
100 Southend-on-Sea
Swindon
20
L O N D O N
Newbury
Reading
50 Bracknell
10 Medway
Towns
3
38 N O R T H   D O W N S Maidstone
20
3 Ashford 15
75
Crawley
S O U T H   D O W N S Hastings
Southampton-
Portsmouth
Poole

twentieth centuries by Ebenezer Howard. During the interwar era an example had been built, Welwyn Garden City, a private venture, 20 miles north of London.

Eight sites were selected (Figure 17–8), and with detailed meticulous plans complete, building got under way in the late 1940s. A public corporation developed each town, constructing houses, factories, neighborhoods, local shopping centers, business areas, social facilities, and schools. By 1962 the combined population of the new towns had reached 265,000, and they were attracting visitors from all over the world. With this experience, Britain began to create other new towns in the industrial northern regions.

In retrospect, the original plans and their execution seemed somewhat doctrinaire. Controls relaxed. But other problems arose. Despite restrictions, an enormous number of people moved into the outer ring beyond the greenbelt; many towns up to 40 miles from the center of London expanded to double their number of inhabitants. The original population ceilings for the new towns became unrealistic.

Even in the mass, people are unpredictable. For example, fertility changes its pattern from time to time, confounding all estimates. The birth rate in England rose during the 1950s and early 1960s. At the same time immigration from overseas increased. Not only were the new towns permitted to admit more than first planned, but a number of selected old towns in southeastern England also experienced planned expansion. Even this failed to solve the problem of redistribution of people and jobs. "Industry has grown rapidly in the New Towns partly as a reflection of the rapid growth in the southeast as a whole; people, especially skilled workers, have come to the New Towns not only from London but from the rest of Britain; the rise in the birth rate is causing unexpected growth both in the New Towns and in London where it creates a new and a continuing overspill problem. Thus the problem of the growth of London, which the overspill policy was designed to solve once for all, has been exported to the New Towns and the ring of countryside within which they lie" (Hall, 1966, 51).

These issues, plus a heightened sense of urgency, led to larger proposals for the near future, including planned new cities with a third of a million or more inhabitants and radical expansion of many older cities and towns (Figure 17–8). The main change in policy concerns not only size, but also distance. The new designs envisage the whole of southeastern England as an interlinked system of settlement focusing on London.

Governmental Structure. The proliferation of governmental units seems at times to be the most intractable of urban problems. In the United States, traditions of local autonomy have resulted in scores (in some city regions, hundreds) of different governmental units, often created for specific purposes (e.g., airports, schools, parks, highways, hospitals). Among the scattered welter of responsibilities, problems grow which, because there is no one to deal with them comprehensively, remain nobody's problem, and thus go unsolved until disaster comes near. Then crash programs must be initiated, with new governmental units to administer them.

Some feel that the only solution is to establish a new order of government with total dissolution of the old, replacing local autonomy with metropolitan or regional control. But there are two reasons why such a radical cure will not do. Past experience shows that the best forms of government blend old ideas with the new. As Chinitz argues: "A community that waits for a whole new order to replace the old, and does not confront the challenge of reconciling the new with the old, runs a serious risk of waiting in vain" (Chinitz, 1965, 138). Further, there is no agreed solution either to metropolitan government or to the application of new technologies to metropolitan problems. It would be foolhardy to go to the extreme and establish a government that might be entirely unsuitable. Informed observers see no immediate solution. Chinitz proposes ". . . that the new order will not be implemented efficiently by private choice, that it cannot be implemented by the substitution of one giant local government where many existed before, and that a way must yet be found to inject a large measure of regional planning and decision" (Chinitz, 1965, 138–139).

Metropolitan governments, whether fragmented or unified, with or without planning machinery, face many issues, a number of which have been discussed in the above pages. In the United States the dominant themes in the late 1960s appear to be: rationalization of local taxation, elimination of poverty and its consequences, disposal of sewage and other wastes, provision of adequate water supplies, elimination of smoke, rebuilding and reconstruction, provision of recreational areas, and solution of internal and external transportation problems. Since a discussion of these issues is beyond the purpose of this book, it must suffice to say that the greatest success in solving them has gone to those city regions that have an adequate and continuing metropolitan planning organization, with enough political power to translate its proposals into action.*

*See, for example, the case of Stockholm, Sweden, where a city planning agency has operated since the seventeenth century. The forward-looking planning policies and actions of Stockholm are described in G. Sidenbladh, 1965.

Citations

Ambassade de France, *France: Town and Country Planning,* New York, 1965. [Map]

Barlow, A. M. (chairman) *Report of Royal Commission on the Distribution of the Industrial Population,* London, 1940.

Broek, J. O. M. *The Santa Clara Valley, California: A Study in Landscape Changes,* Utrecht, 1932. [Map]

Chinitz, B. "New York: A Metropolitan Region," *Scientific American,* 213 (September, 1965): 134–148.

Dickinson, R. E. *City and Region,* London, 1964.

Geddes, P. *Cities in Evolution,* London, 1915.

Glazer, N. "The Renewal of Cities," *Scientific American,* 213 (September, 1965): 195–204.

Gottmann, J. *Megalopolis: The Urbanized Northeastern Seaboard of the United States,* New York, 1961.

Hall, P. *London 2000,* London, 1963.

———. *The World Cities,* New York, 1966.

International Urban Research, *The World's Metropolitan Areas,* Berkeley, Calif., and Los Angeles, Calif., 1959.

Morrill, R. L. "The Negro Ghetto: Problems and Alternatives," *Geographical Review,* 55 (1965): 339–361.

Mumford, L. *The Culture of Cities,* New York, 1938.

———. *The City in History,* New York, 1961.

Park, R. E., Burgess, E. W., and Mackenzie, R. D. *The City,* Chicago, 1925.

Sidenbladh, G. "Stockholm, a Planned City," *Scientific American,* 213 (September, 1965): 107–118.

U.S. Bureau of the Census, *Census of Population: 1960, Subject Reports, Mobility for Metropolitan Areas,* Final Report PC (2), Washington, D.C., 1963. [Map]

Webb, J. W. "The Natural and Migrational Components of Population Changes in England and Wales, 1921–1931," *Economic Geography,* 39 (1963): 130–148.

White, C. L. "Sequent Occupance in the Santa Clara Valley, California," *Journal of the Graduate Research Center,* Dallas, Tex., 34 (1965): 1. [Map]

Further Readings

Abromisov, P., et al. *Construction and Reconstruction of Towns 1945–1957,* 3 vols., the first two in English and Russian, Moscow, 1958.

Borchert, J. R. "The Twin Cities Urbanized Area: Past, Present, and Future," *Geographical Review,* 51 (1961): 47–70.

Burton, I. "A Restatement of the Dispersed City Hypothesis," *Annals of the Association of American Geographers,* 49 (1959): 305–323.

Briggs, A. *Victorian Cities,* London, 1963.

Coppock, J. T., and Prince, H. C. (eds.) *Greater London,* London, 1964.

Dickinson, R. E. "The Geography of Commuting: The Netherlands and Belgium," *Geographical Review,* 47 (1957): 521–538.

Duncan, O. D., et al. *Metropolis and Region,* Baltimore, 1960.

Dyos, H. J. *The Victorian Suburb: A Study of the Growth* of *Camberwell,* London, 1961.

Ekistics, Reviews on the Problems and Science of Human Settlements, (monthly), Athens Center of Ekistics of the Athens Technological Institute, Athens, Greece, 1955–.

Freeman, T. W. *The Conurbations of Great Britain,* Manchester, 1959.

Frolic, B. M. "The Soviet City," *Town Planning Review,* 34 (1963): 285–306.

George, P., and Randet, P. *La région parisienne,* Paris, 1959.

Gibbs, J. P. (ed.) *Urban Research Methods,* Princeton, N.J., 1963.

Gravier, J-F. *Paris et le désert français,* Paris, 1958.

Isenberg, G. *Die Ballungsgebiete in der Bundesrepublik,* Bad Godesberg, 1957.

Mishchenko, G. Ye. "Satellite Towns and Cities of Moscow," *Soviet Geography,* 3 (1962): 35–43.

Murphy, R. E. *The American City: An Urban Geography,* New York, 1966.

Nelson, H. J. "The Spread of an Artificial Landscape over Southern California," *Annals of the Association of American Geographers,* 49 (1959): Supplement, 80–99.

Paris 1960, Paris, 1961.

Pred, A. "Intermetropolitan Location of American Manufacturing," *Annals of the Association of American Geographers,* 54 (1964): 165–180.

Rasmussen, S. E. *London, the Unique City,* London, 1934, 1960.

The Southeast Study, London, 1964.

Thomas, D. "London's Green Belt: The Evolution of an Idea," *Geographical Journal,* 129 (1963): 14–24.

Turner, R. (ed.) *India's Urban Future,* Berkeley, Calif., and Los Angeles, Calif.,1962.

Vernon, R. *Metropolis 1985,* New York, 1960.

Winsemius, J. "Randstad Holland," *Tijdschrift voor Economische en Sociale Geografie,* 51 (1960): 188–199.

Part V. Population Change

Everybody talks about the population problem. Like the weather, it differs from place to place. Unlike the weather, something can be done about it. Birth and death are not mere biologic facts; their incidence reflects cultural values and economic conditions. That is why this discussion of the dynamic aspects of population is placed at the end of this volume, after the reader has become acquainted with the differentiation in culture realms, in developed and underdeveloped countries, in countryside and metropolis.

Part V opens with an analysis of the changing patterns of fertility and mortality, and the resulting natural growth, pointing up the tremendous increases we must expect in Asia, Africa, and most of Latin America. The subsequent chapter surveys the different forms of spatial mobility, from the great transoceanic migrations in the past to current population movements within national borders. The last chapter considers the problems of rapid population growth. Though securing an adequate food supply doubtless is the fundamental and urgent issue, overcrowding the earth's habitable space raises other and equally serious questions concerning the quality of human life.

V. Population Change

Mass meeting in Pakistan. [Josephine Powell]

18. The Differential Growth of Population

Our age is one of great happenings, swift changes, and perplexing problems. Among them is the rapid growth of world population. Its number doubled between 1900 and 1964, and may double again by the turn of the century. This view of the earth as a whole, while important, hides significant variations between the parts. The merit of the geographic approach to the study of population lies in its emphasis on regional differences. Seen in this way, the much-quoted "world explosion of population" divides into a succession of bursts happening at different places at different times. This place-and-time perspective enables us to comprehend current growth patterns and from this vantage point to view the prospects.

Population Growth in the Past

Archeological evidence suggests that man at the end of the last glaciation (about 10,000 B.C.) lived as a roaming gatherer, sparsely scattered over the earth. As he wandered through changing environments and improved his means of acquiring food, his numbers gradually increased. By about 8000 B.C. there may have been some ten million people, widely dispersed throughout the world. Shortly after that date came the first population explosion in consequence of the invention and spread of agriculture, which could support many more than subsistence gathering.

At the opening of the Christian Era the earth's population added up to some 300 million, which means that the annual growth rate (compounded annually) had been only 0.06 percent over the previous 80 centuries. These estimates and the more reliable figures for recent times form the basis for Figure 18–1 and Table 18–1. Modern annual growth rates are phenomenal when compared to those of the past. They rose from 0.29 percent between 1650 and 1750 to about 2.00 percent today.

Prehistoric to Ancient Times. The rimlands of Asia and Nuclear America were the important centers of early farming. These agricultural communities supported five or more persons per square mile, a density many times that possible for gatherers. But the farmers were forced to migrate at irregular intervals, because of soil exhaustion or because their numbers had increased above the carrying capacity of the land.

After 4000 B.C. the rise of city-centered societies, linked with advances in farming, led to a fairly continuous zone of increasing population density which stretched from the Mediterranean Sea across southwestern Asia into India and, by way of the Central Asian oases, to China. However, shifting political power, warfare, and other calamities caused temporal and

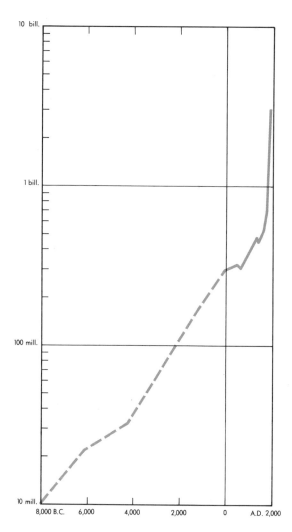

Figure 18–1. WORLD: POPULATION GROWTH FROM 8000 B.C.

This graph is drawn to logarithmic scale.

regional variations in growth. Where and when a strongly centralized empire enforced peace, the population grew rapidly: e.g., during the Persian Empire (550–425 B.C.), the Periclean Age in Athens (fifth century B.C.), the rule of Asoka in India (third century B.C.), the Augus-tan Age of the Roman Empire (first century A.D.), and the Han dynasty in China (202 B.C. to A.D. 220).

Other parts of the earth were but thinly occupied. Pastoral nomadism, particularly in its primitive form, permitted only small bands to roam the vast steppelands of Asia and North Africa. In Europe north of the Alps, until the expansion of the Roman Empire, the tribes practiced a simple agriculture which at best could support only moderate numbers. In the margins of the world where knowledge of farming had not yet penetrated, populations remained scanty.

Reasonably accurate estimates of some populations can be made for the time around the beginning of the Christian Era, when enumerations were conducted in various countries. However, these sources are difficult to interpret. Roman censuses counted only citizens (perhaps only males); Chinese records may not have been complete; those of ancient American empires are obscure in meaning. For other regions no early population data are available, although sometimes inferences can be made from archeological evidence, size of armies, tax lists, and contemporary writings.

The Roman Empire in A.D. 14 totaled about 55 million people, which increased but slightly during the two succeeding centuries (some scholars advocate higher figures). Administrators of the Han dynasty carried out two censuses for China: they yield estimates of 70 million for A.D. 2 and 60 million for A.D. 156. Ancient India left no enumerations, but it is believed that there were from 100 to 140 million during the reign of Asoka. By adding modest numbers for Africa south of the Sahara, northern Europe, central and northern Asia, Oceania, and the Americas, we arrive at a total of 300 million about the year A.D. 1.

Ancient to Modern Times. The earth's population doubled during the first sixteen centuries of the Christian Era, but the growth was neither steady nor evenly distributed. The fall of the Roman Empire led to the wholesale depopulation of some frontier regions in Europe. On the other hand, the Mediterranean lands were gen-

Table 18–1. World Population from 8000 B.C. to the Present

Date	Population, millions		Average annual increase		Number of generations
			Millions	Percent*	
8000 B.C.	10				
		Invention of agriculture, development of trade	.036	0.06	266
A.D. 1	300				
		Varied conditions in densely populated regions	.150	0.04	55
1650	545				
		More peaceful conditions	1.8	0.29	
1750	728				
		Beginning of social and economic revolutions	3.5	0.44	
1800	906				
		Rapid growth of worldwide trading system	5.3	0.51	
1850	1,171				
		Spread of economic growth within European culture area	8.7	0.64	
1900	1,608				
		Continued economic growth and World War I	10.1	0.59	12
1920	1,810				
		Growth and depression; the loaded pause	21.8	1.11	
1940	2,246				
		World War II and its aftermath	24.7	1.05	
1950	2,493				
		Spread of economic and social development	49.1†	1.81†	
1960	2,984				
		Continued economic growth	64.8†	2.15†	
1965	3,308				

* Rates of increase compounded annually.
† Amounts and rates of increase affected by improved collection of data.
SOURCE: Carr-Saunders, 1936, 42; Population Reference Bureau, *World Population Data Sheet,* Washington, 1965.

Four thousand years ago Mesopotamia was the most densely settled region on earth. Arbela (Erbil) was one of its earliest cities. The mound in the center consists of the flattened remains of many generations of buildings in the ancient city. The built-up areas around the mound are of later date. [Aerofilms, Ltd.]

Table 18–2. The Population of Europe: Ancient to Modern Times (millions)

Region	A.D. 1	350	600	800	1000	1200	1340*	1500
Greece and	3.0	2.0	1.2	2.0	5.0	4.0	2.0	1.5
Balkans	2.0	3.0	1.8	3.0			2.0	3.0
Iberia	6.0	4.0	3.6	4.0	7.0	8.0	9.5	8.3
Gaul	6.6	5.0	3.0	5.0				
France-Lowlands					6.0	10.0	19.0	16.0
Italy	7.4	4.0	2.4	4.0	5.0	7.8	9.3	5.5
Germany and	3.5	3.5	2.1	4.0	4.0	7.0	11.0	7.0
Scandinavia							0.6	0.5
British Isles	0.4	0.3	0.8	1.2	1.7	2.8	5.3	4.0
Slavia	4.0	4.8	2.8	6.0				
Poland, etc.					1.0	1.2	1.2	2.0
Russia					7.5	6.0	8.0	6.0
Hungary					1.0	2.0	2.0	2.0

* An estimate of Europe's population in 1400 is 40.7 million, a reduction of the 1340 estimate by 40 percent.

SOURCE: Russell, 1958, 148, with permission.

erally able to absorb the barbarian invaders. During the Dark Ages from the seventh to the tenth century, Europe was periodically ravaged by famine, plague, and the invasions by Arabs from the south, Vikings from the north, and Magyars from the east (Table 18–2).

In the tenth century began a long period of land colonization and a gradual revival of city life. For about three centuries the population increased, then leveled off as farmlands approached their limits of sustenance. In 1346 came another cycle of misery and death from the plague; in some regions the black death took one half of the population. Recovery was hampered by the Hundred Years' War between France and England.

The sixteenth century, on the whole, was a period of growth by which the population attained, then surpassed the level of 1340. There followed new losses, as in Germany during the Thirty Years' War (1618 to 1648), and with occasional outbreaks of bubonic plague. Europe remained at about the 100 million mark throughout most of the seventeenth century.

Southwest Asia and North Africa also lost population during medieval times. Mounted nomads invaded from Central Asia and Crusaders from western Europe, leading to slaughter, destruction, or neglect of irrigation systems. Epidemics of the plague and other diseases decimated the survivors. Not until the nineteenth century did these lands begin to regain their ancient population levels.

Fluctuations also characterized the population history of China, India, and other Asian countries. Numbers increased during periods of peace and order, when water control works expanded and food production rose. In turn, times of internal disorder had the opposite effect. At the beginning of the modern period, China's

Table 18-3. The Populations of the Continents, 1650–1965 (millions)

Date	Africa	Asia (excl. U.S.S.R.)	Europe (incl. U.S.S.R.)	North America	Middle and South America	Oceania	European culture area*
1650	100	327	103	1	12	2	118
1700	98	396	113	1	12	2	128
1750	95	475	144	1	11	2	158
1800	90	597	192	6	13	2	219
1850	125	741	274	26	33	2	335
1900	120	915	423	81	63	6	573
1920	140	967	485	115	92	9	701
1930	155	1,073	530	134	110	10	784
1940	172	1,213	579	144	132	11	866
1950	199	1,376	594	166	162	13	935
1960	254	1,679	641	199	206	16	1,062
1965	311	1,842	677	215	248	18	1,157

Percentage change (compounded annually)

1650–1700	−0.04	0.38	0.19	0.00	0.00	0.00	0.16
1700–1750	−0.06	0.37	0.49	0.00	−0.17	0.00	0.42
1750–1800	−0.11	0.46	0.58	3.41	0.29	0.00	0.65
1800–1850	0.12	0.39	0.72	2.98	2.08	0.00	0.86
1850–1900	0.47	0.44	0.87	2.30	1.65	2.23	1.07
1900–1920	0.77	0.28	0.67	1.73	1.92	2.05	1.01
1920–1930	1.02	1.05	0.89	1.54	1.80	1.06	1.12
1930–1940	1.05	1.24	0.89	0.72	1.84	0.95	1.00
1940–1950	1.47†	1.28	0.26	1.43	2.07	1.69	0.77
1950–1960	2.47†	2.01†	0.77	1.83	2.43†	2.10	1.28†
1960–1965	4.15†	1.95†	1.15	1.45	3.75†	2.60	1.70†

* The European culture area includes American Indian and other indigenous populations.
† Rates of increase affected by improved collection of population data.
SOURCE: Carr-Saunders, 1936; Population Reference Bureau, *World Population Data Sheet,* Washington, 1965.

population may have been in the order of 150 million, that of the Indian subcontinent 140 million.

The civilizations of Nuclear America supported substantial numbers. Estimates differ considerably, but it appears that by A.D. 1500 there were some 15 to 20 million people in the advanced regions from Mexico to north Chile. The Spanish conquests caused the collapse and depopulation of these empires.

V. Population Change

From the Seventeenth to the Twentieth Century. Table 18-3 and Figure 18-2 survey the populations of the continents at various dates from 1650 to 1965, and give average annual growth rates, calculated on a compounded basis. Nearer our own times estimates can be made with greater accuracy. Census enumeration and collection of birth and death data started in northern Europe in the eighteenth century. During the nineteenth century most modernizing countries adopted these procedures. By now nearly all countries have begun them, especially since, first the League of Nations, then the United Nations provided assistance in collecting the data. Carr-Saunders (1936) and Wilcox

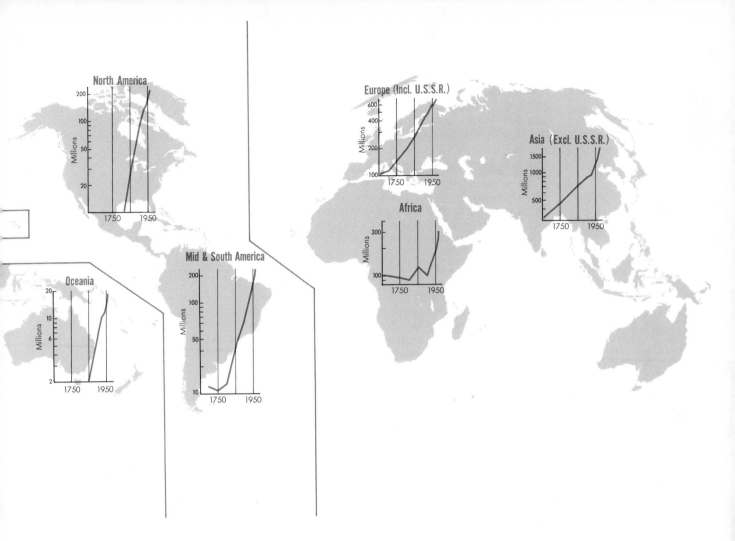

Figure 18–2. POPULATIONS OF THE CONTINENTS SINCE A.D. 1650

The graphs (drawn to logarithmic scales) show rates of population change during the modern era. Note that the slopes of the graphs for Oceania, North America, Middle and South America, and Europe are steeper than those of Asia and Africa, indicating a consistently higher rate of population increase for the European culture area. The very high increase rates in Africa, Asia, and Middle and South America since 1950 are due, in part, to improved data collection.

(1940) sifted available evidence on regional populations up to about 1900; the former's estimates have been used for Table 18–3, modified to include the Asian part of the present-day Soviet Union in the European totals.

The European Culture Realm (Figure 18–3). Two outstanding new departures mark the population geography of the earth since 1650: a sharp acceleration in growth rates, and large-scale long-distance migrations. The latter (discussed in the next chapter) were mainly by Europeans or at their instigation, especially the transportation of Africans as slaves to the Americas.

Adding the populations of the Americas, Siberia, and Oceania to those of Europe gives an approximate figure for the European culture area (Table 18–3). Since 1650 its population has multiplied tenfold. By contrast, Africa and Asia combined have multiplied only fivefold. In the Americas the sustained high rates resulted partly from continual immigration. Especially the second half of the nineteenth century witnessed great numerical advances among European populations. This growth slackened in the twentieth century during wars and economic depression, and only after 1945 resumed higher rates, though with variations between different parts of the Occidental realm.

Asia and Africa. Asia's population increased more than fourfold from the mid-seventeenth century to the mid-twentieth. By 1965, Asia had about 1,850 million—well over half the world's total. In China the founding of the Manchu dynasty (1644–1912) initiated a long period of prosperity and colonization, which led to the tripling of the population between 1650 and 1850. But thereafter the growth rate slowed, as floods, famines, epidemics, and warfare brought higher mortality. After 1950 the march of population resumed with only minor interruptions. Estimates of China's population in the mid-1960s give a total of somewhat over 700 million. Japan now has about 100 million.

South Asia (India-Pakistan-Ceylon) underwent a more gradual growth from the seventeenth through the nineteenth centuries, rising to 255 million in 1871. The rate of growth accelerated during the late nineteenth and early twentieth centuries, checked only once by the severe influenza epidemic after World War I. By the mid-1960s South Asia's population had reached almost 600 million.

In both Southwest and Southeast Asia the growth patterns varied from one oasis, delta land, or island to another. On the whole, they saw only slight increases until the late nineteenth century, when the rates became rapid, often exceeding those of East or South Asia. The island of Java is an exception in that its swiftest increase came during the nineteenth century, when the Dutch administration intensified measures of economic development. From an estimated 5 million in the first decade of the 1800s it grew to 30 million in 1905. In 1931 Java numbered 41.7 million, in 1961 no less than 63 million—all these people, chiefly rural, packed into an area no larger than the state of New York.

North Africa and the southern two-thirds of the continent differed in demographic trends. In North Africa, growth changed from slow to rapid toward the end of the nineteenth century. In contrast, south of the Sahara the ravages of the slave trade caused an actual population decline until about 1800. It has been calculated that slaving operations eliminated as many as 50 million Africans, the greater part by death in warfare and from maltreatment before they reached the embarkation ports (Davidson, 1961). In the nineteenth century the population recovered slowly, and in the present century grew at a faster pace. By the 1960s several Meso-African countries were increasing at a very high rate.

Birth and Death Rates

Natural growth is the positive difference between births and deaths. To compare among nations the fertility and mortality (the incidence of births and deaths), we need some simple yardsticks. The *crude birth rate* is the ratio of the number of live births in a given year to

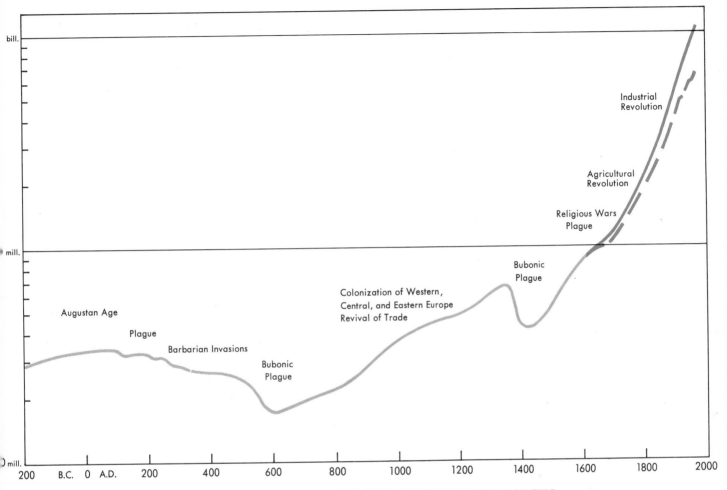

Figure 18–3. THE POPULATION OF EUROPE AND THE EUROPEAN CULTURE AREA SINCE ANCIENT TIMES

After A.D. 1600 the dashed line shows the growth of Europe's population, the solid line that of Europe plus the Americas, Russian Asia, and Oceania. The vertical scale is logarithmic.

the total population, and is usually expressed in numbers per 1,000; for example, in 1965 the rate for the United States was 19.4 and for Mexico 44.2 per 1,000. The *crude death rate* is the ratio of the number of deaths in a given year to the total population; in the United States in 1965 it was 9.4 and in Mexico 9.5 per 1,000. The

crude natural increase rate for the United States in 1965 was 10.0, and for Mexico 34.7 per 1,000.

The Demographic Transformation (Figure 18–4). Analysis of population data for the Occidental culture area reveals that economic development

18. The Differential Growth of Population

429

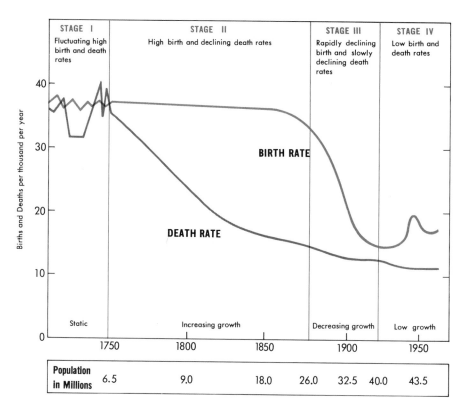

STAGE I	STAGE II	STAGE III	STAGE IV
Fluctuating high birth and death rates	High birth and declining death rates	Rapidly declining birth and slowly declining death rates	Low birth and death rates

BIRTH RATE

DEATH RATE

Births and Deaths per thousand per year

Static   Increasing growth   Decreasing growth   Low growth

Population in Millions	6.5	9.0	18.0	26.0	32.5	40.0	43.5

Figure 18–4. DEMOGRAPHIC TRANSFORMATION IN ENGLAND AND WALES

Huge population increase occurs when the death rate falls and the birth rate remains high. The length of time high increase continues and the amount of increase per year depend on economic and social conditions in individual countries.

was accompanied by a demographic progression through different phases of birth-death relationships. Taking western Europe as example, the first stage was before 1800 when high birth rates and high death rates resulted in static or, at most, slightly increasing numbers. After 1800 the second stage began, when mortality dropped slowly but steadily as the economy expanded and simple health measures found acceptance. Since fertility at first maintained its high level, the growing excess of births over deaths led to a sharp increase in numbers.

The third stage opened when the idea of family limitation began to spread. The need for having many children dwindled as more survived, and as income from child labor decreased. More important, old traditions weakened: A large family came to be felt as an obstacle toward achieving individual aspirations. Effective contraceptives, a product of modern technology, provided the means to reduce family size. As birth rates dropped, at first slowly, then more rapidly, the growth curve flattened out. The demographic transformation ended with the fourth stage: a much higher number of people than at the start and with birth and death rates at low levels.

Observation of these changes in Europe has led to formulation of the hypothesis that all societies of the world will pass through the same demographic transformation as they shift from traditional to modern ways. But this hypothesis, as the word implies, is only a supposition. Is the European experience a reliable guide for predicting what will happen in other culture realms? Their death rates may drop more quickly than in Europe—in numerous cases they have already done so—their birth rates may, or may not, decline rapidly. Depending on these trends, the resulting population increments will differ considerably.

One might ask: Since the death rate in a num-

V. Population Change

430

ber of underdeveloped countries has fallen much faster than in Europe, why cannot a breakthrough to a low fertility level be achieved just as rapidly? The answer is that everyone wants to avoid death, but that the personal decisions regarding family size are governed by a host of social and economic factors. These can change only gradually. Nevertheless, here lies an intriguing and significant issue: Must family planning wait until a society is economically well advanced? Or can it be successfully injected at an early stage? As yet there is no clear answer.

Population Projections. Crude birth and death rates relate fertility and mortality to total population numbers. They are not, however, by themselves accurate predictors of future populations. In western Europe birth rates were so low in the 1930s that demographers forecast the decline of many national populations. By the early 1960s many of the same countries still had birth rates as low, or almost as low, as those of the 1930s; however, there is no talk now of imminent population decline. Why is this? Because the crude birth rate fails to consider the age and sex structure of the population. Populations that pass through the demographic transformation develop variable numbers in different age groups (see the age and sex diagram for Sweden, Figure 18–18). For such countries we need more sophisticated measures of fertility.

A population with an abnormally large proportion of women of childbearing age has a relatively high crude birth rate, even if family size is small; conversely, a relatively small number of potential mothers means low birth rates, even if family size is large. The *gross reproduction ratio,* which relates the number of potential mothers to the number of female children they bear, gives an estimate of the potential size of the next generation. While the precise method of this ratio's calculation need not concern us here, the ratio would be 1.00 if the average 1,000 women between 15 and 45 had 1,000 female children.

However, some girls die young, and there are varying degrees of marriage and motherhood among adult females. We obtain a more exact ratio by taking account of expected deaths among girls between birth and marriage and of expected marriage rates. This is the *net reproduction ratio,* which being more precise is a better predictor of population. A net reproduction ratio of 2.00 would mean that, other things being equal, the next generation of mothers (or parents) would be twice the size of the present generation; a ratio of 0.50 would mean halving the parental population in the next generation. In the United States the net reproduction ratio was below unity in the 1930s, rose rapidly in the late 1940s to a peak in the 1950s, then declined in the early 1960s. Thus, the low crude birth rates in many economically advanced countries result from many factors, among which the number of parents relative to the total population is important.*

Table 18–5 shows for a number of countries the divergence between crude birth rates and net reproduction rates. Some of the figures must be regarded as only provisional, since the raw statistics on which they are based are incomplete. By the 1970s most countries probably will be collecting and publishing vital data of this kind, which will permit more accurate statements and predictions than now possible.

Mortality in the Twentieth Century. To comprehend the population changes now in progress we must look more closely at recent death and birth rates in various regions. The maps depicting the distribution in the 1930s (Figures 18–5 and 18–8) and in the 1960s (Figures 18–6 and 18–9) provide instructive comparisons. Table 18–7 presents the current demographic situation in some 50 countries.

Until recently, the prevalence of death marked all but the most advanced societies. Only a generation ago a list of national death rates clearly showed the distinction between developed and underdeveloped countries (Figure 18–5). For many in the poverty-stricken lands, poor diet and constant exposure to disease led to general debilitation and early death; famine, epidemic, and natural disaster occasionally car-

---

* The net reproduction ratio can be further refined by taking into account the relative number of potential mothers by single or five-year age groups.

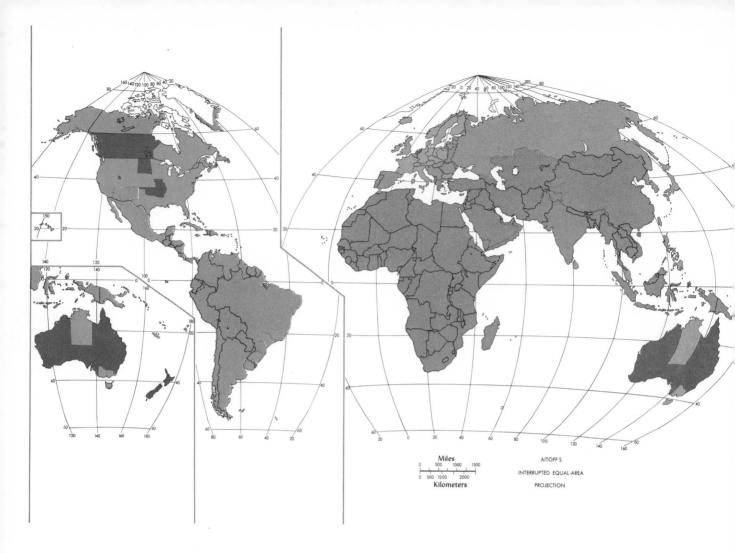

Crude Death Rates, ca. 1935 (per thousand)

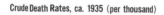

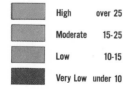

	High	over 25
	Moderate	15-25
	Low	10-15
	Very Low	under 10

Figure 18–5. WORLD: MORTALITY, CIRCA 1935

Many of the death rates shown on the map are estimates, even guesses, for in the 1930s only a few countries outside Europe and North America kept accurate population records.

V. Population
Change

432

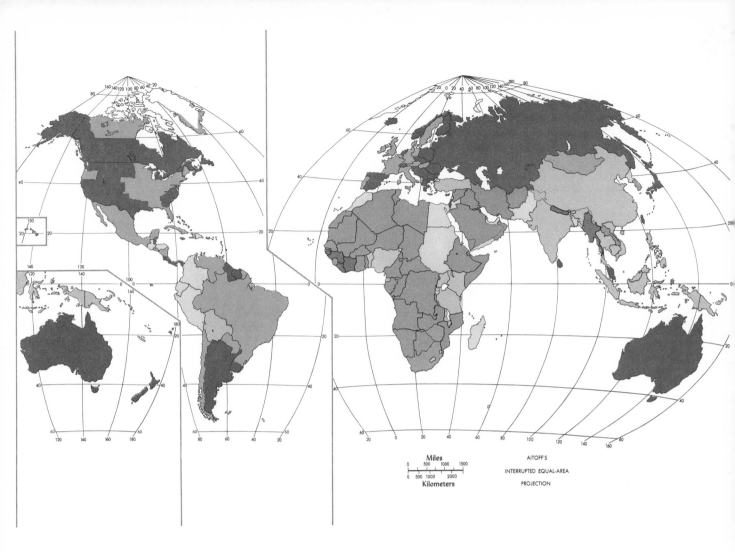

Crude Death Rates, Mid-1960s (per thousand)

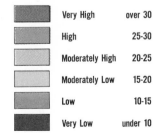

Very High	over 30
High	25-30
Moderately High	20-25
Moderately Low	15-20
Low	10-15
Very Low	under 10

Figure 18–6. WORLD: MORTALITY, MID-1960s

In the last thirty years the systematic collection of population statistics has spread to most parts of the world, allowing a more accurate portrayal of crude death rates than in the 1930s.

18. The Differential Growth of Population

Table 18–4. Mortality Rates and Life Expectancy for Selected Countries

| Country | Crude death rates | | Infant mortality rates | | Life expectancy at birth | | | |
	Mid-1930s	Mid-1960s	Mid-1930s	Mid-1960s	Mid-1930s Male	Female	Mid-1960s Male	Female
United States	11	9	56	25	56	58	67	74
Netherlands	9	8	40	15	66	67	71	75
Italy	14	10	105	40	54	56	64	67
Poland	14	7	135	56	48	51	65	71
Puerto Rico	18	7	115	40	45	47	67	72
Costa Rica	22	9	157	75			55	57
Chile	26	11	251	115	36	38		
Ceylon	23	9	173	55	39	37	60	59
India	32	22	163	145	27	27	42	41

SOURCE: United Nations *Demographic Yearbook; World Population Data Sheet,* 1965.

ried away large numbers. The impact of calamity varied widely. In countries with relatively low death rates (below 15 per 1,000), the worldwide influenza epidemic of 1918 brought only a slight rise in mortality. Sweden, for example, that year had 18 deaths per 1,000 instead of the then normal rate of 14 per 1,000. In contrast, mortality in India rose from the level of about 40 per 1,000 to 85 in 1918.

In the 1930s average life expectancy at birth was only 27 years in India, 33 in Mexico, and 36 in Chile, mostly because so many children died in infancy. In some countries the *infant mortality ratio* (the annual number of deaths among infants under one year per 1,000 live births) was as high as 250. In economically advanced countries, however, life expectancy at birth was more than 60 years and the infant mortality ratio in most cases below 50 (Table 18–4).

By the late 1960s much had changed (Figure 18–6). Most regions have seen the spread of death control through the reduction of disease and rapid mobilization of assistance to disaster areas. Crude death rates in many countries of Asia, Latin America, and east and south Europe sank to the Anglo-American and West European level, or even lower. In some cases death retreated with dramatic suddenness. For instance, in Ceylon the large application of insecticides brought instant suppression of malaria and fly-borne diseases. The crude death rate per 1,000 tumbled from 20 in 1946 to 13 in 1948, and 9 in 1951. In the island of Mauritius the rate dropped in one decade from 27 to 10 per 1,000 (Figures 18–7 and 18–14).

These events and their consequences stand in vivid contrast to the European experience. Mortality reduction in Europe and also in Anglo-America closely coincided with the gradually rising domestic levels of living. The countries now experiencing death control owe it mostly to external aid. It has come with such a rush that quite often the ensuing population explosion finds the economy unprepared to meet the situation, with the result that the people—more people—live as marginally as before.

Fertility in the Twentieth Century. Figure 18–8 shows the distribution of crude birth rates for the mid-1930s. Low fertility was confined to western Europe, Anglo-America, and Australia–New Zealand. Only in small measure was it a response to depressed economic conditions; low rates had already appeared in these countries in the 1920s. Moderate rates prevailed in southern Latin America, central and southern Europe, and Japan. Elsewhere high, or very high, fertility was common, with some parts of Asia and Africa reaching 50 per 1,000.

The situation in the 1960s (Figure 18–9) re-

V. Population Change

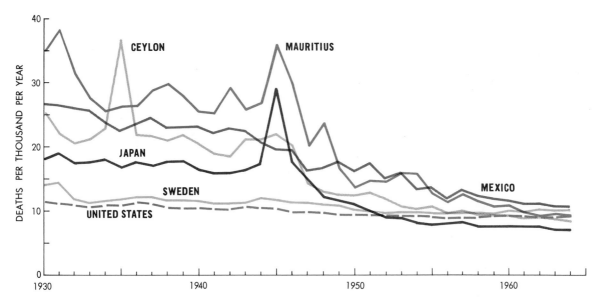

Figure 18-7. DEATH RATES FOR SELECTED COUNTRIES, 1930-1964

mained much the same, though some changes were evident. Some countries with moderate rates in the 1930s had dropped to low rates, such as, for instance, Italy and Japan. Some countries with high fertility in the 1930s had moved to moderate levels, among them Puerto Rico, Taiwan, Hong Kong, and Singapore. Slight declines, though not yet down to our category of "moderate," occurred in several other countries, such as Costa Rica and Ceylon. Lastly, the increasingly affluent modern countries showed a small gain in fertility during the postwar period. This rise, higher and more persistent in Canada, New Zealand, and Australia than in the United States and western Europe, may or may not be a temporary phenomenon (Figure 18-10).

High birth rates are bound to fall for the simple reason that, in the long run, death control is impossible without birth control. The big question, however, is when and how much fertility will decline in the countries where it is still high. Usually a small Westernized minority already practices family limitation, while the remainder of the society retains traditional attitudes. The masses probably will change their values as the modern way of life takes hold, but the process may be very slow, in part because high fertility puts a brake on economic advance. The governments of a number of countries now realize the adverse effect of unbridled population growth. Both India and China now engage in extensive birth-control propaganda.

The Current Demographic Situation. The relation of fertility level to mortality level defines each country's position in the demographic transformation (Table 18-7 and Figure 18-11). The regional differentiation in the 1960s can be summed up as follows:

1. Low fertility and low mortality, with consequently low natural increase, was confined mainly to Europe and Japan.

2. Moderate fertility and low mortality characterized the Soviet Union and the countries of Occidental culture outside Europe. A few others, in the Middle East and elsewhere, were also in this group. Increase in this category was moderate.

3. High, in some places very high, fertility combined with low, even very low, mortality,

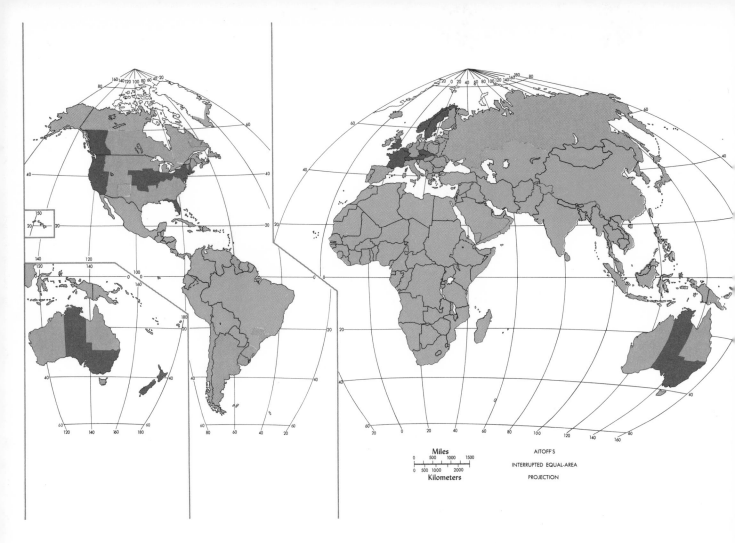

Crude Birth Rates, ca. 1935 (per thousand)

	High	over 40.0
	Moderate	25.0 - 40.0
	Low	17.5 - 25.0
	Very Low	under 17.5

Figure 18–8. WORLD: FERTILITY, CIRCA 1935

Like Figure 18–5, this map is based partly on guesses and estimates.

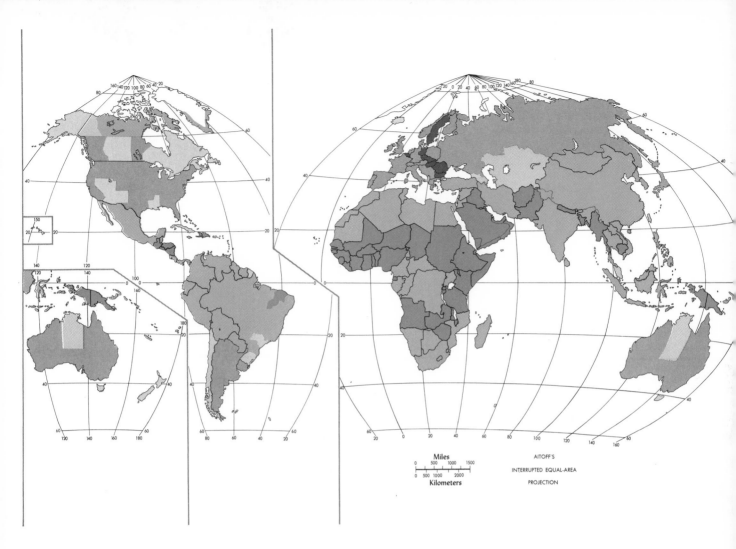

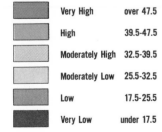

Crude Birth Rates, Mid-1960s (per thousand)

	Very High	over 47.5
	High	39.5-47.5
	Moderately High	32.5-39.5
	Moderately Low	25.5-32.5
	Low	17.5-25.5
	Very Low	under 17.5

Figure 18–9. WORLD: FERTILITY, MID-1960s

Countries with low fertility are in the same regions
as in the 1930s. The lowest rates are in central
Europe, the highest in tropical America and Africa
and some parts of southern Asia.

*18. The Differential
Growth of
Population*

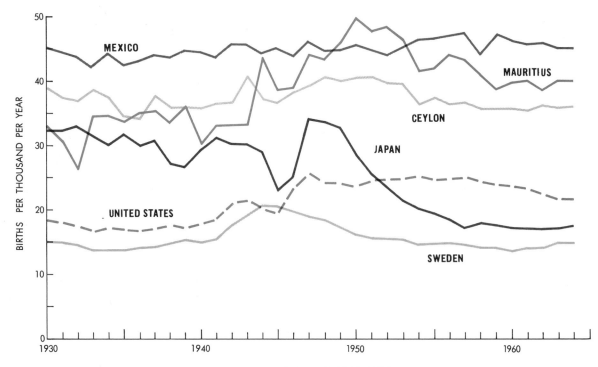

Figure 18–10. BIRTH RATES FOR SELECTED COUNTRIES, 1930–1964

Table 18–5. Crude Birth and Net Reproduction Ratios for Selected Countries

Country	Mid-1930s Crude birth rate	Mid-1930s Net reproduction ratio	Late 1940s Crude birth rate	Late 1940s Net reproduction ratio	About 1960 Crude birth rate	About 1960 Net reproduction ratio	1965 Crude birth rate
United States	16.9	0.98	25.7	1.53	23.7	1.72	19.4
Netherlands	20.2	1.15	27.8	1.64	20.8	1.52	19.9
Italy	23.4	1.13	21.9		22.3		19.2
Poland	26.1	1.11			22.3	1.37	17.4
Puerto Rico	36.9	1.62	42.7		32.3		30.3
Costa Rica	43.6	1.16	53.3	1.54	48.4	2.84	40.8
Chile	33.3	1.12	33.8	1.19	35.4	1.63	32.0
Ceylon	34.4		38.4	1.44	39.1	1.99	37.0
India	46.0	1.25	37.5	1.30	41.0		41.0

SOURCE: United Nations *Demographic Yearbook; World Population Data Sheet*, 1965.

Table 18–6. Forecast of Population Increase, 1965–2000 (millions)

| | Population | | Increase 1965–2000 | |
	1965	2000	Absolute	Percent
Anglo-America	215	388	173	80
Europe	443	571	128	29
Soviet Union	234	402	168	72
Oceania	17	33	16	94
SUBTOTAL	909	1,394	485	53
Latin America	250	756	506	202
Asia	1,840	4,400	2,560	139
Africa	310	860	550	177
SUBTOTAL	2,400	6,016	3,616	151
World population	3,309	7,410	4,101	124

SOURCE: United Nations *Demographic Yearbook,* 1965.

prevailed in Latin America and in some scattered countries in Africa and Asia (e.g., Tunisia, Ceylon, the Malay Federation, and Taiwan). Obviously, increases were very high in these areas. A number of other countries in Asia and Africa experience declining death rates which, in case high birth rates continue, augur very high increases by 1970.

4. Relatively high mortality offsetting high fertility still persists in a few Asian and African countries.

Patterns of Growth. The regional differentiation in population growth for the 1930s and the 1960s is presented in Figures 18–12 and 18–13. Already by the 1930s mankind was experiencing unprecedented increase. During this decade the total rose about 1 percent per year. Figure 18–12 shows that a number of Occidental countries had a low natural gain. South and East Europe, the Soviet Union, Japan, southern South America, and many countries in Middle America increased moderately. Africa, much of Asia, and the remainder of Latin America grew slowly.

In the mid-1960s the world's population was increasing about 2 percent annually, and the growth pattern also differed considerably from that in the 1930s. Central and southern Europe, as well as Japan, had joined western Europe in the group with lowest gains. The Soviet Union, Anglo-America, Australia, and New Zealand had moderate increments. Most of Latin America, Asia, and some parts of Africa had high or very high increases (Figure 18–13).

The Prospect. The key to reducing rates of increase lies in stabilizing death rates and further cutting birth rates. The rapid diffusion of medical technology should stabilize death rates at a low level in all countries within the next decade or two. In some countries mortality is already rising slowly, as those saved from early death grow to middle and old age.

Birth rates may be expected to drop, but the important question is whether they will go to low levels (as in Europe and Japan) or only moderate levels (as in southern Latin America). Evidently, this will make quite a difference in the national increments. At any rate, it is clear that Africa, the rimlands of Asia, and the greater part of Latin America—in short, the underdeveloped countries—pose enormous prob-

18. The Differential Growth of Population

Table 18–7. Countries with over Ten Million Inhabitants: Selected Data, Mid-1960s

Country	Population mid-1965,[a] millions	Crude rates mid-1960s per thousand — Births	Crude rates mid-1960s per thousand — Deaths	Annual population increase 1960-1965, percent[b]	Population projection for 1985[c]	Gross national product 1963 per capita[d]	International trade per capita[e]
Very high population increase (3.0 percent per year or more)							
Brazil	82.2	43–47	11–16	3.25	154.0	195	33
Mexico	42.7	45–46	9–10	3.25	76.0	400	66
Philippines	32.3	44–50	15–20	3.50	64.5	140	51
Turkey	31.1	43–48	14–18	3.00	57.5	230	32
Thailand	30.6	42–48	20–21	3.00	55.0	110	44
Iran	24.8	42–48	23–27	3.00	42.5	215	
North Vietnam	18.5			3.25(?)	35.0		
South Africa	17.9	38–42	12–15	3.00	32.3	490	218
Taiwan (China)	12.4	32–34	5–7	3.25	23.5	170	81
Peru	11.7	42–48	13–18	3.00	21.0	265	117
High population increase (2.0–2.9 percent per year)							
China	710.0	32–38	15–20	2.00(?)	1,055.0	120	10
India	482.5	40–43	20–23	2.50	790.5	85	12
Indonesia	104.5	43–48	19–23	2.25	163.0	80	15
Pakistan	102.9	48–53	20–23	2.25	160.5	80	27
Nigeria	57.2	45–50	20–25	2.00(?)	85.0	100	50
United Arab Republic	29.6	41–44	15–18	2.75	51.0	140	22
South Korea	28.4	40–45	12–16	2.75	49.0	115	19
Burma	24.7	43–50	20–25	2.00	37.0	75	56
Colombia	17.8	42–46	14–17	2.75	28.0	290	22
South Vietnam	16.1	41–48	15–20	2.75	28.0	115	
Afghanistan	15.6	45–53		2.00(?)	23.0	80	40
Congo Republic	15.6	41–46	22–28	2.00	23.2	80	35
Sudan	13.5	50–56		2.75	23.5	100	28
Morocco	13.2	43–49	18–22	2.25(?)	22.0	175	127
Algeria	12.6	45–49	22–25	2.25(?)	19.5	185	
North Korea	12.0			2.75(?)	20.5		
Australia	11.4	19–20	8–9	2.00	17.0	1,735	562
Ceylon	11.2	35–41	8–9	2.50	18.5	145	64
Tanzania	10.6	40–45	20–25	2.00	16.0	70	30

Also: Burundi (population in 1965) 2.9, Cambodia 6.4, Costa Rica 1.4, Dominican Republic 3.6, Ecuador 5.1, El Salvador 2.9, Honduras 2.3, Hong Kong 3.8, Israel 2.6, Ivory Coast 3.8, Jordan 2.0, Kenya 9.4, Malagasy Republic 6.4, Malawi 4.0, Mongolia 1.1, Nicaragua 1.7, Niger 3.4, Panama 1.2, Paraguay 2.0, Rhodesia 4.3, Syria 5.6, Togo 1.6, Venezuela 8.7, Zambia 3.7.

Also: Albania (population in 1965) 1.9, Botswana 0.6, Cameroon 5.2, Central African Republic 1.4, Chile 8.6, Cuba 7.6, Dahomey 2.4, Ghana 7.7, Guatemala 4.3, Guinea 3.5, Guyana 0.6, Haiti 4.7, Laos 2.0, Lebanon 2.3, Sabah 0.5, Sarawak 0.7, Mali 4.6, Mauritius 0.7, New Guinea 1.6, Papua 0.6, Puerto Rico 2.6, Rwanda 3.1, Senegal 3.5, Singapore 1.9, Somalia 2.5, Trinidad 1.0, Tunisia 4.7, Uganda 7.6.

Country	Population mid-1965,[a] millions	Crude rates mid-1960s per thousand — Births	Deaths	Annual population increase 1960-1965, percent[b]	Population projection for 1985[c]	Gross national product 1963 per capita[d]	International trade per capita[e]
Moderate population increase (1.0–1.9 percent per year)							
Soviet Union	234.0	19–20	7–8	1.75	331.0	1,200	70
United States	194.6	19–20	9–10	1.50	262.0	3,080	249
Japan	98.0	17–18	7–8	1.00	119.5	630	169
West Germany[f]	59.0	17–18	11–12	1.25	75.5	1,630	599
France	48.9	17–18	11–12	1.25	62.5	1,560	417
Poland	31.5	17–18	7–8	1.15	39.5	775	145
Ethiopia	22.6	45–55	25–35	1.75(?)	32.0	50	10
Argentina	22.3	20–22	8–9	1.50	30.0	615	120
Canada	19.6	21–22	7–8	1.75	28.0	2,100	763
Yugoslavia	19.5	20–21	8–10	1.12	24.4		116
Netherlands	12.3	19–21	7–9	1.25	16.0	1,205	1,128
Nepal	10.1	45–53		1.75(?)	14.3	60	

Also: Angola (population in 1965) 5.2, New Zealand 2.6, Lesotho 0.7, Bolivia 3.7, Chad 3.4, Congo (Brazzaville) 0.8, Iraq 7.8, Jamaica 1.8, Liberia 1.0, Malaya 7.8, Mozambique 7.0, Portuguese Timor 0.6, Ryukyu Islands 0.9, South-West Africa 0.6, Uruguay 2.7.

Country	Population mid-1965,[a] millions	Crude rates mid-1960s per thousand — Births	Deaths	Annual population increase 1960-1965, percent[b]	Population projection for 1985[c]	Gross national product 1963 per capita[d]	International trade per capita[e]
Low population increase (0.1–0.9 percent per year)							
United Kingdom	54.6	18–19	11–12	0.75	63.5	1,560	529
Italy	51.6	19–20	9–10	0.75	60.0	895	282
Spain	31.6	20–22	8–10	0.80	37.5	480	125
Romania	19.0	14–15	8–9	0.60	21.5	640	115
Czechoslovakia	14.2	16–17	9–10	0.65	16.0	1,275	378
Hungary	10.1	13–14	10–11	0.30	10.5	840	132

Also: Austria (population in 1965) 5.2, Belgium 9.5, Bulgaria 8.2, Switzerland 5.9, Cyprus 0.6, Denmark 4.8, Finland 4.6, Greece 8.6, Ireland 2.9, Norway 3.7, Portugal 9.2, Portuguese Guinea 0.5, Sweden 7.7.

Country	Population mid-1965,[a] millions	Crude rates mid-1960s per thousand — Births	Deaths	Annual population increase 1960-1965, percent[b]	Population projection for 1985[c]	Gross national product 1963 per capita[d]	International trade per capita[e]
Stationary or declining population							
East Germany[g]	17.0	16–17	13–14	−0.20	16.5	1,360	331

[a] Data are given for all countries with over ten million inhabitants in mid-1965. The "also" category lists countries with between half a million and ten million inhabitants.

[b] Usually given to the nearest ¼ percent.

[c] Projection of 1965 population for twenty years compounded annually, using increase rate from 1960 to 1965.

[d] Using current market prices in 1963 dollars (U.S.) for 1963 population and gross national product figures. Figures for Communist countries are unofficial estimates.

[e] Imports and exports in 1965 per capita in United States dollars.

[f] Includes West Berlin.

[g] Includes East Berlin.

SOURCE: *Population Index*, various issues; United Nations, *Monthly Bulletin of Statistics*, various issues; United Nations, *Demographic Yearbook*, various issues; Population Reference Bureau, *World Population Data Sheet*, Washington, 1965.

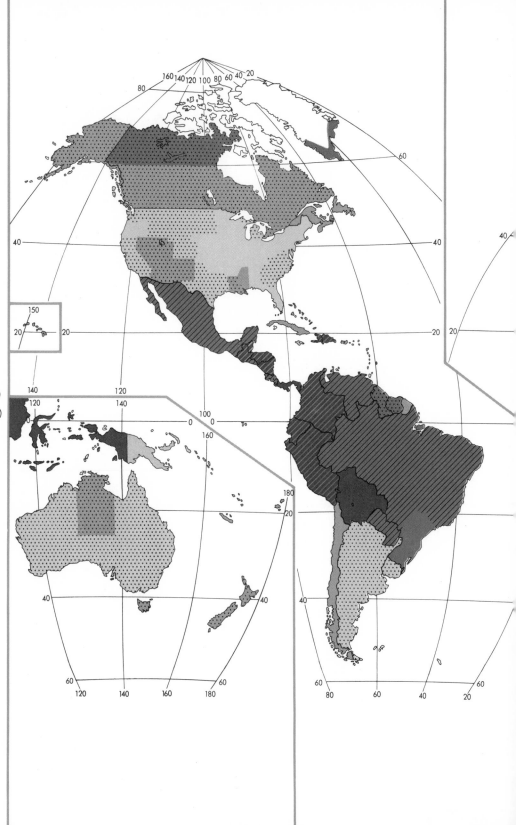

Figure 18–11. WORLD: DEMOGRAPHIC SITUATION IN THE MID-1960s

This map analyzes rates of natural increase by classifying countries according to their combination of birth and death rates. Note that the very high birth rates and very high death rates have special symbols.

Rates per thousand

High Birth Rates (over 35)
High Death Rates (over 25)

High Birth Rates (over 35)
Moderate Death Rates (15-25)

High Birth Rates (over 35)
Low Death Rates (under 15)

Moderate Birth Rates (25-35)
Low Death Rates (under 15)

Low Birth Rates (under 25)
Low Death Rates (under 15)

Very High Birth Rates (over 45)

Very Low Death Rates (under 10)

V. Population Change

442

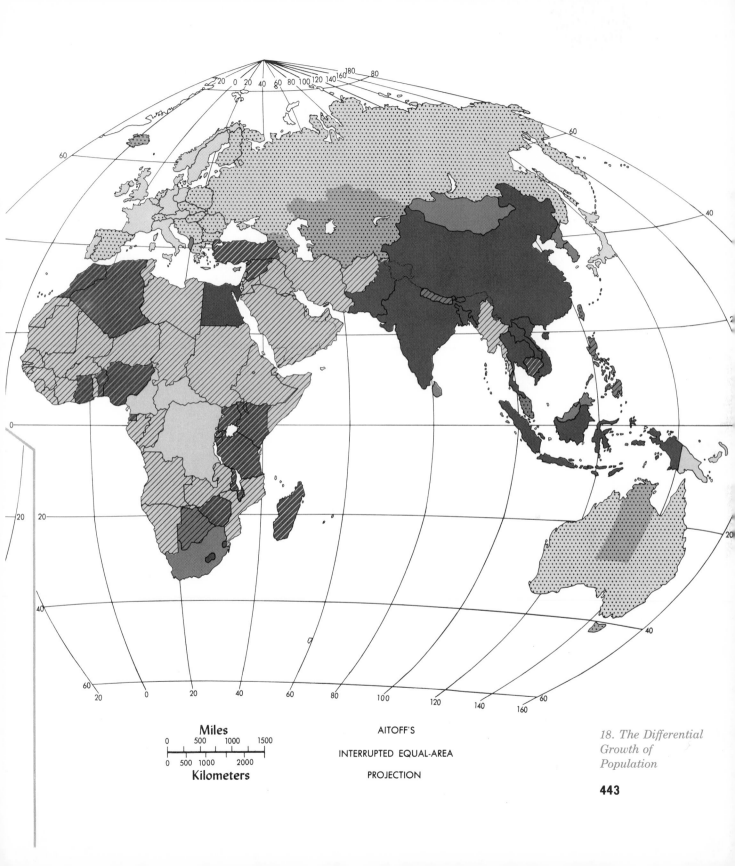

Miles

0   500   1000   1500

0   500   1000   2000

Kilometers

AITOFF'S

INTERRUPTED EQUAL-AREA

PROJECTION

*18. The Differential
Growth of
Population*

443

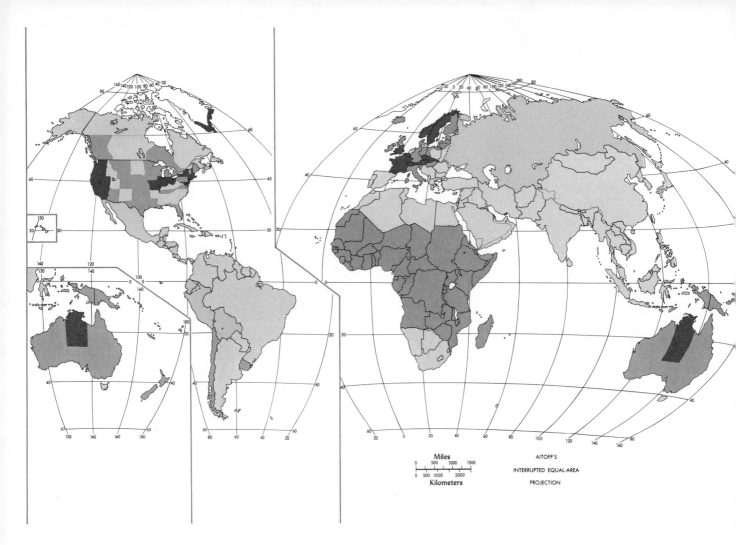

Natural Increase Rates, ca. 1935 (per thousand)

■	High	over 25.0
■	Moderately High	17.5-25.0
■	Moderately Low	10.0-17.5
■	Low	5.0-10.0
■	Very Low	under 5.0

Figure 18–12. WORLD: NATURAL CHANGE, CIRCA 1935

Most countries had moderate or low natural increases a generation ago, those with low death rates having low birth rates, while countries with high birth rates had moderate or high death rates. Only Taiwan (Formosa) had high natural increase. Like Figures 18–5 and 18–8, this map is based on inadequate records.

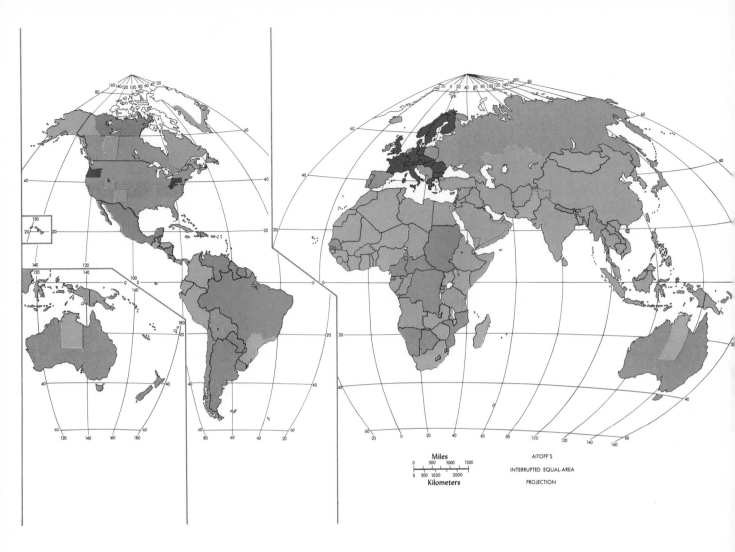

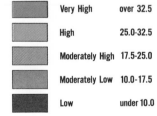

Natural Increase Rates, Mid-1960s (per thousand)

	Very High	over 32.5
	High	25.0-32.5
	Moderately High	17.5-25.0
	Moderately Low	10.0-17.5
	Low	under 10.0

Figure 18–13. WORLD: NATURAL CHANGE, MID-1960s

Very high rates of natural increase are characteristic for most of tropical Latin America, low rates for Europe. On the whole, the underdeveloped countries have higher rates than the developed ones, but there are significant exceptions, especially in underdeveloped countries where high death rates still prevail. See Figure 18–11.

18. The Differential Growth of Population

445

Table 18–8. Population Growth in India and Pakistan, 1921–1965 (millions)

| | 1921–1931 | | | 1931–1941 | | | 1941–1951 | | | 1951–1961 | | | 1961–1965 | | |
	Ten-year increase	Percent yearly	1931	Ten-year increase	Percent yearly	1941	Ten-year increase	Percent yearly	1951	Ten-year increase	Percent yearly	1961	Four-year increase	Percent yearly	1965
India*			278.0	41.1	1.46	319.1	42.5	1.33	361.6	77.6	2.16	439.2	43.3	2.46	482.5
Pakistan			60.2	9.9	1.65	70.1	5.7	0.81	75.8	18.0	2.37	93.8	9.1	2.42	102.9
TOTAL	32.0	1.06	338.2	51.0	1.50	389.2	48.2	1.24	437.4	95.6	2.26	533.0	52.4	2.46	585.4
West Pakistan						28.3	5.5	1.94	33.8	9.1	2.68	42.9			
East Pakistan						41.8	0.2	0.05	42.0	8.9	2.12	50.9			

*Includes Jammu and Kashmir territories, disputed by Pakistan.
SOURCE: *Census of India;* Population Reference Bureau, *World Population Data Sheet, 1965.*

lems not only to themselves, but to the human community as a whole. In these realms—China and India come especially to mind here—massive increases will inevitably occur, even if fertility were to lessen in the near future.

Table 18-6 presents the population in 1965 and a forecast for the year 2000 based on present trends. The figures, given by broad realms, are arranged in such fashion that the top four comprise fairly well the developed countries and the bottom group the underdeveloped countries. The prospect is frightening. In this span of 35 years the world population is expected to increase by 124 percent, but the underdeveloped parts will grow 151 percent. In contrast, the regions with an advanced economy will increase only 53 percent. To put it in another way, the underdeveloped countries, which now constitute 73 percent of the world population, will in the year 2000 comprise 81 percent of a more than twice as numerous world population. While Latin America and Africa are due to have the greatest percentual increases, Asia by far will face the largest absolute gains.

Population predictions are always hazardous. They necessarily are based on certain assumptions which in the course of time may prove wrong. The predictions for the year 1965 made some thirty years ago have turned out to be much too low. Current projections, such as the one presented in Table 18-6, may turn out to be too high. Man differs from other species in that he observes himself, reflects, and acts. The prospect of a tidal flood of additional hungry human beings in the next generation may bring about a drop in birth rates sooner than now foreseen. Some forecasts, anticipating lower fertility rates, arrive at a total of about 6,000 million for the year 2000, more than one billion less than the projection in Table 18-6, based on present trends. Even this lower figure—which may well prove to be more accurate—presents a formidable challenge to the next generation.

Case Studies in Population Geography

The following thumbnail sketches show the diversity of recent population changes and the distinctive problems they pose. The order is not arbitrary: Starting with the area where the issue is most acute, we end with a country that has achieved a balance between quantity of people and quality of living.

India and Pakistan. The fateful race between population and subsistence, which Malthus observed in Europe around 1800, now can be seen in its most dramatic form in the arena of the In-

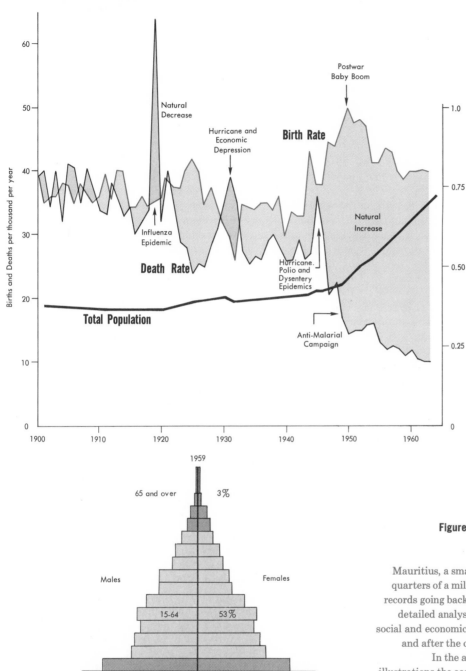

Figure 18–14. MAURITIUS: POPULATION IN THE TWENTIETH CENTURY

Mauritius, a small island in the Indian Ocean with three-quarters of a million inhabitants, has excellent population records going back to the nineteenth century. These permit detailed analysis of fertility and mortality in relation to social and economic conditions and catastrophes both before and after the coming of modern means of death control.

In the age and sex pyramids of this and following illustrations the economically productive age groups (15–64) are shown in gray, the economically dependent age groups (0–14 and 65 and over) in brown. Based on materials in Population Reference Bureau, 1962.

dian subcontinent. An already crowded land with a venerable civilization is experiencing a population surge of such magnitude that catastrophe threatens before the end of this century.

India's growth in the past was slow and sporadic. Famine took terrific toll whenever the monsoon failed to bring rain. In 1866 in Bengal and Orissa 1 million died of hunger, in 1869 in Rajputana 1.5 million, in 1876–1878 in peninsular India 5 million, in 1943 in Bengal 1.5 million. The influenza epidemic of 1918 carried away 15 million or more, some 5 percent of the population.

From 1921 to 1951 growth on the whole was larger and steadier, amounting to 1 percent or more per year (Table 18–8). Although this rate of increase was not exorbitant, it added in three decades 131 million to an already dense and largely agrarian population. There were, of course, regional differences. East Pakistan grew hardly at all between 1941 and 1951, in consequence of the severe famine and community strife.

The decade 1951–1961 brought an unprecedented wave of increase, over 2 percent per year, to both the Indian Republic and Pakistan, a rate which persisted into the 1960s. Its cause is a classic example of the uneven diffusion of Occidental culture traits: Western medical technology and disaster relief cut down mortality, but Western notions of family size hardly made a dent on a social system that encourages copious fertility. Though death rates dropped from over 40 to about 22 per 1,000, birth rates are still 40 to 43—in Pakistan even higher, perhaps 50 per 1,000. Since India's mortality rates are still twice as large as in neighboring Ceylon, further reduction is quite possible, unless countered by a declining level of living.

The Indian Republic in its first Five-year Plan (1951–1956) recognized the need for family limitation as a condition of economic progress. Although India's leading circles support the idea, little has been accomplished so far. To reach most of the population, medical and social workers need to visit 550,000 villages. Communication by other means is difficult because the people are largely illiterate and many villages lack even one radio. Unlike vaccination against a disease, even a simple and cheap means of birth control must overcome massive reluctance if not resistance.

Declining fertility commonly goes together with increasing urbanization. There are, indeed, signs in India that city people are beginning to limit their families. And the proportion of urban population, though small as yet, is rising. This trend, hopeful as it is, will take a very long time to translate itself into a substantial reduction of fertility.

If the present course continues, India will double its population to 965 million in 1996, and Pakistan even faster, reaching 230 million by 1990. There is always that "if." It is possible that some simple device will turn the population tide, and that science, technology, and education will bring economic renewal. In the meantime American grain can keep millions from starvation. But what if—or when—American surpluses run out? And what if modernization comes too slowly, or not at all? Malthus erred on Europe's future; one can only hope that his theory will also prove wrong for the Indian subcontinent.

United Arab Republic. The inhabited, real Egypt lies like a long fertile island amid a sea of sterile desert. In ancient times it was famed not only for its great civilization, but also for its output of food, enough to feed other people as well as its own. Today, with an exceedingly high density, the increasing population has outstripped the gains in food production. There are, however, possibilities of economic growth which may eventually reduce the severe population pressure (Figure 18–15).

Virtually all the people (30 million in 1966) live in the Nile Valley and Delta, on only 3.5 percent of the national territory. The average density of this settled zone is no less than 2,100 persons per square mile. Two-thirds of all Egyptians live in the delta, including those in the big cities, of which Cairo (4.5 million) and Alexandria (1.5 million) are the largest. In all, about 40 percent live in towns and cities, and this proportion rises steadily.

The population numbered 8 million in 1882, climbed at an even pace to 17 million in 1940,

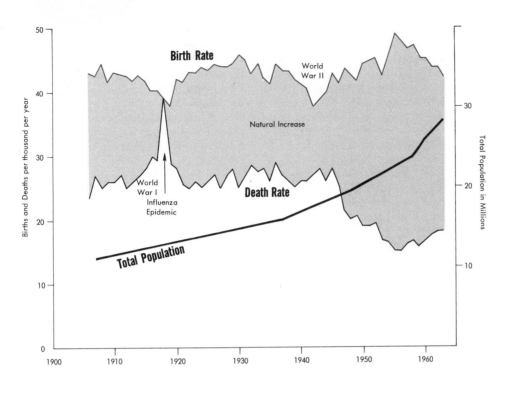

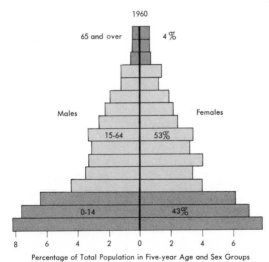

Percentage of Total Population in Five-year Age and Sex Groups

Figure 18–15. UNITED ARAB REPUBLIC (EGYPT): POPULATION IN THE TWENTIETH CENTURY

18. The Differential Growth of Population

and then spurted to 30 million in 1966. Before World War II the crude birth rate was between 45 and 48 and the death rate between 30 and 35 per 1,000.* The population grew at a rate of about 1.4 percent per year. Following the war, fertility remained high (at about 45 per 1,000), but mortality fell to below 20. The annual natural increase rate in recent years thus has been about 2.5 percent. As a result, the country has a very young population—51 percent are younger than twenty years. This puts a heavy burden on government services, especially education. The number of illiterates aged ten and over increased from 10.4 million in 1947 to 12.5 million in 1960 (El-Badry, 1965, 167).

If present birth and death rates persist, Egypt's population will be twice as large by the year 2000. However, since 1955, fertility has declined slightly, especially in the cities. The improved position of women after the revolution may also aid to reduce the birth rate.

Farm production per acre is twice that at the beginning of this century, owing to the extension of double-cropping, the improvement of plant strains, and the use of chemical fertilizer. The Aswan high dam, now nearing completion, and other schemes may expand the arable land by one-half. (This ignores the long-range possibility of irrigating the desert with desalted seawater, prohibitive in cost for years to come.) However, the population will increase much more than farmland, and the rising expectations include much more than food.

Egyptians get more calories now than in the past, but only through buying more wheat abroad; most likely the import of food will remain a considerable item in Egypt's future trade budget. The country earns foreign currency through the Suez Canal tolls and the sale of cotton, but more diversified exports are highly desirable. Egypt's position on the crossroads of the Old World is an asset, and the revolution of 1952 has cleared away many obstacles to using the national potential. In recent years capital injections from abroad have boosted economic development. Nevertheless, the industrial base still remains quite narrow (only 10 percent of the labor force works in industry, compared to 7 percent in 1937), and it needs far more capital to expand substantially. This would be true even if the population were to remain at its present numbers; as it is, the fast rate of growth will be a severe handicap in the struggle toward progress.

Mexico (Figure 18–16). Mexico is undergoing a population boom of singular proportions. Its present annual increase is higher than Egypt's, but while the two countries have many similar problems, their circumstances differ considerably.

Mexican culture roots reach back to both Old and New World origins; Meso-American and Spanish elements continue side by side, exemplifying the many paradoxes of life. Though the revolution of 1910–1911 turned Mexico toward twentieth-century social and political values, much remains that is outmoded and traditional. The national spirit and the institutions it has created are tempered by localism and disregard for the law. The urban exchange economy contrasts with the countryside, where illiterate peasants still live in near-self-sufficient villages. Church and state discords and capitalist versus socialist arguments further reveal the diversities and contradictions in Mexico.

Against this background one must view the population explosion and the economic change which are bringing a new nation into being. Reliable statistics date only from 1930. They show a continuous decline in the death rate from just below 30 to about 10 per 1,000. This results from free medical care for the poor, better public health and sanitation, improved diet, and decreased violence. Infant mortality dropped from about 140 per 1,000 in 1930 to about 60 in 1965. Life expectancy in the early part of the century was less than thirty years, now it is over sixty years.

Fertility remains very high: well over 40 births per 1,000, and over 50 in some years. Mexicans marry at an early age and have large families; in 1960 there were 4.9 children per

* The reported figures, used in Figure 18–15, are somewhat lower than those given here, which are vital rates as corrected by El-Badry, 1965.

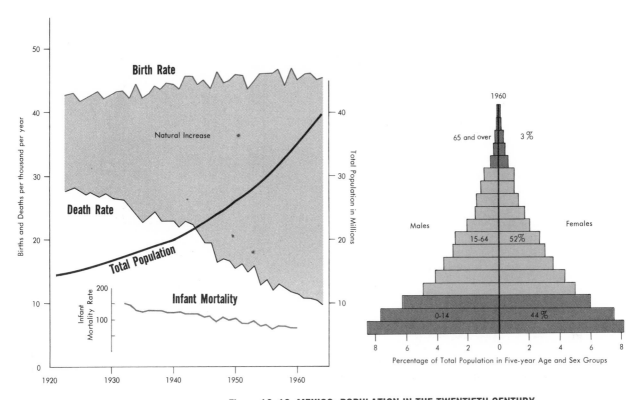

Figure 18–16. MEXICO: POPULATION IN THE TWENTIETH CENTURY

family as against 2.5 in the United States. While the growing middle class does have slightly lower fertility than the lower-income groups, it is unlikely that birth rates will drop substantially within the next decade. The cult of the virile and courageous male—*machismo*—is a powerful stimulus to produce children, and is not likely to fade away soon.

The gap between births and deaths is as wide in Mexico as anywhere, and results in prodigious population increments. From a total of 14 million in 1920 the number climbed to 20 million in 1940 and leaped to 44 million in 1966. The rate of increase has steadily risen as numbers have gone up: 1.7 percent annually in the 1920s, 2.7 percent in the 1940s, 3.4 percent in the 1950s. Between 1960 and 1980 the number of potential mothers will double. By that time Mexico may have as many as 70 million inhabitants. The on-

rush of births has produced a population heavy with dependents. Well over half of all Mexicans are under twenty years of age. Compared with the United States, a relatively small proportion of the citizens must provide for the young.

Fortunately, economic growth has accompanied the population explosion. Mexico is past the take-off stage in economic development. The gross national product grew by 61 percent in the 1950s, and the average income per capita topped $400 in 1963. The returns from the economic renewal, however, are spread quite unevenly: urban dwellers, and especially the upper classes, take the lion's share. In 1963 4.8 percent of all Mexican families received two-fifths of the national income.

There is yet much to be done if the economic advance is to maintain its impetus. Each year one-third of a million new jobs must be created.

18. The Differential Growth of Population

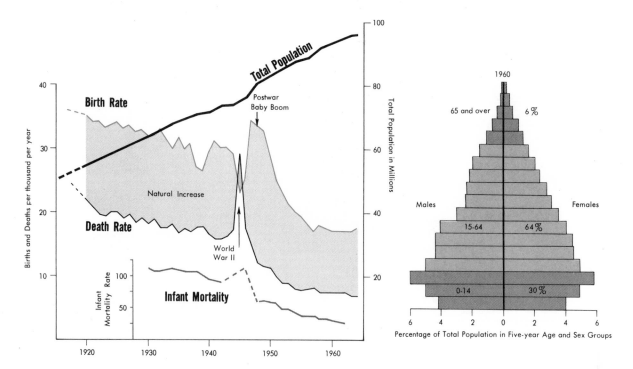

Figure 18–17. JAPAN: POPULATION IN THE TWENTIETH CENTURY

The capital needed to carry development forward will be enormous. Housing, education, and social services must be expanded. Especially the rural people, who still form a majority of the population, must obtain a more equitable share in the benefits of progress. Life in the smaller towns and cities should be made more attractive to encourage industrial decentralization. All in all, these objectives in the face of a fast-rising population are herculean tasks. However, as a recent study concludes: "Mexico has acquired a sense of nationality, purpose, and dignity. Greater maturity and a sense of accomplishment have given Mexico greater confidence in its own strength and an appreciation of its own culture . . . the situation is hopeful for a free . . . well-fed and well-housed people" (Brand, 1966, 150, 152).

Japan (Figure 18–17). Just a century ago Japan started its headlong rush from medieval feudalism into modern industrial capitalism. Its culture today presents an incongruous fusion of Oriental base and Occidental superstructure. That is why superficial similarities with Britain —insular location on the continental periphery, and rapid rise to commercial-industrial hegemony—are misleading. Nor can the transformation of this "Oriental" country serve as a reliable guideline to anticipate similar changes in other rimlands of Asia. Nevertheless, Japan's population history makes a fascinating story of what can happen when East and West meet.

Around 1600 the Japanese, living in an island empire a bit smaller than California, numbered approximately 18 million. This represents a much higher density than that of any European country at that time. During the Tokugawa period (1615–1868) the feudal military dictatorship firmly maintained order, furthered land colonization, and built in strict isolation a cohesive nation. The population grew to between 28 and 30 million, then stagnated at that level until the middle of the nineteenth century. As

V. Population Change

452

More than any other city in the world, Hong Kong suffers from overcrowding in tenements and squatter communities because of the large influx of people from Communist China. The refugees form one-third of the more than three million inhabitants packed together in the small British colony. [Courtesy of United Nations]

18. The Differential Growth of Population

usual in such societies, famine, disease, and natural disaster sporadically took away large numbers. But voluntary population control became a necessity in Japan's closed, self-sufficient economy. Infanticide and abortion were widely practiced, at least during periods of hardship.

The modernization after 1868 had to rely on a very limited natural resource base that resembled Italy's more than Britain's. Japan's greatest asset was its dense population, steeped in the traditional ethos of corporate duties rather than individual rights, willing to sacrifice comfort and even life for the future welfare of the commonweal, and easily regimented into a docile work force for giant industrial firms.

The period until 1900 were the years of the take-off. By that date the population had risen to about 44 million (Table 18–9), but the incomplete vital statistics of the time prevent analysis of the changes in the relation of births to deaths. What shifts there were occurred mainly in cities, because modernization had not yet affected the villages where three-fourths of the people lived. Birth rates may have risen as preventive population checks receded; death rates may have increased under poor sanitary conditions and long working hours in the industrial towns.

The years from 1900 until 1920, although a period of rapid industrialization and urbanization, brought no significant change in fertility and mortality trends. Both appear to have been higher in 1920 than in 1900. A substantial migration from country to city, however, caused a population decline in remote mountain districts.

Industrialization and expansion of cities into great conurbations grew apace after 1920, but new vital trends did not appear until late in that decade: Birth rates as well as death rates began to drop very gradually. Since this happened simultaneously, the rate of increase remained about the same (12 to 14 per 1,000) during most of the thirties.

Japan's leaders of that time, desiring a large population growth for their expansionist aims, forebade all birth-control propaganda. Although this policy did not appreciably boost the birth rate, it may have retarded a steeper decline. Altogether, reduction of fertility came very slowly as compared to that in Western industrialized countries between 1920 and 1940.

Japan's defeat in the Pacific war forced the ruined country to absorb 2 to 3 million returnees from overseas in addition to the 3 million military personnel. New marriages and the reunion of families shot the birth rate up to 34.3 in 1947, while at the same time health measures which the American occupation forces had introduced brought the death rate down to 14.6, and even lower in subsequent years. The result was an unprecedented increase of 20 per 1,000, or 2 percent, per year. In light of the precarious

	1700–1850	1900	1920	1930	1940	1947	1950	1955	1960	1965
Population, millions	28–30	43.8	55.9	64.4	73.1	78.1	83.2	89.3	93.4	97.8
Crude birth rate		32(?)	36	32.4	29.4	34.3	28.4	19.4	17.2	17.7
Crude death rate		23(?)	25	18.2	16.4	14.6	11.0	7.8	7.6	6.9
Rate of natural increase		9(?)	11	14.2	13.0	19.7	17.4	11.6	9.6	10.8

Table 18–9. Japan's Population Growth, 1870–1965*

*Japanese vital statistics are considered quite accurate after 1920.

economic situation, with the island empire shorn of all overseas territories, it is no wonder that the Japanese realized they had to limit their numbers. What is surprising, however, was the speed at which fertility plunged. In 1951 the birth rate sank under the previous low (1939) of 26.6 per 1,000 and in the next ten years fell below 17. The slight upward curve today reflects the marriages of the large postwar baby crop.

The precipitous drop in fertility may at first sight seem to be the cure for all countries suffering from severe population pressure. Further consideration shows, however, that Japan's case is likely to remain unique. First of all, Japan with its well-established industrial and urban economy was far from an underdeveloped country. With widespread literacy and cultural homogeneity, the people were able to understand the serious situation and to agree on this way out of the dilemma. Moreover, control of family size had been common during the Tokugawa period, and some of its practices had persisted within living memory. The latter circumstance explains why there was wide social acceptance of the provisions of the Eugenic Protection Act of 1948. This law sanctioned sterilization and abortion to prevent the birth of abnormal children or to protect the health of mothers. Also, and this is especially significant, it allowed termination of pregnancy for economic reasons. It has been calculated that from 1949 to 1958 female sterilizations prevented 135,000 births, and abortion 7.5 million births (Garry, 1964). Probably deliberate abortion will become less common as the use of effective contraceptives spreads.

Because fertility dropped so rapidly, Japan's age-sex pyramid has taken on a peculiar form: Its base, consisting of the age groups under fifteen years, is narrower than the lower middle part comprising the ages fifteen through thirty-four. Since mortality has also declined, Japan's population still grows at an annual rate of about 10 per 1,000. This means that the country must provide for one million more each year.

Sweden (Figure 18–18). We conclude this series of close-ups with a look at a thoroughly "modern" country which has passed through the demographic transformation.

Sweden, a little over twice the size of Minnesota, has a relatively small population, 7.8 million in 1966. The average density is only 44 per square mile. But most of the country is cold upland with poor soil, covered with forest. Good farmland is limited to the southern part. Agricultural production and its potential, however, are only a minor factor in Sweden's ability to support its population. The nation prospers by exporting iron ore, timber, and manufactured goods, from ships and cars to roller bearings and plywood, and by performing various services in the international web of trade.

It was not always that way, and the vital statistics—recorded over a long time—reflect the changes in society and economy. Figure 18–18 shows the march of birth and death rates since the middle of the eighteenth century. In the early 1800s sporadic peaks of high mortality during hardship years disappeared, as the Swedes insured themselves against famine by improving farming, developing better means of food distribution, and avoiding war. As the nineteenth century wore on, the death rate declined because preventive and remedial medicine and hygiene gradually became available to the mass of the population. Infant mortality fell and life expectancy increased. In this century improved medical care and diet have helped further to lower the death rate to the present 10 per 1,000 (Table 18–10).

Beginning in the late nineteenth century, fertility also fell. Parents (using methods of birth control with the approval of church and state) limited their families, allowing themselves and their children a higher level of well-being. By the 1930s the crude birth rate was below 15 per 1,000. The net reproduction rate (p. 431), which had fallen below 1.00 in 1926, continued its downward trend to a low of 0.74 in 1935 during the depression years. Concern with the very real possibility of depopulation led to propaganda for larger families and government aid to parents with small children. These measures and the economic upswing raised the birth rate to over 20 per 1,000 in the late 1940s. In the late 1950s and early 1960s it dropped again, in

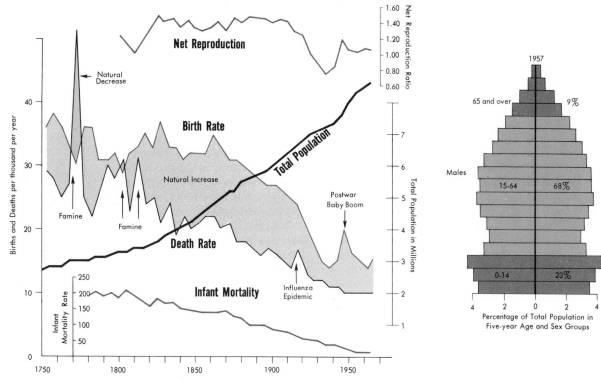

Figure 18–18. SWEDEN: POPULATION SINCE 1750

Table 18-10. The Population of Sweden, 1750–1965

	Range of annual rates per thousand of the population			Per thousand of the population per year	
	Crude birth rate	Crude death rate	Natural change	Net migration	Population change
1750–1799	37–25	53–22	+15--28	-1.5	+5.5
1800–1849	37–28	40–18	+16--11	-1.0	+9.0
1850–1899	35–27	27–15	+17-+5	-3.0	+9.0
1900–1919	27–20	18–13	+10-+3		+7.4
1920–1939	23–14	13–11	+10-+2		+3.7
1940–1959	21–14	11–9	+10-+4		+9.2
1960–1965	15–14	10	+5 -+4		+5.0

SOURCE: Kuczynski, 1928; United Nations *Demographic Yearbook*, various years.

part because there were fewer potential parents, the result of few births in the 1920s and 1930s. Since 1942 the net reproduction ratio has been slightly above replacement level, even though in the 1960s the crude birth rate was as low or lower than in the 1930s. As pointed out before, to measure actual fertility one must take into account the sex and age structure of the population. In Sweden the age classes are almost of equal size, resulting in a diagram quite different from the "pyramid" of countries in the early stage of the demographic transformation. In this situation the crude birth rate does not truly reflect fertility level.

The control of birth and death has caused radical changes in Sweden's population. In the nineteenth century, despite substantial emigra-tion, the number rose steeply. By 1930 the population was nearly stationary; since then, natural increase has been modest, and probably will continue that way. Sweden now even at-tracts a small but continuous flow of immi-grants.

The Swedes enjoy a level of living comparable to that of Americans. The population is highly skilled. Capital is available for investment in industry, commerce, education, and welfare, leading to further advances. The proceeds of the economy are widely distributed throughout Swedish society; there are few conspicuously rich or poor people. Since the population grows only slowly, the economic expansion makes possible a further rise in material well-being.

Citations

Brand, D. D. *Mexico: Land of Sunshine and Shadow,* Princeton, N.J., 1966.

Carr-Saunders, A. M. *World Population: Past Growth and Present Trends,* London, 1936, 1966.

Davidson, B. *Black Mother: The Years of the African Slave Trade,* Boston, 1961.

El-Badry, M. A. "Trends in the Components of Population Growth in the Arab Countries of the Middle East: A Survey of Present Information," *Demography,* 2 (1965): 141–186.

Garry, R. "La Loi de 1948 sur l'eugénisme national et l'évolution de la popula-tion japonaise de 1949 à 1958," *Revue de Géographie de Montréal,* 18 (1964): 87–97.

Kuczynski, R. R. *The Balance of Births and Deaths,* New York, 1928.

Political and Economic Planning, *World Population and Resources,* London, 1955. [Graph]

Population Reference Bureau "The Story of Mauritius," *Population Bulletin,* (1962): 93–115. [Graph]

Russell, J. C. "Late Ancient and Medieval Population," *Transactions of the American Philosophical Society,* Philadelphia, New Series, 48 (1958), part 3.

United Nations *Demographic Yearbook,* New York, 1949 to date.

———. *Statistical Yearbook,* New York, 1949 to date.

———. "Population Growth and the Standard of Living in Underdeveloped Countries," *Population Studies,* no. 20, New York, 1956.

———. *The Determinants and Consequences of Population Trends,* New York, 1953.

Wilcox, W. F. *Studies in American Demography,* New York, 1940.

18. The Differential Growth of Population

Further Readings

Barbour, K. M., and Prothero, R. M. (eds.) *Essays on African Population,* London, 1961.

Beaujeu-Garnier, J. *Géographie de la population,* 2 vols., Paris, 1956–1958.

———. *A Geography of Population,* London, 1966.

Brush, J. E. *The Population of New Jersey,* New Brunswick, N.J., 1958.

Cipolla, C. *The Economic History of World Population,* Harmondsworth, England, 1962.

Clarke, J. I. *Population Geography,* Oxford, 1965.

Davis, K. *The Population of India and Pakistan,* Princeton, N.J., 1951.

Freedman, R. (ed.) *Population: The Vital Revolution,* New York, 1964.

George, P. "Questions de la géographie de la population," Institut d'Etudes Démographiques, *Cahiers de "Travaux et Documents,"* no. 34, Paris, 1959.

Glass, D. V., and Eversley, D. E. C. (eds.) *Population in History: Essays in Historical Demography,* Chicago, 1965.

Hauser, P. M., and Duncan, O. D. (eds.) *The Study of Population: An Inventory and Appraisal,* Chicago, 1959.

Kirk, D. *Europe's Population in the Interwar Years,* Geneva, 1946.

Lorimer, F., et al. *Culture and Human Fertility,* New York, 1954.

Lowenthal, D. "The Population of Barbados," *Social and Economic Studies* (Jamaica), 6 (1957): 445–501.

Peterson, W. *Population,* New York, 1961.

Reinhard, M. R., and Armengaud, A. *Histoire générale de la population mondiale,* Paris, 1961.

Smith, T. E., and Blacker, J. G. C. *Population Characteristics of the Commonwealth Countries of Tropical Africa,* London, 1963.

Stamp, L. D. *The Geography of Life and Death,* London, 1964.

Taeuber, C., and Taeuber, I. *The Changing Population of the United States,* New York, 1958.

Taeuber, I., and Beal, E. G. "The Dynamics of Population in Japan," *Demographic Studies of Selected Areas of Rapid Growth,* Milbank Memorial Fund, New York, 1944, 1–34.

Taeuber, I. B. *The Population of Japan,* Princeton, N.J., 1958.

Thompson, W. S., and Lewis, D. T. *Population Problems,* 5th ed., New York, 1965.

Trewartha, G. T. "The Case for Population Geography," *Annals of the Association of American Geographers,* 44 (1954): 71–97.

United Nations "The Future Growth of World Population," *Population Studies,* no. 28, New York, 1958.

U.S. Bureau of the Census. *Historical Statistics of the United States: Colonial Times to 1957: A Statistical Abstract Supplement,* Washington, D.C., 1960.

Witthauer, K. "Die Bevölkerung der Erde: Verteilung und Dynamik," *Petermann's Geographische Mitteilungen,* supplement 265, 1958.

Wrigley, E. A. *Industrial Growth and Population Change,* London, 1961.

Zelinsky, W. "A Bibliographic Guide to Population Geography," University of Chicago Department of Geography, *Research Paper no. 80,* Chicago, 1962.

———. *A Prologue to Population Geography,* Englewood Cliffs, N.J., 1966.

V. Population Change

19. Population Movements

Introduction

Mobility. Life is movement. The distribution of population at a given moment is like the still from a motion picture. Were a population-dot map of the United States suddenly to spring to life, it would show a kaleidoscopic array of moving particles: short-distance shuttles everywhere, longer-distance oscillations between cities, a diffuse but steady convergence from rural to urban places, broad pulsating streams from one region to another, and small currents and countercurrents across all borders.

The mobility of organisms, including man, so impressed Friedrich Ratzel (1844–1904), one of the founders of modern human geography, that he visualized geography as essentially a *Bewegungslehre*—a science of movement. In man's association with the earth the time span is quite long, but the space limited. From this relationship Ratzel inferred that human groups must have traversed the more accessible parts of the earth over and over again, mixing biologic features and diffusing culture traits.

Spatial mobility takes many forms. Some of these have already been mentioned in previous chapters: nomadism, transhumance, commuting, and recreational travel. The first two are decreasing in significance, the latter two increasing. Another form is the flow of transient laborers who leave home to live a season or even a few years in another place; these temporary moves are commonly called labor migrations. Strictly speaking, the term migration should be reserved for the movement of persons from one place to another for the purpose of permanent settlement. However, the movement of laborers—and also of refugees—intended as a temporary shift may well result in permanent change of residence. Hence, the line between migration proper and some other forms of mobility cannot be drawn sharply.

Migration may be compared with the phenomenon of flow: It goes from a source to a destination; it follows a route over shorter or longer distance; it has a certain composition, volume, speed, and duration. All these components can be expressed, in principle at least, in quantitative form.

"Push" and "Pull." Less measurable are cause and effect of migration. In general, it is useful to think of the region or country of emigration as exerting pressure or "push," while the area of immigration attracts or "pulls." Both push and pull are made up of a number of forces and counterforces. The individual migrant, where free to make the decision, weighs the advantages and the drawbacks of staying put, and compares them with the hopes and fears of building a new life in another country; he may also consider a choice between several countries and the means of reaching them. The way he perceives the situation—that is, his "operational environment"—may differ markedly from the "cognized environment" as others know it to exist in reality. For instance, the government expert in Djakarta notes population pressure on Java and settlement opportunities in Borneo, but the Javanese peasant does not ascribe his meager existence to population pressure and has not heard about Borneo; even if he has, he most likely rejects the thought of exchanging his beloved village for the dreaded pioneer life on another island.

We tend to assign simple causes to the aggregate of individual decisions which express themselves in migration currents. Theoretically one can distinguish various categories of determinants: natural catastrophes (earthquake, crop failure); man-made disasters (war, revolution); economic factors (unemployment or, more general, population pressure); sociocultural forces (the quest for spiritual freedom, the attraction of a mild climate or of urban amenities). But quite often these causes mingle. Drought is a natural event, but the subsequent famine may result from human failure to take the proper preventive action. Or population pressure may be the underlying reason, and crop failure merely the trigger that sets off the outflow of people. Antagonism toward some ethnic group and the wish to oust it may rest on—or at least be reinforced by—envy of its economic superiority. Conversely, an oppressed social group may seek a new home because it expects a better economic life there. The complexity of factors obstructs exact measurement of each variable and limits the validity of broad generalizations on why migrations occur.

Theoretical Approaches. Movements within one country (internal migration) usually reflect the relatively untrammeled interplay of economic factors. Hence, quantitative studies that aim at theoretical constructs find them a more rewarding subject than international migrations. As early as the 1880s the British scholar E. G. Ravenstein analyzed population movements within England. Among the "laws" he formulated, the one best known states that the number of migrants decreases as distance increases.

During recent years Torsten Hägerstrand and associates at the University of Lund, Sweden, developed quite sophisticated theoretical models to account for population movements; several American geographers now also engage in this line of research. Some use gravity models to describe and predict movements between areas in terms of mass (population), distance, and relations between the two. Even these few components are not easy to define nor simple to relate. "Population" hides important qualitative differences and regional variations; "distance" can be measured in various ways. The formula to express interaction is not simply Newton's law, but requires manipulation to fit the empirical data (for a brief overview of the methodology and pertinent literature see Haggett, 1965, 33–40).

Effects of Migration. To give a systematic overview of the consequences of migration would lead too far, but to suggest some lines of inquiry may be useful.

There is, first of all, the effect of migration on the countries of ingress and egress. It raises such questions as these: Has emigration solved, or at least lessened, population pressure in the country of origin (e.g., Ireland)? Has the eviction of an ethnic group harmed or benefited the remaining society (e.g., expulsion of Jews and Moors from Spain)? What does an immigrant group contribute to the culture or economy of the receiving country (e.g., Germans in Brazil, Chinese in Southeast Asia, Indians in Fiji)?

Another set of questions assesses the effect of migration on the migrant. Who moves and who stays home? In other words, what is the selective process of migration? How far must the migrant travel? And does he move in stages, using intervening opportunities? Where does he settle? How does he adjust to the new physical and social environment? What functions in society does he perform? Does he maintain close ties with the homeland? Although the answers to some of these questions may lie beyond the competence of the geographer, they interest him insofar as they aid him to understand the character of a place and its relations with other places.

Palestinian Arab refugee camp in the Gaza strip, between the Mediterranean Sea and Israel. Most of the Arabs who fled or were expelled from Israel in the late 1940s still live in barrack camps in the territories of adjacent Arab states. The United Nations Relief and Works Agency supports the settlement shown here, and many others. [Courtesy of United Nations]

International and Internal Migrations. The distinction between intracountry and intercountry movements reflects the compartmentalization of the modern world into sovereign states. Statistical data adhere to this division because they are derived from national records, which strictly distinguish between the two forms. This duality has merits, but also shortcomings. Boundary changes make time-sequence comparisons difficult, as for instance regarding the outflow from

Poland, once carved up between the surrounding empires, reborn in 1919, and subsequently changed in extent several times.

For migrations in earlier periods, when state territories were ill-defined or nonexistent, the distinction between internal and international movements becomes impossible, even meaningless. In such cases it may be more proper to separate the migrations into those over short and long distance. But even under modern circumstances distance can be an important variable. Of course, the notion of what is near and what is far changes with improvements in transportation. Fifty years ago the countryman who found a factory job in the city 30 miles away would have moved there permanently; his grandson in similar circumstances may commute between his rural home and his work.

Often the distinction between long- and short-distance migration runs counter to that between international and internal migrations. For instance, moving from Quebec to Maine, or from eastern Bengal (Pakistan) to western Bengal (India) is by definition international, though it involves only a short distance. On the other hand, moving from Maine to California or from the Ukraine to the Lena basin is an internal transfer, but much farther than many international migrations.

In spite of the limitations, we classify migrations in this chapter primarily according to their international or internal character. Not only are the statistics poured in this mold, but more important, the move from one country to another usually involves a greater switch in sociocultural environment than one within the national borders.

International Migrations

The following examples illustrate (1) voluntary migrations, (2) forced migrations, and (3) labor movements. After what has been said before, we hardly need to point out that the categories are not sharply defined and may overlap.

Emigration from Europe. One of the great events of modern history is certainly that of

Europeans settling in newly discovered lands. Various estimates place the number who went overseas between 1500 and 1960 at 63 to 72 million. If one subtracts those who returned to Europe, the net number who permanently settled abroad may be put at 50 million or more. Of these, 36 million found a home in the United States. The remainder went to other parts of the Americas, Australia, New Zealand, and South Africa (Figure 19–1).

Until well into the nineteenth century the outflow of Europeans was a mere trickle, bringing to the Americas somewhat over two million people in three centuries. The British Isles, by far the main source in this early period, sent about 1,750,000 migrants overseas, mainly to North America. From Spain a few hundred thousand crossed to its American empire, from France perhaps 25,000 to Quebec and a few thousand to its Caribbean possessions. Over 100,000 migrants left Germany, the only country without colonies to participate significantly in the early settlement of North America.

If these figures seem surprisingly small, it should be remembered that slaves imported from Africa largely filled the labor demand in commercial agriculture. As estimated, by 1800 at least 15 million Africans had been shipped to the Americas, six times as many as the total number of European migrants of that date. Only a fraction of the Africans—less than half a million—came to what is now the United States.

Mass emigration from Europe began in the 1830s. From an annual outflow of over 100,000 in that decade it rose to 1,500,000 per year before World War I. The sources of the flow, too, changed. At first the countries of origin were chiefly in western Europe, but in the course of time, the headwaters of the migration streams reached farther and farther back into south and east Europe. After World War I emigration resumed, but at a lower level. The Soviet regime in Russia soon closed the door to emigrants, a policy extended after World War II to its satellites in east Europe.

Immigration into the United States. The influx into the United States reflected the European outflow until restrictions were put into effect in the 1920s (Table 19–1). As western Europe be-

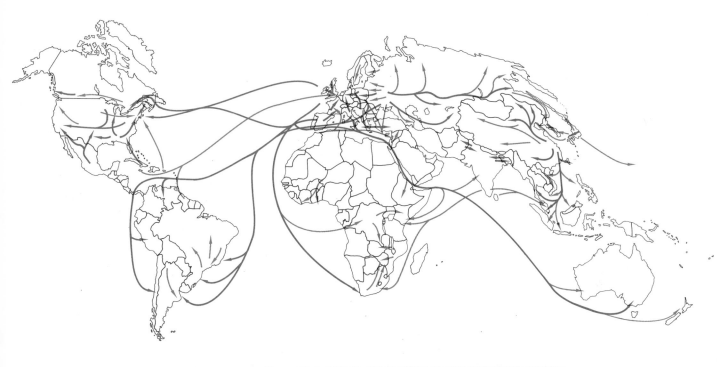

Figure 19-1. WORLD: MIGRATIONS OF THE TWENTIETH CENTURY

came a better place to live in, economically and socially, as well as politically, the lure of America faded. Immigration from western Europe was supplemented and soon surpassed by waves of the poor or oppressed from underdeveloped parts of Europe who had become aware of the opportunities that beckoned overseas (Figure 19-2).

Until 1890 the largest contingents came from the British Isles and Germany, joined by Scandinavians in the 1860s. Small numbers from Italy and the multinational Russian and Austro-Hungarian empires began to arrive in the late 1870s and gained dominance in the 1890s. In the decade 1901–1910, when newcomers averaged 800,000 per year, no less than 71 percent of them came from east and south Europe. Many Americans, alarmed by this drastic shift in ethnic composition, favored restrictive measures. The Act of 1882, which had curbed the

growing stream of Chinese into California, offered a precedent. In 1921 and 1924 Congress passed immigration laws in order "to maintain the cultural and racial homogeneity of the United States by the admission of immigrants in proportions corresponding to the composition in the present population." The national origins provision of the 1924 act, which became effective July 1, 1929, prescribed that the quota should be determined on the basis of the national origin of the total white population as enumerated in the 1920 census. The total annual quota was set at about 154,000, in addition to nonquota immigrants.

Economic depression in the 1930s reduced immigration, and war in the 1940s further disrupted the flow pattern. Since 1945, net immigration (the balance between inflow and outflow) has remained relatively low, averaging about 260,000 per year. Immigration now accounts for

19. Population Movements

463

Table 19–1. Origins of United States Immigrants from Europe by Top-ranking Countries, 1821–1960 (numbers of immigrants per decade in thousands)		
Period	Total from Europe	Top-ranking countries of origin
1821–1830	144	Ireland 51, Great Britain 25, Germany 7
1831–1840	599	Ireland 207, Germany 152, Great Britain 76
1841–1850	1,713	Ireland 781, Germany 435, Great Britain 267
1851–1860	2,453	Germany 952, Ireland 914, Great Britain 424
1861–1870	2,065	Germany 787, Great Britain 607, Ireland 436, Norway 72
1871–1880	2,272	Germany 718, Great Britain 548, Ireland 437, Sweden 116
1881–1890	4,737	Germany 1,453, Great Britain 807, Ireland 655, Sweden 392
1891–1900	3,559	Italy 652, Austria-Hungary 593, Russia 505, Germany 505
1901–1910	8,136	Austria-Hungary 2,145, Italy 2,046, Russia 1,597, Great Britain 526
1911–1920	4,337	Italy 1,110, Russia 921, Austria-Hungary 900, Greece 184
1921–1930*	2,478	Northwest Europe 871, South Europe 565, Central Europe 535, Germany-Austria 445
1931–1940*	348	Germany-Austria 118, Northwest Europe 84, South Europe 83, Central Europe 62
1941–1950*	622	Northwest Europe 263, Germany-Austria 252, South Europe 77, Central Europe 29
1951–1960*	1,318	Germany-Austria 545, Northwest Europe 447, South Europe 261, Central Europe 65

* The postwar boundary changes make strict comparison with previous decades impossible. Northwest Europe includes the British Isles, Scandinavia, Low Countries, France, Switzerland; South Europe: Italy, Greece, Spain, Portugal. Central Europe includes the successor states. The Soviet Union is excluded (immigration 62,000 in 1920–1930, less than 1,000 in later decades).
SOURCE: U.S. Bureau of the Census.

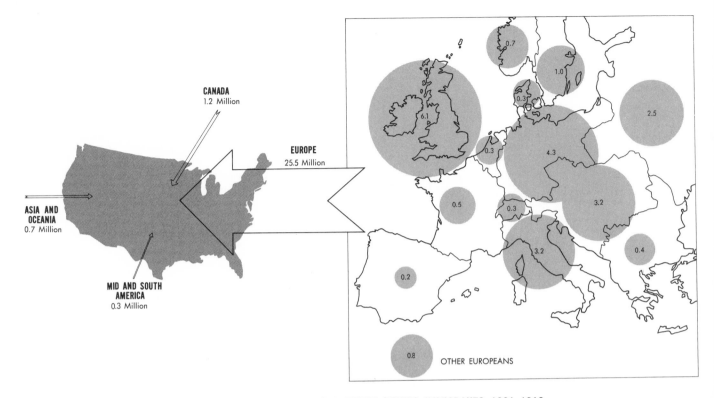

Figure 19–2. UNITED STATES: IMMIGRANTS, 1831–1910

Between 1831 and 1910, 27.7 million persons migrated to the United States.
All except 2.2 million (who arrived from Asia, Oceania, and other parts of the
Americas) came from Europe. The circles on the map of Europe are pro-
portional in area to the number of emigrants to the United States.

only a small part of the population growth of
the United States (Table 19–2).

In summary, from the 1920s to the 1960s immigration into the United States from Europe
no longer reflected population pressures. The
process was selective, favoring that part of Europe with the least need for emigration. Of the
annual quota total, 72 percent was allotted to
Great Britain, Ireland, and Germany. More than
half of their options were never used.

In 1966 Congress abolished the quota system,
but in fact continued it by giving first preference
to relatives of citizens. The new law also reduced
the possible number of immigrants, and barred

those who would take jobs that Americans could
fill.

In the postwar years the composition of immigration changed. The quota system never applied to countries of the Americas. Very few
came from there before World War I, and even
in the 1920s they constituted only one-third of
the total immigration. The majority of them
were from Canada. But in the mid-1960s over
two-fifths of all immigrants—somewhat more
than from Europe—arrived from Latin America,
mainly Mexico, Central America, and the Caribbean islands. This does not include Puerto Rico,
because its status of commonwealth, associated

*19. Population
Movements*

465

Table 19–2. Components of United States Population Growth, 1870–1960 (thousands)

Period	Population			Natural increase		Net immigration	
	Beginning of period	End of period	Increment	Number	Percent	Number	Percent
1870–1880	39,818	50,156	10,337	8,063	78.0	2,274	22.0
1880–1890	50,156	62,948	12,794	8,302	64.9	4,490	35.1
1890–1900	62,948	75,995	13,047	10,516	80.6	2,531	19.4
1900–1910	75,995	91,972	15,978	10,689	66.9	5,289	33.1
1910–1920	91,972	105,711	13,738	10,537	76.7	3,201	23.3
1920–1930	105,711	122,775	17,064	13,974	81.9	3,089	18.1
1930–1940	122,775	131,669	8,894	8,787	98.8	1,067	1.2
1940–1950*	131,669	150,697	19,028	18,153	95.4	875	4.6
1950–1960†	151,326	179,323	27,997	25,337	90.5	2,660	9.5

* Excludes Alaska and Hawaii.
† Includes Alaska and Hawaii.
In comparing Tables 19–1 and 19–2 it should be kept in mind that Table 19–2, aside from slightly different dates, presents *net* immigration from *all* countries.
SOURCE: Population Reference Bureau, *Population Bulletin,* 18 (1962): 140.

with the United States, gives its citizens free access.

The high growth rate of most Latin American countries, coupled with economic underdevelopment, is reminiscent of southern and eastern Europe around 1900. In light of these conditions, plus very high population densities in several Caribbean islands, the inflow of Latin Americans seems likely to increase in years to come unless the new immigration law is so interpreted as to limit their ingress.

Forced Migrations. The international migrations described in the previous section were classed as "voluntary," not because pressures to move were absent, but because, by and large, the migrants on their own account decided to leave their country and settle elsewhere. The present section deals with migrations resulting from coercion, by higher authority or other powerful groups. The historical record of population movements is punctuated by such human crises, among them the Diaspora of the Jews, the expulsion of the Huguenots from France, and the deportation of American Indians from their tribal territories. The slave-hauling from

Africa by Arabs and Europeans, stretching over many centuries, was selective removal rather than a wholesale evacuation, but is no less tragic than the cataclysmic deportations of entire ethnic or religious groups.

Europe. The power of modern governments, together with means of mass transportation, makes possible massive transfers undreamed of in former times. The evidence lies in the events in mid-twentieth century Europe, when some 45 million people were uprooted within a dozen years. The currents and countercurrents of exchange, deportation, expulsion, evacuation, and flight are too complex to describe here (Kulischer, 1953; Proudfoot, 1956). Only some major categories can be mentioned. The Nazis gathered up the Jews, first in Germany, later in occupied territories, and murdered most of them—close to six million. To secure an adequate labor force for its war production, Germany took in eight million laborers from conquered lands and transferred another four million from one country to another. Most of those who survived the hardships of slave labor returned to their homes after the war. Other forced mass movements involved the hapless Estonians, Latvians, and

Lithuanians, caught between the war machines and political designs of Hitler and Stalin. The Balkan countries also experienced various transfers of ethnic groups. Within the Soviet Union at least 1½ million refugees from the war zone were relocated in the Urals and Soviet Asia; a million Volga Germans (suspected of disloyalty to the Soviet state) were moved to Siberia.

The retreat of the German armies from Russia put ethnic Germans to flight from all over eastern Europe. Following the war's end, massive evacuations of Germans took place from Czechoslovakia (2.7 million) and from the territory east of the Oder-Neisse (6.5 million). In addition, over five million Germans escaped from Soviet-occupied East Germany to West Germany. Altogether, Hitler's dream of empire caused, as a direct or indirect consequence, at least 15 million ethnic and Reich Germans to lose their homes. As the Germans withdrew, peoples of Slavic speech moved westward (Figure 19-3). Already before the war many Germans had left agrarian east Germany for jobs in Berlin and the western industrial districts. Their places were filled by poor Poles and Slovaks who came chiefly for seasonal labor, but often stayed for long periods or for good. Hence, it has been argued that the sudden westward shift of Slavs after the war was a climactic expression of an already existing ethnic trend.

Israel. The establishment of a national home for Jewish people in Palestine is so closely linked to coercion in other countries that the immigration into this area is best included under the heading of forced migrations. Moreover, the creation of Israel led to an involuntary outflow of Arabs.

In 1882 some 24,000 Jews lived in Palestine among the largely Arab population. By 1919 natural growth and a small influx had raised their number to somewhat over 70,000. During the British mandate over Palestine (1919 to 1948), 430,000 Jewish immigrants arrived, 90 percent from Europe. These, together with natural growth, brought the total Jewish population in Palestine to 650,000 in May, 1948.

The United Nations' approval of the partition of Palestine in the fall of 1947 led to clashes between Arabs and Jews, which grew into open warfare between the state of Israel, proclaimed in May, 1948, and the neighboring Arab states. In the struggle some 700,000 Arabs fled or were ousted from the territory of the new state. These refugees still live largely in "temporary" camps, close to Israel's borders, in Egypt, Jordan, Syria, and Lebanon.

In accordance with the policy of gathering in the exiles, the "Law of Return" gives every Jew the right to settle in Israel. Moreover, the new state, surrounded by enemies, needs people. The size of the country compares with that of New Jersey, but much of it has an arid climate. The truly remarkable resource development demonstrates what a people with vision, zeal—and generous external financial support—can accomplish in a habitat commonly perceived as "desert." Foremost among its many problems is that of building one nation from the diverse cultural strains of Jews now assembled within Israel's borders.

The registration of November, 1948, showed 873,000 citizens, of whom 717,000 were Jews and 156,000 (18 percent) non-Jews, mainly Moslem Arabs. Of the Jews 35 percent were native-born (chiefly of European parentage), 55 percent immigrants of "Western" origin, and only 10 percent immigrants of "Oriental" origin. Israel uses the term "Oriental" to designate those who come from North Africa and the Middle East, almost all Sephardic Jews.

By 1965 the total population of Israel had grown to slightly over 2.5 million, of whom 280,000 (11 percent) were non-Jews. Almost one million of the increase between 1948 and 1965 was due to net immigration. (Some 129,000 Jews left Israel between 1948 and 1960.) To absorb such a high ratio of newcomers in a short time would strain the social and economic framework of any country. In Israel a shift in the origin of immigrants aggravated the problem. After 1950 more Oriental Jews came than European, so that in 1965 they formed almost one-third of the Jewish population. The new arrivals, from Morocco to Iran and from Egypt to Yemen, generally were illiterate and poor. More significant, they brought along the languages, values, and economic modes of life of the traditional societies whence they came. In almost all re-

19. Population Movements

467

spects there is a broad cultural gap between these newcomers and the industrial-urban society developed by the Western Jews. Moreover, the former grow at a fast pace because Oriental-Jewish mothers average 5 children each compared to the Western-Jewish average of 2.3. The effort and cost of assimilating the new ethnic groups (education, job training, health care, housing, and so on), together with high defense expenditure, impede the country's economic development.

The precarious social status of the 300,000 Oriental Jews who still live outside Israel marks them as potential emigrants to that country, which would reinforce the present trend. Western Jews who fear that the new immigration may change Israel into quite a different society wonder what reservoirs of Western Jewry can be tapped to balance the recent influx. Very few of the 7 million Jews in Anglo-America and Europe west of the Iron Curtain show interest at present in moving to the land of their forefathers. The 2.7 million Jews behind the Iron Curtain, chiefly in the Soviet Union, may not leave. If the bars were removed, many would undoubtedly go to Israel. The only other remaining source of Western Jewry is Latin America. Whether a substantial number of the 700,000 who live there can be induced to move to Israel is not known.

The case of Israel strikingly demonstrates how difficult the process of integration can be, even where the national ideology favors it and the government is firmly committed to carrying out the task. The Israeli citizens of Oriental origin are in virtually all respects worse off than their "European" compatriots. They occupy the lower rungs of the economic ladder, have lower incomes, lower literacy rates, and higher crime rates. They complain bitterly of discrimination, while the Western Jews justify their own higher rank in the pecking order by their alleged merits (Safran, 1965). Yet, "the two Israels" must fuse into one nation and—if the present rate of development is to be maintained—on the Occidental pattern envisaged by the founding generation. If this fails, the ingathering of exiles may well result in a very different Israel from that

V. Population
Change

468

Figure 19–3. EUROPE: MIGRATIONS, 1944–1951

In the aftermath of World War II mass movements occurred in central Europe. Expulsion of German citizens and ethnic Germans from eastern Europe, Italians and Hungarians from some southeastern European countries, and Poles from the Soviet Union was followed by streams of Slavic peoples moving in a generally westward direction. The Russians removed from the Crimea were mainly Tatars. Many Balts fled to the West, others were deported to Siberia. Finns were expelled from the territory annexed by the Soviet Union. Many Turks in Bulgaria were repatriated.

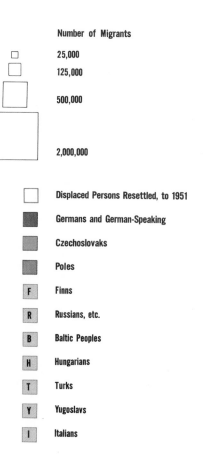

Number of Migrants

25,000

125,000

500,000

2,000,000

Displaced Persons Resettled, to 1951

Germans and German-Speaking

Czechoslovaks

Poles

F Finns

R Russians, etc.

B Baltic Peoples

H Hungarians

T Turks

Y Yugoslavs

I Italians

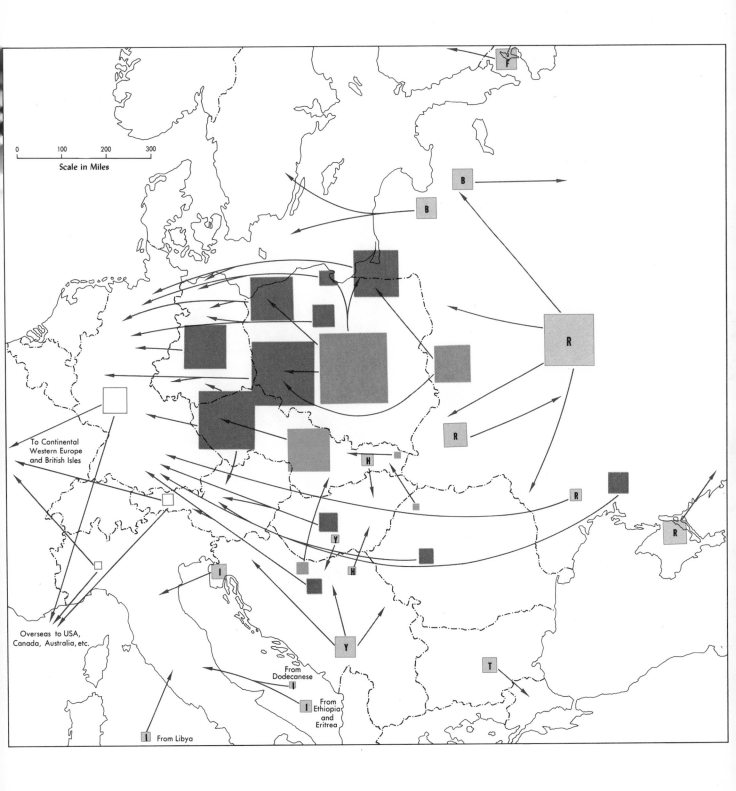

0   100   200   300

Scale in Miles

B

B

R

B

R

R

R

H

R

To Continental
Western Europe
and British Isles

H

Y

H

Overseas to USA,
Canada, Australia, etc.

Y

I

T

From
Dodecanese

Y

I

From
Ethiopia
and
Eritrea

I   From Libya

Israel: "Ship-to-Settlement-Movement." In a number of cases new immigrants
have been moved directly after their debarkation to the new village where
homes are ready to receive them. This agricultural settlement (Shefer) lies on
the southern mountain slopes of upper Galilee, overlooking the Sea of Galilee,
or Lake Kinneret. [Courtesy of Information Department, Jewish Agency, Jerusalem]

expected when the Law of Return was proclaimed.

South and East Asia. The partition of the
British Empire in India, in August, 1947, set off
mass migrations on a scale that rivaled and perhaps surpassed those of Europe. Thousands
were killed in communal riots, and millions fled
in panic across the newly established borders
between India and Pakistan. By March 1948,
6.5 million Moslems had sought refuge in West
Pakistan and some 6 million Hindus and Sikhs
had left it.

A little later in East Pakistan, Moslem out-

bursts drove out 3.5 million Hindus. The reaction in West Bengal sent a counterwave of
Moslems fleeing to East Pakistan. Altogether
these violent displacements involved some 17
million people. Twenty years later the problems
created by the human upheaval were still not
solved; mutual resentment still hangs like a
pall over Indian-Pakistani relations.

At the end of World War II 5.5 million Japanese were repatriated from former Japanese-
held territories; 1.1 million persons, chiefly
Koreans, who had been working in Japan's
mines and factories, were sent home. Another

Figure 19-4. EUROPE: MAJOR SOURCES OF FOREIGN LABOR

The widths of the arrows show the major flows of workers to Europe's industrial countries. Based on a map in *The Economist,* 1966, 723.

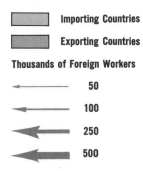

Importing Countries

Exporting Countries

Thousands of Foreign Workers

50

100

250

500

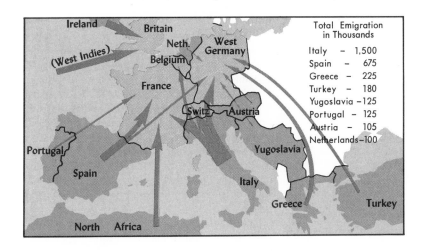

Total Emigration in Thousands	
Italy	1,500
Spain	675
Greece	225
Turkey	180
Yugoslavia	125
Portugal	125
Austria	105
Netherlands	100

example is that of Indochina after the French defeat and the division of Vietnam in 1954, when some two million people, mostly Catholics, fled to the South.

International Labor Movements. *General Considerations.* Shortage of labor in one country and a surplus in others set strong currents of people into motion. If the distance is great, transportation costly, and the home situation repellent, the migrant packs up without hope or intention to return. However, when distance becomes a minor matter and ties with the homeland are strong—or if the receiving country discourages permanent settlement—the worker departs for a limited stay ranging from a season of road construction or farm work to a few years of mine or factory employment. Or he may merely be a daily commuter with his home on one side of the border and his job in the industrial district on the other. Hence, the number of foreign workers who live temporarily at the place of employment increases in comparison to those who migrate for the purpose of permanent settlement. This greater mobility causes an extraordinarily complex pattern of oscillations. New workers stream to areas of

labor shortage, brushing past compatriots on the way home after their stint abroad. But not all go home; a number prefer the life abroad, assimilate into the foreign society, and become permanent residents; or they may move on to another country.

At the same time the nation that takes in unskilled aliens at the bottom of the labor pool may lose its top specialists to a more advanced country, temporarily or for good (e.g., the "brain drain" from Great Britain). To catch in statistical form this anthill-like to-and-fro travel is often a frustrating task.

Labor Movements in Europe. In Europe the tragic forced transfers of people during the war and postwar years have been succeeded by broad currents of workers who freely seek better opportunities. Similar movements occurred before World War II: Poles and Slovaks served as farmhands on the estates in eastern Germany or in the mines of western Europe; Italians constructed roads in Switzerland; Spaniards helped with the harvests in France. But these and other travels were a minor phenomenon compared to the massive flows today (Figure 19-4).

The general economic upswing in Europe during the 1950s and 1960s was especially steep in

19. Population Movements

471

its commercial-industrial core. It soon attracted labor from the agrarian periphery, where open or disguised unemployment and low wages prevail, that is, in the countries of Italy, Spain, Ireland, Greece, Turkey, Yugoslavia, Portugal, and Austria. (The Netherlands too experienced a loss of workers—a consequence of its postwar policy of winning markets abroad by keeping wages down—but influx from elsewhere partly offset this.) Workers from the Soviet Union and its satellites do not participate in these movements, not because they are better off, but because their governments virtually prohibit emigration.

The main receiving countries of intra-European labor migrations are France and West Germany, each with 1.25 to 1.5 million foreign workers within its borders in 1965. France draws its labor supply mainly from Spain, Italy, and North Africa, but West Germany also from southeast Europe. Britain's number of foreign workers equals those of France or West Germany; most come from Ireland and the Commonwealth countries, especially the Caribbean and West Pakistan. Switzerland harbors over three-fourths of a million migrant workers, the bulk of them Italian, who form almost one-third of the Swiss labor force, a proportion higher than in any other country.

Over the last twenty years the areas supplying migrant workers have expanded. To take West Germany again as an example: Until the early 1950s over four-fifths of all sojourners were Italians. To fill its increasing labor demands, West Germany imported growing numbers of Spaniards and Greeks and, since 1960, also Turks. In 1966 Italians constituted only two-fifths of the alien labor force, the remainder about equally divided between Spaniards, Greeks, and Turks.

As economic conditions in Italy improve, the native of the indigent South has a better chance to find employment in his own country. Indeed the movement of Italians abroad shows signs of slackening. The outflow from Spain and Greece probably will continue for some years at a fairly high rate if the West European economy keeps up its pace, and that from Turkey probably will increase markedly. In the near future, Portugal, which so far has sent out a rather modest number (mostly to France), may well participate significantly in the intercountry labor movements.

Most of the migrants are unskilled or semi-skilled. They fill whatever less desirable jobs the local men vacate as they move up the social ladder by qualifying as technicians or foremen in industry or by taking positions in the expanding service sector. For instance, West Germany in the middle sixties had 84 percent of its foreign employees in mining, industry, and construction. However, the import of aliens does not cut costs. Because the national unions want no competition from sweated labor, the migrants receive the prevailing wages. They send home a substantial part of their pay—which unfavorably affects the balance of payments of the employer country. The entrepreneur, who usually foots the transportation bill, finds that it takes some weeks before the newcomers can adjust to the new environment and their tasks. Moreover, these foreign workers have a much higher rate of turnover than the local ones.

From the business point of view it would be advantageous to induce the foreigner to remain, have his family come over, and settle down as permanent resident. However, this raises questions of assimilation and integration which the European nations have not yet solved. The Common Market countries have pledged to remove all barriers to free circulation of workers and to give domestic and foreign labor equal treatment. To implement these principles takes time. Moreover, with the exception of Italy, the big labor reservoirs lie outside the Common Market. Nor is Switzerland, a substantial importer of labor, a member of this group. The Swiss have already severely restricted the influx of foreign manpower because the immigration from Italy brought unfavorable social repercussions. Several countries welcome the temporary worker, but do not wish to admit his family. If the time away from home is relatively long, this breakup of family life has harmful consequences.

The sending countries, too, have mixed feelings about labor migration. The remittance of earnings is a very welcome addition to the national income. The skills most of the returnees have gained aid the developing economy. Precisely for this reason these countries do not wish to see the industrial lands to the north cream off their energetic young men permanently. Greece is particularly worried about the drain abroad. So far, only one Greek returns home for every four who leave (Foreign Workers, 1966, 723). In 1965 the number of emigrants from Greece to all countries—temporary and permanent—exceeded the natural increase by 50 percent. This efflux especially affects the already sparsely populated border areas.

In summary, Europe's new labor mobility—outside the Soviet sphere—brings benefits as well as problems. Although a portion of the migratory workers may settle for good in the new land, the far greater part considers the time abroad a temporary expedient. Governments of sending and receiving countries alike favor temporary movements over permanent mass migrations. International treaties and domestic laws, taking cognizance of this new phenomenon, must provide rules that protect the migrants and their families, and at the same time serve the interests of the diverse national economies.

Labor Movements in Africa. Migratory labor commonly occurs in traditional and tribal societies whenever Occidental enterprises settle amid villages geared to subsistence agriculture. The foreign entrepreneur needs labor; the worker, after initial indifference or reluctance, accepts the chance to earn cash, but does not want to give up the relationship with his village, clan, or tribe. Thus he vacillates between two modes of life at intervals of a few months to several years. At mine or plantation, as employee of Western business, he participates in the money economy; in his own community he shares as part-time villager in the social system, including the rights and obligations of kinship and land cultivation. This compromise between the old and the new, the indigenous and the alien worlds, takes on many forms in Latin America, South and Southeast Asia, and Africa.

Africa illustrates especially well the various facets of current labor movements. Opening up Africa's interior in the latter part of the nineteenth century brought discoveries of rich mineral deposits: diamonds in Orange Free State, Transvaal, South-West Africa, and later Tanzania; gold at the fabulous Witwatersrand; copper, uranium, zinc, lead, chrome, asbestos, and other metals in Katanga (southern Congo), Zambia (formerly North Rhodesia), and Rhodesia (formerly South Rhodesia). The tribesman within his self-sufficient economy had no incentive to perform wage labor for European enterprises. Since slavery had been abolished—at least by law—the British used taxation as indirect coercion. The taxes had to be paid in money; this forced many Africans to work awhile at the mines. A second stage was to recruit labor, still practiced to some extent, particularly for the Rand gold mines, which employ some 300,000 workers. In most areas the economic incentives to seek employment are now sufficiently strong to ensure adequate labor through voluntary migration, in some cases assisted by free transportation and accommodations along the way.

Since the mining areas lack an adequate local labor force, most of the workers must come from other parts of the same country or from adjoining territories, a number even from quite distant countries. The South African Republic draws on its own native reservations, but also on Botswana (Bechuanaland), Lesotho (Basutoland), and Mozambique (Portuguese East Africa). Zambia, which in addition to its mines has many tobacco farms, depends for over half of its labor needs on external sources, mainly Malawi and Mozambique. Rhodesia, four-fifths self-sufficient in labor, imports the balance from Malawi, Tanzania, and Angola.

Although the African laborer supposedly is free to accept or decline work in European enterprises, it would be naïve to believe that there is no coercion. During the initial period working conditions, wages, housing, and other social provisions left much to be desired. Governments gradually issued rules to protect workers and regulated, by international conventions, the traffic of migratory workers across borders. In the course of time these measures have done away with the worst features of labor migrations. Nevertheless, serious problems remain and they go well beyond the welfare of the migratory worker.

First and foremost the native peasant in south and south central Africa produces foodstuffs for his own use. He obtains cash mainly through wage labor away from his village. As need for money increases so does mobility. Going off to work is now generally accepted as part of normal young male behavior. But his tribal village remains his home. Hence arises the assumption that the African is a visitor, a transient, in urban areas. In several southern African countries this attitude is reflected in the legal position of the African: He belongs in a tribal area; he sojourns in a European town only as an employee. In consequence, few if any urban areas provide African families with adequate permanent residence. This impedes the adjustment to city life and reinforces the pull of the tribal areas (Mitchell, 1961, 236–239).

As population increases and standards of living rise, the tribal lands fill to capacity. Many Africans, whether they—and the Europeans—like it or not, must find a permanent niche in town. This requires, however, a more stable economic basis, including a broader range of urban employment than is now available in the mining towns. It also demands that the African develop more specialized interests and skills. Obviously such a socioeconomic transformation is a slow and often painful process.

Internal Migrations

We have already considered in other contexts some forms of internal mobility: frontier settlement, the flow toward metropolitan areas, and the journey to work. In this sector we call attention to interregional migrations within China, the Soviet Union, and the United States.

China.   From the dawn of Chinese civilization in the lands of the Huang Ho gradual expansion southward has been a persistent theme of Chinese history. On the north flank the attitude long remained defensive: The Great Wall was the divide between agrarian China and pastoral nomadism. In time, nevertheless, small numbers of Chinese farmers gradually moved beyond the wall into the coastal margin of Manchuria, even though the Manchu emperors of China opposed this trespass onto the grazing lands of their compatriots.

Around 1900 an entirely new situation was created when the Russians completed the Trans-Siberian Railway with its branch line southward through Manchuria to Port Arthur. Now it became possible to use the fertile soils for commercial agriculture and to exploit the mineral wealth of the region. Although in the subsequent 50 years Manchuria became a "cradle of conflict" between Russia, China, and Japan, the imperial shifts of fortune hardly affected the basic trend of development: Capital investment created a demand for wage labor, and North China was the obvious reservoir. Initially the migratory movement was seasonal, and the net permanent immigration small. As the economy of Manchuria expanded, more and more Chinese settled there on farms and in cities. In the late 1920s when the Chinese government concentrated on building strength in Manchuria against possible aggression, the influx of Chinese reached one million per year. In 1931 Japanese occupation stopped the tide, but later immigration resumed, although on a more moderate level, as Japanese industrialists in the puppet state of Manchukuo needed labor for their expanding mineral and industrial production.

There are no exact figures available on Manchuria's annual number of migratory workers, permanent settlers, and returnees, nor on the composition, origin, and destination of the population movement. But the vast wave of immigration is suggested by these figures: In 1900 the population of Manchuria was estimated at 10 million, consisting of Chinese in the very south and Manchu nomads elsewhere. In 1911 the number of inhabitants was 15 million, mainly Chinese; in 1930 it had doubled to 30 million; in 1950 it was over 40 million, 95 percent Chinese.

After World War II China incorporated Manchuria as its new northeastern provinces. Industrial development in the People's Republic of China mainly centers in this region, which must have attracted many workers from other parts of China. The present population of the northeastern provinces is estimated at over 50 million, mostly living along the north-south axis from Harbin via Shenyang (Mukden) to Talien (Dairen).

The confrontation of China with Russia across their lengthy common border, a fact of long standing, has recently taken on an increasingly ominous character. Both the Soviet Union and the People's Republic strive to remove uncommitted indigenous tribes from the border zone, replacing them by ethnic Russians and Chinese. Transportation development and land reclamation in (Chinese) Inner Mongolia and Sinkiang serve strategic as well as economic objectives. The population transfer associated with this frontier settlement involves substantial numbers of Chinese. According to estimates of Western scholars, the number of ethnic Chinese in Sinkiang has risen between 1949 and 1965 from about 200,000 to 2.5 million, of a provincial population of roughly 7 million in 1965.

The rapid population increase of mainland China may well cause its leaders to speculate on outlets beyond the present borders. The Soviet Far East and eastern Siberia adjacent to China are sparsely populated lands, rich in mineral resources and capable of further agricultural development in spite of the harsh climate. They may well become a new cradle of conflict.

Soviet Union. In the middle of the sixteenth century, while western Europe was turning toward the ocean, Muscovy began its expansion east across the Ural Mountains. Advancing by rivers and across portages, Cossacks and traders swiftly traversed Siberia and reached the Sea of Okhotsk in 1647. Although the conquest yielded great profits in furs and gold, the Russian colonists by 1800 still numbered less than 600,000.

The flow increased in the first half of the nineteenth century, in part through large deportations from Russia proper. After serfdom had been abolished in 1861, many peasants moved into western Siberia, mainly to the open woods and grasslands south of the boreal forest. The building of the Trans-Siberian Railway during the last decade of the nineteenth century brought greater mobility and economic opportunity. The influx became a mass migration. An estimated total of seven million Russians moved east across the Urals between 1801 and 1914, two-thirds of them in the last two decades of that period. World War I and the revolution stemmed this flow.

In the mid-1920s the Soviet government undertook to develop its Asian frontier in conjunction with the overall planning of the Soviet economy. In contrast to czarist days, industrial growth received the emphasis. Migration was directed toward the new mining and manufacturing centers in the Kuznetsk Basin, the Far East, and Central Asia, instead of western South Siberia. Between 1926 and the German invasion of 1941, some six million people were transferred from Soviet Europe to Soviet Asia. To these must be added unrevealed but vast numbers of "politically abnormal" citizens and other delinquents who, in the old Russian tradition, were sent to labor camps in the least attractive parts of Siberia to work in mines, forests, and on railroad and road construction. During the war two or more millions of refugees and deportees were resettled across the Urals. The exploitation of the "virgin lands" brought a new wave to Kazakhstan in the 1950s.

Immigration since 1926, combined with a moderately high natural growth, has greatly increased the population of Russia beyond the Urals. In 1926 the area contained 27 million; it is estimated that forty years later the number had just about doubled. The shift from agricultural to industrial development caused the urban population to rise much faster than the rural population.

Soviet colonization policy has deeply affected the ethnic composition. Even in districts where indigenous peoples are still in the majority—chiefly in Central Asia—economic and political leadership is in the hands of the immigrants. The Russian cultural impact is profound.

United States. To be "on the go" characterizes the typical American. Quite apart from the hectic to-and-fro of commuters and travelers for business or pleasure, people in the United States change residence with remarkable frequency. According to recent census data one out of five Americans one year old and over moves to a new address each year. About 13 percent of the population move within counties; the 7 percent who cross county lines are about equally divided between those who move to a new home within the state and those who go to a different state. This order reminds one of

19. Population Movements

Ravenstein's dictum that migration volume relates inversely to distance. Most leave the countryside or small service centers for cities or change residence within metropolitan areas.

The movement between states, or more broadly between regions, deserves special attention (Figure 19–5). Though people move in large numbers from almost every state, their goals are concentrated in a few. Many states in the North Central region and in the South experienced during the 1950s and 1960s a net out-migration (Figure 19–6). However, in all but Mississippi, Arkansas, and West Virginia, the natural increase more than offset the loss of

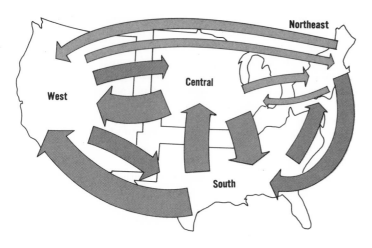
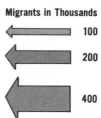

Figure 19–5. UNITED STATES: INTERREGIONAL MIGRATION, 1960–1965

Flow-line widths are proportional to the number of interregional migrants. Based on a map in U.S. Department of Commerce, 1966.

Migrants in Thousands

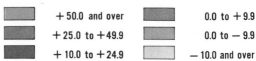

100

200

400

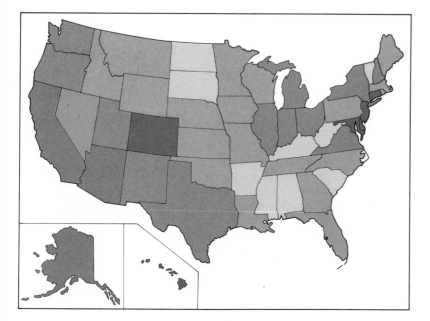

Figure 19–6. UNITED STATES: NET MIGRATION BY STATES, 1950–1960

Net migration is the difference between in-migration and out-migration. In the 1950s, net out-migration characterized the Old South, the Great Plains states, the northern Rocky Mountain region, and parts of New England; net in-migration was evident in Megalopolis, in the industrial Midwest, and especially in Florida, the Southwest, and the Far West. SOURCE: same as for Figure 19–7.

Percentage of the 1950 Population

+ 50.0 and over

+ 25.0 to + 49.9

+ 10.0 to + 24.9

0.0 to + 9.9

0.0 to − 9.9

− 10.0 and over

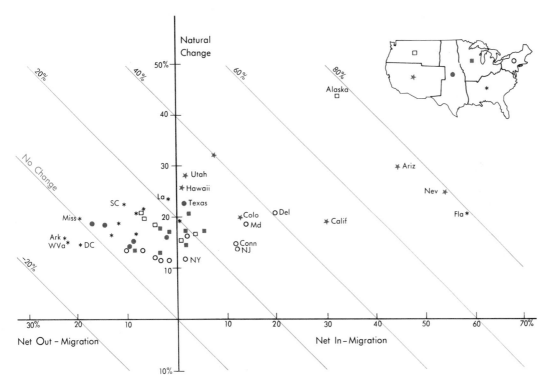

Figure 19–7. UNITED STATES: COMPONENTS OF POPULATION CHANGE, 1950–1960

This figure shows for each state (1) natural change on the vertical axis, (2) net migrational change on the horizontal axis, (3) population change, the resultant, on the diagonal axis, between 1950 and 1960, expressed as a percentage of the 1950 population. The states are distinguished by regional symbols. States identified by name on the graph do not conform to the general population change pattern of their region. Data are from U.S. Bureau of the Census, *Current Population Reports,* Series P-25, No. 304, "Revised Estimates of the Population of States and Components of Population Change: 1950 to 1960." Washington, D.C., 1965, table 4. Also see Figure 19–6.

migrants. At the other extreme, California, Nevada, Arizona, and Florida gained more from migration than from natural increase. These states grew at the annual rate of over 3 percent between 1960 and 1965, more than twice the 1.5 percent of the entire country. In these same five years the South increased only a little above average. Compared to the 1950s, net migration

from the South (largely to the industrial areas in the North and West) appears to have slowed down. The Northeast and North Central regions on the whole grew at a rate below the national average, the chief exception being Megalopolis, which continued to grow at a rate well above the mean (Figure 19–7).

The "West," as defined by the census, was

19. Population Movements

the only region in the 1950s and 1960s to register a net gain from migration, while all the others lost. This underscores the common observation that the westward movement continues, though the frontier vanished over sixty years ago. From 1960 to 1965 "an average of one million persons per year moved into the West from other regions, while 600,000 migrated from the West, a ratio of 5 in-migrants to 3 out-migrants. Nearly a third of the total inter-regional migration had the West as its destination, with the largest streams of in-migrants coming from the South and the North Central regions" (U.S. Department of Commerce, 1966, 17).

It would lead too far to examine here the demographic and economic characteristics of the migrants. Sufficient to say, young people in their twenties comprise the most mobile segment of the population. Also, the Negro out-migration from the South has greatly changed their distribution. In 1950 only one-third of them lived outside the South, now one-half of them do.

Conclusion

People do not move to empty lands; they move toward better opportunities. This point needs emphasis because it is a common error to translate the unique experience of the nineteenth century agricultural frontier into a general rule.

The "better opportunities" are not necessarily of an economic nature. The American Negro leaves the South to escape a caste society; the Moslem Indian flees from Hindu domination; the Middle Westerner seeks the more attractive climate of California or Arizona; rural youth everywhere are attracted by the excitement of the big city.

The time of free international migration is past. The few countries that admit substantial numbers of people carefully screen them on their merits. Even if racial discrimination were unknown, hardly a state in the world would throw its doors open to illiterate and unskilled masses. Yet mass migration would be necessary to give even temporary relief to the mounting pressures in South and East Asia. For example, India's population grows 11 million per year. If only half were to depart for other countries, 15,000 per day would have to leave India's ports. Quite apart from the question of where they would go, the sheer logistics of transportation staggers the imagination. Asia's population increases by 40 million annually; it took Europe over a century to send that many people abroad. Obviously migration offers no cure for dense and rapidly growing populations. Instead, each country must solve its dilemma by internal development, international trade, and drastic birth control. Among the Asian countries, Japan has done all three, and is reaping the benefits of its policy.

The end of great intercontinental migrations does not mean lesser mobility. To the contrary, Anglo-America and Europe demonstrate how facility of movement allows people to take advantage of economic opportunities within the national or continental framework. As the Industrial Revolution, including mass transportation, spreads to the underdeveloped countries, they too will profit from greater mobility.

Citations

"Foreign Workers: Europe's Prop," *The Economist,* May 14, 1966, 722–723.

Haggett, P. *Locational Analysis in Human Geography,* New York, 1965.

Kulischer, E. M. *The Displacement of Population in Europe,* Montreal, 1953.

Mitchell, J. C. "Wage Labour and African Population Movements in Central Africa," in Barbour, K. M., and Prothero, R. M. (eds.) *Essays on African Population,* London, 1961, 193–248.

Proudfoot, M. J. *European Refugees, 1939–1952: A Study in Forced Population Movement,* Evanston, Ill., 1956.

V. Population Change

Ravenstein, E. G. "The Laws of Migration," *Journal of the Royal Statistical Society,* 48 (1885): 167–235; 52 (1889): 241–305.

Safran, N. "Israel Today: A Profile," *Headline Series* no. 170, The Foreign Policy Association, New York, 1965.

U.S. Department of Commerce, *Americans at Mid-decade,* Washington, D.C., 1966. [Map]

Further Readings

Bowman, I. *The Pioneer Fringe,* American Geographical Society, Special Publication no. 13, New York, 1931.

Brondsted, J. *The Vikings,* London, 1960.

Buck, P. H. *Vikings of the Sunrise,* New York, 1938. [Polynesia]

Cook, R. C. "Israel: Land of Promise and Perplexities," *Population Bulletin,* 21 (1965): 101–134.

Dominedo, F. M. "How Migration Affects the Country of Immigration," *Migration,* 2, 2 (1962): 49–60.

Elston, D. R. *Israel: The Making of a Nation,* London, 1963.

Foster, P. W. "Migrations and Agriculture," U.S. Department of Agriculture, *Farmer's World,* Yearbook of Agriculture, Washington, D.C., 1964, 22–29.

Freeman, T. W. "Population and Emigration," in *Pre-famine Ireland: A Study in Historical Geography,* Manchester, England, 1957.

Goodrich, C., Allin, B. W., and Hayes, M. *Migration and Planes of Living, 1920–1934,* Philadelphia, 1935.

Hannerberg, D., Hägerstrand, T., and Odeving, B. (eds.) "Migrations in Sweden: A Symposium," *Lund Studies in Geography, Series B, Human Geography,* 13 (1957).

International Labor Office *International Migration, 1945–1957,* Geneva, 1959.

International Migration (periodical), 1962–.

Joerg, W. L. G. (ed.) *Pioneer Settlement,* Cooperative Studies by Twenty-six Authors, American Geographical Society, Special Publication no. 14, New York, 1932.

Johnson, H. B. "The Location of German Immigrants in the Middle West," *Annals of the Association of American Geographers,* 41 (1951): 1–41.

Kant, E. "Classification and Problems of Migration," translated from Swedish in Wagner, P. L., and Mikesell, M. W. (eds.) *Readings in Cultural Geography,* Chicago, 1962, 342–354.

Kindleberger, C. P. "Mass Migration, Then and Now," *Foreign Affairs,* 43, 4 (1965): 647–658.

Lowenthal, D., and Comitas, L. "Emigration and Depopulation: Some Neglected Aspects of Population Geography," *Geographical Review,* 52 (1962): 195–210.

Mikesell, M. W. "Comparative Studies in Frontier History," *Annals of the Association of American Geographers,* 50 (1960): 62–74.

Rochgau, G. "Die innereuropäischen Arbeiterwanderungen," *Geographische Rundschau,* 18 (1966): 121–128.

19. Population Movements

Rose, A. J. "The Geographical Pattern of European Immigration in Australia," *Geographical Review,* 48 (1958): 512–527.

Schechtman, J. *Postwar Population Transfers in Europe, 1945–1955,* Philadelphia, 1962.

Sorre, M. *Les Migrations des peuples: Essai sur la mobilité géographique,* Paris, 1955.

Stouffer, S. A. "Intervening Opportunities: A Theory Relating Mobility and Distance," *American Sociological Review,* 5 (1940): 845–867.

Thornthwaite, W. *Internal Migration in the United States,* Philadelphia, 1934.

Toniolo, A. R. "Studies of Depopulation in the Mountains of Italy," *Geographical Review,* 27 (1937): 473–477.

United Nations, Department of Social Affairs, *Analytical Bibliography of International Migration Statistics, 1925–1950,* New York, 1955.

Velikonja, J. "Postwar Population Movements in Europe," *Annals of the Association of American Geographers,* 48 (1958): 458–481.

Wheeler, J. O., and Brunn, S. D. "Negro Migration into Rural Southwestern Michigan," *Geographical Review,* 58 (1968): 214–230.

20. Problems of Population Growth

Controversial Views

All organisms must adapt to their environment or perish. Man faces the curious paradox that as he creates more and more of his environment, he becomes increasingly vulnerable to catastrophe. For example, unlocking nuclear energy promises enormous benefits if wisely used, but if uncontrolled threatens to extinguish mankind. Another instance—the theme of this chapter—is the antithesis between the modern means to assure a long and healthful life and the danger that mankind will be smothered by its own numbers.

Population growth and its implications have been discussed since ancient times. Plato stressed the quality of man, and actually estimated the optimum population size of his ideal city-state. Aristotle expressed concern with more materialistic aspects of excessive population growth, and advocated birth control to prevent poverty. On the other hand, Roman authors favored large and increasing numbers to provide manpower for the expanding empire. These two opposing philosophies cropped up in later times, but not until 1800 did the relation between population growth and welfare become a major issue.

Malthus, Marx, and Modern Thought. The idea of human progress came to the fore late in the eighteenth century. Thomas R. Malthus (1766–1834) took issue with the social philosophers who thought that rational man could rapidly perfect his existence through social reforms. In his famous *Essay on the Principle of Population* (1798), he declared population growth the prime and inevitable cause of poverty. He pointed out the conflict between two immutable processes: (1) "the passion between the sexes" which would double the population in one generation, or about twenty-five years, and (2) the much slower expansion of food production. Actually he stated that population, when unchecked, tends to increase in a geometrical ratio $(1 - 2 - 4 - 8 - 16 -$ etc.) while "subsistence" (a term he used alternately with "food") can increase only in an arithmetical ratio $(1 - 2 - 3 - 4 -$ etc.). One may assume that Malthus intended the comparison of the ratios merely to demonstrate in theory the race between the hare of reproduction and the tortoise of food production.

The pressure of population on subsistence made death the chief brake on population growth. Famine, disease, and war were the main "positive checks" that kept a population down to its food supply. In addition there were "preventive" or "prudential checks" which operated to reduce the birth rate: postponement of marriage and continence. However, these preventive measures never would be sufficiently strong to eliminate the pressure of population on subsistence. Consequently, Malthus considered social reforms and emigration mere palliatives bringing only temporary relief from the struggle for existence.

The second edition of the *Essay* (1803), virtually a new and much longer book, was based on extensive study, including much travel in Europe. Although he did not alter his basic position, he recognized that newly settled lands such as the United States could expand food production rapidly, and even double it in twenty-five years. He also observed that "in modern Europe the positive checks to population prevail less and the preventive checks more than in past times, and [more than] in the more uncivilized parts of the world." Although contraception was practiced to some extent in western Europe by 1800, Malthus never mentioned it in the second and later editions which he prepared. He probably regarded it as immoral "and hence overlooked the possibility that it might, under certain conditions, make subsistence relatively more available by adjusting the rhythm of man's growth in numbers to the growth of his subsistence" (Thompson and Lewis, 1965, 30). For the Europe of his day Malthus was essentially correct in assessing the relation between population and food; by extension, his reasoning applies to other traditional societies, even at present. But he was wrong in declaring his propositions to be laws, universally valid for all times and places. His own observations should have alerted him to the significance of cultural difference and cultural change, but he insisted that they were only minor deviations from inexorable laws.

Karl H. Marx (1818–1883) held a view diametrically opposed to Malthus. He asserted that the laboring masses were the foundation of society and the ultimate source of wealth; thus, society could only benefit by an increase in numbers. Marx believed that imperfections in the capitalistic system caused the poverty of the masses. He advocated a socialistic society with full employment and balanced use of natural resources, thus leading to rising welfare for increasing numbers.

Experience has repudiated the sweeping statements of both Malthus and Marx. Modern "capitalistic" countries show population and living standards increasing concurrently, and equal to if not faster than in a "socialistic" society like the Soviet Union. In spite of official adherence to the Marxist doctrine, birth control is widely practiced in the Soviet Union, and is encouraged by the People's Republic of China, ostensibly to protect the health of mothers. Nevertheless, Marx's point—contrary to Malthus's—that political and economic reforms can raise standards of living is certainly valid.

Although Malthus and Marx failed to discover universal laws and cures, others keep on trying. Some say that growing population density reduces fecundity (the physiological capacity to reproduce). Well-documented studies of animal behavior under increasing density conditions point in that direction, but transferring such conclusions to man is dangerous. More important, demographic data do not support the hypothesis. Another scholar, noting that the nations with low birth rates have high protein diets, concluded that protein causes low fecundity (de Castro, 1952). Hence, providing all peoples with substantial amounts of protein would solve the population problem. If this were true, the Eskimos long ago should have eaten themselves into extinction.

Still others, especially conservationists, paint a picture more gloomy than that of Malthus in his first essay (Osborn, 1948; Vogt, 1948). They claim that modern man destroys his habitat. Thus future generations will be caught in the vise of growing numbers and diminishing natural resources. One can fully agree with the need for wise resource management, yet wonder where the authors found the evidence pointing toward decreasing food production.

Each of these theories selects and emphasizes only one factor. Yet experience shows that human affairs have multiple causes. The geographer is particularly aware of this, because he constantly deals with the variety of cultures in diverse habitats.

Usually the discussion of population growth centers on how many people the earth can feed. However, even if this problem were solved, the more important issue would remain: the quality of human life. "The revolution of rising expectations" expresses the idea that man all over the world no longer is willing to live by bread or rice alone. Taking into account higher living standards—a cultural concept—greatly complicates the calculations regarding the potential number of people which parts of the earth may support.

Population Pressure. It is easy to talk about population pressure, but hard to define it. Like the concept of density, it seems to have been derived from physics. Knowing the density of a gas at a given temperature is sufficient to make accurate statements about some of its other properties. But can the same be said of population density? Take, for example, the mathematical density of a region, that is, the average number of inhabitants per specified unit of area, usually a square kilometer or mile. It is a common notion—perhaps as a carry-over from the days when agriculture was the mainstay of life—that "teeming millions" crowded in space spell poverty. The facts quickly disprove this naïve notion. The northeastern United States has a higher average income per capita than the Great Plains. In Central Africa the people are poor, in Australia well off, though both lands are sparsely settled. The Netherlands, one of the most densely populated countries in the world, rates among the more prosperous nations.

If mathematical (or crude) density is inadequate to measure the pressure of population on land, are there better yardsticks? Among those proposed is the physiological or nutritional density, that is, the number of inhabitants per unit of agricultural land. The calculation may be based on cultivated (or arable) land only, or may include permanent pastures (Table 20–1). These figures, though quite interesting in themselves, do not tell much about population pressure. It will be noted that physiological densities in East Asia, the Caribbean, and western Europe are of the same order of magnitude, yet the European is far more successful in his struggle for life than the inhabitants of the other areas. The measure would have validity only if all nations had similar agricultural economies, and each were self-sufficient in food production.

The term "carrying capacity of the land" has a broader connotation because it recognizes other resources than agriculture. Still, it is too restrictive: its focus remains on the relationship, or potential relationship, between the environmental content of an area and its population. Is it really meaningful to speak of "the carrying capacity" of Singapore Island, of Hong Kong, or of the Netherlands? As we grope to comprehend the nature of population pressure, its definition continues to recede.

Higher productivity per worker is a key factor in raising levels of living. It is not only related to the level of technology, but also to social, economic, and political organization. Resources obviously are important too, but as pointed out before, they are cultural achievements and are thus intricately linked to the society that exploits them. All these factors are interrelated; they are causes, but also consequences. How do population numbers fit into this complex? For one type of society, a fast rate of population growth may stimulate, for another it may seriously impede economic development.

These considerations suggest the difficulty of precisely defining population pressure. Yet there is no denying it exists, and in many countries presents a problem of growing urgency. It shows up clearest where people live close to the bare level of subsistence. When food consumption per capita goes down while the number of people goes up, it is reasonable to blame severe population pressure. Such conclusions may not fit more advanced societies. In the 1930s the United States, like many other countries, experienced a severe economic depression. Many blamed population pressure, or "overpopulation," for the distress. Yet the 130 million at that time were only a few million more than in prosperous 1928, and far fewer than at present.

Level of living relates to existing conditions, standard of living to the cultural image of what the level ought to be (the norm). This distinction helps to understand the true nature of population pressure in many underdeveloped countries. Even if their production of the bare necessities of life keeps up with population growth, awareness that other peoples live at higher levels makes them want the same and creates a sense of deprivation. To alleviate these

20. Problems of Population Growth

Table 20–1. Man-Land Ratios for Selected Countries

Country	Persons per square mile 1964	Persons per square mile of arable land[a]	Persons per square mile of agricultural land[b]	Agricultural workers[c] per square mile of agricultural land
Australia	3	86[e]	6	0.3[g]
Congo (Democratic Republic)	18	80	76	27[h]
Argentina	21	290	41	27
Liberia	23	86[f]	86	21
Mozambique	23	893	39	7
Soviet Union	26	256	98	17
Sweden	44	597	515	17
Mexico	52	424	98	30[i]
United States	54	251	105	3[j]
Egypt (United Arab Republic)	75	2,925	2,925	455[k]
France	228	597	365	30
Poland	259	501	397	85[l]
Philippines	269	721[f]	721	136
India[d]	401	744	685	201
Italy	440	853	641	63
United Kingdom	575	1,887	714	15[m]
Japan	679	4,124	3,565	486
Puerto Rico	751	1,845	1,086	72
Netherlands	935	3,195	1,376	51

[a] Arable land includes land under crops (double-cropped areas are counted only once), land temporarily fallow, temporary meadows for mowing or pasture, land under market and kitchen gardens (including cultivation under glass), and land under fruit trees, vines, shrubs, and rubber plantations.

[b] Agricultural land includes arable land as defined above plus permanent meadows and pastures.

[c] "Agricultural workers" in this table means "population engaged in agricultural occupations," as defined in Food and Agriculture Organization, *Production Yearbook*, 1965, 461.

[d] Data relate to reporting area and include Jammu and Kashmir.

[e] Includes cultivated grassland (about 44 million acres).

[f] Based on total agricultural area.

[g] Excludes full-blooded aborigines.

[h] Indigenous populations only.

[i] Workers twelve years old and over.

[j] Workers fourteen years old and over.

[k] Workers six years old and over, but excluding nomad population and foreigners.

[l] Data based on a 5 percent sample tabulation of the 1961 census, excluding persons living in collective dwellings, and on an enumeration of 370,000 persons.

[m] Workers fifteen years old and over.

SOURCE: United Nations *Demographic Yearbook*, 1965, table 2; and Food and Agriculture Organization *Production Yearbook*, 1965, tables 1 and 6A. The data as reported refer to different years, most of them within the period 1960–1964.

feelings requires greater production per capita, well above mere provision of food. But if fast population growth absorbs the gains in production, it dashes all hopes for a more comfortable life. Such frustrations easily lead to social unrest, even war.

In passing we referred to "overpopulation." The layman is quick to use this term to explain poverty in crowded countries. The population expert is more reluctant: Before he can speak of overpopulation or underpopulation, he must decide what the optimum (or best) number is for the country. The French demographer Sauvy neatly summed up the relativity of the concept when he defined optimum population as "that which best assures the realization of a predetermined objective" (Sauvy, 1952, vol. 2, 221).

The difficulties of defining optimum population have led others to propose that attention be turned to another measure—the optimum *rate* of growth. This provides a more practical and useful tool because it relates annual population increase to index figures for production, capital formation, consumption, or facilities such as housing, schools, and other social services. This procedure allows a clearer view of what is optimal population growth, because it links it to the immediate objectives of progress. Nevertheless, there remains the arguable assumption that in each country the "national goals" are agreed upon by the entire population.

Nutrition

The average American spends less than one-third of his income on food, and for this modest part of his money obtains not only an ample amount, but a rich variety. In contrast, people in India on the average devote four-fifths of their wretchedly low income to purchase food and cannot afford much else than a daily ration of cereals. Other nations lie somewhere between these poles of abundance and poverty, the largest number by far crowded on the lower end of the scale.

Plants, through the process of photosyn-thesis, transform sunlight, water, carbon dioxide, and minerals into organic materials containing in various proportions carbohydrates, proteins, and fats. Animals convert plants into proteins and fats. Because they eat vegetable matter that man cannot digest, they broaden his food supply. If animals eat plants that man can use directly, he may forego the consumption of the carbohydrates to gain the greater nutritive value of animal protein, even though it contains only a fraction, say one-seventh, of the energy originally in the plants. Obviously, this conversion of energy is not efficient. It explains—apart from cultural food avoidances—why densely populated, poor countries do not take the detour of producing meat, but rely mainly on direct consumption of vegetable matter.

The human diet contains carbohydrates, proteins, fats, minerals, and vitamins. Each food yields a certain number of calories per gram when combustion changes it into energy. Amount of adequate food intake varies with conditions. In year-round warm climates a person requires fewer calories than in the mid-latitudes, other things being equal. Small persons need fewer calories than large ones. These differences must be kept in mind when comparing the average caloric intake in Anglo-America with that in Indonesia or Ecuador.

Within a given population, individual food requirements also differ markedly, depending on activity, sex, and age. For example, the Food and Nutrition Board of the National Research Council recommends the following daily quantities of calories: children of 4 to 6 years, 1,600 calories, men of 25, 3,200 calories; men of 45, 2,900 calories. The figures for comparable classes of females are substantially lower. Of course, a man in a sedentary job needs far fewer than a farmer or miner. This differentiation must be taken into account when comparing national nutrition data. A young population largely employed in physical labor eats more—or should eat more—than one with a high proportion of white-collar workers and elderly citizens.

In most parts of the world people consume enough food for basic energy needs. But often the quality of intake is inadequate even where the quantity is sufficient. In such cases the stomach is filled, but "hidden hunger" for proteins, minerals, or vitamins remains. This is malnutrition. The body tissues do not receive the elements necessary to function properly, and this inevitably leads to various diseases. Malnutrition also causes apathy. In turn, apathy reduces the worker's productivity and thus tends to make a vicious circle of poverty and malnutrition.

The sad thing is that most countries with low food quantity also have low quality (Figure 20-1). Grains, roots, and tubers, which are rather easy to produce, contain principally starches—carbohydrates that fuel the body. In contrast, the foodstuffs that contain protective elements—meat, fat, vegetables, fruits—are on the whole much more expensive. Hence, in poor countries many people are not only "on the eternal compulsory fast" (as Gandhi said of India's masses), but in addition suffer from malnutrition. There are exceptions, of course. In some countries with a relatively low quantitative diet, the consumption of protein is fairly adequate: Japan, the Philippines, Syria, Venezuela, and Paraguay. On the other hand, the Soviet Union and Spain, which report over 2,900 calories per person, have less protein in their diet than other nations in the top group. Unfortunately, reliable data are lacking for many of the less-developed countries, including mainland China. Among those reporting to the United Nations, the following five are at the bottom of calories per capita: the Philippines (1,800), Jordan (1,830), Ecuador (1,970), India (2,000), and Ceylon (2,000).

Unequal population growth intensifies inequalities of nutrition. By and large, the nutritional have-nots yearly add the greatest number of mouths. In South and Southeast Asia since before World War II, food production has risen less than population. Whether mainland China has done better is not clear. Food production in most of Latin America and Africa also is slipping behind population growth. However, increasing dependence on food import may signify an advance in the economy. After all, most developed countries buy food with money earned through specialty production or services. But many underdeveloped countries do not have the money to buy food in foreign markets for their hungry people. On the other side, the countries that were the first to have the most— Anglo-America, western Europe, Australia, and New Zealand—show a marked increase of food output. Some, especially the United States, could yield far more if production had not been purposely throttled down.

Malnutrition and Disease.   Malnutrition has its own disease patterns. Moreover, gross deficiencies in diet are likely to lower resistance to other diseases. Among the disorders that malnutrition causes, we note first of all those due to protein deficiencies. Most underdeveloped countries in the tropics and subtropics have a high incidence of nutritional edemas and *kwashiorkor*. The latter is the most severe and widespread nutritional disease, caused by lack of protein. Commonly it is found among young children; their growth after weaning is retarded; abdomen, face, and extremities swell with fluid, the hair loses color and curl. Among Africans it becomes silky and reddish—hence the name of the disease, literally meaning "the little red boy." Only twenty years ago it was discovered that many ailments which had been described in medical journals under various names all were what now is called kwashiorkor. The victims all have a diet consisting mainly of sweet potato, yam, cassava, or banana, with almost no meat or fish or dairy foods.

Goiter is caused by insufficient intake of iodine. The Great Lakes region of the United States, which has very little iodine content in its drinking water and food, has been called "the goiter belt." Actually, the zone stretches westward along the United States–Canadian border to the Columbia River. Switzerland, interior China, and southern Brazil also are well known for the prevalence of goiter. The use of iodized table salt is an effective preventive. Coastal regions where seafood is easily available have a low incidence of goiter.

The distribution of vitamin deficiencies of one

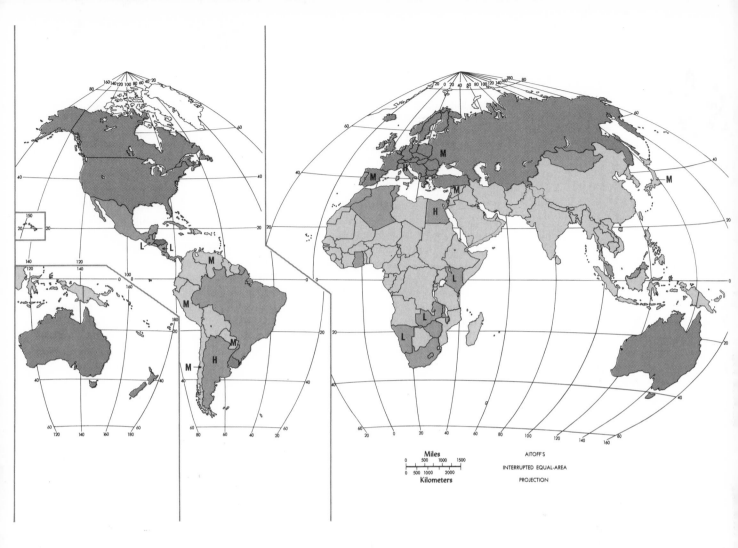

Low Calories (Under 2500)
Low Protein (Under 60 grams)

Medium Calories (2500 – 2900)
Medium Protein (60-80 grams)

High Calories (Over 2900)
High Protein (Over 80 grams)

L   Low Protein

M   Medium Protein

H   High Protein

**Figure 20–1. WORLD: CALORIC AND PROTEIN
INTAKE PER CAPITA**

The nutritional levels are shown by calories and
grams of protein per capita per day. Data are from
United Nations *Statistical Yearbook, 1964,* New
York, 1965, table 137.

*20. Problems of
Population
Growth*

487

kind or another shows high correlation with that of low incomes (Figure 20–2). In Europe lack of vitamins shows up in the Mediterranean countries and eastern Europe. Each region has its own type of vitamin deficiency diseases, depending on what particular foods are not available or too expensive. In West Africa the scarcity of niacin (a B vitamin) in the local food supply causes widespread pellagra. In West Pakistan and north India the lack of vitamin D and vitamin B is responsible for much rickets and pellagra, respectively. South Indians, on the other hand, get little vitamin C, causing scurvy, and little vitamin A, resulting in night blindness. In the rice-eating countries of southeastern Asia, consumption of polished rice results in beriberi, because the vitamin B_1 has been discarded with the husk.

These examples suggest the seriousness of nutrition problems in much of the world. It is said sometimes that the advanced countries could produce enough food to avert famine everywhere, at least for the next ten or twenty years. However, if true, this could only refer to the provision of cereals. It might ease undernutrition, but could not significantly alleviate malnutrition.

Infectious Diseases

Man is part of a complex food system. He eats plants and animals, while in turn he is the host to invading microorganisms that exploit his body for their own existence. Some are harmless, others cause severe damage. An infectious disease, then, is a disease caused by the entrance, growth, and multiplication of a foreign organism within the body.

Infectious diseases illustrate well the process of interaction between different orders of phenomena. There is first of all man as host—never as a mere organism, but as a member of a culture with all that this implies. Then there are the pathogens (disease-causing organisms), each with its own life requirements and often traveling via intermediate hosts (vectors) from one human or animal to another. And finally there

Figure 20–2. WORLD: DISEASES

The shaded parts are major areas of occurrence, the crosses indicate minor areas. On the cholera map the arrows show the spread of the disease during the epidemics identified by date. SOURCE: May, 1956.

is the physical environment with its specific climate, soil, and water supply (the latter two resources often changed by man, with unforeseen biological consequences), favoring or restricting certain life forms (Figure 20–2).

Many diseases are *endemic*—that is to say, a state of equilibrium exists between man and microorganism whereby the latter is widespread in a community without causing extensive death. For instance, tuberculosis and syphilis may be regarded as endemic in the United States and western Europe. An *epidemic* is a sudden and virulent outbreak; if it spreads worldwide, as influenza did after World War I, it is called *pandemic*. Diseases to which Europeans had developed considerable immunity, such as smallpox and measles, spread like wildfire among the American Indians and the island peoples of the Pacific after they had been "discovered."

Diseases that rely on indirect methods of transmission do not move so easily, since they need suitable intermediate hosts. A good example is the African sleeping sickness, which is restricted to the range of the tsetse fly vectors. But malaria occurs widely because the approximately 35 species of *Anopheles* mosquitoes that can act as vectors of plasmodia—the disease-causing protozoa—live in tropical climates as well as those with fairly warm summers.

During the last thirty years sulfa drugs and antibiotics have greatly diminished the fatal effects of many bacterial diseases: tuberculosis, pneumonia, typhoid fever, bacterial dysentery, rheumatic fever, syphilis, yaws, and cholera. Some virus diseases also have declined because of immunization by vaccination (smallpox, polio), others are controlled by eradication of mosquito vectors as well as by vaccination (e.g., yellow fever); but viruses of the influenza group

PLAGUE (Occurences 1900-1952)

CHOLERA

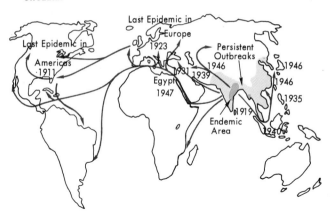

Last Epidemic in
Europe
1923

Last Epidemic in
Americas
1911

Persistent
Outbreaks
1946

1931 1939

Egypt
1947

1946

1946

1935

1919

Endemic
Area

1940

YELLOW FEVER (Endemic Areas According to World Health
Organization, 1952)

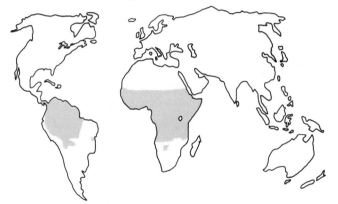

YAWS (Including Pinta and Bejel)

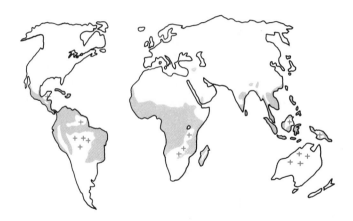

HOOKWORM

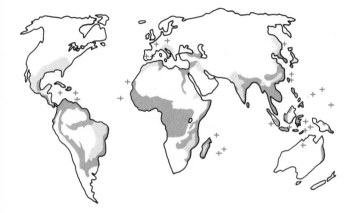

VITAMIN DEFICIENCY DISEASES (Rickets-D, Beri-beri-B, Scurvy-C, etc.)

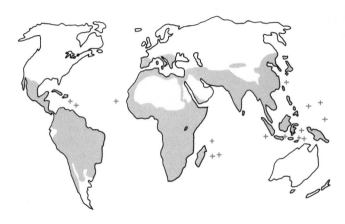

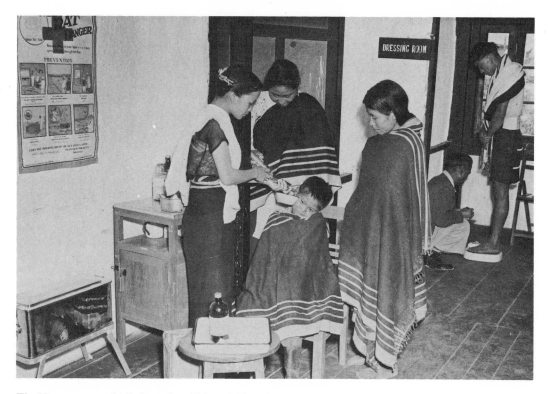

The Naga, a group of tribal peoples of Mongoloid stock, speaking Tibeto-Burmese languages, live in the mountains of India's northeast frontier, between Assam and Burma. They are reluctant to accept Indian rule. One of the ways the government employs in pacifying the area is by providing free health services. [Courtesy of Press Information Bureau, Government of India]

and the common cold still enter the human body freely. In some parts of the world, diseases caused by parasitic worms (hookworm, trichina worm, flukes) have been virtually eradicated, while elsewhere they debilitate and kill large numbers.

Our interest is not in the medical aspects of disease control, but in the areal differentiation of this control, and how it affects population growth. In modern societies of the Western world the death rate declined gradually as medical knowledge advanced, public health expanded, and notions of sanitary conduct spread among the population. The introduction of sulfa drugs in the 1930s and of antibiotics in the

1940s only depressed further an already low mortality. Death now for the greater part is caused by disorders that result from structural changes or damage in the body, such as cancer, and malfunctioning of the circulatory system, particularly the heart.

The course of events was very different in the underdeveloped countries. By the 1930s modern medical science and public health, although present in only rudimental form, had somewhat lowered the death rate, but progress had been slow. It seemed then that—apart from vaccination for a few diseases—great advances would depend on the cooperation of the local people in accepting public and private cleanliness. It was realized, of course, that this would take much time. Asking people to observe the hygienic rules of Western medicine is asking them to change their customary way of life. Moreover, sanitary conduct usually requires money, even if only for soap or sandals, which may mean sacrificing food or other immediate necessities for an uncertain future benefit.

Wonder drugs and insect sprays, developed shortly before and during World War II, opened new perspectives on the control of infectious diseases in underdeveloped lands. DDT and other insecticides can be applied over wide areas without the active participation of the local populace. As for the drugs, they are essentially curative in character. The person who feels ill is much more willing to submit to an injection or take a dose than one who is told that a shot will prevent future sickness. Since the results are readily apparent, news of the miracle drug spreads quickly and people flock to the clinics. The new confidence soon extends to preventive inoculations, which further reduce death from infectious diseases.

This happened in the underdeveloped countries after the war, although not everywhere to the same degree. What took the Western countries a century to accomplish in the fight against death can now be done elsewhere in one generation or less. However, if birth rates remain high and food production fails to increase rapidly, the retreat of death simply will mean that more people will live out their longer lives in misery.

Future Food Supply

Most of the present 3,400 million people are poorly nourished. By about the year 2000 the earth is expected to carry over 6,000 million. How can they be fed? Will their diet be better than that today? Essentially there are two ways to make this possible, given our current technology: expand the area under cultivation, or wrest higher yields from lands now in use. Actually it is not an "either-or" choice. Let us first consider the possibilities of "horizontal" expansion.

More Food from More Land? Some 3,500 million acres are now in cropland and orchards, and 6,350 million in permanent meadows and pastures. Together they form what we shall call agricultural land: 9,850 million acres, constituting 29.5 percent of the land surface, excluding Antarctica.

If the population were to double in thirty-five years and it had to be fed at present levels of consumption by expanding the agricultural land area, another 9,850 million acres would have to be added to the area now in use. Thus, in 2000 there should be 19,700 million acres, or 59 percent of the land surface, in crops or permanent pasture. Improving the diet would certainly require still more agricultural land, perhaps another 5 to 10 percent of the land surface, raising the total to 64 or 69 percent. But where is this new agricultural land to be found?

Many geographers have tried to answer this question. Since there is no reliable inventory of the earth's resources, calculations must be based on rough estimates of regional environmental qualities such as temperature, precipitation, soil, and slope conditions. Furthermore, one must make assumptions regarding the future state of agricultural technology and the price levels. To illustrate, the frontier moves poleward as quick-ripening crops develop, and desertward with new drought-resistant crops. But how far such expansion actually will reach depends on the financial returns to the farmer. Evidently, estimates of potential agricultural land will differ widely, depending on the assumptions. The calculations of various experts, referring mainly to the total of arable land available, range from 11,000 million to 17,000 million acres, the highest figure representing 51 percent of the land surface.

In terms of climate about 25 percent of the land surface is too cold for agriculture as now practiced; it comprises the ice cap, the tundra, and the subpolar forest zone. Arid climates cover some 18 percent, semiarid climates another 20 percent of the land surface. Expansion of agriculture in these dry lands is possible through irrigation and better use of the steppelands, although enormous capital investment would be required to overcome nature's obstacles. Tropical rainy climates extend over 10 percent of the earth. The possibilities of expanding agriculture in this zone are hotly debated. Its sparse use so far suggests the manifold difficulties man faces in such an environment. These areas with climates unfavorable to agriculture add up to 73 percent of the land surface. Most of the present agricultural production is concentrated in the remaining 27 percent. What lands are not yet in use here are marginal in quality or worse. Mountains and hills have steep slopes and stony soils, which discourage food production. Part of the more favorable terrain suffers from infertile soils or poor drainage. Growing cities, roads, parks, and other forms of nonagricultural occupance utilize ever more space, usually in the fertile plains. One must conclude that expansion of farmland, while feasible in some areas, offers no solution for the food needs of the next generation.

Higher Productivity per Acre. Instead of basing our hope on agricultural ventures in unfamiliar climate and terrain, we can turn with more confidence to lands of proven value. We have already seen (Chapter 12) what strides modern agriculture has made in the industrial countries of Anglo-America and West Europe. Japan shows what can be done in the East Asian context. The accomplishments so far are only the beginning of a new era. For instance, the recent breakthrough in the knowledge of the gene structure opens up vistas of plant and animal breeding far beyond present methods. But speculation concerning the future aside, it is clear that widespread adoption of modern farming methods would increase the world's food production tremendously, even without adding an acre to the land now in use.

The late L. Dudley Stamp, an outstanding British geographer and expert on land utilization, has suggested that in regard to land productivity, Northwest Europe is a better model for imitation than the United States. Indeed, if greater food production per acre—not per farmer—is the objective, agriculture as practiced in Denmark, for instance, is best. In Northwest Europe approximately 1 acre of cultivated land yields enough food to feed one person. Stamp points out that by this standard the really "underdeveloped" countries are Anglo-America, southern South America, Australia, New Zealand, and also the Soviet Union (Stamp, 1952). To support his view he quotes yields per acre in Denmark, the Netherlands, Belgium, England, and West Germany, which are indeed far above those of the United States and similar countries. His argument might be countered by observing that the high level of living in Anglo-America, or Australia, has been reached by great productivity per worker rather than per unit area, a goal to which other countries should aspire instead of wresting the last bushel of wheat from an acre.

Somewhere between the divergent objectives of productivity-per-acre and productivity-per-worker must lie a feasible compromise. Recent increases in American yields per acre resulting from more fertilizer and improved plants and animals show what can be done in a country where the main objective is high income per worker. On the other hand, Danish or English farmers are hardly peasants tending their fields with backbreaking labor to feed their poverty-stricken families. They combine a high degree of mechanization with high acre yields and enjoy a fairly good income. These considerations lead to the conclusion that the mid-latitudes offer far greater capability of supporting more people than do the uncertain riches of the tropics.

Stamp's estimate that one acre of improved farmland can support one human being translates into surprisingly large potentials for what he calls the "underdeveloped countries." According to his standard, the arable land currently in use in the United States could support some 500 million, Canada 100, Argentina 75, Australia 70, and the Soviet Union 560 million, a total of 1,305 million people versus a present population in these countries of less than 500 million. Whether these figures need correction or even are desirable objectives is not at issue here.

The wet tropical and subtropical countries need not be written off as incapable of higher yields. Japan has achieved a rice production per acre three times as large as that of the southeast and south Asian countries. This suggests the possibility that the tropical countries can substantially increase their food supplies.

More productive agriculture is inextricably bound up with other sectors of modern life: science, technology, mechanical energy, manufacturing, transportation, and so on. No less does it require that the farmer change his attitude. This transformation comes with relative ease in the backward parts of the Occidental realm because they are essentially similar to the advanced countries (with the possible exception of Latin America, where the hidalgo complex is hard to crack). Significant progress in East Asia proves that the West holds no monopoly on the modern economy. Almost everywhere else traditional culture patterns (including high birth rates) slow down the advance of the modern economy, and thus of agriculture. In short, science and technology hold great promise of more food, but the fulfillment depends on whether a nation is able to adjust its way of life to the new challenge. There is no time to lose. The next thirty years will be the critical period in the race between population and food.

The Seas. There are other ways to improve and increase the food supply. The urgent need for more animal protein calls attention to the promise of the sea (McElroy, 1961). So far the sea has retained the nature of a hunting and gathering ground. With better knowledge of the regional ecology, it should be possible to manipulate the oceans as farmers do their environments: select the best habitat for each useful fish species, breed better strains, weed out harmful interlopers, provide more plankton for feeding, and so on.

But all this must wait until the intensive oceanographic research, now getting under way, can lay a sound foundation for the agriculture of the sea. In the meantime the technology of large-scale fishing is making great strides, threatening to destroy a rich resource before it can be developed as an enduring crop. Naturally, the industrial nations are the ones with the means to build the ocean-going fleets. The

countries that most need the animal protein lack the capital and know-how for bringing in the big catch.

Beyond Food

The overriding concern with questions of subsistence almost makes one forget that man to be truly human needs more than food. To insist on quality is today as important as it was in the time of Plato. Seen in this light, population pressures may—and do—exist in countries with ample food supply. Some writers who argue that the United States has a population problem point to the insufficiency of schools and hospitals, the scarcity of community recreation facilities, the traffic congestion, soil, water, and air pollution. There can be no doubt that the rapid population growth of recent years, coupled with rising standards among all groups, puts heavy pressure on social as well as economic space. Especially noticeable is the strain in metropolitan areas, which have had to absorb the tremendous postwar influx. Although some of these tensions and troubles may be no more than temporary maladjustments characteristic of an era of swift change, many thoughtful people have misgivings about the future.

In densely populated—overdeveloped?—West Europe the crisis of space shortage is already at hand. Cities expand and—because of higher standards—much faster than their population. For instance, Amsterdam's population increased between 1930 and 1960 by 20 percent, but its built-up area more than doubled. For 1980 the plan foresees an increase of 7.5 percent, but another doubling of the built-up area. In addition, new industrial plants and expansion of port facilities eat up vast tracts of farmland. As demands for water increase, it becomes short in supply, even in an amphibious province like Holland, partly because cities and industries pollute the streams, partly because seawater penetrates inland as it replaces the drawn-off fresh groundwater.

Open spaces for recreation within reasonable

20. Problems of Population Growth

493

Smog-bound Metropolis. [The New York Times]

distance from urban areas are getting scarce; hordes of visitors trample the reality as well as the illusion of being "in nature." It has been calculated that the magnificent beaches along the Dutch coast afford each citizen only 1 linear inch. Quite apart from recreational space, the general absence of "elbow room" affects people in many subtle ways. If it is hard to define economic population pressure, it is even harder to know what constitutes its psychic counterpart. Biologists have observed stress syndromes as they appear in animal populations when their density becomes too high. This suggests the possibility of pathological behavior in equivalent human situations. At any rate, crowding demands discipline, which if not voluntarily adhered to, must be maintained by regimentation, easily subverted into authoritarianism.

It becomes more and more difficult to be alone. Not all societies equally appreciate the privilege of solitude, even if they can afford it (a comparison between the United States and Europe is instructive in this respect). Nevertheless, in the modern world the lack of privacy is a frustrating experience for the individual and signifies a flaw in his environment.

Citations

Castro, J. de, *The Geography of Hunger,* Boston, 1952.

Food and Agriculture Organization, *State of Food and Agriculture* (annual), Rome, 1948–.

May, J. M. (comp. and ed.) *Atlas of Distribution of Diseases,* American Geographical Society, New York, 1956, 17 plates reprinted from *Geographical Review,* 1950–1955.

McElroy, W. D. "The Promise of the Sea," *Johns Hopkins Magazine,* 12 (May–June 1961): 20–23.

Osborn, F. *Our Plundered Planet,* Boston, 1948.

Sauvy, A. *Théorie générale de la population,* 2 vols., Paris, 1952, 1954.

Stamp, L. D. *Land for Tomorrow: The Underdeveloped World,* Bloomington, Ind., 1952.

Thompson, W. S., and Lewis, D. T. *Population Problems,* 5th ed., New York, 1965.

Vogt, W. *Road to Survival,* New York, 1948.

Further Readings

Ackerman, E. A. "Population and Natural Resources," in Hauser, P. M., and Duncan, O. D. (eds.) *The Study of Population: An Inventory and Appraisal,* Chicago, 1959, 621–648.

Bates, M. *The Prevalence of People,* New York, 1955.

Demangeon, A. *Problèmes de géographie humaine,* Paris, 1942.

Deshler, W. "Livestock Trypanosomiasis and Human Settlement in Northeastern Uganda," *Geographical Review,* 50 (1960): 541–554.

Francis, R. G. (ed.) *The Population Ahead,* Minneapolis, Minn., 1958.

Ginsburg, N. "Natural Resources and Economic Development," *Annals of the Association of American Geographers,* 47 (1957): 196–212.

20. Problems of Population Growth

Howe, G. M. *National Atlas of Disease Mortality in the United Kingdom,* New York, 1963.

Kamerschen, D. R. "On an Operational Index of 'Overpopulation,'" *Economic Development and Cultural Change,* 13, 2 (1965): 169–187.

Kariel, H. C. "A Proposed Classification of Diet," *Annals of the Association of American Geographers,* 56 (1966): 68–79.

Learmonth, A. T. A. "Medical Geography in India and Pakistan," *Geographical Journal,* 127 (1961): 10–26.

Lee, D. H. K. *Climate and Economic Development in the Tropics,* New York, 1957.

May, J. M. "Medical Geography: Its Methods and Objectives," *Geographical Review,* 40 (1950): 9–41.

———. *Ecology of Human Disease,* New York, 1959.

———. *The Ecology of Malnutrition in the Far and Near East: Food Resources, Habits, and Deficiencies,* New York, 1961.

———. *Studies in Disease Ecology,* New York, 1961.

———. *The Ecology of Malnutrition in Five Countries of East and Central Europe,* New York, 1963.

Prothero, R. M. *Migrants and Malaria,* London, 1965.

Rodenwalt, E., and Jusatz, H. (eds.) *Welt-Seuchen Atlas,* 3 vols., Hamburg, 1952–1961.

Russell, E. J. *World Population and Food Supplies,* London, 1954.

Simmons, J. S. *Global Epidemiology: A Geography of Disease and Sanitation,* 3 vols., Philadelphia, 1944–1954.

Simoons, F. J. *Eat Not This Flesh: Food Avoidances in the Old World,* Madison, Wis., 1961.

Sorre, M. "The Geography of Diet," in Wagner, P. L., and Mikesell, M. W. (eds.) *Readings in Cultural Geography,* Chicago, 1962, 445–456. Originally published in French in *Annales de Géographie,* 61 (1952): 184–199.

Spilhaus, A. "Control of the World Environment," *Geographical Review,* 46 (1956): 451–459.

Stamp, L. D. "The Measurement of Land Resources," *Geographical Review,* 48 (1958): 1–15.

———. *Some Aspects of Medical Geography,* New York, 1964.

Woeikof, A. "La Géographie de l'alimentation humaine," *La Géographie, Bulletin de la Société de Géographie,* 20 (1909): 225–240, 281–296.

Woytinsky, W. S., and Woytinsky, E. S. *World Population and Production: Trends and Outlook,* New York, 1953.

Epilogue

The Differentiation of Mankind

While Americans and Russians ready spaceships for the moon voyage, primitive groups in New Guinea and Australia are just emerging from the Stone Age. What causes this wide range in development? Why do peoples behave in so many ways? Such questions can be answered from several viewpoints. First and oldest is the theological one: Divine will has ordained the fate of earth and humanity. Second is the biological concept of evolution, introduced in the nineteenth century: Organisms, including man, diverge through selection in their natural environment. This book reflects a third thought, which has come to the fore in the present century. It shifts the emphasis from environmental influences to cultural relationships. It does not discard physical environment and evolution. To the contrary, both receive deeper meaning by relating them to culture. The evolutionary process of Homo sapiens operates through cumulative transmission of collective experience rather than anatomical change. "Mankind does not live in a state of nature, but in history."

The environmentalists' error lay in conceiving the physical environment as the dominant independent variable to which man—the selfsame creature everywhere—had to adjust. The modern view, in contrast, takes the position that each society projects its own common set of meanings and goals onto its habitat. To quote the geographer George H. T. Kimble: "The most potent geographical factors in the world are not climate, soils, . . . or any other objective 'environmental' circumstance, but rather the shape these circumstances assume in the mind's eye, and the willingness of the mind to do something about them."

Civilizations

Sir Julian Huxley once characterized civilizations as "successful idea-systems," forming the steps in the stairway of cultural evolution. Each new civilization builds on the heritage of others, but derives its singular character from a mental breakthrough—a breakthrough somewhat like a mutation in an organism, creating a different variety. The new attitudes transform the societal structure, and realign the ties between the people and their land. Exactly what causes a civilization eludes us. Certainly no great one ever grew in quiet backwaters. Rather, it emerged at the turbulent confluence of many currents, some of native, many of foreign origin.

But civilizations fade away and others succeed them, usually rising in other locations. In western Eurasia, the crest of civilization moved from Middle East to Mediterranean, and then to northwestern Europe. South and East Asia, as well as pre-Columbian America, experienced similar relocations. There is no reason to think that progress has found its final home in the North Atlantic community.

Although the dynamic culture hearths have shifted, they have so far been confined to relatively small segments of the earth surface. None have evolved in polar and subpolar regions, in equatorial lowlands, or in the mid-latitudes of the southern hemisphere, mainly, it would seem, because of environmental handicaps or peripheral location.

The present four major culture realms are the East Asian, Indic, Islamic, and Occidental. Their historical kinship is evident in the common economic roots: plow agriculture of grains, which has transformed the habitat into a man-made steppe landscape; domesticated herd animals; commerce and urban centers. Their superstructures are more diverse, although here too old links are apparent. Each has its spiritual basis in an ethical and religious ideology that demands supratribal if not worldwide adherence. Each has a written-down legacy of great thoughts and deeds that fosters awareness of its historic *raison d'être*. And each has its political basis in concepts of statehood and law.

Cultural Unity or Diversity?

Some five hundred years ago European civilization was simply one among several, and not a particularly distinguished one at that. Since then it has rapidly forged ahead, assuming since the Industrial Revolution the character of a hyperdynamic force. It is altering humanity as decisively as did the introduction of agriculture, some ten thousand years ago. Its influence has expanded in three ways. Through emigration and settlement the European has overwhelmed the weak cultures in the temperate lands of North and South America, southern Siberia, Oceania, and the south tip of Africa. Through colonial rule Occidental culture has affected in various degrees most of the remainder of the world. And third, even those countries not politically controlled by Europeans or their descendants, have borrowed many Western traits, especially technical and economic ones.

The passing of the colonial era, while signifying political withdrawal, has not stopped the spread of Occidental culture. Quite to the contrary, the newly independent peoples need to develop their technology, economic organization, and social structure if they want to move forward. This means more, not less, Westernization. However, each country must fit the alien ideas, institutions, and gadgets into its own culture pattern. In doing this, the independent country has more freedom in choosing what to accept and what to reject than

Epilogue

was possible under a colonial administration. Moreover, it is not even desirable that Western culture, like a bulldozer, flatten out all that came before. The philosopher Alfred N. Whitehead puts it this way: "Diversification among human communities is essential for the provision of the incentive, and material for the Odyssey of the human spirit. Other nations of different habits are not enemies: they are godsends. Men require of their neighbors something sufficiently akin to be understood, something sufficiently different to provoke attention, and something great enough to command admiration."

Different cultures, even the most humble ones, may harbor idea strains that could prove highly valuable in breeding new institutions to cope with as yet unforeseen situations. Burmese statesman U Thant's plea "to make the world safe for diversity" has meaning for the present as well as the future.

Forces of Our Times

The great forces that currently affect mankind are nationalism, progress, population growth, and urbanization.

Nationalism is the all-pervading political propellant of our era. It takes on many forms as it interacts with other ideologies—religion, capitalism, democracy, socialism, communism, racism, and so on—but, under whatever guise, it determines the present organization of earth space. Its positive value lies in transcending parochial interests and quarrels by uniting local communities into a greater whole and by inspiring them to common efforts for the general good.

But nationalism also has a negative side. At its worst it leads to wars on a much wider scale than tribal strife, and at least impedes the international cooperation that the shrunken and interdependent world needs today. The trend seems to lead toward larger, multinational regional frameworks—and eventually, perhaps, world federation. Whatever the future, the sovereign nation-state is as yet the accepted mold of political organization. Europe set the example; we now witness other culture realms in their slow and often painful process of nation building.

Progress through science, technology, and new forms of economic organization is the hallmark of modern Western civilization. Like the Occidental concept of the nation-state, the idea of material advance is now spreading throughout the world. But economic development requires more than importing machinery. It demands changes in social organization, and above all, changes in attitude. Moreover, the ultimate goal must be to serve the social aims of each society. These intertwined means and ends defy efforts to formulate a universally valid model for progress. Some countries will advance rapidly, others slowly, some through peaceful evolution, others by ruthless revolution. In the meantime, the Occident will race ahead with exploration of outer space, use of nuclear energy, industrial automation, and other applications of the computer's mechanical brain. One can but dimly perceive the opportunities—and dangers!—that mankind may encounter in these new ventures. Thus, while the West enters a phase which not long ago seemed mere science fiction, many societies just now are escaping the confines of a Babylonian technology.

Epilogue

499

Economic development, then, is a relative matter. Measured against the front-runners of the West, many backward countries climb uphill at an unbearably slow pace, but measured on their own ground, against their starting line only a generation or two ago, they may have covered a remarkable distance.

However, it cannot be taken for granted that progress is inevitable and automatic. History offers numerous cases of societies that disintegrated when confronted by an aggressive alien culture. Other peoples have tried, at least for a time, to ward off "the contagion of ideas" by building either visible or invisible walls. At present we cannot be sure that all societies really wish to modernize, whatever their Westernized leaders claim. Reluctance to give up cherished ways of life, or incompetence to guide the transformation, may effectively block economic development. The economist Kenneth E. Boulding once said of India that development is difficult because its people have become so well adjusted to poverty.

Impatience with peoples who stubbornly refuse to abandon obsolete habits should be tempered by the thought that the "brave new world" of the Occident shows a wide—and widening?—gap between control over nature and man's control over himself.

Rapid population growth in underdeveloped countries is now generally recognized as a major obstacle to their progress. While Western medical technology has curbed their death rates, traditional attitudes toward reproduction still prevail. Their governments must use a substantial part of the national savings to provide for the massive increase in population instead of investing in enterprises that will propel the economy forward. But again, one must guard against overgeneralization. Some countries, especially in Latin America and Africa, have large resource potentials which, if wisely used, should ease the pressure. Others, mostly in Asia, may double their already crowded and hungry populations in about thirty years. The last part of this century will be the critical period, either of successful transition to controlled well-being, or of decline to such depth of destitution that any upward move of the economy becomes virtually impossible.

Finally, there is the process of *urbanization*. For the last five thousand years cities have served as the mainsprings of creative thought and action. One can hardly think of a culture worthy of being called a civilization if it lacks urban centers. The difference, however, between traditional and modern societies is that while city life in the former can support only a fraction of the total population, in the latter it is the mode of life for the majority.

Evidently, the city is going to be the physical environment for most of humanity. Man has always transformed his habitat, but never before has he been confronted with so stupendous a task of creating a vast artificial milieu for such multitudes. The nagging problem of population growth is magnified by the urban squeeze. Housing, transportation, recreation, education, water supply, sewage disposal, and other public facilities demand careful planning and tremendous investments. But this entire mechanical framework is only the means to serve cultural ends. An objective look at our own cities makes us realize the inadequacy of the material base and the confusion about the spiritual goals. If this is true for a wealthy nation with room to spare, it holds even more for poor and crowded countries without an urban tradition. Jean Gottmann, contemplating the American Megalopolis, wrote that it "gives one the feeling of looking at the dawn of a new stage in human evolution." No wonder we have as yet only a blurred vision of the scope and quality of tomorrow's city.

These great forces of our era all have Occidental roots. Interrelated among themselves, they also interact in many ways with indigenous cultures existing in different environments, thereby creating variations on the general theme of change.

The geographer cannot lay aside his work and write "finis." Continuous change in societies and their habitats permits only tentative, interim conclusions. Old facts, too, show unexpected facets when reexamined with sharper analytical tools or viewed from a new angle. Beyond the horizon of present knowledge there is always the challenge of the unknown, spurring on to further exploration.

But the pleasures and rewards of being curious about peoples and places are not reserved for the professional circle. Anyone who has learned how to observe the earth as the home of man, and how to perceive order in its diversity, has made a compact with geography that will prove stimulating and fruitful throughout his life.

Index

Numbers in italics refer to maps and figures.

Migrations, in China, 474, 475
  and distance, 462
  effects of, 460
  from Europe, 59, 60, 462, 464
  forced, 466–471
  of Germans, *161*, 162
  of Indo-Europeans, 99, 109
  internal, 474–478
  international, 461–474
  and labor movements, 459, *471*, 471–474
  metropolitan, *92*, 404, 405, *407*
  net, 476
  of nonspecialized foragers, 217
  and opportunities, 459, 460
  of pastoral nomads, 254–257
  and population problems, 478
  prehistoric, *82*
  of Slavic peoples, 133
  in South Asia, 170
  in Soviet Union, 475
  of specialized hunters, 218
  theoretical approaches to, 460
  transhumance, 256
  trans-Pacific contacts, 56
  to U.S., 462–466, *465*
  within U.S., 475–478, *476*, *477*
  of West Indians, 91–93
Milk, markets for, 270–272, *271*
Milpa agriculture, 53, 225
Minneapolis-St. Paul, 16, *17*
Minnesota, population density, *8*
  urban functions, *385*
Minoans, 48
Minorities, in cities, 406–408
  in nation-states, 154, 155, 169, 170
Mirow, N. T., *220*
Mitchell, J. C., 474
Mitteleuropa, 162
Moa hunters, 221
Mobility, 459
  of Americans, 475–478
  of horse and camel riding nomads, 256
Modern societies, 211, 212, *213*
  agriculture in, 261–284, *266*, *267*
    integration into industrial economy, 261–263, *263*, *264*, 280
    productivity of, 261, 262, 280, 281
  cities in, 375–388, 391–416
  control of nature and, 57

Modern societies, crop farming in, 272–277
  dairy farming in, 270–272
  death control in, 431–434
  forms of economy in, *213*
  land tenure in, 262–264
  land use in, 212, 214
  livestock ranching in, 277–280
  mixed farming in, 264–270
  population changes in, 429, 430, 455–457
  technological origins of, 57–66
  transportation in, 57–63
Mohawk Valley, 299
Moluccas, 59
Mongolia, pastoral nomadism, 257
Mongoloid peoples, 80–85
  merging with Caucasoids, 81, 84, 85
  spread of genes, 81–85
Mongols, 257
Monophysites, 134, *135*
Montagu, M. F. A., 78, 85, 86
Montenegro, 160
Montesquieu, 24
More, Thomas, 326
Mormon Church, *139*, 140
Mormon villages, *354*, 356, 357
Morrill, R. L., 407
Mortality, 431–434
  infant, 434
Moscow, 308, *309*
Motor vehicles, *63*
Mourant, A. E., *et al.*, 77
Mulatto, 193
Mumford, L., 31, 371, 403
Murphey, R., 374
Muscovy, 196, *197*
Mutual aid, 211, 245
Myrdal, G. O., 334, 335
Myres, J. N. L., 99
Mysore, 171

Nairobi, Kenya, 14
Nation, 153–182
  (*See also* Nation-state)
National income, 319
National populations, *34*, *35*
Nationalism, 153, 154, 499
  as inconography, 154
  and interdependence, 166, *167*